DRAMA
for Students

DRAMA for Students

Presenting Analysis, Context, and Criticism on Commonly Studied Dramas

Volume 11

Elizabeth Thomason, Editor

Detroit
New York
San Francisco
London
Boston
Woodbridge, CT

National Advisory Board

Dale Allender: Teacher, West High School, Iowa City, Iowa.

Dana Gioia: Poet and critic. His books include *The Gods of Winter* and *Can Poetry Matter?* He currently resides in Santa Rosa, CA.

Carol Jago: Teacher, Santa Monica High School, Santa Monica, CA. Member of the California Reading and Literature Project at University of California, Los Angeles.

Bonnie J. Newcomer: English Teacher, Beloit Junior-Senior High School, Beloit, Kansas. Editor of KATE UpDate, for the Kansas Association of Teachers of English. Ph.D. candidate in information science, Emporia State University, Kansas.

Katherine Nyberg: English teacher. Director of the language arts program of Farmington Public Schools, Farmington, Michigan.

Nancy Rosenberger: Former English teacher and chair of English department at Conestoga High School, Berwyn, Pennsylvania.

Dorothea M. Susag: English teacher, Simms High School, Simms, Montana. Former president of the Montana Association of Teachers of English Language Arts. Member of the National Council of Teachers of English.

Drama for Students

Staff

Editor: Elizabeth Thomason.

Contributing Editors: Anne Marie Hacht, Michael L. LaBlanc, Ira Mark Milne, Jennifer Smith.

Managing Editor: Dwayne Hayes.

Research: Victoria B. Cariappa, *Research Manager.* Cheryl Warnock, *Research Specialist.* Tamara Nott, Tracie A. Richardson, *Research Associates.* Nicodemus Ford, Sarah Genik, Timothy Lehnerer, *Research Assistants.*

Permissions: Maria Franklin, *Permissions Manager.* Sarah Tomasek, *Permissions Associate.*

Manufacturing: Mary Beth Trimper, *Manager, Composition and Electronic Prepress.* Evi Seoud, *Assistant Manager, Composition Purchasing and Electronic Prepress.* Stacy Melson, *Buyer.*

Imaging and Multimedia Content Team: Barbara Yarrow, *Manager.* Randy Bassett, *Imaging Supervisor.* Robert Duncan, Dan Newell, *Imaging Specialists.* Pamela A. Reed, *Imaging Coordinator.* Leitha Etheridge-Sims, Mary Grimes, *Image Catalogers.* Robyn V. Young, *Project Manager.* Dean Dauphinais, *Senior Image Editor.* Kelly A. Quin, *Image Editor.*

Product Design Team: Kenn Zorn, *Product Design Manager.* Pamela A. E. Galbreath, *Senior Art Director.* Michael Logusz, *Graphic Artist.*

Copyright Notice

Since this page cannot legibly accommodate all copyright notices, the acknowledgments constitute an extension of the copyright notice.

While every effort has been made to secure permission to reprint material and to ensure the reliability of the information presented in this publication, Gale neither guarantees the accuracy of the data contained herein nor assumes any responsibility for errors, omissions, or discrepancies. Gale accepts no payment for listing; and inclusion in the publication of any organization, agency, institution, publication, service, or individual does not imply endorsement of the editors or publisher. Errors brought to the attention of the publisher and verified to the satisfaction of the publisher will be corrected in future editions.

This publication is a creative work fully protected by all applicable copyright laws, as well as by misappropriation, trade secret, unfair competition, and other applicable laws. The authors and editors of this work have added value to the underlying factual material herein through one or more of the following: unique and original selection, coordination, expression, arrangement, and classification of the information. All rights to this publication will be vigorously defended.

Copyright © 2001
Gale Group, Inc.
27500 Drake Road
Farmington Hills, MI 48331-3535

All rights reserved including the right of reproduction in whole or in part in any form.

ISBN 0-7876-4085-9

ISSN 1094-9232

Printed in the United States of America.

10 9 8 7 6 5 4 3 2 1

Table of Contents

GUEST FOREWORD
 "The Study of Drama"
 by Carole L. Hamilton ix

INTRODUCTION xi

LITERARY CHRONOLOGY xv

ACKNOWLEDGMENTS xvii

CONTRIBUTORS xxi

ABE LINCOLN IN ILLINOIS
 Robert E. Sherwood 1

THE AMEN CORNER
 James Baldwin 21

DANCING AT LUGHNASA
 Brian Friel 38

DRIVING MISS DAISY
 Alfred Uhry 58

GHOSTS
 Henrik Ibsen 77

THE GREAT GOD BROWN
 Eugene O'Neill 108

HARVEY
 Mary Chase 126

INDIAN INK
 Tom Stoppard 146

THE INSECT PLAY
    Josef Capek and Karel Capek 162

M. BUTTERFLY
    David Henry Hwang 182

SAINT JOAN
    George Bernard Shaw 206

SHADOWLANDS
    William Nicholson 224

SLAVE SHIP
    Amiri Baraka 242

THE SLEEP OF REASON
    Antonio Buero Vallejo 260

SPIKE HEELS
    Theresa Rebeck 273

GLOSSARY OF LITERARY TERMS 287

CUMULATIVE AUTHOR/TITLE INDEX . 321

NATIONALITY/ETHNICITY INDEX . . . 325

SUBJECT/THEME INDEX 329

The Study of Drama

We study drama in order to learn what meaning others have made of life, to comprehend what it takes to produce a work of art, and to glean some understanding of ourselves. Drama produces in a separate, aesthetic world, a moment of being for the audience to experience, while maintaining the detachment of a reflective observer.

Drama is a representational art, a visible and audible narrative presenting virtual, fictional characters within a virtual, fictional universe. Dramatic realizations may pretend to approximate reality or else stubbornly defy, distort, and deform reality into an artistic statement. From this separate universe that is obviously not "real life" we expect a valid reflection upon reality, yet drama never is mistaken for reality—the methods of theater are integral to its form and meaning. Theater is art, and art's appeal lies in its ability both to approximate life and to depart from it. By presenting its distorted version of life to our consciousness, art gives us a new perspective and appreciation of reality. Although, to some extent, all aesthetic experiences perform this service, theater does it most effectively by creating a separate, cohesive universe that freely acknowledges its status as an art form.

And what is the purpose of the aesthetic universe of drama? The potential answers to such a question are nearly as many and varied as there are plays written, performed, and enjoyed. Dramatic texts can be problems posed, answers asserted, or moments portrayed. Dramas (tragedies as well as comedies) may serve strictly "to ease the anguish of a torturing hour" (as stated in William Shakespeare's *A Midsummer Night's Dream*)—to divert and entertain—or aspire to move the viewer to action with social issues. Whether to entertain or to instruct, affirm or influence, pacify or shock, dramatic art wraps us in the spell of its imaginary world for the length of the work and then dispenses us back to the real world, entertained, purged, as Aristotle said, of pity and fear, and edified—or at least weary enough to sleep peacefully.

It is commonly thought that theater, being an art of performance, must be experienced—that is, seen—in order to be appreciated fully. However, to view a production of a dramatic text is to be limited to a single interpretation of that text—all other interpretations are for the moment closed off, inaccessible. In the process of producing a play, the director, stage designer, and performers interpret and transform the script into a work of art that always departs in some measure from the author's original conception. Novelist and critic Umberto Eco, in his *The Role of the Reader: Explorations in the Semiotics of Texts,* explained, "In short, we can say that every performance offers us a complete and satisfying version of the work, but at the same time makes it incomplete for us, because it cannot simultaneously give all the other artistic solutions which the work may admit."

Thus Laurence Olivier's coldly formal and neurotic film presentation of Shakespeare's *Hamlet* (in which he played the title character as well as directed) shows marked differences from subsequent adaptations. While Olivier's Hamlet is clearly entangled in a Freudian relationship with his mother, Gertrude, he would be incapable of shushing her with the impassioned kiss that Mel Gibson's mercurial Hamlet (in director Franco Zeffirelli's 1990 film) does. Although each of the performances rings true to Shakespeare's text, each is also a mutually exclusive work of art. Also important to consider are the time periods in which each of these films were produced: Olivier made his film in 1948, a time in which overt references to sexuality (especially incest) were frowned upon. Gibson and Zeffirelli made their film in a culture more relaxed and comfortable with these issues. Just as actors and directors can influence the presentation of drama, so too can the time period of the production affect what the audience will see.

A play script is an open text from which an infinity of specific realizations may be derived. Dramatic scripts that are more open to interpretive creativity (such as those of Ntozake Shange and Tomson Highway) actually require the creative improvisation of the production troupe in order to complete the text. Even the most prescriptive scripts (those of Neil Simon, Lillian Hellman, and Robert Bolt, for example), can never fully control the actualization of live performance, and circumstantial events, including the attitude and receptivity of the audience, make every performance a unique event. Thus, while it is important to view a production of a dramatic piece, if one wants to understand a drama fully it is equally important to read the original dramatic text.

The reader of a dramatic text or script is not limited by either the specific interpretation of a given production or by the unstoppable action of a moving spectacle. The reader of a dramatic text may discover the nuances of the play's language, structure, and events at their own pace. Yet studied alone, the author's blueprint for artistic production does not tell the whole story of a play's life and significance. One also needs to assess the play's critical reviews to discover how it resonated to cultural themes at the time of its debut and how the shifting tides of cultural interest have revised its interpretation and impact on audiences. And to do this, one needs to know a little about the culture of the times which produced the play as well as the author who penned it.

Drama for Students supplies this material in a useful compendium for the student of dramatic theater. Covering a range of dramatic works that span from the fifth century B.C. to the 1990s, this book focuses on significant theatrical works whose themes and form transcend the uncertainty of dramatic fads. These are plays that have proven to be both memorable and teachable. *Drama for Students* seeks to enhance appreciation of these dramatic texts by providing scholarly materials written with the secondary and college/university student in mind. It provides for each play a concise summary of the plot and characters as well as a detailed explanation of its themes and techniques. In addition, background material on the historical context of the play, its critical reception, and the author's life help the student to understand the work's position in the chronicle of dramatic history. For each play entry a new work of scholarly criticism is also included, as well as segments of other significant critical works for handy reference. A thorough bibliography provides a starting point for further research.

These inaugural two volumes offer comprehensive educational resources for students of drama. *Drama for Students* is a vital book for dramatic interpretation and a valuable addition to any reference library.

Source: Eco, Umberto, *The Role of the Reader: Explorations in the Semiotics of Texts,* Indiana University Press, 1979.

Carole L. Hamilton
Author and Instructor of English
Cary Academy
Cary, North Carolina

Introduction

Purpose of Drama for Students

The purpose of *Drama for Students* (*DfS*) is to provide readers with a guide to understanding, enjoying, and studying dramas by giving them easy access to information about the work. Part of Gale's "For Students" literature line, *DfS* is specifically designed to meet the curricular needs of high school and undergraduate college students and their teachers, as well as the interests of general readers and researchers considering specific plays. While each volume contains entries on "classic" dramas frequently studied in classrooms, there are also entries containing hard-to-find information on contemporary plays, including works by multicultural, international, and women playwrights.

The information covered in each entry includes an introduction to the play and the work's author; a plot summary, to help readers unravel and understand the events in a drama; descriptions of important characters, including explanation of a given character's role in the drama as well as discussion about that character's relationship to other characters in the play; analysis of important themes in the drama; and an explanation of important literary techniques and movements as they are demonstrated in the play.

In addition to this material, which helps the readers analyze the play itself, students are also provided with important information on the literary and historical background informing each work. This includes a historical context essay, a box comparing the time or place the drama was written to modern Western culture, a critical overview essay, and excerpts from critical essays on the play. A unique feature of *DfS* is a specially commissioned overview essay on each drama by an academic expert, targeted toward the student reader.

To further aid the student in studying and enjoying each play, information on media adaptations is provided, as well as reading suggestions for works of fiction and nonfiction on similar themes and topics. Classroom aids include ideas for research papers and lists of critical sources that provide additional material on each drama.

Selection Criteria

The titles for each volume of *DfS* were selected by surveying numerous sources on teaching literature and analyzing course curricula for various school districts. Some of the sources surveyed included: literature anthologies; *Reading Lists for College-Bound Students: The Books Most Recommended by America's Top Colleges;* textbooks on teaching dramas; a College Board survey of plays commonly studied in high schools; a National Council of Teachers of English (NCTE) survey of plays commonly studied in high schools; St. James Press's *International Dictionary of Theatre;* and Arthur Applebee's 1993 study *Literature in the Secondary School: Studies of Curriculum and Instruction in the United States.*

Input was also solicited from our expert advisory board (both experienced educators specializing in English), as well as educators from various areas. From these discussions, it was determined that each volume should have a mix of "classic" dramas (those works commonly taught in literature classes) and contemporary dramas for which information is often hard to find. Because of the interest in expanding the canon of literature, an emphasis was also placed on including works by international, multicultural, and women playwrights. Our advisory board members—current high school teachers—helped pare down the list for each volume. If a work was not selected for the present volume, it was often noted as a possibility for a future volume. As always, the editor welcomes suggestions for titles to be included in future volumes.

How Each Entry Is Organized

Each entry, or chapter, in *DfS* focuses on one play. Each entry heading lists the full name of the play, the author's name, and the date of the play's first production or publication. The following elements are contained in each entry:

- **Introduction:** a brief overview of the drama which provides information about its first appearance, its literary standing, any controversies surrounding the work, and major conflicts or themes within the work.

- **Author Biography:** this section includes basic facts about the author's life, and focuses on events and times in the author's life that inspired the drama in question.

- **Plot Summary:** a description of the major events in the play, with interpretation of how these events help articulate the play's themes. Subheads demarcate the plays' various acts or scenes.

- **Characters:** an alphabetical listing of major characters in the play. Each character name is followed by a brief to an extensive description of the character's role in the plays, as well as discussion of the character's actions, relationships, and possible motivation.

  Characters are listed alphabetically by last name. If a character is unnamed—for instance, the Stage Manager in *Our Town*—the character is listed as "The Stage Manager" and alphabetized as "Stage Manager." If a character's first name is the only one given, the name will appear alphabetically by the name.

  Variant names are also included for each character. Thus, the nickname "Babe" would head the listing for a character in *Crimes of the Heart,* but below that listing would be her less-mentioned married name "Rebecca Botrelle."

- **Themes:** a thorough overview of how the major topics, themes, and issues are addressed within the play. Each theme discussed appears in a separate subhead, and is easily accessed through the boldface entries in the Subject/Theme Index.

- **Style:** this section addresses important style elements of the drama, such as setting, point of view, and narration; important literary devices used, such as imagery, foreshadowing, symbolism; and, if applicable, genres to which the work might have belonged, such as Gothicism or Romanticism. Literary terms are explained within the entry, but can also be found in the Glossary.

- **Historical and Cultural Context:** This section outlines the social, political, and cultural climate *in which the author lived and the play was created.* This section may include descriptions of related historical events, pertinent aspects of daily life in the culture, and the artistic and literary sensibilities of the time in which the work was written. If the play is a historical work, information regarding the time in which the play is set is also included. Each section is broken down with helpful subheads.

- **Critical Overview:** this section provides background on the critical reputation of the play, including bannings or any other public controversies surrounding the work. For older plays, this section includes a history of how the drama was first received and how perceptions of it may have changed over the years; for more recent plays, direct quotes from early reviews may also be included.

- **For Further Study:** an alphabetical list of other critical sources which may prove useful for the student. Includes full bibliographical information and a brief annotation.

- **Sources:** an alphabetical list of critical material quoted in the entry, with full bibliographical information.

- **Criticism:** an essay commissioned by *DfS* which specifically deals with the play and is written specifically for the student audience, as well as excerpts from previously published criticism on the work.

In addition, each entry contains the following highlighted sections, set separate from the main text:

- **Media Adaptations:** a list of important film and television adaptations of the play, including source information. The list may also include such variations on the work as audio recordings, musical adaptations, and other stage interpretations.

- **Compare and Contrast Box:** an "at-a-glance" comparison of the cultural and historical differences between the author's time and culture and late twentieth-century Western culture. This box includes pertinent parallels between the major scientific, political, and cultural movements of the time or place the drama was written, the time or place the play was set (if a historical work), and modern Western culture. Works written after the mid-1970s may not have this box.

- **What Do I Read Next?:** a list of works that might complement the featured play or serve as a contrast to it. This includes works by the same author and others, works of fiction and nonfiction, and works from various genres, cultures, and eras.

- **Study Questions:** a list of potential study questions or research topics dealing with the play. This section includes questions related to other disciplines the student may be studying, such as American history, world history, science, math, government, business, geography, economics, psychology, etc.

Other Features

DfS includes "The Study of Drama," a foreword by Carole Hamilton, an educator and author who specializes in dramatic works. This essay examines the basis for drama in societies and what drives people to study such work. Hamilton also discusses how *Drama for Students* can help teachers show students how to enrich their own reading/viewing experiences.

A Cumulative Author/Title Index lists the authors and titles covered in each volume of the *DfS* series.

A Cumulative Nationality/Ethnicity Index breaks down the authors and titles covered in each volume of the *DfS* series by nationality and ethnicity.

A Subject/Theme Index, specific to each volume, provides easy reference for users who may be studying a particular subject or theme rather than a single work. Significant subjects from events to broad themes are included, and the entries pointing to the specific theme discussions in each entry are indicated in **boldface.**

Each entry has several illustrations, including photos of the author, stills from stage productions, and stills from film adaptations.

Citing Drama for Students

When writing papers, students who quote directly from any volume of *Drama for Students* may use the following general forms. These examples are based on MLA style; teachers may request that students adhere to a different style, so the following examples may be adapted as needed.

When citing text from *DfS* that is not attributed to a particular author (i.e., the Themes, Style, Historical Context sections, etc.), the following format should be used in the bibliography section:

"Our Town," *Drama for Students.* Ed. David Galens and Lynn Spampinato. Vol. 1. Farmington Hills: Gale, 1997. 8–9.

When quoting the specially commissioned essay from *DfS* (usually the first piece under the "Criticism" subhead), the following format should be used:

Fiero, John. Essay on "Twilight: Los Angeles, 1992." *Drama for Students.* Ed. David Galens and Lynn Spampinato. Vol. 1. Farmington Hills: Gale, 1997. 8–9.

When quoting a journal or newspaper essay that is reprinted in a volume of *DfS,* the following form may be used:

Rich, Frank. "Theatre: A Mamet Play, 'Glengarry Glen Ross'." *New York Theatre Critics' Review* Vol. 45, No. 4 (March 5, 1984), 5–7; excerpted and reprinted in *Drama for Students,* Vol. 1, ed. David Galens and Lynn Spampinato (Farmington Hills: Gale, 1997), pp. 61–64.

When quoting material reprinted from a book that appears in a volume of *DfS,* the following form may be used:

Kerr, Walter. "The Miracle Worker," in *The Theatre in Spite of Itself* (Simon & Schuster, 1963, 255–57; excerpted and reprinted in *Drama for Students,* Vol. 1, ed. Dave Galens and Lynn Spampinato (Farmington Hills: Gale, 1997), pp. 59–61.

We Welcome Your Suggestions

The editor of *Drama for Students* welcomes your comments and ideas. Readers who wish to suggest dramas to appear in future volumes, or who have other suggestions, are cordially invited to contact the editor. You may contact the editor via

E-mail at: **elizabeth.thomason@galegroup.com.**

Or write to the editor at:

Editor, *Drama for Students*
The Gale Group
27500 Drake Rd.
Farmington Hills, MI 48331-3535

Literary Chronology

1828: Henrik Ibsen is born on March 20 in Skein, on the east coast of Norway.

1856: George Bernard Shaw is born in Dublin on July 26.

1887: Josef Capek is born in Male Svatonovice, Bohemia (now part of Czechoslovakia).

1888: Eugene O'Neill is born on October 16 in New York City.

1889: *Ghosts* makes its world debut in Chicago; it is not produced in Ibsen's homeland, Norway, until 1898.

1890: Josef's brother and future writing partner, Karel Capek, is born on January 9, also in Male Svatonovice, Bohemia.

1896: Robert Sherwood is born on April 4.

1906: Ibsen dies from complications brought on by a series of strokes on May 23 in Norway.

1907: Mary Coyle Chase is born in Denver, Colorado.

1916: Antonio Buero Vallejo is born on September 29 in Guadalajara, Spain.

1921: *The Insect Play* is published in its original Czech.

1923: *Saint Joan* is produced in New York City.

1924: James Baldwin is born on August 2 in New York City.

1926: *Great God Brown* opens at the Greenwich Village Theatre on January 23.

1929: Brian Friel is born near Omagh, County Tyrone, in Northern Ireland, on January 9.

1934: Amiri Baraka is born as Everett LeRoi Jones on October 7 in Newark, New Jersey.

1936: Alfred Uhry is born in Atlanta, Georgia.

1937: Tom Stoppard is born on July 3 in Zlin, Czechoslovakia, with the name Tomas Straussler.

1938: Sherwood's play, *Abe Lincoln in Illinois*, is produced and earns him his second of four Pulitzer Prizes.

1938: Karel Capek dies of pneumonia on December 25 in Prague, Czechoslovakia.

1944: Chase's Pulitzer-Prize winning *Harvey* opens on Broadway.

1945: Josef Capek dies.

1948: William Nicholson is born in England.

1950: Shaw dies on November 2 in Ayot Saint Lawrence, Hertfordshire, England.

1953: O'Neill dies of pneumonia on November 27 in Boston, Massachusetts.

1955: Sherwood dies on November 14.

1957: David Henry Hwang is born on August 11 in Los Angeles, California.

1965: *The Amen Corner*, although written in the 1950s, isn't produced until now on a professional stage, and isn't published until 1968.

1967: *Slave Ship* is produced.

1970: *The Sleep of Reason* is produced in Madrid.

1981: Chase dies of a heart attack on October 20 in Denver, Colorado.

1987: Uhry finishes *Driving Miss Daisy*.

1987: Baldwin dies of stomach cancer on November 30 or December 1 in St. Paul de Vence, France.

1988: *Driving Miss Daisy* wins the Pulitzer Prize for Drama.

1989: *Shadowlands* debuts in England on October 5.

1989: *M. Butterfly* is produced and wins the Tony Award for Best Play of the Year.

1990: *Spike Heels* is first staged in New York.

1990: *Dancing at Lughnasa* is staged at the Abbey Theater in Dublin.

1994: *Indian Ink* is published.

2000: Buero Vallejo dies of a stroke on April 29 in Madrid, Spain.

Acknowledgments

The editors wish to thank the copyright holders of the excerpted criticism included in this volume and the permissions managers of many book and magazine publishing companies for assisting us in securing reproduction rights. We are also grateful to the staffs of the Detroit Public Library, the Library of Congress, the University of Detroit Mercy Library, Wayne State University Purdy/Kresge Library Complex, and the University of Michigan Libraries for making their resources available to us. Following is a list of the copyright holders who have granted us permission to reproduce material in this volume of *Drama for Students (DfS)*. Every effort has been made to trace copyright, but if omissions have been made, please let us know.

COPYRIGHTED EXCERPTS IN *DfS*, VOLUME 11, WERE REPRODUCED FROM THE FOLLOWING PERIODICALS:

Commonweal, v. 121, January 28, 1994. Copyright © 1994 Commonweal Publishing Co., Inc. Reproduced by permission of Commonweal Foundation.—*Los Angeles Times Book Review,* v. 3, November 3, 1996. Copyright, 1996, Los Angeles Times. Reproduced by permission.—*The New Republic,* v. 197, September 28, 1987. © 1987 The New Republic, Inc. Reproduced by permission of The New Republic.—*New York Magazine,* v. 20, May 4, 1987, Copyright © 1987 PRIMEDIA Magazine Corporation. All rights reserved. Reproduced with the permission of New York Magazine.—*The New Yorker,* November 26, 1990 for "Shady Doings" by Mimi Kramer. © 1990 by The New Yorker Magazine, Inc. All rights reserved. Reproduced by permission of the author.—*The Spectator,* v. 260, June 18, 1988. © 1988 by The Spectator. Reproduced by permission of The Spectator.—*Time,* New York, v. 136, November 19, 1990; v. 142, December 27, 1993. Copyright 1990, 1993 Time Warner Inc. All rights reserved. Both reproduced by permission from Time.

COPYRIGHTED EXCERPTS IN *DfS* VOLUME 11, WERE REPRODUCED FROM THE FOLLOWING BOOKS:

Andrews, Elmer. From *The Art of Brian Friel: Neither Reality Nor Dreams.* St. Martin's Press, 1995. © Elmer Andrews 1995. Reprinted with permission of St. Martin's Press, LLC. In the UK by permission of Macmillan, London and Basingstoke.—Berlin, Normand. From *Eugene O'Neill.* Grove Press, 1964. Copyright © 1982 by Normand Berlin. All Rights Reserved. Reproduced by permission of Macmillan, London and Basingstoke.—Bogard, Travis. From *Contour in Time: The Plays of Eugene O'Neill.* Oxford University Press, 1972. Copyright © 1972, 1988 by Oxford University Press, Inc. Used by permission of Oxford University Press, Inc.—Brown, John Mason. From *The Worlds of Robert E. Sherwood.* Harper & Row, 1965. Copyright © 1962, 1965 by John Mason Brown. Reprinted by permission of

HarperCollins Publishers, Inc.—Brown, Lloyd W. From *Amiri Baraka.* Twayne Publishers, 1980. Copyright © 1980 by G.K. Hall & Co. All Rights Reserved. Reproduced with the permission of Macmillan Library Reference USA, a division of Ahsuog, Inc.—Carpenter, Frederic L. From *Eugene O'Neill.* Twayne Publishers, 1964. Copyright © 1964 by Twayne Publishers, Inc. All Rights Reserved. Reproduced by permission of the Gale Group.—Collis, John Stewart. From ''Religion and Philosophy'' in *The Genius of Shaw: A Symposium.* Edited by Michael Holroyd. Holt, Rinehart and Winston, 1979. Copyright © 1979 by George Rainbird Limited. All rights reserved. Reprinted by permission of Henry Holt and Company, LLC.—Elam, Jr., Harry J. From *Taking It to the Streets: The Social Protest Theater of Luis Valdez and Amiri Baraka.* University of Michigan Press, 1997. Copyright © by the University of Michigan 1997. All rights reserved. Reproduced by permission.—Fergusson, Francis. From *The Idea of a Theater: A Study of Ten Plays: The Art of Drama in Changing Perspective.* Princeton University Press, 1949. Copyright, 1949, by Princeton University Press. Renewed 1976 by Francis Fergusson. Renewed 1977 by Princeton University Press. Reproduced by permission.—Hill, Eldon C. From *George Bernard Shaw.* Twayne Publishers, 1978. Copyright © 1978 by G.K. Hall & Co. All Rights Reserved. Reproduced by permission of the Gale Group.—Macebuh, Stanley. From *James Baldwin: A Critical Study.* The Third Press, 1973. Copyright © 1973 by The Third Press, Joseph Okpaku Publishing Co., Inc. Reproduced by permission.—Northam, John. From *Ibsen: A Critical Study.* Cambridge at the University Press, 1973. Reproduced with the permission of Cambridge University Press and the author.—Olaniyan, Tejumola. From *Scars of Conquest/Masks of Resistance: The Invention of Cultural Identities in African, African-American, and Caribbean Drama.* Oxford University Press, 1995. Copyright © 1995 by Tejumola Olaniyan. Used by permission of Oxford University Press, Inc.—Pratt, Louis H. From *James Baldwin.* Twayne Publishers, 1978. Copyright © 1978 by G.K. Hall & Co. All Rights Reserved. Reproduced by permission of the Gale Group.—Uhry, Alfred. From the preface to *Driving Miss Daisy.* Theatre Communications Group, 1986. Preface copyright © 1988 by Alfred Uhry. Reproduced by permission.

PHOTOGRAPHS AND ILLUSTRATIONS APPEARING IN *DfS* VOLUME 11, WERE RECEIVED FROM THE FOLLOWING SOURCES:

Baldwin, James. AP/ Wide World Photos. Reproduced by permission.—Baraka, Amiri, standing in a doorway, photograph. AP/Wide World Photos. Reproduced by permission.—Capek, Karel with Joseph Capek, photograph. © Bettmann/CORBIS. Reproduced by permission.—Chase, Mary Coyle, photograph. AP/Wide World Photos. Reproduced by permission.—Chase, Mary Coyle with James Stewart, on set of the film ''Harvey,'' 1950, photograph. AP/Wide World Photos. Reproduced by permission.—From a theatre production of Brian Friel's ''Dancing at Lughnasa'' from Dublin's Abbey Theater, August 21, 1991 with Catherine Byrne, Brid Nineachtain and Brid Brennan, photograph. AP/Wide World Photos. Reproduced by permission.—Friel, Brian, photograph by Bobbie Hanvey. Reproduced by permission of Bobbie Hanvey.—Streep, Meryl with Brid Brennan and Sophie Thompson, in the movie ''Dancing at Lughnasa,'' 1998, photograph by Jonathon Hession. The Kobal Collection. Reproduced by permission.—Hwang, David Henry, 1988, photograph by Rick Maiman. AP/Wide World Photos. Reproduced by permission.—Hopkins, Anthony and Glenn G. Goei, in a scene from the theatrical production of ''M. Butterfly,'' 1989, photograph. © Donald Cooper/Photostage. Reproduced by permission.—Irons, Jeremy with John Lone, in a scene from the film ''M. Butterfly,'' 1993, photograph. Geffen CO/Warner Brothers. The Kobal Collection. Reproduced by permission.—Ibsen, Henrik, photograph. Culver Pictures, Inc. Reproduced by permission.—Beale, Simon Russell with Jane Lapotaire, in a scene from the theatrical production of ''Ghosts,'' 1993, photograph. © Donald Cooper/Photostage. Reproduced by permission.—Fairleigh, Lynn and Simon Chandler, in a scene from the theatrical production of ''Ghosts,'' 1984, photograph. © Donald Cooper/Photostage. Reproduced by permission.—Hawthorne, Nigel, on stage as C. S. Lewis in a production of ''Shadowlands'' at Queens Theatre, London, England, photograph. © Donald Cooper/Photostage. Reproduced by permission.—Hopkins, Anthony with Debra Winger, in a scene from the film ''Shadowlands,'' 1993, photograph. Spelling/Price/Savoy. The Kobal Collection. Reproduced by permission.—O'Neill, Eugene, photograph. AP/Wide World Photos. Reproduced by permission.—A playbill from from the theatrical production of Eugene O'Neill's ''The Great God Brown,'' at the Coronet Theatre. PLAYBILL ® is a registered trademark of Playbill Incorporated, N. Y. C. All rights reserved. Reproduced by permission.—A playbill from the April, 1965 theatrical production of James Baldwin's ''The Amen Corner,'' at the Ethel Barrymore Theatre. PLAYBILL ® is a registered trademark of Playbill Incorporated, N. Y. C. All rights reserved. Reproduced by permission.—A playbill from the February, 1970 theatrical production of "Harvey," at the Anta Theatre. PLAYBILL ® is a registered trademark of Playbill Incorporated, N. Y. C. All rights reserved. Reproduced by permission.—Playbill title page insert for production of the play "Spike Heels" by Theresa Rebeck, directed by Michael Greif, at the Second Stage Theatre, New York. PLAYBILL ® is a registered trademark of Playbill Incorporated, N.Y.C. All rights reserved. Reproduced by permission.—Shaw, George Bernard, photograph. The Library of Congress.—Seberg, Jean with Richard Widmark and two other men, in a scene from the film "Saint Joan," 1957, photograph. The Kobal Collection. Reproduced by permission.—Widmark, Richard with others, in a scene from the film "Saint Joan," 1957, photograph. The Kobal Collection. Reproduced by permission.—Sherwood, Robert E., photograph. AP/Wide World Photos. Reproduced by permission.—Massey, Raymond with Ruth Gordon, in a scene from the film "Abe Lincoln in Illinois," 1940, photograph. RKO. The Kobal Collection. Reproduced by permission.—Massey, Raymond with Ruth Gordon (seated in carriage), in a scene from the film "Abe Lincoln in Illinois," 1940, photograph. RKO. The Kobal Collection. Reproduced by permission.—Kendal, Felicity with Flora Crewe, Art Malik, and Dominic Jephcott, in "Indian Ink," photograph. © Donald Cooper/PHOTOSTAGE. Reproduced by permission.—Stoppard, Tom, photograph. AP/Wide World Photos. Reproduced by permission.—Uhry, Alfred, photograph. AP/Wide World Photos. Reproduced by permission.—Hyman, Earle, photograph. Martha Swope Associates/Carol Rosegg. Reproduced by permission.—Freeman, Morgan with Jessia Tandy and Dan Aykroyd, in a scene from the film "Driving Miss Daisy," 1989, photograph. Warner Bros. The Kobal Collection. Reproduced by permission.—Buero Vallejo, Madrid, Spain, 1986, photograph. AP/Wide World Photos. Reproduced by permission.

Contributors

Bryan Aubrey: Aubrey, Ph.D., has published many articles on literature and drama. Entry on *M. Butterfly*. Original essay on *M. Butterfly*.

Greg Barnhisel: Barnhisel holds a Ph.D. in American literature. Entry on *Spike Heels*. Original essay on *Spike Heels*.

Liz Brent: Brent has a Ph.D. in American Culture, specializing in cinema studies, from the University of Michigan. She is a freelance writer and teacher of courses in American cinema. Entries on *The Amen Corner*, *Dancing at Lughnasa*, *Indian Ink*, and *Slave Ship*. Original essays on *The Amen Corner*, *Dancing at Lughnasa*, *Harvey*, *Indian Ink*, *The Insect Play*, *M. Butterfly*, and *Slave Ship*.

Sheldon Goldfarb: Goldfarb has a Ph.D. in English and has published two books on the Victorian author William Makepeace Thackeray. Entry on *Saint Joan*. Original essay on *Saint Joan*.

Carole Hamilton: Hamilton is an English teacher at Cary Academy, an innovative private school in Cary, North Carolina. Original essays on *Indian Ink* and *Spike Heels*.

Joyce Hart: Hart, a former college professor, is a freelance writer. Original essay on *The Insect Play*.

Kirsten Herold: Herold has a Ph.D. and specializes in the history of dramatic literature. Original essay on *Harvey*.

David J. Kelly: Kelly is a professor of English at College of Lake County, IL. Entries on *Abe Lincoln in Illinois*, *Ghosts*, and *Harvey*. Original essays on *Abe Lincoln in Illinois*, *Ghosts*, and *Harvey*.

Rena Korb: Korb has a master's degree in English literature and creative writing, and has written for a wide variety of educational publishers. Entry on *Driving Miss Daisy*. Original essays on *Driving Miss Daisy* and *Spike Heels*.

Wendy Perkins: Perkins, an Associate Professor of English at Prince George's Community College in Maryland, has published articles on several twentieth-century authors. Entry on *Great God Brown*. Original essay on *Great God Brown*.

Annette Petrusso: Petrusso is a freelance author and screenwriter from Austin, TX. Entries on *The Insect Play* and *Shadowlands*. Original essays on *The Insect Play* and *Shadowlands*.

Daniela Presley: Presley has an M.A. in Germanic Languages and Literature. Original essay on *Indian Ink*.

Leah Ryan: Ryan is a writer and a teacher of dramatic writing with an MFA in playwriting. Original essay on *Dancing at Lughnasa*.

Chris Semansky: Semansky holds a Ph.D. in English from Stony Brook University, and teaches writing and literature at Portland Community College in Portland, OR. His collection of poems *Death, But at a Good Price* received the Nicholas Roerich Poetry Prize for 1991 and was published by Story Line Press and the Nicholas Roerich Museum. Semansky's most recent collection, *Blindsided*, has been published by 26 Books of Portland, OR. Entry on *The Sleep of Reason*. Original essay on *The Sleep of Reason*.

Abe Lincoln in Illinois

ROBERT E. SHERWOOD

1938

Abe Lincoln In Illinois presents a vision that fits in with the legends of the sixteenth president that have been told to generations of American school children, but it gives these legends a human face. The play deals with Lincoln's formative years. It focuses in particular on Lincoln's growth from a shy, uneducated backwoodsman who was more willing to accept the enslavement of blacks than to accept war to the man who would lead half of the nation against the other half in the name of justice. When Sherwood's play was brought to the stage in 1938, its parallels to the international political situation were obvious. Adolf Hitler had established himself as the dictator of Germany and had started his expansion across Europe, and the people of America, an ocean away, found themselves faced with questions about whether to fight for justice or maintain peace. As the play continued to run on Broadway, Hitler invaded more countries, raising more and more support for America's entry into the war, giving audiences even more empathy for Lincoln's dilemma. Today, it stands as a reminder of the responsibilities that come along with power and of the sort of person that Lincoln must have been. Among constitutional scholars, historians, and average citizens, he is still the country's most respected president, and Robert Sherwood's play offers a well-rounded view of Lincoln's flaws as well as his greatness.

AUTHOR BIOGRAPHY

Robert E. Sherwood was a popular American playwright and novelist of the twentieth century. His works reflected the concerns of the generation that had lived through the First World War. They often explored the horrors of modern warfare and the moral choices that were required of those who participated in war. Sherwood was born on April 4, 1896, and attended Milton Academy, graduating from Harvard with a bachelor of arts degree in 1917. When he tried to enlist in the American army during World War I, he was rejected, and so he joined the Canadian infantry. During the war, he was wounded and was sprayed with toxic mustard gas. On his return from the war, he became a magazine movie reviewer, first for *Vanity Fair* and then for *Life*. He was, in fact, one of the country's first serious film critics. By the mid-1920s, he was an editor for *Life* and was doing some screenwriting for Hollywood studios. In 1926 his first screenplay, an adaptation of Victor Hugo's *The Hunchback of Notre Dame*, was produced. The following year had the opening of his first stage play, *The Road to Rome*. He wrote several movies and plays during the twenties and thirties. His works were not praised for their artistry, but they were considered well crafted and effective and generally pleased the public.

In 1934 Sherwood divorced his first wife and remarried. The following period found him at the peak of his artistic powers. *The Petrified Forest*, from 1935, was a commercial success and is considered his most successful artistic piece. The following year, his *Idiot's Delight* won a Pulitzer Prize for drama. He won a second Pulitzer in 1938, when *Abe Lincoln in Illinois* was produced and a third in 1940 for *There Shall Be No Night*. It was through *Abe Lincoln in Illinois* that he began a friendship with Eleanor Roosevelt, the wife of the president of the United States, Franklin Delano Roosevelt. His friendship led to several government appointments during World War II, including Special Assistant to the Secretary of War in 1940, director of the oversees branch of the Office of War Information in 1942, and Special Assistant to the Secretary of the Navy in 1945. It also led to a book about the president called *Roosevelt and Hopkins,* which won Sherwood yet another Pulitzer Prize in 1948. Sherwood is most remembered today for his work in Hollywood where he wrote some of the finest screenplays of the thirties and forties. These screenplays include the adaptations of his own stage works and the script for *The Best Years of Our Lives,* which won numerous Academy Awards in 1946. Sherwood died on November 14, 1955.

PLOT SUMMARY

Act I

The first act of *Abe Lincoln in Illinois* is comprised of the play's first three scenes. They take place in the vicinity of New Salem, Illinois, in the 1830s.

Scene 1 is set in the cabin of Mentor Graham, who is tutoring young Abraham Lincoln in the use of the English language. Lincoln, who would have been in his early twenties, discusses the financial troubles he has had and his desire to move out to the open territory out West to escape his failures. Mentor Graham tells him to "just bear in mind that there are always two professions open to people who fail at everything else: there's school teaching, and there's politics."

A major theme of *Abe Lincoln in Illinois* is introduced when Lincoln tells Graham that he thinks often about death, describing his mother's death and her burial. Among the examples that Graham has Lincoln read from are a speech by Daniel Webster, a leading politician and noted orator of the time, about keeping the states united, and a poem by John Keats entitled "On Death."

Scene 2 takes place at the Rutledge Tavern, in New Salem. Lincoln is the local postmaster. This scene helps to establish his fine reputation among the uneducated country people. It begins with Judge Bowling Green and Joshua Speed, two friends of Lincoln's, bringing the governor's son, Ninian Edwards, to meet him. They buy drinks for an old veteran of the Revolutionary War, and they discuss the fact that Ann Rutledge, the daughter of the tavern owner, has become engaged to a man who ran off on her, much to her shame and horror. A gang of local toughs enters, and their leader, Jack Armstrong, threatens to fight with Edwards until Lincoln shows up. Armstrong knows that Lincoln is the only man in the territory who can beat him in a fight; Lincoln jokes with him so that Armstrong can back out of fighting with honor. Green, Speed, and Edwards explain to Lincoln their real reason for coming to see him. Knowing the prestige he has in the community, they want him to run for the state assembly. Lincoln, who owes fifteen hundred dollars because of a failed business venture, says that he will consider it. In the mail that he has brought to the tavern, there are two letters of significance. The first is from Seth Gale, with whom Lincoln had planned to move West, which says that Gale has to return home to the family farm. The second letter comes to Ann Rutledge, from her fiancé, announcing that he will not return to her. Lincoln announces that he is in love with Ann, and, to improve himself and earn her love, he goes off to find Bowling Green to accept the political nomination.

In Scene 3, Lincoln has been elected and is back from the state assembly in Vandalia because Ann Rutledge is ill. The action in this scene takes place in the home of Bowling Green, where Lincoln is staying while visiting. Green, his wife Nancy, and Josh Speed discuss Lincoln, how much he loves Ann Rutledge, how he has failed in business, and how unimpressive he is in the legislature. When Lincoln enters, he is crushed because Ann has died. He wants to go out, but his friends convince him to go upstairs and go to bed.

Robert E. Sherwood

Act II

The action of the play's second act takes place in the 1840s, in and around Springfield, which became Illinois' state capitol in 1837. Lincoln, at thirty-one, is a lawyer. Scene 4 takes place in his law office, on the second floor of the courthouse. He and his clerk, Billy Herndon, discuss the issue of slavery, with Lincoln taking the issue that free states should respect the sovereignty of the states that allowed slavery. Bowling Green and Josh Speed stop in to visit, and, in a general discussion of the South's threat to quit the union and form their own nation, Lincoln explains that his position is one of pacifism: he could not support fighting over it. Ninian Edwards comes in and invites them all to a party at his house where he hopes that Lincoln and the town's other eligible bachelors, including Stephen Douglas, will meet his unmarried sister-in-law, Mary Todd.

In Scene 5, Elizabeth Edwards objects to her sister Mary's choice of Abe Lincoln for a husband, though Ninian points out his promising career as a politician. When Mary enters, she explains that she sees Lincoln as a man with great potential, one who has not fenced himself in with the illusion of security. Lincoln enters and says that he is going to represent Duff, the son of Jack Armstrong, who tried to fight with Ninian in Scene 2. Duff is accused of murder, and Lincoln thinks he is clearly guilty, but he will represent him for old time's sake.

The action returns to Lincoln's law office in Scene 6, a few weeks later. Lincoln has his friend Josh Speed read a letter that Lincoln intends to send to Mary, breaking off their engagement. He has been to Bowling Green's funeral that morning, and it has made him philosophical about life. Ninian Edwards tells Lincoln to be careful of Mary's ambition: "My wife tells me that even as a child she had delusions of grandeur—she predicted to one and all that the man she would marry would be President of the United States." Josh throws Lincoln's letter to Mary in the fireplace. Even Billy Herndon, who does not like Mary much, agrees that it would be wrong to call off the wedding; he is a staunch abolitionist and sees the move as Lincoln's way of ducking his social responsibility.

Scene 7 is set outdoors, near New Salem. Lincoln has been traveling over the prairie for almost two years since breaking his engagement. Seth Gale, who was forced to move back to the family farm, is now free and traveling with his wife and son to the West, but his son has become ill. Jack Armstrong is with the family, and Lincoln has been looking for a doctor. When Lincoln arrives, there is some talk about whether the new states opening in the West will have slavery. His friends convince Lincoln to say a prayer over the sick boy, and he does so, showing the oratory skills he is remembered for today.

Scene 8 is very brief. Lincoln returns to the Edwards' house and explains to Mary what he has learned about life, responsibility, and destiny by encountering his friends moving into the new territory and the threat to the child's life. He asks her to marry, giving his promise that he will not run from his responsibility again.

Act III

Act III takes place in Springfield. Scene 9 presents one of the famous Lincoln-Douglas debates of 1858, with Stephen Douglas arguing that the North should tolerate slavery in the South and Lincoln arguing that the country cannot continue as it has been, half slave and half free, and that the South cannot be allowed to separate itself from the United States.

Lincoln and his family—Mary and his three sons, the oldest one a student at Harvard—are visiting the Edwards' house in Scene 10. Lincoln tells the boys about the time, depicted in scene 7, when he went for a doctor for the sick boy on the prairie. When Mary finds out that a committee of politicians is coming to the house to discuss the possibility of running for president, she is in a fit of rage because the house is dirty. The members of the committee have different ideas of Lincoln as a candidate. Sturveson, a businessman, questions whether Lincoln would be good for business interests because he supports the common people. Barrick, a clergyman, is bothered because Lincoln is not affiliated with any church. But Crimmin, a political operative, is impressed with the way that Lincoln handles their hostility and feels that he could win the election.

Scene 11 takes place at Lincoln's campaign headquarters on election night, 1860. In the tension of the vote count that shows Lincoln trailing but gaining, Mary becomes upset, and Lincoln angrily curses her. He apologizes almost immediately, but it is too late: "This is the night I dreamed about, as a child. . . . This is the night when I'm waiting to hear that my husband has become President of the United States. And even if he does—it's ruined, for me. It's too late." As the election results continue, Lincoln wins. Almost immediately a security officer, Kavanagh, attaches himself to Lincoln, to protect him from Southerners who have sworn to kill him. The security guards place themselves between Lincoln and the people who elected him.

In Scene 12, Lincoln boards the train that will take him to Washington. Kavanagh discusses the danger that Lincoln is in (foreshadowing the assassin's bullet that eventually killed him), and Lincoln, in a final speech to the people of Illinois, talks about the struggle to hold the Union together, even if war is the result. The crowd sings as his train pulls away.

CHARACTERS

Jack Armstrong

Armstrong is the leader and the most aggressive of the Clary's Grove Boys, a gang of bullies in New Salem. When the gang enters the Rutledge Tavern, Armstrong speaks roughly to Ann Rutledge and tries to pick a fight with Ninian Edwards. He stops when Lincoln enters, though. He respects Lincoln, in part because Lincoln is a man of the people and not a rich sophisticate like Edwards, but mostly he respects Lincoln because Lincoln is the only man in the territory who can beat him in a fight. Lincoln shows respect for Armstrong, too, preferring to joke with him rather than threaten him. Years later, Lincoln mentions that he is defending Armstrong's son Duff on a murder charge, even though Duff seems to be hopelessly guilty. Armstrong is the one to bring Lincoln to the aid of Seth Gale when Jimmy Gale falls sick as the family is passing through New Salem.

Billy

See William Herndon

Stephen A. Douglas

Douglas was a politician who ran against Lincoln for the Senate. He was a skilled orator, only slightly less persuasive than Lincoln. The series of debates that the two men had in 1858, primarily over the issue of slavery, became national news, giving Lincoln the fame that he needed across the land to run for president. Scene 9 presents one of those debates.

Ninian Edwards

Edwards is the son of the governor of Illinois. Although he comes from a wealthy background, he is not afraid to stand up for himself and fight Jack Armstrong, if necessary, although it is likely he would lose. He is the one to introduce Lincoln to his sister-in-law, Mary Todd. During the debate between Lincoln and Stephen Douglas in Scene 9, Ninian Edwards is the narrator.

Seth Gale

At the very start of the play, Seth Gale plans to move with Lincoln out to the open territory west of the Mississippi river, where land is cheap and political systems are not yet established. He has to drop out of the plan, though, when he receives a letter saying that his father is ill and that he has to return to run the family farm. Ten years later, when his parents are dead, Seth finally does move west. While passing through New Salem with his wife, child, and a free Negro servant, Gale's son Jimmy becomes ill, and Lincoln and Jack Armstrong help out his family. Seth's family is an inspiration to Lincoln, who sees how important it is to stop slavery before it spreads to the new territory, so that people like the Gales do not have to worry about what kind of morals with which their children will be raised.

Gobey

A free Negro who works for Seth Gale's family. His father had been a slave, but was freed by Seth's father twenty years earlier. While they lived in Maryland, there was always the danger that kidnappers might abduct Gobey and take him to the South, where they would sell him as a slave.

Mentor Graham

Mentor Graham only appears in the first scene, tutoring Lincoln. The examples that he uses reflect the political attitudes that Lincoln shows later in the play, particularly the selection from Senator Daniel Webster about whether the South has a right to secede from the Union.

Bowling Green

One of Lincoln's oldest friends, Green is a judge whose influence guides Lincoln's early political career. He brings Edwards, the son of the state's governor, to see Lincoln and to consider him as a possible candidate for the state assembly. It is partially because of his grief when Bowling Green dies that Lincoln breaks off his engagement to Mary Todd and goes off for nearly two years to think.

William Herndon

A young clerk in Lincoln's law office in Springfield, Herndon is driven by two strong compulsions. The first is alcohol; there is not a scene in which he

MEDIA ADAPTATIONS

- *Abe Lincoln in Illinois* was adapted as a film in 1940, starring Raymond Massey in the title role, with Ruth Gordon and Gene Lockhart. Sherwood wrote the screenplay, which was adapted by Grover Jones; John Cromwell directed. Available from Turner Home Video's RKO Collection.

- There is a 41-minute audio cassette version of the play entitled *Abe Lincoln in Illinois: Robert Sherwood's Political Drama of a Lincoln Few People Knew.* Released by the Center for Cassette Studies in 1971.

is not either drunk or on his way to get himself a drink. Lincoln notes in Act IV that when Herndon leaves to take some papers to the clerk's office, which is downstairs in the same building, he takes his hat, which is a sign that he intends to go to the saloon. Herndon's other driving passion is his staunch opposition to slavery. He functions as Lincoln's conscience on the slavery issue. While Lincoln himself takes a tolerant attitude toward the laws of the South, Herndon is more radical, constantly pushing him to speak out against slavery, to refuse to associate with slaveholders or with supporters of slavery. Although Lincoln privately opposes slavery, he resists Herndon's efforts to get him to speak out against it at political gatherings.

Kavanagh

Kavanagh is a secret service agent who moves in to protect Lincoln immediately after he is elected president. His presence indicates the way that the office distances the man from the men who helped him get there. Immediately after the election returns are announced, Kavanagh moves in, coming between Lincoln and the people, walking before Lincoln through doorways to look for assassins. His concern is not just a matter of paranoia; as he points out, there were many threats on Lincoln's life by Southerners who felt that he would endanger their right to own slaves. Audiences, of course, know that Lincoln was killed by an assassin, so all of Kavanagh's precautions have an element of prophecy to them.

Abe Lincoln

This play is about the formative years of Abraham Lincoln, explaining how he grew in outlook and popularity from a simple country man to the president of the United States. As a result, every scene of the play either has Lincoln in it or has people talking about him. In the beginning, Lincoln is in his early twenties and being tutored in English grammar at night, using a variety of texts for examples. Even at such a young age, he is financially destitute, having invested in a business with a man who ran away with all of the funds and feeling responsible for paying back all creditors. He is already haunted by death, having helped his father make a coffin for his mother when she died out in the prairie wilderness. He is popular with the men of New Salem, where he delivers mail. He is in love with Ann Rutledge, but when her fiancé drops her and Lincoln has a slight chance with her, she dies. After Lincoln begins practicing in Springfield, he becomes engaged to Mary Todd, whose ambitions for his political career are greater than his own. On the day of his wedding, though, he runs away from her, and stays away for two years, until a chance encounter with an old friend and his family makes him think about responsibility, both to his family and to the country. He returns and marries Mary.

In the late 1850s, while they both are running for the United States Senate, he and Stephen A. Douglas have a series of debates on the subject of slavery: these debates receive much attention and make Lincoln's name a household word. A committee of civic leaders comes to him to ask if he is interested in running for president. The final chapter of the play presents his farewell speech to the people of Illinois. Lincoln is not entirely enthusiastic about being the president—he tells friends that he expects to die, and he feels cut off by security measures from the people he knows best, the common people. He and Mary Todd are both unhappy in their marriage, but both are driven toward the presidency.

Ann Rutledge

Ann is the daughter of the owner of Rutledge Tavern, a meeting place in New Salem. She is forced to take orders from the tough local people who order her around when they want drinks. Lincoln has a crush on her, but he is not able to say so because she is engaged, and also because he is a homely man with financial debt and no social prestige. In Act II, a letter comes from Ann's fiancé, Mr. McNiel, and Lincoln recognizes the handwriting and the fact that it has come from New York State. Seeing that it has upset her, he asks and finds out that McNiel probably is not coming back. Because Ann is upset about what people will say about her when they find out that her fiancé has dropped her, Lincoln declares his love for her, hoping that she could use an engagement with him to explain breaking up with McNiel. She tells him that she has never thought of him like that, and that she would have to consider his proposal. In the following scene, Lincoln's political patrons, Green and Speed, discuss the fact that his romance with her might hinder Lincoln's political career, but Lincoln arrives soon after with the startling news that she has died of a sickness that they all thought she would easily survive.

Joshua Speed

Described in Scene 2 as "quiet, mild, solid, thoughtful, well-dressed," Speed is from Springfield, and is a member of the Whig party who knows the small local towns like New Salem well enough to think of Lincoln when asked who might be a good candidate for the state assembly. He is full of admiration for Lincoln, but has doubts about his ability for success: "he has plenty of strength and courage in his body," Speed tells Bowling and Nancy Green, "but in his mind he's a hopeless hypochondriac." Speed is usually present in meetings for political planning, but he is not very instrumental, usually limiting his input to asking questions and giving encouraging advice. In a decisive moment, he destroys the letter that Lincoln has written to Mary to break off their engagement.

Mary Todd

Mary is a willful woman, a bright, well-connected socialite, the daughter of the president of the Bank of Kentucky. She has many suitors, including Stephen Douglas, but to the surprise of her sister, Elizabeth Edwards, she chooses to marry Lincoln. Her choice is carefully thought out; she sees him, of all of the eligible bachelors around, to be the one with the greatest potential. She does not want social prestige or financial comfort and would live in poverty, "so long as there is forever before me the chance for high adventure—so long as I can know that I am always going forward, with my husband, along that road that leads to the horizon." On the day of their wedding, Lincoln gets cold feet and runs away, but when he returns two years later Mary accepts him back and marries him. Mary becomes very status conscious when she is married to him, which causes strain in their marriage. She is horrified that he has invited several politicians over without telling her, because she feels that the house is not sufficiently clean. She refuses to let him smoke in the house, and so, when one of the politicians lights a cigar, Lincoln encourages him, telling him to bring it along as he comes to the dining room. On the night of his election to the presidency, they have a serious fight. Nervous about the changing results, Mary becomes hysterical and shouts, "You only want to be rid of me! That's what you've wanted ever since the day we married—and before that. Anything to get me out of your sight, because you hate me!" Lincoln calmly asks the other people to leave the room before shouting back at her. Even though he immediately apologizes, Mary declares that he has ruined the most important day of her life.

THEMES

Death

Lincoln's life, as it is presented in this play, was ruled by his feelings about the deaths that he witnessed. Lincoln's issues with death begin early, in the first scene, when Lincoln tells Mentor Graham that he thinks about death often "because it has always seemed to be close to me—as far back as I can remember." He then describes helping build a coffin for his mother, who died when he was young, relating it to the men he saw in New Orleans who "had murder in their hearts." The theme of death is continued with his loss of Ann Rutledge, the woman that he loved, who was socially and physically out of his league. Her death causes him to retreat from his political rise. He explains to Bowling and Nancy Green, "I couldn't give any devotion to one who has the power of death, and uses it"—a statement referring to prayer, but with implications to the responsibilities he will accept as president, sending troops off to war. Just as Ann's death drives him away from political involvement, the death of his longtime friend Bowling Green makes him retreat from his planned marriage to Mary Todd. It is the near-death of young Jimmy Gale, though, that pulls him back into a sense of responsibility in both political and personal arenas. His prayer at the end of Scene 7 relates life to freedom and death to imprisonment and shows Lincoln shifting from despair to hope. Throughout the whole play, one element of death remains constant. His expectation of his own early death is present in the first scene, with his fear of the city, and is still present in the final scene, when, as Elizabeth points out, he always prefaces his plans with, "If I live . . ."

Doubt and Ambiguity

Abe Lincoln in Illinois offers audiences a new way to look at Lincoln. Popular conception, based on his decisive actions during the Civil War, remember him as a man with a vision, who could see the necessity of fighting to preserve the Union no matter what the cost, and historical studies almost unanimously praise him for making the right choices. What Sherwood presents in this play, however, is a view of Lincoln as an uncertain man who in no way felt that he knew the right thing to do and who did what he could to avoid the responsibility of making decisions about the lives of others. From the moment when it is first suggested that he might run for political office, in Scene 2, he comes up with various excuses why the people would not want to vote for him, and why he himself is unfit for the position. His run for the presidency is just as clouded by doubt. "I'm afraid I can't go quite that far in self-esteem," he tells the committee that comes to offer him the nomination. In addition, he is never confident in romance, humbly asking Ann Rutledge to consider him in spite of his faults, and later backing out on his marriage to Mary Todd on their wedding day because, as his letter puts it, their marriage "could only lead to endless pain and misery for them both." In his notes, Sherwood points out that the real Lincoln did not seem so ambiguous, especially regarding his own political career; while the play presents him as someone who has to be dragged to action, he was actually a much more active participant in his own fate. For the sake of drama, this man, who is known all over the world as a fearless leader, is presented as growing into his fearlessness and confidence in his early, formative years.

War and Peace

Lincoln's entire presidency was engulfed by the Civil War. Some Southern states split away from the country before he even took office. The war began when Southern troops fired on Fort Sumter, just over a month after he was inaugurated, and he was assassinated five days after the South surrendered. It is ironic that he is so closely associated with war, when Lincoln, as presented in this

TOPICS FOR FURTHER STUDY

- Read the text of the Lincoln-Douglas debates and rate each speaker in terms of how well he argues his point.

- Research the life of a rural postmaster in the 1830s and write out an agenda that would show what a typical day was like.

- The tension between Lincoln and his wife, Mary, in Scene 9 is just a slight example of their tumultuous relationship. Write a scene that shows them arguing at home during the last year of his presidency, using historic facts to support your characterizations.

- Write a brief report on the Underground Railroad, which helped blacks escape from slavery in the South into freedom.

- Much is made in this play of how the Supreme Court's decision in the Dred Scott case changed the rights of slave owners and mobilized the opposition to slavery. Find testimony from people of the 1850s (besides Lincoln) stating what this decision meant to their lives.

- Lincoln had less than a half year of formal schooling in his life. Find out what level of education has been attained by recent presidents, from the 1940s on.

- The "milksick" that Lincoln's mother died of was later diagnosed as a disease that came from drinking the milk of cows that had ingested white snakeroot. Find out the story behind how this was discovered and how this illness affects the body.

- Write a paper that imagines what the United States would have been like if Lincoln had allowed the Confederate states to secede from the Union.

---

play, is a man who supported peace at almost any cost. Throughout much of the play, Lincoln opposes slavery, but he does not oppose it strongly enough to support open hostility over it. In Scene 4, he speaks with disgust about seeing slaves shackled together, but when he is asked to participate in a rally against slavery he dismisses the opponents of slavery as "a pack of hell-roaring fanatics." He equates opposition to slavery with violence, and so he cannot condone it. He feels that the abolitionists who are fighting to abolish slavery are agitators who should be put in jail for disturbing the peace. "I am opposed to slavery," he tells his friends. "But I'm even more opposed to going to war."

By the time of his debate against Stephen Douglas in Scene 9, he is more in favor of involvement. He opposes his own former policy, saying that the fundamental virtues of democracy are threatened by the institution of slavery: "I believe most seriously that the perpetuation of those virtues is now endangered, not only by the honest proponents of slavery, but even more by those who echo Judge Douglas in shouting, 'Leave it alone!'" On election night, Billy Herndon points out two facts that are evident to everybody: Lincoln will go to war against any states that try to secede, and that they will secede upon his election. Horrible as the prospect of war is, he has come, throughout the course of the play, to accept it as the only right thing to do.

STYLE

Structure

Most full-length plays are divided into two or three acts, or, as in the case of most of Shakespeare's works, into five. Each of these acts is further divided into scenes, usually two or three per act. Very few dramas reach the level of twelve scenes, as *Abe Lincoln in Illinois* does. In addition, very few are written for a cast as large as this, which has more than thirty performers. This is a work of epic scope, fitting three decades of Lincoln's life into a few hours onstage. It incorporates many familiar moments and expressions that are part of the Lincoln legend, as well as new ones that were fabricated by Sherwood to dramatize the aspects of Lincoln's character that he thought were most important. There is no consistency in the lengths of the individual acts, nor is there any pattern used in the play's structure to remind readers of things that came before. For instance, Scene 8 is the shortest scene, just a little more than four pages, which is a length not approached by any other scene. It is not part of any larger repeating pattern, either; there is no real relationship between Scene 8, which ends Act II, and either of the scenes that end the first or third acts. The structure of this play is not aimed at any measurable sense of style, it is aimed at making sure that all of the important parts of the Lincoln legend have been taken into account.

Because it is a biography, the most obvious structure, the one that Sherwood used, is chronological, following the order of time. Other plays use devices such as flashbacks, to tell what happened earlier in time, or tricks of lighting to show action that happens in two different places at once. *Abe Lincoln in Illinois* starts when Lincoln is twenty-one and progresses straight through to his election to the presidency. It would be a simple structure, if not for the many scene changes and characters involved.

Setting

The setting of this play is crucial to its message. It is a play about Lincoln's formative years, how he came to be the president that he was. It does not focus solely on his formative years in the wilderness, but presents Lincoln within a period of transformation. In the early scenes around New Salem, in the first act, he is light-hearted, good-natured, well liked, but unsure. His attitude is changed by the death of Ann Rutledge, who succumbs to "the brain sickness." Like Seth Gale's son Jimmy, who is overcome in Scene 7 with "the swamp fever," and Lincoln's own mother, whom he describes as having died of "the milksick," people out in the prairie were susceptible to disease and early death. When Lincoln moves to Springfield, the issues examined by the play take on a more political nature. His rise in politics coincides with scenes that are set in offices and homes. In these settings, political issues are discussed, especially the burning issue of the day: slavery. This follows naturally because Lincoln is a politician, but it also is more expected that people in town would be aware of national political issues than people in remote villages like New Salem, where the news is delivered once a week. A turning point in Lincoln's life comes when he discusses the issue of slavery with the Gale family on the prairie, as they are passing from the sophisticated, crowded East Coast to the unsettled space in the West, and he realizes that slavery affects people in all areas of the country, no matter how remote.

The importance of this play's prairie setting can be seen in the fact that it ends when Lincoln leaves Illinois. In part, this change is required by the play's title—it only promises to tell audiences about his life in Illinois—but it also makes thematic and psychological sense to consider a chapter of his development complete and fulfilled.

HISTORICAL CONTEXT

The Abolitionist Movement

Slavery existed in the United States from the earliest colonial days, with settlers first using captured Native Americans to do the heavy labor of cultivating and then importing poor people from Europe to work as indentured servants, a position almost equal to slavery. In the 1680s, southern landowners began importing slaves from Africa. From colonial times, laws defined black slaves and their children as property, to be owned for life. The invention of the cotton gin in 1793 made it easier to process cotton and increased the demand for cotton. In the South, which had the soil and climate for cotton production, slavery became an institution and a necessary part of the economy.

The Abolitionist Movement, which fought to abolish slavery, is generally considered to have started in 1831, when the newspaper *The Liberator* began publication in Boston. A few years later, in 1833, which is the year of the first act of *Abe Lincoln in Illinois,* delegates from all over the country met in Philadelphia to form the American Anti-Slavery Society, which was to become the principle organization for fighting for slaves' freedom. It was a time of vocal opposition to injustice, especially in the New England states. There were movements to encourage the government to adapt free schooling, workers rights, and voting rights for women, and groups that wanted the government to put an end to slavery, consumption of alcohol, and imprisonment for debt. Out of this rash of social movements, the Abolitionist Movement was to be-

COMPARE & CONTRAST

- **1837:** Chicago is incorporated as a city.

  1938: At a time when freight is moved by rail and barges, Chicago is the country's second largest city, only losing that title to Los Angeles in the 1990s.

  Today: Although they are still in the same state, Chicago has little in common with rural downstate towns like New Salem and Vandalia.

- **1830s–60s:** Most black people in Southern states are slaves. Blacks living in states that bordered the Southern states are sometimes kidnapped and forced into slavery. The Supreme Court rules in 1857 that blacks can never become U. S. citizens.

  1938: Although slavery is technically over when the Civil War ends in 1865, a series of laws passed in the South, known as Jim Crow Laws, keep blacks from enjoying their rights as citizens. Difficult IQ tests are given at polls to keep blacks from voting, and the charade of offering ''separate but equal'' accommodations leave blacks with inferior housing, food, and education.

  Today: The Civil Rights Act of 1964 threatens serious federal punishment for anyone who discriminates on the basis of race.

- **1830s:** The economic depression, which begins in 1837, is eventually overcome with new resources acquired by expanding the nation westward.

  1938: The economic depression, begun in 1929, is eventually overcome by an increase in manufacturing when America enters World War II in 1941.

  Today: The economic recession of the 1980s is eventually overcome, in part by the new business resources made available by the growth of the Internet.

- **1830s:** A message going from rural Illinois to Washington, D. C. has to be carried by train or horseback, and takes more than a week.

  1938: Telephones are common in most households; verbal messages can span the continent almost immediately. A written message takes a few days, unless sent by airplane with a special courier.

  Today: A message can be sent via fax or e-mail attachment almost immediately.

- **1830s:** Food has to be eaten fresh or else preserved with salt, limiting how far people can live from farms.

  1938: Precooked frozen meals become available from Birdseye, which has been offering frozen vegetables since 1931.

  Today: Foods are sealed in packages so that they can be kept fresh in cabinets or desk drawers without refrigeration.

---

come one of the largest and most lasting. Its members, like Billy Herndon in *Abe Lincoln in Illinois,* were passionate in their opposition to slavery, and they kept pressure on the government to limit the spread of slave ownership as the country grew.

The Kansas-Nebraska Act

Throughout this play, Abraham Lincoln becomes increasingly conscious of how slavery affects his life, even though he lives in a free state and would rather ignore the issue altogether. One of the reasons that Americans were so aware of slavery in the 1830s to 1860s was that the country was still expanding westward, and when each new territory applied to become a state, there had to be a decision about whether it would be free or slave. The issue was settled for a long time by the Missouri Compromise, which was a series of legislative measures enacted in 1820. To get around Southern opposition to Maine entering the Union as a free state and Northern opposition to Missouri entering as a slave state, Congress decreed that future slavery states would be limited to those south of a line near 36 degrees latitude. By the 1850s, though, activists on both sides of the issue were becoming angry about the gains that were being made on the other side. Congress passed a new law, the Kansas-Nebraska Act, which superseded the Missouri Compromise.

Some politicians, led by Illinois Senator Stephen A. Douglas (who appears as a character in this play), fought for measures that would allow new territories to vote on whether they wanted to be free states or slave states as they entered the Union. When the Kansas Territory was opened for settlement in 1854, the Kansas-Nebraska Act was passed, allowing the issue of slavery to be settled by popular vote. Thousands of settlers crossed the border from pro-slavery Missouri, and, to counter their votes, thousands of Abolitionists came from the Northeast. The violence that followed was extreme, earning the territory the nickname "Bloody Kansas." Compromise measures to end the killing were suggested, voted upon, and rejected, until Kansas finally was admitted to the Union as a free state in 1861. In the meantime, though, the country had seen that emotions on the slavery issue were so strong that they could not be ignored or be left to settle themselves in a spirit of cooperation. The face of politics had changed: the Whig party, which had existed since the country was formed, was so divided that it eventually dissolved, and in its place rose a new party: the Republicans. When the Democrats nominated Douglas as their presidential candidate in 1860, southern Democrats objected, putting forward their own candidate instead. The split in the Democratic party allowed Lincoln to win the election in 1860.

Theater in the 1930s

The Great Depression began in 1929, two years after the first commercially successful sound movie. During the 1930s, audiences shifted their attention to movies, which cost a fraction of what plays cost and were able to bring the biggest stars to small towns all across America, all at the same time. Theater became more of an isolated pursuit, written for and enjoyed by an educated class. At the same time, intellectual circles, disappointed by the failure of the American economy, began experimenting with other forms of government, such as communism and socialism. In some ways, this new social consciousness resembled the rise of the social movements like the abolitionists in New England in the 1830s. Some theater groups were formed on socialist principles, with equal rights granted to all players and decisions made by group consent. For instance, the members of the American Laboratory Theater not only worked together, but lived together, as well, and the members of the Mercury Theater staged *The Cradle Will Rock* without any sets or costumes after the government withdrew its support money, claiming that its pro-union stance was too controversial.

Abe Lincoln in Illinois was the first production of the Playwrights' Company, a group that Sherwood and several other writers formed in response to the mishandling of their plays by members of the Dramatists' Guild. They felt that the Guild was too wrapped up with making petty decisions about casting and rights for movie adaptations to present their works properly, so they decided to form their own group. Sherwood, Elmer Rice, Maxwell Anderson, Sidney Howard, and S. N. Behrman founded the Playwrights' Company in 1938. At the time, Sherwood had almost completed *Abe Lincoln in Illinois,* so he presented it to the others in the group, and it was the first play that they staged, with great success.

CRITICAL OVERVIEW

Critics have considered Robert E. Sherwood's drama *Abe Lincoln in Illinois* to be a labor of love, and an important part of the mythology that defines the American character, but the general consensus among serious critics is that it is not a very well-crafted piece. Even before this play was produced, Eleanor Flexner identified several repetitive aspects of Sherwood's plots. "A man—wise, cynical, and charming—finds the answer to his quest for the meaning of life, in a woman; suddenly he falls in love, no less suddenly his life is wrenched from its old pattern, and in three cases out of four he goes gallantly to his death in consequence." She went on to identify the background of war as a device that Sherwood used for sustaining tension, "a device forced upon him by his inability to construct a play in which the suspense will arise from the actions of the characters themselves." Flexner found these plot elements overextended in 1938, and it is unlikely that she would have found much changed in *Abe Lincoln In Illinois,* from the title character's doomed but ennobling love for Ann Rutledge to his own impending fate.

When the play was produced, critical responses were mixed. It was immensely popular, running on Broadway for 472 performances, longer than any of Sherwood's other works, and it was successfully adapted to a movie in 1940, for which Sherwood wrote the script. Many critics accepted it, as audiences did, as an entertaining dramatization of the old legends, and these critics endorsed the play enthusiastically, but with the slightly condescending sense that viewing it would be one's civic duty. More thoughtful critics, however, held the play to a higher standard, and these writers seemed to find it their reluctant duty to point out its flaws. Even Carl Sandburg, whose three-volume biography of Lincoln was one of Sherwood's main biographical sources, seemed to choose his words of praise very carefully. Instead of saying that Sherwood has done a fine job of translating Lincoln's life to the stage, Sandburg tells readers that Sherwood was conscious of using good sources and also of the fact that he needed to change some facts for dramatic purpose. The introduction continued with further evasion, telling readers that Sherwood's play "carries some shine of the American dream," that it "delivers great themes of human wit, behavior and freedom." What was lacking, in this discussion of Sherwood's methods, was any statement that it is consistently good.

Sandburg implied that the play bends reality too much for the sake of popularity—his only criticism of a more accurate drama is that people might not go "to see or value it as a drama." Other critics, in contrast, have found that Sherwood did not take enough dramatic license with his biographical material. Francis Fergusson, writing in the *Southern Review,* felt that the play offered a succession of elements of the Lincoln legend without ever coming together as a unified work of art. "We never get the immediate sense of actuality which good drama gives and which comes from the vitality and dramatic necessity of each character and the imaginative consistency of the whole," he wrote. The facts of Lincoln's life, Fergusson wrote, just were not enough to tell the story: "they may be history, they may be souvenirs, but they are not drama." He noted that Sherwood's supporting characters, such as Mary Todd and Joshua Speed, "owe their existence to the books, they have no life of their own." They are "perfunctory, like the Martha Washington in the school pageant."

After Sherwood's death, a critical biography by R. Baird Shuman was able to look at the context of all of his works. "If Robert Sherwood were to be remembered for any one of his plays," Shuman wrote, "it is likely that the play which would fix his name in the galaxy of the immortals is *Abe Lincoln In Illinois.* The Lincoln play is not his best drama, but more people have probably seen it and been affected by it than by any of his other productions." Like most critics, Shuman was willing to admit that his own misgivings about the play's artistry must give way to its immense popularity.

In 1970, Walter J. Meserve came close to defining that exotic mixture of talent and popular sensibility that made Sherwood's work difficult for critics to either love or ignore. "It is easy enough to describe the part that Sherwood did not play," he wrote. "He was not an experimenter nor an innovator, nor was he an influential dramatist in the developing American theatre. He was not a theorist; in fact, one of his friends and directors stated that he did not have a theory of drama.... He was, of course, a dramatist who naturally and frankly dealt with the emotions that America wanted to feel, who knew how to express them in good theatre." With the benefit of looking back in time, Meserve was able to summarize Sherwood's career and mixed accomplishments with respect but not flattery: "Never a great playwright, he spoke intensely and with wit and integrity during a period in history when such plays as his were needed."

CRITICISM

David Kelly

Kelly is an instructor of Creative Writing and Script Writing at two colleges in Illinois. In the following essay, he discusses the inherent limitations of writing biographical drama.

One of the most respected of all American historical biographies for the stage is Robert E. Sherwood's play *Abe Lincoln in Illinois.* It is a difficult piece to judge objectively, since it concerns a president who, more than most, is key to how Americans see themselves. Lincoln was a man of the people, a pioneer who came to be president without a law degree or much formal schooling at all. He was a compassionate man, willing to face up to a force as powerful as the Confederacy to end slavery. There are folktales about Lincoln, and there are

Raymond Massey (as Abraham Lincoln) and Ruth Gordon (as Mary Todd Lincoln) in a scene from the film adaptation of Abe Lincoln in Illinois.

many witticisms attributed to him, whether he said them or not.

Sherwood was right to realize the dramatic potential inherent in the story of Abraham Lincoln, right to realize that the story of Lincoln's life before his presidency had enough dramatic potential to captivate audiences. One thing that he might not have been right about, though, is the labor and responsibility involved in constructing a biographical work for the stage. The version of Lincoln that Sherwood presents is reverent and accurate, but Sherwood does not imbue his character with the kind of fire and consistency needed to make him come to life. The problem does not seem to be in Sherwood's writing, which is, at the least, craftsmanlike, but in the very nature of what he is trying to do.

Biographies have always been written, and they always will be. They represent one of the most basic functions of literature, the opportunity to look at other people's lives and compare them to one's own. Biographies are treated with a level of respect above that allowed to fiction because they are, in some ill-defined way, considered to be "real." In

WHAT DO I READ NEXT?

- Critics consider *The Petrified Forest* to be Sherwood's most successful play. It is about an intellectual war veteran facing a dangerous gangster in a diner out in the desert. It is available from the Dramatist's Play Service.

- Much of Sherwood's information about Lincoln comes from the poet Carl Sandburg's thorough biography, *Lincoln: The Prairie Years*, which is often bound with the other volume of his biography, *The War Years*.

- Lincoln was very secretive about his family life. The source that most historians begin with for biographical information is the writings of William Herndon (who appears in the play as Billy Herndon). His biography is available as *Herndon's Life of Lincoln: The History and Personal Recollections of Abraham Lincoln*. A 1997 collection called *Herndon's Informants: Letters, Interviews and Statements about Abraham Lincoln* explores Herndon's own sources of information.

- One of the few book-length studies of Sherwood is John Mason Brown's critical biography *The Worlds of Robert E. Sherwood: Mirror to His Times, 1896–1939*. Missing from this work is Sherwood's career during World War II.

- This play presents the formation of Lincoln's sense of responsibility. The resultant sensibilities are examined in Mark E. Neely, Jr.'s 1992 Pulitzer Prize-winning study *The Fate of Liberty: Abraham Lincoln and Civil Liberties*.

- Gore Vidal's novel *Lincoln* is like Sherwood's version in that it is an entertaining, speculative work, based in fact but stretched to tell an interesting story. It was reissued in a 1998 paperback edition.

- Historians have long relied on Harvey Lee Ross' book *The Early Pioneers and Political Events of the State of Illinois*, first published in 1899. It was reprinted in 1970 by Stevens Publishing Co. of Astoria, IL.

---

this modern age of made-for-television movies and rampant lawsuits, the nuances involved with representations of reality are commonplace. Almost everybody knows that "based on a true story" is different than "based on actual events," which is different than "inspired by actual events." The number of variations on the theme of reality is a testimony to the great value placed by our culture on real-life drama.

Western culture has come to some sort of understanding with biographical books, which are just naturally assumed without much thought to be mostly true, perhaps around ninety percent or more based on what actually happened. Biographies sit in their own sections of libraries and bookstores, comfortably nestled between the textbooks, which ought to be one hundred percent true, and the novels, which tell made-up stories. Recently, political biographies have played around with the form and have upset the assumption of truth. One writer has presented Edward Kennedy's private thoughts, which the writer could of course only have guessed at, as if they were verifiable facts. Another said that he could find no way of writing his biography of president Ronald Reagan without including himself as a character—not just as someone passing by in the background, but as a boyhood friend who in fact never existed. The very fact that these experiments upset the traditional notion of biography is an indication that, in general, readers feel comfortable with their understanding of how much in biographical books is true.

The same cannot be said about movies and plays, where the biographical subject has to be portrayed by someone else. While it represents just a slight shift from the "textbook" frame of mind to a written biography, in terms of how much truth can be expected, there is a leap of abstraction when one person recreates what another person did.

Art is artifice. Theater is one of the most artificial forms of art, asking its audience to believe that people are in places, as strange as a boat or a log cabin, when they are in fact just steps away. If viewers stop suspending their disbelief for a moment, they become aware of the untruth of it all, of the actors in costumes who actually share the same reality as the ticket rippers, the lighting system, and all of the rest of the trappings.

It seems that playwrights should count themselves lucky enough when their audiences are willing to pretend that the people they are seeing are real people, in real situations. The playwright who wants viewers to believe that the people on stage are in fact reproducing actions and situations that have actually occurred before in the world is really stretching credibility thin. The Abe Lincoln in Carl Sandburg's three-part biography is likely to resemble how Lincoln really was, his essence captured in the poet's words. William Herndon's biography of Lincoln has been praised for being less likely than the writings of the president's other friends to hide his unsavory characteristics, achieving a level of truth greater than the sugar-coated version. Robert Sherwood's Lincoln, however, will always be whoever is portraying him—Raymond Massey, in the case of the Broadway production and the subsequent film.

Drama lacks accuracy—it cannot record events, but only reproduce them. Biography is, though, at its core an accurate record. At its best, drama can give its audience some sense of the essence of a person, a truer philosophical feel for personality than simple, recorded historical fact. Audiences understand things that are not shown outright, like an optical illusion that arranges black dots on a white page to make the viewer see another dot that is not really there. With *Abe Lincoln in Illinois,* it is not enough to present a series of events from Lincoln's life. The question that every reviewer has to ask when considering Sherwood's script is whether it at least gives a complete portrait of who Lincoln might have been.

The straightforward chronological structure of *Abe Lincoln in Illinois* is the first clue that Sherwood may have allowed his play to be ruled by reality as readers know it, rather than his artistic reality. In common reality, childhood is followed by adolescence, which is followed by adulthood, then old age. There is no reason why a narrative has to

"AT ITS BEST, DRAMA CAN GIVE ITS AUDIENCE SOME SENSE OF THE ESSENCE OF A PERSON, A TRUER PHILOSOPHICAL FEEL FOR PERSONALITY THAN SIMPLE RECORDED HISTORICAL FACT."

follow such a structure, though. It depends on what point the writer is trying to make. In the case at hand, Sherwood's point might be to examine how the cumulative weight of events built, year after year, to make Lincoln into the man he was when he boarded the train out of Illinois, shown in the last act. The chronological structure, though, is reason enough for at least suspecting that Sherwood might lack imagination and/or an artistic vision.

This is not to say that Sherwood, or anyone involved in the original Broadway production, did not do the best job possible, only that the thing they were trying to do may have been self-defeating. By all accounts, *Abe Lincoln in Illinois* was not something that Robert E. Sherwood dashed off quickly. According to his biographer, John Mason Brown, Sherwood worked the structure repeatedly in his mind, cutting scenes, adding, struggling to turn his Lincoln into an American archetype. The supplemental notes that are usually printed with the play should be sufficient indication that this play is no sloppy piece of work. It is, however, stiff, the sort of presentation that has audiences leaving the theater feeling more like they have been taught a lesson than that they have been entertained.

This question of whether Sherwood might have given his audience too much historical record at the expense of offering up an actual play has been a point of contention since *Abe Lincoln in Illinois* was first produced. The play did win the Pulitzer when it debuted, and it basked in the glow of critical support, overall, although some critics found it too stifled by the greatness and familiarity of the subject to ever take on a personality of its own.

It is either ironic or a sign that Sherwood worked the issue to the finest balance that could be achieved to see that both sides, cheering and dismissing his achievement, have been supported by one writer—John Mason Brown, the aforementioned biographer. In his original review of the play, Brown was one of the few critics to stray from the consensus, which was that Sherwood had done the country a great service with his portrayal of Lincoln. His original review complained that the play wasn't really Sherwood's at all, or at least wasn't solely Sherwood's accomplishment: to be honest, he would, according to Brown, have to give half of the credit to Lincoln himself, or, more specifically, to the text of the Lincoln-Douglas debates, from which he had taken so much of his dialog. He also commented on how much the play relied, not on its own dramatic situation, but on the audience's knowledge of events that were to happen in Lincoln's life after the events presented on stage.

In future years, though, Brown came to reverse his judgment. In *The Worlds of Robert E. Sherwood: Mirror to His Times,* he looked back on his old review and wrote, "I was rotten, and wrong, though not entirely so. I had some points to make which were not without their validity, though they now seem to me academic, ungrateful, and carping." Having had access to Sherwood's diaries while working on his biography, Brown had come to realize how much effort Sherwood had put into controlling the incredible amounts of information he had compiled, how he struggled to keep the process from being "too much reading, too much homework, and too little playwriting by Sherwood himself."

The background information may have helped Brown understand his subject and how his subject, Sherwood, understood his own subject, Lincoln. Still, it is almost impossible to take seriously a reviewer who takes back what he has said on the grounds of having been "ungrateful." Reviewers owe authors nothing more than an honest appraisal. One gets the sense that Brown felt he had been an ungrateful citizen for not appreciating the service done for the American populace with this portrayal of a president. But this is not a standard for artistic criticism, any more than a work of art can be judged by how "nice" its main character is.

If this country's citizens can get beyond national pride for Abraham Lincoln, who historians (Northern ones, at least) constantly rank among the two or three greatest American presidents, it does in fact seem that Sherwood's play is too focused on Lincoln as a historical figure, turning Lincoln the human being into an emblem. It could use some firmer control. Lincoln needs to be more of a character in the play, less of a caricature. This is what Shakespeare did with his histories, and England's national honor was in no way compromised by his decision to let go of some of "the truth" in order to better present the spirits of his subjects. Drama relies on the human thought processes and interactions that may not have been part of the public record, but are necessary for the playwright to really convey the nature of his subject. *Abe Lincoln in Illinois* retells old stories about the great man, and Sherwood certainly put his heart into arranging those old tales in a way that would make a larger point, but it makes for a clumsy play, so uncomfortable with itself that even readers and viewers who aren't familiar with the legends can pick out the lines that come from Lincoln himself, because they are so unevenly worked into the story.

There is no way for a play to function as a documentary, because theater, of all visual media, works on an abstract level that does not allow the use of original material. Documentary films can show viewers actual participants, or play their voices, or at least show locations where events occurred. Books have been used for conveying information for so long that most readers have a sense of how much reality to expect from them. On stage, the subject of a biography cannot speak for him- or herself, which leaves the playwright with the awful responsibility of choosing just what parts of reality to include and how to organize the facts. No one has ever raised the charge that Robert E. Sherwood was anything less than diligent in his duties as an author, but still *Abe Lincoln in Illinois* suffers from not having its own individual identity as a work of art, even though it does provide a fine overview of the most interesting facts of Lincoln's life.

Source: David Kelly, in an essay for *Drama for Students,* Gale Group, 2001.

John Mason Brown

In the essay, "Bob Sherwood in Illinois" John Mason Brown describes Abraham Lincoln as Sherwood's "hero," which was the reason for the creation of the play.

Why Abe Lincoln? Had Sherwood been a small man, he said he might, instead, have written a play about Napoleon. But Lincoln was a tall man outside and a giant within, and Sherwood a taller man who was growing inside year by year. This inner growth readied him for *Abe*—this plus the fact that, with the challenges to freedom multiplying throughout the world, Lincoln moved into the present with a new

A scene from RKO Studios' 1940 film adaptation of Abe Lincoln in Illinois.

timeliness as "a man of peace who had had to face the issue of appeasement or war."

We say much about ourselves in our choice of heroes. They are the mirrors not only of what we would like to be but a reflection in part of what we are. From his youth Lincoln had occupied a special place among Sherwood's idols. As early as 1909, when he was twelve, he submitted an essay to a nationwide school children's contest commemorating the centennial of the President's birth. For some weeks he haunted the Fifth Avenue jeweler's window in which the prize medals were on display, confident that one of them would be his. He was genuinely surprised to learn when the awards were announced that he had not received even an honorable mention.

He saw Lincoln then and for many years thereafter through the usual fog of reverence, saw him as the myth not the man, as a statue that had somehow been alive. No other hero in our history reached so deep into Sherwood's heart as this figure of sadness, suffering, homely humor, and compassion. There was a kinship between them of temperament and beliefs, of bafflement and courage, and loneliness and eloquence. Like many another, Sherwood had been stirred by John Drinkwater's *Abraham Lin-*

> "NO OTHER HERO IN OUR HISTORY REACHED SO DEEP INTO SHERWOOD'S HEART AS THIS FIGURE OF SADNESS, SUFFERING, HOMELY HUMOR, AND COMPASSION. THERE WAS A KINSHIP BETWEEN THEM OF TEMPERAMENT AND BELIEFS, OF BAFFLEMENT AND COURAGE, AND LONELINESS AND ELOQUENCE."

coln, which he saw several times in 1920 and admired greatly as a "beautiful play." Two years later even the newsreel pictures of the opening of the Lincoln Memorial in Washington moved him, he confessed in Life, to a "state of maudlin lachrymosity."

He had read much on Lincoln, first learning the details of his early life from Ida M. Tarbell and of his period from Albert Bushnell Hart. His love for him grew as his knowledge increased. It was not, however, until he read Carl Sandburg's The Prairie Years that Sherwood "began to feel the curious quality of the complex man who, in his statement of the eternal aspirations of the human race, achieved a supreme triumph of simplicity." Sandburg introduced him to a new and human Lincoln and made him eager to know more about the forces, interior and external, which "shaped this strange, gentle genius."

For some fifteen years Sherwood had talked vaguely of writing a play about Lincoln's early life. The Prairie Years (1926), which he reread again and again during the next decade, eventually strengthened his determination to do so. "Can't open this wonderful book without feeling a rush of emotion to the imagination." Sandburg gave him an understanding he had not had before of the intricacies and contradictions of Lincoln's character and served as an invaluable guide to "the main sources of Lincoln lore."

This copious lore cracked for him the marble of Lincoln as a public statue, thereby permitting the man to emerge, flesh, blood, and fallibility, and all the greater for being human. Sherwood came to see, and state conqueringly in his episodic drama, the importance of Lincoln's frailties to his virtues. More and more he realized that, however heretical any admission of Lincoln's faults might seem to those who saw him only in Daniel Chester French or Gutzon Borglum terms, these faults were a part of his size. As he put it, the doubts and fears that tormented Lincoln "could not have occurred to a lesser man" and his ultimate triumph over them was "in many ways the supreme achievement of his life."

In the winter of 1936 Sherwood began to write a play on Lincoln. At a Child's Restaurant on 48th Street he wrote the prayer for the recovery of a sick boy (really a prayer for America) which Lincoln speaks in the seventh scene. But he could get no further. His play had not formed in his mind nor his Lincoln come into focus. He needed more time in which to brood and plan and absorb. And greater and more intimate knowledge, too. Accordingly, led by Sandburg, he went to work in earnest.

Earnest in his case meant furious application. Never a decent student at school or college, Sherwood was always a painstaking researcher when, as a writer, he dealt with history. Before taking the license to which he was entitled as a dramatist, he had to know the facts from which he was departing. Hannibal, Richard Coeur de Lion and the Crusades, and Periclean Athens—all these he had read about with a scholar's zeal before handling them in his own unscholarly way. But never, until he wrote Roosevelt and Hopkins, did he immerse himself so deeply in history as when preparing to write Abe Lincoln in Illinois.

His supplementary notes, wisely printed not as an introduction but as a postscript to the play, are staggering in their thoroughness. Stephenson, Beveridge, Barton, Lord Charnwood, Evans, Baringer, the Dictionary of American Biography, Herndon and Weik (especially Herndon), and, above all, Lincoln himself as revealed in Nicolay and Hay's compilation of his Complete Works were among the sources upon which Sherwood drew with easy familiarity. He knew there were hundreds of other books which he could mention but did not, because, as he said in typical Sherwood fashion, "I haven't read them."

He had no desire in his notes to set himself up as a "learned biographer." But he was learned about Lincoln, drawn to his knowledge not only by the instinctive understanding he felt for him but by his theory of what a play about Lincoln should be. No one was more aware than Sherwood that "the playwright's chief stock in trade is feelings, not facts." A dramatist, he believed, was "at best, an interpreter, with a certain facility for translating all that he has heard in a manner sufficiently dramatic to attract a crowd." He felt, however, that in a play about the development of Lincoln's character a strict regard for the plain truth was both obligatory and desirable. "His life as he lived it was a work of art, forming a veritable allegory of the growth of the democratic spirit, with its humble origins, its inward struggles, its seemingly timid policy of 'live and let live' and 'mind your own business,' its slow awakening to the dreadful problems of reality, and its battles with and conquest of those problems."

His conviction was that, just as Lincoln's life needed no adornments to make it pertinent, his character needed "no romanticizing, no sentimentalizing, no dramatizing." To a reporter he said that, before he began, he made up his mind "not to have a line of hokum in the play. I love hoke in the theatre," he went on, "but this time I decided that, while they might say the play was dull, they couldn't say it was 'theatre.'"

To his Aunt Lydia he confided that he was "not concerned with Abraham Lincoln's position in history—because no one needs to elaborate on that. It was his remarkable character. It seems to me that all the contrasted qualities of the human race—the hopes and fears, the doubts and convictions, the mortal frailty and superhuman endurance, the prescience and the neuroses, the desire for escape from reality, and the fundamental, unshakable nobility—were concentrated and magnified in him as they were in Oedipus Rex and in Hamlet. Except that he was no creation of the poetic imagination. He was a living American, and in his living words are the answers—or the only conceivable answers—to all the questions that distract the world today."

Sherwood's shadowing of Lincoln when he was pondering his play did not stop with history or biography. Language, Lincoln's language public and private, the language of his period and of the authors who, having fed the hungers of his mind, helped to shape his style, became Sherwood's natural concern. To give authenticity to the dialogue in his scenes about the young Lincoln, he bought an English grammar of 1816. For periods flavor he savored the *Pickwick Papers* and, to catch the swing and phraseology of common speech along the Mississippi, he reread *Huckleberry Finn.* Again and

"HE HAS SO IMMERSED HIMSELF IN LINCOLN'S STYLE OF SIMPLE, DIRECT, RUGGED SPEECH THAT YOU PASS FROM SHERWOOD'S WORDS TO LINCOLN'S WITH NO SENSE OF CHANGE."

again he searched the Bible, Shakespeare, Jefferson, and Whitman for an appropriately somber passage with which the student Lincoln could conclude the opening scene. Finding none, he used Keats' "On Death" as being right in spirit even if there was no record of Lincoln's having read it. The poem contained a phrase in "his rugged path" which stuck in Sherwood's mind, For a while he considered *The Rugged Path* for the title of his Lincoln play, which earlier he had thought of calling *The First American,* then *An American.*

Source: John Mason Brown, "Bob Sherwood in Illinois," in *The Worlds of Robert E. Sherwood,* Harper & Row, 1965, pp. 367–71.

Edith J. R. Isaacs

Edith J. R. Isaacs reviews Sherwood's style and language, linking it to the success of the play.

Abe Lincoln in Illinois says what all Sherwood's other serious plays and serious prefaces have tried to say, and says it so well and so convincingly that audiences rise to their feet to applaud it. Much of *Abe Lincoln* is in Lincoln's own words—his homely phrases, his anecdotes, his famous speeches; but the play is none the less Sherwood's creation. He has so immersed himself in Lincoln's style of simple, direct, rugged speech that you pass from Sherwood's words to Lincoln's with no sense of change. Every speech is in character as Sherwood has recreated Lincoln, and within that character a great man, a national hero with all of a nation's legend behind him, lives and moves as a man among men. To create such a figure out of history may seem an easier task than to mold a character out of a dramatist's own fresh clay. Indeed it is far harder, as the whole history of such endeavor shows. Great historic figures already live double lives, one of which is in the minds of their audience, and a dramatist who tries to put his own portrait of the man into words stands constantly at the edge of a precipice. Raymond Massey, who plays the part of Lincoln with a devotion to the character he represents almost equal to Sherwood's, and with a surprising personal likeness, deserves all the acclaim he has had for his performance. But you have only to read Sherwood's script before seeing the play to know that it is the dramatist who has given this Lincoln the spark of life.

Abe Lincoln in Illinois carries through three periods of Lincoln's life—in and about New Salem, Illinois, in the 1830's; in and about Springfield, Illinois, in the 1840's; the years 1858 to 1861 to the day when Lincoln, as President-Elect, parted with his neighbors at the railroad station to go on his honored and lonely way:

'Let us live to prove that we can cultivate the natural world that is about us, and the intellectual and moral world that is within us, so that we may secure an individual, social and political prosperity, whose course shall be forward, and which, while the earth endures, shall not pass away.'

Which is a good speech for a dramatist to end on.

Source: Edith J. R. Isaacs, ''Man of the Hour,'' in *Theatre Arts*, Vol. 23, 1939, pp. 31–40.

SOURCES

Brown, John Mason, *The Worlds of Robert E. Sherwood: Mirror to His Times*, Harper & Row Publishers, 1962.

Fergusson, Francis, ''Notes on the Theatre,'' in *The Southern Review*, Winter 1940, p. 560.

Flexner, Eleanor, *American Playwrights, 1918–1938*, Simon and Schuster, 1938, pp. 272–82.

Meserve, Walter J., *Robert E. Sherwood: Reluctant Moralist*, The Bobbs-Merrill Company, Inc., 1970, pp. 221–222.

Sandburg, Carl, ''Forward,'' in *Abe Lincoln in Illinois*, Charles Scribner's Sons, 1939, pp. xi–xii.

Shuman, R. Baird, *Robert E. Sherwood*, Twayne Publishers, 1964, p. 83.

FURTHER READING

Drennan, Robert E., *The Algonquin Wits*, Replica Books, 2000.
As a member of the famous Algonquin Round Table, a group of literary wits who met at the Algonquin Hotel in New York in the 1920s and 30s, Sherwood was engaged in intense intellectual competition.

Fehrenbacher, Don E., ed., *Abraham Lincoln: Speeches and Writings, 1832–1858*, Library of America, 1989.
The Library of America editions are painstakingly researched, checked for authenticity and thoroughness. This edition covers the same years as the play and gives Lincoln's own words to compare to Sherwood's portrayal.

Holzer, Harold, ed., *The Lincoln-Douglas Debates: The First Complete, Unexpurgated Text*, HarperCollins, 1993.
Edited and introduced by Harold Holzer, one of the leading historians in the field of Lincoln studies, this text gives a sense of drama that is like that of the play.

Smith, Wendy, *Real Life Drama: The Group Theatre and America, 1931–1940*, Grove Press, 1992.
The Playwrights Company, which had its debut with *Abe Lincoln in Illinois*, was patterned on the Group Theater.

Wilson, Douglas, *Lincoln Before Washington: New Perspectives on the Illinois Years*, University of Illinois Press, 1997.
Covering the same period of Lincoln's life as Sherwood, this scholarly work is particularly concerned with the historical truth of William Herndon's biography.

The Amen Corner

JAMES BALDWIN

1968

The Amen Corner, the first dramatic play by the now much-celebrated African-American novelist, essayist, and playwright James Baldwin, was written during the 1950s, first performed on the professional stage in 1965, and first published in 1968.

The Amen Corner takes place in two settings: a ''corner'' church in Harlem and the apartment dwelling of Margaret Anderson, the church pastor, and of her son, David, and sister Odessa. After giving a fiery Sunday morning sermon, Margaret is confronted by the unexpected arrival of her long estranged husband, Luke, who collapses from illness shortly thereafter. Their son, David, along with several elders of the congregation, learn from Luke that, while Margaret had led everyone to believe that he had abandoned her with their son years ago, it was in fact Margaret who had left Luke in pursuit of a purely religious life. This information precipitates confrontations between Margaret and her son, her congregation, and her estranged husband, regarding what they see as the hypocritical nature of her religious convictions, which she uses to justify the breakup of her family. After an important conversation with his dying father, David informs Margaret that he is leaving home to pursue his calling as a jazz musician. On his deathbed, Luke declares to Margaret that he has always loved her, and that she should not have left him. Finally, Margaret's congregation decides to oust her, based on their perception that she unjustly ruined her own family in the name of religion. Only after losing her son, her

husband, and her congregation, does Margaret finally realize that she should not have used religion as an excuse to escape the struggles of life and love, but that ''To love the Lord is to love all His children—all of them, everyone!—and suffer with them and rejoice with them and never count the cost!''

The Amen Corner addresses themes of the role of the church in the African-American family, the complex relationship between religion and earthly love, and the effect of a poverty born of racial prejudice on the African-American community.

AUTHOR BIOGRAPHY

James Baldwin was born on August 2, 1924, in New York City, to David Baldwin, a factory worker and clergyman, and Emma (Jones) Baldwin. Baldwin was the eldest of nine children, whom he spent much of his childhood helping to raise and care for amidst the poverty of black Harlem. During his high school years, the young Baldwin became a revivalist minister for the Fireside Pentecostal Assembly. He graduated from De Witt Clinton High School in 1942, after which he began working in the defense industry in New Jersey. In 1942, when his stepfather died, Baldwin decided to become a writer and moved to Greenwich Village, New York, to pursue his goal. There he took on various unskilled odd jobs while working on his first novel. In 1944, he met the celebrated black novelist Richard Wright, who aided Baldwin's career by helping him to get an Eugene F. Saxton Fellowship. Finding the racism in the United States more and more unbearable, Baldwin in 1948 moved to Paris, where he gained experience and insight crucial to his writing career, his sense of racial heritage, and his sexual identity.

It was during this period that his first two novels, *Go Tell It on the Mountain* (1953) and *Giovanni's Room* (1956), were published. Returning to the United States in 1957, Baldwin became an important public speaker and activist in the burgeoning civil rights movement, a political role he maintained throughout his life. He continued to be a world traveler, living for various periods in France and other countries, as well as in the Untied States. Baldwin wrote distinguished works in several forms. Important essays on racial issues are collected in *Notes of a Native Son* (1955), *Nobody Knows My Name: More Notes of a Native Son* (1961), and *The Fire Next Time* (1963). Notable fiction, besides his first novels, includes *Another Country* (1962) and *If Beale Street Could Talk* (1974). *The Amen Corner* (1955) and *Blues for Mr. Charlie* (1964) are his most celebrated dramas. Baldwin died of stomach cancer on November 30 or December 1 (sources vary), 1987, in St. Paul de Vence, France.

PLOT SUMMARY

Act I

Act I takes place ''on a Sunday morning in Harlem.'' It begins with a church service, led by Margaret Anderson, the pastor of a ''corner'' church. The singing of hymns, accompanied by Margaret's eighteen-year-old son, David, on the piano, is an important element of the service. At one point, Mrs. Ida Jackson, a young woman, walks up to the pulpit holding her sick baby; she asks Margaret what she should do to save her baby, and Margaret advises her to leave her husband, but Mrs. Jackson asserts that she doesn't want to leave her husband.

After the service, Margaret, her sister Odessa, David, and three elders of the church, Sister Moore, Sister Boxer, and Brother Boxer, congregate in Margaret's apartment, which is attached to the church. Margaret's long estranged husband, Luke, arrives unexpectedly at the apartment. In front of David and the church elders, Luke confronts Margaret with the fact that, while she had led everyone to believe that he had abandoned her with their son years earlier, it was in fact Margaret who had left Luke. After an infant of theirs had died, Margaret had blamed Luke for the tragedy, and had abandoned him to pursue a purely religious life. Luke then collapses from illness and is taken to lie down on a bed in Margaret's apartment. Although David and the others plead with Margaret to stay and care for the dying Luke, Margaret leaves for a brief trip to Philadelphia for the purpose of aiding another church.

Act II

Act II is set the following Saturday afternoon. In the first scene, Odessa, Sister Boxer, and Sister Moore sit in the kitchen of the apartment, discussing Sister Margaret's role in the church, given this new information that she had abandoned her own husband. The church elders express some discontent with Margaret's use of the church funds and with her treatment of the congregation, as well as the hypocrisy they perceive in her years of lying about her relationship with her husband. In the next scene,

David enters the room where his father, Luke, lies ill. David and Luke discuss David's ambitions to become a jazz musician and his father's life as a jazz musician. Luke explains to David that being abandoned by Margaret had ruined his life. Luke encourages David to pursue jazz, but also explains to him that music is nothing if a man doesn't have the love of a woman in his life.

During the next scene, in the church, several of the church elders and other congregation members gather to discuss Margaret's position as pastor of the church. They criticize Margaret for her use of church funds, her treatment of her husband, and her seeming hypocrisies in regard to what she preaches versus how she lives her own life. They all break into a hymn, during which Margaret enters the church, just back from Philadelphia. She explains that the Philadelphia congregation will be coming to join their service the next day. They all sing a hymn and then say a prayer.

In the following scene, David brings a record player into the room where Luke lies and plays a record of Luke playing the trombone. Margaret enters the bedroom, and David leaves with the record player. Margaret and Luke then have a conversation about their relationship and the role of religion in Margaret's life, but the two come to no understanding. Odessa then enters and warns Margaret that the church is about to have a business meeting in which they will be discussing Margaret's position as pastor.

Act III

Act III takes place the following Sunday morning. In the first scene, Margaret and Mrs. Jackson talk in the church; Mrs. Jackson's baby has died, but she resists Margaret's religious advice about the matter and insists that she is more concerned with her husband than with religion. In the kitchen of the apartment, Margaret and her sister Odessa discuss Margaret's relationship with Luke. Later in the church, Odessa joins the church elders, who are again discussing their plans to oust Margaret from her post as pastor. Odessa attempts to defend Margaret against this decision. In the apartment, David confronts Margaret with the fact that he has decided to leave home to pursue his calling as a jazz musician.

Margaret enters the bedroom where Luke lies dying, and they discuss David's decision to leave. Margaret and Luke finally make peace with one another and admit that they still love each other; as they embrace, Luke dies. Margaret then enters the

James Baldwin

church and speaks to the congregation, although she knows that they have chosen to oust her from her position. Margaret tells the congregation that she is "just now finding out what it means to love the Lord." She concludes that "To love the Lord is to love all His children—all of them, everyone!—and suffer with them and rejoice with them and never count the cost!" The congregation breaks into a hymn as Margaret steps down from the pulpit, enters the room where Luke lies dead, and falls beside his body on the bed.

CHARACTERS

David Alexander

David is the eighteen-year-old son of Margaret and Luke. David plays the piano in the church during Margaret's sermons, and his mother wants him to pursue a life of devotion to religion, utilizing his musical talents for that purpose only. David, however, has enrolled in a music school, and has been secretly sneaking out to jazz clubs and playing in a jazz band. One night, he sneaks out to hear his estranged father, Luke, also a musician, play at a jazz club. When Luke arrives at Margaret's house, David learns that it was his mother who had left his father, and not his father who had abandoned them, as she had led him to believe. While Margaret had wanted David to accompany her to Philadelphia, David chooses to stay home with his dying father. David and Luke have an important discussion about the family history, his parents' relationship, and jazz music. When Margaret returns from Philadelphia, David confronts her with the decision that he is leaving home to pursue a career as a jazz musician. David tries to explain to his mother that he can make a better contribution to the world through pursuing his own musical calling, pleading with her that "Maybe I can say something—one day—maybe I can say something in music that's never been said before."

Luke Alexander

Luke is the estranged husband of Margaret, and the father of David. Luke arrives unexpectedly at Margaret's house and collapses from illness. He confronts Margaret with the fact that she had left him after blaming him for the death of their infant child years earlier. Margaret is unsympathetic to his pleas of love for her, and leaves for a brief trip to Philadelphia, despite the fact that he lies dying in a bed in her home. While Margaret is gone, Luke has an important conversation with their son, David, in which he tries to explain to David his perspective on his relationship with Margaret. After Margaret returns from Philadelphia, Luke again confronts her with the fact that she had unfairly blamed him for the death of their infant and had used religion as an escape and an excuse to leave him. He tells her that David's decision to leave is a decision to "live," not a moral lapse on his part. Most of all, Luke pleads with Margaret that he loved her and needed her and that she should never have left him. Luke then dies, after which Margaret finally realizes the truth of what he has said.

Margaret Alexander

Margaret Alexander is the pastor of a church. In the first scene of the play, she gives a sermon. She then prepares to leave for a brief trip to Philadelphia to aid another church. As she is about to leave, her estranged husband, Luke, arrives unexpectedly and collapses from illness. Several members of Margaret's congregation learn that while she had lead everyone to believe that Luke had abandoned her with their son, David, in fact it was Margaret who left Luke. Despite the fact that Luke lies on his deathbed in her home, Margaret leaves for Philadelphia anyway. While she is gone, members of her congregation meet to discuss their various dissatisfactions with Margaret's position as pastor of their church. They question her use of church funds as well as the new information that she had abandoned her own husband. When Margaret returns, she is confronted by her son, her estranged husband, and her congregation. David informs her that he has been secretly playing in a jazz band and is going to leave home to pursue a career as a jazz musician. Luke confronts her with the fact that she had blamed him for the death of their infant child years ago and had abandoned him in the name of the service of God; Luke points out Margaret's hypocrisy in using religion as an excuse to escape life. Finally, Margaret's congregation confronts her on similar grounds. Having lost her son, her husband, and her congregation, Margaret finally realizes that religion should not have been an excuse for her to break up her family but a reason for her to stand by her man.

Brother Boxer

Brother Boxer is an elder of Margaret's church who resents her for insisting that it is sinful of him to take a job driving a liquor delivery truck.

Sister Boxer

Sister Boxer is an elder of Margaret's church who criticizes Margaret for insisting that it is sinful for her husband, Brother Boxer, to take a job driving a liquor delivery truck.

Ida Jackson

Ida Jackson is a young woman who steps up to the pulpit during Margaret's sermon with a plea for help for her sick baby. Margaret advises her to leave her husband, but Mrs. Jackson protests that she doesn't want to leave her husband. Later, Mrs. Jackson returns to Margaret for consolation after her baby has died. Again, Mrs. Jackson protests Margaret's religious explanations and consolations, asserting instead that "I just want my man and my home and my children." Margaret tells her that she needs to pray, but Mrs. Jackson disagrees, maintaining that she is going home to her husband instead. Margaret finally realizes that Mrs. Jackson is right to stand by her man, rather than abandon him in the name of religion, telling her, "Get on home to your husband. Go on home, to your man."

Sister Moore

Sister Moore is an elder of Margaret's church who is instrumental in having Margaret ousted from her position as pastor.

Odessa

Odessa is Margaret's sister, who lives with Margaret and David. Odessa is supportive of Margaret, and defends her against the criticism of the members of her congregation.

THEMES

Religion

Religion is a central theme in Baldwin's play. The first seventeen pages of the play are taken up with a Sunday morning church sermon, led by the pastor, Sister Margaret Anderson. Baldwin has noted that this material was in part based on his own experiences as a young minister. Baldwin also wished the theater audience to be swept up in the experience of actually attending a church service. The role of religion in Margaret's life is examined and questioned by various characters throughout the play. While Margaret presents herself as a pure, holy woman who has been abandoned by her husband, others point out that she has used religion as an excuse to escape from the problems of the material world. It is Luke who finally impresses upon Margaret the idea that she has misinterpreted the significance of religion. Luke points out that human love is not at odds with religion, but is in fact an important element of religion. It is only after she has lost her son, her husband, and her congregation that Margaret is able to appreciate Luke's words. Her final words to her congregation confirm her understanding.

Poverty

Although not one of the play's most prominent themes, the impact of poverty permeates the play as an underlying condition of the lives of the characters. Margaret berates Brother Boxer for taking a job driving a liquor delivery truck, asserting that it is sinful of him to spend his day providing liquor to people. Sister Boxer, Brother Boxer's wife, however, complains that Margaret is not taking into account the importance of earning a living and supporting a family. In other words, it is economic necessity, based on the limited availability of jobs to African-American men during that time period, which requires that Brother Boxer accept the best job he can find. Poverty is also an underlying theme in the death of Margaret's infant, years before the play takes place, and the death of Mrs. Ida Jackson's infant. It is made clear that these babies became sick and died due to poor nutrition (and perhaps inadequate medical care) because of their poverty. Reference is also made to the limited availability of jobs for African-American women, as one character refers to her work as a maid in the home of a white woman. Thus, while there are no white characters who appear in the play, the black community is presented within a broader context of racial inequality in which African-American women have little choice but to work in positions of servitude to white women, and African-American men are compelled to accept whatever jobs may be available to them.

Love

Many critics have noted that one of the recurring themes throughout Baldwin's fiction is that of love. Baldwin states in his "Notes" to the published play that the first line he wrote was Margaret's in Act III: "It's an awful thing to think about, the way love never dies!" Margaret throughout most of the play has made the mistake of substituting religion for the love of her own husband. Luke insists that he still loves her, and yet she continues to deny her own feelings of love for him. Through the character of Luke, the love of a woman is presented as a necessity to the survival of black men in a racist society; Luke's downfall is attributed to Margaret's withholding of love from him. It is only at the end, just before Luke dies, that Margaret is able to understand the power of love: "Maybe it's not possible to stop loving anybody you ever really loved. I never stopped loving you, Luke. I tried. But I never stopped loving you." Baldwin explains that although Margaret, by the end, "has lost everything," she "also gains the keys to the kingdom." He goes on to say that "The kingdom is love, and love is selfless, although only the self can lead one there. She gains herself."

TOPICS FOR FURTHER STUDY

- In addition to plays and novels, Baldwin has been celebrated for his essays on issues of race in America. Read one of Baldwin's essays, such as from his collections: *Notes from a Native Son* (1955), *Nobody Knows My Name* (1961), or *The Fire Next Time* (1963). What are some of Baldwin's central concerns with the issue of race in America? What solutions does he suggest for addressing issues of racial inequality? In what ways are these concerns addressed in his play *The Amen Corner*?

- Pick a particularly moving or important scene from *The Amen Corner* to perform with another student (or students). How does performing a scene from the play help you to understand the motivations of certain characters or to illuminate key thematic concerns of the play? In what ways could different performance choices affect the meaning, effect, or impact of that particular scene?

- Baldwin's play addresses issues of race and poverty in terms of the significance of the black church to an African-American family. Learn more about the role of the church in the history of African-American culture and the struggles of African Americans for racial equality in America. In what ways has religion and the institution of the church been an important factor in African-American history and African-American communities?

- Baldwin's play focuses on the role of the wife and mother in an African-American family. Another important and much celebrated African-American playwright who addresses the role of African-American women in the black family is Ntozake Shange, who is best known for her play *for colored girls who have considered suicide when the rainbow is enuf*. Learn more about this playwright and her works. In what ways does she address similar issues to those addressed by Baldwin in his play? In what ways does she provide a different perspective on male-female relationships in the African-American community?

STYLE

Staging

Baldwin wrote this play with a very specific stage set in mind. The two main parts of the set are the church and the adjoining apartment. The positioning of the church in relation to the apartment is symbolic of the role of the church in the life of the family. The stage notes indicate that "The church is on a level above the apartment and should give the impression of dominating the family's living quarters." This is meant to symbolize the dominating influence of the church on Margaret's family. The set design within the church is also a key element of Baldwin's vision for this play. The stage notes indicate that the church "is dominated by the pulpit, on a platform, upstage." Thus, within the church itself, Margaret, as the pastor giving sermons, is the dominant figure. This set design emphasizes the extent to which the church is an arena in which Margaret holds a great deal of power, as opposed to the rest of the world, in which she is an impoverished single black woman. The program notes also mention that on the platform on which the pulpit sits is "a thronelike chair." The implication is that, in the world of her congregation, Margaret reigns supreme, as if she were royalty. This again emphasizes, by way of contrast, the extent to which, in the rest of the world, Margaret as a poor African-American woman is virtually powerless. Finally, Baldwin wanted the stage set of the church to position the audience of the play itself as if they, too, were members of the congregation, listening to Margaret's sermons. This positioning of the audience is key to one of Baldwin's central goals in writing this play: to suggest a parallel between theatrical elements of performance and audience participation in the black church with that of the theater.

Sermons

A central element of Baldwin's play is the church sermons led by Pastor Margaret. As he has stated in his "Notes" which preface the published edition of the play: "I knew that out of the ritual of the church, historically speaking, comes the act of the theatre, the communion which is the theatre. And I knew that what I wanted to do in the theatre was to recreate moments I remembered, as a boy preacher, to involve the people, even against their will, to shake them up, and, hopefully, to change them." The long service that begins the play alternates the singing of hymns with a fiery sermon by Sister Margaret. Margaret's sermon is written in the highly developed and stylized oratory style of African-American ministers. This oratory style is most easily recognized by the use of repetition of key phrases and the use of black English vernacular. The civil rights activist Reverend Martin Luther King, Jr. has been widely noted for his skill and mastery of this oratory style, particularly as exemplified by his famous "I Have a Dream" speech.

HISTORICAL CONTEXT

African-American Literary Movements

Twentieth-century African-American literature has been characterized by two important literary movements: the Harlem Renaissance and the Black Arts Movement. The Harlem Renaissance, also referred to as the New Negro Movement, designates a period during the 1920s in which African-American literature flourished among a group of writers concentrated in the Harlem section of New York City. Important writers of the Harlem Renaissance include James Weldon Johnson, who wrote the novel *Autobiography of an Ex-Colored Man* (1912); Claude McKay, who wrote the best-selling novel *Home to Harlem* (1928); Langston Hughes, who wrote the poetry collection *The Weary Blues* (1926); and Wallace Thurman, who wrote the novel *The Blacker the Berry* (1929). This period of incredible literary output diminished when the Great Depression of the 1930s affected the financial status of many African-American writers. The Black Arts Movement, also referred to as the Black Aesthetic Movement flourished during the 1960s and 70s, and embodied values derived from black nationalism and promoted politically and socially significant works, often written in Black English vernacular. Important writers of the Black Arts Movement include Imamu Amiri Baraka (also known as LeRoi Jones), Eldridge Cleaver, Angela Davis, Alice Walker, and Toni Morrison.

Black Theater

Dramatic works by African-American writers in the nineteenth century include *King Shotaway* (1823), by William Henry Brown, the first known play by an African-American writer; *The Escape: or, A Leap for Freedom* (1858), by William Wells Brown, the first play by an African-American writer to be published; and *Rachel* (1916), by Anglina W. Grimke, the first successful stage play by an African-American writer. Important literary movements, such as the Harlem Renaissance and the Black Arts Movement, influenced dramatic works and stage productions by African Americans in the twentieth century. The development of Black Theater in the first half of the twentieth century was inspired by the Harlem Renaissance, and included the establishment of theaters devoted to black productions in major cities throughout the United States. The most prominent black theaters by mid-century were the American Negro Theater and the Negro Playwrights' Company. In the post-World War II era, black theater became more overtly political and more specifically focused on celebrating African-American culture. One of the most prominent works to emerge from this period was the 1959 play, *A Raisin in the Sun*, by Lorraine Hansberry. The Black Arts Movement, which emerged in the 1960s, led to the establishment in 1965 of the Repertory Theater of Harlem, initiated by Amiri Baraka (still LeRoi Jones at that time). Baraka's award-winning 1964 play, *The Dutchman,* is among the most celebrated dramatic works of this period. Ntozake Shange's 1977, *for colored girls who have considered suicide, when the rainbow is enuf,* utilized an experimental dramatic format to address issues facing African-American women. In the 1980s, August Wilson emerged as an important African-American playwright with his *Ma Rainey's Black Bottom* (1985), about a blues singer and her band, set in Chicago in the 1920s.

CRITICAL OVERVIEW

In his "Notes" for the first publication of *The Amen Corner* in 1968, Baldwin recalls that writing the

COMPARE & CONTRAST

- **1920s:** The Harlem Renaissance characterizes a period of flowering of African-American literature.

  1960s: The Black Arts Movement, also called the Black Aesthetic Movement, inspired in part by the Civil Rights Movement, represents the cutting edge of African-American artistic and literary style and philosophy.

  1990s: A new generation of African-American writers and artists have been greatly influenced by the legacy of the Black Arts Movement.

- **1950s:** The most prominent Black theaters in the United States include the American Negro Theater and the Negro Playwrights' Company.

  1960s: Inspired by, and in part an initiator of, the Black Arts Movement, Amiri Baraka establishes the Black Repertory Theater in Harlem.

  1990s: Numerous black theaters have been established throughout the United States, with many mainstream stages also featuring black theatrical productions.

- **1954:** In the decision of *Brown* vs. *the Board of Education*, the Supreme Court declares that racially segregated schools are unconstitutional. This initiates the desegregation of public schools in the United States.

  1955: Rosa Parks initiates the Montgomery bus boycott in protest against seating segregation on public buses.

  1961: Over 70,000 college students, in what are called "Freedom Rides," travel to the South to register black voters.

  1964: An extensive Civil Rights Act is passed by Congress, declaring various forms of racial discrimination illegal.

  1965: The Voting Rights Act is passed to protect African Americans against discriminatory tactics in regard to voting.

- **1963:** President John F. Kennedy is assassinated.

  1964: Martin Luther King, Jr., is awarded the Nobel Peace Prize for his achievements in the Civil Rights Movement.

  1965: Black Muslim leader Malcolm X, who promoted Black Nationalism, is assassinated.

  1966: The Black Panther Party, a revolutionary organization of African Americans, is founded by Huey Newton and Bobby Seale.

  1968: Martin Luther King, Jr., is assassinated.

  1980s: The Black Panther party is essentially disbanded.

---

play was "a desperate and even rather irresponsible act." With one published novel to his name (*Go Tell It on the Mountain*), Baldwin was not in a strong position to succeed with his first play. As his agent at the time informed him, "the American theatre was not exactly clamoring for plays on obscure aspects of Negro life, especially one written by a virtually unknown author whose principal effort until that time had been one novel." Nevertheless, Baldwin forged ahead, and *The Amen Corner*, written in the 1950s, was first produced on the campus of Howard University, then in Los Angeles, before opening on Broadway in 1965. While it won the 1964 Foreign Drama Critics Circle Award, the play was not published in book form until 1968.

Critics have commented on the artistic success of Baldwin's play as a dramatic stage production. Carlton W. Molette, writing in 1977, stated that *The Amen Corner* "is one of the most successful Afro-American plays that I have seen." Molette asserts that "The first professional production was moving as theater ought to be but seldom is." Carolyn Wedin Sylvander, asserting that "*The Amen Corner* is a better play than its production history or critical attention would seem to indicate," especially praises the play for its qualities as a stage production, particularly in Baldwin's use of music: "the play is certainly constructed in such a way as to truly 'come alive' on the stage. Much of that liveliness and power to involve is transmitted through the music. Group singing, individual singing, instrumental accompaniment, jazz (Luke on record), all provide choral commentary on character and conflict."

Several critics have noted the play's embodiment of aesthetic values put forth by the Black Arts Movement of the 1960s. Darwin T. Turner explains that "*The Amen Corner* seems more clearly designed as a drama written about black experience for a black audience. In this respect, it resembles Black Arts drama, in which the dramatist presumes that he must write without concern for the white spectator, who exists outside the black experience and without comprehension of it. I do not wish to imply that Baldwin consciously designed the play for the education of a black audience. Instead, I am suggesting that he found strength in writing meaningfully about an experience he knew while assuming that his audience would be equally familiar with that experience." Turner concludes that Baldwin's "success, I feel, did not result solely from his recreation of a church setting that was familiar to him but from his presumption that his audience required no interpretation, no modification, because it already knew the cultural setting. Thus Baldwin achieved an artistic freedom rarely granted a black dramatist except when he works within the theater of a black community." Molette provides a similar assessment of Baldwin's play in terms of the ways in which it addresses its audience: "*The Amen Corner* does not protest to whites; it informs, educates, illuminates blacks.... It is not self-consciously black. The play assumes that there are some elementary aspects of black culture that do not require explanation within the body of the play. It assumes, in effect, a black audience. It is not an anti-white play, it is an a-white play."

Molette, however, does note that "the play is not perfect," pointing out that "Ironically, *The Amen Corner* is at its worst as a play precisely when it is at its best as literature. There are several two-character scenes between the members of the Alexander family that are true literary gems. They are also the scenes of greatest character revelation. They actually tell us too much about the characters. Now, all that is told needs to be told; but some of it ought to be told through means other than words." Molette goes on to criticize scenes that are particularly static and lacking in drama when seen on stage.

Playbill cover from the 1965 production of Baldwin's The Amen Corner *at the Ethel Barrymore Theatre.*

For example, in Act II, "the action slows down, and the words become far more important than the deed. In the theater, that usually means trouble. This is especially a problem with the scenes that involve the father (Luke), because he is confined to his sickbed, making visual interest through movement very difficult to achieve, as well."

Fred L. Standley praises the play, along with other works by Baldwin, for his treatment of "a variety of thematic concerns: the historical significance and the potential explosiveness in black-white relations; the necessity for developing a sexual and psychological consciousness and identity; the intertwining of love and power in the universal scheme of existence as well as in the structures of society; the misplaced priorities in the value systems in America; and the responsibility of the artist to promote the evolution of the individual and the society."

Trudier Harris criticized Baldwin's portrayal of female characters in a number of his works, asserting that "Few women in Baldwin's works are able to move beyond the bounds of the traditional roles that have been cut out for them and in which the use of their bodies is the most important factor." Harris offers both criticism and praise, however, of Baldwin's representation of women through the character of Margaret in *The Amen Corner*. She states that Sister Margaret "is most like the women in the fiction in her desire and ability to serve.... In her adherence to scripture, she is one of the most fanatical of Baldwin's black women characters. Yet in her recognition of the unrelenting antagonism between males and females, she voices the plight of all of the church-based women." Harris concludes, however, that, in Baldwin's fiction and drama, "for all this growth and progression, for all this freedom of action and movement, the women are still confined to niches carved out for them by men whose egos are too fragile to grant their equality."

CRITICISM

Liz Brent

Brent has a Ph.D. in American Culture, specializing in film studies, from the University of Michigan. She is a freelance writer and teaches courses in the history of American cinema. In the following essay, Brent discusses the motif of jazz music in Baldwin's play.

Music plays a central role in expressing key themes within Baldwin's play. The play is structured thematically around two types of music: church music and jazz music. On one level, church music and jazz music are symbolic within the play of opposing sets of values, represented on each side by Luke and Margaret: church music represents Margaret's religious fervor and convictions, while jazz music represents Luke's insistence on embracing life through human love. David, the eighteen-year-old son of Margaret and Luke, is caught between the opposing sets of values held by his mother and father. He is torn between his mother's insistence that he continue as a church musician and his own desire to follow in his father's footsteps by pursuing a career as a jazz musician. By the end of the play, however, as Luke dies in her arms, Margaret realizes that life (as symbolized by jazz) and religion (as symbolized by hymns) do not embody opposing values of sin and purity—but actually encompass one another as expressions of love—love of life and other human beings, as well as love of the Lord.

The role of actual music in the performance of the play thus expresses the struggle between these opposing viewpoints and sets of values. The predominant musical motif throughout the play is church music. The production notes state that, even before the curtain rises, David's piano music, emanating from the church, can be heard underneath the random street noises. The opening scene of the play is essentially a church service, alternating Margaret's sermon with the singing of hymns by the congregation, accompanied by David's piano. In addition, throughout the play, members of the congregation spontaneously break into the singing of hymns.

Before Luke's unexpected arrival at Margaret's apartment, David has already chosen a path away from church music and toward jazz music. Although he has told his mother that he has enrolled in a local music school, he has also been secretly sneaking out at night to attend jazz clubs and play in a jazz combo. It is later revealed that he had gone one night to watch his father, whom he hadn't seen in years, play trombone in a jazz band. Jazz music, however, while central to the play thematically, is only actually heard on the stage during a few key scenes. When Luke first appears unexpectedly in Margaret's apartment, the stage directions indicate that "Jazz version of 'Luke's Theme' begins." Luke thus symbolically brings the values associated with jazz into Margaret's realm of church music. When David brings a phonograph into the room where Luke lies dying and plays a record of Luke's trombone music, the sound of jazz music provides the audience with a visceral contrast to the hymnal music which has, up to this point, dominated the play. The playing of this record is furthermore an important point of contact between father and son; it represents David's decision to follow in his father's footsteps in the pursuit of a career as a jazz musician. David's association of his father with jazz music is in fact what led him to pursue music; he tells Luke that "I remembered how you used to play for me sometimes. That was why I started playing the piano. I used to go to sleep dreaming about the way we'd play together one day, me with my piano and you with your trombone." This exchange between David and Luke furthermore provides a point of connection between father and son in which David rejects his mother's system of values (as represented by church music) and takes on his father's system of values (as represented by jazz music). For David, entering the world of jazz leads to a loss of religious faith. He tells Luke that, after he was asked to join a jazz combo, he "stopped praying," and that, eventually, "I stopped believ-

WHAT DO I READ NEXT?

- *Blues for Mr. Charlie* (1964), Baldwin's most noted play, was performed on Broadway in 1964 and received a Foreign Drama Critics Award. "Mr. Charlie" is a name used to refer to the white man.

- *Notes of a Native Son* (1955) is Baldwin's first collection of essays on issues of race in America.

- *Nobody Knows My Name: More Notes of a Native Son* (1961) is Baldwin's second collection of essays on racial relations in America.

- *The Fire Next Time* (1963) is an essay by Baldwin based on an article published in the *New Yorker* magazine in 1962, and addresses issues of racial relations in America.

- *Go Tell It on the Mountain* (1953) is Baldwin's first novel and the work for which he is best known and most celebrated. It is an autobiographical account of Baldwin's childhood and early religious influences.

- *Giovanni's Room* (1977) is Baldwin's second novel and concerns a young man in Paris struggling with his sexual identity.

- *Native Son* (1955) is a novel by the celebrated African-American writer Richard Wright, who was an important role model for Baldwin and important early influence on his writing career.

---

ing—it just went away." Luke admits that he, himself, never found religious faith.

When David comes home one morning smelling of whiskey, Margaret associates his pursuit of jazz with "wickedness" and "sin"; she particularly associates it with sex, as she accuses David of "stinking of whiskey and some no-count, dirty, black girl's sweat." For David, however, playing jazz music is a calling, equivalent to a religious calling. He tells Margaret that, while he "can't play piano in church no more," playing jazz is something he's "got to do!" For David, playing jazz is equivalent to a religious calling in the sense that he feels he's got "work to do" in the world, by "speaking for" his fellow African Americans through his music. He tells Margaret: "I've got my work to do, something's happening in the world out there, I got to go! I know you think I don't know what's happening, but I'm beginning to see something. . . . Who's going to speak for all of us? I can't stay home. Maybe I can say something—one day—maybe I can say something that's never been said before." Thus, while Margaret associates jazz music with "wickedness" and "sin," David perceives jazz to be essentially equivalent to religion in the sense of having an important, positive effect on the world.

The conflict between Margaret's associations of jazz with wickedness and sin and David's associations of jazz with a religious calling is representative of the seemingly conflicting associations jazz music has acquired through history. According to *Encyclopedia Britannica,* while jazz developed in the twentieth century in the urban settings of brothels and bars, it's musical roots are firmly planted in the "spirituals" born of the adaptation by African slaves in America to Christian hymnals:

> This vast influence of Africanized church music on the development of jazz underlines one more fallacy about the music, which is that it was always linked irrevocably to the lowlife. Its connections with the brothels of Louisiana and the saloons of Chicago tell only half the story, for jazz has been concerned with sanctity as well as with sin, has been a sacred music as well as a profane one. Its links with Christianity and particularly with the act of worship and the rituals of birth, marriage, and death have proved so durable that they remain unbroken to this day.

Thus, while Margaret associates jazz only with the profane, David is more accurate in his association of jazz with a religious calling and positive

> "FOR DAVID, PLAYING JAZZ IS EQUIVALENT TO A RELIGIOUS CALLING IN THE SENSE THAT HE FEELS HE'S GOT 'WORK TO DO' IN THE WORLD... THROUGH HIS MUSIC."

social force. Furthermore, the historic and musical relationship of jazz music to church music is indicated by Margaret's decision to allow "drums and trumpets" to be played during a church service. When Sister Rice asks if these instruments "seem kind of worldly," Margaret responds: "Well, the evil ain't in the drum, Sister Rice, nor yet in the trumpet. The evil is in what folks do with it and what it leads them to. Ain't no harm in praising the Lord with anything you get in your hands." Brother Boxer then suggests that, while David hasn't been to services in a week, these "drums and trumpets," instruments associated with jazz music, will "bring Brother David out to church again, I guarantee you that." While she herself is not aware of it, Margaret's decision to allow these more flamboyant instruments into her church is indicative of the common musical ancestry of jazz and church music. Furthermore, her statement that "Ain't no harm in praising the Lord with anything you get in your hands," suggests that David's ultimate decision to pursue jazz rather than church music may constitute his own form of "praising the Lord" through the expression of his musical gifts.

From Luke's perspective, as from David's, jazz music represents a positive life force, associated with human love. When Margaret tells Luke that David has gone to pursue life as a jazz musician, Luke responds that "He's gone into the world. He's into the world! ... He's in the world, he's living.... He's living. He's living." The association of Luke with jazz, as representative of life, and human love, is evoked when, in their final interaction before Luke dies, Margaret and Luke are symbolically remarried. He tells Margaret, who is wearing her white robe for conducting church service, "You all in white. Like you was the day we got married. You mighty pretty." Margaret recalls that they were married on a sunny day, to which Luke responds, "They used to say, 'Happy is the bride the sun shines on.'"

In the final minutes of the play, Luke dies in Margaret's arms, just as she has finally admitted to herself and Luke that she still loves him and has always loved him: "Maybe it's not possible to stop loving anybody you ever really loved. I never stopped loving you, Luke. I tried. But I never stopped loving you." As Margaret and Luke embrace, the music of "The Old Ship of Zion," sung by the congregation, is heard emanating from the church, where Sister Moore is leading the sermon. As Luke dies, the mouthpiece to his trombone falls out of his hands to the floor. Margaret sees the mouthpiece and picks it up. As the congregation sings "I'm Gonna Sit at the Welcome Table," Margaret then enters the church, "Still holding Luke's mouthpiece clenched against her breast." Luke's trombone mouthpiece symbolizes jazz music and the values of life and human love he espoused. Margaret's gesture of holding the mouthpiece "clenched against her breast" symbolizes her decision to embrace Luke, her human love for him, and "life." Margaret's changed perspective, whereby she comes to understand that human love is not opposed to religion, but is in fact embraced by religion, is expressed through her final words to the congregation, which has decided to oust her as their pastor: "I'm just now finding out what it means to love the Lord. ... To love the Lord is to love all His children—all of them, everyone!—and suffer with them and rejoice with them and never count the cost!" As Margaret steps down from the pulpit (presumably still holding Luke's mouthpiece), Sister Moore leads the congregation in a "final song of jubilation." Walking away from the church and sounds of the hymn to enter the bedroom where Luke lies dead, Margaret symbolically distances herself from her former religious convictions and moves toward Luke's jazz world of life and human love. Margaret's final act of removing her white robe and falling beside Luke on the bed also carries sexual connotations; after years of renouncing earthly love, Margaret has finally returned to her marriage bed.

Source: Liz Brent, in an essay for *Drama for Students,* Gale Group, 2001.

Louis H. Pratt

Discussed within this essay is the viewpoint that The Amen Corner *is strictly a "religious drama."*

Sometimes the phrase "religious drama" is applied by Baldwin's critics to his first dramatic effort, *The Amen Corner*. This meaningless and inappropriate epithet reflects a superficial grasp of the more significant aspects of the drama. It is a categorization which precisely points up the reason many critics are unable to analyze the broader philosophical aspects that dominate the play. They cannot view the *whole* drama of conflict because religion, the *part,* has obscured their view. Perhaps also, the critics have fallen victim to the idea that the black man's world is a sphere of religious and racial consciousness, and therefore it is expected that the theme of religion should dominate his writings in the instances where race has failed to prevail. I suggest that *Amen* is not a "religious drama" but rather a drama of interpersonal conflict, set against the background of a storefront Holy Roller church in Harlem. Only if we view the drama from this perspective can we discover the deeper human emotions and involvements with which the playwright is concerned.

Near the opening of *The Amen Corner* it becomes obvious that Margaret Alexander, the church's pastor, has fled the world of reality to take refuge—not in religion—but in illusion and self-deception. We find her in the midst of a homiletic rejoinder to the congregation's concepts of religion: "Some of you say, 'Ain't no harm in reading the funny papers.' But children, *yes,* there's harm in it. While you reading them funny papers, your mind ain't on the Lord. And if your mind ain't stayed on Him, every hour of the day, Satan's going to cause you to fall. Amen! Some of you say, 'Ain't no harm in me working for a liquor company. I ain't going to be drinking the liquor, I'm just going to be driving the truck!' But a saint ain't got no business delivering liquor to folks all day . . . "

This admonition raises the ancient, yet valid question of whether or not some objects can be considered intrinsically good or evil apart from their social context. Obviously, Margaret's response would be affirmative. But illusion suggests confusion, and even Margaret is not always consistent in her attitude. When she is questioned about the "worldliness" of the drums and trumpets that the Philadelphia church members plan to bring to New York, she tells Sister Rice that "the evil is in what folks do with [the drum or trumpet] and what it leads them to. Ain't no harm in praising the Lord with anything you get in your hands".

But that "anything" does not include a liquor truck. Sister Boxer recognizes this incongruity and continues her challenge: "Well, ain't a truck a *thing?* And if it's all right to blow a trumpet in church, why ain't it all right for Joel to drive that truck, so he can contribute a little more to the house of God?''. Margaret replies simply that there is "all the difference in the world." She can clearly see that a musical instrument has no intrinsic moral significance, but she fails to regard the liquor truck in that same light.

Another theme in the play concerns the perversion of one of the basic concepts of Christianity: humanitarianism. The foundation of Christian doctrine rests on the compassion and sympathy of one human being for another—the saved and the unsaved—and we would expect that one as holy as Margaret would practice what she preaches. Yet we are struck by a merciless, hypocritical piety which becomes apparent when Luke returns home and collapses. In spite of her husband's need, Margaret refuses to postpone her trip to Philadelphia because "the Lord made me leave that man in there a long time ago because he was a sinner. And the Lord ain't told me to stop my work . . . ". Here we have the curious paradox of the woman of God who refuses to help an unsaved brother—her husband—precisely because he is a "sinner." Margaret has other souls to save.

When we consider the allusions to fancy cars and good times which the Philadelphia congregation seems to enjoy, the ostensible purpose for her visit lies open to question. This is particularly true in light of the apparent neglect of her own congregation, as seen when Sister Moore raises the question of Margaret's visit to Sister Rice's mother while Sister Boxer listens. The two women begin to empathize with Margaret because the Philadelphia visits have left her with her "hands full," but Sister Boxer recognizes the hypocrisy inherent in their pastor's priorities and counters, "She got her hands full right down there in her own house. Reckon she couldn't get over to pray for your mother, Sister Rice, she couldn't stay here to pray for her own husband''.

The social significance of the play, as I have suggested, is paramount. On this level the familiar Baldwin theme of the search for identity becomes apparent. Fred L. Standley's succinct analysis of the significance of this quest in Baldwin's writings provides a context for my consideration here:

This search or quest for identity is indispensable in Baldwin's opinion, and the failure to experience such is indicative of a fatal weakness in human life.

The quest for identity always involves a man with other men—there can be no self-perception apart from or outside the context of interpersonal relationships. Only within the dynamic interplay of personalities can men become profoundly aware of the significance of being a man. Baldwin sees the lack of interpersonal relations as explicitly related to the breakdown of communication between persons—specifically 'the breakdown of communication between the sexes'. . . .

Luke appears in Act I, and we soon discover that David believes his father had abandoned him. But it is Margaret who is guilty of desertion. She had interpreted the death of their second baby as a sign from the Lord to leave her husband and find a "hiding place." She finds sanctuary in the church because all other doors are closed to her, and she begins her quest for self as a minister of God. But, as Standley's comments indicate, Margaret has made a tragic mistake which is revealed when Mrs. Jackson comes forward to have Margaret pray for her ailing baby:

MARGARET: Maybe the Lord wants you to leave that man.

MRS. JACKSON: No! He don't want that!

Mrs. Jackson refuses Margaret's advice because she has already discovered that her identity can only be achieved through an open line of communication with her husband. Margaret has yet to realize this.

The parallel story of the two women becomes even more significant when we consider the sharp contrast which Baldwin makes. In Act III, after her baby has died, Mrs. Jackson tells Margaret, "I ain't like you, Sister Margaret. I don't want all this, all these people looking to me. I'm just a young woman, I just want my man and my home and my children''. Margaret, too, had lost a child when she was a young woman but instead of standing by Luke, she nagged him to drink because she felt that he was responsible for the baby's death. She deprived Luke and David of the family relationship which each needed so badly, though no more than she herself required. And as Mrs. Jackson stands alone in the church—a young woman who has just lost her second child—she is bewildered and perplexed. Margaret, however, begins to see her own mistake from the past. Realizing that she has taken the wrong road, Margaret reverses the advice that she had given to Mrs. Jackson prior to the baby's death.

"Go on home to your husband," she advises compassionately. "Go on home to your man".

In all probability, Luke is the most sensitive and perceptive character in the play. In one of the most memorable scenes, he describes his suffering, and we are moved to empathy and pity. He tells David that he has failed in his quest for identity—not because of his music—but because he has been denied the most basic human quality—love: "I don't believe no man ever got to . . . [who he is inside] without somebody loved him. Somebody *looked* at him, looked *way* down there and showed him to himself—and then started pulling, a-pulling of him up—so he could live". Luke realizes that Margaret's distorted sense of reality has precluded the extension of her love and understanding, thereby denying David the pursuit of his manhood. He knows that any efforts either to prescribe the terms of that quest or to protect him from its consequences can only result in the pain and misery of failure which he himself knows only too well. Luke has learned that a man must strike out, against the odds, if necessary, to discover the meaning of his own life. And he encourages David to take the first step toward reaching that goal.

Baldwin skillfully uses the contrasting qualities of vision and blindness to symbolize Margaret's lack of inner sight as compared to that possessed by Luke. This juxtaposition becomes particularly significant near the end of the drama, as the two parents discuss the boy—Margaret as if he were dead, Luke affirming that he is alive:

MARGARET: He's gone.

LUKE: He's gone into the world. He's gone into the world!

MARGARET: Luke, you won't never see your son no more.

LUKE: But I seen him one last time. He's in the world, he's living.

MARGARET: He's gone. Away from you and away from me.

LUKE: He's living. He's living. Is you got to see your God to know he's living?

The references to "dark" and "white" further serve to draw our attention to the contrasting moods and heighten our awareness of these two different reactions to the boy's departure:

MARGARET: Everything—is dark this morning.

LUKE: You all in white. . . .

Luke's subsequent death occasions Margaret's remorse and enhances the cognizance of her own identity. She is forced into a reexamination of those values that have precipitated her misfortune, and she emerges in the final scene with a fuller understanding of the error of her ways: ''Her triumph . . . is that . . . although she has lost everything, [she] also gains the keys to the kingdom. The kingdom is love, and love is selfless, although only the self can lead one there. She gains herself''.

Source: Louis H. Pratt, ''The Darkness Within,'' in *James Baldwin,* Twayne Publishers, 1978, pp. 83–87.

Stanley Macebuh

Stanley Macebuh's essay offers a brief look into the background of James Baldwin and touches on the making of The Amen Corner.

James Baldwin's continuous attempts to come to terms with his inheritance in the Western world have earned him a certain genteel notoriety in the history of American letters. The passionately apocalyptic vision, the pained discomfiture in the realm of morals, the evangelistic fervour and the biblical rhetoric are elements in his writings that ultimately derive from his long apprenticeship and briefer ministry in the Black Church in Harlem. From a more technical perspective, also, the extent to which he has so far shown an ability to control the fictional form is clearly not unrelated to the rhetorical practices of the Black Ministry; but beyond the generalized and now somewhat mandatory notices that have been made between the mood of his writings and his personal history, little serious attempt has so far been made to identify the precise manner in which his religious background has been for him both a source of creative inspiration and of conceptual and psychological constraint.

Students of the history of the Black Church in America are agreed that the practice of Black Christianity has always been ambiguous in its objectives; they will admit that while its joyless rejection of the things of the world in favour of a hypothetical paradise was more akin to the dreams of the early Christians, its very faith in the possibility of another, better world was in itself a subjective response to the actual condition of its members. While, that is, the rhetoric of the city of God may have been a somewhat impractical indulgence, the very mythology of Black Christianity, with its curiously appropriate analogies to the biblical accounts of the Jewish exile, may also be seen as a strategy of guarded political protest. For those who are overwhelmed by the often fatal inequities of their social condition, there is an understandable temptation to reject the real world as evil, and this rejection is often accompanied by a feverish anticipation of the millennial Eden, of an age in which there shall be neither pain nor injustice.

> "To a people without circumstantial hope", Reuben Sheres has written, "(the Black Church) offered the hope of the by and by . . . The circumstances of the existing world were bad enough that (sic) they needed to be denied or rejected . . . and in their place was substituted the hope of the world to come".

The oppressed, it is true, cannot make any exclusive claims to the knowledge of evil, but it is also true that when understood as much in its social as in its metaphysical meaning, evil is a reality with which they are only too familiar. That the congregations of the Black Church should thus have been preoccupied with the celestial city is, therefore, quite understandable, but it should also be emphasized that its millennialism was, almost by definition, equally a strategy of protest, an expression of dissatisfaction with the real condition of the members of these congregations. Indeed, the very transformation of the Church from an 'invisible institution' to an established and transparently Black organization was, in itself, an act of moderate defiance, a gesture of denunciation of the inhumanity of the older, white churches; and the long line of ministers and preachers who, through the history of this church have seen and taken advantage of the possibilities of social leadership offered by it is, clearly, an indication of its political significance.

Nevertheless, despite the implication of 'protest' that is involved in any definition of utopianism, religious or political, it must be observed that the true strength of the Black Church lay rather in the power of its metaphorical evocations than in any actual confrontations it may have had with white oppression. Lawrence Jones' observations in this regard are no doubt well-meaning enough, but he rather strains credibility when he claims that

> "AT FOURTEEN HE ENTERED THE CHURCH IN SEARCH OF SAFETY, HAVING CONVINCED HIMSELF THAT SAFETY WAS 'SYNONYMOUS WITH GOD'."

. . . viewed through the prism of present rhetoric, it becomes clear that one of the issues being contested in the founding of the Black Churches was Black Power.

The Black minister, it is true, occasionally managed to acquire a measure of actual political influence in proportion to the size of his congregation, as shown by the more recent example of Martin Luther King's meteoric career; but in general, political protest in the Black Church was a matter of analogical references to biblical history. The generic white man was Pharaoh, from whose oppression a black Moses was some day to arise to rescue his brethren, and America was Egypt, the land of sin and evil and godlessness that was doomed to suffer the brunt of God's fiery vengeance. There were compelling practical reasons for this preference for indirect imagery. The certainty of furious reprisals, of the white backlash, ensured that the 'protest' of the Black Church should be couched in such terms as to render it lame and largely unavailing. And in a world in which terror and suffering were more real than the possibility of ideal justice in society, the feverish anticipation of bliss in heaven became a more rewarding exercise than any attempt to confront the evil in the actual world.

The millennialism and the metaphorical protest in Black Christianity are two major elements that were later to be dramatized in Baldwin's writings, but there was a third element which, in our opinion, is even more significant for an understanding of Baldwin's career so far. We have seen how, in response to the actual suffering of its members, the Black Church evolved a theology in which the promise of the celestial city took on a lurid fascination for them, and we have suggested that practical considerations of safety contributed to the rhetorical extravagances of this theology. For the preacher who contemplated the plight of his congregation, safety, the evasion or assuagement of white anger, lay in metaphor, in indirect statement. He could offer them citizenship in heaven, and he could inveigh against the corruption of Sodom and Gomorrah, against the oppression of the Pharaohs with far more impunity than he could decry, in straightforward language, their real suffering. But he knew also, with a chill puritan certainty, that not all his flock would automatically gain entrance into heaven. Promising them the city of God, he also reminded them of the visitation of God's anger on all who chose the path of evil and sin. And since he knew how much more accessible the path of damnation was, his predictions of doom were even more passionate than his promises of divine intervention. And so he left in the minds of his congregation an indelible fear, a vision of their corruption, of the dangers they courted if they were ensnared by the temptations of the white man's world.

Such was the theology of Baldwin's adolescence in America. Everywhere he turned he saw the manifestations of sin. The Harlem of his boyhood was, and still is, as close to an illustration of the contours of hell as could be found anywhere in the real world. At home, his father was a discontented, imperious patriarch whose single-minded religious fervour was as formidable as his permanent rage; at school and on the streets, he saw only omens of his own personal corruptibility. Under such conditions, it was not inevitable that Baldwin should see the social horror around him primarily as a paradigm of metaphysical evil; but given the pervading squalor, both of spirit and of environment that he saw around him, it is perhaps understandable that he should have felt he had no right to expect to be spared the fate of his friends and playmates. At fourteen he entered the church in search of safety, having convinced himself that safety was 'synonymous with God'. Four years later he was out of the church; it had given him little more than the illusion of safety, and it had sought to curtail both his freedom of action and of imagination. It was at this time that he took the curiously not unrelated decision of becoming a writer.

Source: Stanley Macebuh, "The Amen Corner," in *James Baldwin: A Critical Study,* Third Press, 1973, pp. 29–33.

SOURCES

Baldwin, James, "Notes" to *The Amen Corner,* Dial Press, 1968, pp. xv–xvi.

Harris, Trudier, *Black Women in the Fiction of James Baldwin,* University of Tennessee Press, 1985, pp. 9–11.

Molette, Carlton W., "James Baldwin as Playwright," in *James Baldwin: A Critical Evaluation,* edited by Therman B. O'Daniel, Howard University Press, 1977, pp. 184–86.

Standley, Fred. L., "James Baldwin as Dramatist," in *Critical Essays on James Baldwin,* edited by Fred L. Standley and Nancy V. Burt, G. K. Hall, 1977, p. 302.

Sylvander, Carolyn Wedin, *James Baldwin,* Frederick Ungar Publishing Co., 1980, pp. 91, 96.

Turner, Darwin T., "James Baldwin and the Dilemma of the Black Dramatist," in *James Baldwin: A Critical Evaluation,* edited by Therman B. O'Daniel, Howard University Press, pp. 192, 194.

FURTHER READING

Baraka, Amiri (LeRoi Jones), *The Dutchman and the Slave Ship: Two Plays,* Morrow, 1964.

> These two plays are critically acclaimed pieces by one of the leading writers of the Blacks Arts Movement.

Harris, Trudier, *Black Women in the Fiction of James Baldwin,* University of Tennessee Press, 1985.

> This book is a critical assessment of the female characters in Baldwin's fiction.

Jones, LeRoi (Imamu Amiri Baraka) and Larry Neal, eds., *Black Fire: An Anthology of African-American Writing,* Morrow, 1968.

> This text is an important collection of works emanating from the Black Arts Movement of the 1960s and 70s.

Leeming, David Adams, *James Baldwin: A Biography,* Knopf, 1994.

> Leeming's book is a recent and highly enjoyable biography of Baldwin.

Shange, Ntozake, *for colored girls who have considered suicide, when the rainbow is enuf: A Choreopoem,* Scribner Poetry, 1997.

> Shange's play is an important experimental dramatic work (first published in 1977) that emerged from the Black Arts Movement. It addresses issues of African-American women in terms of racism and sexism.

Dancing at Lughnasa

BRIAN FRIEL
1990

Dancing at Lughnasa, by Brian Friel, one of Ireland's most important playwrights, was first performed at the Abby Theater, in Dublin, in 1990, and garnered the 1991 Olivier Award. In 1998, *Dancing at Lughnasa* was adapted to the screen in a film directed by Pat O'Connor and starring Meryl Streep.

Dancing at Lughnasa opens with a monologue by Michael, who introduces his nostalgic memories of the summer of 1936, when he was seven years old, and the five Mundy sisters, who raised him in rural Ireland, acquired their first wireless radio. Their older brother, Michael's Uncle Jack, had just returned from twenty-five years spent as a missionary in a leper colony in Uganda. Michael was born out of wedlock to Chris, the youngest of the Mundy sisters, and Gerry Evans, who deserted her and the child and only returns every couple of years to see her. The radio, which breaks down more than it works, unleashes unarticulated emotions in the five women, who spontaneously break into song and dance, with or without its aid. By the end of the year, as the older Michael explains in monologue, two of the sisters, Rose and Agnes, had run off, never to return, and Uncle Jack had died of a heart attack.

Friel's play employs the central motif of dancing and music to explore themes of Irish cultural identity, nostalgia, historical change, and pagan ritual.

AUTHOR BIOGRAPHY

Brian Friel was born near Omagh, County Tyrone, in Northern Ireland, on January 9, 1929, to Patrick, a teacher, and Christina (MacLoone) Friel. When he was ten, the family moved to Londonderry, where his father became the principal at Long Tower School, and the young Friel attended St. Columb's College from 1941 to 1946. In 1946, he enrolled in a seminary at St. Patrick's college in Maynooth, from which he graduated with a B.A. in 1948. Friel subsequently abandoned his plans to enter the priesthood, and entered St. Joseph's Teacher Training College in Belfast, which he attended from 1949 to 1950.

From 1950 to 1960, Friel worked as a teacher in Londonderry, during which time many of his short stories were published in the *New Yorker*. Encouraged by this success, Friel quit teaching in 1960 to become a full-time writer of short stories and radio plays, as well as stage plays, which were produced at the Abbey Theater in Dublin. In 1954, he married Anne Morrison, with whom he had five children. To learn more about the theater, Friel spent six months in 1963 at the Tyrone Guthrie Theater in Minneapolis, Minnesota.

This experience was followed by the production of his first internationally successful stage play. *Philadelphia, Here I Come!* garnered critical and popular acclaim, first at the Dublin Theater Festival, in 1964, and then in New York and London. The play concerns the thoughts and memories of a young Irishman shortly before he leaves Ireland to emigrate to America. *Philadelphia, Here I Come!* ran for over 300 performances at the Helen Hayes Theater, Broadway's longest run of an Irish play. Friel subsequently produced approximately one play per year, garnering such awards at the New York Drama Critics Circle Award for best foreign play, 1989, for *Aristocrats,* and the Olivier Award, 1991, for *Dancing at Lughnasa*.

In 1980, Friel, along with Stephen Rea, founded the Field Day Theater Company in Northern Ireland to provide Irish playwrights with an outlet for works of social and political significance. Friel's most critically acclaimed play, *Translations,* was performed at the Field Day Theater that same year. Friel has lived in Donegal, Ireland since 1973.

PLOT SUMMARY

Act I

Act I is set "on a warm day in early August, 1936," in the "home of the Mundy family, two miles outside the village of Ballybeg, County Donegal, Ireland." The play opens with a monologue by Michael, who introduces the play as a nostalgic memory of the summer when he was seven years old. The family of five sisters who raised him have just acquired their first wireless radio. The sisters, most of them in their thirties, include Kate, Maggie, Rose, Agnes, and Chris (Michael's mother). In addition to the arrival of the radio, Michael's Uncle Jack, who has been a missionary in a leper colony in Uganda for the past twenty-five years, has returned home. Michael explains in this opening monologue that he was a child born out of wedlock, and had only seen his father, Gerry Evans, a few times.

The action of the play opens as the five sisters do chores while occasionally breaking into singing and dancing, inspired by their new radio. Michael, as a boy, discusses with his aunts the kites he is building. Agnes suggests that they all attend the upcoming local harvest dance, to which Maggie, Rose, and Chris respond enthusiastically. But Kate vetoes the idea, saying that they are all too old to attend the dance. The sisters discuss a local boy who is suffering from severe burns that he got while attending the Festival of Lughnasa, a pagan tradition. When the radio, which only works intermittently, is turned on again, the sisters all break into a frenzied dance together, which only ends after the radio breaks down again and the music is cut off. Looking out the window, they see Gerry Evans, Michael's father, who has not paid them a visit for over a year, approaching the house. Despite the disapproval of her sisters, Chris approaches Gerry in the yard, where they both talk and laugh. Gerry tells Chris that he has gotten a job selling gramophones, and that he will soon be joining the military to fight in Spain. Gerry spontaneously takes Chris into his arms and dances with her. Later, Uncle Jack explains rituals and ceremonies in which he participated in Uganda, without regard to his Christian profession. Act I ends with Jack re-enacting a ritual dance and drumbeat from Uganda.

Act II

Act II takes place "in early September, three weeks later." In the opening scene, Maggie is doing

Brian Friel

chores in the kitchen, and Michael sits writing what he says is a letter to Santa Claus when Uncle Jack enters, about to take one of his many walks of the day. Jack describes at length a ritual ceremony he participated in Uganda, which included the sacrifice of animals. Jack then leaves for his walk. Chris and Gerry enter, as Gerry explains that he has just signed up for military duty in Spain. Gerry climbs a tree in an attempt to fix the radio by working on the antenna. Agnes returns home, carrying pails of blackberries that she has picked. It is discovered that Rose, who had told Agnes she wasn't feeling well and was going home to rest, is not home. Rose then returns home, and explains that she had arranged to go on a boat ride with Danny Bradley, the married man with whom she is in love.

The adult Michael then provides a long monologue that explains the fate of most of the characters. Agnes and Rose left the family and never returned; twenty-five years later, Michael discovered that they had gone to London, where they became destitute, and eventually died. Michael also learned, after Gerry's death, that his father had maintained a legitimate wife and three children in Wales, which Chris never knew about. Uncle Jack died suddenly of a heart attack within a year of his return to Ireland.

The scene returns to the kitchen in September, 1936, where the women are doing chores and talking amongst themselves. Gerry looks at the completed kites the child Michael has made; each have "a crude, cruel, grinning face, primitively drawn, garishly painted."

The adult Michael ends with a monologue in which he states that, with Agnes and Rose gone, and Uncle Jack dead, "much of the spirit and fun had gone out of their lives; and when my time came to go away, in the selfish way of young men I was happy to escape." Michael goes on to express the significance of music and dance to his nostalgic memories of that summer of 1936.

CHARACTERS

Gerry Evans

Gerry Evans, thirty-three, is the father of the illegitimate son Michael, whose mother is Chris. Gerry and Chris were never married, and Gerry had abandoned her with their child years earlier. Gerry appears unexpectedly every year or so, and Chris, despite herself, is charmed by him all over again each time. But Gerry is unreliable, and has a new idea for a career path with each visit. He does leave to fight in Spain, where he is injured in a motorbike accident that leaves him with a limp. He continues to visit Chris and Michael every year or so, but disappears around the time of World War II. After Gerry's death, Michael learns that his father had a wife and three children in Wales throughout all those years, unbeknownst to Chris.

Uncle Jack

See Jack Mundy

Agnes Mundy

Agnes, thirty-five, is the middle of the five sisters, and knits mittens to support them. After a local knitting factory makes their home knitting work obsolete, Agnes and her sister Rose eventually leave the family home, never to return. Twenty-five years later, Michael locates Rose and Agnes in London, where Agnes has died, and Rose soon dies in a hospice for the destitute.

Chris Mundy

Chris, twenty-six, is the youngest of the five sisters. Her son, Michael, was born out of wedlock, her love child with Gerry Evans. When Gerry returns after more than a year's absence, he charms Chris all over again, despite herself and her sister's disapproval. Gerry jokes with her, makes her laugh, and frequently breaks into a dance with her. Chris is repeatedly taken in by Gerry's unreliable promises, believing him when he says he will return soon, and that he has purchased a bicycle for Michael. Three weeks later, Gerry does return briefly, during which time he and Chris enjoy a rejuvenation of their romance before he leaves for military work in Spain. Chris never learns of Gerry's legitimate family in Wales.

Jack Mundy

Jack, fifty-three, also referred to by Michael as Uncle Jack, is the brother of the five women, and uncle of Michael. He spent twenty-five years as a missionary priest in a leper colony in Uganda, and has recently returned to Ireland, sick with malaria. It turns out that Jack was asked to leave the priesthood for participating in local, non-Christian ceremonies and rituals in Uganda. In Ireland, he seems mentally confused, as well as physically ill. He cannot keep the names of his five sisters straight, and has trouble remembering English words, having spoken mostly Swahili during his years in Uganda. The character of Uncle Jack highlights Friel's theme of paganism, as he frequently refers to local spiritual practices in Uganda, and seems to have strayed far from his Christian faith. Kate helps Uncle Jack to reinvigorate his health with long walks several times a day. Michael explains in a monologue toward the end of the play that Jack died suddenly of a heart attack within a year of returning to Ireland.

Kate Mundy

Kate is the oldest of the five sisters. She is forty years old, and was once a schoolteacher. Kate is the most resistant to the changes taking place around her, and is especially critical of the "pagan" singing and dancing that the radio has brought into her household.

Maggie Mundy

Maggie, thirty-eight, is the second oldest of the five sisters, and works as the cook and housekeeper of their home. Michael describes his Aunt Maggie as "the joker of the family." She is the one who suggests naming the new wireless radio Lugh, after the "old Celtic god of the Harvest."

MEDIA ADAPTATIONS

- *Dancing at Lughnasa* was adapted to the screen in a 1998 film produced by Colombia TriStar, directed by Pat O'Connor, and starring Meryl Streep.

Michael Mundy

Michael, as a young man, functions as a narrator and describes the action of the play through direct monologue to the audience, in the form of a nostalgic reminiscence of a time of his childhood when he was only seven years old. Michael is the illegitimate child of Chris and Gerry, and only sees his father about once a year. The child Michael in the flashbacks is primarily intent on making and painting a series of kites; only toward the end of the play are his paintings displayed to the audience, when they reveal a series of faces expressing strong emotions.

Rose Mundy

Rose, thirty-two, is the second youngest of the sisters, and works knitting mittens to support the family. Rose is in love with Danny Bradley, a married man with three children, with whom she sneaks off for a boat ride one afternoon.

THEMES

Memory

A central theme of Friel's play is memory. The action of the play, which takes place in the later summer of 1936, is framed as a depiction of Michael's memories of his childhood. In his closing monologue, the character of Michael as a young man explains the significance of these memories:

> And so, when I cast my mind back to that summer of 1936, different kinds of memories offer themselves to me. But there is one memory of that Lughnasa time that visits me most often; and what fascinates me about that memory is that it owes nothing to fact. In

TOPICS FOR FURTHER STUDY

- Friel's play takes place in Ireland in 1936. Learn more about the history of Ireland in the twentieth century. What are the major historical events of the era? What is the significance of this historical context to the concerns expressed in the play?

- In Friel's play, Michael's Uncle Jack has just returned from twenty-five years in Uganda as a missionary priest. Learn more about the history of European missionary efforts in Africa during the nineteenth and twentieth centuries. What were the conditions of the Christian missionary efforts in Africa? In what ways were missionaries significant to the history of colonial Africa?

- The initial incident that sparks the changes in the lives of the characters in Friel's play is the acquisition of a wireless radio, which broadcasts a variety of musical features throughout the play. Learn more about the history of the radio and its effect on cultural history. When did radios first become popular in private homes? What was the content of early radio broadcasts? How has the role of the radio in mass culture changed over history?

- Friel is considered the most important Irish playwright of his generation. Learn more about the history of Irish drama and theater. Who are some of the major Irish playwrights of the twentieth century? To what extent are social and political concerns central to the literary traditions of the Irish theater?

---

that memory atmosphere is more real than incident and everything is simultaneously actual and illusory. In that memory, too, the air is nostalgic with the music of the thirties.

Friel is interested in personal memory not as a means of reproducing factual incidents, but as a means of recapturing the atmosphere of the memory. Thus, for Friel, memory is "simultaneously actual and illusory," because it is true to the emotional content of the memory without necessarily being true to the actual events that took place. Music is central to Friel's play because of the extent to which he associates nostalgic memories with "the music of the thirties."

Change

Friel's play is concerned with the theme of change. The acquisition of the wireless radio in the Mundy household represents a turning point in the make-up of the family, as well as in rural Irish cultural history. The radio in 1936 is a newfangled technology that brings mass-produced popular culture into the home. The entry of this variety of music into the Mundy home unleashes repressed urges in the five single women who live there. The radio is also a harbinger of more significant historical and socioeconomic changes; namely, the Industrial Revolution. The opening of a knitting factory replaces the cottage industry by which Rose and Agnes had supported themselves by hand knitting at home. Kate, the oldest of the five sisters, expresses her anxiety at the realization that change is in the air:

> You work hard at your job. You try to keep the home together. You perform your duties as best you can—because you believe in responsibilities and obligations and good order. And then suddenly, suddenly you realize that hair cracks are appearing everywhere; that control is slipping away; that the whole thing is so fragile it can't be held together much longer. It's all about to collapse.

This anxiety over change is also raised by the introduction of pagan practices and ideas into the Mundy home. Because she is the most resistant to change, Kate is especially dubious of the singing of pagan songs, and the explanations of pagan rituals from Uganda, which Uncle Jack describes at length.

Paganism

Paganism and pagan ritual are central themes of Friel's play. The play is set during the festival of

Lughnasa, a local pagan harvest ritual of which Kate is disdainful. Furthermore, Friel presents all dancing and singing, which permeate the action of the play, as a form of pagan ritual. Uncle Jack brings back from Uganda a wealth of experiences with non-Christian ceremonies and rituals, including sacrifice of animals and native dances. Kate makes the connection between paganism, or non-Christian belief, and the music brought into the household by the radio when she exclaims: "D'you know what that thing has done? Killed all Christian conversation in this country." In an Act II monologue, Michael explains that Jack's recollections of his experiences in Uganda continued to bring more "revelations" regarding pagan rituals and ceremonies. Michael explains that "each new revelation startled—shocked—stunned poor Aunt Kate." But Kate makes some peace with Jack's expressions of paganism when she "finally hit on the phrase that appeased her: 'his own distinctive spiritual search.'" Friel seems to be celebrating such a personal "distinctive spiritual search," as expressed through the pagan rituals of music, song, and dance by the various characters.

STYLE

Setting

Friel's play is set in "the home of the Mundy family, two miles outside the village of Ballybeg, County Donegal, Ireland, in 1936." While County Donegal is a real geographic location (where Friel himself resides), the village of Ballybeg is Friel's fictional creation, utilized as a setting in many of his plays. Act I takes place in early August, and Act II takes place three weeks later, in early September. The historical setting of 1936 is significant for several reasons. The family's acquisition of their first wireless radio provides the novelty of modern technology and popular culture during that time. The historical setting is also relevant to the intrusion of the Industrial Revolution on rural Ireland. At the beginning of the play, Agnes and Rose support the family by knitting at home. A knitting factory, however, is opened nearby, and the supplier for whom they work loses all of her business to the larger company. The cottage industry by which Agnes and Rose had earned their living becomes obsolete before their very eyes. As Michael explains in monologue, "the Industrial Revolution had finally caught up with Ballybeg." This event is significant to Friel's theme of nostalgia for the rural Ireland of his childhood, as well as the theme of historical changes in Irish culture.

Monologue

The character of Michael as a young man appears in the play addressing the audience directly in a series of monologues that introduce, explain, and conclude the play. The entire play is thus presented as a depiction of Michael's nostalgic memories of this particular period in his childhood. Through this monologue, Michael explains to the audience the circumstances and history of his family, the eventual fate of each of the characters, and the significance of these memories.

Music

Music is a central theme of this play, in which the new wireless radio in the Mundy household represents an agent of change. The dialogue is thus interspersed with music coming from the radio, as well as the musical outbursts of the various characters. Specific song lyrics and types of music are therefore significant to the meaning of the play. Friel provides very specific descriptions of the radio music in the stage directions. For example, at one point the radio is turned on while the Mundy sisters do chores in the kitchen: "The music, at first scarcely audible, is Irish dance music—'The Mason's Apron,' played by a ceili band. Very fast; very heavy beat; a raucous sound. At first we are aware of the beat only. Then, as the volume increases slowly, we hear the melody." The Mundy sisters then slowly break into a frenzied dance that only partially matches the music, and is expressive of their repressed desires. At other points, characters break into snatches of popular songs, as well as folk songs, which Kate refers to disdainfully as "pagan songs." Music is associated with "pagan," or non-Christian, ritual again when Uncle Jack breaks into a rhythmic dance he learned in Uganda, beating two sticks together for musical accompaniment; the stage directions state that: "Jack picks up two pieces of wood . . . and strikes them together. The sound they make pleases him. He does it again—and again—and again. Now he begins to beat out a structured beat whose rhythm gives him pleasure."

HISTORICAL CONTEXT

Abbey Theatre

Friel's early plays were performed at the famous Abbey Theatre in Dublin. The Abbey Theatre, established in 1904, has been an important influence in the history of twentieth-century Irish drama. In 1899, the poet William Butler Yeats and other Irish writers established the Irish Literary Theatre to promote Irish dramatic works. In 1902, this organization became subsumed under the Irish National Dramatic Society, which in 1903 was renamed the Irish National Theatre Society. The Abbey Theatre was located in an old theater on Abbey Street in Dublin, thanks to the financial contribution of a wealthy Englishwoman. In 1904, it opened with a series of plays by Yeats, Lady Gregory, and John Millington Synge. Synge's controversial satiric work, *Playboy of the Western World,* first staged at the Abbey in 1907, lead to rioting and violent protest by outraged audiences in Dublin, New York, and Philadelphia. After a period of difficulty, the Abbey Theatre became state subsidized in 1924. In the 1950s, the Abbey Theatre was destroyed in a fire, and was relocated to the Queen's Theatre, until 1966, when a new theater was built at the original location on Abbey Street.

Uganda and Swahili

In Friel's play, Michael's Uncle Jack has recently returned from twenty-five years spent as a missionary in a leper colony in Uganda. During that time, Uncle Jack spoke Swahili with the local population, and has forgotten many English words. Uganda is a country in Africa which, during the mid-nineteenth century, was subjected to "exploration," first by Arab traders in search of ivory and slaves in the 1840s, and then by Egyptian and Sudanese slave traders in the 1860s. In 1856, Mutesa I became the ruler of Buganda, a state within the region now called Uganda. The famous British explorer, Henry Morton Stanley, arrived in the region in 1875, and persuaded Mutesa to allow Christian missionaries to enter Buganda. In 1877, the first missionaries, from the Church Missionary Society, arrived, followed in 1879 by missionaries from the Roman Catholic White Fathers Mission. Missionaries became influential in the region and were responsible for the establishment of schools in the early 1900s. In 1890, the British declared the region to be under their rule; that same year, a treaty between the Imperial British East Africa Company and Buganda's new leader, Mwanga, secured Buganda as a region under British influence. In 1894, the British government declared Buganda a "protectorate." After several revolts in 1897, the Buganda Agreement of 1890 determined that local chiefs would maintain power while agreeing to operate under British authority. During the interwar years of the 1920s and 30s, the power of local chiefs receded under British intervention. After periods of civil unrest during the post-World War II era, however, Uganda was granted national independence in 1962. The Swahili language spoken by Uncle Jack in Uganda is the mother tongue or "lingua franca" of many countries along the Eastern Coast of Africa. Swahili originated from the arrival of Arab traders in Africa, and was originally written in Arabic (although it is now written in the Roman alphabet). It was first adopted by Bantu-speaking tribes, and is similar in grammar to Bantu languages. The use of Swahili eventually spread further into Africa via the Arab ivory and slave trade. European traders and colonists in Africa also began to use Swahili in their contact with African peoples. Today, Swahili is spoken in Tanzania, Kenya, and Uganda.

CRITICAL OVERVIEW

Brian Friel is one of the leading Irish playwrights of the twentieth century. Friel's works have been praised for their skillful focus on Irish cultural identity. Referring to Friel as a "modern master," and "Ireland's most important contemporary writer," Richard Pine praises the playwright who "has maintained a tradition of Irish literature by addressing local themes which have universal significance." Pine goes on to describe the thematic concerns of Friel's dramatic settings in Ireland:

> Friel's Ireland, if it exists at all, is a complexity of loyalties, horrors, hopes, confused time sequences, hostilities of the sacred and the profane, a constant probing of its role as victim, a continual belief in the restoration of a way of living and thinking which was beneficent and provident but which has somehow turned tragic and punitive.

Critics particularly note Friel's use of language as a means of expressing issues of Irish nationalism. F. C. McGrath notes that, in *Dancing at Lughnasa,* "The language . . . is intensely lyrical." Richard Pine asserts that "Friel has provided us with a new language, an Irish-English more powerful than English-English, to express . . . 'concepts of Irishness.'" Alan J. Peacock states that several of Friel's plays

A scene from the 1991 production of Dancing at Lughnasa *at Dublin's Abbey Theater.*

"make exhilaratingly explicit a preoccupation with the dubieties, the duplicities, limitations and simultaneous analytical, expressive and transcendent qualities of language which is ubiquitous in Friel's drama." Peacock goes on to list some of the thematic concerns addressed by Friel's use of language:

> The power of naming and its political or metaphysical consequences; the problematics of self-definition through language and the tyranny of imposed definitions at a personal, social or national level; emotional inarticulacy at the individual level and cultural aphasia at the national; authentic and inauthentic narrative—these are the kind of themes which insistently feature in Friel's drama.

His 1990 play, *Dancing at Lughnasa,* is one of Friel's most popular and most critically acclaimed. It has garnered many awards, including the Evening Standard, Writers Guild, Plays and Players, and Olivier, as best play of the 1990–91 season, as well as the Tony and the New York Drama Critics Circle award for best new play of the 1991–92 season. Critics especially note the scene in Act I during which the Mundy sisters spontaneously break into expressionistic dance, inspired by the music from their new radio. Claire Gleitman asserts that "This scene, so quickly famous, is strikingly effective in its invocation of the repressed impulses that lie beneath the sisters' calm exteriors." Gleitman goes on to explain that "For a brief moment, the play modulates from Friel's characteristic naturalism into an expressionistic interlude that reveals, with breathtaking compression, the subterranean lives of the characters." Christopher Murray concurs that "The most extraordinary scene in the play, as anyone who has seen *Lughnasa* on stage can testify, is the spontaneous dance which erupts in Act One, as the five sisters join in a wild response to traditional Irish music on the radio." Fintan O'Toole agrees that "The play's most vibrant moments—the wild dance in the first act—are moments of surrender by the sisters to the force of music, the urge of the dance, a force at once joyous and tyrannical, a dance of grief and liberation." Peacock refers to this scene in the Abbey Theater production as "a piece of pure theatre: Ireland's finest theatrical *writer* had brought off the core scene in his drama entirely in non-verbal terms."

Friel's first critical and popular success was the production of *Philadelphia, Here I Come!* (1964), which garnered the author immediate international acclaim. It became the longest running Irish play on Broadway, playing over 300 performances at the Helen Hayes Theater. Friel followed this success with approximately one play per year for the next ten years. In *The Loves of Cass McGuire* (1966), an eighty-nine-year old Irish woman returns to Ireland after living in America for thirty-four years. This production was followed by *Lovers* (1967), *Crystal and Fox* (1968), and *The Mundy Scheme* (1970), a political satire that met with resounding failure; according to June Schlueter, in the *Dictionary of Literary Biography*, "The play's inadequacies were confirmed by its unhappy reception on Broadway . . . where it closed after only four performances." *The Gentle Island* (1971) centers on the Sweeney family, the only remaining inhabitants on the island of Inishkeen, off the coast of Ireland. *The Freedom of the City* (1973) is set in the aftermath of Bloody Sunday, when, in 1970, British troops killed three civil rights demonstrators in Northern Ireland. Subsequent plays by Friel include *Volunteers* (1975), *Living Quarters* (1977), *Faith Healer* (1979), and *Aristocrats* (1979).

In 1980, Friel and actor Stephen Rea founded the Field Day theater, devoted to Irish plays of social and political significance. The first production of the Field Day was Friel's masterpiece, *Translations* (1980). *Translations* takes place in Donegal, Ireland, in 1833, and focuses on the closing of Irish schools by English authorities, who imposed English language schools on the local Irish populations, in spite of their protests. Schlueter comments that "The contemporary struggle in Northern Ireland resonates in Friel's sensitive treatment of the collision between the English and the Irish." In *Wonderful Tennessee* (1993), Friel focuses on a group of characters as they await a ferry that never comes. *Molly Sweeney* (1994), is about a forty-one-year-old blind Irish woman who regains her sight after an operation. Friel's most recent play to date is *Give Me Your Answer, Do!* (1997).

CRITICISM

Liz Brent

Brent has a Ph.D. in American Culture, specializing in film studies, from the University of Michigan. She is a freelance writer and teaches courses in the history of American cinema. In the following essay, Brent discusses the motif of song and dance in Friel's play.

Song and dance are major motifs of Friel's *Dancing at Lughnasa*. They symbolize the play's central thematic concerns with paganism and societal change. The instrument of change in the Mundy household is the acquisition of the family's first wireless radio. The presence of the radio, which functions only sporadically, inspires in the Mundy sisters a spirit of freedom and expressiveness heretofore repressed within their traditional Irish Catholic household. The setting of the play during Ireland's pagan tradition of the Festival of Lughnasa provides a backdrop of pagan dance, music, and ritual, which is (inadvertently) inspired in the Mundy sisters by the radio. Throughout the play, various characters spontaneously break into song and dance, more often than not, at times when the radio itself is broken. Various references to the technology that made possible the spread of popular musical culture to a mass audience, such as the radio and gramophone, are included. References to American movie stars, such as Fred Astaire, Ginger Rogers, Shirley Temple, and Mae West, known for their song and dance routines, as well as references to specific song lyrics from Broadway and Hollywood musicals, elaborate the play's central thematic concerns.

Act I of Friel's play takes place during a Festival of Lughnasa, in rural Ireland. Elmer Andrews explains that Lughnasa "was one of the four major pre-Christian, Celtic festivals. . . . Basically a harvest festival, Lughnasa was celebrated over fifteen days in honour of the god Lugh, one of the most important Irish gods." Andrews goes on to conclude that "Thus, Lughnasa is traditionally associated with sexual awakening, rebirth, continuances. . . ." Andrews points out that "These motifs of sexual awakening and magical transformation are central to Friel's play." Furthermore, the association of the ritual of Lughnasa with pagan song and dance is significant within the play because the sexual awakening of the Mundy sisters is inspired by the similarly pagan music emanating from their newly acquired radio.

In Friel's play, changes in both family dynamics and traditional Irish culture are represented by the arrival of the Mundy family's first wireless radio in 1936. The Mundy sisters dub their new radio, "Marconi because that was the name emblazoned on the set." A brief history of radio broadcasting helps to put this key element of the play into a broader context. The first radio broadcast was transmitted in the United States in 1906, and included music, poetry, and a talk. The first radio station, however, was not founded until 1921, but soon led to the opening of many other radio stations across

WHAT DO I READ NEXT?

- *Waiting for Godot* (1952) is the masterpiece of the absurdist playwright Samuel Beckett, to whose works Friel's are frequently compared.

- *The Glass Menagerie* (1944) by Tennessee Williams is a "memory play" to which *Dancing at Lughnasa* has often been compared. A man narrates the play as a memory of his mother, sister, and father who has abandoned them, addressing the audience directly, as in Friel's play. The lines, "I give you truth in the pleasant disguise of illusion," and "In memory everything seems to happen to music," echo similar sentiments as expressed in Friel's play.

- *Philadelphia, Here I Come!* (1964) was Friel's first commercially and critically successful stage play. It is about the thoughts of a young Irish man about to emigrate to America.

- Friel's *Aristocrats* (1979) is about an aristocratic Irish Catholic family on the verge of decline. In 1989 this play won the New York Drama Critics Circle Award for best foreign play.

- Friel's *Translations* (1980) is considered by some critics to be his best stage play. It focuses on the theme of Irish national identity in the wake of British governmental policy in Ireland.

- *The Diviner: Brian Friel's Best Short Stories* (1983) is a selection of Friel's short stories previously published in the *New Yorker* and other collections.

- *Molly Sweeney* (1994) is another Friel play about a blind forty-one-year-old woman whose sight is unexpectedly restored, altering her relationship with her husband.

- *Give Me Your Answer, Do!* (1997) is Friel's most recent play. Set in Friel's fictional country of Donegal, this play concerns an author, Tom Connolly, and his alcoholic wife, Daisy, who are visited in their rural home by a scholar, another author, and Daisy's parents.

---

the United States. In the United Kingdom, the first radio broadcast, which was transmitted from Ireland, was not made until 1919. Throughout the early 1920s, the opening of radio stations, and the acquisition of radios in private homes, spread rapidly throughout the world. In the United Kingdom, the Post Office banned non-government-sponsored radio broadcasts until 1921, when it granted the Marconi Company the right to broadcast for fifteen minutes per week. In 1922, the Marconi House established a radio station in London. Radio broadcasts were regulated in the United Kingdom, beginning in 1922, by the British Broadcasting Company, until 1927, when the British Broadcasting Corporation (BBC), a public regulatory organization under the supervision of Parliament, took its place. The presence of the Marconi brand radio in Friel's play links technological advances to the spread of popular culture (in the form of music), which inspires the performance of pagan rituals of song and dance in a spiritually repressed family and society.

Michael's father, Gerry Evans, who stops by the Mundy household every few years to visit Chris, Michael's mother, embodies the free-spirited, pagan rituals of song and dance. Gerry tells Chris that he has gotten a job selling gramophones. "This country is gramophone crazy," Gerry tells Chris. "People thought gramophones would be a thing of the past when radios came in. But they were wrong." The gramophone was an early phonograph player, which eventually developed into the modern hi-fi record player, and has, since the 1980s, given way to the compact disk player. The first phonograph recording can be dated to Thomas Edison's experimental success at recording onto a wax cylinder in 1877. In 1887, Emile Berliner patented the gramophone, which utilized a disk for phonographic

> "... TECHNOLOGICAL ADVANCES IN THE FORM OF RADIO BROADCAST AND MASS-PRODUCED MUSIC REPRODUCTION INSPIRE A MASS AUDIENCE TO GET BACK IN TOUCH WITH TRADITIONAL PAGAN EXPRESSIONS OF SPIRITUALITY THROUGH SONG AND DANCE."

recording. In 1898, a branch of the Gramophone Company was established in London, and eventually branches spread throughout Europe. In the 1890s, phonograph recordings were a novelty of public entertainment, but by the 1910s, phonographs were popular in private homes. The popularity of the newly developed radio in the mid-1920s, however, resulted in a significant decline in popularity of phonographs. But in the early 1930s, several mergers reinvigorated the industry. In Friel's play, Gerry's mention of, and association with, the gramophone links his character to the pagan rituals of popular song and dance inspired by newly developed technologies of mass culture, such as the gramophone.

Thus, in Friel's play, while technological advances in the form of the newly erected knitting factory result in the death of tradition (in the form of the cottage industry of knitting), technological advances in the form of radio broadcast and mass-produced music reproduction inspire a mass audience to get back in touch with traditional pagan expressions of spirituality through song and dance.

Friel's play makes reference to the famous dance duo of classic Hollywood musicals, Fred Astaire and Ginger Rogers. In Act I, after the five Mundy sisters break out into a frenzied song and dance, inspired by music from the radio, Maggie lights a cigarette and says, "I'll tell you something, girls: this Ginger Rogers has seen better days." In Act II, toward the end of the play, Michael explains in monologue that, "The last time I saw [my father] was dancing down the lane in imitation of Fred Astaire, swinging his walking stick, Uncle Jack's tricorn at a jaunty angle over his left eye." Fred Astaire (1899–1987) and Ginger Rogers (1911–1995) became an enormously popular dance duo in Hollywood's musical comedies throughout the 1930s, beginning with their first film together, *Down to Rio,* in 1933. Subsequent Astaire-Rogers films included *The Gay Divorcee* (1934), *Top Hat* (1935), and *Swing Time* (1936). During the time in which Friel's play is set—1936—Astaire and Rogers would have been well known for their song-and-dance routines both in these films and through the mass marketing of recorded music and radio broadcasts.

In Act II, Gerry first dances with Agnes, then asks Chris to dance with him. When she refuses, Maggie enthusiastically blurts out, "I'll dance with you, Gerry!" In preparation to dance, Maggie kicks off her shoes, saying, "Stand back there, girls. Shirley Temple needs a lot of space." Shirley Temple (born 1928) was an enormously popular child movie star during the 1930s, known for her tap-dancing routines that were accompanied by song and music. Perhaps her most famous routine is "On the Good Ship Lollipop," and some of her better known films include *The Little Colonel* (1935), and *Wee Willie Winkie* (1937). It is significant that Maggie associates herself with both Ginger Rogers and Shirley Temple, as her character seems to embrace, perhaps more so than some of the other sisters, the pagan spirit of song-and-dance.

References to Hollywood movie stars known for their song-and-dance routines are just one link between the medium of mass-produced popular culture to the pagan spirit of song-and-dance that preoccupies the Mundy household in Friel's play.

At various points in the play, characters sing lyrics from "Anything Goes," the title song of the Broadway musical, *Anything Goes* (1934), which features songs by the famous musical composer Cole Porter (1892–1964). Porter composed an incredible string of hit musicals for both Broadway, including *Gay Divorcee* (1932), *Anything Goes, Red, Hot and Blue* (1934), and *Silk Stockings* (1955). Many of these were adapted to the screen and became hit Hollywood musicals as well, including *Anything Goes* in 1936, which starred Astaire and Rogers. Many popular hit songs emerged from Porter's successes on the stage and screen, including "I Get a Kick out of You," "I've Got You Under My Skin," and "Just One of Those Things," as well as "Anything Goes." In addition to his association with the popular entertainment forms of Broadway and Hollywood musicals, Cole Porter was known for his nontraditional relationships, such as his open homosexuality in conjunction with his open marriage to a wealthy divorcee. (A musical tribute to Cole Porter was compiled in the 1990 album release, *Red, Hot, and Blue,* which features Cole Porter songs as performed by various pop musicians.) Reference to a song by Porter in Friel's play indirectly invokes the free-spirited lifestyle that Porter led, as well as the free-spirited sexual implications of his famously risqué song lyrics. It is this free-spirited quality that Friel associates with the pagan ritual of song and dance.

The specific lyrics to the song "Anything Goes," sung by characters in Friel's play, further develop the themes of popular culture both supplanting tradition and inspiring paganistic spirituality. While dancing with Agnes, Gerry sings several stanzas from "Anything Goes":

> In olden times a glimpse of stocking Was looked on as something shocking . . . anything goes. Good authors, too, who once knew better words Now only use four-letter words Writing prose, Anything goes. If driving fast cars you like, If low bars you like, If old hymns you like, If Mae West you like, Or me undressed you like, Why, nobody will oppose. When ev'ry night, the set that's smart is in—'truding in nudist parties in Studios, Anything goes.

These lyrics pick up on several key motifs and central themes of Friel's play. The basic gist of the song is that social morals in the modern world have loosened to such a great extent that "anything goes"—particularly, open expressions of sexuality are referred to in the song as characteristic of changing times: "a glimpse of stocking," exposing a woman's leg; the use of "four-letter words" even in print; even nudity, as indicated by the phrases "me undressed" and "nudist parties." These changing times are also associated with the development of modern technology, as referred to in the song through the mention of "fast cars." In Friel's play, as well, the release of sexual repression and other pagan impulses as a result of changing times is associated with the development of modern technology in the form of the radio. This is significant in that the five Mundy sisters, at the beginning of the play, are characterized by a deep sexual repression that is only unleashed with the arrival of popular music via the radio.

The reference to Mae West (1893–1980) in Cole Porter's lyrics furthers develops the focus of the song on outward sexual expression as an acceptable facet of modern times. Mae West is best known for her outward display of female sexuality on both the Broadway stage during the 1920s, and in Hollywood movies during the 1930s. On Broadway, West was given greater artistic freedom, and became enormously popular for the character Diamond Lil, whom she created through a musical that she both wrote and starred in. The degree of controversy aroused by West is indicated by her arrest in 1926 for her role as a prostitute in her play *Sex*. After her film debut in 1932, West became equally popular and controversial for her Hollywood movies, such as *She Done Him Wrong* (1933), *I'm No Angel* (1933), and *Belle of the Nineties* (1934), in which her characters were often based on Diamond Lil. West became a target of Catholic organizations pushing for greater censorship in Hollywood movies, a battle that they effectively won with the institution and enforcement of the Motion Picture Production Code in 1934. West was especially known, on both stage and screen, for her sexual innuendoes, as expressed in her musical numbers, dialogue, and bodily gestures. The significance of a reference to West in Friel's play is to invoke the image of a woman famous for her outward expression of female sexuality as a means of contrast to the sexually repressed Mundy sisters. West's risqué expression of sexuality through her song-and-dance numbers once again suggests that the Mundy sisters experience a form of sexual awakening through song and dance.

Source: Liz Brent, in an essay for *Drama for Students,* Gale Group, 2001.

Leah Ryan

Leah Ryan is a writer and a teacher of dramatic writing with an MFA in playwriting. In the following essay, Ryan examines the effect of the loss of meaningful ritual in the lives of the characters in Dancing at Lughnasa.

Friel's *Dancing at Lughnasa,* written in 1990, surrounds the lives of five grown sisters in rural Ireland in 1936. Though the eldest sister, Kate, struggles to maintain a hard-working, god-fearing Catholic household, Ireland's pagan origins beckon constantly, and the tension between the two ideologies threatens the family's already tenuous harmony. The characters have many unrequited longings (such as romantic love and material possessions) but the lack of religious or spiritual ritual is conspicuous.

Brian Friel was born the son of a Catholic teacher in County Tyrone, Ireland in 1929. He is known not only as a playwright but also as a theatre director and a short story writer. He now lives in

Meryl Streep (as Kate Mundy), Brid Brennan (as Agnes Mundy) and Sophie Thompson (as Rose Mundy) in a scene from the 1998 film adaptation of Dancing at Lughnasa.

County Donegal, which is also the setting for *Dancing at Lughnasa*.

The five Mundy sisters keep chickens and knit gloves to support themselves. Kate, the oldest sister, earns the only steady wage in the household as a schoolteacher. Economic hardship and isolation are taken for granted. The only males present are Michael, age seven, the son of Chris (the youngest sister), and Father Jack, the Mundy sisters' only brother, a priest who has just returned from a twenty-five year mission in Africa.

Lughnasa is not a place, as the title might suggest, but a pagan festival of the harvest, complete with roaring bonfires, ritual chants, and animal sacrifice. The fires of Lughnasa seem to burn off in the distance throughout the play; we're always aware of their presence. The Mundy household, though, is not a place where such revelry is enjoyed. Not only is it limping along financially, but sibling relationships are strained to a breaking point. Kate, as the eldest and the wage-earner, feels obliged to be the arbiter of everyone else's moral conduct. This positioning of the sisters is clear from the first scene, when Chris muses that she might begin wearing lipstick, and Agnes retorts, "As long as Kate's not around. Do you want to make a pagan of yourself?" All things forbidden are associated with paganism.

Dancing at Lughnasa is a memory play. Our window into this world is provided by Michael. He appears to us as an adult and takes us through the story like a narrator, but also plays the role of the seven-year-old Michael, making us ever aware that we are looking backward into childhood through the eyes of an adult.

The play opens with a monologue by Michael, in which he prepares us for the world we are about to enter. He explains that this is the summer his Uncle Jack, whom he had never before met, came home from Africa. He tells us that this is also the summer the family got their first wireless radio set. The set is less than reliable, but its effect on the household is dramatic. His mother and aunts have launched a spontaneous dance in the kitchen, something Michael has never seen before. Michael explains that the radio has been named like a family pet; first Lugh, after the Celtic God of the harvest, but that name was nixed by the pious Kate and they finally just called it Marconi (the name stamped on the front of the set). Though he's only seven, he's somehow aware that the life he has come to know is on the verge of change: "I know I had a sense of unease, some awareness of a widening breach between what seemed to be and what was, of things changing too quickly before my eyes, of becoming what they ought not to be."

Almost as an afterthought, Michael explains that this was the summer his father Gerry came home for a brief visit. This event seems no more or no less important than the arrival of the wireless in his memory.

While Michael delivers his speech, he flies a kite, and the other characters stand behind him in a formal tableau. A tableau can freeze the world of the play and its characters like a painting. The use of tableau at the opening of the play also underscores the concept of the memory play. The characters are frozen in the midst of an activity that well represents them, much as the mind can capture a long-ago memory in a kind of single-frame snapshot. In this case, Father Jack (Michael's Uncle) and Gerry (Michael's father) are dressed in ceremonial uniforms. We learn that Father Jack was a chaplain in the military, and that Gerry is on his way to join the war in Spain. In this memory tableau, their uniforms might suggest the occasional (and mythic) role of men in Michael's life.

The Marconi, again, is unreliable, flickering on and off without warning. So, it seems, is Father Jack's conscious grasp on reality. Twenty-five years in Africa (first as a military chaplain, then as a missionary priest in a leper colony) have left him physically weak and mentally unhinged. His return has had an uneasy affect on everyone. Michael, who has heard Father Jack described in resplendent terms, is disappointed and confused by the first sight of his wasted, disoriented uncle. Jack seems to forget where he is rather easily, which unnerves his tightly wrapped sister Kate. He refers to Michael (whose parents are not married) as a "love-child" and says that in Africa it's good to have "love-children"; he goes so far as to encourage the other sisters to have one too. Jack often slips and refers to his sisters by the name of his African houseboy. But most unsettling is the fact that he seems to have come to regard the African rituals he witnessed (and participated in) for several decades as perfectly harmless and commonplace, giving no offense to his Catholic sensibilities. Father Jack's level of comfort with paganism is ultimately a catalyst to the household's disintegration.

> "THROUGHOUT THE PLAY, THE SISTERS DISCUSS THE LUGHNASA FESTIVAL THAT THEY KNOW ONLY FROM RUMOR. A LOCAL BOY HAS BEEN BURNED IN THE BONFIRE. HOW DID IT HAPPEN? ARE ANIMALS ACTUALLY SACRIFICED?"

The sisters have a kind of marriage (to each other), and have worn comfortable (if unsatisfying) grooves into their daily lives. Agnes and Rose earn a little money by knitting gloves, until eventually they're put out of business by a nearby factory. Maggie's job seems to be to keep the peace and make everyone laugh. Kate's role resembles that of an iron-fisted patriarch. She earns the wages and makes the rules. Agnes, along with her knitting, takes care of the house and does the cooking. Though all the women seem to help, it's clear that Agnes is relied upon to make sure it all gets done, and that Rose is her right hand. It's clear, also, that she feels taken for granted by Kate. Agnes finally says, "What you have here, Kate, are two unpaid servants." Agnes and Kate bicker like an unhappily married couple whose union is one of necessity. The forces pulling them apart are stronger than those holding them together.

Chris is the youngest of the sisters, and is also Michael's mother. When Michael's father arrives unexpectedly to see Chris, all the other sisters are as watchful and protective as young parents on their teenage daughter's first date. Kate is sure that Gerry is going to break Chris' heart again, and furious that he does not contribute financially to his son's upbringing. While some of the other sisters have affection for him, all are wary of the effect Gerry will have on their lives. For his part, Gerry is casual about his comings and goings, and is completely out of touch with his son, to the point where he invents a reality for Michael. He asks Chris how Michael is enjoying school, and when Chris tells him that Michael doesn't have much to say about it, Gerry quickly replies, "He loves it. He adores it. They all love school nowadays." It's clear that though Gerry feels a guilty twinge here and there, he feels no real sense of obligation, and has no moral dilemma telling Chris that he'll be gone again for an indeterminate period. Gerry and his son have no shared memories, no family traditions, no father-son rituals.

The women have created a home, something solid and constant. It's a place for Father Jack to come home to, and a place for Michael to grow up. Gerry seems quite comfortable abandoning the care of his son not just to Chris, but to the household created by Chris and her sisters. But of course this home is not as stable as it seems.

Rose, who is thought of as "simple," is constantly alluding to her fascination with a certain man in town named Danny Bradley, a man of whom all the sisters disapprove. Danny is a married father of three, and Rose's assertion that his wife has left and gone to England does little to reassure her sisters. Though she's not the youngest, Rose is the innocent of the family, and it seems that any man who preyed upon her would arouse the family's suspicions.

Meanwhile, the lack of male companionship has created an almost palpable sense of longing in the house. Long-ago suitors and missed chances at love hang in the air like ghosts. At one point, the women discuss attending the annual harvest dance, which none of them have gone to in years, but which was once the site of much youthful revelry. Briefly, the women enjoy a discussion of what they will wear and how much they love to dance. Kate, though momentarily swayed by the idea, forbids them all from attending, complaining that household expenses demand any extra money that would be spent on frivolities such as dances and fixing the wireless. It's dancing, though, that transcends their differences. In dancing, they find a sense of release and of belonging, which resembles religious ecstasy.

Kate denies herself everything she denies her sisters. The one man in town who seems to interest her, Austin Morgan, the shopkeeper, marries someone else. Kate is held together by work and a sense of order and obligation. All this begins to unravel when she loses her job (the implication being that Jack's African rantings do not befit a Catholic schoolteacher's household) and finally when Agnes and Rose leave home.

Throughout the play, the sisters discuss the Lughnasa festival that they know only from rumor. A local boy has been burned in the bonfire. How did it happen? Are animals actually sacrificed? Kate forbids discussion of the ceremonies but curiosity still hovers. Though the women appear to be practicing Catholics, there is a conspicuous lack of religious ritual in their lives. Religion functions more as a set of rules and admonishments than as a source of strength and spiritual renewal. Perhaps it's not the faith they yearn for, but the ceremony.

Father Jack tells of animal sacrifices in Africa. He struggles to describe the rituals and finds himself at a loss for words. He has to grope for the word "ceremony." He suggests that in the realm of ritual, spoken language is unnecessary. Like the Celtic-inspired dance that the Mundy sisters seem ready to burst into at any moment, ritual transcends language and intellect. "Coming back in the boat there were days when I couldn't remember even the simplest words," he says. "Not that anybody seemed to notice."

In the final scene, Father Jack emerges in the uniform he wore in the opening tableau, but now it is worn and soiled. He hands off his hat to Gerry. Michael's kites have primitive, mask-like faces on them, suggesting that something pagan has taken hold for Michael to carry into the next generation. In his final speech, Michael talks about the disintegration of the household, and of his own departure: "In the selfish way of young men, I was happy to escape."

Like all the men before him, he can come and go without a sense of obligation. But Michael is self-aware and can name his own selfishness. He's also able to name the importance of ceremony and ritual, the dancing that his mother and aunts have denied themselves. The play ends with dance music reverberating over a dark stage. The music has the final word.

Source: Leah Ryan, in an essay for *Drama for Students,* Gale Group, 2001.

Elmer Andrews

Elmer Andrews presents a detailed analysis of the characters and the importance of their "individual experiences" in the play.

Friel's play is set in 1936, in the months when De Valera was drawing up his Catholic Constitution for a Catholic people. 'Will you vote for De Valera, will you vote?' sings Maggie to Rose's song about Abyssinia. These women are the victims of an oppressively Catholic ethos, shortly to be enshrined in a Constitution which recognised 'the Family as the natural primary and fundamental unit group of society' and 'the special position of the Holy Catholic and Apostolic Roman Church as the guardian of the faith professed by the great majority of its citizens'. Responding to a demand in the country at the time for traditional Catholic social teaching in matters of marriage and family law, the Free State outlawed divorce, contraception and abortion. De Valera's programme, writes Robert Kee, was characterised by a 'homely narrowness' and 'pious dogmatism':

> Conservative in social and economic outlook, paying limited attention to problems such as housing, slum clearance and social welfare in general, safely—some would say smugly—steeped in the orthodox moral and social teachings of the Catholic Church of that day, it offered little in the way of inspiration to the young. Emigration, so long held by nationalists to have been one of the evils of English rule and to have been caused by the lack of freedom, continued. A strict literary censorship banned at different times almost all the best modern writers, including Irish ones.

Terence Brown refers to 'an almost Stalinist antagonism to modernism, to surrealism, free verse, symbolism and the modern cinema', which combined with 'prudery (the 1930s saw opposition to paintings of nudes being exhibited in the National Gallery in Dublin) and a deep reverence for the Irish past'. Summarising the attitude of Irish writers of the 1930s and 1940s, Brown continues:

> Instead of de Valera's Gaelic Eden, the writers revealed a mediocre, dishevelled, often neurotic and depressed petit-bourgeois society that atrophied for want of a liberating idea. O'Faolain's image for it, as it was James Joyce's before him, is the entire landscape of Ireland shrouded in snow: 'under that white shroud, covering the whole of Ireland, life was lying broken and hardly breathing.'

The repressive Catholic ethos may have helped to consolidate a sense of identity, but it certainly left little room either for modernism and cosmopolitan standards or for the instinctual needs of ordinary people or for the least remnants of 'pagan' tradition. . . .

Kate objects to levity, playfulness and novelty for they are threats to her fragile order. The hair cracks, we recognise early on, are caused not just by external forces over which the sisters have no control, but by equally unruly forces within the family itself, within consciousness (even Kate's). The greater the effort of repression, it would seem, the stronger the insurrectionary pressures. The great merit of the play is the unmistakable tension which we feel between the very human desire for order and stability and the equally strong desire for excitement and new experience. This tension has various forms. On one level, it is a struggle between Christianity and paganism, on another, it is the challenge

> "THE GREAT MERIT OF THE PLAY IS THE UNMISTAKABLE TENSION WHICH WE FEEL BETWEEN THE VERY HUMAN DESIRE FOR ORDER AND STABILITY AND THE EQUALLY STRONG DESIRE FOR EXCITEMENT AND NEW EXPERIENCE."

offered to civilised value by an irruption of repressed libidinal energy, at yet another, it is the harassment of the symbolic order of 'ordinary' language and fixed structure by a semiotic force outside language which disrupts all stable meanings and institutions.

Dancing is the play's central image for a contravention and violation of 'normal' reality. It is Friel's new expression of the secret life which before he had represented verbally (in the character of, say, Private Gar) but which we know in actuality never formulates itself in words, even in the mind. The dancing is the play's chief 'opening' activity which is disturbing because it represents a break in the acknowledged order, an irruption of the inadmissible within the usual routine, a ritualised suspension of everyday law and order. In the repressive climate of the 1930s, dancing was regarded with some suspicion as representing a species of moral decadence and a threat to the morals of the nation's youth. These puritanical attitudes were reflected in the Public Dancehalls' Act of 1953 which required licensing of dance-halls. This pleased rural businessmen and the clergy for it did away with open-air dancing at crossroads and dances held in private houses. But it was a measure which contributed to the dying out of many traditional customs, though ironically the government which enacted it was officially pledged to a revival of Irish folklore and Irish traditional music and dancing.

When Agnes suggests that the sisters all go to the harvest dance, Rose quickly launches into 'a bizarre and abandoned dance' while Kate 'panics'. . . .

In reacting to the dancing as she does, Kate is reacting to the *id,* to the assertion of the spermatic principle, the free imagination, the buried impulse. She represents the repressive force of Christianity inhibiting full and free embracement of this primitive, pagan, secret life of Pan. 'Just look at yourselves!' she shouts at her sisters, 'Dancing at your time of day. That's for young people with no duties and no responsibilities and nothing in their heads but pleasure'. In Kate's eyes, dancing is 'pagan', associated with a kind of sexual freedom which contravenes her strict Catholicism: 'Mature women dancing? What's come over you all? And this is Father Jack's home—we must never forget that'.

Later, when Irish dance music comes over the radio, Kate's remonstrations are ignored by all the other sisters who, one by one, succumb to the music's strange enchantment. Friel comments that 'there is a sense of order being consciously subverted'. Their dancing, as Julia Cruickshank notes, is both an expression of individual identity and an affirmation of collectivity, the five sisters dancing as a family but still preserving their own distinctive personalities. Maggie's features 'become animated by a look of defiance' and she emits 'a wild, raucous "Yaaaah!"'. She draws her flour-covered hand down her cheek, patterning her face 'with an instant mask'. Described as a 'white-faced, frantic dervish', she is associated with the Ryangan natives amongst whom Father Jack has lived and who paint their faces with coloured powders and then 'dance— and dance—children, men, women, most of them lepers, many of them with misshapen limbs, with missing limbs'. Similarly, the Mundy sisters find momentary release from harsh reality in the ecstasy of the dance. Maggie is joined by a transfigured Rose, Agnes and Chris. Agnes moves 'gracefully, most sensuously' while Rose dances wildly, her 'wellingtons pounding out their own erratic rhythm'. Eventually, even Kate, who has been watching the scene with unease, suddenly leaps to her feet, flings her head back, and utters a loud 'Yaaaah!'. Kate, the most repressed of the sisters, dances alone. Her dancing, we are told, is 'ominous of some deep and true emotion', but it is 'totally concentrated, totally private'. When the music stops, the sisters self-consciously and awkwardly recollect themselves, and the old routines are resumed....

The pagan connotations of the sisters' dancing is emphasised by relating it to the dancing which is a part of the festival of Lughnasa taking place in the 'back hills'. The play, that is, concerns itself with the collective as well as personal memory. Just as the sisters' dancing expresses their individual private feelings so the dancing in the 'back hills' is the manifestation of a hidden, submerged culture which neither colonial influence nor Christian teaching has been able to extinguish. When Maggie and Rose first break into song—the appropriately exotic 'Abyssinia' song—and dance around the kitchen, Agnes's comments again playfully echo Kate: 'A right pair of pagans the two of you'. Rumours of what has been going on at the Lughnasa festivities infiltrate the Mundy household. Kate, the guardian of Christian value, is appalled when she hears the story of how a local boy has been badly injured when, during the drinking and dancing, he fell into the bonfire. Young Sweeney becomes her prime example of the dire consequences of yielding to 'pagan' and dissolute impulses and letting slip the properties of civilised order. The boy's name links him with the ancient Irish archetype of pagan disobedience and impiety, the legendary Sweeney who defied the Christian authorities and was punished by being condemned to fly around like a bird for the rest of his life. Young Sweeney is a denizen of the 'back hills', the *pagus*, the wilderness beyond the bounds of civilisation. It is to these same 'back hills' that the sinister Danny Bradley later takes Rose courting. Kate claims to know the people who live there: 'And they're savages! I know those people from the back hills! I've taught them! Savages— that's what they are!

Any good reference work on Irish myth and legend will provide information about the meaning and origins of 'Lughnasa'. It was one of the four major pre-Christian, Celtic festivals, the others being Oimelc, Samhain and Beltaine. Basically a harvest festival, Lughnasa was celebrated for fifteen days in honour of the god Lugh, one of the most important Irish gods. In Peter Berresford Ellis' *A Dictionary of Irish Mythology* we find that Lugh, cognate with Welsh Lleu and Gaulish Lugos, was a sun god, known for the splendour of his countenance, and god of all arts and crafts. Over the years this mighty god's image diminished in popular folk memory until he was simply known as 'Lugh-chromain', which became Anglicised as Leprechaun....

The dancing in the play is associated not only with the pagan festival of Lughnasa but also with African tribal rituals. As Cruickshank observes, the Celtic and Ryangan worlds are both small, neglected communities on the fringes of civilisation; both are ex-colonies, both are cultures rich in dance and ritual. Jack admires the Ryangan 'capacity for fun, for laughing, for practical jokes—they've such open hearts! In some respect they're not unlike us'.

And so, like the Sweeney boy, Jack has 'gone native', attracted by ancient ritual and wordless ceremony. Jack's lapse from Christian orthodoxy is synonymous with his loss of language ('My vocabulary has deserted me'), the primary tool of the rational western mind. What Jack particularly values in Ryangan culture is the fact that there is 'no distinction between the secular and the religious'. The Ryangans allow the spiritual and the sensual to interpenetrate each other: 'almost imperceptibly the religious ceremony ends and the community celebration takes over'. Ryangan primitivism emphasises both the sensuous and the communal life. In Ryanga 'women are eager to have love children', Jack informs a horrified Kate who earlier, we may recall, sought to discourage Chris's participation in the festival dance by reminding her of her maternal role: 'You have a seven-year-old child. Have you forgotten that?'. Like Father Chris, the returned missioner in the early play, *The Blind Mice,* Jack is forced to reassess conventional piety in the light of his experience of the 'alien' and the 'Other'. Repatriated to Ballybeg, he seeks to create a new, more congenial 'home' for himself than the one he has inherited. Michael remembers him as 'a forlorn figure ... shuffling from room to room as if he were searching for something but couldn't remember what'. . . .

In the play, dancing signifies a freeing of human behaviour from predetermining norms and motivations and an attunement of the individual to his or her deepest impulses, to the rest of the group and, ultimately, to the cosmic forces symbolically (and actually) transmitted through the music on the radio, 'Marconi's voodoo'. It is Gerry to whom the sisters turn when their radio keeps breaking down. He is the one who tries to fix their aerial so that they can tune in again to the 'dream music'. He is their link with the 'Other', with the world beyond their usual, stifling routines. He leads them out of themselves and helps them to discover the submerged parts of their own being. Not only is he a professional dancer, he is also one of the birdmen of the play, one of those adept at flying. Aloft in the sycamore tree tinkering with the radio aerial, he sways and sings, '"He flies through the air with the greatest of ease ... That daring young man on the flying trapeze"', while down below Agnes covers her eyes in terror, unable to watch the daredevilry of the dashing risk-taker, the 'clown' amongst the branches. Gerry is linked with the ancient Sweeney and, by extension, with the young pagan celebrant from the 'back hills'. He is also linked with the boy Michael, another 'flyer', who throughout the play is engaged in making and trying to fly two kites. Michael's kites are decorated with grotesquely painted, savage faces, which recall the painted faces of Jack's Ryangan dancers. In the complex web of parallels and correspondences which we find in the play, there is a connection between flying, dancing and pagan ceremonial. All of these activities are forms of release from the tyranny of routine and the pressure of the fact. Recalling earlier 'flying' motifs—Cass's 'winged armchair' or Manus's 'airplane seat'—we remain uncomfortably aware that flying can all to easily become mere avoidance, delusion, escapism. . . .

The play would seem to emphasise lost opportunities, tragic waste, failure, a gradually diminishing life. And yet the feeling one is left with is not at all as simple as that. The play doesn't end with the narrator's blunt account of the ultimately tragic ends of the characters. Even knowing the destiny of his aunts, Michael remains 'fascinated' by the hypnotic, magical power of memory. 'The stage is lit in a very soft, golden light so that the tableau we see is almost, but not quite, in a haze'. This is the space somewhere between the real world and fairyland, where the Actual and the Imaginary may meet. Life retains its aura of enchantment. The play refuses pessimism. Unlike Maggie, Michael is conscious of change—change for good as well as bad. He acknowledges the sordid deaths of Agnes and Rose, but also registers the survival of young Sweeney. In the closing tableau, 'the characters are now in positions similar to their positions at the beginning of the play—*with some changes*'. Michael's kites may never have flown in the course of the play, but they are still 'boldly' displayed, the savage faces on them 'grinning' defiantly. One of the kites stands between Gerry and Agnes, the other between Agnes and Jack, for the failure of Agnes's flight has to be balanced by the perpetually buoyant quality of Gerry's life and the freedom which Jack discovered. As Michael begins his final speech, Friel directs that the music—'It is Time to Say Goodnight'—should be 'just audible' in the background. 'Everybody sways very slightly from side to side—even the grinning kites. The movement is so minimal that we cannot be quite certain if it is happening or if we imagine it'. Like memory, our experience of the play itself is ambivalent. The liminal movement and sound act to undermine our sense of a solid, fixed reality. We are put in the position of Private Gar who, thinking of his childhood fishing trip with his father, 'wonders now did it really take place or did he imagine it'. Friel explores that space between objective fact and subjective imagining, that 'limbo' in which, as Michael puts it, 'everything is simultaneously actual and illusory'. Michael's final speech powerfully asserts a ghostly presence, an 'atmosphere . . . more real than incident', 'a mirage of sound—a dream music'—which mesmerically leads people out of themselves, even out of the prison-house of language. The play ends with Michael's vivid memory of 'dancing as if language had surrendered to movement—as if this ritual, this wordless ceremony, was now the way to speak, to whisper private and sacred things, to be in touch with some otherness'. In his opening speech of the play, Michael speaks of a rite of passage, indicating how, on one level, this is a play about growing up, about the transition from innocence to experience: 'I had a sense of unease, some awareness of a widening breach between what seemed to be and what was'. The stability and solidity of his childhood world have been disturbed: 'That may have been because Uncle Jack hadn't turned out at all like the resplendent figure in my head. Or maybe because I had witnessed Marconi's voodoo derange those kind, sensible women and transform them into shrieking strangers'. He comes to recognise a deep mystery in life. He has seen frustration, break-up, unbearable drudgery, failure, but he also becomes aware of a force for change which, though it may threaten the 'safe' world of childhood, is also the ground of hope and aspiration. His final tableau rearranges the opening one and the most abiding memory he is left with is of 'atmosphere', of 'dream music', 'dancing'—of a mysterious libidinal energy. The significance of this intuitive, illogical, level of experience is finally articulated verbally, in Michael's powerful, lyrical closing narration.

The play enacts an ideal balance—between narration and enactment, the rational and the irrational, language and music, the religious and the secular, past and present. To live in one sphere alone is inadequate. As Julia Cruickshank observes, Rose may be the one 'not educated out of her emotions', but she perishes away from the security of the family. On the other hand, Kate, the one most alarmed by instinct and irrationality, makes a strenuous effort to adapt and come to terms with Jack's 'nativism'. Michael can't help but be amused by her valiant struggle to accept. 'Startled', 'stunned' and 'shocked' as Kate is by the change in Jack, 'finally she hit on a phrase that appeased her: "his own distinctive spiritual search"', "Leaping around a fire and offering a little hen to Uka or Ito or whoever is not religion as I was taught it and indeed know it," she would say with a defiant toss of her head. "But then Jack must make his own distinctive search."' Ballybeg, too, is faced with the challenge of adapting to change in the form of the knitting factory. As in *Translations,* the community's survival depends on its ability to move with the times. Frank Rich, the influential—even feared—*New York Times* critic, commenting on the success of the Abbey Theatre production of the play at Broadway's Plymouth Theatre in October 1991, concluded his review with these words of appreciation of Friel's complex vision:

> Even knowing that he (Michael) knows and what everyone knows about life's inevitable end, he clings to his vision of his childhood, a golden end-of-summer landscape in the production's gorgeous design, for what other antidote than illusions is there to that inescapable final sadness? *Dancing at Lughnasa* does not dilute that sadness—the mean, cold facts of reality, finally, are what its words are for. But first this play does exactly what theatre was born to do, carrying both its characters and audience aloft on those waves of distant music and ecstatic release that, in defiance of all language and logic, let us dance and dream just before night must fall.

If in *Faith Healer Friel* takes us to the very edge of the postmodern Apocalypse, in *Dancing at Lughnasa* he recollects himself to affirm the vitality and dialogue of individual experience even when we are aware of what the future holds. Just as Chris's and Agnes's dancing is not simply socialised as Gerry's is, their story is not merely a chronicling of events. Like Father Jack's spirituality which cannot be held by the words of the Mass, it is fluid. The ultimate image of Friel's drama is of a space where 'language surrendered to movement'. The almost imperceptible fluidity of the play's closing tableau is a celebration of the power of theatre to renew and reveal, and a rejection of 'fossilised' history.

Source: Elmer Andrews, "Body," in *The Art of Brian Friel: Neither Reality Nor Dreams,* St. Martin's Press, 1995, pp. 220–234.

SOURCES

Andrews, Elmer, *The Art of Brian Friel: Neither Reality Nor Dreams,* St. Martin's Press, 1995, pp. 226–27.

Gleitman, Claire, "Negotiating History, Negotiating Myth: Friel Among His Contemporaries," in *Brian Friel: A Casebook,* edited by William Kerwin, Garland, 1997, p. 237.

Kerwin, William, ed., *Brian Friel: A Casebook,* Garland, 1997, p. 237.

McGrath, F. C., *Brian Friel's (Post)Colonial Drama: Language, Illusion, and Politics,* Syracuse University Press, 1999, p. 247.

Murray, Christopher, "'Recording Tremors': Friel's *Dancing at Lughnasa* and the Uses of Tradition," in *Brian Friel: A Casebook,* edited by William Kerwin, Garland, 1997, p. 36.

O'Toole, Fintan, "Marking Time: From Making History to Dancing at Lughnasa," in *The Achievement of Brian Friel,* edited by Alan J. Peacock, Colin Smythe, 1993, p. 214.

Peacock, Alan J., ed., *The Achievement of Brian Friel,* Colin Smythe, 1993, pp. xviii, xv.

Pine, Richard, *Brian Friel and Ireland's Drama,* Routledge, 1990, pp. 1, 4, 5, 8.

Schlueter, June, *Dictionary of Literary Biography,* Volume 13: *British Dramatists Since World War II,* edited by Stanley Weintraub, Gale Group, 1982, pp. 179–85.

FURTHER READING

Chekhov, Anton, *Anton Chekhov's Three Sisters: A Translation,* translated by Brian Friel, Gallery Books, 1981.
> Friel's translation of the Chekhov play to which *Dancing at Lughnasa* has sometimes been compared provides further insight into Friel's perspective on the two dramas.

Grene, Nicholas, *The Politics of Irish Drama: Plays in Context from Boucicault to Friel,* Cambridge University Press, 1999.
> This text provides critical discussion of the historical and political significance of major Irish playwrights.

Kerwin, William, ed., *Brian Friel: A Casebook,* Garland, 1997.
> Kerwin's book is a collection of critical essays on Friel's drama and fiction.

Pine, Richard, *Brian Friel and Ireland's Drama,* Routledge, 1990.
> Pine's work discusses Friel's stage plays in the context of the history and literary traditions of the Irish stage.

Driving Miss Daisy

ALFRED UHRY

1987

Alfred Uhry had already been writing for musical theater for twenty-five years when his first nonmusical play *Driving Miss Daisy* became a surprise smash hit. Originally slated to run for five weeks at a small theater in New York City, demand for tickets was so high that it moved to a larger theater where it ran for about three years. Uhry also won the Pulitzer Prize in 1988. In his preface to the published play, Uhry commented on the experience.

> When I wrote this play I never dreamed I would be writing an introduction to it because I never thought it would get this far.... When I wonder how all this happened ... I can come up with only one answer. I wrote what I knew to be the truth and people have recognized it as such.

Indeed, the numerous critics who lauded the play displayed remarkable similarity in their comments. They liked the play's sincerity, dignity, and honesty. Dealing with issues that plague all people—white or African American, northern or southern—the appeal of *Driving Miss Daisy* is universal.

Driving Miss Daisy went on to become an equally successful movie, winning best picture, best actress, and best screenplay adaptation for Uhry. Uhry's surprise success has also given him the freedom to continue pursuing his writing. In plays and musicals since *Driving Miss Daisy,* Uhry has continued to explore issues of concern to southern Jews, but his work is essentially about basic humanity.

AUTHOR BIOGRAPHY

Alfred Uhry was born around 1936 to an upper-middle-class German-Jewish family. He grew up in Atlanta, Georgia, where his father was a furniture designer. He left the South in 1958 to attend Brown University in Rhode Island, and he graduated with a degree in English. Uhry next moved to New York to begin his career in show business. He began collaborating with the composer Robert Waldman. Their play *The Robber Bridegroom* (1975) was their most successful, earning Uhry a Tony nomination and a Drama Desk nomination. It is a musical based on the southern writer Eudora Welty's novella. Uhry wrote the book and the lyrics. The play was a surprise hit Off-Broadway and moved to Broadway for the 1976–77 season.

He continued to work on other musicals, many of which closed on opening night or soon thereafter, or never even opened. To earn a living, he also wrote lyrics for television shows and commercials and also taught English and drama at a New York high school. In 1984, Uhry was struggling to get a workshop production of a musical about Al Capone off the ground and thinking about leaving theater. Suddenly, the idea came to him to write a play instead.

The characters in *Driving Miss Daisy* (1987) are based on people that Uhry knew growing up, including his grandmother and her African-American chauffeur. The play, Uhry's first, was an instant success, quickly moving from the 74-seat Studio Theatre to another larger Off-Broadway theater and winning for Uhry another Drama Desk nomination. The play ran for three years. It was produced in regional theaters, by a national touring company, and in London, England. In 1988, it won a Pulitzer Prize.

It was also made into a movie. Uhry wrote the adaptation, for which he won an Academy Award. He had prior screenplay experience, having helped finish the script for the 1988 film *Mystic Pizza*. The film, *Driving Miss Daisy*, also won the 1990 Academy Award for best picture.

After his surprise hit, Uhry was approached by the Olympic Games Cultural Olympiad to produce a play for the 1996 Olympic Games that would be held in Atlanta. The play he wrote, *The Ghost of Ballyhoo*, won him another Tony Award the following year. In 1998, he wrote the book for the musical *Parade*, which played at Lincoln Center in New York.

PLOT SUMMARY

The play spans a period of twenty-five years in an unbroken series of segments. At the beginning of the play, Daisy Werthan, a seventy-two-year-old, southern Jewish widow, has just crashed her brand-new car while backing it out of the garage. After the accident, her son Boolie insists that she is not capable of driving. Over her protests, he hires a driver—Hoke Coleburn, an uneducated African American who is sixty. At first, Daisy wants nothing to do with Hoke. She is afraid of giving herself the airs of a rich person, even though Boolie is paying Hoke's salary. She strongly values her independence, so she also resents having someone around her house.

For the first week or so of Hoke's employment, Daisy refuses to let him drive her anywhere. He spends his time sitting in the kitchen. One day, however, he points out that a lady such as herself should not be taking the bus. He also points out that he is taking her son's money for doing nothing. Daisy responds by reminding Hoke that she does not come from a wealthy background, but she relents and allows him to drive her to the grocery store. She insists on maintaining control, however, telling him where to turn and how fast to drive. On another outing, she gets upset when he parks in front of the temple to pick her up, afraid that people will thinking she is giving herself airs.

One morning Boolie comes over after Daisy calls him up, extremely upset. She has discovered that Hoke is stealing from her—a can of salmon. She wants Boolie to fire Hoke right away. Her words also show her prejudice against African Americans. Boolie, at last, gives up. When Hoke arrives, Boolie calls him aside for a talk. First, however, Hoke wants to give something to Daisy—a can of salmon to replace the one he ate the day before. Daisy, trying to regain her dignity, says goodbye to Boolie.

Hoke continues to drive for Daisy. She also teaches him to read and write. When she gets a new car, he buys her old one from the dealer.

When Daisy is in her eighties, she makes a trip by car to Alabama for a family birthday party. She is upset that Boolie will not accompany her, but he and his wife are going to New York and already have theater tickets. On the trip, Daisy learns that this is Hoke's first time leaving Georgia. Suddenly, Daisy realizes that Hoke has taken a wrong turn. She gets

Alfred Uhry standing beneath a marquee promoting his Pulitzer Prize-winning play, Driving Miss Daisy.

frantic and wishes aloud that she had taken the train instead. The day is very long. It is after nightfall that they near Mobile. Hoke wants to stop to urinate, but Daisy forbids him from doing so as they are already late. At first Hoke obeys her, but then he pulls over to the side of the road. Daisy exclaims at his impertinence, but Hoke does not back down.

Hoke is exceedingly loyal to Daisy, but not so loyal that he does not use another job offer as leverage to get a pay raise. He tells Boolie how much he enjoys being fought over. One winter morning, there is an ice storm. The power has gone out and the roads are frozen over. On the telephone, Boolie tells Daisy he will be over as soon as the roads are clear. Right away, however, Hoke comes in. He has experience driving on icy roads from his days as a deliveryman. When Boolie calls back, Daisy tells him not to worry about coming over because Hoke is with her.

In the next segment, Daisy is on her way to temple, but there is a bad traffic jam. Hoke tells her that the temple has been bombed. Daisy is shocked and distressed. She says the temple is Reformed and can't understand why it was bombed. Hoke tells his own story of seeing his friend's father hanging from a tree, when he was just a boy. Daisy doesn't see why Hoke tells the story—it has nothing to do with the temple—and she doesn't even believe that Hoke got the truth. She refuses to see Hoke's linkage of prejudice against Jews and African Americans. Though she is quite upset by what has happened, she tries to deny it.

Another ten years or so has passed. Daisy and Boolie get into an argument about a Jewish organization's banquet for Martin Luther King, Jr. Daisy assumes Boolie will go with her, but he doesn't want to. He says it will hurt his business. Daisy plans on going, nonetheless. Hoke drives her to the dinner. At the last minute, she offhandedly invites Hoke to the dinner, but he refuses because she didn't ask him beforehand, like she would anyone else.

As Daisy gets older, she begins to lose her reason. One day Hoke must call Boolie because Daisy is having a delusion. She thinks she is a schoolteacher and she is upset because she can't find her students' papers. Before Boolie's arrival, she has a moment of clarity, and she tells Hoke that he is her best friend.

In the play's final segment, Daisy is ninety-seven and Hoke is eighty-five. Hoke no longer drives; instead, he relies on his granddaughter to get around. Boolie is about to sell Daisy's house—she has been living in a nursing home for two years. Hoke and Boolie go to visit her on Thanksgiving. She doesn't say much to either of them, but when Boolie starts talking she asks him to leave, reminding him that Hoke came to see her. She tries to pick up her fork and eat her pie. Hoke takes the plate and the fork from her and feeds her a small bite of pie.

CHARACTERS

Hoke Coleburn

Hoke is sixty years old when the play begins. He is an unemployed, uneducated African American. He has worked as a driver and deliveryman previously. He is pleased when Boolie hires him, both for the job and because he likes to work for Jews. He is extremely patient with Daisy and tolerant of her barely disguised prejudices. He also is not afraid to speak up to her, always, however, in a quiet, respectful manner. When his dignity is at stake, he speaks up for his rights. His integrity

MEDIA ADAPTATIONS

- Uhry wrote the screenplay adaptation for 1989's *Driving Miss Daisy*. The movie starred Jessica Tandy, Morgan Freeman, and Dan Ackroyd. Bruce Beresford directed it. Warner Home Video released it in 1990.

teaches Daisy how to be a more humane person. Hoke also develops as a result of their friendship, for instance, Daisy teaches him to read. Perhaps most importantly, the financial security Hoke obtains over the twenty-five years brings him greater self-confidence and self-respect.

Daisy

Daisy is a seventy-two-year-old widow living alone when the play opens. She is independent and stubborn, but her son Boolie insists on hiring a driver for her after she crashes her car while backing out of the garage. Daisy deeply resents Hoke and the implication that she is no longer able to control her own life. However, Hoke's mild manner eventually wins her over, and she finally allows him to drive her to the market. He serves as her driver for the next twenty-five years. Through her friendship with Hoke, Daisy loses some of her deep-rooted prejudice against African Americans and even comes to consider herself a supporter of civil rights. Although she becomes unable to care for herself as she gets older, eventually moving to a nursing home, she never loses her determination or her sense of self. Some of the characteristics that identified her at the beginning of the play, such as her bossiness or her sense of humor, are with her as strongly at the end of the play.

Boolie Werthan

Boolie is Daisy's son. He is forty years old when the play begins. He has taken over his father's printing company, and, over the course of the play, he develops into one of the city's leading business figures. As the years pass, he becomes more conscious of how he will be perceived by society, and, consequently, does not want to attend the United Jewish Appeal banquet for Martin Luther King, Jr. Boolie takes good care of his mother, but he sometimes neglects her feelings. When her opinion disagrees with his, he generally overrides her without thinking about what she really wants or why she wants it. However, he humors his mother's stubbornness rather than try to understand it.

Florine Werthan

Although Boolie's wife Florine is never seen by the audience, she is still a lively character. She is Jewish but socializes with the Christian community and surrounds herself with Christian trappings, such as Christmas decorations. She has high social aspirations and is a member of many organizations. She values social status and symbols more than she does family, and primarily because of this, Daisy thinks she is shallow and foolish.

THEMES

Race and Prejudice

Race and prejudice are important themes in the play. Prejudice is demonstrated against both African Americans and Jews. Several brief statements remind readers of the situation for African Americans in the South. Hoke tells Boolie that he has had a hard time finding a job, for "[T]hey hirin' young if they hirin' colored." Years later, Hoke refers to the fact that African Americans cannot use white facilities. Prejudice against Jews is demonstrated through the bombing of the temple and Boolie's reference to businessmen who dislike and stereotype Jews. He recognizes their belief that "as long as you got to deal with Jews, the really smart ones come from New York." Hoke also specifically mentions the way many Southerners feel toward Jews: "People always talkin' 'bout they stingy and they cheap, but doan' say none of that roun' me."

Daisy, herself a Jew, feels prejudice against African Americans, though she denies it. When the play opens, Daisy refers to African Americans as "them," which does not escape Boolie's notice. After she is convinced that Hoke is stealing from her, she becomes more aggressive in her accusations. "They all take things, you know," she tells Boolie. Later in the same scene, she even says, "They are like having little children in the house. They want something so they just take it. Not a smidgin of manners. No conscience." She also mimics the speech of uneducated African Americans like Hoke: "'Nome,' he'll say." Daisy's accusations, which indict all African Americans, backfire when Hoke brings her a new can of salmon. She can no longer hold his actions against an entire race. Throughout the course of the play, however, Daisy begins to lose her prejudices. She even argues with Boolie about their presence at a banquet honoring civil rights leader Martin Luther King, Jr.

Despite this change, she still does not see the prejudiced world around her clearly, and does not understand that some white Southerners dislike Jews as much as they dislike African Americans. When the temple is bombed, she is certain it must be a mistake—"I'm sure they meant to bomb one of the conservative synagogues or the orthodox one. The temple is reform"—or that Hoke misheard the police officer. Hoke, however, understands better than Daisy. "It doan' matter to them people," he says. "A Jew is a Jew to them folks. Jes' like light or dark we all the same nigger." Daisy refuses to believe this, for even though she makes great strides in combating her prejudice, she still feels superior to Hoke, for many reasons: she is wealthier, she is his employer, and she is white. Because of this innate feeling, she does not invite Hoke to attend the King banquet with her until virtually the last minute. Hoke pridefully refuses, knowing that it is only because she takes him for granted that she did not speak with him about it sooner.

Friendship

The relationship between Daisy and Hoke is at the heart of this play. When Daisy first meets Hoke, she dislikes him, both because he is African American and because she resents his presence in her home. Over the years, she comes to grow fond of Hoke, though her gruff speech would not indicate this. Both Hoke and Daisy, however, understand the feelings that they share. On the day of the ice storm, Hoke drives to her home despite the slick roads. He wants to be there for Daisy, whom he knows will be alone. Although Daisy is "*[T]ouched*" and calls his actions "sweet," she still reproves him for tracking dirt into her kitchen. Hoke says, "Now Miz Daisy, what you think I am? A mess?" Though Daisy responds in the affirmative, the stage directions note, "*This is an old routine between them and not without affection.*" It is not until Daisy is much older—and getting occasionally confused—that she puts her feelings into words. "You're my best friend," she tells Hoke, and she takes hold of his

TOPICS FOR FURTHER STUDY

- One way that actors "get into" their roles is to imagine their characters in situations that are implied but not included in the play. Try to imagine these characters in other situations and write another short scene for inclusion in the play.

- Imagine that Hoke overheard the conversation between Boolie and Daisy in which she implies that all African Americans are dishonest. How do you think he would react to such statements?

- Conduct research to find out more about how racial relations have changed in the South from the 1940s to the present day. Write a paragraph about your findings.

- Imagine that you are from another country and know nothing about race relations in the twentieth-century South. What might be your impression of race relations based solely on *Driving Miss Daisy*?

- Read another play that portrays a Southern point of view and Southern issues. Tennessee Williams' *A Streetcar Named Desire* would be a good choice. How does the image of the South differ in the two plays? How is at alike?

- Toward the end of the play, Daisy exclaims to Boolie, "I've never been prejudiced and you know it!" How do you think Hoke would respond? How would you respond?

---

hand. It seems likely that she wants to express her feelings for Hoke while she is still able to do so.

Growing Old

An important theme in the play is growing old. The play spans twenty-five years. By its end, Daisy is ninety-seven, Hoke is eighty-five, and Boolie is sixty-five. The characters all experience changes over the years. Daisy becomes more liberal, while Boolie becomes more conservative. Daisy and Hoke also become good friends. The two share the knowledge of the difficulties of aging. When Daisy grows confused, thinking that she is still a teacher, she says to Hoke, "I'm being trouble. Oh God, I don't want to be trouble to anybody." She realizes that her aging is making her more difficult, and she is afraid that she will become a burden. Hoke points out that she at least has the benefit of aging in comfort. "You want something to cry about, I take you to the state home, show you what layin' out dere in de halls."

Eventually, Boolie puts Daisy in a nursing home. The stage directions note that "*[S]he seems fragile and diminished, but still vital.*" Her aging has not made her unwilling to speak her mind. "Go charm the nurses," she tells Boolie when she wants him to leave. Though she is unable to feed herself very well, she still has her mind.

For his part, Hoke has changed too. He can no longer drive and, instead, must rely on his granddaughter to chauffeur him around. Through Hoke's inability to drive, the play also demonstrates that as people get older, they lose their independence, in a sense, becoming more like children again. Hoke is unable to visit Daisy often because the bus doesn't go to the nursing home. Hoke admits that "It hard [to visit Daisy], not drivin'." At this point in their lives, people like Daisy and Hoke must rely on others for almost everything—even for the maintenance of cherished friendships.

STYLE

Symbolism

Daisy's automobiles (of which there are many) are central symbols in the play. For Daisy, driving her own car represents freedom. This freedom is taken away from her when Boolie hires Hoke. For

Hoke, Daisy's cars—the Oldsmobile that he purchases used from the dealer after Boolie gets Daisy a new car—represents a rise in social status. "Keep them ashes off my 'polstry,'" he warns Boolie, as the two men drive to the dealership. For Boolie, however, the car is just an object, a large, dangerous object in the hands of his mother, which he places in the hands of a driver he can trust.

Even when Daisy relents and allows Hoke to drive her car—in a sense, take away her freedom—she does her best to continue to assert herself. On their first trip together, Daisy tries to instruct Hoke on the route to take. "I want to go to it [the Piggly Wiggly] the way I always go," she says, demonstrating her fixation with being in charge of herself. Hoke, however, rejects her orders, refusing to turn as she tells him to, because he knows a better route to the store. This exchange shows each person's basic nature: Daisy's stubborn insistence on denying that change can occur, and Hoke's quiet yet resolute manner of teaching Daisy to accept change.

Daisy's house also has symbolic meaning. Like the car, it symbolizes her independence. She feels she should be in charge of her house, thus when Boolie hires Hoke, her control of this sphere is undermined. The other characters recognize what the house means to Daisy. Boolie does not sell it until she has been in the nursing home for several years and will never come home. "It feels funny to sell the house while Mama's still alive," he says to Hoke, "I know I'm doing the right thing." He looks to Hoke for affirmation, which he finds, but he also admits that he is not going to tell his mother what he is doing. Hoke also agrees with this decision. Both men know that Daisy will not idly abide the only symbol of her independent adulthood being taken away.

Setting

Almost the entire play takes place in Atlanta, Georgia. Daisy has spent her life in the city, though she grew up in a much poorer section of town. She is a part of Atlanta's Jewish community. She belongs to a temple and takes part in Jewish cultural events. Boolie has also spent his life in Atlanta. He has taken over his father's printing business, and he becomes a leading figure in the city's circle of businessmen. Though his wife, Florine, is also Jewish, she socializes within the Christian community because it gives her higher status.

Even though Atlanta is a thriving city, the atmosphere is more that of a small town. The people within Daisy's social circle are all well acquainted. Even Hoke has a connection to the Werthans prior to working as Daisy's chauffeur. He used to work for a Jewish judge whom Boolie knows.

Although Daisy leads an insular life, she does get out of the city. Boolie, as well, takes trips to New York. Hoke, however, has never left Georgia before he drives Daisy to attend a funeral in Alabama. Hoke originally comes from a farm near Macon, and his recollection of the lynching of his friend's father serves as a reminder of the racial violence that regularly took place in the rural South. Although his family also lives in Atlanta, they clearly belong to the generations of African Americans who leave the South, or if staying there, make the choice to do so. His daughter, married to a train porter, has visited northern cities such as New York and Detroit and urges her father to do so. His granddaughter still lives in Atlanta, but she is an educated scientist, teaching at an African-American college.

Structure

The play has no specific acts and scenes. Instead, it is divided up into segments, some of which flow one into the other, others that do not. The play also spans twenty-five years, so sometimes large amounts of time pass between segments. This structure frees the action of the play from time or plot constraints. Uhry can create exactly which incidents he believes will be the most evocative. The structure also emphasizes the compactness of the characters' lives. Though the fluid structure would seem to indicate that little changes over the course of twenty-five years, that is not the play's reality.

HISTORICAL CONTEXT

The 1940s

After the end of World War II, American society and economy saw significant changes. During the war, many women, Mexican Americans, and African Americans were employed in defense factories. After the war ended, however, as government measures encouraged employers to hire veterans, many of these people lost their jobs. Congress even abolished the Fair Employment Practices Committee, which had protected African Americans from job discrimination. Overall, however, unemployment remained low, and incomes increased. Even though the economy experienced dramatic inflation, many Americans, who had scrimped dur-

COMPARE & CONTRAST

- **1950s:** Of a total U.S. population of close to 164.3 million in 1955, around 7.4 million are aged between 65 and 79, or 4.5 percent.

  1990s: Of a total U.S. population of 273.9 million in 1998, just over 18 million are aged between 65 and 79, or 6.6 percent.

- **1950s:** In 1956, the Supreme Court rules that segregated transportation systems are illegal.

  1960s: In 1960, the Supreme Court rules that segregation in certain public facilities is illegal.

  1970s: In 1971, the Supreme Court upholds affirmative actions programs in schools and businesses.

  1990s: In 1996, the Supreme Court hears a case involving allegations that federal prosecutors in Los Angeles selectively pursued and charged blacks in crack cocaine cases. The Court finds that the African-American defendants are unable to prove the allegations, so the guilty charge stands.

- **1950s and 1960s:** African Americans stage numerous boycotts, marches, and sit-ins to protest segregation laws in the South.

  1990s: Since passage of the Civil Rights Act of 1964, discrimination in employment and in public accommodations has been illegal.

- **Mid-1960s:** In 1964, less than 6 percent of eligible African Americans in Mississippi are registered to vote.

  Late 1960s: By 1968, 59 percent of African Americans in Mississippi are registered to vote.

  1990s: In 1990, 31.5 percent of African Americans of voting age in Mississippi are registered to vote.

- **1960s:** In 1969, only about 1,500 African Americans hold elected office.

  1970s: By the end of the decade, more than 4,500 African Americans hold elected office.

  1990s: In 1997, there are 8,617 elected African-American officials throughout the United States.

- **1960s:** In 1964, only about 200,000 African Americans attend college.

  1970s: By the end of the decade, more than 800,000 African Americans attend college.

  1990s: In 1994, about 36.7 percent of African Americans, out of a total population of 32.5 million, attended two- or four-year colleges.

---

ing the war years, were eager to spend their savings. Rising consumerism helped lead to a new era of prosperity.

President Harry S. Truman ran for reelection in 1948. His stand on civil rights became an important issue in the campaign. Two years earlier, in 1946, African-American civil rights groups had urged Truman to act against racism. African Americans faced segregation and discrimination in housing and employment. African Americans in many areas continued to be lynched, a crime that the courts ignored. Also, Southern African Americans were prevented from voting through the use of poll taxes.

In 1948, Truman banned racial discrimination in the military and in federal jobs. In response, Southern Democrats formed their own party, one that called for continued racial segregation. Despite these party divisions, Truman won the presidency.

The Civil Rights Movement

African Americans began taking a more active stance in the 1950s to end discrimination in the United States. During the 1950s, the Supreme Court ordered the desegregation of schools and transportation systems. President Dwight Eisenhower signed the Civil Rights Act of 1957. The first civil rights law passed since Reconstruction, this act made it a federal crime to prevent any qualified person from voting. The Reverend Martin Luther King, Jr., also emerged as an important civil rights leader. He urged the use of nonviolent resistance to bring about the end of racial discrimination. King was assassinated in 1968.

In the 1960s, civil rights activists continued to challenge racist policies in interstate transportation and voter registration. The Civil Rights Act of 1964 was passed, barring discrimination in employment and public accommodations, and giving the Justice Department the power to enforce school desegregation. Congress also passed the Voting Rights Act of 1965, which put the voter registration process under federal control. Within three years, over half of all eligible African Americans in the South had registered to vote.

Despite these successes, many African Americans grew to question the effectiveness of nonviolent protest. Some felt they should use violence for self-defense, while others did not want to integrate into white society at all. These African Americans adopted the slogan ''Black Power,'' which became widely used by the late 1960s. They wanted greater economic and political power and even complete separation from white society.

Throughout the 1970s, African Americans, as well as other minority groups, continued to fight for equal rights. President Richard Nixon, however, vowed to not ask for any new civil rights legislation. When the Supreme Court ruled in 1971 that busing could be used to integrate schools, he denounced their decision. By the middle of the decade, more African Americans were enrolling in college, holding professional jobs, and serving in public office. African-American political leaders formed strong alliances and effective lobbies.

Women and Society

Although popular culture in the 1950s presented the ideal woman as a full-time suburban homemaker, many women in that decade held jobs outside the home. By the 1960s, the women's movement was experiencing a widespread revival. Betty Friedan's 1963 book *The Feminine Mystique* vehemently rejected the popular notion that women were content with fulfilling the roles of wife, mother, and homemaker. Friedan charged that many women felt stifled by this domestic life. The National Organization for Women, a women's rights group, was formed in 1966, and more and more women joined the movement throughout the 1970s.

The National Women's Political Caucus, founded in 1971, encouraged women to run for political office. Women's leaders believed that women in public office would contribute to the shaping of public policy in favor of equal rights. In 1972, Congress passed the Education Amendments Act, which outlawed sexual discrimination in higher education. Many all-male schools began to allow women to enroll. The women's rights movement, however, failed to win passage of the Equal Rights Amendment, or ERA, a constitutional amendment barring discrimination on the basis of sex. Although Congress passed the ERA in 1972, not enough states ratified the bill, therefore it never became a law.

The Aging Population

Several measures contributed to a changing lifestyle for elderly Americans. President Lyndon B. Johnson initiated the Medicare program in 1965, which offered national health insurance to people over the age of 65. Americans were living longer, so by the 1970s, the aging population contributed to a dramatic rise in U.S. spending on health care—from $74 billion in 1970 to around $884 billion in 1993.

CRITICAL OVERVIEW

Driving Miss Daisy was the first play that Alfred Uhry wrote and he based it on people he had known growing up in the South, particularly his grandmother and her driver. The play's original schedule called for it to run for five weeks at Playwrights Horizon, a New York nonprofit theater that seated an audience of seventy-four. When the five-week run was up, the play was extended another five weeks, and when that was up, the play moved to a bigger theater. A year and a half later, the show was still playing in New York, and also around the country. Uhry also won the Pulitzer Prize.

Audiences and critics immediately responded to the play, even when its premise seemed distinctly unpromising. In *American Theatre,* Don Shewey recalls his experience.

> I remember trudging upstairs . . . to see a play that sounded distinctly unpromising. It was about—gads!—an elderly white woman and her black chauffeur. On one hand, it sounded politically unsavory: Have we progressed no further than portraying African-Americans onstage as servants. On the other hand, it sounded

Frances Sternhagen and Earle Hyman in scene from a stage production of Driving Miss Daisy.

theatrically too dreary for words: How could it be anything but a parade of predictable Sunday-school pieties about how we're all alike under the skin and we should all get along? I personally resisted every inch of the way the feeling I left the theatre with that night: Wow, [this] is a good play!

Critics commented on the play's appeal, in fact, often using that very word. In the *New York Times,* Mel Gussow refers to the play's "homespun appeal" and its "renewed sincerity." Robert Brustein writes in the *New Republic* that the play "has both appealing brevity and considerable quality." He calls viewing the play "an experience of considerable power and sensitivity." These critics, along with others, responded to the play's basic humanity and the truths it told. "It is the work of decent people," writes Brustein, "working against odds to show how humans still manage to reach out to each other in a divided world." Judy Lee Oliva, in *Contemporary Dramatists,* says that "*Driving Miss Daisy* is a play about dignity in which all the characters strive to hold onto their personal integrity."

The play deftly presents an overview of the changing values and times in the South. Spanning from 1948 to 1972, the play alludes to important themes of the twentieth century, such as racism and prejudice. Its focus on the relationship between two people allows for a more personalized view of historical realities. Oliva notes that the play is "representative of a time in history and tells about that time via this one story." However, as Gussow points out, "history remains background. The principal story is the personal relationship, the interdependence of the two irrevocably allied Southerners."

Critics overwhelmingly warmed to the characters, who carried this play smoothly along: the crusty Daisy and the restrained but prideful Hoke. Gussow declares that the play sometimes "seems more like an extended character sketch or family memoir than an actual drama." Even Florine, the invisible character, emerges, "deftly characterized by the playwright," writes Brustein, "with simple strokes through Daisy's attitude toward her."

Uhry's subtlety of writing was also appreciated. Oliva calls Uhry "a master of understatement." Notes Gussow, "The play remains quiet, and it becomes disarming, as it delineates the characters with almost offhand glimpses." He uses Hoke's casual declaration "The first time I left Georgia was 25 minutes ago" as an example of this technique. Oliva further believes that *Driving Miss Daisy* was distinguished from other plays of the decade by "the subtlety with which the playwright empowers his dramaturgy, enabling him to address issues of race and ethnicity and to explore conflicts of old versus young, rich versus poor, Jew versus gentile, while maintaining the emphasis on the very human relationship that develops between Daisy and Hoke.''

Even after its New York run ended, *Driving Miss Daisy* remained with the American audience. Uhry adapted it into a film that came out in 1989. Like the play, it garnered numerous positive reviews including one from Vincent Canby of the *New York Times* who declared it to be ''the most successful stage-to-screen translation'' since *Dangerous Liaisons*. *Driving Miss Daisy* went on to win Academy Awards for best actress, best screenplay adaptation, and best film.

CRITICISM

Rena Korb

Korb has a master's degree in English literature and creative writing and has written for a wide variety of educational publishers. In the following essay, she compares Daisy and Hoke, discussing fundamental similarities that contribute to their friendship as well as differences that influence their actions.

More than twenty years after Alfred Uhry arrived in New York with dreams of becoming a lyricist, he made a surprise hit with his first original play, *Driving Miss Daisy*. Uhry had actually made the decision to leave the theater for good when, as he told a reporter for the *Chicago Tribune*, he suddenly decided to write a play about his grandmother. Lena Guthman Fox was a former schoolteacher who insisted on driving long after she could safely do so, so her family hired Will Coleman, an African-American chauffeur. Uhry believed that exploring their friendship could, at the least, counter misperceptions about racial relations in the South. *Driving Miss Daisy* took New York's theater-going crowd by storm and played Off-Broadway for three years.

Daisy Werthan is the play's title character, but she shares the stage and the audience's respect with Hoke Coleburn, the illiterate African-American man, twelve years her junior, who nevertheless becomes her ''best friend.'' The two older people, though of vastly different backgrounds and socioeconomic classes, are able to establish a valuable relationship. They share crucial similarities, yet their differences allow them the opportunity to learn from each other and enrich their lives.

The play opens with Daisy's refusal to acknowledge that she is no longer capable of driving safely. ''It was the car's fault,'' she declares, speaking of her accident. She longs for her old car. ''You should have let me keep my La Salle. . . . It never would have behaved this way,'' she tells Boolie. Daisy wants to be in control of her own life. Don Shewey, writing in *American Theatre,* points out some of the reasons for Daisy's stubbornness. ''Her physical and social vulnerability, because of her age and because she's Jewish in an overwhelmingly Christian society, only exacerbates the sharpness with which she hides her fear and fragility.''

Hoke also suffers the same vulnerability, because of his age, but primarily because of his racial background. Unlike Daisy, he admits to this insecurity. When Boolie comments that Hoke has been out of work for a long time, he frankly replies, ''Well, Mist' Werthan, you try bein' me and looking for work. They hirin' young if they hirin' colored, an' they ain' even hirin' much young, seems like.''

Though Daisy is white and Hoke is black, they both have preconceived notions of race. Daisy holds deep-seated prejudices against African Americans, but she does not acknowledge them, for they are simply the fabric of her society. For instance, a missing can of salmon provides all the opportunity she needs to denounce his race: ''They want something so they just take it,'' she says to her son, Boolie. Over the years, Hoke's quiet honesty and dignity force Daisy to rethink her ideas.

Hoke also has strong notions about Jews. Unlike Daisy, however, his prejudices are positive. ''I'd druther drive for Jews,'' he tells Boolie during his interview. ''People always talkin' 'bout they stingy and they cheap, but doan' say none of that roun' me.'' He holds Jews in higher esteem than their Christian counterparts for no truly valid reason—the same way that Daisy's prejudices have no basis.

Both Daisy and Hoke are formidably stubborn, but they have different ways of showing this trait. Daisy tends toward verbal protestation, as when Boolie tells her that he is going to hire a driver. Though she speaks loudly and vehemently, the play aptly demonstrates Daisy's habit of eventually succumbing, though she acts like she is not doing so even while it is happening. She also attempts to maintain control of her own life by placing herself

WHAT DO I READ NEXT?

- Uhry's second play, *The Last Night of Ballyhoo* (1997) tackles the unexplored aspects of southern anti-Semitism. Uhry again returns to the affluent Jewish community in Atlanta.

- Carson McCuller's novel *The Heart is a Lonely Hunter* (1940) draws on the Southern gothic tradition of American literature. The novel's protagonists—including a man who is deaf and mute, an African-American doctor, and a widower—all live in a Georgia mill town and are drawn together by their outsider status.

- Lorraine Hansberry's three-act play *A Raisin in the Sun* (1959) explores what happens in 1940s Chicago when an African-American family attempts to move into an all-white neighborhood. This drama reflects Hansberry's own experiences of racial harassment.

- Evan O'Connell's novel *Mrs. Bridge* (1959) chronicles the adult life of Mrs. Bridge, a well-off Midwestern matron. Though she enjoys life's comforts, Mrs. Bridge feels isolated from her husband and her three children.

- Uhry's first theatrical success was based on the musical adaptation of Eudora Welty's novel *The Robber Bridegroom* (1942). This fairy tale tells the story of a highwayman who masquerades part-time as a gentleman. He kidnaps a planter's daughter, and she falls in love with him. The novel contains gothic horror, mystery, and magic.

- *Fried Green Tomatoes at the Whistle Stop Cafe* (1987) by Fannie Flagg tells the extraordinary friendship of two Southern women. After helping her friend escape from an abusive marriage, Idgie and Ruth set up a small cafe where everyone was welcome. The story is told through reminiscences of aging characters as well as in the small-town past.

---

in charge of the unimportant details that comprise her surroundings, including the speed at which Hoke drives. Hoke, in contrast, speaks little but takes firm action. He sums up his strategy for getting his way in the initial job interview: "I hold on no matter what way she run me. When I nothin' but a little boy down there on the farm above Macon, I use to wrastle hogs to the ground at killin' time, and ain' no hog get away from me yet." The following exchange, which takes place on their first car ride together, typifies each character's determination:

> DAISY: ... Where are you going? HOKE: To the grocery store. DAISY: Then why didn't you turn on Highland Avenue? HOKE: Piggly Wiggly ain' on Highland Avenue. It on Euclid, down near the— DAISY: I know where it is and I want to go to it the way I always go. On Highland Avenue. HOKE: That three blocks out of the way, Miz Daisy. DAISY: Go back! Go back this minute! HOKE: We in the wrong lane! I cain' jes'— DAISY: Go back I said! If you don't, I'll get out of this car and walk! HOKE: We movin' You cain' open the do'! DAISY: This is wrong! Where are you taking me? HOKE: The sto'. DAISY: This is wrong. You have to go back to Highland Avenue! HOKE: Mmmm-hmmmm. DAISY: I've been driving to Piggly Wiggly since the day they put it up and opened it for business. This isn't the way! Go back! Go back this minute! HOKE: Yonder the Piggly Wiggly. DAISY: Get ready to turn now. HOKE: Yassum.

The exchange also shows their manner of dealing with each other. Daisy quite vocally makes demands. Hoke, quietly, ignores them and continues on his chosen path. To get her way, Daisy makes threats ("I'll get out of this car and walk.") and validates her superior knowledge ("I've been driving to the Piggly Wiggly since the day . . . they opened it for business."). As her futile protests grow more frantic, Hoke responds by not responding ("Mmmm-hmmmm."). When Daisy finally accedes that Hoke has gotten his way ("Yonder the Piggly Wiggly."), she again grasps control of the situation ("Get ready to turn now."), at which point

> "DAISY AND HOKE ARE... DRAWN TOGETHER PARTIALLY BECAUSE THEY BOTH RESIDE OUTSIDE THE NORM OF SOUTHERN SOCIETY."

Hoke is smart enough to let her salvage her pride (''Yassum.''). This pattern repeats itself over the years, but becomes increasingly shortened. Decades later, Hoke is driving Daisy to a banquet for Martin Luther King, Jr.:

> DAISY: You forgot to turn. HOKE: Ain' this dinner at the Biltmo'? DAISY: You know it is. HOKE: Biltmo' straight thissaway. DAISY: You know so much. HOKE: Yassum. I do. DAISY: I've lived in Atlanta all my life. HOKE: And ain' run a car in onto twenty years.

Both Hoke and Daisy know that, despite their age or race, they have basic human rights. As Daisy points out to Boolie at the very beginning of the play, ''I am seventy-years old as you so gallantly reminded me and I am a widow, but unless they rewrote the Constitution and didn't tell me, I still have rights. And one of my rights is the right to invite who I want—not who you want—into my house.'' Daisy, of course, loses this argument, primarily because it is theoretical and really has little meaning in her daily life. In the grand scheme, Daisy's rights are not trodden upon to any significant extent.

Hoke has a different experience. Though Daisy does not realize it, she continually questions his human dignity, and the audience can gather, other whites in Southern society do just the same. On the trip to Alabama, Hoke needs to urinate. When Daisy tells him that ''there's no time to stop'' and that they will ''be in Mobile soon,'' Hoke also feels compelled to remind Daisy of his rights—and follow up on his declaration:

> HOKE: Yassum. (He drives a minute then stops the car.) Nome. DAISY: I told you to wait! HOKE: Yassum. I hear you. How you think I feel havin' to ax you when can I make my water like some damn dog? DAISY: Why, Hoke! I'd be ashamed! HOKE: I ain' no dog and I ain' no chile and I ain' jes' a back of the neck you look at while you goin' wherever you want to go. I a man nearly seventy-two years old and I know when my bladder full and I getting' out dis car and goin' off down de road like I got to do. And I'm takin' de car key dis time. And that's de end of it.

Unlike Daisy, Hoke must stick to his resolution because much higher stakes are involved.

Although Hoke makes points such as this, and even though Daisy comes to move away from her prejudice and to accept Hoke as a friend, she still cannot bring herself to treat him as an equal. The Martin Luther King, Jr., banquet best shows Daisy's struggle. She wants Hoke to accompany her but waits until the last minute to tell him, ''Boolie said you wanted to go to this dinner with me tonight.'' With pride, Hoke refuses to attend: ''next time you ask me someplace, ask me regular.'' Only at the end of the play is Daisy able to treat Hoke in a way consistent with her feelings: she takes his hand.

Daisy and Hoke are also drawn together partially because they both reside outside the norm of Southern society. Daisy, not surprisingly, refuses to acknowledge this truth. The temple bombing perfectly illustrates this concept. Daisy can't believe that her synagogue has been the object of attack. ''Well, it's a mistake. I'm sure they meant to bomb one of the conservative synagogues or the orthodox one. The temple is reform.'' Hoke understands the mindset of prejudiced people: ''It doan' matter to them people. A Jew is a Jew to them folks. Jes' like light or dark, we all the same nigger.'' This ''otherness'' help Daisy and Hoke to form a meaningful, lasting friendship that is mutually beneficial. Daisy strengthens Hoke's inner world, giving him access to the tools that will bring greater self-respect, such as a steady income, a car, and the ability to read. Hoke strengthens Daisy's outer world, helping her to become a better person, one who can move beyond her proscribed point of view and embrace concepts, such as civil rights, that will bring positive change to others. At the end of the play, their cohesiveness is demonstrated by this simple act: ''*(He cuts a small piece of pie with the fork and gently feeds it to her. Then another as the lights fade slowly out.).*''

Source: Rena Korb, in an essay for *Drama for Students,* Gale Group, 2001.

Christopher Edwards

Christopher Edwards portrays Driving Miss Daisy *as a ''sentimental'' and ''comfortable'' play in the following review.*

Hay fever (the ailment not the play) prevented me from writing a column last week. Here are a couple of the more interesting productions that opened in the last two weeks.

Comfortable is one word for Alfred Uhry's Pulitzer Prize-winning play *Driving Miss Daisy.* Sentimental is another. What has become of this American award? I had just begun to think that if David Mamet could win it (for *Glengarry Glenn Ross*) then perhaps we could start taking it seriously again. Mamet was an original talent, without any doubt. This piece is an example of cosy American liberalism murmuring reassuring noises to itself. Purring is general, all over Broadway.

It is 1948. Rich, crusty old Atlanta Jewess (Wendy Hiller as Daisy) is persuaded by long-suffering son Boolie (Barry Foster) to employ poor illiterate old black chauffeur Hoke (Clarke Peters). Daisy, in her seventies, is unfit to drive, but wishes to soldier independently on (hurray for indomitable old bats like Daisy). The last thing she wants is an old black in the house (boo, but we know she will learn), least of all one who might disturb her frank idea of the stereotype nigger ('they all take things'). But the author has a stereotype of his own in store. Enter Hoke, as honest as the day is long (hurray again), quietly dignified (goes without saying, but more cheers), loyal to his old charge and full of homely Deep South insight; oppression breeds wisdom in a black man's soul, yessir.

It is not the message that deprives the piece of bite so much as its user-friendly serrations; an autumnal glow just will bathe every prejudice in sight. And of course there is the utter predictability of the play's ending. Twenty-five years on, in 1973, shared racial suffering and common humanity have sealed a geriatric concord. At the end, old Hoke visits older Daisy in the nursing home to feed her Thanksgiving pie.

Both lead actors are excellent. The considerable virtues of the production lie in the playing. Clarke Peter's Hoke is sparky, outspoken and engagingly ingenuous. Wendy Hiller completely eschews the Jewishness of Daisy, but that which would be unforgivable on Broadway is not much missed in the West End. Her cantankerous hauteur manages to be funny, vilely prejudiced and quaintly heroic—*virtu* refusing to give any quarter. But experience and old age bring her round. Her style of tight, crusty humour, of inarticulate expressiveness, does its best to cut across sentimentality. This is most notable in the scene where Hoke is driving her

Morgan Freeman (as Hoke Colburn), Jessica Tandy (as Daisy Werthan), and Dan Aykroyd (as Boolie Werthan), starred in the 1989 film adaptation of Driving Miss Daisy.

to the synagogue, burnt down by anti-semites. The event prompts Hoke's own youthful memories of lynched blacks dangling from trees. Daisy's tears at this point confirm a sense of identity with Hoke that her snobbery has been resisting throughout. Wendy Hiller ages so touchingly, and accurately, too (she is into her nineties by the end)—making faint, fluttering, expressive gestures of protest and despair with her hands. In fact both actors manage to create an air of simple, characterful spontaneity that almost overcomes the formulaic promptings of the text.

Source: Christopher Edwards, "Southern Comfort," in *Spectator,* Vol. 260, No. 8345, June 18, 1988, pp. 38–39.

Robert Brustein

Robert Brustein presents a review in which he expresses that Driving Miss Daisy *is an "experience of considerable power and sensitivity."*

New American plays, banished from New York's main stem, are cropping up in out-of-the-way quarters in modest productions. I belatedly popped in on two such works of reputation, both of them set in the

South. My seat was warm for only one act of Robert Harling's *Steel Magnolias* at the Lucille Lortel Theatre—an excruciatingly cute concoction in the Beth Henley manner about a bunch of gabby women in a beauty parlor trading artificial wisecracks (sample: ''I'm not crazy—I've just been in a bad mood for forty years''). At the John Houseman Theatre, however, Alfred Uhry's *Driving Miss Daisy,* which might sound equally unappealing in bare outline, proved to be an experience of considerable power and sensitivity.

It was also exquisitely acted and directed, one of those rare moments in theater when every aspect of production seems to be controlled by a single unifying imagination, *Driving Miss Daisy* plays for about 90 minutes without intermission, further documenting my only formula for popularity on the stage these days—that critics and audiences will embrace most warmly those productions that last an intermissionless hour and a half. (Paradoxically, they are only slightly less enthusiastic about those lasting between four and nine hours with breaks for lunch and dinner.) I can't say why this is so—perhaps it is a consequence of the fast forward buttons on our VCRs. I only know that brevity now seems to have become a more important factor than quality in determining theatrical success.

Driving Miss Daisy has both appealing brevity and considerable quality. It is a first play by Uhry, who has hitherto been associated with musicals (he wrote book and lyrics for *The Robber Bridegroom*). If his talent holds against the inevitable pressures, we have another gifted playwright in our midst. Uhry comes from a German-Jewish family in Atlanta. His play is apparently autobiographical, a series of vignettes about the relationship between an aging Southern Jewish matriarch (presumably his grandmother) and her only slightly less venerable black chauffeur. Having once again totaled her car, Daisy Werthan is now considered too feeble to drive. Her son, Boolie, employs Hoke Coleburn to transport her back and forth to the supermarket, the synagogue, the cemetery where her husband is buried—invariably over Daisy's contentious objections. The play concerns the evolving intimacy between these two aged people, the gentle, bemused black man and the cranky Southern Jewess who resists his services—a kind of *I'm Not Rappaport* without the jokes. The old alliance between Jews and blacks is somewhat strained these days. It was already strained in the South during the period of the play, 1948 to 1973. Although ''Miss Daisy'' (as Hoke calls her, using the common form of subordinate Negro address) persists in believing that she feels no bigotry toward blacks, she is deeply opposed to Hoke's presence in her house, and not just because he reminds her of her helplessness. Daisy embodies all the racial prejudices of her class toward the ''other'' that Hoke represents.

Including an assumption about thieving black people. Daisy complains to her son that she is missing a can of salmon, having found the empty can under the coffee grounds. Hardly a generous spirit, she assumes that Hoke has stolen this 33-cent item and wants him dismissed. Hoke enters, offering her another can of salmon, to admit he helped himself because the pork chops she gave him were ''stiff.''

But Hoke, though unfailingly courteous, is not merely a passive image of virtue. It takes him six days to persuade Daisy to let him drive her car (''the same time it took the Lord to make the world''), and when he finally gets her in the Oldsmobile, grumbling and complaining, driving becomes an occasion for a battle of wills. ''Hold on, you're speeding,'' she tells him, as he hurtles along at 19 miles per hour; they have a quarrel about the proper route to the supermarket; she complains that he parked the sedan in front of the synagogue (''like I was Queen of Romania'') instead of at the side entrance. A former teacher, Daisy is sensitive about being wealthy (''I don't want you, I don't need you, and I don't like you saying I'm rich''), while Hoke tries to persuade her there's nothing wrong with having a little money.

They disagree about everything and Hoke spends his days moping in the kitchen, a talkative man deprived of conversation. Only when they drive to visit her husband's grave does some intimacy spring up between them. Unable to make out the writing on the gravestone, Hoke arouses Daisy's tutorial instincts by admitting he's illiterate. Before long she is teaching him to read phonetically, and later gives him a handwriting copy book as a gift.

Daisy denies this is a Christmas present. She disapproves deeply of Jews who observe that holiday, chief among them her daughter-in-law, Floreen, whose idea of heaven on earth, she says, is ''socializing with Episcopalians.'' Floreen is an invisible character, deftly characterized by the playwright with simple strokes through Daisy's attitude toward her. Floreen puts reindeer in her trees, a Christmas wreath in every window. (''If I had [her] nose,'' snorts Daisy, ''I wouldn't go around saying Merry

Christmas to anyone.'') Despite her nose, Floreen ends up as a Republican National Committeewoman, the type of woman who goes to New York to see *My Fair Lady* rather than attend the funeral of Daisy's brother in Mobile.

The trip to Mobile inspires tender and nostalgic memories in Daisy, who recalls tasting salt water on her face at her brother's wedding. As for Hoke, he admits to having never left Georgia before, and ''Alabama ain't lookin' like much so far.'' Yet even this intimate journey inspires arguments. Hoke has to pass water; Daisy wants him to wait until they reach a Standard Oil gas station. But colored people aren't allowed to use white rest rooms and Hoke, shouting he will not be treated like a dog, stops the car and disappears into a bush. Her small piping ''Hoke?'' signifies a belated realization of just how much she needs him.

Going to the synagogue one morning, both of them see a big mess in the road. The temple has been bombed. By whom? ''Always the same ones,'' says Hoke. Daisy is convinced the hoodlums meant to bomb the conservative synagogue, but as Hoke observes, ''A Jew is a Jew—just as in the dark we're all the same nigger.'' This shared suffering moves Hoke to speak of a time when the father of his friend was lynched, his hands tied behind his back and flies all over his body. ''Why did you tell me that story?'' asks Daisy. ''Stop talking to me.''

By the time she's nearing 90, and extremely feeble, Daisy has developed enough social conscience to help organize a United Jewish Appeal banquet honoring Martin Luther King Jr. Now it is her son, a successful banker with business to conduct with a racist clientele, who is hesitant about public demonstration of Jewish-black friendship. But Daisy persists. ''Isn't it wonderful the way things are changing?'' she says to Hoke, who grumbles, ''Things ain't changed that much.'' Daisy has waited until the very day of the King memorial to invite him to join her at the banquet—and with quiet pride he refuses.

Growing senile in her 90s, confused and rambling, convinced she's teaching school again, Daisy realizes, with a start, that Hoke, the black man, is her best friend. And when her son and Hoke come to visit her in the nursing home, it is Hoke she wishes to talk to. ''How old are you?'' he asks. ''I'm doing the best I can.'' ''Me too,'' he responds, ''. . . that's all there is to it.'' In the final action of the

> *DRIVING MISS DAISY* IS ALL OF A PIECE, COMBINING ELEMENTS OF SENSE AND SENSIBILITY, NOT TO MENTION GENEROUS PORTIONS OF PRIDE AND PREJUDICE.''

play, a sweet, delicate moment, he feeds her two pieces of pie.

This odd love story, though it never underestimates the difficulty of intimacy between the races, could easily grow mawkish. It is a tribute to Uhry's discreet understatement that the sentiment does not grow into corn—or into *The Corn Is Green*. It is also a testimony to the gracefully detailed direction of Ron Lagomarsino and the splendid acting performances of Dana Ivey as Daisy Werthan and Morgan Freeman as Hoke Coleburn. (Ray Gill, playing Boolie like a portly young Charles Durning, is also effective in a more sketchy role.) The way Ivey and Freeman each age 25 years in the course of the action has been widely admired, and it should be. This is not a technical stunt, but the achievement of two gifted actors fully inhabiting their roles. Padded and spectacled in her flowered dress and lace collar, Ivey gives Daisy a growing fragility, inwardness, and snappishness that personifies perfectly realized old age, while Freeman's gray-haired, hatchet-faced, stooped, vaguely cadaverous Hoke is a portrait of a dignified, endearing soul. When he simulates driving the car, sitting on a stool, gently turning the wheel, and raising his eyes as if to watch his passenger in a rearview mirror, he creates a space filled with serenity.

The economy of the acting is matched by that of the production. Thomas Lynch's setting consists of a scrim, a few sticks of furniture, and two stools that represent the front and back seats of the car. Arden Fingerhut's lighting enhances the multiple scene changes. And Robert Waldman's string trio composition—viola, cello, and banjo—blends atmospheric music with the twangy sounds of the South. *Driving Miss Daisy* is all of a piece, combining elements of sense and sensibility, not to mention generous portions of pride and prejudice. It is the work of decent people, working against odds to show how humans

> "I CANNOT THINK OF ANOTHER ACTOR WHO COULD GET SUCH EMOTIONAL VARIETY FROM MERE 'YES'M'S, OR WHOSE LAST-DITCH SELF-ASSERTION COULD BE MORE QUIETLY COMMANDING."

still manage to reach out to each other in a divided world.

Source: Robert Brustein, "Elegy for Old Age," in *New Republic,* Vol., 197, No. 3793, September 28, 1987, pp. 28–30.

John Simon

In the following review, John Simon offers an illustration of the main characters in the play Driving Miss Daisy.

There is a kind of play as redolent of the good old days as 5-cent beer and about as likely to make a comeback. What a sweet surprise, then, to find *Driving Miss Daisy,* a two-and-a-half-character play by Alfred Uhry (author and lyricist of *The Robber Bridegroom,* which I missed), at the tiny upstairs theater of Playwrights Horizons; it is full of an old-style unpretentiousness, coziness, and—despite genuine emotions—quietude. It concerns Miss Daisy Werthan, a crotchety, parsimonious, monumentally stubborn 72-year-old Atlanta widow, who, while insisting she can still drive, has to bow to the combined wills of her son, Boolie, and all the insurance companies in the land and accept a black chauffeur, Hoke, whom Boolie has hired for her.

Hoke is delighted that the Werthans are Jews, whom, in the past, he has found much easier to work for than Baptists. But he has never met the like of Miss Daisy for taciturn intractability, almost whimsical orneriness. He himself is a proud and determined man, respectful but never servile, possessed of amusingly ingenious ways to drive an iceberg as well as a car. The play covers, in bright but unflashy episodes, twenty-five years in these two lives, with Boolie providing an intermittent, droll or exasperated, obbligato to a duet that progresses from discord to close harmony in small, credible steps.

It is to Uhry's credit that there is no cheating. Miss Daisy, in her prosperity, never forgets her hard, impecunious childhood and struggling schoolteacher days; though she is not exactly a champion at the other virtues (except perhaps at propriety), in the generosity sweepstakes she was left at the starting gate. Her always-offstage maid, Idella, has come to terms with this; Boolie, who pays Hoke out of his pocket ("highway robbery," Daisy calls his modest salary), plays along with it; it is Hoke who, slowly, good-humoredly, dismantles Daisy's suspiciousness and isolation, even if he can never quite get her 'ungivingness' to give.

Still, Daisy teaches Hoke to read and write even as he teaches her about human rights and wrongs, and a prickly (on her part) and wary (on his) affection develops between them, the limits of which she will not overstep even after she, well into her nineties and after many changes in cars and conditions, declares him her best friend. Even more than a delicate miniaturist's talent, the playwright exhibits tact: He milks neither the sentiment nor the humor of the situation, and also resists, without avoiding the issues of racism and anti-Semitism, giving us a social tract. Neither the bombing of the synagogue to which Hoke has been regularly driving her nor the testimonial dinner for Martin Luther King Jr. that, despite her son's cautious abstention, she insists on attending can induce Miss Daisy to accept Hoke as her equal in every way.

The dialogue is savory and spirited, and although not a moment of *Driving Miss Daisy* becomes momentous, not a minute of its 80 is boring. Even the predictable, in Uhry's hands, manages to be idiosyncratic enough to be palatable, and connoisseurs of filigree pleasures should feel snugly ensconced here. Those pleasures are vastly enhanced by a tastefully trimmed-down production, smartly and unfussily directed by Ron Lagomarsino and designed with elegant economy by Thomas Lynch (scenery), Michael Krass (costumes), and Ken Tabachnick (lights). But the evening's jewel is the acting. Dana Ivey, in splendid command of the accent, gives a performance exemplarily clean of outline yet rich in detail. I am not wholly sure that (without a chance for elaborate makeup) she really reaches 97 in the end, a feat even more rare on the stage than in life. And Ray Gill infuses the almost incidental role of Boolie with uncommon restraint and suggestiveness.

Primus inter pares, however, is Morgan Freeman. A specialist in tough, violent, often malign parts, he plays Hoke with an easygoing steadfastness both ironic and overwhelmingly humane. His pliability is strength in action, his sarcastic muttering cauterizes as much as it cuts, his wry warmth is as devoid of self-abnegation as of self-righteousness, and his overarching shrewdness is always clearly at the service of decency and good sense. I cannot think of another actor who could get such emotional variety from mere ''Yes'm''s, or whose last-ditch self-assertion could be more quietly commanding. A magnificent performance.

Source: John Simon, ''Daisy and Miller,'' in *New York,* Vol. 20, No. 18, May 4, 1987, pp. 122, 124.

Alfred Uhry

In this article, Alfred Uhry describes his inspiration for creating the three characters in his play.

There was a real Miss Daisy. She was a friend of my grandmother's in Atlanta, back in the forties when I was a child. She was a ''maiden lady'' as we called it then, the last of a big family, and she lived in what I remember as a spooky old Victorian house. There was a Hoke, too. He was the sometime bartender at our German-Jewish country club, and, I believe, he supplemented his income by bartending at private parties around town. And Boolie . . . well, I didn't really know him, but he was the brother of my dear Aunt Marjorie's friend Rosalie. They were real people, all right, but I have used only their names in creating the three characters in *Driving Miss Daisy.* I wanted to use names that seemed particular to the Atlanta I grew up in. The actual characters, though, are made of little bits and pieces of my childhood. Quite a bit of my grandmother, Lena Guthman Fox, and her four older sisters have gone into Miss Daisy herself. And I guess my mother, Alene Fox Uhry, is in there too. Hoke is based on my grandmother's chauffeur, Will Coleman, but also on Bill and Riley and Marvin and Pete and other black chauffeurs I knew in those days. And Boolie is so many pieces of so many men I know (including me, I suppose) that it would be hard for me to say what exactly comes from what.

I find that there is unusual interest in my offstage character Florine, Boolie's wife. Many people have said (by mail or in person) that they know Florine, she is their aunt, their cousin, their old friend from home, etc., etc., etc., and who was she really? I will never tell.

When I wrote this play I never dreamed I would be writing an introduction to it because I never

> **"WHEN I WONDER HOW ALL THIS HAPPENED...I CAN COME UP WITH ONLY ONE ANSWER. I WROTE WHAT I KNEW TO BE THE TRUTH AND PEOPLE HAVE RECOGNIZED IT AS SUCH."**

thought it would get this far. The original schedule was a five-week run at Playwrights Horizons, a New York nonprofit theatre, in the spring of 1987, and I made sure various family members from Atlanta would get to town during that period. The theatre seated seventy-four people. Just the right size, I thought, for a little play that could surely have appeal only to me, my family, and a few other southerners. To my amazement, the appeal was much wider. When the five weeks was up, the engagement was extended for another five weeks, and by then the demand for tickets was so great that we had to move to a bigger theatre.

Flash forward a year and a half. Now there are several companies playing and many more productions planned in all parts of the world. I am in the process of writing the screenplay. I have won the Pulitzer Prize. Even as I write these words they seem unbelievable to me. When I wonder how all this happened (which I do a lot!) I can come up with only one answer. I wrote what I knew to be the truth and people have recognized it as such.

And I have been remarkably lucky. My wife, Joanna, has believed in me for thirty years. How can you ever thank somebody for that? And my daughters, Emily, Elizabeth, Kate and Nell, have always been loving and understanding about what I do for a living. Flora Roberts, my agent for twenty-five years, has always been my friend too, as well as a wonderful sounding board. I must also thank Jane Harmon, Robert Waldman, Andre Bishop, Ron Lagomarsino, Dana Ivey, Morgan Freeman, and Ray Gill for caring so much.

This has been one helluva ride!

Source: Alfred Uhry, ''Preface,'' in *Driving Miss Daisy,* Theatre Communications Group, 1986, pp. vii–ix.

SOURCES

Brustein, Robert, Review of *Driving Miss Daisy* in *New Republic,* Vol. 197, No. 13, September 28, 1987, pp. 28–30.

Canby, Vincent, "'Miss Daisy,' Chamber Piece from the Stage" in *New York Times,* December 13, 1989, p. C19.

Gussow, Mel, Review of *Driving Miss Daisy* in *New York Times,* April 16, 1987, p. C22.

Oliva, Judy Lee, "Alfred Uhry: Overview," in *Contemporary Dramatists,* 5th ed., edited by K. A. Berney, St. James Press, 1993.

Shewey, Don, "Ballyhoo and Daisy, Too" in *American Theatre,* Vol. 14, April, 1997, p. 24–27.

Uhry, Alfred, Preface to *Driving Miss Daisy,* Theatre Communications Group, 1986.

FURTHER READING

Shewey, Don, "Ballyhoo and Daisy, Too," in *American Theatre,* April, 1997, p. 24–27.

> This article surrounds a talk between Shewey and Uhry about several of his plays, providing a unique look at Uhry's perspective of his work.

Sterritt, David, "A Voice for Themes Other Entertainers Have Left Behind," in *Christian Science Monitor,* July 29, 1997, p. 15.

> This article discusses Uhry's work in relation to prevailing attitudes toward morality in the United States.

Ghosts

HENRIK IBSEN
1882

Henrik Ibsen's *Ghosts* surprises modern audiences with some of the issues that it discusses, including out-of-wedlock children, venereal disease, incest, infidelity, and euthanasia. It is the story of a woman, Mrs. Alving, who is preparing for the opening of an orphanage in memory of her husband, Captain Alving, on the tenth anniversary of his death. The captain was an important and respected man in his community, and Mrs. Alving plans to raise this one great memorial to him so that she will not have to ever again speak of him. She wants to avoid the awful truth: that he was a cheating, immoral philanderer whose public reputation was a sham. Their son Oswald has come home from Paris with the news that he is dying of syphilis, which he contracted in the womb, and planning to marry the family's maid. He hopes that she can nurse him as his illness progresses, and Mrs. Alving has to tell him that the maid is actually Captain Alving's illegitimate daughter.

The "ghosts" in this play are the taboo topics that cannot be openly discussed. This drama is one of Ibsen's most powerful works, but also one of his most controversial. Its initial publication sold only a few copies, with most of those printed returned to the publisher and no new edition printed until thirteen years later. It was not performed in Ibsen's native Norway for almost a decade after its world debut in Chicago. In 1898, at a dinner in Ibsen's honor at the Royal Palace in Stockholm, King Oscar II expressed the opinion that *Ghosts* was not a good

play, and that Ibsen should not have written it. After a moment of silence, the playwright replied, "Your majesty, I had to write *Ghosts*."

AUTHOR BIOGRAPHY

Henrik Ibsen was born in 1828 to a wealthy family in Skien, on the east coast of Norway. His father's ancestors had been seafarers; his mother came from a family of the most prominent merchants in the town. During the early years of his life, Ibsen grew up in luxury. His father owned one of the most prosperous stores in Skein, and the family had servants and a stable of horses and a house in the country. That changed early in the author's life, in 1835, when a drop in timber prices forced his father into bankruptcy. The store was lost, the house was sold at auction, and the family had to move to a rented house outside of town. Many critics point to the sudden reversal in his family's fortune as a key to Ibsen's later cynicism about the social order.

After the family's fall from social prestige, life became difficult in the Ibsen household. His father became a hot-tempered bully, constantly shouting and arguing. His mother, whom Ibsen adored, became silent and moody. Henrik became withdrawn, interested in reading and in producing puppet shows. He did not get along with many of the neighboring children, but when he did it was more often with the girls than with the boys.

Ibsen dropped out of school at age fifteen and worked for several years as a pharmacist's assistant. He went to Christiana (which has since become known as Oslo) in 1850 and attempted to enroll in Christiana University, only to be rejected after failing the entrance exams in mathematics and Greek. He became an assistant stage manager at the National Theater in Bergen: one of his duties was to write patriotic plays that celebrated the national character of Norway. This was the beginning of his playwriting career.

Critics often divide Ibsen's plays into three groups or stages. The first stage of his writing, from the 1850s through the end of the 1860s, is marked by dry, traditional, nationalistic plays. These plays were often based in Norwegian legends, such as tales of the Vikings. *Ghosts* belongs to the second period, which is considered to be the most artistically productive. Starting from 1863, and for twenty-seven years after, he lived abroad in Italy and Germany, returning to Norway only once. The plays in this second period are realistic, driven by dialog and not theatrical conventions, while challenging social morality. Also included in this stage are the well-known plays *A Doll's House* (1879) and *An Enemy of the People* (1882). This phase of realism hit its high point with *Hedda Gabler* in 1890. The plays of his last period, during the 1890s, depart from the theme of the individual against society and deal with the individual alone. The most successful of these plays is *The Master Builder* from 1892, which many critics consider Ibsen's most autobiographical work. In 1901, Ibsen's writing career came to an end when he suffered the first of a series of paralyzing strokes. He died in Norway, on May 23, 1906, from complications from the strokes.

PLOT SUMMARY

Act I

Ghosts takes place in the library of the country house of Helena Alving, a wealthy widow. It opens with Mrs. Alving's maid, Regina Engstrand, being visited by Jacob Engstrand, who often reminds her that he is her father, although she seems to doubt it—he tells her that the church register can prove it. Engstrand has been working nearby as a carpenter, helping to build an orphanage, and when he returns to town, he wants Regina to go with him because he plans on using the money he has earned to open a boarding house for sailors and a tavern; and he wants a woman around: "But there must be a petticoat in the house. . . . For I want to have it a little lively in the evenings, with singing and dancing, and so forth." When Engstrand leaves, Pastor Manders enters. Engstrand has confided with the pastor about the drunken life he has led, and the pastor supports his new plan and thinks that Regina should be supportive of her father.

Mrs. Alving enters and discusses the plans of the orphanage with the pastor, who is her financial advisor. She is building the orphanage as a memorial to her late husband, who was an honored member of the community. The pastor suggests that the orphanage not be insured, because insuring it might make people doubt her trust in God.

Mrs. Alving's son Oswald, a painter, enters. He shocks the pastor with talk about couples living together and having children in Paris, where he has recently lived. When he steps out, Pastor Manning tells Mrs. Alving that she should be a better mother.

He reminds her that she left Chamberlain Alving early in their marriage, but that after the pastor convinced her to return to her husband, Alving turned out to be a fine husband. She tells him that Alving was never faithful, that he had an affair with the maid, who was Regina's mother. At the end of the scene, she hears Oswald in the next room, making sexual advances toward Regina.

Act II

Later the same day, after dinner, Mrs. Alving and Pastor Manders talk about ending the flirtation between Oswald and Regina, who are brother and sister. She does not want to send Regina to live with Engstrand, who married a pregnant girl and raised her child for money. Engstrand enters and asks the pastor to lead a prayer meeting at the new orphanage. When Manders asks Engstrand about Regina, he explains that he did not personally profit, that the money given to Regina's mother was all spent on the child's education. He asks for the pastor's help with his planned home for sailors: "[I]t too might be a sort of orphanage, in a manner of speaking. There are many temptations for seafaring folk ashore. But in this Home of mine, a man might feel as under a father's eye, in a manner of speaking."

When they leave, Mrs. Alving talks to Oswald. He has been diagnosed with a disease—the play does not use the word syphilis, but the symptoms indicate it. A doctor has told him that the disease was probably with him since birth, although he does not believe that because he was raised to think that his father was morally correct. On his last visit, he says, he casually mentioned taking Regina to Paris for a trip, and on returning he has found out that she has planned her whole life around it. Mrs. Alving invites Regina to sit down with them and drink champagne with them just as Pastor Manders returns from the prayer at the orphanage. He is about to tell Oswald and Regina that they are related, but they look out the window and see that the orphanage is on fire.

Act III

Engstrand says that he saw Pastor Manders start the fire, that he snuffed out a candle and threw it among wood shavings, although the pastor does not remember even having held a candle. Mrs. Alving says that she has no intention of rebuilding the orphanage, that the pastor can do what he wants with the leftover money, and Engstrand suggests he

Henrik Ibsen

use it to support the sailors' home. Mrs. Alving tells Oswald and Regina that Chamberlain Alving was Regina's father, and Regina is not surprised; instead, she turns out to be selfish, wanting to leave as soon as she knows that she cannot marry Oswald, unwilling to spend her days caring for a sick man. Mrs. Alving tells her that she is always welcome to return if she ever needs a home, and Regina responds that there is one place she knows she will always have a right to: the sailors' home.

> MRS ALVING: Regina—now I see it—you're going to your ruin. REGINA: Oh, stuff! Good-bye.

After Regina has gone, Mrs. Alving muses over the idea that she might not have been the victim of Chamberlain Alving's terrible behavior, but rather the cause of it, making him live in a small provincial town when he might have been more suited for a large city. She promises to take care of Oswald in his illness. Oswald shows her some pills that he was going to tell Regina to poison him with if the next attack of his illness destroyed his brain. As the sun comes up, he sits in a chair, facing away from the window, and says, "Mother, give me the sun." After that, he does not move and only repeats, "The sun. The sun." Mrs. Alving takes the box of pills from his pocket, and before she gives them to Oswald, the curtain falls.

CHARACTERS

Mrs. Helena Alving

Mrs. Alving is the widow of Captain Alving, a well-respected man in the community who has been dead for ten years. She is preparing to open an orphanage named after him to serve the nearby town. When Pastor Manders accuses her of failing to provide Oswald with enough moral guidance, he reminds Mrs. Alving that she has left her husband during her first year of marriage, but that he turned out all right after she returned to him. This prompts Mrs. Alving to tell the truth that she had kept hidden. Captain Alving was an awful man who was unfaithful throughout their marriage. The orphanage is to be built with all of the money Captain Alving had when he married her, and she will live on the money that she made from managing their investments after their marriage; in this way, she hopes to free herself of anything to do with him.

In the course of this play, Mrs. Alving loses her connection with conventional morality. She feels that social convention is false, and that she can put pretense behind her when she distances herself from Captain Alving's memory after naming the orphanage after him. In the last act, though, her view on life is turned around. Instead of seeing herself as a long-silent victim of Captain Alving's hedonistic ways, she sees that he was a victim of her.

Oswald Alving

Oswald is Mrs. Alving's son, who came home the day before the play begins. He has been living in Paris, where his work as an painter has been successful enough to earn coverage in the local Norwegian papers.

While Oswald was growing up, Mrs. Alving attempted to protect him from his father's bad influence by sending him away to school at an early age. The one memory of his father that Oswald talks about in the play is when he was a very young boy, and Captain Alving took him up on his knee and gave him his pipe to smoke. Seeing him smoking his father's pipe, Pastor Manders is shocked by how much Oswald looks like Captain Alving. Oswald has, in fact, grown up to be quite a lot like his father, in spite of his mother's attempts to prevent such a fate. He smokes, and he drinks, and he has relations with women outside of marriage. Soon after Mrs. Alving tells the pastor about her husband's affair with their maid, she finds Oswald carrying on with the present maid, just as his father did.

Jacob Engstrand

In some ways, Engstrand is the mirror image of the late Captain Alving, who is frequently talked about in this play but who died ten years before the play's time. Both men are drinkers and opportunists, willing to lie to secure their good names in society.

Mrs. Alving has hired Jacob to work on the orphanage, and he plans to use the money that he has earned to open a business in town. The purpose of the place changes—early in the first act, he refers to it as a "tavern" for sailors, though by the last act, when he is asking for funding from the pastor, he talks about the place as if it were a rest home for retired sailors, "sort of an Orphanage," which he presents as a charity by naming it "Captain Alving's Home." In an ironic reflection on the immorality of both himself and the unfaithful Captain Alving, he describes the home as the sort of place where "a man might feel under a father's eye."

Regina Engstrand

During the course of this play, Regina's character changes from that of the doting servant who is in love with the master of the house to that of a cold manipulator. She is the first character on the stage. When Engstrand comes in, she shows concern for Oswald, who is napping upstairs. Engstrand wants to include Regina in his scheme to open a tavern, offering her money to be made and the opportunity to marry a rich man, or to be paid off by a rich man who gets her pregnant, and Regina is offended by the offer. When Mrs. Alving invites Regina to sit down and have some champagne with her and Oswald at the end of Act II, Regina thinks she is being treated as one of the family because she is to marry Oswald, unaware that she is part of the family because she is Oswald's sister.

In the last act, when she is told that she is the daughter of Captain Alving, Regina immediately asks to leave. Her concern for Oswald turns out to have been built on what he could do for her, and so she has decided immediately that there is nothing to help her ambitions.

Pastor Manders

Throughout the play, the pastor speaks for conventional morality, even though he does not seem to deeply believe in the course of action that convention would require. This is made most clear in his deliberation over whether or not to insure the orphanage. He says that he would not have any problem with insuring it, but that it might cause a scandal among people who might see insurance as a sign that he does not have enough faith in God to keep the building safe. He is so afraid of the prospect of scandal that he advises against insurance.

Reality is not of primary concern to Pastor Manders. In Act II, when Mrs. Alving has regrets about not having told Oswald how disreputable his father was, Manders takes the position that it was more important to give the boy ideals than to tell him the truth. This concern for inner serenity over understanding what actually happened may account for why he so adamantly denies the attraction that Mrs. Alving says once was mutual.

Because he is more concerned with appearance than with true moral behavior, Pastor Manders is a dupe for Engstrand, who address the pastor humbly as "your Reverence" and pretends to defer to Manders, all the while having his way. As a result of not being able to see when Engstrand is being false, Manders actually believes that he has struggled against being a lazy drunkard, although he has no evidence of this except Engstrand's word. In the end, he believes Engstrand's claim that he saw Manders start the fire with the candle, even though the pastor does not remember holding a candle in his hand, and he runs away from all of his responsibilities in the town, rather than face up to the possible negative opinion that would follow from the fire.

MEDIA ADAPTATIONS

- *Ghosts* was adapted as a silent film in 1915, starring Erich von Stroheim and Mary Alden. It was produced by D. W. Griffith.

- There is a modern version, produced in 1986, with Judi Dench as Mrs. Alving, Kenneth Branagh as Oswald, and Natasha Richardson as Regina. Elijah Moshinsky directed.

- An unabridged audio cassette, with Flo Gibson reading it as text (not "performing" it as a play) was released in 1993 by Audio Book Contractors of Washington, D. C.

THEMES

Deception

The main conflict of this play stems from the fact that Mrs. Alving feels remorse for her part in helping to deceive the world about what sort of man Captain Alving was. She feels that she should have told the truth to Oswald long ago. If she had been honest with him all along, the disease that he inherited from his father may still have been unavoidable, but she could have saved him the confusion that he felt upon finding out that his father, who he thought was morally pure, had syphilis. His own character might have been less cynical if the truth about his father had not come as such a shock.

For his part, Pastor Manders supports the idea of deception. When Mrs. Alving talks about truth, he counters her with talk about ideals. He tells her that, regardless of what the true facts are, Oswald needs to have ideals, that she should not sour his image of his father if that is something that Oswald thinks he can believe in.

In the end, the pastor's belief in deception turns against him. Because his own ideal is that Engstrand is basically a decent, if weak, person, he is more willing to believe what Engstrand says about the fire at the orphanage than what he himself remembers. Pastor Manders falls for a simple deception almost willingly because his grasp on truth is so completely flexible.

Loyalty

In *Ghosts,* the only true loyalty is between Mrs. Alving and her son. All other instances of loyalty seem pure, but they are actually based in social usefulness. The first example of this sort of insincere loyalty is in the early scene between Engstrand and Regina. He asks her to help him with the sailors' home, making a feigned attempt to be concerned about her because she is his daughter. He is not intelligent enough, however, to stick with his case and eventually admits that he wants her there because it would be good for business to have a woman around. Later, he is just as transparently insincere about his loyalty when he tells Manders,

TOPICS FOR FURTHER STUDY

- Parallels have been drawn between this play's treatment of syphilis and the current AIDS epidemic. Make a list of suggestions of changes that would have to be made to *Ghosts* if it were to be played as if Oswald had AIDS.
- Write a short scene taking place between Captain Alving and Mrs. Alving, giving your audience a sense of the tension in their household when she was trying to control his cheating.
- When Pastor Manders says that Johanna was a fallen woman when she was married, Mrs. Alving points out that, using the same reasoning, Captain Alving was a fallen man. In small groups, discuss how much people make such sexists distinctions in contemporary America.
- The last scene of *Ghosts* deals with mercy killing, a subject that has become even more pertinent as medicine has learned to extend the lives of terminally ill people. Research outside sources that have weighed in on the euthanasia debate and write a paper explaining what you think Mrs. Alving should do about Oswald.
- Research the world of Parisian artists in the 1870s and 1880s. Was their worldwide reputation for loose morals deserved? Give some examples that Ibsen might have had in mind when he was writing this play.

"Jacob Engstrand may be likened to a guardian angel, he may, your Reverence." The danger that he professes to "guard" the parson against is the charge that he burned down the orphanage, which is a charge that Engstrand himself made up.

Manders claims to be loyal to the sanctity of marriage. When discussing the time when Helena Alving came to his home after leaving his husband, though, his main focus is on the possible scandal that could have ensued. He's less motivated by loyalty to religious and social doctrine than by fear of repercussions.

Oswald pretends to be loyal to Regina, the maid, but later on, after he reveals the facts about his disease, he talks about how he has counted on her to look after him when his disease makes him an invalid. Regina, for her part, professes her loyalty to Oswald until she finds out that they cannot be married and that he is ill. These are good reasons to not marry him and to realize that they will not have the relationship that she thought they would have, but she is extreme in tossing her loyalty aside, making plans to leave the house the very minute that she hears the news.

Moral Corruption

Ibsen uses Oswald's disease to symbolize the corruption that is handed down from previous generations. When he tells his mother about being diagnosed, Oswald even quotes the doctor as making a statement that indicates a moral judgment beyond his medical one: "The sins of the fathers are visited on the children." This makes sense because, in a strictly physical sense, it is Captain Alving's blood that infected his unborn son. It makes just as much sense in a completely moral frame, too, because Oswald, after finding out that his father was sexually active, took on many of the same qualities. The facts that he smokes his father's pipe, that he drinks constantly, and especially that he flirts with the family maid, just as his father did, are all directly related to being his father's son. Ibsen uses the transmission of the syphilis infection to represent the fact that immorality passes from generation to generation as if it were a genetic condition.

The way that morality is carried through a family is also examined in the example of Regina. Throughout much of the play, she behaves as her mother did: she is a maid, conspicuously at the same house where her mother worked, and she is willing to be the mistress of a wealthy man to get what she wants. When she finds out that she is Captain Alving's daughter, she refers to the Sailor's Home that is named after him as "one house where I've every right to a place." It is not a decent place for a woman, but her connection with Engstrand and with the Captain make it her birthright.

Pastor Manders worries that Mrs. Alving will be morally corrupted by reading new, free-thinking ideas, but the readings that he finds dangerous make her feel more secure. Rather than corrupting her, they just let her know that she is not alone in the way she sees things: as she tells him, "I seem to find explanation and confirmation of all sorts of things that I myself have been thinking."

Victim and Victimization

Ibsen's style of realism does not allow for even the most downtrodden of characters to look like a victim. The most tragic figure in the play is Oswald, who suffers from a disease that was contracted by his father and who did not know that he was infected, did not even think that he could be infected, for much of his life. Still, his condition cannot be called victimization because his is not a decent personality that is being taken advantage of. At heart, Oswald is self-centered. He hates the thought of being ill because it will incapacitate him, and he is full of life. His attitude toward his mother is best summarized when he says, "you can be so very useful to me, now that I'm ill." His relationship with Regina, too, is based on what she can do to help him in his illness. In a sense, the victim of the inherited venereal disease uses his misfortune to justify victimizing everyone around him.

In the course of the play, Mrs. Alving comes to reconsider her relationship with Captain Alving. At first, she tells Pastor Manders of the ways in which she was the captain's victim. She describes her life with and without him, as a life and death struggle to keep Oswald from knowing his father's true nature, although she later calls herself a coward for not telling him the truth. She describes the measures that she took to keep him home nights, so that he would not ruin his reputation by going to town and chasing women. She later regrets her actions, taking the responsibility on herself instead of blaming him for her actions; in fact, by the final act she sees him as her victim, because she suppressed "the overpowering joy of life that was in him."

STYLE

Realism

Realism, as a literary movement, flourished in the United States and Europe in the late 1800s, which is when *Ghosts* was written. In response to romanticism, which presented a version of reality that was twisted through human perception, realism marked an attempt to capture the truth about life, especially the ugly elements of truth that people would rather ignore. Realist literature is often associated with suffering, with disease and corruption, because these are the elements of life that romantic literature shied away from. *Ghosts* comes from a period in Ibsen's career that is considered his realist period, during which he wrote about social issues that disturbed him and his audience, with the hope that examining such unpleasant truths would lead to social change. In this play, he is unmasking the hypocrisy that is usually behind memorials to great civic leaders, looking at the damage that a man with a great reputation might leave in his wake, the "ghosts" that linger.

Setting

All three acts of this play take place in the same setting: the garden-room of Mrs. Alving's house. Keeping the action contained to this one place gives the play several distinguishing aspects. First, the small, enclosed, limited set keeps audiences' attention focused on the characters and how they are interacting with one another. The human drama takes precedence over the exterior trappings that are necessary, but incidental.

This one particular location is meaningful because it is where the past, which affects the present in a ghostly way, took place. This house is where Captain Alving lived; through the doors is the dining room where Helena Alving saw him accost the maid; the bleak fjords on the landscape outside of the windows have defined Mrs. Alving's world for most of her life. No other set would convey as much about what life was like in that house thirty years earlier, when the Alvings were newlyweds, when the trouble all began. If ghosts haunt this family, this specific setting is the locus of their haunting ground.

Symbolism

A writer of Ibsen's caliber will always present objects that resonate with meaning beyond their actual function in the play. In *Ghosts,* several stand out as particularly noteworthy. The most obvious is the orphanage. An orphanage is, of course, a place for children who are left alone in the world without parents. By erecting an orphanage as a memorial, Mrs. Alving is able to accomplish two aims at once. She creates a public institution that benefits the community and enhances the prestige of the person it is named after, but, in making the memorial an orphanage, she also creates a subtle, sarcastic commentary on how the captain treated his own children. In the course of the play, the orphanage, which was to be a tribute to a man who did not deserve one, burns down, indicating that such deception is destined to fail.

The second most important symbolic element is Oswald's disease. Although the script does not name it, the symptoms match those of syphilis. Two aspects of syphilis make it symbolically important in a story like this. The first is the fact that it is spread through intercourse; Captain Alving would never have had the disease if he had been the morally proper man that he and those around him pretended he was. The second aspect is that it can be passed down from parents to unborn children—as Oswald quotes his doctor, "The sins of the father are visited upon the children." There is also a biblical reference to the doctrine of Original Sin, which states that all humans are born sinful because of the sin of the first human, Adam. The doctor, after examining him, told Oswald, "You have been worm-eated from your birth."

A minor, but significant, object that has meaning beyond its actual existence is the champagne glass. In Act II, Regina is invited to drink champagne with Mrs. Alving and Oswald. Because she is the maid, she is apprehensive, but since she does have hopes of marrying Oswald she can believe that the invitation is legitimate. Before they can drink, though, they are interrupted, first by the entrance of Pastor Manders and then by the orphanage burning in the distance. When they come back from the fire, the champagne bottle is still unopened, and Mrs. Alving tells Oswald and Regina that he is her brother. Before leaving the house, Regina takes a bitter glance at the champagne that she was not able to have and remarks, "I may come to drink champagne with gentlefolks yet." Although she lived there and, as she tells Engstrand in the first act, was "treated almost as a daughter here," drinking champagne represents a class barrier that she has been unable to cross.

HISTORICAL CONTEXT

Norway in the 1880s

Ibsen lived away from Norway from 1863 to 1891. Rather than distancing him from the character of the Norwegian people, though, critics note that this separation helped him understand his native land better. Throughout the 1800s, Norway was a land of peaceful self-assurance, left alone to rule itself while still formally under the control of Sweden. This period of independence was a result of the Napoleonic Wars, which changed the organization of Scandinavia as much as they changed almost all of Europe's political structure. Norway had been a province of Denmark for several centuries, from 1381 to 1814, but was taken from Norway, which supported Napoleon, and given over to Swedish rule because Sweden had supported the Russians, who eventually defeated the French. Sweden allowed Norway a great deal of independence. The Norwegian constitution, drafted in 1815, gave more political power to the Norwegian king's council than to ministers from Sweden, whose power was limited to advising. Norway came to be one of Europe's most independent and also one of its wealthiest countries, with the third largest merchant navy on the planet.

One result of this peace, prosperity, and independence was that social issues were examined with greater seriousness than they were in countries just struggling for subsistence. Issues of moral conduct were examined by radical social organizations that would have been outlawed in stricter countries. Also, questions of marriage and sexuality, which would have been left to church decree in the Catholic countries of Europe, were open to discussion in Norway, which was predominantly Lutheran. *Ghosts* was still a shock to Norwegian audiences when it debuted, but it would have been unthinkable to raise some of the issues it raises in a less progressive country.

Realism

Ibsen is considered one of the most important figures in the realist movement that came to dominate literature in Europe and America in the last half of the 1800s. Realism was a reaction to romanticism, which dominated the first half of the century. The romantic movement was about individual freedom—the most important writers of that period generally shared the belief that reality was flexible, subject to human interpretation. Beauty was assumed to have its own distinct existence, aside from the world people live in, and it was assumed that people had the power to interpret reality as they saw fit. Leading romantic writers were the poets Keats and Shelly, the essayist Henry Wadsworth Longfellow, and Edgar Allan Poe. After a while, romantic idealism came to be seen as too dependent on wishful thinking and not connected strongly enough to reality. The realist movement took romantic principles and, in effect, reversed them.

Realism recognized that individuals do not control their environment, but most struggle with it constantly. Realist ideas are evident in *Ghosts* in the way that the reality of disease puts a stop to Oswald's artistic ambitions, and the ways that social expectations put limits on what Mrs. Alving is able to do

COMPARE & CONTRAST

- **1882:** German engineer Gottlieb Daimler invents the first internal combustion engine.

  Today: Automobiles are so common that they create constant problems of crowding and pollution in urban and suburban areas around the globe.

- **1882:** Major industrial areas, such as New York and London, are experimenting with electrical lighting to replace gas lights.

  Today: Most areas in the world have been reached with electrical cables from huge nuclear or hydroelectric generators.

- **1882:** The first birth control clinic in the world is opened in Amsterdam by Aletta Jacobs, who is the first woman to practice medicine in Holland.

  Today: Birth control is still a controversial subject, even in areas where the rates of birth to single mothers have skyrocketed.

- **1882:** Six years after Alexander Graham Bell develops the first working telephone, Western Electric began producing telephone units.

  Today: Wireless telephones and e-mail devices that use the same radio waves are among the most popular consumer products.

- **1882:** The romantic image of the western outlaw is developed after the death of Jesse James, a bank robber who was killed by his cousin for reward money.

  Today: Criminal figures are still romanticized in popular culture, particularly in rap music.

- **1882:** Chicago, where *Ghosts* premiered, installs its first mechanized form of public transportation: electric cable cars that can travel twenty blocks along a straight street in half an hour.

  Today: Underground trains and elevated trains can take passengers out of the city to the airport in that same amount of time.

---

with her life. It was a time when the invisible rules of social interaction were being explored. Charles Darwin's theory of evolution defined the capabilities of the body and drew attention to heredity; Karl Marx proposed the principles of historic inevitability; Sigmund Freud worked at mapping the unseen mechanism of the mind. In the arts, realists like Ibsen, Tolstoy, and Zola did not shy away from showing the miseries that followed when the free-thinking individual was hemmed in by society, but they usually showed misery for a purpose, to shake up old expectations and move people to demand change.

Syphilis

Syphilis is an infectious disease, seldom fatal today but incurable in Ibsen's time. It is usually spread by sexual intercourse with an infected person; because the spirochete that carries the disease cannot live very long in the open, it is almost impossible for syphilis to be transmitted without an exchange of bodily fluids. The first known cases of syphilis in Europe occurred in 1493, leading medical historians to believe that the disease was brought back to the continent by the crew of Christopher Columbus' first expedition to the Americas in 1492. In the following decades, it became a major disease. Its symptoms are similar to those of other diseases, which led to constant confusion about its characteristics before a blood test for diagnosing the disease was developed in 1905. Ibsen's use of the disease in *Ghosts* shows several misconceptions about syphilis, most notably the idea that a child born with it can develop symptoms as late as his twenties; infected newborns sometimes do not develop symptoms until a few weeks after birth, but it does not lie dormant for years.

The first effective treatment for syphilis was developed in 1909, when German-born bacteriologist Paul Ehrlich found that the compound Salvarsan was effective in killing off the spirochete that caused it. Unfortunately, Salvarsan contained arsenic, a deadly poison. In 1943, penicillin was found highly effective as a treatment, and that method is used today. Using an antibiotic program centered on penicillin, doctors have the power to contain syphilis, but in treating the disease scientists are confronted with public attitudes. People with the disease sometimes put off treatment, afraid or ashamed because of its connection with sexual promiscuity. As a result, not all treatable cases are reported to doctors early enough to be cured.

CRITICAL OVERVIEW

At the time when he wrote *Ghosts,* Ibsen's career had eased into a phase of social criticism. His previous work, *A Doll's House,* was met with some objection, but it is easily his most popular and influential play to date. Today, critics consider Ibsen one of the most important playwrights of the modern period, pivotal in introducing a new, realistic way of presenting life on the stage. With the publication of *Ghosts,* though, his career almost came to a grinding halt.

Of all of Ibsen's dramas, *Ghosts* is easily the most controversial, crammed tight with social and sexual themes that challenged the conventional morality. Readers rejected the play and refused to buy it when it was released in book form. Theatrical companies also found it too dangerous to risk offending their local communities. Most of the copies printed in the first edition were returned to the publisher, and they did not all sell for thirteen years. As Ibsen biographer Hans Heiberg explains in a chapter titled, ''The Great Scandal'':

> From December 1881 and throughout the whole of 1882, a hurricane continued to blow all through Scandinavia over Ibsen's new play. And it was not only the conservatives who let out a howl. The liberals, too, and most radicals, were so shaken by the explosion that they neither realized what a masterpiece it was, nor that there was balance in it. Most people thought that Ibsen, through the mouth of Mrs. Alving, wanted to legalize incest and advocate sexual license and nihilism.

Scandanavian theaters would not put the play on, and its debut occurred across the ocean, in Chicago, which had a large Norwegian population. Eventually, a company directed by August Lindberg had success with the play in Helsinki, and their subsequent tour met with increasing popularity.

In the following decade, Ibsen's reputation as a masterful playwright who challenged conventions had become even more solidified by his successes with *An Enemy of the People* (1882) and *Hedda Gabler* (1890). William Archer, Ibsen's contemporary, recognized *Ghosts*' power in capturing reality, and dismissed its critics for trying to limit what an artist can write about. ''If art is ever debarred from entering upon certain domains of human experience,'' he wrote in 1889, ''then *Ghosts* is an inartistic work. I can only say, after having read it, seen it on the stage, and translated it, that no other modern play seems to me to fulfill so entirely the Aristotelian ideal of purging the soul by means of terror and pity.'' The unpleasant elements, in other words, were good for audiences, who could free themselves of their own problems through the act of watching.

Because of his strongly-stated political views, Ibsen became a favorite of political activists, who advocated change in almost all areas of life, from woman's rights to socialism to sexual freedom. Early in the twentieth century, Ibsen's works, especially *Ghosts,* were hailed as heroic achievements, as political unrest against the status quo swelled in Europe and in America. A prime example is Emma Goldman, possibly America's most famous anarchist, who devoted considerable space to the play in her 1914 book *The Social Significance of Modern Drama.* ''The social and revolutionary significance of Henrik Ibsen is brought out with even greater force in *Ghosts* than in his preceding works,'' Goldman wrote. ''Not only does this pioneer of modern dramatic art undermine in *Ghosts* the Social Lie and the paralyzing effect of Duty, but the uselessness and evil of Sacrifice, the dreary Lack of Joy and of Purpose in Work are brought to light as most pernicious and destructive elements of life.'' The end of her review was filled with just as much praise, bordering on hyperbole:

> The voice of Henrik Ibsen in [this play] sounds like the trumpets before the walls of Jericho. Into the remotest nooks and corners reaches his voice, with its thundering indictment of our moral cancers, our social poisons, our hideous crimes against unborn and born victims. Verily a more revolutionary condemnation has never been uttered in dramatic form before or since the great Henrik Ibsen.

Simon Russell Beale (as Oswald Alving) pleading with Jane Lapotaire (as Mrs. Helen Alving) in a scene from the 1993 production of Ghosts, *performed at London's The Other Place Theatre.*

Martin Esslin, one of the most respected and influential contemporary writers about drama, notes in his book about Ibsen that the great German playwright Bertolt Brecht considered *Ghosts* to have been rendered obsolete by 1928, owing to medical developments in suppressing syphilis. The play has continued, however, because audiences do not look at it as an old-fashioned criticism of our time, as Brecht might have, but as a work that was surprisingly ahead of its own time, that has kept its edge by emphasizing human attitudes over situations. Esslin emphasizes how Ibsen changed the performing world by having characters express their motivation gradually and indirectly through dialogue and action. This is something that audiences take for granted today, but the style of Ibsen's contemporaries called for characters whose motivations were obvious the moment that they stepped out on stage. Esslin traces the development of this technique of spontaneity from Ibsen through Chekhov and the Moscow Theatre to modern avant-garde filmmakers like John Cassavettes and Robert Altman, as well as playwrights like Eugene Ionesco and Harold Pinter, whose characters rely on more than just their words to convey who they are.

CRITICISM

David Kelly

Kelly teaches creative writing and scriptwriting at two colleges in Illinois. In the following essay, he examines the life of Helena Alving, the main character in Ibsen's Ghosts, *in terms of one haunting, definitive moment in her past.*

In any of Henrik Ibsen's plays there will be layers of characterization, complicated by the lingering presence of events that occurred to the characters years before what is seen presented on the stage. This is especially true of *Ghosts* with its focus on the ways in which people and events that are long gone continue to resonate, how they stay alive from one generation to the next. The most obvious ghosts are those of Johanna the maid and Chamberlain Alving. But they have been dead for years when, seeing her son, Oswald, touching Johanna's daughter Regina in the same dining room where her husband had made a pass at Johanna a generation earlier, Mrs. Alving blurts out the play's title. "I almost think we're all of us Ghosts, Pastor Manders," Mrs. Alving says later, recalling that moment. "It's not

WHAT DO I READ NEXT?

- Ibsen's play *An Enemy of the People* was started before *Ghosts* but was not finished until after the latter play. It is a scathing indictment of social standards, as a doctor who points out contamination of a town's water supply goes from hero to enemy when his revelation upsets the local economy. Viking Press has a 1987 edition edited by Arthur Miller, the author of *Death of a Salesman*.

- At the same time that Ibsen wrote in Norway, August Strindberg was the leading playwright in Sweden. Both playwrights explored the new realistic forms. *Miss Julie*, Strindberg's 1888 drama about an aristocratic girl and her affair with her conniving butler, is considered his best.

- The Russian author Anton Chekhov is considered one of the greatest authors of short stories and dramas in history. He cited Ibsen as one of his main influences. All of Chekhov's plays are important, but *The Cherry Orchard* (1904) in particular examines some of the same themes as *Ghosts*.

- Irish playwright George Bernard Shaw was a supporter of moderate Socialist ideas. His political analysis of Ibsen is printed as a book, *The Quintessence of Ibsenism*, available in a 1994 Dover Books edition.

- Ibsen's life and ideas come alive in the 1970 publication *Correspondence of Henrik Ibsen*, edited by Mary Morrison.

- The way that writers treat the weaknesses of the body, like Ibsen's use of syphilis to represent the decadence that is passed down from one generation to the next, was examined in Susan Sontag's classic essay *Illness as a Metaphor*, which is now published in one volume (1995) with its sequel, *AIDS and Its Metaphors*.

- Stella Adler is one of the great teachers of actors in America, having been instrumental in the training of Marlon Brando, Robert DeNiro, Al Pacino, and others. In 1999, Barry Paris edited a series of her lectures into one cohesive book, *Stella Adler on Ibsen, Strindberg and Chekhov*.

---

only what we have inherited from our father and mother that 'walks' in us. It's all sorts of ideas, and lifeless old beliefs, and so forth. . . . There must be Ghosts all the country over, as thick as the sands of the sea. And then we are, one and all, so pitifully afraid of the light.''

As Mrs. Alving understands it, ghosts are not just the specters of people. Actions cast shadows. Emotions cast shadows. The difficult job for the playwright is to show how long and how deeply an isolated moment from the past can continue to affect one's life.

In *Ghosts,* many of the events of the past twist around another, braided like a rope, but one event in particular seems to be at the center of the Alving family's tragedy: it is the brief moment, nearly thirty years earlier, when Mrs. Alving presented herself to Pastor Manders with the words, ''Here I am. Take me.'' The pastor, of course, did not take her, even though there is every reason to believe that he wanted to. At that brief moment in the past, all of the play's major concerns—love, lust, repression, honor, freedom and possibility—intersected, and the results of that lost moment are every bit as important as anything in these unfulfilled lives.

This moment in Mrs. Alving's life came when she had been married to Captain Alving for a year and had already learned to regret it. She had been young and fatherless, practically a child, talked into marriage by her mother and aunts who believed that marriage to the dashing young sailor would be glamorous to young Helena because she had no better prospects in her life. Their encouragement was, however, based on the assumption that marriage would change the captain from a sailor to a husband, which in fact it did not. He continued to live like a bachelor—Mrs. Alving describes his behavior in the play as "dissolute," a word that defines a lack of moral restraint by emphasizing the fact that his spirit is dissolved, uncontrolled, unfocused. As she says later, the town "had no joys to offer him—only dissipations."

To Pastor Manders, the bride he had married to the sailor a year earlier must have looked, as she stood on his doorstep, less like the possibility for romantic love than like trouble incarnate. He tells her that going to him was "incredibly reckless," wording that in itself shows more his terror of being found with a woman than fear of the danger to her mortal soul. There is every reason to believe that he did not take her seriously, that he just thought of her as a discontent bride who was not willing to accept the unglamorous parts of marriage. Pastor Manders is, after all, presented as a man of duty, a "poor instrument in a Higher Hand," to use his own words. To such a person, anyone not driven by duty would seem to lack proper seriousness. He may have seen young Helena Alving as socially greedy, like Regina Engstrand, who rejects her father's scheme to put her to work as a virtual prostitute in his sailors' home because "Sailors have no *savoir vivre*.

Did he love her, when she showed up at his door saying, "Take me"? If he ever thought in terms of love and hate, then he may have, but the pastor's mind, focused on duty, had no room for emotions. Ideally, a person in his position just would not have any emotions that could cloud his moral judgment. He was human, though, and so, in pursuit of that ideal, he tried throughout his life to quash the emotions that he did have. When Mrs. Alving implies that there was once an emotional bond between them, he is emphatic about his version of the past, so emphatic that he seems to be struggling to turn the version he hoped for into reality. "Never," he says, and then repeats, "never in my most secret thoughts have I regarded you otherwise than as another's wife." Whether or not he is sincere, Mrs. Alving certainly does not take his claim too seriously, responding bemusedly with, "Oh!—indeed?" The pastor considers his "victory over myself" to be his greatest victory, while Mrs. Alving considers his denial of his own urges to be his greatest defeat.

That moment, twenty-eight years earlier, defined Mrs. Alving's life to come, sending her on a secret search for innocence. If she had offered

> THE DIFFICULT JOB FOR THE PLAYWRIGHT IS TO SHOW HOW LONG AND HOW DEEPLY AN ISOLATED MOMENT FROM THE PAST CAN CONTINUE TO AFFECT ONE'S LIFE."

herself to him and had been rejected because of her looks, her life might have become a crusade against superficial standards of beauty; if she had been rejected as too poor, she might have become a socialist. When Pastor Manders followed what was "law" instead of his own feelings, Mrs. Alving begins to consider the personal losses one may suffer by doing so and wonders whether sometimes it is better to follow one's own truth rather than what others define as right and acceptable behavior.

The horror of Mrs. Alving's life is that she had to lock herself up in the house in the country, giving in to the captain's "secret orgies" and preserving his bogus reputation, in the quest for the truth. The social world that Manders flung her back into when he rejected her was a sort of maze that she had to wind her way through before reaching her moment of truth. Mrs. Alving needed to learn how to stop living the lies that her role in society forced upon her. Mrs. Alving challenges society's view of her in several ways. She begins reading nonconformist, free-thinking books; raises her son with the sort of sensibilities more comfortable in the artistic community of Paris than provincial Norway; and, raises a memorial to Captain Alving, leaving her free to pursue less reputable inquiries. As she explains to Pastor Manders, her quest for truth began "when you forced me under the yoke you called Duty and Obligation; when you praised as right and proper what my whole soul rebelled against as something loathsome."

With the orphanage that she has erected, Captain Alving's false image as a humanitarian is supposed to take on a life of its own, so that it can leave her alone to pursue her own interests; instead, her acceptance of this fraud destroys her, proving that a future of truthfulness cannot be built upon a past of lies. Seeing Oswald with Regina, Mrs.

Alving declares that she should never have withheld the truth about the captain's character. Finding out how confused Oswald's life has been since he found out that the man he considered a saint passed a venereal disease to him, she is even more remorseful about her deception. From beyond the grave, Captain Alving's sinful life appears to reach out to the one she loves more than her own life, her son, first in the form of a forbidden love and then as death.

What seems to be the ghostly force of the late captain's character, though, is actually the same fascination with "Duty and Obligation" that drove Helena Alving to the pastor's door so long ago. Her dream that she could ever, at any set time, be relieved of her responsibility to her husband, turns out to just be wishful thinking. When she tells Pastor Manders that she should give Oswald the truth, he counters that she owes her son ideals, not truth. He may be on the opposite side of the argument from her, but it is by mutual consent that his side balances hers. Before the threat of an incestuous relationship between Regina and Oswald, before the fact of Oswald's disease is known, Mrs. Alving's truth and Pastor Manders's ideals hold equal footing, if not for the audience then for the two of them.

As late as the last act, Pastor Manders's morality is still affecting her, exerting a gravitational pull. Having despised her husband when he was alive and survived ten years since his death with her hatred undiminished, she suddenly sees that she may have been responsible for the ruin of Captain Alving's life. She feels that she may have been too concerned about "duties," draining the "joy of life" from him. She is seeing that part of Pastor Manders that she has in herself. The same call to duty that she believed that she was only putting up with for a short while turns out to be deeply imbedded within her personality.

Pastor Manders and Mrs. Alving have complimentary personalities, but by the time that the play begins, their roles within the dynamic of their relationship have reversed. She came to him once as a girl, offering him the adult position of responsibility, authority, and control. When she watches him falling naively for the lies that Engstrand tells him, she sees that she is much more qualified to deal with the duplicity of the real world. "I think you are, and will always be, a great baby, Manders." When she recognizes at last that she has always had the power in their relationship by realizing that his command to return to her husband was a command that she did not need to follow, she is almost giddy with her sense of freedom. She puts her hands on his shoulders, threatens to kiss him, which terrifies him, so he grabs his things and leaves. It is possibly the one true moment of their relationship, where she acts out the truth of his fear and weakness and displays her attraction to acting on one's impulses.

This attraction, which for that one moment seemed to border on sweetness, comes back as an echo—a ghost—in the bitter tragedy of the play's last scene. First, it is applied to the captain, who is the official ghost of the play. Mrs. Alving's delight at seeing the pastor as a "great baby" makes more sense to audiences when she shows the same attraction to that aspect in her late husband's character, "child of joy as he was—for he *was* like a child at that time." But when that childishness shows itself in a real person, Oswald, who is the captain's physical manifestation in the play, then the figure of her imagination turns grim.

Oswald describes the condition that his disease will leave him in even before it happens in the play. He will be "helpless, like a new-born baby, impotent, lost, hopeless, past all saving." In the play's last lines, when this state has actually descended upon him, the Alving family has come full circle. Helena, who once laid herself at the mercy of another person, grew such strength because of the pastor's rejection that she now ends up having to make the ultimate decision. She has overcome her own weakness to appreciate the weakness in others, until her own son slides back into it with the stated wish that she take his life.

Ghosts' detractors have pointed out that it is an incomplete drama, with the concluding act left to occur after the final curtain has fallen, out of view of the audience. This reading of the play assumes that knowing whether Mrs. Alving gives Oswald the poison would conclude the play. Looking at it from another angle, though, it is complete. In the end, Helena Alving, who wanted so much when she was young to give herself over to a man of morals, now has a grave moral choice in her hand. It does not matter how she acts; what matters is that the identity of the person who once said "take me" has been completely reversed by the circumstances her personality has created in her life.

Source: David Kelly, in an essay for *Drama for Students*, Gale Group, 2001.

Lynn Fairleigh and Simon Chandler star as mother and son, Helen and Oswald Alving, in the Shaw Theatre's 1984 production of Ghosts.

John Northam

John Northam focuses on Mrs. Alving in Ghosts, *placing her in the context of the society depicted in the play. According to him, Mrs. Alving "has always been at war" with her society, which subtly coerces women to sacrifice their "personal integrity to social demands."*

The ironies compressed into [the final scene of *Ghosts*] are likely to be almost as unendurable for the audience as for Mrs. Alving. She worked so hard to create for her son a corner of health and sanity in a corrupt world; that son is mentally diseased. She planned to clear the house of all other but herself and her beloved child; she has succeeded, but only in this appalling travesty. She thought that she could bring the long, hateful comedy to a neat end, scaling off all consequences, but she has unwittingly written a final act which is tragic. She worked to preserve a life and must now decide whether to destroy it.

The sum of these reversals to her expectations amounts to a condemnation of Mrs. Alving; not for her trying, but for the mode of her trying. The essential quality in her is ambiguity, that strangely constant mingling within the one woman of radical and conformist; she is strong enough to try to think for herself, but too cowardly to act in any other way than that required by the society she has, in part, seen through. Her radicalism itself is never complete; it may, under Oswald's influence, expand, but at no point can she fully liberate herself from the influence upon her, acknowledged or unacknowledged, of dead social habits. All that can be said of her at the end of the play is that at least at that moment she is being forced to face facts as they really are; what she will make of the experience we cannot know.

Thus the play could be taken as the trial and condemnation of a misguided, inadequate woman. If Mrs. Alving had been true to her own feelings she would not have married Alving, or remained with him once married; had she been true to her own sense of the genuine, she would not have decided to rectify the disaster of her life by preserving appearances, whose falsity she recognised, in order to appease society. It is a strong indictment and the play undoubtedly levels it at her; and yet an account that stopped there would seem to me not to acknowledge much else that is offered.

For all her misguidedness, Mrs. Alving remains in the imagination as a splendid woman. This im-

> "IBSEN CAN SEE... THAT NO INDIVIDUAL, NOT EVEN ONE WITH THE BASIC INTEGRITY OF A MRS. ALVING, CAN ESCAPE PERMEATION BY THE VERY CORRUPTION BY SOCIETY THAT THEIR INTEGRITY MAKES THEM IDENTIFY AND OPPOSE."

pression comes partly from her personality and character taken by and for themselves. She has been so strong, to have coped with a life like that without weakness and to have coped alone. She must have had nerves and a will of steel to have conceived and carried out a plan of such complexity and long duration without losing heart. She always fights to control and shape events, never allowing herself to be passively overwhelmed. She is indeed a strong woman. And we can only admire the direction in which her strength is constantly directed. Misguided or not, blinkered though she may be in ways unsuspected by herself, she is always trying to see through pretence and hypocrisy to the truth behind it. She often fails to get through, and she initially fails to act on the truth that she has discovered, but that is the direction her bent of mind leads her in. And out of her private understanding she hopes for one single thing: to create the possibility of a decent life.

There is an element of selfishness in all this, yet even that is forgiveable in a mother. She wants her boy to herself. But she is no child-devourer; Oswald has always been free to come and go; but for his illness he could return to Paris; Mrs. Alving relishes the thought of his staying but she has never suggested it, still less demanded or engineered it.

The element of maternal selfishness is minor compared with the selflessness that has made her sacrifice her own happiness to her son's well-being. Everything that she has done has been directed towards that.

Thus even on a narrow view of Mrs. Alving as a character in isolation she seems to merit deep respect and not mere blame. For the full assessment we need to see her in her context.

In simple terms, Mrs. Alving has always been at war with society. Her stature, and her achievements, must be gauged in relation to her antagonist. And here the play creates a force of peculiar horror. Society is presented as an openly coercive force, but that is not its chief characteristic. We see it in action upon Manders and through him upon Mrs. Alving. The coercion is strong, certainly not negligible, but it is not remarkable.

Society's real power lies in its unobtrusiveness. The trap it lays for Mrs. Alving is one into which she and millions of other women have slipped without recognising that it was a trap. There is nothing openly coercive about the advice of relations when it comes to choosing a husband. Mrs. Alving was not aware of facing a great crisis in her life when she decided that Alving was the best catch in social terms; and yet in that choice she subdued her own feelings to the criteria created by society. The essential falsification occurred then, yet who could have identified such a crisis in so commonplace a decision? Part of the power of society in *Ghosts* is that it works through small-scale events which do not proclaim their real significance at the moment of occurrence. Brand could identify his crises; Mrs. Alving could not.

Yet once in, the consequences are fatal and inescapable. From the initial falsification all others flow; and these too hide their significance in unobtrusiveness. When Mrs. Alving sent Oswald away from home and made arrangements for Regine and so on, she was being false to her knowledge of the truth, but she was conditioned by society to accept without question that this was the reasonable way to act. Her plans were reasonable submissions to society that followed from her first reasonable submission. And she has gone on living for years without having much reason to recognise that such submission of personal integrity to social demands could be critical and fatal.

And yet in the end the magnitude of crisis must become clear. To submit, to the extent that Mrs. Alving has, to society is to cause terrible corruption to set in. Oswald's disease is the outward and spectacular sign of the corruption, of its secretiveness and of its fatal inevitability, but it is not the only form of corruption. There is corruption of will, corruption of courage, corruption of integrity, of relationships—indeed a creeping invasion through many different veins and arteries of the play simultaneously. In *Brand* the sequence of events was linear; Brand moved on from one crisis and its consequences to the next. In *Ghosts* the various streams of corruption move apparently independently and in unsuspected ways towards the one moment of dissolution.

Perhaps Ibsen's greatest discovery in *Ghosts* was the way in which his protagonist must necessarily be involved in modern society. Falk, in *Love's Comedy,* by virtue of his favoured status as student, was allowed to stand outside the social structure he condemned. Though affected by his antagonism to his surroundings, he was not contaminated by them. Nor was Brand; even though he was woven into his community far more intimately than Falk, his small parish can serve only as an emblem of real modern social existence; and he too, Ibsen seemed to imagine, could preserve his spiritual integrity.

Mrs. Alving cannot preserve hers entirely from the corruption she later comes to identify. However clearly she may, by the time the play begins, recognise that she married for the wrong reason, may have acted wrongly since, may need to revise and enlarge her sense of truth and honesty, she constantly reveals that society continues to influence her ways of thought and action. Ibsen can see now that no individual, not even one with the basic integrity of a Mrs. Alving, can escape permeation by the very corruption by society that their integrity makes them identify and oppose. Significantly one of the images of that permeation is the gloom which envelops, as an all-pervasive natural force, the action of so much of the play.

This is Mrs. Alving's antagonist, and it is in its peculiar fashion powerful enough to explain and justify total submissiveness in all the individuals who compose it. Mrs. Alving is conditioned; she is partly submissive, deliberately and unconsciously; but she is never totally subdued. And this refusal to give up trying to discover what is the truth and the right way to respond to it is again significantly defined through the image of a great natural force, the sun. Notwithstanding her wounds and blemishes, indeed because of them, Mrs. Alving emerges as a great fighter against a terrible opponent.

In *Ghosts,* then, Ibsen has entered more deeply into the nature of modern society and its relationship to the heroic individual; he has also created a dramatic form for embodying his vision. Whatever else it may be, *Ghosts* cannot reasonably be assessed as a mere surrender on Ibsen's part to theatrical expediency or as a betrayal of the poetic copiousness of *Love's Comedy, Brand,* and *Peer Gynt* to the seductions of naturalism. Its form is essential to the vision.

The language, for instance, is limited in range because this is one of the effects society has on its members. It educates them to think decorously and to express themselves with conventional neatness. Anyone who tries to break these limitations must create his own language and in Oswald's shapeless rhetoric the impression of overemphasis, of straining after effects not to hand in the common use of language, is indicative not of Ibsen's verbal impoverishment but of the spiritual impoverishment of the society that cannot accommodate Oswald; and, as we have seen, Mrs. Alving's reduction of his vision to the careful patterning that she has been educated in illuminates the same point from a different angle. Ibsen can no longer imagine for his modern hero that degree of mental and spiritual autonomy that allowed Falk and Brand to be fully articulate poets. Their significance lies in their being poets of living, men with a vision of a finer life than society offers, but their ability to be poets in words, to speak out with full-blooded rhetoric to expound, explore, define their visions, is one way of asserting that they are spiritually free men. But they were so only because Ibsen had not, at that time, really sensed the power of modern society: Falk can stand outside it, Brand encounters a simplified version, an emblem. Nobody, not even Mrs. Alving, can preserve his autonomy in the face of the complexity of power that society now represents for Ibsen, and the language is one means of expressing this fact.

The same is true of the setting. Mrs. Alving's handsome room may be less spectacular than Brand's mountains and ice-church but it is not to be despised for its ordinariness. The set mirrors Ibsen's conviction that it is by its unobtrusiveness, by its very reasonableness and seemliness, that society is able to exercise its power; the very decency of appearances helps him emphasise the horror of discovering that the attractive setting is a monstrous snare, and the limiting of the action to one room takes away the illusion, still preserved in *Love's Comedy* and *Brand,* that there is somewhere else to go. In modern society, as Ibsen sees it, there is nowhere else; the great battles must be fought out amongst comfortable furniture in a handsome house; the mountains offer no escape to Mrs. Alving: they are remote images of ultimate truth, not to be trodden as they were by Falk and Brand. The setting is an essential part of Ibsen's harsher vision.

The setting is created partly by verbal, partly by visual imagery. Both kinds indicate further advances beyond the artistry and vision of his earlier works. The extremity of imagery in *Brand*, those blatant and massive symbols of opposition—storm, mountains, ice-church, narrow dale, sunshine and so forth—help create what amounts to an almost comforting sense of clarity. The opposed values are identified for us; the crises that arise out of the opposition are made manifest not merely to us but to the protagonist. In *Ghosts* everything is made less precise. Instead of storm, steady drizzle and mist, not a challenge so much as an enervating atmosphere; instead of miserable dale, Mrs. Alving's country house, outwardly a haven. There are no sharp indices of crisis; we have to discover them as Ibsen now sees them, as latent and lurking. Out of this lack of clarity comes a further virtue. Instead of establishing his imagery *ab initio* [from the beginning], as he does in *Love's Comedy* and in *Brand*, and then working by repetition, Ibsen allows his imagery to grow organically, establishing itself and its significance progressively. He works not by massive and blatant groupings but by small affinities gradually discovered. Yet he holds all this together, more successfully than in *Brand*, by creating a feeling of tempo, of inevitable movement towards a climax. All of the imagery is ultimately controlled by the image of Oswald's disease and by the image of day dispersing night. Thus Ibsen can represent deviousness and cryptic consequence without losing his sense of the essential unity of the action or of the pace in which the action moves. There is little feeling of development or progression in *Love's Comedy*; in *Brand* there is progression of a relatively simple linear kind, with little feeling of tempo; *Ghosts* moves much more impressively.

In *Ghosts* the vision is enriched and the form for its expression brought almost to perfection. Not quite to perfection because there are signs, here and there, that the effort to elucidate for himself the pattern that underlies the seemingly petty detail of modern living led him into oversimplification, both of vision and form, in the interests of clarity. Some of the cross-weaving of images into patterns is of this kind—the equation of the drizzle with the spiritual climate, or of Oswald with the Orphanage, does not need the kind of emphasis it is given. Manders need not be as inadequate as he is to give a reasonable representation of society's inadequacies.

Ghosts has its imperfections but it is a great play for all that. Though different in kind it is arguably a finer dramatic poem than *Brand*, if by poem we mean an imaginatively organised structure of imagery constituting a profound and unified vision. Less debatably, Mrs. Alving is a more convincing kind of hero than Brand, by virtue of her fuller involvement in a society more fully understood and represented. From *Love's Comedy* and *Brand* we gain insight into the issues that govern the quality of living; in *Ghosts* the issues are played out upon our nerves and feelings as we experience, with Mrs. Alving, what it feels like to be a woman like that condemned to live in such a world. *Ghosts* is, above all, an experience, immediate and immensely painful. And yet, for all its greatness, it marks only Ibsen's entry into artistic maturity; the greatest works are amongst those that follow.

Source: John Northam, Excerpt from *Ibsen: A Critical Study,* Cambridge at the University Press, 1973, p. 237.

Robert W. Corrigan

Corrigan views Mrs. Alving in Ghosts *as divided between her intellectual ideals and an "emotional inheritance" over which she has no control.*

Ghosts created the biggest stir in Europe of all of Ibsen's plays. It was the hallmark of the Free Theatre movement. Antoine at the Théâtre Libre, Brahm at the Freie Buehne, and Grein at the Independent Theatre in London all produced this play as a symbol and a harbinger of their freedom. But the play was violently received. It shocked respectable middle-class audiences everywhere; it was condemned and banned; for the young turks of liberalism it was a banner to be waved on high. From the beginning the play had a notoriety that Ibsen only partially intended.

Fortunately, *Ghosts* is now seen in clearer perspective and we tend to be amused by the critical reaction of the Nineties. But *Ghosts* is still a controversial play. The number of respectable interpretations currently making the rounds is large and when you get on the subject of *Ghosts* as tragedy—well, it is one of those plays, like [Arthur Miller's] *Death of a Salesman,* it just won't stay settled and is always good for an argument. The four major interpretations of the play usually advanced are: First, Ibsen wrote *Ghosts* as an answer to the objections raised by Nora's flight from her husband and children in *A Doll's House.* Tied to a worse husband than Helmar, Mrs. Alving, instead of leaving him, had decided to stay, and to cover up the "corpse" of her married life with respectable trappings. Second: Mrs. Alving and Oswald are the victims of a two-fisted fate which takes the form of the laws of heredity in a mechanistic world and the stultifying and debilitating conventions of respectability. Third: Hereditary disease was for Ibsen the symbol of all the determinist forces that crush humanity, and, therefore, he sought to put in opposition to these forces the strongest of all instincts—maternal passion. And, finally, there is a fourth group of critics who dismiss the play as irrelevant except as an historical landmark. They argue that although the play may have been revolutionary in its day, today any dramatic conflict which presents suffering and a shot of penicillin as its alternatives is not very convincing. All of these interpretations—and they have been persuasively argued by responsible critics—seem to me to be either misreadings of the play or beside the point. They are comments about the play, but they are ancillary and fail to recognize the underlying conflict of the play. For this reason most modern commentaries on *Ghosts* fail to describe and interpret the central action which Ibsen is imitating, and this has resulted in many limited or erroneous discussions of the play as a tragedy. It is this central action and its tragic implications which I wish to discuss, and this can best be done by first turning to Ibsen the man and the artist.

Ibsen's biography is a study in conflict and contradiction. The gadfly of bourgeoisie morality was helplessly bourgeois; the enemy of pietism was a guilt-ridden possessor of the worst kind of "Lutheran" conscience; the champion of the "love-life of the soul" was incapable of loving; the militant spokesman against hypocrisy and respectability was pompous and outraged at any breach of decorum. Ibsen's life is the contradiction of those values affirmed in his plays. This should not confuse us, however, if we will look even briefly at some of the significant events in a life that was really quite dull. . . .

In short, Ibsen became a "pillar of society" in his last days; he was a regular speaker at the Norwegian equivalents of the Rotary Club, the AAUW, Labor Unions, and the Better Business Bureau. In his speeches he praised all of these groups and gratefully accepted their adulation and honors. His study walls were covered with plaques and certificates from civic organizations and only a bust of [August] Strindberg—a bust that captured the penetrating and demonic quality of Strindberg's gaze—acted as an antidote to this display of middle-class self-righteousness. On March 15th, 1900 Ibsen had a stroke, and another in the following year. These paralytic strokes were followed by amnesia and for six years he lay helplessly senile. He died on May 23rd, 1906, at the age of seventy-eight.

> THE GHOSTS OF PLOT AND SYMBOL ARE THE MANIFESTATIONS OF MRS. ALVING'S STRUGGLE WITH THE GHOSTS WITHIN. IT IS THIS INTERNAL CONFLICT. . .THAT IS THE PLAY'S CENTRAL ACTION."

The clue to the meaning of all Ibsen's plays lies in this strange biography. Ibsen's plays are a continuous act of expiation. Certainly, it is significant that bankruptcy and the resultant rejection by society appears in four of his plays; the desire to restore the family honor is central to two more; and there are illegitimate children in eight plays. Thematically, the plays are, almost without exception, patterned in a similar way: a hidden moral guilt and the fear of impending retribution. Structurally, the plays are epilogues of retribution. All of the plays after *Peer Gynt,* begin on a happy note late in the action. In each case the central figure has a secret guilt which is soon discovered. As the play progresses, by series of expository scenes (scenes which delve into the past and are then related to the present condition of the characters), a sense of the foreboding doom of impending retribution envelops the action and each of the plays ends with justice, in the form of moral fate having its way. And finally, beginning with *Ghosts,* Ibsen introduces the theme of expiation. In every play following *Ghosts,* at least one of the central characters feels the need to exorcise his guilt, doubt, or fear by some form of renunciation.

Perhaps more important is the fact, that as Ibsen's art developed these themes and attitudes changed in tone and form. The guilt, which had been specific in the early days—Bernick's lie [in *The Pillars of Society*], Nora's forgery [in *A Doll's House*], Mrs. Alving's return—becomes more and more abstract, nebulous, and ominous as best evidenced in the nameless guilt of Solness [in *The Master Builder*] and Rosmer [in *Rosmersholm*]. The fear, which in the early plays had been the fear of discovery, becomes a gnawing anxiety. Self-realization, which in *Brand* is presented in terms of the Kierkegaardian imperative of either/or is realized in the later plays in an ambiguous kind of self-destruction. And finally, significant action on the part of the characters has tendencies towards becoming a frozen stasis of meaningless activity and contemplation.

Ibsen's life and his work are closely interwoven. Ibsen, rejected from society as a young man, had good reason to see the blindness of bourgeois respectability in his exile. And yet his sharp criticism of society is always balanced by his desire to be a part of that very society he saw and knew to be false. Over and over again in his plays and letters he condemns the hypocrisy, the intellectual shallowness, and the grim bleakness of his Scandinavian homeland. But he returned to it in pomp and circumstance. Herein lies the crux to an understanding of Ibsen's art in general and *Ghosts* in particular. More and more we see that both in Ibsen the man and in the characters of his plays the basic struggle is within.

Ibsen lived in a time of revolution; he was a maker of part of that revolution; and he knew full well that all the things he said about bourgeois society were true. But despite his rational understanding, his intellectual comprehension of this fact, he was driven by deeper forces within him not only to justify himself to that false society, but to become a part of it. It is this struggle within himself between his rational powers and the Trolls of the Boyg that best explains his life and work. Ibsen's plays are his attempts to quell the guilt he felt for desiring values which he knew to be false. In support of this point, I call attention to two important bits of evidence: the first is a letter written by Ibsen to Peter Hanson in 1870:

> While writing *Brand,* I had on my desk a glass with a scorpion in it. From time to time the little animal was ill. Then I used to give it a piece of soft fruit, upon which it fell furiously and emptied its poison into it—after which it was well again. Does not something similar happen to us poets? The laws of nature regulate the spiritual world also. . . .

The second is a short poem entitled "Fear of Light" (presently, I shall relate the significance of that title to *Ghosts*):

> What is life? a fighting
> In heart and brain with Trolls.
> Poetry? that means writing
> Doomsday-accounts of our souls.

I contend that Ibsen's plays were attempts—attempts that were bound to fail, just as Mrs. Alving's attempts were bound to fail—to relieve Ibsen of his guilt and at the same time were judgments of his failure to overcome the Trolls (which first appear as Gerd in *Brand*), those irrational forces and powers within man over which he has no control.

Keeping these facts in mind, let us now turn to *Ghosts*. One does not have to be a very perceptive student of the theatre to realize that the "ghosts" Ibsen is talking about are those ghosts of the past that haunt us in the present. In fact, Ibsen has often been criticized for using his ghost symbolism with such obviousness, such lack of subtlety, and so repetitiously. Certainly, when reading the play we feel this criticism is justified. Oswald's looking like Captain Alving; his interest in sex and liquor; his feelings toward Regina; his syphilitic inheritance; Pastor Mander's influence over Mrs. Alving, the orphanage, and the fire are only a few of the "ghosts" that Ibsen uses as analogues to his theme. Alrik Gustafson puts it this way [in "Some Notes on Themes, Character, and Symbol in *Rosmersholm*," *Carleton Drama Review* I, No. 2]:

> Symbols are, of course, a commonplace in Ibsen's dramas, but in his early plays before *The Wild Duck* he uses symbolistic devices somewhat too obviously, almost exclusively to clarify his themes. Any college sophomore can tell you after a single reading of *Pillars of Society, A Doll's House,* or *Ghosts* what the symbols expressed in these titles mean. The symbols convey *ideas*—and little else. They have few emotional overtones, are invested with little of the impressive mystery of life, the tragic poetry of existence. They tend to leave us in consequence cold, uncommitted, like after a debate whose heavy-handed dialectic has ignored the very pulse-beat of a life form which it is supposed to have championed.

But *Ghosts* is concerned with more than the external manifestations of an evil heritage. In those oft-quoted lines that serve as a rationale for the play, Mrs. Alving says:

> I am half inclined to think we are all ghosts, Mr. Manders. It is not only what we have inherited from our fathers and mothers that exists again in us, but all sorts of old dead ideas and all kinds of old dead beliefs and things of that kind. They are not actually alive in us; but there they are dormant, all the same, and we can never be rid of them. . . . There must be ghosts all over the world. . . . And we are so miserably afraid of the light, all of us . . . and I am here, fighting with ghosts both without and within me.

The ghosts of plot and symbol are the manifestations of Mrs. Alving's struggle with the ghosts within. It is this internal conflict, a conflict similar to Ibsen's personal struggle, that is the play's central action.

To define this action more explicitly, I would say that Ibsen is imitating an action in which a woman of ability and stature finds her ideals and her intellectual attitudes and beliefs in conflict with an inherited emotional life determined by the habitual responses of respectability and convention. As the play's form evolves it becomes apparent that the values Mrs. Alving affirms in intellectual terms are doomed to defeat because she has no control over her emotional inheritance—an inheritance of ghosts which exists, but which cannot be confined to or controlled by any schematization of the intelligence.

Every significant choice that Mrs. Alving has ever made and the resultant action of such a decision is determined by these ghosts of the past rather than by intellectual deliberation. To mention but a few instances: Her marriage to Captain Alving in conformity to the wishes of her mother and aunts; her return to her husband; her reaction to the Oswald-Regina relationship; her acceptance of Manders after she has seen and commented upon the hypocrisy of the scene with Engstrand; her failure to tell Oswald the "straight" truth about his father; the horror of her reaction when Oswald is indifferent to his father's life; and finally, the question mark with which the play ends. All of these scenes are evidence that Mrs. Alving's ideals of freedom and her rhetorical flights into intellectual honesty are of no use to her when it comes to action. Perhaps, I can make my point more clear by briefly developing two of the above mentioned episodes.

As the second act opens, Mrs. Alving comes to a quick decision about Oswald's relationship with Regina: "Out of the house she shall go—and at once. That part of it is clear as daylight." I will return to the relationship of light to enlightenment, but for the moment we see that Mrs. Alving's decision is based upon an emotional response determined by her inheritance of respectability. Then, Mrs. Alving and the pastor begin to talk; and Mrs. Alving always talks a good game. After better than four pages of dialogue, Mrs. Alving is finally able to exclaim: "If I were not such a miserable coward, I would say to him: 'Marry her, or make any arrangement you like with her—only let there be no deceit in the matter.'" The pastor is properly shocked when Mrs. Alving gives him the "face the facts of life" routine; but her liberation, which is only verbal, is short lived! Manders asks how "you, a mother, can be willing to allow your . . ." This is Mrs. Alving's reply: "But I am not willing to allow it. I would not allow it for anything in the world; that is just what I was saying."

Or to take another situation. In Act I, Mrs. Alving tells Manders what her husband was really like: "The truth is this, that my husband died just as great a profligate as he had been all his life." In Act II, she is telling Manders of all the things she *ought* to have done and she says: "If I had been the woman I ought, I would have taken Oswald into my confidence and said to him: 'Listen, my son, your father was a dissolute man.'" In the third act circumstances have forced Mrs. Alving to tell Oswald the truth about his father: "Your poor father never found any outlet for the overmastering joy of life that was in him. And I brought no holiday spirit into his house, either; I am afraid I made your poor father's home unbearable to him, Oswald."

When we come to see the big scenes in this way, we then recall the numerous small events that create the network of the action and give the play its texture. Such things come to mind as Mrs. Alving's need of books to make her feel secure in her stand, and the neat little bit in the first act where Mrs. Alving reprimands Oswald for smoking in the parlor, which Ibsen then underscores by making it an issue in the second act.

Ibsen's plays are filled with such incidents; those little events that tell so much. I am of the persuasion that Ibsen is not very good at making big events happen; as appealing as they may be to a director, they tend to be theatrically inflated; they are melodramatic in the sense that the action of the plot is in itself larger than the characters or the situation in the play which create such events. Ibsen is the master of creating the small shocking event, or as Mary McCarthy puts it: "the psychopathology of everyday life." Nora's pushing off the sewing on the widow Christine [in *A Doll's House*]; Hjalmer letting Hedwig do the retouching with her half-blind eyes as he goes off hunting in the attic; his cutting of his father at Werle's party [in *The Wild Duck*]; and the moment when Hedda intentionally mistakes Aunt Julia's new hat for the servant's [in *Hedda Gabler*], are all examples of this talent. These are the things we know we are capable of! This is the success (and the limitation) of the naturalistic convention "which implies a norm of behavior on the part of its guilty citizens within their box-like living rooms."

But to return to the main business at hand: the conflict for Mrs. Alving, then, is not how to act. She just acts; there is no decision, nor can there be, for she has no rational control over her actions. Herein lies the conflict. Just because Mrs. Alving has no control over her actions, does not mean she escapes the feelings of guilt for what she does and her inability to do otherwise. Her continual rhetoricizing about emancipation and her many acts of renunciation are attempts to satisfy these feelings of guilt. For example, and I am indebted to Wiegand here [Hermann Weigand, *The Modern Ibsen,* 1925], the explicit reasons she gives for building the orphanage do not account sufficiently for her use of the expression, ''the power of an uneasy conscience.'' There is a big difference between fear that an ugly secret will become known and an evil conscience. Mrs. Alving's sense of guilt is the result of an intellectual emancipation from the habits of a lifetime; it is an emancipation from those values which she emotionally still accepts. It is precisely for this reason that her attempts at expiation are never satisfactory—they are not central to and part of her guilt.

To put it another way, Mrs. Alving's image of herself as liberated from outworn ideas is at odds with what in fact she is, a middle-aged woman bound by the chains of respectability and convention. It is for this reason, in a way similar to [Jean-Paul] Sartre's characters in the hell of *No Exit,* that she suffers. She is aware of the disparity between image and fact: ''I ought'' is a choric refrain that runs through her conversation; and she constantly looks for ways to affirm her image and assuage her guilt. And yet, the very fact that she accepts the image of herself as free, when experience has proven otherwise time and time again, explains why she is defeated in every attempt at atonement.

The sun finally rises. Ibsen has been preparing for this from the beginning. As the past is gradually revealed in the play and as the issues of the action come into sharper focus, ''light'' becomes more and more important in Ibsen's design. The play opens in the gloom of evening and rain; Mrs. Alving, at least according to Ibsen's stage directions, plays most of her important revelation scenes at the window, the source of light; as Mrs. Alving decides to quell Oswald's ''gnawing doubts,'' she calls for a light; Oswald's big speech about the ''joy and openness of life'' uses the sun as its central metaphor; the light that reveals—tells the truth—how impossible it is for Mrs. Alving to atone for her guilt has its source in the flames of the burning orphanage; and, finally, it is the sun, the source of all light, that reveals the meaning of the play's completed action. Mr. Alving is still trapped within the net of her own inheritance. She, as she has already told us and as Ibsen tells us in his poem, ''Fear of Light,'' is afraid to face the real truth about herself. This fear is something over which she has no control.

If we can empathize with Mrs. Alving, and I think we can, we have been lead to feel, as she believes, that as the light comes out of darkness, as the pressures of reality impinge upon her with unrelenting force, she will be capable of an act of freedom. We want to believe that she will affirm the image that she has of herself as a liberated human being by an action that is expressive of that freedom, even if that action is the murder of her own son. We want to feel that the light and heat of the sun will have the power to cauterize the ghosts of her soul. But if we have been attentive to the developing action, if we but recall what events followed the ''lesser lights;'' then we realize that there can be no resolution. Mrs. Alving can give only one answer, ''No!''

Mrs. Alving, like Oswald, who is the most important visible symbol of the ghosts, is a victim of something over which she has no control. We are reminded of Oswald's famous speech in the second act: ''My whole life incurably ruined—just because of my own imprudence. . . . Oh! if only I could live my life over again—if only I could undo what I have done! If only it had been something I had inherited—something I could not help.'' We have known all along that Oswald is a victim, so Ibsen is telling us for a purpose. The reason, as a study of his other plays will attest, is that for Ibsen the external is always the mirrored reflection of what's within. Mrs. Alving is also a victim! Like Oswald, she is doomed just by being born. And since she never comes to understand herself; since she never realizes and accepts the disparity of her image of herself and the truth about herself, she can never—in a way that Oedipus, a similar kind of victim, can—resolve the conflict.

For Mrs. Alving the sun has risen and just as she cannot give Oswald the sun, so the light of the sun has not been able to enlighten her. This, I believe is the conflict in the play and the developed meanings of this conflict form the play's central action.

But is this action tragic? How, if at all, is *Ghosts* a tragedy? It seems to me that there are two possible answers to these questions and the answer will depend largely on which interpretation of the play one accepts. The prevalant interpretation is the one which claims that this is a play of social protest and reform. The adherents of such a view can gather together a great deal of evidence in support of their case: all of Ibsen's plays from *League of Youth* to *The Wild Duck*; passages from the play themselves, like Oswald's speech on the freedom of Europe; numerous of Ibsen's public speeches, and several of his letters. With this interpretation the play is saying that if man would only see how hypocritical and outmoded his values were then the disasters that occur in the play need never have taken place. This view has as its fundamental premise that social evils can be cured and that when they are man is capable of living with a "joy of life." But if this is true, if all you have to do is be honest with yourself—and such a view assumes this is possible—and if men would see the falseness of social conventions and change them, then it seems to me the eternal elements of tragedy are dissolved in the possibility of social reform. Tragedy is concerned with showing those destructive conflicts within man that exist because man is a man no matter what age he may happen to be a part of, and no matter what kind of a society he may live in. John Gassner puts it this way [in *The Theatre in Our Times,* 1954]:

> Tragedy requires an awareness of "life's impossibilities," of limitations imposed upon man by the nature of things and by the nature of man, which cannot be poetically dissolved by sentiment or "reformed" out of existence.

In some ways, I think Ibsen did intend *Ghosts* to be a play of social reform, but if this is the case, he created more than he planned. In all of his early plays, the plays we think of as the social reform plays, Ibsen is much like Mrs. Alving; he believed intellectually in freedom and wrote and talked a good deal about it, but is this the whole story? The disassociation of the ideals men live by and the facts of their living is a central theme in Ibsen's work, but it is interesting to note that even in *Ghosts* the possibility of the "happy illusion" is presented. It is a hint that Ibsen is coming to feel that the conflict between truth and ideals can never be reconciled. By the time of *Rosmersholm,* even the free souls are tainted, the reformers are corrupt, and the man trying to redeem himself is shown to be capable only of realizing that he cannot be redeemed. Rosmer's death is an act of expiation, but suicide is decided upon only after Rosmer discovers the impossibility of redemption within society by means of freer and more honest views and relations.

Thus, while it is true that Ibsen, both in his public pronouncements and in his plays prior to *Ghosts,* gives us evidence that he believes optimistically in the possibility of social reform; that he believes that finally the sun will rise and continue to shine if man works long and diligently at facing the truth, I wonder if Ibsen is in fact whistling as he walks in the night through a graveyard. I wonder if Ibsen, even as early as *Ghosts,* isn't being a Mrs. Alving. Certainly this passage from a letter written during the composition of *Ghosts* permits us to wonder:

> The work of writing this play has been to me like a bath which I have felt to leave cleaner, healthier, and freer. Who is the man among us who has not now and then felt and acknowledged within himself a contradiction between word and action, between will and task, between life and teaching on the whole? Or who is there among us who has not selfishly been sufficient unto himself, and half unconsciously, half in good faith, has extenuated this conduct both to others and to himself?

The alternative interpretation of *Ghosts* is the one which I have outlined in this essay. Mrs. Alving is a victim in a conflict over which she has no control. What are the implications of such a view to tragedy?

In 1869 Ibsen wrote a significant letter to the critic George Brandes. In this letter he says:

> There is without doubt a great chasm opened between yesterday and today. We must continually fight a war to the knife between these epochs.

What Ibsen meant in this letter was that to live in the modern world is to be, in many important ways, different from anyone who ever lived before. Now this doesn't mean that man has changed; human nature is still the same, but Ibsen felt that the modern way of looking at man had changed in a way that was significantly new.

Joseph Wood Krutch pursues this problem in his recent book, *"Modernism" in the Modern Drama.* Krutch develops his argument by pointing out that since Greek times the Aristotelian dictum that "man is a reasoning animal" had been pretty universally accepted. This view did not deny man's irrationality, but it did assert that reason is the most significant human characteristic. Man is not viewed as pre-eminently a creature of instincts, passions, habits, or conditioned reflexes; rather, man is a creature who differs from the other animals precisely in the fact that rationality is his dominant mode.

The modern view assumes the opposite premise. In this view men are not sane or insane. Psychology has dissolved such sharp distinctions; we know that normal people aren't as rational as they seem and that abnormal people don't act in a random and unintelligible way. In short, the dramatist of our age has had to face the assumption that the rational is relatively unimportant; that the irrational is the dominant mode of life; and that the artist must realize, therefore, that the richest and most significant aspects of human experience are to be found in the hidden depths of the irrational. "Man tends to become less a creature of reason than the victim of obsessions, fixations, delusions, and perversions." [Krutch].

It is this premise that all of the great dramatists at the end of the 19th century, beginning with Ibsen, had to face. How is one to live in an irrational world? How is one to give meaning to life in a world where you don't know the rules? How are human relationships to be meaningfully maintained when you can't be sure of your feelings and when your feelings can change without your knowing it? Ibsen's plays, beginning with *Ghosts*, dramatize man destroyed by trying to live rationally in such a world. But to accept irreconcilable conflict as the central fact of all life; to make dissonance rather than the harmony of reconciliation the condition of the universe is to accept as a premise a view of life which leads in drama, as in life, to a world in which men and women, heroes and heroines, become victims in a disordered world which they have not created and which they have no moral obligation to correct.

It is this process, which began in the drama when Ibsen came to see man as a victim of irrational powers, of the Trolls, over which he has no control, that leads to the sense of futility that so completely dominates a great deal of modern drama. This is the kind of futility that is expressed in our text from Ecclesiastes (as it is in Hemingway's novel); but is this sense of futility generative of what we traditionally associate with tragedy?

The traditional forms of tragedy have been affirming in the sense that they celebrated man's ability to achieve wisdom through suffering. Such tragedy saw man as a victim, to be sure, but it also saw man as having those heroic qualities and potentialities which permitted him to endure his suffering and be significantly enlightened by them in such a way that victory was realized even in defeat.

The central conflict of *Ghosts* is not peculiar to the modern world. The disassociation of fact and value is a common theme in all tragedy. But there is a significant difference when this theme is used before Ibsen. Traditional tragedy celebrates the fact that, although most of us are incapable of it, the values men wish to live by can, if only for a moment, be realized through the actions of the tragic hero. It celebrates the fact that man's capacity for greatness is often expressed in the committing of an action which is horrifying and ought not to happen and yet which must happen. In this way the possibility that man's actions and his values can be in harmony is realized. This is the affirmation of tragedy; this is the meaning of the sun that resolves so many traditional tragedies. In this kind of tragedy the hero goes through the "dark night of the soul" with all its pain, suffering, doubt, and despair; but man is viewed as one responsible for and capable of action, even if that action is a grasping for the sun. Because of this fundamental difference in view, in traditional tragedy the dark night passes away and the sun also rises on the rebirth and affirmation of a new day.

This sunrise of traditional tragedy, which celebrates the "joy and meaning of life," is not the sunrise of futility. It is not the sunrise which sheds its rays as an ironic and bitter joke on a demented boy asking his equally helpless mother: "Mother, give me the sun, The sun—the sun!"

Perhaps Mrs. Alving is more tragic than Oedipus, Hamlet, or Lear; but if she is, her tragedy must be evaluated by new canons of judgment; for she differs from her predecessors in kind and not degree.

Source: Robert W. Corrigan, "The Sun Always Rises: Ibsen's *Ghosts* as Tragedy?" in *Educational Theatre Journal*, Vol. XI, No. 3, October, 1959, pp. 171–80.

Francis Fergusson

In his discussion of Ghosts, *Fergusson detects elements of three conflicting types of drama in the work: a formulaic "well-made" thriller, a realist "thesis play" about a specific social question, and a traditional tragedy.*

The Plot of Ghosts: Thesis, Thriller, and Tragedy

Ghosts is not Ibsen's best play, but it serves my purpose, which is to study the foundations of modern realism, just because of its imperfections. Its power, and the poetry of some of its effects, are evident; yet a contemporary audience may be bored with its old-fashioned iconoclasm and offended by the clatter of its too-obviously well-made plot. On the surface it is a *drame à thèse* [thesis play], of the kind [Eugène] Brieux was to develop to its logical conclusion twenty years later: it proves the hollowness of the conventional bourgeois marriage. At the same time it is a thriller with all the tricks of the Boulevard entertainment: Ibsen was a student of Scribe in his middle period [Augustin Eugène Scribe was the originator of the "well-made play"]. But underneath this superficial form of thesis-thriller—the play which Ibsen started to write, the angry diatribe as he first conceived it—there is another form, the shape of the underlying action, which Ibsen gradually made out in the course of his two-years' labor upon the play, in obedience to his scruple of truthfulness, his profound attention to the reality of his fictive characters' lives. The form of the play is understood according to two conceptions of plot, which Ibsen himself did not at this point clearly distinguish: the rationalized concatenation of events with a univocal moral, and the plot as the "soul" or first actualization of the directly perceived action.

Halvdahn Khot, in his excellent study *Henrik Ibsen,* has explained the circumstances under which *Ghosts* was written. It was first planned as an attack upon marriage, in answer to the critics of *A Doll's House.* The story of the play is perfectly coherent as the demonstration and illustration of this thesis. When the play opens, Captain Alving has just died, his son Oswald is back from Paris where he had been studying painting, and his wife is straightening out the estate. The Captain had been accepted locally as a pillar of society but was in secret a drunkard and debauchee. He had seduced his wife's maid, and had a child by her; and this child, Regina, is now in her turn Mrs. Alving's maid. Mrs. Alving had concealed all this for something like twenty years. She was following the advice of the conventional Pastor Manders and endeavoring to save Oswald from the horrors of the household: it was for this reason she had sent him away to school. But now, with her husband's death, she proposes to get rid of the Alving heritage in all its forms, in order to free herself and Oswald for the innocent, unconventional "joy of life." She wants to endow an orphanage with the Captain's money, both to quiet any rumors there may be of his sinful life and to get rid of the remains of his power over her. She encounters this power, however, in many forms, through the Pastor's timidity and through the attempt by Engstrand (a local carpenter who was bribed to pretend to be Regina's father) to blackmail her. Oswald wants to marry Regina and has to be told the whole story. At last he reveals that he has inherited syphilis from his father—the dead hand of the past in its most sensationally ugly form—and when his brain softens at the end, Mrs. Alving's whole plan collapses in unrelieved horror. It is "proved" that she should have left home twenty years before, like Nora in *A Doll's House*; and that conventional marriage is therefore an evil tyranny.

> *GHOSTS* IS NOT IBSEN'S BEST PLAY, BUT IT SERVES MY PURPOSE, WHICH IS TO STUDY THE FOUNDATIONS OF MODERN REALISM, JUST BECAUSE OF ITS IMPERFECTIONS."

In accordance with the principles of the thesis play, *Ghosts* is plotted as a series of debates on conventional morality, between Mrs. Alving and the Pastor, the Pastor and Oswald, and Oswald and his mother. It may also be read as a perfect well-made thriller. The story is presented with immediate clarity, with mounting and controlled suspense; each act ends with an exciting curtain which reaffirms the issues and promises important new developments. In this play, as in so many others, one may observe that the conception of dramatic form underlying the thesis play and the machine-made Boulevard entertainment is the same: the logically concatenated series of events (intriguing thesis or logical intrigue) which the characters and their relationships merely illustrate. And it was this view of *Ghosts* which made it an immediate scandal and success.

But Ibsen himself protested that he was not a reformer but a poet. He was often led to write by anger and he compared the process of composition to his pet scorpion's emptying of poison; Ibsen kept a piece of soft fruit in his cage for the scorpion to sting when the spirit moved him. But Ibsen's own spirit was not satisfied by the mere discharge of venom; and one may see, in *Ghosts,* behind the surfaces of the savage story, a partially realized tragic form of really poetic scope, the result of Ibsen's more serious and disinterested brooding upon the human condition in general, where it underlies the myopic rebellions and empty clichés of the time.

In order to see the tragedy behind the thesis, it is necessary to [turn] to the distinction between plot and action, and to the distinction between the plot as the rationalized series of events, and the plot as "the soul of the tragedy." The action of the play is "to control the Alving heritage for my own life." Most of the characters want some material or social advantage from it—Engstrand money, for instance, and the Pastor the security of conventional respectability. But Mrs. Alving is seeking a true and free human life itself—for her son, and through him, for herself. Mrs. Alving sometimes puts this quest in terms of the iconoclasms of the time, but her spiritual life, as Ibsen gradually discovered it, is at a deeper level; she tests everything—Oswald, the Pastor, Regina, her own moves—in the light of her extremely strict if unsophisticated moral sensibility: by direct perception and not by ideas at all. She is tragically seeking; she suffers a series of pathoses and new insights in the course of the play; and this rhythm of will, feeling, and insight underneath the machinery of the plot is the form of the life of the play, the soul of the tragedy.

The similarity between *Ghosts* and Greek tragedy, with its single fated action moving to an unmistakable catastrophe, has been felt by many critics of Ibsen. Mrs. Alving, like Oedipus, is engaged in a quest for her true human condition; and Ibsen, like Sophocles, shows on-stage only the end of this quest, when the past is being brought up again in the light of the present action and its fated outcome. From this point of view Ibsen is a plotmaker in the first sense: by means of his selection and arrangement of incidents he defines an action underlying many particular events and realized in various modes of intelligible purpose, of suffering, and of new insight. What Mrs. Alving sees changes in the course of the play, just as what Oedipus sees changes as one veil after another is removed from the past and the present. The underlying form of *Ghosts* is that of the tragic rhythm as one finds it in [Sophocles's] *Oedipus Rex*.

But this judgment needs to be qualified in several respects: because of the theater for which Ibsen wrote, the tragic form which Sophocles could develop to the full, and with every theatrical resource, is hidden beneath the clichés of plot and the surfaces "evident to the most commonplace mind." At the end of the play the tragic rhythm of Mrs. Alving's quest is not so much completed as brutally truncated, in obedience to the requirements of the thesis and the thriller. Oswald's collapse, before our eyes, with his mother's screaming, makes the intrigue end with a bang, and hammers home the thesis. But from the point of view of Mrs. Alving's tragic quest as we have seen it develop through the rest of the play, this conclusion concludes nothing: it is merely sensational.

The exciting intrigue and the brilliantly, the violently clear surfaces of *Ghosts* are likely to obscure completely its real life and underlying form. The tragic rhythm, which Ibsen rediscovered by his long and loving attention to the reality of his fictive lives, is evident only to the histrionic sensibility. As Henry James put it, Ibsen's characters "have the extraordinary, the brilliant property of becoming when represented at once more abstract and more living": i.e., both their lives and the life of the play, the spiritual content and the form of the whole, are revealed in this medium. A Nazimova, a Duse, could show it to us on the stage. Lacking such a performance, the reader must endeavor to respond imaginatively and directly himself if he is to see the hidden poetry of *Ghosts*.

Mrs. Alving and Oswald: The Tragic Rhythm in a Small Figure

As Ibsen was fighting to present his poetic vision within the narrow theater admitted by modern realism, so his protagonist Mrs. Alving is fighting to realize her sense of human life in the blank photograph of her own stuffy parlor. She discovers there no means, no terms, and no nourishment; that is the truncated tragedy which underlies the savage thesis of the play. But she does find her son Oswald, and she makes of him the symbol of all she is seeking: freedom, innocence, joy, and truth. At the level of the life of the play, where Ibsen warms his characters into extraordinary human reality, they all have moral and emotional meanings for each other; and the pattern of their related actions, their partially blind struggle for the Alving heritage, is consistent and very complex. In this structure, Mrs. Alving's changing relation to Oswald is only one strand, though an important one. I wish to consider it as a sample of Ibsen's rediscovery, through modern realism, of the tragic rhythm.

Oswald is of course not only a symbol for his mother, but a person in his own right, with his own quest for freedom and release, and his own anomalous stake in the Alving heritage. He is also a symbol for Pastor Manders of what he wants from Captain Alving's estate: the stability and continuity of the bourgeois conventions. In the economy of the play as a whole, Oswald is the hidden reality of the whole situation, like Oedipus' actual status as son-husband: the hidden fatality which, revealed in a series of tragic and ironic steps, brings the final peripety [reversal] of the action. To see how this works, the reader is asked to consider Oswald's role in Act I and the beginning of Act II.

The main part of Act I (after a prologue between Regina and Engstrand) is a debate, or rather agon [conflict], between Mrs. Alving and the Pastor. The Pastor has come to settle the details of Mrs. Alving's bequest of her husband's money to the orphanage. They at once disagree about the purpose and handling of the bequest; and this disagreement soon broadens into the whole issue of Mrs. Alving's emancipation versus the Pastor's conventionality. The question of Oswald is at the center. The Pastor wants to think of him, and to make of him, a pillar of society such as the Captain was supposed to have been, while Mrs. Alving wants him to be her masterpiece of liberation. At this point Oswald himself wanders in, the actual but still mysterious truth underlying the dispute between his mother and the Pastor. His appearance produces what the Greeks would have called a complex recognition scene, with an implied peripety for both Mrs. Alving and the Pastor, which will not be realized by them until the end of the act. But this tragic development is written to be acted; it is to be found, not so much in the actual words of the characters, as in their moral-emotional responses and changing relationships to one another.

The Pastor has not seen Oswald since he grew up; and seeing him now he is startled as though by a real ghost; he recognizes him as the very reincarnation of his father: the same physique, the same mannerisms, even the same kind of pipe. Mrs. Alving with equal confidence recognizes him as her own son, and she notes that his mouth-mannerism is like the Pastor's. (She had been in love with the Pastor during the early years of her marriage, when she wanted to leave the Captain.) As for Oswald himself, the mention of the pipe gives him a Proustian intermittence of the heart: he suddenly recalls a childhood scene when his father had given him his own pipe to smoke. He feels again the nausea and the cold sweat, and hears the Captain's hearty laughter. Thus in effect he recognizes himself as his father's, in the sense of his father's *victim;* a premonition of the ugly scene at the end of the play. But at this point no one is prepared to accept the full import of these insights. The whole scene is, on the surface, light and conventional, an accurate report of a passage of provincial politeness. Oswald wanders off for a walk before dinner, and the Pastor and his mother are left to bring their struggle more into the open.

Oswald's brief scene marks the end of the first round of the fight, and serves as prologue for the second round, much as the intervention of the chorus in the agon between Oedipus and Tiresias punctuates their struggle, and hints at an unexpected outcome on a new level of awareness. As soon as Oswald has gone, the Pastor launches an attack in form upon Mrs. Alving's entire emancipated way of life, with the question of Oswald, his role in the community, his upbringing and his future, always at the center of the attack. Mrs. Alving replies with her whole rebellious philosophy, illustrated by a detailed account of her tormented life with the Captain, none of which the Pastor had known (or been willing to recognize) before. Mrs. Alving proves on the basis of this evidence that her new freedom is right; that her long secret rebellion was justified; and that she is now about to complete Oswald's emancipation, and thereby her own, from the swarming ghosts of the past. If the issue were merely on this rationalistic level, and between her and the Pastor, she would triumph at this point. But the real truth of her situation (as Oswald's appearance led us to suppose) does not fit either her rationalization or the Pastor's.

Oswald passes through the parlor again on his way to the dining room to get a drink before dinner, and his mother watches him in pride and pleasure. But from behind the door we hear the affected squealing of Regina. It is now Mrs. Alving's turn for an intermittence of the heart: it is as though she heard again her husband with Regina's mother. The insight which she had rejected before now reaches her in full strength, bringing the promised pathos and peripety; she sees Oswald, not as her masterpiece of liberation, but as the sinister, tyrannical, and continuing life of the past itself. The basis of her rationalization is gone; she suffers the breakdown of the moral being which she had built upon her now exploded view of Oswald.

At this point Ibsen brings down the curtain in obedience to the principles of the well-made play. The effect is to raise the suspense by stimulating our curiosity about the facts of the rest of the story. What will Mrs. Alving do now? What will the Pastor do—for Oswald and Regina are half-brother and sister; can we prevent the scandal from coming out? So the suspense is raised, but the attention of the audience is diverted from Mrs. Alving's tragic quest to the most literal, newspaper version of the facts.

The second act (which occurs immediately after dinner) is ostensibly concerned only with these gossipy facts. The Pastor and Mrs. Alving debate ways of handling the threatened scandal. But this is only the literal surface: Ibsen has his eye upon Mrs. Alving's shaken psyche, and the actual dramatic form of this scene, under the discussion which Mrs. Alving keeps up, is her pathos which the Act I curtain broke off. Mrs. Alving is suffering the blow in courage and faith; and she is rewarded with her deepest insight: ''I am half inclined to think we are all ghosts, Mr. Manders. It is not only what we have inherited from our fathers and mothers that exists again in us, but all sorts of dead ideas and all kinds of old dead beliefs and things of that kind. They are not actually alive in us; but they are dormant all the same, and we can never be rid of them. Whenever I take up a newspaper and read it, I fancy I see ghosts creeping between the lines. There must be ghosts all over the world. They must be as countless as the grains of sand, it seems to me. And we are so miserably afraid of the light, all of us.'' This passage, in the fumbling phrases of Ibsen's provincial lady, and in William Archer's translation, is not by itself the poetry of the great dramatic poets. It does not have the verbal music of [Jean] Racine, nor the freedom and sophistication of Hamlet, nor the scope of the Sophoclean chorus, with its use of the full complement of poetic and musical and theatrical resources. But in the total situation in the Alving parlor which Ibsen has so carefully established, and in terms of Mrs. Alving's uninstructed but profoundly developing awareness, it has its own hidden poetry: a poetry not of words but of the theater, a poetry of the histrionic sensibility. From the point of view of the underlying form of the play—the form as ''the soul'' of the tragedy—this scene completes the sequence which began with the debate in Act I: it is the pathos-and-epiphany following that agon.

It is evident, I think, that insofar as Ibsen was able to obey his realistic scruple, his need for the disinterested perception of human life beneath the clichés of custom and rationalization, he rediscovered the perennial basis of tragedy. The poetry of *Ghosts* is under the words, in the detail of action, where Ibsen accurately sensed the tragic rhythm of human life in a thousand small figures. And these little ''movements of the psyche'' are composed in a complex rhythm like music, a formal development sustained (beneath the sensational story and the angry thesis) until the very end. But the action is not completed: Mrs. Alving is left screaming with the raw impact of the calamity. The music is broken off, the dissonance unresolved—or, in more properly dramatic terms, the acceptance of the catastrophe, leading to the final vision or epiphany which should correspond to the insight Mrs. Alving gains in Act II, is lacking. The action of the play is neither completed nor placed in the wider context of meanings which the disinterested or contemplative purposes of poetry demand.

The unsatisfactory end of *Ghosts* may be understood in several ways. Thinking of the relation between Mrs. Alving and Oswald, one might say that she had romantically loaded more symbolic values upon her son than a human being can carry; hence his collapse proves too much—more than Mrs. Alving or the audience can digest. One may say that, at the end, Ibsen himself could not quite dissociate himself from his rebellious protagonist and see her action in the round, and so broke off in anger, losing his tragic vision in the satisfaction of reducing the bourgeois parlor to a nightmare, and proving the hollowness of a society which sees human life in such myopic and dishonest terms. As a thesis play, *Ghosts* is an ancestor of many related genres: Brieux's arguments for social reform, propaganda plays like those of the Marxists, or parables *àla* [Leonid Nikolaivich] Andreev, or even [Bernard] Shaw's more generalized plays of the play-of-thought about social questions. But this use of the theater of modern realism for promoting or discussing political and social ideas never appealed to Ibsen. It did not solve his real problem, which was to use the publicly accepted theater of his time for poetic purposes. The most general way to understand the unsatisfactory end of *Ghosts* is to say that Ibsen could not find a way to represent the action of his protagonist, with all its moral and intellectual depth, within the terms of modern realism. In the attempt he truncated this action, and revealed as in a brilliant light the limitations of the bourgeois parlor as the scene of human life.

The End of Ghosts: The Tasteless Parlor and the Stage of Europe

Oswald is the chief symbol of what Mrs. Alving is seeking, and his collapse ends her quest in a horrifying catastrophe. But in the complex life of the play, all of the persons and things acquire emotional and moral significance for Mrs. Alving; and at the end, to throw as much light as possible upon the catastrophe, Ibsen brings all of the elements of his composition together in their highest symbolic valency. The orphanage has burned to the ground; the Pastor has promised Engstrand money for his ''Sailor's Home'' which he plans as a brothel; Regina departs, to follow her mother in the search for pleasure and money. In these eventualities the conventional morality of the Alving heritage is revealed as lewdness and dishonesty, quickly consumed in the fires of lust and greed, as Oswald himself (the central symbol) was consumed even before his birth. But what does this wreckage mean? Where are we to place it in human experience? Ibsen can only place it in the literal parlor, with lamplight giving place to daylight, and sunrise on the empty, stimulating, virginal snow-peaks out the window. The emotional force of this complicated effect is very great; it has the searching intimacy of nightmare. But it is also as disquieting as a nightmare from which we are suddenly awakened; it is incomplete, and the contradiction between the inner power of dream and the literal appearances of the daylight world is unresolved. The spirit that moved Ibsen to write the play, and which moved his protagonist through her tragic progress, is lost to sight, disembodied, imperceptible in any form unless the dreary exaltation of the inhuman mountain scene conveys it in feeling.

Henry James felt very acutely the contradiction between the deep and strict spirit of Ibsen and his superb craftsmanship on one side, and the little scene he tried to use—the parlor in its surrounding void—on the other. "If the spirit is a lamp within us, glowing through what the world and the flesh make of us as through a ground-glass shade, then such pictures as Little Eyolf and John Gabriel are each a chassez-croisez of lamps burning, as in tasteless parlors, with the flame practically exposed," he wrote in *London Notes*. "There is a positive odor of spiritual paraffin. The author nevertheless arrives at the dramatist's great goal—he arrives for all his meagerness at intensity. The meagerness, which is after all but an unconscious, an admirable economy, never interferes with that: it plays straight into the hands of his rare mastery of form. The contrast between this form—so difficult to have reached, so 'evolved,' so civilized—and the bareness and bleakness of his little northern democracy is the source of half the hard frugal charm he puts forth."

James had rejected very early in his career his own little northern democracy, that of General Grant's America, with its ugly parlor, its dead conventions, its enthusiastic materialism, and its "non-conducting atmosphere." At the same time he shared Ibsen's ethical preoccupation, and his strict sense of form. His comments on Ibsen are at once the most sympathetic and the most objective that have been written. But James's own solution was to try to find a better parlor for the theater of human life; to present the quest of his American pilgrim of culture on the wider "stage of Europe"

as this might still be felt and suggested in the manners of the leisured classes in England and France. James would have nothing to do with the prophetic and revolutionary spirit which was driving the great continental authors, Ibsen among them. In his artistry and his moral exactitude Ibsen is akin to James; but this is not his whole story, and if one is to understand the spirit he tried to realize in Mrs. Alving, one must think of [Søren] Kierkegaard, who had a great influence on Ibsen in the beginning of his career.

Kierkegaard (in *For Self-Examination*) has this to say of the disembodied and insatiable spirit of the times: ". . . thou wilt scarcely find anyone who does not believe in—let us say, for example, the spirit of the age, the *Zeitgeist*. Even he who has taken leave of higher things and is rendered blissful by mediocrity, yea, even he who toils slavishly for paltry ends or in the contemptible servitude of ill-gotten gains, even he believes, firmly and fully too, in the spirit of the age. Well, that is natural enough, it is by no means anything very lofty he believes in, for the spirit of the age is after all no higher than the age, it keeps close to the ground, so that it is the sort of spirit which is most like will-o'-the-wisp; but yet he believes in spirit. Or he believes in the world-spirit (*Weltgeist*) that strong spirit (for allurements, yes), that ingenious spirit (for deceits, yes); that spirit which Christianity calls an evil spirit—so that, in consideration of this, it is by no means anything very lofty he believes in when he believes in the world-spirit; but yet he believes in spirit. Or he believes in 'the spirit of humanity,' not spirit in the individual, but in the race, that spirit which, when it is god-forsaken for having forsaken God, is again, according to Christianity's teaching, an evil spirit—so that in view of this it is by no means anything very lofty he believes in when he believes in this spirit; but yet he believes in spirit.

"On the other hand, as soon as the talk is about a holy spirit—how many, dost thou think, believe in it? Or when the talk is about an evil spirit which is to be renounced–how many, dost thou think, believe in such a thing?"

This description seems to me to throw some light upon Mrs. Alving's quest, upon Ibsen's modern-realistic scene, and upon the theater which his audience would accept. The other face of nineteenth century positivism is romantic aspiration. And Ibsen's realistic scene presents both of these aspects of the human condition: the photographically accurate parlor, in the foreground, satisfies the requirements of positivism, while the empty but stimulating scene out the window—Europe as a moral void, an uninhabited wilderness—offers as it were a blank check to the insatiate spirit. Ibsen always felt this exhilarating wilderness behind his cramped interiors. In *A Doll's House* we glimpse it as winter weather and black water. In *The Lady from the Sea* it is the cold ocean, with its whales and its gulls. In *The Wild Duck* it is the northern marshes, with wildfowl but no people. In the last scene of *Ghosts* it is, of course, the bright snow-peaks, which may mean Mrs. Alving's quest in its most disembodied and ambivalent form; very much the same sensuous moral void in which Wagner, having totally rejected the little human foreground where Ibsen fights his battles, unrolls the solitary action of passion. It is the "stage of Europe" before human exploration, as it might have appeared to the first hunters.

There is a kinship between the fearless and demanding spirit of Kierkegaard, and the spirit which Ibsen tried to realize in Mrs. Alving. But Mrs. Alving, like her contemporaries whom Kierkegaard describes, will not or cannot accept any interpretation of the spirit that drives her. It may look like the *Weltgeist* when she demands the joy of living, it may look like the Holy Ghost itself when one considers her appetite for truth. And it may look like the spirit of evil, a "goblin damned," when we see the desolation it produces. If one thinks of the symbols which Ibsen brings together in the last scene: the blank parlor, the wide unexplored world outside, the flames that consumed the Alving heritage and the sunrise flaming on the peaks, one may be reminded of the condition of Dante's great rebel Ulysses. He too is wrapped in the flame of his own consciousness, yet still dwells in the pride of the mind and the exhilaration of the world free of people, *il mondo senza gente*. But this analogy also may not be pressed too far. Ulysses is in hell; and when we explore the Mountain on which he was wrecked, we can place his condition with finality, and in relation to many other human modes of action and awareness. But Mrs. Alving's mountains do not place her anywhere: the realism of modern realism ends with the literal. Beyond that is not the ordered world of the tradition, but *Unendlichkeit*, and the anomalous "freedom" of undefined and uninformed aspiration.

Perhaps Mrs. Alving and Ibsen himself are closer to the role of Dante than to the role of Ulysses, seeing a hellish mode of being, but free to move on. Certainly Ibsen's development continued beyond *Ghosts*, and toward the end of his career he came much closer to achieving a consistent theatrical poetry within the confines of the theater of modern realism. He himself remarked that his poetry was to be found only in the series of his plays, no one of which was complete by itself.

Source: Francis Fergusson, "*Ghosts* and *the Cherry Orchard:* The Theater of Modern Realism," *The Idea of a Theater: A Study of Ten Plays,* Princeton University Press, 1949, pp. 146–77.

SOURCES

Archer, William, "Ibsen and English Criticism," in *Fortnightly Review,* Vol. 46, No. 271, July, 1889, pp. 30–37.

Derry, T. K., *A History of Scandinavia,* University of Minnesota Press, 1979.

Esslin, Martin, "Ibsen and Modern Drama," in *Ibsen and the Theater: The Dramatist in Production,* New York University Press, 1980, pp. 71–82.

Goldman, Emma, *The Social Significance of Modern Drama,* Gorham Press, 1914.

Heiberg, Hans, in *Ibsen: A Portrait of the Artist,* translated by Joan Tate, University of Miami Press, 1987, p. 217.

FURTHER READING

Archer, William, ed., *From Ibsen's Workshop: Notes, Scenarios and Drafts of the Modern Plays,* translated by A. G. Charter, Scribner, 1978.
  This reprint of the 1913 study shows the process of development of Ibsen's most important works. Included is an introduction by Archer, who was one of Ibsen's most knowledgeable critics.

Clurman, Harold, "In Full Stride," in *Ibsen,* Macmillan Publishing Co., 1977.
  A chapter in Clurman's critical survey of Ibsen, which covers *Ghosts* and *A Doll's House.* This analysis examines the approach actors need to take in order to fully understand the characters in the play.

Joyce, James, "Ibsen's New Drama," from *The Critical Writings of James Joyce,* Viking Penguin, 1959.
  Originally published in 1900, this review of a minor, seldom-discussed Ibsen piece, *When We Dead Awaken,* touches on all of the plays in the author's long career.

Lebowitz, Naomi, *Ibsen and the Great World,* Louisiana State University Press, 1990.
  This book is an in-depth look at how Ibsen's environment shaped his characterizations. Difficult and rich.

MacFarlane, James, ed., *The Cambridge Companion to Ibsen,* Cambridge University Press, 1994.

An indispensable guide, with cross-references to all of Ibsen's major works and annotations about the references made in them. MacFarlane, who oversaw the publication, is one of the world's great authorities on Ibsen.

Meyer, Hans Georg, "Ibsen's Dramatic Technique," in *Henrik Ibsen,* Frederick Ungar Publishing Co., 1972, pp. 9–18.

Focuses mostly on the earlier plays *Brand* and *Peer Gynt* to draw generalizations about how Ibsen's style evolved throughout the different phases of his life.

Salome, Lou, *Ibsen's Heroines,* Black Swan Books, 1985.

For thorough appreciation, the chapter about the main character of *Ghosts* should be read along with Salome's analyses of Ibsen's other important female characters.

Theoharis, Constantine, *Ibsen's Drama: Right Action and Tragic Joy,* St. Martin's Press, 1996.

Theoharis delves deeply into the underlying psychology of each of the characters and how their interlocking needs hold the plays together.

The Great God Brown

EUGENE O'NEILL
1926

When *The Great God Brown* opened at the Greenwich Village Theatre in New York on January 23, 1926, Eugene O'Neill presented the audience with a new kind of theatrical experience. Other playwrights had previously used masks on stage, but none had presented them in such an innovative way. While opening night reviews were mixed, the audience's appreciation of the play kept it running for 283 performances. Many viewers were excited by the play's bold expressionistic technique—specifically O'Neill's experimental use of masks. The play focuses on the lives of three main characters: Dion Anthony, a failed artist; his wife, Margaret; and Billy Brown, a successful architect and friend to Dion and Margaret. Throughout the play, these characters wear masks that serve several purposes. They help the characters hide and thus protect their vulnerable inner selves while, at the same time, allowing them to project pleasing public images in an attempt to restore their confidence in themselves. Yet, ultimately, the tensions that result from not being able to reveal their true selves cause the characters to suffer and further isolate themselves from each other. *The Great God Brown* presents a penetrating study of the inner workings of the human psyche as it struggles to cope with betrayal, failure, and a search for identity.

AUTHOR BIOGRAPHY

Eugene O'Neill was born on October 16, 1888, in New York City, to James and Mary Ellen O'Neill. The O'Neills led a transient life as the family followed James' stage career. O'Neill's father was a celebrated actor who became famous for his performance in *The Count of Monte Cristo*. The constant traveling and the life of the theatre caused tensions between O'Neill's parents, exacerbated by Mary's addiction to morphine, a habit she started after her son's difficult delivery. Their decidedly dysfunctional family had an enormously negative effect on Eugene and his brother Jamie. After surviving his expulsion from Princeton, a suicide attempt, a bout of tuberculosis, and a failed marriage, O'Neill determined to devote his life to writing for the theatre. Familial tensions would become the subject of several of O'Neill's plays, including his most successful, *Long Day's Journey into Night*. In 1914, with his father's help, O'Neill published *Thirst and Other One Act Plays*. The first staging of one of his plays did not occur until after his involvement with the Provincetown Players in Massachusetts in the summer of 1916. Their summer theater premiered his *Bound East for Cardiff*, which enjoyed solid reviews.

O'Neill's successful playwriting continued for three decades and secured him the reputation as one of the world's greatest dramatists. He won the Pulitzer Prize four times: in 1920 for *Beyond the Horizon*, in 1922 for *Anna Christie*, in 1928 for *Strange Interlude*, and in 1957 for *Long Day's Journey into Night*. Other awards included the Gold Medal from the National Institute of Arts and Letters in 1923, a Litt.D. from Yale University in 1923, the Nobel Prize in literature in 1936, and, for *Long Day's Journey into Night*, the New York Drama Critics Circle Award in 1957. He died of pneumonia on November 27, 1953, in Boston, Massachusetts.

PLOT SUMMARY

Prologue and Act One

The play opens on the night of the high school commencement dance. Billy Brown stands on the pier with his parents, who decide that Billy will go to college to study architecture and that he will eventually become a partner in his father's firm. Soon after the Browns leave, the Anthonys approach the pier. Dion walks behind them "as if he were a stranger."

Eugene O'Neill

Mr. and Mrs. Anthony argue about sending Dion to college. His father says he doesn't believe in it, declaring, "let him slave like I had to! . . . College'll only make him a bigger fool than he is already." However, when Mrs. Anthony tells him that Billy will be going to college to become an architect and afterward will work in the contracting firm he and Mr. Brown jointly own, Dion's father changes his mind, insisting that Dion will go to college and become a better architect or he will turn his son "out in the gutter without a penny."

Later, Margaret and Billy come out on the pier. Margaret takes off her mask, which is an accurate replica of her own face, and declares her love for Dion as Billy declares his own feelings for her. After she ignores his pronouncements, Billy feels despondent but wishes her happiness and insists that he will always be her best friend. The focus then shifts to Dion, standing alone. He takes off his mask, revealing "his real face . . . shrinking, shy and gentle, full of a deep sadness." He asks himself questions that reveal his sensitivity and insecurity. When Billy approaches and sees Dion, he is at first resentful and then becomes the "good loser." Dion admits to Billy his fear of loving Margaret since he doesn't know himself. When he removes his mask, a mocking reflection of Pan, his face appears "torn and transfigured by joy." He soon decides that her love will allow him to discard his mask. Yet later, when Margaret does not recognize him without it, he puts it back on.

After his father dies, Dion sells his share of the firm to Billy and marries Margaret. The two live for a time in Europe, where Dion tries but fails to become a successful artist. After seven years, they return home. Dion's failures have turned him into an alcoholic. While his "real face has aged greatly, grown more drained and tortured but at the same time, in some queer way, more selfless and ascetic, more fixed in its resolute withdrawal from life," his mask has become more "defiant and mocking, its sneer more forced and bitter, its Pan quality becoming Mephistophelian." Dion searches for spiritual consolation but finds none. Recognizing that her family, which now includes three children, is quickly running out of money, Margaret convinces Dion to take a job with Billy, who now runs his father's firm. Cybel, a young woman who finds Dion passed out on her doorstep, offers maternal support and comfort. Dion is able to remove his mask and reveal his true self when he is with her. Billy also turns to Cybel for comfort after Dion starts working for him.

Act Two

Dion's face behind the mask continues to get gentler and more spiritual over the next seven years. One evening, he tells Margaret that he is lonely and frightened, and is going away. He begs her to look at him when he tears off his mask, his face "radiant with a great pure love for her and a great sympathy and tenderness" as he asks her forgiveness for his lack of support for her and for their children. However, she cannot bear to look at his "ghostlike" face. Later that night Dion appears in Billy's library, insisting that he is "the devil come to conclude a bargain." Dion's masked face "has a terrible deathlike intensity, its mocking irony becomes so cruelly malignant as to give him the appearance of a real demon, tortured into torturing others." He relates his memory of an incident that occurred when he was four, when Billy, jealous over Dion's artistic talent, betrayed his friend's trust. Dion explains that from that moment, he became "silent for life and designed a mask of the Bad Boy Pan in which to live and rebel against that other boy's God and protect myself from His cruelty." At first he expresses anger toward Billy, but then begs him to take care of Margaret and the boys. Dion's face without the mask becomes that of a Christian martyr, and he dies. Believing that he could now gain Margaret's love, a triumphant Billy puts on Dion's mask and clothes and so assumes his friend's identity.

Act Three

One month later, Margaret appears in Billy's office looking for her husband. She no longer needs to wear her mask since Billy, in his guise as Dion, has made her feel secure and happy. When she asks Billy where Dion is, Billy breaks down and tears off his "Billy" mask, revealing "a suffering face that is ravaged and haggard . . . tortured and distorted by the demon of Dion's mask." When he declares his love for her, Margaret runs out of his office. Later that night, Margaret tells Billy (as Dion) that Billy had confessed his love for her. Billy responds, "I'll murder this God-damned disgusting Great God Brown who stands like a fatted calf in the way of our health and wealth and happiness." When Margaret is shocked by his behavior, he tells her, "Don't worry, "Mr. Brown is now safely in hell. Forget him."

Act Four and Epilogue

One month later, Brown calls out to God to give him the strength to destroy himself. When Margaret and his clients appear in his office, Billy, in an increasingly frenzied state, changes back and forth from his mask to Dion's. When he disappears, his draftsmen go in his office, find Billy's mask, and declare him dead. All but Margaret assume that Dion killed him. Later that evening, the police come to his home and shoot him in Dion's mask. When Margaret arrives, she picks up Dion's fallen mask and grieves for her dead husband. As Billy dies, he tells Cybel he has found God. Four years later, Margaret and her children stand on the same dock where she and Dion had stood at the beginning of the play. She implores them to never forget their father and promises her husband her eternal love.

CHARACTERS

Dion Anthony

O'Neill introduces his protagonist, Dion Anthony, as "lean and wiry, without repose, continually in restless nervous movement." When he first appears at the dock, Dion's face is masked. The mask is a "fixed forcing of his own face—dark, spiritual, poetic, passionately supersensitive, helplessly unprotected in its childlike, religious faith in life—into the expression of a mocking, reckless, defiant, gaily scoffing and sensual young Pan." The audience discovers later that Dion began wearing the mask after his friend Billy Brown betrayed him. He explains that from that moment he became "silent for life and designed a mask of the Bad Boy Pan in which to live and rebel against that other boy's God and protect myself from His cruelty." Throughout the play his insecurities tear at him and cause him to hide behind a mask of cruel indifference. At one point he asks himself a series of questions that reveal his anguish:

> Why am I afraid to dance, I who love music and rhythm and grace and song and laughter? Why am I afraid to live, I who love life and the beauty of flesh and the living colors of earth and sky and sea? Why am I afraid of love, I who love love? Why must I pretend to scorn in order to pity? Why must I hide myself in self-contempt in order to understand? Why must I be so ashamed of my strength, so proud of my weakness? Why must I live in a cage like a criminal, defying and hating, I who love peace and friendship. Why was I born without a skin, oh God, that I must wear armor in order to touch or to be touched.

Several times he tries to remove the mask and reveal his true self to Margaret, but she is unable to gaze at his acute vulnerability. As a result of his artistic failings and Margaret's inability to accept the reality of his suffering, he tries to harden himself against life.

Throughout the play, Dion fights a battle between his sensitive nature and his growing cynicism about life. He often prays to God for salvation but is not able to find it. At one point when he reads from the Bible, "Come unto me all ye who are heavy laden and I will give you rest," he cries out, "I will come—but where are you, Savior?" He feels forsaken by all, including God. He explains, "I got paint on my paws in an endeavor to see God. But that Ancient Humorist had given me weak eyes, so now I'll have to foreswear my quest for Him and go in for the Omnipresent Successful Serious One, the Great God Mr. Brown, instead." His cynicism and bitterness often emerge in his dealings with Billy whom he blames in part for his suffering. Ultimately though, his kind, sensitive nature allows him to forgive Billy and ask, "God forgive me the evil I've done him." When he tells Cybel that he lacks strength to endure his suffering on his own, she insists, "you're not weak. You were born with ghosts in your eyes and you were brave enough to go looking into your own dark—and you got afraid." After alcoholism ravages his body, he dies like a "Christian martyr," asking Billy to take over his role as husband and father.

Margaret Anthony

When the play opens, Margaret, almost seventeen, is a "pretty and vivacious, blonde, with big romantic eyes, her figure lithe and strong, her facial expression intelligent but youthfully dreamy." Like Dion, Margaret also wears a mask, but hers is "an exact almost transparent reproduction of her own features." The mask gives her "the abstract quality of a Girl instead of the individual, Margaret." She loves Dion deeply but is not strong enough to look beneath his mask and face his vulnerabilities. She regards Dion as a "crazy child" and attempts to mother him. When she insists that he has the talent to be a great painter, Dion says of her, "her blindness surpasseth all understanding—or is it pity?" After enduring Dion's failures and his inattention to her and their three sons, Margaret's mask and face change. Her mask becomes "the brave face she puts on before the world to hide her suffering and disillusionment." When Dion dies, Margaret swears her love for him will be eternal.

Mr. Anthony

Mr. Anthony is a "tall lean man of fifty-five or sixty with a grim, defensive face, obstinate to the point of stupid weakness." Dion admits that he and his father were "aliens" to each other. Dion's estrangement from his father becomes apparent at the beginning of the play when he walks alone behind his parents "as if he were a stranger." His father's critical nature and lack of support for his son surface when he initially rejects his wife's pleas to send Dion to college. Mr. Anthony insists, "let him slave like I had to.... College'll only make him a bigger fool than he is already." However, after Mrs. Anthony reveals Billy Brown's plans for college and his future in the company owned jointly by the Anthonys and the Browns, Mr. Anthony's ambition causes him to change his mind. He now declares that Dion will go to college and become a better architect than Billy, or, he warns him, "I'll turn you out in the gutter without a penny."

Mrs. Anthony

Mrs. Anthony is a "thin frail faded woman, her manner perpetually nervous and distraught, but with a sweet and gentle face that had once been beautiful." Dion's supportive mother continually tries to build up his confidence in his artistic talent. During the opening conversation among the family on the pier, she proudly tells Dion, "you've always painted pictures so well." Yet, she shows weakness in not defending her son more forcefully against his father's verbal abuse. Dion alludes to both her pride and her weakness when, after his father insists that he will go to college, he declares, "I thank Mr. Anthony for this splendid opportunity to create myself in my mother's image, so she may feel her life comfortably concluded." Dion describes his mother as "a sweet, strange girl, with affectionate, bewildered eyes as if God had locked her in a dark closet without any explanation." Her death becomes almost unbearable for Dion since, he admits, "her hands alone had caressed without clawing."

Billy Brown
See William Brown

Mr. Brown
Readers only get a glimpse of Billy's parents at the beginning of the play. Billy's father "is fifty or more, the type of bustling, genial, successful provincial business man, stout and hearty in his evening dress." He owns an architect firm with Dion's father. His wife's lack of respect for his business angers him. He has set goals for his son that he expects him to follow without question.

Mrs. Brown
Billy's mother appears as "a dumpy woman of forty-five, overdressed in black lace and spangles." Her insistence on addressing her son only in the third person reveals her lack of maternal instincts. When she is discussing Billy's future with his father, Billy stands "like a prisoner at the bar, facing the judge." Her words reveal her "yearning for the realization of a dream." She announces her determination that Billy will go to college and study for a profession, and then she gains agreement from her husband. Her primary concern appears to be her social status. She has been disappointed in her role in life and so pins her hopes to move up in society on her son. When Billy joins the firm as an architect, the company and the family will gain higher status in the community.

William Brown
When readers are first introduced to Billy Brown, he is a handsome, tall, and athletic boy of nearly eighteen. He is blond and blue-eyed, "with a likeable smile and a frank good-humored face, its expression already indicating a disciplined restraint. His manner has the easy self-assurance of a normal intelligence." Throughout the play, he harbors an intense love for Margaret that she returns only when he "becomes" Dion by putting on his mask. After he takes over his father's business and expands it through his talent as an architect, he grows "into a fine-looking, well-dressed, capable, college-bred American business man, boyish still and with the same engaging personality." Billy's unrequited love for Margaret and his jealousy over Dion's artistic talents, however, become the impetus for his moral collapse. His betrayal of Dion when the two were boys is one of the primary causes of Dion's vulnerability and thus his subsequent failures. After Billy talks Dion into working with him, Billy takes credit for his friend's creativity. He also tries to weaken him in an effort to win Margaret's love. Knowing that Cybel offers Dion much needed comfort, Billy tries to persuade her to stop her contact with him. He also offers the alcoholic Dion drinks. Toward the end of the play, Dion tells Billy that he is "unloved by life . . . a successful freak, the result of some snide neutralizing of life forces—a spineless cactus." When Billy insists that he is satisfied with his life, Dion contradicts him, arguing that Billy has "piled on layers of protective fat, but . . . he feels at his heart the gnawing of a doubt!"

After he assumes Dion's identity, Billy is forced to face his own shortcomings. His own "suffering face" has become "ravaged and haggard . . . tortured and distorted by the demon of Dion's mask." He admits, "you're dead, William Brown, dead beyond hope of resurrection. It's the Dion you buried in your garden who killed you, not you him." Later when Margaret tells him as Dion that Billy confessed his love for her, Billy laments, "Poor Billy, Poor Billy the Goat. I'll kill him for you. . . . I'll murder this God-damned disgusting Great God Brown who stands like a fatted calf in the way of our health and wealth and happiness." When Margaret becomes apprehensive about his response, he tells her not to worry since "Mr. Brown is now safely in hell. Forget him." Eventually Billy turns, like Dion had, to God for comfort and salvation. He asks, "Why must the demons in me pander to cheapness—then punish me with self-loathing and life-hatred. Why am I not strong enough to perish—or blind enough to be content. Give me the strength to destroy [the mask]—and myself—and him—and I will believe in thee." At one point he loses faith, claiming, "God has become disgusted and moved away to some far ecstatic star where life is a dancing flame!" Yet, as he is dying, he appears to find peace when he tells Cybel that he hears God speak to him.

Cybel

Cybel is a "strong, calm, sensual blonde girl of twenty or so, fresh and healthy." She brings Dion into her home after he passes out on her steps. Although she wears the mask of a prostitute, beneath it she is "like an unmoved idol of Mother Earth" who offers maternal comfort for Dion and Billy. When she and Billy are together, they are each able to take off their masks.

THEMES

Identity

In O'Neill's masterpiece, *Long Day's Journey into Night,* Mary Tyrone insists, "None of us can help the things life has done to us. They're done before you realize it, and . . . they make you do other things until at last everything comes between you and what you'd like to be, and you've lost your true self forever." Like *Long Day's Journey into Night, The Great God Brown* focuses on the search for identity and the devastating consequences for those who are unable to discover a true sense of self.

Betrayal

Dion loses his sense of self at a young age when his best friend, Billy Brown, betrays him. He explains that when he was four, Billy "sneaked up behind when I was drawing a picture in the sand he couldn't draw and hit me . . . and laughed when I cried." Consequently, his trust in his friend and humanity was shaken and, as he notes, "I became silent for life and designed a mask of the Bad Boy Pan in which to live and rebel against that other boy's God and protect myself from His cruelty." Ironically though, the mask further isolates Dion and prevents him from allowing others to gain a glimpse of his inner self. The act of betrayal turns an ashamed Billy into "the good boy, the good friend, the good man." The two also commit acts of betrayal against themselves. When they wear masks that project false, public personalities, they essentially betray their true natures.

Success and Failure

While Dion and Billy experience public success, they both suffer with inner failures, which eventually destroy them. Dion's dream is to gain divine inspiration and to become a successful artist. Yet, he considers himself a failure as he notes to his mother when she tells him "you've always painted

TOPICS FOR FURTHER STUDY

- Research Freud's theories on the subconscious, especially his definition of the ego, the id, and the super ego and apply them to the characters and their use of masks in *The Great God Brown.*

- Investigate the history of the use of masks in the theater. Explain whether O'Neill's use of masks in the play is traditional or innovative.

- Read O'Neill's *Long Day's Journey into Night* and compare its themes to those in *The Great God Brown.*

- Explore biographical details about O'Neill, especially those that concern his relationship with his family. What autobiographical elements can you find in the play?

pictures so well." He responds, "why must she lie? Is it my fault? She knows I only try to paint." At that point, he has some confidence in his future as an artist, admitting that "some day" he will be able to produce works of art. He returns from Europe, however, despondent over his lack of success and drowns his sorrow in alcohol.

American Dream

Billy's vision of success is tied up in the American Dream. He achieves his goal of being a successful architect and grows into "a fine-looking, well-dressed, capable, college-bred American business man." However, his unrequited love for Margaret has prevented him from establishing a lasting relationship. He also has become soulless as noted by Dion who tells him he is "unloved by life . . . merely a successful freak, the result of some snide neutralizing of life forces—a spineless cactus." When Billy insists that he is satisfied with his life, Dion points out that "he's piled on layers of protective fat, but . . . he feels at his heart the gnawing of a doubt."

Billy convinces Dion to join his firm and gain his own piece of the American Dream to provide a better life for Margaret and his sons. Ironically, Dion's artistic talent causes him to be a successful architect, but joining "The Great God Brown" in his materialistic quest leaves him with a sense that he has sold out, which ultimately destroys him.

Change and Transformation

All the main characters, and often their masks, go through transformations during the course of the play. Dion's despondency over his artistic failures and his subsequent withdrawal from her and their family has transformed Margaret from "a pretty and vivacious" young girl to a world-weary woman with "an uncomprehending hurt in her eyes." Consequently, her mask has also changed to a "brave face she puts on before the world to hide her suffering and disillusionment." Dion's inability to gain divine inspiration in his art changes him outwardly into a satanic figure filled with a "cruelly malignant, mocking irony." Yet beneath the mask, he becomes "gentler, more spiritual, more saintlike and ascetic." Unfortunately, Margaret is unable to face the vulnerability of his true self, which contributes to his eventual destruction. Billy tries to take on the most radical change when he impersonates Dion. After he puts on Dion's mask, his own face becomes "ravaged and haggard" as he faces his own shortcomings. Adopting Dion's identity forces Billy to look into his own soul, and, as a result, he becomes filled with "self-loathing and life-hatred," which ultimately becomes unbearable for him.

STYLE

Combining Realism and Expressionism

O'Neill combines elements of realism—a style that makes things look like they would in real life—and expressionism—a style that distorts things to look like they might come from the point of view of the characters—in *The Great God Brown*. Expressionistic plays often employ masks to either hide the characters' inner emotions or reflect them. The masks used by the main characters in the play objectify the public images they want to portray and at the same time hide their inner psychological and emotional turmoil. The masks also work effectively to isolate the characters from each another. George H. Jensen, in his article on O'Neill for *Dictionary of Literary Biography*, writes, "The mask is a defense, a pose, a lie that a character presents to the world to protect the vulnerable self beneath it. Only rarely can a character feel secure enough to unmask and reveal his true self. The mask, O'Neill felt, was an unfortunate necessity. It protects the self, but maintaining a mask (the strain of living a lie) dissipates, haunts, and isolates the self." Dion and Billy are ultimately destroyed by wearing masks.

O'Neill employs these nonrealistic devices in a realistic setting. For example, when Billy assumes Dion's identity, he not only starts wearing his mask, he also dresses in his friend's clothes. Billy's wearing of Dion's clothes helps him fool people in the office. The nonrealistic device is set in a realistic setting where realistic events occur. O'Neill also forces Billy to frantically switch back and forth between his own identity and that of Dion's. When Margaret appears at the office, she will not discover what has happened to her husband. It would be unrealistic if everyone in the office just accepted Billy as Dion when he wasn't wearing Dion's clothes.

Symbolism

O'Neill uses mythological symbolism in *The Great God Brown* to illustrate the psychology of his characters. Dion Anthony and William Brown represent two opposite figures in Greek mythology: Apollo and Dionysus. Apollo was the messenger of the gods and the presiding deity of music, medicine, and youth. Dionysus was the god of vegetation and wine. In the latter part of the nineteenth century, Nietzsche used the terms Apollonian and Dionysian to note the distinction between reason and culture (Apollonian), on the one hand, and instinct and primitiveness (Dionysian), on the other. Many authors in the twentieth century were influenced by Nietzsche's discussion of these opposing forces. D. H. Lawrence, for example, employed Apollonian/Dionysian symbolism in his works to illustrate the theme of intellect versus instinct. O'Neill uses this tension of opposites in his representation of the relationship between Billy and Dion. Billy represents the controlled intellect that is incapable of experiencing any kind of creative inspiration. Dion, whose name echoes Dionysus, symbolizes instinct and the liberation of the senses in an effort to release divine creativity.

Another Greek god O'Neill symbolizes in his play is Pan, the pastoral god of fertility and mischief. In Greek mythology, he was depicted as a sometimes merry, sometimes ill-tempered jokester with the horns and the legs of a goat. Later, he became associated with Dionysus. Dion's mask represents the figure of Pan, and when he and Billy wear it, they take on his personality. This Pan-like mask, however, takes on Mephistophelian characteristics as Dion's artistic ambitions are continually thwarted. When Billy takes the credit for Dion's architectural creativity, his growing sense of betrayal prompts him to condemn his friend. Yet, as the mask increases its satanic distortion, Dion's face becomes more spiritual. Here O'Neill begins to employ more Christian symbolism. Dion's last name, Anthony, suggests Saint Anthony, who, according to tradition, resisted every temptation the devil could devise for him. By the end of the play, Dion becomes a martyred Saint Anthony, rejecting the temptations of alcohol and the urge to punish Billy for his betrayal of him.

HISTORICAL CONTEXT

The Emergence of the American Theatre

At the end of the nineteenth century, a group of playwrights, which included James A. Herne, Bronson Howard, David Belasco, Augustus Thomas, Clyde Fitch, and William Vaughn Moody, started breaking away from traditional melodramatic forms and themes. Consequently, American theatre began to establish its own identity. These and other playwrights in the early part of the twentieth century were inspired by the dramatic innovations of Henrik Ibsen, August Strindberg, and George Bernard Shaw. During this period, experimental theatre groups made up of dramatists and actors encouraged new innovative American playwrights. In 1914, Lawrence Langner, Helen Westley, Philip Moeller, and Edward Goodman created the Washington Square Players in New York, and playwright Susan Glaspell, in 1915, helped start the Provincetown Players in Massachusetts. The most important member of this latter group was Eugene O'Neill, who wrote plays with a uniquely American voice. George H. Jensen, in the *Dictionary of Literary Biography,* notes that "before O'Neill began to write, most American plays were poor imitations or outright thefts of European works." Jensen insists that O'Neill became the "catalyst and symbol . . . of the establishment of American drama."

Realism

In the late nineteenth century, playwrights turned away from what they considered the artificiality of melodrama to a focus on the commonplace in the context of everyday contemporary life. Their work, along with much of the experimental fiction written during that period, adopted the tenets of realism, a new literary movement that took a serious look at believable characters and their sometimes problematic interactions with society. In order to accomplish this goal, realistic drama focuses on the commonplace and eliminates the unlikely coincidences and excessive emotionalism of melodrama. Dramatists like Henrik Ibsen discarded traditional sentimental theatrical forms as they chronicled the strengths and weaknesses of ordinary people confronting difficult social problems, like the restrictive conventions suffered by nineteenth-century women. Dramatists who embraced realism used settings and props that reflected their characters' daily lives and realistic dialogue that replicated natural speech patterns.

Expressionism

Dramatists during the early decades of the twentieth century also adopted the techniques of another new literary movement. Expressionism eschewed the realists' attention to verisimilitude and instead employed experimental methods that tried to objectify the inner experiences of human beings. Influenced by the theories of Freud, playwrights like August Strindberg used nonrealistic devices that distorted and sometimes oversimplified human actions in order to explore the depths of the human mind. Eugene O'Neill's long career reflected the shifting styles of the American theatre at the end of the nineteenth century and the beginning of the twentieth. His early plays were unsuccessful attempts at melodrama. He then turned to realistic depictions of men at sea and later of the interactions between family members. In the 1920s, he experimented with expressionism, most notably in *Emperor Jones* and *The Great God Brown.*

CRITICAL OVERVIEW

When *The Great God Brown* premiered on January 23, 1926, at the Greenwich Village Theatre in New York, the opening night reviews were mixed. Many critics praised O'Neill's daring experimentalism and psychological themes in the play. Others, though, found fault with those same qualities. Public response was strong enough to run the play for 283 performances. Since then, assessments of the play have remained mixed.

On opening night, E. W. Osborn in his review for *New York World* praised the play's bold innovations, commenting that "the unexpected is again

COMPARE & CONTRAST

- **1926:** Joseph Stalin becomes dictator of the Soviet Union. His reign of terror will last for twenty-seven years.

   1991: On December 17, President Mikhail Gorbachev orders the dissolution of the Soviet Union, and a new Commonwealth of Independent States is formed by the countries that formerly made up the Soviet Union.

- **1926:** *The Theory of the Gene* by Columbia University zoologist Thomas Hunt Morgan lays the groundwork for future genetic research.

   1984: Veterinarian Steven Willadsen divides sheep embryos and, as a result, clones a sheep.

- **1926:** *Don Juan*, starring John Barrymore becomes the first film to be accompanied by electrically recorded sound. This process, called Vitaphone, is created by Western Electric.

   1980: Videocassettes recorders are a hot item for American consumers. As a result, the rental and sale of videocassettes generate a profitable industry.

---

introduced and spells wonderful.'' In his *New York Times* opening night review, Brooks Atkinson ignores claims that the play was at times confusing but applauds O'Neill's experimentalism. A few years after the play debuted, Barrett H. Clark in *Drama* argues that *The Great God Brown* is the ''highest development of O'Neill's genius we have seen. Like all poets, he writes ahead of us.'' Clark thought that the play should be awarded the Pulitzer Prize. Focusing on O'Neill's technique, Rose Bogdanoff writes in *Drama,* ''O'Neill's use of the mask is the finest in modern theatre, as much a part of the play as the lines themselves.''

Other reviewers, however, find fault with O'Neill's technique in the play. In her opening night review for *Women's Wear Daily*, Kelcey Allen writes, ''The transfer of personality is unacceptable, and far-fetched Expressionism and symbolism must have some relationship to the sphere of logic; there is mask switching to the point of strangulation. A laboratory experiment not good for the theatre.'' J. S. Metcalfe in the *Wall Street Journal* adds another criticism of the play's technique, commenting, ''the masks hinder instead of help, making some speeches seem laughable.'' Thus, Metcalfe concludes, ''O'Neill is no longer the great dramatist of realism and low-life characters.'' Robert Coleman faulted the play's presentation of themes, insisting that it is an ''ineffective and tedious psychological study,'' and the ''despairing dirge of a puzzled pessimist.''

Most critics praised O'Neill's attempts at experimentation but argued that the play achieved only a partial success. David Carb in *Vogue* writes that the play is a ''subtly conceived symbolic tragedy, finely imagined, written with glowing loveliness. It fails to succeed only because of a physical device.'' A reviewer in *New York Graphic* finds a ''strength and beauty of lines,'' but warns theatergoers that they will ''go home mystified and bored.'' Frank Vreeland in *New York Telegram* writes that the play reveals ''O'Neill at both his best and his worst.'' John Anderson echoes this assessment in his review for the *New York Post,* commenting, ''O'Neill has ventured everything and achieved a superb failure.... The play eventually drowns magnificently in the seething theories of the writer.'' Don Carle Gillette, who writes about the play for *Billboard,* notes that O'Neill is an acquired taste for audiences and calls the play a ''glorious confusion.'' John Mason Brown in *Theatre Arts* agrees with this assessment but insists that the first two acts are successful, and that ''in an otherwise dull season, this comes as an utterly different experiment.'' In his review for the *New York Sun,* Gabriel Gilbert admits to being ''hot but troubled'' for O'Neill's ''most poetic and penetrating play,'' and insists that the author ''does not write for popularity but for posterity. One will remember the play whatever he thinks of it.''

Some scholars discuss the play in comparisons of O'Neill's work with that of other dramatists. Brooks Atkinson, in his article on Ibsen and O'Neill for the *New York Times,* finds similarities in the two writers' plays, especially in their ''emotional sensitiveness and philosophy,'' but ultimately concludes that *The Great God Brown* is almost ''unintelligible.'' In her article, ''Masks, Their Use by Pirandello and O'Neill,'' Grace Anschutz compares the style of the two writers and determines that Pirandello's use of masks is more successful than O'Neill's.

CRITICISM

Wendy Perkins

Perkins, an Associate Professor of English at Prince George's Community College in Maryland, has published articles on several twentieth-century authors. In the following essay, she examines The Great God Brown *as an illustration of Friedrich Nietzsche's theory of the Apollonian and the Dionysian impulses in human nature.*

In the closing pages of Thomas Mann's novel, *Death in Venice,* Aschenbach, the main character, condemns the role of the artist and the artistic impulse: ''the training of the public and of youth through art is a precarious undertaking which should be forbidden. For how, indeed, could he be a fit instructor who is born with a natural leaning towards the precipice?'' In *The Great God Brown*, O'Neill offers a more sympathetic view of his main character than does Mann, but he communicates a similar portrait of the artist ''leaning towards the precipice.'' Dion Anthony, in fact, falls into this void of despair and self-destruction, his super-sensitive artistic soul unable to cope with the hostile world he inhabits. The psychological theory O'Neill tests in *The Great God Brown* (as did Mann in his novel) is based on Friedrich Nietzsche's paradigm of the two opposing ''gods'' in human nature: the Apollonian and the Dionysian. O'Neill illustrates these forces in the play through the characterizations of Dion Anthony and Billy Brown. Each character expresses only one impulse. Billy represents the controlled voice of reason through much of the play, while Dion expresses the emotionality and creativity of the artist. Each man is ultimately destroyed by his inability to develop and embrace the opposing impulse and thus strike a harmonious internal balance.

Playbill cover from a 1959 production of O'Neill's The Great God Brown.

According to Nietzsche, an ideal state can be achieved by a balancing of these two conflicting impulses—the Dionysian irrational, creative, primal being controlled by Apollonian order, reason, and repose. However, O'Neill suggests that the two main characters in *The Great God Brown* have been unable to develop this duality in their natures and, as a result, are unable to fulfill their dreams. George H. Jensen, in his article on O'Neill for the *Dictionary of Literary Biography* explains, ''Surrounded by disappointment, O'Neill acquired what might be termed a 'tragic sense of life' that people are doomed to suffer intensely, mocked by dreams they cannot attain.'' O'Neill transferred this tragic sense to the characters in his plays.

Dion Anthony's extreme sensitivity and inability to find a reasoned order for his life prevent him from coping with the failure of his dream to become a successful artist. Since he was a child, Dion, whose name echoes Dionysus—the Greek god of vegetation and wine—has tried to focus his artistic talents but has been continually thwarted by others' lack of consideration for his needs as well as his

WHAT DO I READ NEXT?

- In the philosophic essay *The Birth of Tragedy* (1872) Friedrich Nietzsche outlines his vision of the tensions between the Apollonian and Dionysian impulses and discusses the uses of masks in Greek tragedy (paperback editions from Dover and Oxford University Press).

- August Strindberg's surrealistic *A Dream Play*, which opened in 1902, became the forerunner of modern expressionism and influenced a new generation of dramatists, including Eugene O'Neill (widely available).

- A collection of Sigmund Freud's work can be found in *The Ego and the Id (The Standard Edition of the Complete Psychological Works of Sigmund Freud)*. This volume presents Freud's theories of the subconscious (in paperback from W. W. Norton, 1990).

- *Long Day's Journey into Night*, first performed in 1956, is O'Neill's finest study of domestic interaction and offers insight into O'Neill's own tragic relationship with his family (widely available).

---

own fragile sensibilities. The first obstacle Dion faced occurred when he was four. He explains that Billy:

> sneaked up behind when I was drawing a picture in the sand he couldn't draw and hit me on the head with a stick and kicked out my picture and laughed when I cried. It wasn't what he'd done that made me cry, but him. I had loved and trusted him and suddenly the good God was disproved in his person and the evil and injustice of Man was born. Everyone called me crybaby, so I became silent for life and designed a mask of the Bad Boy Pan in which to live and rebel against that other boy's God and protect myself from His cruelty.''

Dion wears a cynical, ironic mask throughout most of the play in an effort to shield himself from the harsh realities of his life. Jenson argues that in the play "The mask is a defense, a pose, a lie that a character presents to the world to protect the vulnerable self beneath it. Only rarely can a character feel secure enough to unmask and reveal his true self. The mask, O'Neill felt, was an unfortunate necessity. It protects the self, but maintaining a mask (the strain of living a lie) dissipates, haunts, and isolates the self.'' In his book on O'Neill's plays, Travis Bogard notes the irony in the author's use of masks in *The Great God Brown,* as they "reveal the human individuality as directly and profoundly as possible. The mask being removed from Dion Anthony, what the spectator is supposed to see and what O'Neill astonishingly set himself to characterize is the human soul itself.'' Yet Dion's soul is too fragile, even as he hides behind his mask.

When the play opens, the audience gains a glimpse of Dion's vulnerable nature and his efforts to shield that nature. He appears on the stage walking separately from his parents, "as if he were a stranger.'' O'Neill illuminates the probable cause of this tension when the audience hears his father verbally abuse him. In this scene, Dion also reveals his insecurity about his artistic abilities coupled with a capacity for hope. When his mother insists that he has "always painted pictures so well,'' he counters with, "Why must she lie? Is it my fault? She knows I only try to paint. But I will some day.''

Dion expresses his sensitive artistic soul in a private moment that night. When he takes off his mask, he reveals "his real face . . . shrinking, shy and gentle, full of a deep sadness.'' He questions his need to withdraw from his world, asking:

> Why am I afraid to dance, I who love music and rhythm and grace and song and laughter? Why am I afraid to live, I who love life and the beauty of flesh and the living colors of earth and sky and sea? Why am I afraid of love. Who loves love. . . . Why must I hide myself in self-contempt in order to understand. Why must I be so ashamed of my strength, so proud of my weakness? Why must I live in a cage like a criminal, defying and hating, I who love peace and friendship. Why was I born without a skin, oh God, that I must wear armor in order to touch or to be touched.''

When he challenges Margaret to accept his true self without its armor, she does not recognize him and glares at him contemptuously when he tells her he loves her. Even after the two marry, Margaret refuses to peer beneath his mask, unable to face his intense vulnerability.

After failing to gain artistic success in Europe, Dion cannot find a reasonable order or purpose for his existence and, as a result, drowns himself in alcohol. Recognizing his failures as a husband and a father, Dion considers himself to be "sniveling, cringing, [and] life-denying." Finally, under Margaret's prompting, he attempts to gain success as an architect. While working with Billy in their fathers' firm, Dion releases his artistic energies and gives life to Billy's designs. However, when Billy takes all the credit for the work and Dion feels he has sold out to the god of materialism, Dion falls into the void of despair.

Billy also is unable to temper the dominant impulse of his nature. When the play opens, his parents reveal their plans for his future, which include him eventually becoming a partner in his father's firm. While he agrees with his parents, he appears in their presence "like a prisoner at the bar, facing the judge." Yet, his expression already indicates "a disciplined restraint." Billy adopts his parents' vision of the American dream and becomes a successful architect, evolving into "a fine-looking, well-dressed, capable, college-bred American business man."

Billy, however, is not content with his life. Bogard notes that "Brown cannot create, for creation depends on vision, and Brown moves in the dark." He has been unable to develop a creative sensibility, which causes him to envy that quality in Dion. Bogard comments, "What [Billy] cannot possess, he destroys, as in childhood he destroyed Dion's sand castle, and as he finally destroys himself." Billy's unrequited love for Margaret and his jealousy over Dion's artistic talents become the impetus for his moral collapse. After Dion begins working in the firm, Billy takes credit for his friend's creativity. Then, when Dion dies, Billy tries to assume his identity in an effort to win Margaret's love and to develop a creative energy in his work. Yet trying to adopt Dion's persona only forces Billy to recognize his own shortcomings. A "ravaged and haggard" Billy calls out to God at the end of the play, asking "Why must the demons in me pander to cheapness-then punish me with self-loathing and life-hatred. Why am I not strong enough to perish-or blind enough to be content."

Jensen echoes reviewers' mixed assessment of *The Great God Brown* when he praises O'Neill's innovations in the play but ultimately considers it to be a "failed experiment." Yet, most critics applaud the play's psychological intensity. O'Neill's poetic presentation of Nietzsche's theory of the Apollonian and the Dionysian impulses and the consequences of a lack of balance between those impulses illuminates the complex inner workings of the human psyche.

> "ACCORDING TO NIETZSCHE, AN IDEAL STATE CAN BE ACHIEVED BY A BALANCING OF THESE TWO CONFLICTING IMPULSES—THE DIONYSIAN IRRATIONAL, CREATIVE, PRIMAL BEING CONTROLLED BY APOLLONIAN ORDER, REASON, AND REPOSE. HOWEVER, O'NEILL SUGGESTS THAT THE TWO MAIN CHARACTERS IN *THE GREAT GOD BROWN* HAVE BEEN UNABLE TO DEVELOP THIS DUALITY IN THEIR NATURES, AND AS A RESULT, ARE UNABLE TO FULFILL THEIR DREAMS."

Source: Wendy Perkins, in an essay for *Drama for Students*, Gale Group, 2001.

Travis Bogard

In the following essay. Bogard analyzes how O'Neill perceives "man as a prisoner in his body" and presents how that relationship is shown in The Great God Brown.

In *The Great God Brown,* O'Neill sees man as a prisoner in his body. His only escape is in an inner direction toward the roots of God he holds in himself. In all the world, there is no human being he can comprehend or whose comprehension enables him to unmask himself, and thus be freed of loneliness....

In *The Great God Brown,* however, such a union is seen to be impossible, and man is condemned to the cell of self until his death.

To the outer, hostile world, he must turn a face that will not startle by revealing the terrifying agony within him. It must be an expressionless face, bland and unchanging except as it is inevitably eroded by the ravages of his hidden struggle. Wearing the mask is not a matter of choice. Like the Mask Maker

> "TO THE OUTER, HOSTILE WORLD, HE MUST TURN A FACE THAT WILL NOT STARTLE BY REVEALING THE TERRIFYING AGONY WITHIN HIM. IT MUST BE AN EXPRESSIONLESS FACE, BLAND AND UNCHANGING EXCEPT AS IT IS INEVITABLY ERODED BY THE RAVAGES OF HIS HIDDEN STRUGGLE."

in Marceau's great pantomime, man is trapped in the mask, by circumstances, by his own fear and inhibitions, by his need to find some communion with the world beyond his cell. Edmond Dantes telegraphed by tapping on the rocks of his prison wall. In a prison that is not physical, the mask is man's only means of communication, its mouth the only means of crying across the void that separates him from all other human beings. Only by his mask may he be known. . . .

In *The Great God Brown,* however, the mask is used to attain precisely the opposite value, to reveal the human individuality as directly and profoundly as possible. The mask being removed from Dion Anthony, what the spectator is supposed to see and what O'Neill astonishingly set himself to characterize is the human soul itself. This use of the mask is O'Neill's innovation, one which, as he suggested, follows necessarily from the development of psychological theories in the twentieth century, but one which was not characteristic of the theatre of his time.

The consequences of experimentation in this direction were severe. The problem was not in the theatrically fascinating use of masks, but in the development of a language that could accompany such a direct look into the soul. What O'Neill means by a "drama of souls" is really not communicable directly by any verbal device. The "soul" is subverbal, and the great dramatist can do little else than to suggest it by the referential qualities of his poetry. Nietzsche's claim that the mask is a way of expressing the inexpressible essence of nature sheds significant light on O'Neill's use, where, once the mask is removed, the essence itself must be projected. O'Neill's mistrust of the superficial and misleading "surface symbolism" of realism is a sign that he wishes now to present directly on his stage *without symbolism* the naked essence of being. In *The Great God Brown* there are no important symbols, if a symbol is to be taken as a referential device for the expression of an inexpressible truth. Instead, the drama of souls is enacted before its audience as if it were a realistic drama, an impossible state of affairs since once the inexpressible is expressed, it is without meaning.

The Great God Brown, despite its devices, is tied to the realistic theatre. It moves in space and time in a coherent and essentially realistic way, and its setting is sociological, rather than psychological, a space, complete with doors, windows, telephones and all the other accoutrements of daily living. O'Neill, indeed, reveals at several points a certain strain in handling his characters in the realistic context of the play. For instance, in III, i, Margaret must be brought to Brown's office for the crucial scene, in which Brown, unmasked, declares his love for her. As she enters the office, however, O'Neill is forced to have her develop a reason for her presence, a necessity only to a totally realistic drama: "I forgot to tell him something important this morning and our phone's out of order." A similar problem develops in IV, i, when Brown switches frantically between his own mask and that of Dion's, which he has usurped. Brown, as Brown, rushes from the room and returns wearing Dion's mask, but there has been no time for a costume change for the actor. As a realist, O'Neill worries about the matter and has Margaret note the fact that Brown and the supposed Dion are dressed alike: "Why, Dion, that isn't your suit. It's just like . . ." Evidently, if its concern for the color of Brown's pants is an indication, *The Great God Brown* is something less than a "drama of souls." There is here a reminiscence of the quick change of disguise and the dashing in and out of doors of a bedroom farce or of such melodramas as *Dr. Jekyll and Mr. Hyde.* At best the play is a realistic, somewhat overwrought narrative complete with a police chase. Whatever they were intended to do, the masks play a not completely fulfilled part.

In his early play, *Bread and Butter,* O'Neill had treated the same subject matter, indeed had there written what might well be considered a first draft of *The Great God Brown.* The 1914 version considered the fate of the artist in a small Connecticut town. Its hero, John Brown, is a thinly disguised self-portrait, and the play's narrative is a conventional piece of autobiographical speculation that extrapolated certain domestic possibilities lying before the young O'Neill into a condemnation of marriage and of American philistinism that combined the most obvious aspects of Strindberg and Sinclair Lewis.

In *The Great God Brown,* O'Neill altered the story of *Bread and Butter*—it is no longer so directly autobiographical—but he kept most of its essentials. The play's statement is only superficially enlarged by the addition of the masks or of the Nietzschean material. In the earlier work, the hero's confidant was his teacher, the painter Eugene Grammont, a wise and sympathetic counselor. The role is retained in *The Great God Brown* but given to the prostitute Cybel, who makes explicit the sensitive hero's desire to reach the creative core of nature itself—a point implied in the early work by Brown's painting, particularly a seascape and a landscape, the sole vestiges of his artist's life that he retains in his marital bondage. The Faustian implications of *Bread and Butter,* suggested in the hero's willingness to sell his artistic soul for the sake of a woman, are developed more fully in the religious implications of Dion Anthony's name—a combination of Dionysus and St. Anthony—and in the name of Margaret, by which O'Neill wished to recall the Marguerite of *Faust.* The parallels with *Faust* are augmented by the gradual transformation of the Pan mask of Dion into the mocking face of Mephistopheles, at the same time as his true face becomes more saint-like and ascetic.

The most important change in the later play was O'Neill's development of the character of the materialist, William Brown. In his earlier treatment of such figures, in Andrew Mayo or the cartooned Marco Polo, O'Neill had seen him chiefly as what might be called an "anti-poet," the adversary of the sensitive self-portraits. Now, O'Neill developed fully what the figure of Marco Polo had partly suggested to him: the anguish of the uncreative man, the despair of the man who cannot dream. As its title suggests, *The Great God Brown* holds the materialist up to crucial inspection and shows that like the poet, he has a capacity to suffer. Suffering comes to him, when, with the death of Dion, he moves into the play's focal position, attempting to live his life in Dion's mask. As O'Neill explained this turn in his drama:

> Brown has always envied the creative life force in Dion—what he himself lacks. When he steals Dion's mask of Mephistopheles he thinks he is gaining the power to live creatively, while in reality he is only stealing that creative power made self-destructive by complete frustration. This devil of mocking doubt makes short work of him. It enters him, rending him apart, torturing and transfiguring him until he is even forced to wear a mask of his Success, William A. Brown, before the world, as well as Dion's mask toward wife and children. Thus Billy Brown becomes not himself to anyone. And thus he partakes of Dion's anguish—more poignantly, for Dion has the Mother, Cybele—and in the end out of this anguish his soul is born, a tortured Christian soul such as the dying Dion's, begging for belief, and at the last finding it on the lips of Cybel.

The explanation both of Dion and of Brown leaves something to be desired. O'Neill described Brown as "the visionless demi-god of our new materialistic myth—a Success—building his life of exterior things, inwardly empty and resourceless, an uncreative creature of superficial preordained social grooves, a by-product forced aside into slack waters by the deep main current of life-desire." In conceiving of Brown as a "by-product" of the "life-desire," O'Neill has somewhat altered his view of the materialist. Both Andrew Mayo and John Brown became what they were because they denied their rightful heritage. Billy Brown, however, is created without a soul, and there is no explanation for this deformity. In truth, it appears, that O'Neill began by using Brown as a typical opposition for Dion, feeling no need to explain an epitome. Only when he began to concentrate on Brown as his protagonist in the latter half of the play did he ask the important questions about him, and then he did not always find the essential answers.

Source: Travis Bogard, "The Great God Brown," in *Contour in Time: The Plays of Eugene O'Neill,* Oxford University Press, 1972, pp. 264–73.

Normand Berlin

Berlin talks about the significance of the mask and it's underlying theme in the play.

The Great God Brown (written 1925, produced 1926) is O'Neil's first play of the late twenties, and the last play to be produced by the triumvirate of Kenneth Macgowan, Robert Edmond Jones, and O'Neill, thereby ending their five-year association. The play mystified its audience because of O'Neill's complex use of masks, but managed to please many reviewers, even those who found the play puzzling, and ran for 283 performances. Because the audiences and reviewers did not understand the play, O'Neill presented many comments on the play's meaning, explaining what he intended to accomplish. The gap between his intentions and the play's accomplishment is very wide indeed, and the reasons for this gap are not difficult to discern.

O'Neill's use of the mask, the play's most important dramatic device, became a kind of 'cause' for O'Neill, who was very much influenced by the book of his fellow producer, Macgowan's *Masks and Demons,* which emphasized the importance of masks for theatre as well as religion. O'Neill believed that masks 'can express those profound hidden conflicts of the mind which the probings of psychology continue to disclose to us.' They allow for 'a new kind of drama.' For O'Neill the new psychology was essentially 'a study in masks, an exercise in unmasking.' Not satisfied, it seems, with 'a realistically disguised surface symbolism'—that is, the kind of symbolism he himself used in his realistic plays—O'Neill wished to present more directly 'a drama of souls.' In *The Great God Brown* he literally offers 'an exercise in unmasking,' whereas in the realistic and expressionistic plays that preceded it, the 'unmasking' was more subtle, more indirect. The device of masks in *The Great God Brown* too explicitly bares the human soul on stage, trying in vain, as Travis Bogard suggests, to express the inexpressible. Admittedly the conflicts within the human soul or psyche have been directly dramatized in morality plays of the past, but those anonymous dramatists of the Middle Ages never attempted to present believable human characters at the same time that they presented the psychomachia. O'Neill's intention, as he explained to a bewildered public in a newspaper article, was to present 'recognizable human beings' within the larger context of conflict 'in the soul of Man,' but this was misunderstood by audiences who paid more attention to the scheme and the large context than to the 'human beings.'

In *The Great God Brown* O'Neill confronts Mystery head-on, but he does so with the aid of 'expressionistic' masks (which objectively present inner reality) on a realistic stage; the result is confusion. The play provokes a multitude of questions, but not the questions produced by rich ambiguity; rather, the questions arising from genuine puzzlement. What exactly are we to think of Dion Anthony? A 'recognizable human being' or the allegorical representation of Dionysus and St. Anthony? Both? When William Brown, now wearing Dion's mask, is killed at the end of the play, is it a double death, or is it the death of one 'Man,' to use Cybel's word, the two sides of whom are Dion Anthony and William Brown? Or should we recognize three sides to Man because Dion Anthony himself has two sides, Dionysus and St Anthony? Does the equation work in both allegorical and human terms? And how does the composite of Woman—Margaret and Cybel—fit into the pattern? And *is* William Brown the empty materialist O'Neill intends him to be? Doesn't he seem more 'alive' than Dion, who is praised for being alive? Are we meant to take Brown as a satirical portrait of American business? Does the allegory, therefore, have a social as well as a philosophical dimension?

All along, of course, even if we concede that the allegory works and that these questions, and many more, can be answered with some assurance, the audience is engaged in a cerebral exercise, trying to fit together pieces of a puzzle *while* witnessing the 'living drama' of 'recognizable human beings.' O'Neill's *literal* exercise in unmasking produces much thought, but little emotion. We pay attention to the 'philosophy' but we do not respond emotionally to the people. We receive Nietzschean messages and we know something profound and big, even mystical, is being confronted, but we have no deep interest in the bearers of those messages. We see the mask, but it covers no recognizable face, it responds to no beating heart. The mask points to the 'vision' of a serious, sincere dramatist who seems more interested in his thesis, in his ideas on Life and God, than in the characters who present the ideas. In short, *The Great God Brown* is an artistic failure because 'the drama of souls' is essentially undramatic.

O'Neill was especially fond of *The Great God Brown*. 'Of all the plays I have written, I like *The Great God Brown* best. I love that play.' He wrote to Macgowan that the play was 'grand stuff, much deeper and poetical in a way than anything I've done before.' His enthusiasm undoubtedly reflects his belief that *The Great God Brown,* by means of masks, successfully placed Mystery within the reach of the stage. His autobiographical closeness to the play may also explain his fondness for it. The qualities he gave to the poet-artist Dion Anthony were his own—alone, sensitive, unable to reveal his true 'self' to the world, ever aware of the masks people wear to protect themselves from others and from themselves, always in need of a Mother (what both Cybel and Margaret represent), 'born with ghosts in your eyes,' as Cybel tells Dion. Another reason for his enthusiasm is that he uses his favorite source, Nietzsche, more directly in *The Great God Brown* than in any of his other plays, with the possible exception of *Lazarus Laughed.* Nietzsche hovers over the play not only in the Dionysian aspects of Dion Anthony's character, but also in the doctrine offered by Cybel near the play's end—'Always spring comes again bearing life! Always again! Always, always forever again!—Spring again!—life again! summer and fall and death and peace again! ... but always, always, love and conception and birth and pain again—spring bearing the intolerable chalice of life again! ... bearing the glorious, blazing crown of life again!'—and in O'Neill's general preoccupation with mystery. O'Neill considered Nietzsche's *The Birth of Tragedy* the 'most stimulating book on drama ever written.' His use of quotations from that book in the playbill of *The Great God Brown* testifies to its importance, and probably helps to explain O'Neill's stated confidence in the play's depth. But neither O'Neill's enthusiasm for the play nor his explanations of the meanings he intended can erase the judgement that *The Great God Brown* is a bold but bewildering experiment which does not work, what the reviewer of *Billboard* called 'glorious confusion.'

Source: Normand Berlin "The Late Twenties," in *Eugene O'Neill*, Grove Press, 1964, pp. 85–89.

Frederic I. Carpenter

In The Great God Brown *O'Neill attacks the "materialism of modern society." Carpenter examines this aspect through O'Neill's use of symbolism throughout the play.*

The Great God Brown magnified this American dualism of the materialistic and the romantic to universal proportions. William A. Brown—like his contemporary American, George F. Babbitt—became the "god" of our materialism. But in rejecting this false American "god," O'Neill's hero again rejected American democracy: Dion turned away from "the rabble" because "he hated to share with them fountain, flame and fruit." That is, his romantic idealism became wholly negative. Like other Americans, he even began to worship the devil because God would not grant him his absolute ideal: "When Pan was forbidden the light and warmth of the sun he grew sensitive and self-conscious and proud and revengeful—and became Prince of Darkness." And so Dion the romantic dreamer turned against the American world in which he lived....

After completing *Desire Under the Elms,* O'Neill worked simultaneously on two plays; but he completed *The Great God Brown* before *Marco Millions,* and the play was both published and produced first. Both plays carried forward his attack on the

> "WE PAY ATTENTION TO THE 'PHILOSOPHY' BUT WE DO NOT RESPOND EMOTIONALLY TO THE PEOPLE. WE RECEIVE NIETZSCHEAN MESSAGES AND WE KNOW SOMETHING PROFOUND AND BIG, EVEN MYSTICAL, IS BEING CONFRONTED, BUT WE HAVE NO DEEP INTEREST IN THE BEARERS OF THOSE MESSAGES."

materialism of modern society. Brown (as O'Neill specifically explained) "is the visionless demi-god of our new materialistic myth—a Success—building his life on exterior things, inwardly empty...." *Marco Millions* would translate this "new materialistic myth" to the ancient Orient. But "Billy Brown" was one hundred percent American.

The Great God Brown is one of the most interesting but also one of the most confusing of O'Neill's plays. It contains some of his most challenging dramatic ideas and some of his most original characters. Moreover, it achieved success at the time of production, and it was both praised and reproduced throughout the civilized world. It marks a milestone in O'Neill's career, and it also prepared the way for his later triumphs. But it remains a strangely artificial play. Mixing dramatic experimentation with self-conscious poetry, genuine insight with bookish theory, this play attempted everything, but achieved final success with nothing. At the time it seemed greater than *Desire Under the Elms,* but now its fireworks seem contrived.

The element of artificiality in *The Great God Brown* is illustrated by the simple summary of its plot. The first two acts describe the tragedy of Dion Anthony—the sensitive artist who finds himself in conflict with a materialistic society. He has married, and the need of supporting a wife and three sons has forced him to give up his painting and he takes to drink. His wife gets him a job as a draftsman in the architectural office of his old classmate, William A. Brown. But he feels humiliated, and seeks solace

> MIXING DRAMATIC EXPERIMENTATION WITH SELF CONSCIOUS POETRY, GENUINE INSIGHT WITH BOOKISH THEORY, THIS PLAY ATTEMPTED EVERYTHING, BUT ACHIEVED FINAL SUCCESS WITH NOTHING."

and understanding in the arms of Cybel, the eternal prostitute. Lacking the true love of his wife and the true appreciation of his old friend and employer, he finally drinks himself to death.

The second two acts then describe the second tragedy—that of William A. Brown. After Dion's death, Brown assumes the "mask" of his former friend and employee, Dion Anthony. And with this mask he inherits Dion's ability to create, so that his architectural designs win him even greater success than before. With the mask he also wins the love of Dion's wife, who identifies him with her husband. But with the mask he tragically inherits Dion's bitter honesty and insight into the truth. And this honesty compels him to denounce the artistic falsity of his own architectural designs and to recognize the inner duplicity of his own divided personality. Finally, abandoning the "mask" of the insensitive William A. Brown, he also flees to the arms of Cybel, where the police find only the "mask" of Dion Anthony, whom they now accuse of "murdering" Billy Brown. The eternal artist and the eternal materialist have destroyed each other. At the end the police captain asks: "Well, what's his name?" And Cybel, the Earth Mother, replies: "Man!"

Taken together, Dion Anthony and Billy Brown represent the divided personality of modern man. They are, in one sense, two separate and opposing characters; in another, they are the conflicting aspects of the single character, "Man." Both the complexity and the confusion of the play lie in its uncertainty concerning these two alternatives. Dion Anthony and Billy Brown are brothers under the skin. But do they have two skins, or one? Are they really two people, or are they the conflicting halves of one person? And does *The Great God Brown* really consist of two plays, of two acts each? Or is it one play of four acts?

The Great God Brown became famous for its daring use of masks to suggest the conflicting personalities of each of its characters. Earlier *The Hairy Ape* had painted on masks to emphasize the artificial "faces" of people in "Society." And later *Lazarus Laughed* used formal masks to define type characters. But in *The Great God Brown* all the characters used masks to dramatize the contrast between their external, or public selves, and their inner, or private selves. And this new use of masks suggested psychological complexities beyond the scope of the old, realistic drama.

But the trouble with *The Great God Brown* lies in the confusing ambiguity of its use of masks. At the beginning Dion's *"mask is a fixed forcing of his own face."* But as his tragedy develops, this mask becomes (first) the mask of "Pan," and (finally) the mask of "Mephistopheles." And after his death, Brown is able to assume at will Dion's "mask" (which one?). Meanwhile Brown wears no mask at first, but (at the end of the second act) he assumes Dion's; and (at the end of the fourth act) he discards his own *"mask of William Brown,"* and permanently assumes Dion's. Thereupon his associates proclaim that "Mr. Brown is dead!" And they *"return, carrying the mask of William Brown, two on each side, as if they were carrying a body by line legs and shoulders."* If this seems brilliantly imaginative, it is also dramatically confusing. The manipulation of a variety of masks tends to become mere hocus-pocus.

The Great God Brown succeeded on the stage in spite of its strange plot, and it continues to fascinate the reader despite its confusing use of masks. Its occasional excellence derives partly from its author's autobiographical insight, reflected in the action, and partly from his creative use of his wide reading. Dion's tragedy is clearly an allegory of O'Neill's own. Cybel tells him: "You're not weak. You were born with ghosts in your eyes and you were brave enough to go looking into your own dark." And at the other extreme, this "Dion Anthony" is clearly a mixture of Nietzsche's Dionysus and of Saint Anthony; "Cybel" is a mixture of the goddess Cybele, the earth mother, and the eternal prostitute; and Dion's wife Margaret is a modern embodiment of Faust's Margaret. At its best, the play partly realizes a modern myth; at its worst, it becomes a self-conscious allegory.

But if *The Great God Brown* suffers from artificiality of plot, from confusing use of masks, and from self-consciousness of allegory, it manages finally to make a virtue of these very faults. In the last analysis, the play achieves its moments of tragic greatness by means of its very incongruities and confusions. Cybel, for instance, *"chews gum like a sacred cow forgetting time with an eternal end."* And this grotesque mixture of incongruous metaphors suggests the confusion of the modern world—which, of course, the title of the play also suggests. Finally, a speech by Billy Brown, after he has "murdered" his former self, also suggests the final insight of the play into the confusion of the modern world: "Sssh! This is Daddy's bedtime secret for today: Man is born broken. He lives by mending. The grace of God is glue." The final "grace" of *The Great God Brown*, perhaps, lies in its symbolic joining of dissociated fragments of experience by the glue of the creative imagination.

Source: Frederic I. Carpenter, "The Pattern of O'Neill's Tragedies," and "From *The Ape* to *Marco*: Reaction," in *Eugene O'Neill*, Twayne Publishers, 1964, pp. 70–71, 109–12.

SOURCES

Allen, Kelcey, "*Great God Brown* by O'Neill Unique," in *Women's Wear Daily*, January 25, 1926.

Anderson, John, "Another O'Neill Play Comes to Town," in *New York Post*, January 25, 1926.

Anschutz, Grace, "Masks, Their Use by Pirandello and O'Neill," in *Drama*, Vol. 17, April, 1927, p. 201.

Atkinson, Brooks, "Ibsen and O'Neill," in *New York Times*, January 31, 1926, p.1.

Atkinson, Brooks, "Symbolism in an O'Neill Tragedy," in *New York Times*, January 25, 1926, p.26.

Bogard, Travis, *Contour in Time: The Plays of Eugene O'Neill*, Oxford University Press, 1972.

Bogdanoff, Rose, "Masks, Their Uses Past and Present," in *Drama*, Vol. 21, May, 1931, p. 21.

Brown, John Mason, "Doldrums of Midwinter," in *Theatre Arts*, Vol. 10, March 1926, pp. 145–46.

Carb, David, "*The Great God Brown*," in *Vogue*, Vol. 67, March 15, 1926, p. 106

Clark, Barrett H., "Fin de Saison on Broadway," in *Drama*, Vol. 16, May, 1926, pp. 289–90.

Coleman, Robert, "God Brown Tedious," in *New York Mirror*, January 25, 1926.

Gilbert, Gabriel, "All God's Chillun Got Masks," in *New York Sun*, January 25, 1926.

Gillette, Don Carle, "The Great God Brown," in *Billboard*, Vol. 38, February 6, 1926, p. 43.

Jensen, George H., "Eugene O'Neill," in *Dictionary of Literary Biography, Volume 7: Twentieth-Century American Dramatists*, Gale, 1981. pp. 139–65.

Metcalfe, J. S., "A Plea in Defence," in *Wall Street Journal*, January 25, 1926.

Osborn, E. W., "The Great God Brown," in *New York World*, January 25, 1926.

Review in *New York Graphic*, January 25, 1926.

Vreeland, Frank, "The Masked Marvel," in *New York Telegram*, January 25, 1926.

FURTHER READING

Anderson, John, Review in *Literary Review of the New York Evening Post*, April 10, 1926, p. 2.
  Anderson offers a mixed review of the play in his focus on O'Neill's technique.

Cohn, Ruby, "Eugene O'Neill: Overview," in *Reference Guide to American Literature*, 3rd ed., edited by Jim Kamp, St. James Press, 1994.
  Cohn examines the tragic nature of O'Neill's plays.

Marsh, Leo, Review in *New York Telegraph*, January 25, 1926.
  Marsh examines the play's "clinical experiment" in structure.

Review in *New Yorker*, Vol. 1, February 6, 1926, p. 26.
  This reviewer criticizes O'Neill's use of masks but praises the play's presentation of a "nutritious fluid of a deeply digested idea."

Harvey

MARY CHASE

1944

Mary Coyle Chase's *Harvey* has been an American favorite since it was first brought to the Broadway stage in 1944. Before it opened, there were not very high expectations: the author had only written one play previously, which had been a quick failure. Harold Lloyd, Edward Everett Horton, Robert Benchley, and Jack Haley all turned down the lead role before Frank Fay accepted it. Fay, a retired vaudeville actor, astounded the critics with his performance. The play won the Pulitzer Prize for drama in 1944, and its initial run lasted for four years—1,775 performances. It has continually been revived around the globe since then. It was also adapted to film in 1950, starring Hollywood legend James Stewart, and has become one of Stewart's best-loved films.

The story is about Elwood P. Dowd, a good-natured, mild-mannered eccentric who is known in all of the cafeterias and saloons in his small town. Elwood is polite and cheerful and always friendly toward any strangers he might encounter, and he has just one problematic character trait: his best friend is an invisible six-foot-tall rabbit, Harvey. Wherever he goes, he brings an extra hat and coat for Harvey, and he buys theater tickets and railroad tickets in twos so that they can go everywhere together. His sister and her daughter try to have Elwood committed to the local sanitarium, where the behavior of the prominent psychologist and his staff raise the age-old question of who is more dangerous to society: the easy-going dreamer with a vivid imagination or

the people who want him to conform to the accepted version of reality.

AUTHOR BIOGRAPHY

When she was a little girl, Mary Chase's three Irish uncles, Pete, Tim, and Jamie, amused her with stories from Celtic mythology of pookas and banshees. Chase was born in 1907 in Denver, Colorado, which is probably the model for the "western town" where *Harvey* takes place. She attended college in Denver and married Robert Lamont Chase, a newspaper reporter, in 1928. Chase herself worked as a newspaper reporter at that time, first for the *Rocky Mountain News* and then as a freelance correspondent for United Press and International News Service. She gained reputation for being one of the best "picture stealers" in the Denver news business, visiting households of victims or criminals and walking away with stolen photographs of the involved person from the family's collection.

Chase's first play was *Me Third,* which was produced in 1936 for the Federal Theater Project, a government agency aimed at keeping writers employed during the Depression. *Me Third* was brought to Broadway in 1937, under the title *Now You've Done It;* it was an immediate failure. Her next play, *A Slip of a Girl,* never even made it to New York. When Chase had the idea that was to become *Harvey,* she went to the producer, Brock Pemberton, who had produced *Now You've Done It.* Despite her weak record, Pemberton recognized the value of the property and put it into production.

It took Chase two years to write *Harvey.* She meticulously constructed a miniature stage on the dining room table in her house in Denver, so that she could imagine the characters' movements. Over the course of those years, the play underwent at least fifty rewrites, some of them quite significant. Originally, when it was entitled *The Pooka,* Harvey was a six-foot-tall parakeet. In a later version, *The White Rabbit,* Harvey was identifiable as audiences today know him, but the lead was a woman.

After *Harvey* became a critical and financial success on Broadway and in the movies, earning Chase a Pulitzer Prize, she continued to write plays, but only with marginal success. Her most famous post-*Harvey* work was *Mrs. McThing* in 1955. That, and another play, *Bernadine,* were adapted to movies, but none came anywhere near *Harvey*'s success.

She went on to publish two children's books, *Loretta Mason Potts* in 1958 and *The Wicked Pigeon Ladies in the Garden* in 1968. Mary Chase died of a heart attack in Denver on October 20, 1981.

PLOT SUMMARY

Act I

Harvey is a play about forty-seven-year-old Elwood P. Dowd, whose best friend is an invisible, six-foot-tall rabbit named Harvey. Dowd and his rabbit friend are well-known and liked in the taverns around town, but his relatives, who have come to live with him, are embarrassed by his behavior and try to have him committed to an insane asylum. The first scene opens with Dowd's sister, Veta Louise Simmons, and her daughter, Myrtle Mae, throwing a luncheon for the older society matrons of the town. They count on Dowd being out, but he comes home suddenly, talking to Harvey and holding doors for him, and, worse, introducing him to the ladies at the party. As the party clears out, Veta swears that he will not disgrace the family again, and she asks him to wait in the den, which he does happily, while she goes to make arrangements for him to be committed.

Scene II takes place at the mental institution, Chumley's Rest. Nurse Ruth Kelly, who is young and good-looking, interviews Veta about her brother, who is waiting outside in the taxi cab. When Elwood comes in, Kelly has an orderly take him upstairs. When the psychiatrist on duty, Dr. Sanderson, interviews Veta, he gets the impression that she is the one who has hallucinated Harvey (she admits to having seen him sometimes), and so he has her locked up. When he finds out that Elwood Dowd has been locked up, he assumes that a mistake has been made, and Dowd is brought down to the office, where Sanderson and Kelly apologize profusely, fearing that the sanitarium will be sued. Dowd, oblivious to the fact that he had been incarcerated in the first place, invites them both to have drinks with him later.

After Dowd leaves the scene (to explore the sanitarium where he has been told his sister is to be committed), Dr. Chumley, the esteemed director of the facility, enters and discovers that Dowd has left a hat with holes cut in the top. The hospital staff exits, then Dowd returns, just as Dr. Chumley's wife, Betty, enters, and he tells her that he is looking for Harvey, explaining that Harvey is a pooka—a

Mary Coyle Chase

mythological spirit. After he leaves, she tells the others that he was looking for Harvey, and they realize that it was he, not Veta, who had delusions. They understand that the hat is Harvey's, that the holes are for his rabbit ears. At the end of the scene, Wilson, the orderly, looks up "pooka" in the dictionary and reads out loud the definition that somehow, mysteriously, appears there: "A wise but mischievous creature. Very fond of rum-pots, crackpots, and how are you Mr. Wilson?"

Act II

Scene I of Act II takes place in the library of the Dowd house. Myrtle is having the house appraised, planning to sell it as soon as Dowd is committed. Judge Gaffney has come to the house because he received a call from Veta, who was frantic. Veta arrives, distraught, telling of being handled roughly at the sanitarium when they tried to commit her, accusing the people who run the place of having unnatural interest in sex, and instructing the judge to sue them. Wilson and Dr. Chumley arrive from the sanitarium, looking for Dowd, with a list of bars and firehouses that they have been to in their search. When Judge Gaffney and Dr. Chumley leave together, discussing Veta's impending lawsuit, Wilson and Myrtle flirt. They go off to the kitchen together, and Dowd comes in. He sees a flat parcel that Myrtle brought out of the garage to show Judge Gaffney, as evidence of David's madness: a painting of himself and a large rabbit, in a polka-dot collar and red necktie. Putting the picture on the mantle, in front of his mother's portrait, he leaves. Veta and Dr. Chumley enter, and he asks about the portrait over the fireplace and she, not looking, answers as if his questions were about her mother's picture. Dowd phones, looking for Harvey, but while he is on the phone he says that Harvey just stepped in the door, so Veta determines that he is at a bar called Charlie's.

Scene II of Act II takes place at the sanitarium again. Dr. Sanderson, having been fired for falsely committing Veta, is packing his belongings. He and Nurse Kelly discuss having seen each other out on dates the previous Saturday, indicating that they are jealous, although neither is willing to openly declare affection. Dowd enters and gives Kelly a bunch of flowers—Dr. Chumley's prize dahlias. He is under the impression that Kelly and Dr. Sanderson are going to join him for a drink at a bar, and when Wilson enters, Dowd invites him, too. He tells them that he was out at the bar with Dr. Chumley earlier, that after a few drinks the doctor saw Harvey also. Near the end of this scene, Nurse Kelly asks Dowd about his life, and he explains in a long speech how he and Harvey make the acquaintance of strangers when they sit in bars:

> Soon the faces of the other people turn toward mine and smile. They are saying: "We don't know your name, Mister, but you're a lovely fellow." Harvey and I warm ourselves in these golden moments. We have entered as strangers—soon we have friends. They come over. They sit with us. They drink with us. They talk to us. They tell us about the big terrible things they have done. The big wonderful things they *will* do. Their hopes, their regrets, their loves, their hates. All very large because nobody ever brings anything small into a bar. Then I introduce them to Harvey. And he is bigger and grander than anything they offer me. When they leave, they leave impressed.

At the end of this scene, Dr. Chumley enters, nervously, as if someone is following him. He goes into his office and closes the door, and, soon after, the door opens and closes again, as if by itself.

Act III

Dr. Chumley, who was last seen locking himself in his office, is knocking at the sanitarium door; when Wilson answers, he explains that he slipped out of the window of his office and went around. He is terrified. Myrtle and Judge Gaffney arrive. She still wants Dowd committed, but the judge has evidence that there might actually be a Harvey. Reading from a note pad, he describes Veta's testimony that she saw Harvey in her kitchen one morning, calling to her, and she chased him away by shouting, "To hell with you!" Myrtle says that Dowd, claiming Harvey's help, is able to predict events in the future, such as the unexpected arrival of a neighbor's aunt. Nurse Kelly and Dr. Sanderson arrive, behaving like a couple in love, and Dr. Chumley tells Sanderson that he isn't fired after all. Sanderson suggests that Dowd should receive shock treatment with an injection of Doctor Chumley's formula 977.

When Dowd arrives, Dr. Chumley asks to speak with him alone. They discuss Harvey's power to stop time, which leads the doctor to fantasize about running off to a campground outside of Akron for two weeks with a strange girl who will stroke his head and say, "Poor thing! Oh, you poor, poor thing!" At Veta's request, Dowd agrees to take an injection of formula 977, even though he would not be able to see Harvey any more. While he is in the next room for the injection, the cab driver who brought Veta comes in to collect his fare. She cannot find her change purse and so has to ask Dowd for money. The cab driver, noticing what a nice person Dowd is, remarks that he will not be so nice after the injection, that people he brings to the sanitarium always are nice until they are "cured." Thinking about it, Veta realizes that she does not want Dowd changed, and she races in and stops the injection. Her change purse shows up before she leaves, and she realizes that Harvey had hidden it. The whole family leaves, with Elwood P. Dowd waiting a moment for Harvey to catch up with him.

CHARACTERS

Ethel Chauvenet

Mrs. Chauvenet is an old friend of the family. She is a member of the town's social circle, which Veta wants Myrtle to break into, and so they both flatter her and curry her favor. She is delighted to see Elwood, whom she has not seen in a while, until he introduces her to Harvey: then, suspecting his sanity, she hastily apologizes and leaves.

Betty Chumley

Dr. Chumley's wife shows up just briefly in Act I, Scene II. Like Veta, she is more concerned with socializing than with science: told that her husband

MEDIA ADAPTATIONS

- The 1950 film of *Harvey* has become a classic of the American cinema, containing two great performances: James Stewart as Elwood P. Dowd, and Josephine Hull, who played Veta on Broadway and won an Academy Award for her performance as Veta in the film. The screenplay, by Mary Chase and Oscar Brodney, was directed by Henry Koster. Available from MCA/Universal Home Video.

has to examine a patient, she tells him, "Give a little quick diagnosis, Willie—we don't want to be late to the party." She has a conversation with Elwood while he is looking for Harvey, and then later, when everyone at the sanitarium thinks that it is Veta who believes in the imaginary rabbit, she mentions his friend Harvey, making them all realize that they have mistakenly committed the wrong person.

Dr. William B. Chumley

Chumley is an esteemed psychiatrist and the head of the sanitarium, "Chumley's Rest," to which Veta has Elwood taken. He is a difficult, exacting man, feared by his subordinates, unwilling to tolerate his mistakes. After a night out drinking with Elwood, though, Dr. Chumley comes to see Harvey, and after that, he discusses Harvey's attributes with Elwood. Told that Harvey can stop time, allowing one to leave their ordinary life for some time and go somewhere else, he describes an elaborate fantasy that has apparently been fomenting in his mind for a long time. In his fantasy, he would go to a campground outside of Akron, Ohio, and live with a beautiful woman, who would drink beer with him and listen to all of his innermost secrets and stroke his head and say, "Poor thing! Oh, you poor, poor thing!"

Elwood P. Dowd

Elwood P. Dowd is the central character of the play, a friendly eccentric who spends his days and nights in the taverns of his unnamed town. Elwood's best friend is Harvey, an invisible six-foot-tall rabbit. The play leaves open several possibilities regarding exactly what Harvey is, whether he is a figment of Elwood's imagination, as the psychiatrists would like to believe, or he is, as Elwood asserts, a supernatural being known as a pooka. The relevant events in Elwood's past that would account for his relationship with an imaginary, giant rabbit are only hinted at. No information is given about any job he may have ever been employed at, only that he took care of his mother until the time that she died and that she left "all of her property" to him, which implies that the family is rich and that he may have never worked.

Elwood is a charmer, always pleasant when talking to people, even those who, like Wilson, address him gruffly. He has a stack of calling cards in his pocket and takes one out to offer to each new person he meets. He invites strangers to dinner at his house, including a woman who calls selling magazine subscriptions and a cab driver who brings Elwood's sister, Veta, out to the sanitarium. He is gallant toward Nurse Kelly, picking flowers for her and complimenting her on her beauty.

There are hints that Elwood has known disappointment in his life, and that Harvey may be a manifestation of this. He is clearly displeased with his past when he says to Nurse Kelly, "For you I would do anything. I would almost be willing to live my life over again. Almost." Speaking of the choice between being smart or pleasant, he tells Dr. Chumley, "For years I was smart. I recommend pleasant," indicating a break with the past. The most significant indication of his self-image comes in Act II Scene II, when he describes the "golden moments" that he has with strangers in taverns, who tell him about the big things they have done and that they intend to do, and then, as he sees it, they are impressed with Harvey because he is "bigger and grander than anything they offer me." Harvey gives Elwood hope when he thinks about all of the things that he has not done while wasting his life away drinking.

Judge Omar Gaffney

The judge is an old family friend of the Dowds, a representative of the people in town who are accustomed to seeing Elwood talking to Harvey and who do not think anything of it. He is the family's lawyer; so, when Veta wants to commit Elwood, it is up to Judge Gaffney to arrange the commitment papers, and when Veta wants to sue Chumley's Rest for wrongly committing her, it is also his case to file.

Miss Johnson

Miss Johnson is listed in the Cast of Characters as "a cateress," but her dialog in the play is tagged "Maid." She only appears briefly in the first act: when Veta asks if she has seen the guest list, she says, "No, I haven't Mrs. Simmons," and leaves promptly.

Ruth Kelly

Nurse Kelly is a sympathetic character, a pretty young woman who appears to have some sort of love/hate relationship with Dr. Sanderson. Describing him to Veta, she exclaims, "He's really wonderful"—(*Catches herself.*) "to the patients." When it seems that they have incarcerated the wrong person, Kelly apologizes and offers to take the blame, but Sanderson meets her concern with sarcasm: "Beautiful—and dumb, too. It's almost too good to be true." When they are trying to stall Elwood from leaving, Sanderson suggests that she can captivate him with her good looks, telling her to "go into you old routine—you know—the eyes—the swish—the works." She is simultaneously flattered and insulted. Of the people at the sanitarium, it is Nurse Kelly that Elwood responds to—he holds her hand (asking permission first) and recites love poetry to her. Although the play offers no actual conclusion to her flirtation with Sanderson, there is the implication that Elwood's interests will make her more self-confident in the future.

E. J. Lofgren

At the end of the play, it is the cab driver, Lofgren, who makes Veta realize that the treatment that is supposed to make Elwood stop seeing Harvey might drain him of his kind personality. He explains that all of the people that he drives out to Chumley's Rest for treatment are kind and cheerful on the way out, but on the way back, after their treatment, they are angry, mean, and no fun. "Lady," he tells her, "after this, he'll be a perfectly normal human being and you know what bastards they are!"

Dr. Lyman Sanderson

Dr. Sanderson is young, for a psychiatrist, but very qualified—Dr. Chumley has picked him out of the twelve possible assistants that he tried. He is just as infatuated with Nurse Kelly as she is with him, but he only reveals his concern indirectly. When she tells him to tell Dr. Chumley that the mistake of locking up Elwood was her fault, he says out loud, "I never mention your name," but then adds, when he has moved away from her, "except in my sleep." At the beginning of Act II, Scene II, the two of them have their most direct confrontation, discussing the dates that they saw each other with the previous weekend, but Dr. Sanderson continues to insist that his interest in Nurse Kelly is purely as a psychiatrist.

Myrtle Mae Simmons

Myrtle is a young woman, the daughter of Veta. The main reason why she and her mother are concerned about their standing in the community is that they both are concerned that Myrtle find a man to marry. They are afraid that prospective suitors will be frightened away when they find out that Elwood has an imaginary friend. Myrtle is less charitable about Elwood's odd behavior than Veta, expressing the wish that he might be hit by a truck and making arrangements to sell the house as soon as he is taken off to the sanitarium. Ironically, Myrtle finds a man who is attracted to her because of Elwood's case; she and Wilson, the hospital orderly, fall in love before the play is over. She does have some awareness of Harvey's supernatural existence, because she is the one who explains that whatever Elwood says Harvey predicted actually comes to pass; however, Myrtle is too concerned with herself and her own prospects to think that there is anything too odd about this.

Veta Louise Simmons

Elwood's sister, Veta, is an important character in this play because she joins the play's two opposing forces, logic and imagination. It is her embarrassment with Elwood and her fear that her daughter, Myrtle, will not be able to land a suitable husband because of his eccentricities, that has her take him to Chumley's sanitarium to be committed. Veta throws society functions that are covered by the local newspaper, and she is terrified that her social position will be subject to ridicule or scandal. Elwood embarrasses her. But Veta is a comic character and is just as unstable in her own way as is her brother. In fact, Veta admits at one point that she has actually seen Harvey on a few occasions, indicating that she and her brother share a common state of mind. When she tries to explain Elwood's condition to Dr. Sanderson, she describes Harvey in such a confusing way that the doctor thinks that she is the one who imagines him, and so he has Wilson capture her and lock her up. Veta enlists an old family friend, Judge Gaffney, to sue the sanitarium, but her threat is eventually forgotten. She does, however, empathize with her brother in the end, after the cab driver has told her that the sanitarium's treatment will stop his eccentricity but make him mean and dull, and she interrupts the treatment before it can change him.

Wilson

Wilson is the muscle of Chumley's Rest, a devoted orderly responsible for handling the patients who will not cooperate voluntarily. When Dr. Sanderson thinks that Veta is supposed to be committed, Wilson captures her, carries her upstairs, and undresses her in order to put her in the "hydro-tub" for therapy. He is vulgar and crude and completely devoted to Dr. Chumley, almost frantic with concern when he thinks that Elwood may have hurt the doctor. When he goes to the Dowd house looking for Elwood, Wilson flirts with Myrtle—she seems interested in him. When he asks her out in the last scene it is her mother, Veta, who turns him down.

THEMES

Friendship

The friendship between Elwood P. Dowd and Harvey is implied in the way that Dowd carries an extra coat and hat for Harvey, in the way that he opens doors and lets him walk through and reads to him. Except for the fact that one of the participants is imaginary, it seems like an ideal friendship. When Dowd tells Nurse Kelly about how he spends his days in bars, or when he promises his sister that he will go to the Western Slope Water Board to apply, he always includes his friend, saying "Harvey and I. . . ." Several times in the play, he phones places looking for Harvey when he is not around. He commissioned a portrait of them together, which is something that only the closest of friends would do. It is clear that this relationship is the most important thing in Dowd's life, and that, like the best friendships, Elwood P. Dowd enjoys being with his friend Harvey, is proud of him, and wants to spend as much time with him as he can.

The play does not answer the question of why Dowd finds the company of an imaginary friend so fulfilling. There seems to be a clue in the fact that he took responsibility for caring for his mother, and then she died. That, according to Veta, is when she first noticed that he was hanging around with Harvey, and it would make sense that caring for an

TOPICS FOR FURTHER STUDY

- Many of the recent breakthroughs in psychiatry have been in the use of drugs to help with mental conditions. Research one such behavior-altering drug, such as Prozac or Lithium, and determine whether you think that, like formula 977 in the play, it would make Elwood P. Dowd quit seeing Harvey.

- At one of the early rehearsals of this play, the producers tried having Harvey appear on stage, with an actor in a rabbit costume crossing the stage for six seconds. Discuss whether you think this would be an effective staging technique or not.

- Describe what you would do if Harvey could overcome time and space and any objections for you.

- With decreasing tolerance for drunk drivers, the public is less and less inclined to see a chronic drinker as childlike or free-spirited. Do you think that modern audiences would be able to appreciate *Harvey* as much as audiences did when it was first staged in the 1940s?

- There is something about Elwood P. Dowd that makes this pooka appear to him as a rabbit. Pick some public figures from politics, sports or entertainment and explain what sort of pookas would appear to them and why.

- Stage plays often rely on music to represent something that cannot be explicitly shown. Often, unseen characters, such as ghosts, have specific music associated with them, so that audiences know when they are present. Play an original or prerecorded song to your class that you think could represent Harvey and explain why.

---

invalid would isolate him from a real social life and drive him deeper into his imagination. But Judge Gaffney, talking to Myrtle in Scene I of Act II, gives the impression that Dowd lost his real friends because he took up with Harvey. When she asks if it is true that he was liked by other men and women, the Judge replies, "Oh, not since he started running around with this big rabbit. But they did once."

Dr. Sanderson, suspecting that Harvey might be a replacement for some friend in his past that Dowd lost, asks him, "Dowd, when you were a child you had a playmate, didn't you? Someone you were very fond of—with whom you spent many happy, carefree hours?" Chase's script is not willing to allow his attraction to Harvey to be understood in such simplistic psychological terms: his childhood friend was not named Harvey, but Vern McElhinney.

Sanity and Insanity

This play raises the question of whether believing in something as unlikely as a six-foot-tall rabbit actually qualifies as insanity. At first, the members of the psychiatric profession, represented by the staff at Chumley Rest, think so, and they are willing to commit Elwood and then Veta against their wills, on the suspicion of holding such a belief. According to Dr. Chumley, "the function of a psychiatrist is to tell the difference between those who are reasonable, and those who merely talk and act reasonably." The fact that Dowd is initially considered "reasonable" by the psychiatrists and that his sister is deemed unstable, only to have the diagnoses reversed almost immediately, is an indication that the standards about sanity at Chumley's Rest are none too solid.

The question of sanity is pushed even further when the play offers proof that Harvey actually does exist, as when doors open and close by themselves or the dictionary that Wilson consults has the phrase, "and how are you Mr. Wilson?" If Harvey actually does exist as a supernatural being, then there is nothing at all wrong with the way that Elwood Dowd behaves. In raising this possibility, readers are challenged to not easily accept the notion that talking to an invisible friend equals insanity.

Dr. Chumley, an eminent psychiatrist, believes in Harvey by the last act of the play, and furthermore his belief in Harvey expands his imagination, giving him the freedom to daydream beyond his everyday life. His dream of what he would do with Harvey's help is very specific, down to the name of the girl he would spend his time with and what they would drink (beer, he insists, but not whiskey). If believing in an invisible, six-foot-tall rabbit is to be considered a sign of insanity, then insanity can be considered a sign of a liberated mind that has gotten beyond the troubles of the mundane world. If imagination is insanity, then it seems to benefit the psychiatrist who is supposed to be the gatekeeper of sanity.

Science and Technology

Dr. Chumley's formula 977 is expected to shock Dowd back into reality, so that he does not see Harvey anymore. For his family and friends, this cure offers the hope that Dowd can be returned to normal and can live among other people once again, hold down a job, and become a productive member of society. "If this shock formula brings people back to reality, give it to him," Judge Gaffney recommends. "That's where we want Elwood." All of the characters agree that this would be the best way to treat the problem until they find out that the treatment is not specific. As the cab driver explains, it would not only remove Dowd's hallucinations but also it would remove the pleasant part of his personality as well. Science is unable to distinguish between the part of the mind that hallucinates and the part that makes a person take time to look at sunsets and watch birds. In the end, Veta decides to ignore the recommendation of the scientists and to accept the opinion that is implied in the cab driver's speech, that it is better to have her brother with both his sweet disposition and Harvey than to obliterate them both.

STYLE

Setting

The scenes in this play alternate between the library of the Dowd mansion and the foyer of the sanitarium. These two settings help to accentuate the different possible ways of looking at Elwood P. Dowd's eccentricities.

Within his home environment, Dowd's behavior almost makes sense. The big, ornate mansion with relics of an earlier time, which the set direction describes as "faded grandeur," gives readers an understanding of his personality even before Dowd arrives. He is a throwback, courtly and generous, with all of his real human relations behind him. In many ways the charade of Veta and Myrtle hosting the Wednesday Forum is as delusional as his association with an invisible rabbit. The way that the ladies scurry out of the society tea when Dowd starts introducing Harvey around, which is odd but not really offensive, is a hint at how distant a dream it is to hope that Myrtle will be accepted into society. The Dowd mansion setting is appropriate to Dowds, but not to others.

At the sanitarium, the mood is not as desperate for social acceptance, but is steeped in scientific objectivity. The actual events that go on there, though, are just as nonsensical at times. The seriousness of the hospital setting is contrasted most sharply in the end by Dr. Chumley, the leader of the institution, cowering in fear of a giant invisible rabbit.

Both sets are described by the script to include several doors. This allows for a chaotic mood, as characters continually enter and leave the stage. The flow of characters kept in constant motion is in keeping with the central question of stability and instability.

Symbolism

Thanks to this play, and the popularity of the subsequent movie adaptation of it, the giant white rabbit has come to represent child-like imagination in American culture. Characters, usually ghosts, that are only seen by select characters almost always symbolize something in literature, such as suppressed guilt or fear or longing. The end of the second scene of Act II of *Harvey* goes to great lengths to eliminate possible ideas that the large rabbit might symbolize to Elwood P. Dowd. It is not a substitute for his father or for a lost childhood friend. The author, Mary Chase, makes sure to show readers that Harvey is not a desperate substitute for something that is missing in Dowd's life. Instead, he functions as the response of a quiet, polite middle-aged man who has always lived at home to the great crimes and accomplishments of others. This makes sense in terms of what Harvey actually is. Rabbits are not thought of as violent or aggressive creatures, and his size, as Dowd explains to Kelly, is a match for anything that others bring into bars with them, "bigger and grander than anything they offer me."

Harvey is somewhat of a childish idea because, as the oil painting of him shows, Dowd sees him wearing a collar and tie: he is not so much like a real rabbit as a cartoon or puppet, which, again, is more symbolic of imagination than of neurosis.

Climax

This play has a false climax and then an even grander climactic moment. At first, it seems that the play has reached its highest point when Elwood Dowd agrees to accept the injection that will make him stop seeing Harvey. The whole play, after all, is focused on their relationship, and his willing participation in shock therapy signals the end of that. The entrance of the cab driver, E. J. Lofgren, seems almost inconsequential at first, because audiences have their attention directed toward what is happening to Dowd.

As it turns out, though, the climactic choice made in *Harvey* is not Dowd's after all, but Veta's. It becomes clear after she stops the injection that this has not been a play about whether Elwood P. Dowd would change, but whether the people in his family would accept him as he is. Looking at it this way, all of the elements lead toward the climax, with the characters in the play divided between those sympathetic ones like Judge Gaffney and Nurse Kelly, who appreciate Dowd and accept his delusion, and those like Myrtle and Wilson, who feel that something must be done about him.

HISTORICAL CONTEXT

Shock Therapy

Sigmund Freud, considered to be the father of modern psychiatry, became well-known to the American public during the 1920s. His fame started when intellectuals, who heard about the research he was doing in Europe, began undergoing psychoanalysis themselves. From their writings and their life stories, the general populace became familiar with Freud's ideas about the subconscious, an idea that would have perplexed people of earlier centuries, when eccentric behavior was treated as harshly as criminal behavior. Freud's work became familiar, but it was also considered something of a luxury, a hobby that the wealthy could afford to indulge in. In the more extreme cases of mental disorder, science hurried past trying to understand patients and went right for effective treatment of behavior. For severe depression in particular, this meant "shock treatment" (referred to today as "Electroconvulsive Therapy," or "ECT"). ECT proved to have quicker and more certain effects than psychotherapy. It has been controversial since its inception in the 1930s: its supporters claim that ECT offers relief for patients who suffer from emotional instability, while opponents point to side effects—deadening of the personality and weakening of the memory. During the 1950s, psychiatry turned to anti-psychotic drugs to help patients cope with delusions, but these too have proven to have negative effects after long-term use. In recent years, a more controlled form of ECT is used in conjunction with drug therapy, showing positive effects with few of the negative ones.

Small Town America

In the 1940s, American culture experienced a notably large population shift away from small towns and toward big cities. This sort of shift had happened before, most notably during the Industrial Revolution of the 1870s and the economic boom of the 1920s, when descendants of farmers were drawn to big cities by wealth. During tight economic times, such as the Great Depression of the 1930s, there was no more attraction to moving to cities than there was to staying put. When America entered World War II in 1941, a need for large quantities of manufactured goods arose, and there was a labor shortage because much of the work force was in the armed service. Large cities drew workers again.

This sort of shifting population is what creates the impersonal attitude that is associated with large urban areas. The small town where Elwood P. Down lives in *Harvey* is large enough to support all of the businesses that he mentions (Charlie's, Blondie's Chicken Inn, Bennie's Drive-In, and so on, not to mention two cab companies and a sanitarium), but it is small and stable enough for a colorful local character to be accepted as part of the scenery. Dowd and his family live off of the accomplishments of a past generation—their mother arrived in an ox team and was one of the town's founders. Audiences feeling the pressures of urban growth in 1944 could be nostalgic about a slower pace, where eccentrics could peacefully while their time away in the dusty library of an old Victorian mansion.

World War II

This play was produced at a time when the Second World War had the nation's attention every day. The war had been going on for several years,

COMPARE & CONTRAST

- **1944:** Most of the nations of the world have direct or indirect involvement in the Second World War, which has been going on in Europe for five years.

  Today: The nations of the world sometimes become involved in smaller conflicts by contributing peacekeeping forces to group efforts by the United Nations or NATO, but, especially in the United States, war is not the central concern of many.

- **1944:** Excessive drinking is viewed as a harmless pastime that is frowned upon by prudes.

  Today: Alcoholism is recognized as a serious, chronic disease.

- **1944:** People fear that the use of drugs to control psychological abnormalities will leave patients as zombies, void of personality.

  Today: Even though the use of drug therapy is more widespread than ever before, people still fear that psychologists will prescribe psychoactive drugs unnecessarily.

- **1944:** People receive their daily news from newspapers and the radio. Once a week, they may be able to see film of important events in the newsreels that run at theaters along with movies.

  Today: Global link-ups allow instantaneous television broadcasts from anywhere in the world to anywhere in the world.

- **1944:** The National System of Interstate Highways is established by an act of Congress, making it possible to travel across the country quickly by automobile.

  Today: Because of the pollution associated with burning fossil fuels, government regulations try to discourage automobile use and encourage the use of public transportation.

- **1944:** Most telephone calls are placed by talking to an operator and telling her who you were trying to reach.

  Today: Many telephone calls involve picking options off of a service menu, with no contact to a live person ever being made.

---

and the Allies, led by American troops, were starting to win victories. Germany was being assaulted with bombing raids. D-Day, the huge assault by American and British troops to chase the Axis troops out of France, took place on June 6th of that year. This push went through the summer of 1944, with Paris finally liberated from the Germans. The first signs of the horrors of the Nazi Holocaust became apparent when the Allies entered Maidauck, a concentration camp in Poland, and found gas chambers and crematoriums that were responsible for taking one and a half million lives. *Harvey* opened on Broadway on November 1st of that year.

Popular entertainment served as a distraction from the terrors of the war. Some plays and films, such as Alfred Hitchcock's *Lifeboat,* worked the war into their plots, but since the outcome was far from determined, most works steered away from the subject, offering audiences lighter, happier fare. Romantic comedies such as those starring Alfred Lunt and Lynne Fontanne were popular on Broadway, while movies favored comedies like *Arsenic and Old Lace* and suspense stories like *Double Indemnity. Harvey* is a good representative of the type of escapist plays produced during World War II as a diversion from news of the war.

CRITICAL OVERVIEW

Harvey was a hit with both the public and the critics when it opened on November 1, 1944. One reason that was often cited was the casting of the actors. Critics were especially impressed with Frank Fay, who was an old vaudeville actor who came out of retirement to take the role of Elwood P. Dowd, and with Josephine Hull, who played his sister, Veta Louise Simmons. As Russell Rhodes put it in a review in 1944, "For the remarkable performance of these two, the author and producer should rub Harvey's foot every night in gratitude. Even if he *is* a pooka."

John L. Toohey's book, *A History of the Pulitzer Prize*, gives a brief summation of some of the notices that ran when *Harvey* first ran on Broadway. Toohey quotes John Chapman in the *New York Daily News* who could hardly contain his excitement: "*Harvey* is the most delightful, droll, endearing, funny and touching piece of stage whimsy I ever saw, and in it Frank Fay gives a performance so perfect that forever hence he will be identified with the character he plays." Toohey also referred to a review in the *Herald Tribune*, in which Howard Barnes noted that "The new play is as wise as it is witty; as occult as it is obvious. It is full of laughter and delicate meaning. It is stage sorcery at its whimsical best." Barnes went on to note that "Frank Fay's performance of the bum is memorable; Josephine Hull's daffy dowager is a performance not to be missed." Toohey also cites an unsigned review in the *New Yorker:* "A work of pure enchantment—touching, elegant, and lit with a fresh, surprising humor that has nothing to do with standard comedy formulas. The funniest play in town." Most critics agree that it was a splendid piece of theater art, although there are a few who question its winning the Pulitzer Prize for drama in 1944: that year saw the debut of Tennessee Williams's *The Glass Menagerie,* which has survived as one of the most important works written by one of America's most important playwrights.

There were a few negative criticisms, but even these were put within an overall context of reviewers' delight. In an issue of *PM* immediately after the play's opening, Louis Kronenberger noted that the script has given "something funny to the theater, and something fresh," and for that he is willing to forgive "some pretty serious sins—a first act that keeps going way too long, and a last act that, in a sense, can't keep going at all." Kronenberger gave credit to Chase for carrying out "the classic theme of humorists that in wackiness lies the greatest wisdom and the truest happiness." His greatest praise for her, though, is for her creation of Elwood P. Dowd. As with other reviewers, Kronenberger found Fay's performance of Elwood faultless: "Somehow Fay manages to transfix the audience and touch them."

Today, however, the role of Elwood is associated with the actor James Stewart, who played the role briefly in a 1949 revival before committing it to film in a 1950 version that was co-written by Mary Chase. Audiences remember his film performance as one of the best of his long career. Hull repeated her role as Veta for the film, but Frank Fay retired, and is largely forgotten today. David Mermelstein, of *Mr. Showbiz,* identifies the movie as "among the most beloved (pictures) of its era." He gives Mary Chase "a lot of credit," but attributes the picture's success to Stewart's warmhearted performance.

Harvey is still performed regularly today, mostly in community theaters and school productions. The play is seldom studied as a work of literature or included in the anthologies that are used as school texts, but it has not gone out of print. Small theaters are attracted to the play's immediate name recognition, its manageable cast and stage requirements, and its opportunity for at least the two leads, playing Elwood and Veta, to shine.

CRITICISM

David Kelly

David Kelly is an instructor of creative writing and drama at two colleges in Illinois. In the following essay, he examines the aspects of Harvey *that its author has left open to mystery and how unattached, unexplained ideas help to bolster the play's central idea.*

Mary Chase's time-honored play *Harvey* is a fun play to read and to perform. It isn't the type of literary work that cries out to be interpreted. In some ways, the play strains to defy interpretation. One of its central subthemes is that interpretation is a hangup that fun-loving people need to ignore. The play shows an eminent psychiatrist and his staff trying to figure out the reason why Elwood P. Dowd, a mild-mannered drunkard, thinks he sees a giant, invisible rabbit, but it gives its audience enough evidence to believe that he sees it because the rabbit, a mystical spirit, actually exists. There isn't any interpretation called for in explaining Harvey the rabbit, just belief.

There is an element to *Harvey* that goes beyond supernatural explanation, though. Chase teases audiences to see if they can make sense of Elwood's mental state. While there isn't enough evidence to explain why he has turned out to be the way he is, there are a lot of loose ends. There are events that might have no significance if *Harvey* occurred in real life but that have to have *some* meaning, because the audience knows that the author put them there. They aren't enough to build a complete psychological profile. They are, however, compelling enough to make readers want to sit down and take another look at the play, pondering what went on in Elwood's life before the action on stage began.

Of all of the strange and seemingly pointless elements that Chase chose to leave in her play, the one that most defies interpretation must be the business of Elwood's calling card. Whenever he meets a new person, he hands them his card. In most cases, as he hands the card over he points to the phone numbers on it, indicating one number—the "old one"—that the recipient should not call and one that they should.

But why does he have a defunct phone number on his card at all? If the cards had been reprinted since his phone number changed, then he could have left the old number off, and if the new number is just written in by hand then he could have, while writing it, scratched the old one off. And why did he change to a new number anyway?

Most likely, it has something to do with his sister and niece coming to live in his house, but this is only a weak guess that is based on a shortage of other possibilities. He's not likely to have changed phone numbers because of financial reasons, because his finances seem fine and untouched. The fact that he doesn't see his old friends any more since taking up with Harvey appears to be their idea, not his—there is no indication that Elwood has ever tried to distance himself from them or shut them out—so it is unlikely that he would change his phone number to keep old friends from reaching him. The play only accounts for two important changes in Elwood's life, other than the appearance of Harvey. His mother died, which may well have had great impact on Elwood's psyche—as Veta explains, "he was always a great home boy"—but that would be no reason to change his phone number. The only other possible explanation is that he changed his number when new people started inhabiting part of his house, even though there are no

Playwright Mary Coyle Chase and actor James Stewart pose with the giant rabbit featured in the 1950 film adaptation of Harvey.

other hints that he felt any need to protect his privacy against Veta Louise and Myrtle Mae.

It is interesting that Elwood draws attention to the number when he hands his card to Nurse Kelly and Betty Chumley (saying "If you should want to call me."), but in the last act, giving it to the cab driver, he only mentions the address printed on it. This may indicate nothing more than Chase's losing interest in the line, although, for balance, she really ought to follow through with what is started and repeat the line every time that he hands the card out. It might be that Elwood is either chivalrous or romantic by inviting women, but not men, to call him if they should want. One thing is for sure, though, and that is that there is something to this pattern, whether Chase was conscious of it or not. The "new number" is mentioned twice, and that makes it significant.

Even though we are not told what has changed in his telephone situation, we know that something has, and the idea of change in this home boy's life is at the center of the story's dramatic interest. Another big clue to Elwood's mind comes in the

WHAT DO I READ NEXT?

- Ken Kesey's 1963 novel, *One Flew Over the Cuckoo's Nest*, also raises questions about whether the people running psychiatric asylums are necessarily more sane than their patients. Kesey's novel shows the cynicism that developed in the twenty years between it and *Harvey*: its protagonist is more like a dangerous sociopath than a lovable eccentric, while Kesey's asylum is a place where victims are mirthlessly drained of all personality.

- *Arsenic and Old Lace* is another comedy about eccentrics that appeared about the same time (it was made into a movie the year *Harvey* appeared on Broadway). It is about two old aunts who invite lonely bachelors home and poison them. The script is available in a 1995 edition, from Dramatists' Play Service.

- John Patrick Shanley is a contemporary playwright who shares a sense of the whimsical and the imaginative with Mary Chase. His best works are collected in *13 by Shanley* (1992), available from Applause Theater Book Publishers.

- The famous Irish poet William Butler Yates looked into Celtic mythology with his 1892 collection, *Irish Fairy and Folktales*, which may have been one of Chase's sources for information about the pooka. Yates' book is available in a 1995 paperback edition from Barnes and Noble Books.

- Shakti Gawain's book *Creative Visualization* (1983) is one of the most influential "self-help" books available, based on the idea that serves Elwood P. Dowd in this play: benefiting from turning the imaginary into reality.

---

second scene of the second act. Nurse Kelly and Dr. Sanderson try to get to the bottom of Elwood's relationship with Harvey, whom they assume is a figment of his imagination. The doctor's attempt to find out why Elwood's mind would project such an imaginary figure fails, of course, because, as the audience is shown several times throughout the play, Harvey is in fact real, not projected. The nurse does better by listening to Elwood and getting him to talk about what Harvey means to him. Elwood's speech about how his invisible friend overshadows the hopes, regrets, and accomplishments of the other bar patrons tells more about the mysteries of Elwood P. Dowd than any therapeutic baths and psychoanalysis that the hospital has to offer him. It may not be clear why Harvey, the magical creature, appears to him, aside from his great, child-like sincerity, but it is clear that having a giant rabbit has been a tremendous boost to Elwood's self-esteem.

There is one more perplexing clue to what Elwood thinks. Early in the play, he makes a mysterious reference to a psychological condition, but Dr. Sanderson passes over the moment quickly, treating it as a joke. It is in the second scene, after Elwood has been institutionalized and then released. Sanderson, fearing that he might sue the asylum, is nervous and eager to please, which may account for his letting go of what seems a very significant hint. Sanderson is trying to explain what "trauma" is, and as an example he offers up "the birth trauma": "the shock to the act of being born."

"That's the one we never get over," Elwood responds. Sanderson, trying to be agreeable, compliments his astuteness and lets the matter drop, missing a chance to really understand what really drives Elwood P. Dowd. Psychiatrists explain that the "birth trauma" is a discomfort felt by all human beings throughout their entire lives, a response to the sudden shock of going from gloating in a sack of warm amniotic fluid to being brought out into the cold air, cut from the umbilical cord, slapped on the bottom, and thrown into an environment of bright lights and harsh sounds. For most people, it is a trauma that is eventually accepted, forgotten, or buried, although psychiatrists might insist that it affects all aspects of life. It certainly means much to Elwood P. Dowd, who accepts the concept as being natural and obvious. To him, perpetual trauma is the normal state of being.

And so the play *Harvey* presents us with an Elwood Dowd who professes to be familiar with the feelings of the birth trauma, whether he has actually ever heard the concept expressed in words or not. He is a homebody who, according to his old friend Judge Gaffney, "was always so calm about any change in plans," to such an extent that it made the judge suspicious. And he is someone who, for whatever reason, probably the arrival of new people in his house, has changed his phone number, with whatever disruption of his routine is implied with that. This isn't much of a psychological profile, and it certainly does not explain Harvey as a hallucination, but it is enough to explain Elwood's fondness for his big, invisible friend.

And if Harvey's function, not just in the play but in the whole world at large, is not clear enough, Chase shows her audience the effects that he has on people other than Elwood P. Dowd. Among the play's great unexplained oddities, for instance, is Veta's relationship with Harvey. Why does she see him only sporadically, and why is her shouting, "To hell with you," so effective in getting rid of him? Obviously, if Harvey represents childlike freedom, Veta has a childish streak that she is generally able to repress, but not completely. Shouting out an obscenity might seem completely out of character for her, but it is effective precisely because it is so crass, so extreme. The fact that she is as desperate to not see the pooka as Elwood is to see him serves to establish for readers how fearful people usually are of standing out.

The other character who sees Harvey is Dr. Chumley. Like Veta, it is important to Chumley that people not know he sees the invisible rabbit—even more so for him, since his career as a noted psychiatrist could be threatened if there were any suspicion about his sanity. Unlike Veta, but like Elwood, the doctor's relationship with Harvey is brought about by heavy drinking. In Dr. Chumley's past, Chase hints at the same sort of personal mysteries that are vaguely insinuated with Elwood. Most telling is his fantasy about what he would do if Harvey overcame time and space and objection for him. He has a particular place in mind, a cottage camp outside of Akron, Ohio—it isn't a common vision of paradise, but it is his own. He has a woman in mind, one who

> "IT MAY NOT BE CLEAR WHY HARVEY, THE MAGICAL CREATURE, APPEARS TO HIM, ASIDE FROM HIS GREAT, CHILD-LIKE SINCERITY, BUT IT IS CLEAR THAT HAVING A GIANT RABBIT HAS BEEN A TREMENDOUS BOOST TO ELWOOD'S SELF-ESTEEM."

would not know his name and would not speak, indicating that the pressure of his professional fame is a burden. She would feel sorry for his burdens and stroke his head in pity. And he would drink only beer, which is a weak alcoholic stimulant, instead of going for the powerful inebriation of strong liquor. Without any more telling background than his professional reputation, these strange, distinct facts paint a touchingly pathetic portrait of Dr. Chumley.

Dr. Chumley is at the center of one of the oddest mysteries in the play, one that nearly matches Elwood's new telephone number in terms of its obscurity. Describing his night out with Chumley, Elwood says that the distinguished psychiatrist began disturbing "a beautiful blonde woman—a Mrs. Smethills." The doctor claimed to have met her in Chicago, Elwood says, and her escort (conspicuously, he does not refer to the man as Mr. Smethills) issues an implied threat. Nothing more is made of Chicago or Mrs. Smethills or of their relationship. Like other loose ends in this play, the facts given serve to establish a mood, not to weave a web of reality.

Harvey is full of allusions that shoot out into space, not returning to connect with other points in the play. In another work, this would be a flaw, a sign that the playwright has not fulfilled her mission completely. She seems to have included such details at her own whim, not to complete an artistic design. Whimsy is what this play is all about, though. This is a play about mystery, though, not certainty; about magic, not scientific knowledge; about being pleasant, not smart. Something has to be left beyond the reach of reason, and the disjointed facts that Mary Chase weaves into this play serve to open its audience up to the wonders of possibility that could actually make a giant invisible rabbit exist.

A 1970 playbill cover for Harvey *featuring actors Helen Hayes and Jimmy Stewart, who starred in the Anta Theatre's 1970 production of the Pulitzer Prize-winning play.*

Source: David Kelly, in an essay for *Drama for Students*, Gale Group, 2001.

Liz Brent

Brent has a Ph.D. in American culture, specializing in film studies, from the University of Michigan. She is a freelance writer and teaches courses in the history of American cinema. In the following essay, Brent discusses the theme of fantasy versus reality in Chase's play.

The classic comedy play *Harvey*, by Mary Ellen Chase, met with instant popularity on stage, and has remained, along with the movie adaptation, an audience favorite. The six-foot white rabbit who accompanies the wealthy, amiable drunk, Elwood Dowd, has become a staple of American culture, referred to by Stanley Richards as "part of our theatrical folklore." The presence of Harvey is a focal point of the play's central thematic concern with the realm of dreams and the imagination versus the realm of facts and reality. The element of fantasy, and the question of reality, which hovers around the "character" of Harvey, is in part indicated by the differing interpretations offered by critics in regard to Harvey's existence. Richards points out that critics interpreted the existence of Harvey in a variety of ways: "some critics referred to Harvey as an invisible rabbit; others as a rabbit seen only by Elwood; and still others, as an imaginary rabbit." The fact that Harvey is never seen by the audience is important to the effect of the play in maintaining the ambiguity of Harvey's existence. Interestingly, Chase originally included a scene in Act II in which the giant white rabbit actually appears on stage, but was persuaded to rewrite it so that Harvey remains invisible to the audience throughout the performance. Richards describes the last-minute change in staging of this scene:

> Since the stage directions specifically stated that Harvey crosses the stage and enters Dr. Chumley's office, an actor garbed in a rabbit's costume played the scene, somewhat to the detriment of the fantasy. Finally, producer Brock Pemberton convinced the author that the rabbit should not be visible to the audience, strengthening the theory that even literal-minded playgoers might accept the idea that Elwood could persuade others to believe in his pooka. In the New York production, the effect of Harvey's crossing the stage was attained by having a door open, followed by a pause of about eight seconds, then having the opposite door to Dr. Chumley's office open. It became one of the play's more memorable moments.

The decision to maintain Harvey's status as invisible is key to developing the theme of fantasy versus reality in the play. Harvey, clearly, represents the realm of dreams and fantasy, as he is invisible only to those who are dead set on living only in the world of facts and reality. Throughout the play, Harvey's effect on people—those who actually see him or who are otherwise affected by his presence—is to free them from the bind of facts and reality and to release them into the world of their own imagination. Harvey certainly has this effect on Elwood, who sees him all the time, but also on Dr. Chumley, Dr. Sanderson, Kelly, and even Veta.

Harvey represents the realm of the imagination, dreams, hopes, art, poetry, love, and romance, as opposed to the realm of reality, facts, and science. Elwood clearly values the realm of the imagination above the realm of reality. When Dr. Sanderson tells Elwood that "We all have to face reality . . . sooner or later," Elwood responds that "I wrestled with reality for forty years, and I am happy to state that I finally won out over it." Elwood's ability to see Harvey represents the triumph of his imagination over reality. Elwood and Harvey are also associated with the realm of the imagination as expressed through art and poetry. They are associated with art through the oil painting of the two of them together, which Elwood brings home and places on the mantle piece. This painting later becomes the basis of a discussion on the importance of "dreams" in art (discussed below). Elwood is also associated with the imaginative realm of poetry when he recites a line from Ovid's "Fifth Elegy" to Miss Kelly, "'Diviner grace has never brightened this enchanting face!'" Elwood comments that "Ovid has always been my favorite poet."

Because the audience is not acquainted with Elwood before the arrival of Harvey in his life, one cannot say definitely in what ways the giant white rabbit affected him. However, since Elwood is closely associated with Harvey, it is fair to speculate that Elwood's character represents Harvey's potential effect on other people as well. While Elwood's family sees Harvey as an embarrassment, and others who are introduced to Harvey generally respond to Elwood with something like "horrified fascination," the audience is presented with the character of Elwood as extremely amiable and friendly. Harvey thus seems to bring out in Elwood an openness and warmth toward other people, which dispenses with the usual social barriers of propriety. Elwood responds to everyone he encounters with an immediate offer of warmth, friendship, and companionship, always offering his "card" with the expression, "If you should want to call me—." Elwood even does his best to make friends with someone, who he believes has mistakenly called the wrong number, over the telephone. In Act I, while he is in the library, a phone solicitor calls with the intention of selling membership to a club along with several magazine subscriptions. Elwood responds with, "Oh, you've got the wrong number. But how are you, anyway?" After agreeing to order several subscriptions, Elwood addresses the person on the other end with affection and an offer of friendship, telling her, "I hope I will have the pleasure of meeting you some time, my dear." Furthermore, Elwood's expressions of friendship to everyone he meets are not just kind words; he always makes a point of inviting everyone he meets to join him on a specific date. After the woman on the phone makes what would normally be an empty gesture of telling Elwood that she would like to meet him, he insists, "When? When would you like to meet me, Miss Greenawalt? Why not right now?" Elwood's warmth and openness toward others is in part what made it possible for him to "see" Harvey in the first place,

> WHEN DR. SANDERSON TELLS ELWOOD THAT 'WE ALL HAVE TO FACE REALITY . . . SOONER OR LATER,' ELWOOD RESPONDS THAT 'I WRESTLED WITH REALITY FOR FORTY YEARS, AND I AM HAPPY TO STATE THAT I FINALLY WON OUT OVER IT.'"

as well as to become his "best friend." Harvey thus represents this approach to social interaction, which values relationships with other people above all else.

To some extent, the power of the imagination of any individual character in the play is proven by his or her ability to "see" Harvey. Those who are in touch with their own imagination can see Harvey, while those who are cut off from their imagination cannot. In addition, a whole cluster of values is associated with this power of imagination. Elwood, or course, represents the character in the play with the strongest imagination. This quality makes him the most likable character in the play. He is warm, kind, and generous to everyone, only seeing the best in them, even if they are rude or unpleasant to him; he considers everyone his friend and treats them as such. Elwood's sense of imagination is further associated with the ability to dream, with the creative element of the imagination, such as painting and poetry, and even with the capacity for love and romance. At Chumley's Rest sanitarium, Elwood encounters the young Dr. Sanderson and his nurse assistant, Miss Kelly. Miss Kelly is clearly in love with Dr. Sanderson, but Dr. Sanderson fails to "see" her in this light. The cluster of values that oppose the imagination are that of reality, facts, and science. Dr. Sanderson, a psychiatrist, is so preoccupied with the realm of the science of psychology that he fails to use his imagination in his relationship to Miss Kelly. The influence of Elwood, and, by association, Harvey, on Dr. Sanderson is to open his eyes to the potential romance between himself and Miss Kelly. Because Elwood has a strong sense of imagination, he immediately notices and attends to Kelly's feminine charms—but only in a very gentlemanly way. When he enters the waiting room at Chumley's Rest, and Kelly offers him a magazine to look at, he responds that "I would much rather look at you, Miss Kelly, if you don't mind. You really are very lovely." Referring to Dr. Sanderson, Kelly responds that "Some people don't seem to think so." Elwood then comments that "Some people are blind. That is often brought to my attention." Clearly, Elwood is referring to the fact that "some," if not most, people fail to "see" Harvey. He is also indicating that many people lack the imaginative powers to "see" the finer things in life, such as love and romance. Elwood's imaginative powers, particularly in the realm of love and romance, lead him so far as to misinterpret what Kelly and Dr. Sanderson are talking about, to the extent that he thinks they are referring to a romantic encounter that he believes has already occurred between the two of them. In fact, they are attempting to apologize for accidentally committing Elwood to the sanitarium, when they believe they were supposed to have committed his sister, Veta. Miss Kelly and Dr. Sanderson, however, do not even realize that Elwood is interpreting the situation in romantic terms:

> Sanderson: . . . Miss Kelly and I have made a mistake here this afternoon, Mr. Dowd, and we'd like to explain it to you. Kelly: It wasn't Doctor Sanderson's fault, Mr. Dowd. It was mine. Sanderson: A human failing—as I said. Elwood: I find it very interesting, nevertheless. You and Miss Kelly here? [They nod] This afternoon—you say? [They nod. Elwood gives Harvey a knowing look] Kelly: We do hope you'll understand, Mr. Dowd. Elwood: Oh yes. Yes. These things are often the basis of a long and warm friendship.

Although at this point, though Elwood's perception is a misunderstanding, it demonstrates his insight into their true feelings toward each other. In Act III, Elwood finally has the effect of opening Dr. Sanderson's eyes to his love for Kelly and to her love for him.

Dr. Chumley, the head psychiatrist of Chumley's Rest, while representing the pinnacle of a scientific mind, eventually finds that he, too, sees Harvey. Being able to see Harvey allows Dr. Chumley to get in touch with his imagination in terms of his dreams and fantasies. When this happens, Dr. Chumley regards Harvey as a "miracle." He tells Myrtle, "I've been spending my life among fly-specks while miracles have been leaning on lampposts on Eighteenth and Fairfax," where Elwood first met Harvey. Dr. Chumley later learns from Elwood that Harvey can indeed make it possible for people to live out their own dreams and fantasies. Elwood explains that Harvey has the capacity to "stop clocks," and allow people to "go away as long as you like with whomever you like and go as far as you like." Dr. Chumley then describes to Elwood his fantasy dream of drinking a cold beer under a tree in Akron, Ohio, with a strange young woman, "Cold beer at Akron and one last fling!" Seeing Harvey thus allows Dr. Chumley access to his own imagination, which brings forth dreams and fantasies which have been denied by his scientific grip on reality. Dr. Chumley even attempts to steal Harvey away from Elwood, hoping that Harvey will allow him to live out this fantasy.

Until Dr. Chumley finally sees Harvey, Veta is the only other character in the play, besides Elwood, who does so. Veta, however, only sees Harvey occasionally. This suggests that she has a potentially strong sense of imagination, but that she does her best to cling to "reality" in denying to others the existence of Harvey. Veta's ultimate belief in Harvey, and thus in the importance of the realm of the imagination, is expressed at two key points in the play. In fact, Veta most clearly expresses the significance of Harvey to the meaning of the play. She does this during a conversation with Dr. Chumley, after he has just seen the oil painting portrait of Elwood with Harvey. During this exchange, Veta's back is turned to the portrait, which she has not yet seen. And yet, she inadvertently expresses the significance of Harvey's image in the portrait:

> I took a course in art this last winter. The difference between a fine oil painting and a mechanical thing like a photograph is simply this: a photograph shows only the reality; a painting shows not only the reality but the dream behind it—. It's our dreams that keep us going. That separate us from the beasts. I wouldn't even want to live if I thought it was all just eating and sleeping and taking off my clothes. Well—putting them on again—

The portrait of Elwood with Harvey expresses exactly what Veta has been describing: the "dream" (represented by Harvey) behind the "reality" (represented by Elwood). In the painting, Harvey literally stands behind Elwood, who sits in a chair. Despite this insight, however, Veta continues to deny Harvey's presence in talking to others; her problem is thus not a lack of imagination, but being overly concerned with what other people would think of her if she admitted that she, too, sees Harvey at times.

In the final scene of the play, Veta, Myrtle, the Judge, Dr. Sanderson, and Dr. Chumley prepare to inject Elwood with "formula 977," in order to restore him back to reality. Again, Elwood's imaginative abilities to see Harvey are contrasted with such dull aspects of reality as "responsibilities" and "duties." The Judge tells Elwood that, once given the injection, "you won't see this rabbit any more." And Sanderson adds, "But you will see your responsibilities, your duties—" Elwood, however, replies that he "wouldn't care for it." Nonetheless, Veta decides to go ahead with the injection. The cab driver, however, explains to them the effect of "formula 977," which is, essentially, to remove any sense of imagination, leaving people with only a dull and unpleasant grip on "reality." The cab driver explains that, on the way to the sanitarium, before receiving the injection, "they sit back and enjoy the ride. They talk to me. Sometimes we stop and watch the sunsets and look at the birds flyin'. Sometimes we stop and watch the birds when there ain't no birds and look at the sunsets when it's rainin'. We have a swell time." The cab driver goes on to explain that, after receiving the injection, these people become fixated on reality and no longer enjoy life; they "crab, crab, crab. They yell at me to watch the lights, watch the brakes, watch the intersections. They scream at me to hurry. . . . It's no fun." The cab driver concludes that, after receiving the injection, Elwood will be "a perfectly normal human being and you know what bastards they are!" At this point Veta, who has been ashamed of Elwood's insistence on Harvey's existence, realizes that Harvey represents what she likes most about her brother, and other people: their capacity to be imaginative. She concludes that she doesn't want Elwood to be given the injection and forced to exist only in the realm of reality, because "I don't want Elwood that way. I don't like people like that."

Source: Liz Brent, in an essay for *Drama for Students,* Gale Group, 2001.

Kirsten Herold

Herold has a Ph.D. and specializes in the history of dramatic literature. In the following essay, Herold discusses how Mary Chase's Harvey *recycles familiar comic elements, drawing in particular on the ideas of Northrop Frye.*

For a four year old boy to have an invisible friend is nothing extraordinary. However, when the "boy" is a forty-seven year old alcoholic bachelor with a horrified set of relatives, comedy ensues. This simple formula is complicated when other supposedly sane characters also admit to occasionally seeing the invisible friend, a six-foot white rabbit named Harvey. By the end of the play, the question is, who is better off, the sane but anxious Myrtle May or the deluded, pleasant, gentle Elwood? A big audience success, recipient of the prestigious Pulitzer Prize, and mostly glowing reviews, *Harvey* baffles the careful reader by somehow working, in spite of its flimsy premise, creaky construction, and poorly sketched minor characters. Indeed, as Kappo Phelan complained in *Commonweal,* the play could clearly have used another careful revision. Still, more than fifty years later, the play remains popular in amateur and summer stock productions. After all, as one recent review suggests, the central question of the play, "just what is 'normal,' anyway? [*Harvey*] resonates even more with audiences today than it did when the show was new" (Craig).

Written in 1944 during the dark years of World War II, Mary Chase's *Harvey* was intended as pure escapist entertainment, with no deeper meaning whatsoever. The literary student will search in vain for Freudian symbols or profound socio-historic significance. However, like all top-notch comedies (Shakespeare's *A Midsummer Night's Dream* or Oscar Wilde's *The Importance of Being Earnest* come to mind), the play pokes fun at social mores as well as manages to raise important questions about the nature of perception and reality. In fact, one way to explain the success of the play is that it adheres to conventions as old as comedy itself.

In the words of literary critic Harry Levin, all "comedy recycles the oldest devices." Whether a cartoon, a TV sitcom, a comic novel, or a dramatic entertainment, comedy uses elements as old as the form itself. Character types such as foolish parents, young lovers, braggarts, or clever servants are first found in the comedy of ancient Greece and Rome and have survived to the present day. Psychiatrists like Dr. Chumley, who turn out to be as crazy as their patients, may be a more recent invention, but they are as familiar to any fan of *New Yorker* cartoons as are the ancient characters. Comic targets like pomposity, self-importance, and hype are equally common in the plays of fourth century B.C. Greek dramatist Aristophanes or this week's episode of *Saturday Night Live.* Plots and deeper structures have also remained the same. *Harvey* is part of that tradition, and a knowledge of the traditional elements of comedy will enhance the reader's understanding of this play's enduring popularity.

Certainly, the play has many aspects familiar to students of comedy, in drama and fiction alike. The efforts of the mother, Mrs. Veta Louise Simmons, to introduce her unpromising, plain, and acerbic daugh-

> *HARVEY*, LIKE ALL COMEDY, IS A CELEBRATION OF PLEASURE: A VICTORY OF LOVE OVER DUTY, FREEDOM OVER RESTRICTIONS, FELLOWSHIP OVER HARD WORK, COMMUNITY OVER ISOLATION."

ter, Myrtle Mae, into polite society with marriage as the final goal, are familiar from such works as Austen's *Pride and Prejudice*. In fact, early on, Myrtle Mae is shaping up to be the heroine familiar from countless romantic comedies, whose ability to marry is blocked by the opposing patriarchal force of her uncle Elwood, who controls the family home and fortune. However, this formula is quickly reversed since Myrtle quickly turns out not to be the heroine at all but instead the blocking force. In her single-minded anxiety to marry—anyone, at any cost—she becomes absurd, as she tries to force her family into line with her obsession and evict her uncle, whom she despises, from his own house. Veta Louise, on the other hand, is equally horrified but also genuinely fond of her gentle brother. Thus, this play cleverly reverses the comic cliché that parents are the conservative proponents of law and order and the children the rebellious advocates of freedom. Here, the older characters are far more tolerant and able to entertain ambiguity than the young, self-righteous characters such as Myrtle Mae, Kelly, and Doctor Sanderson.

The play also pokes some familiar fun at the so-called high society (at least in its own estimation) of the unnamed western city (presumably Chase's Denver) in which they live. To meet eligible young men, Myrtle Mae has to sit demurely through tedious afternoons with old ladies, in hopes of an eventual introduction to their grandsons. In the meantime, she is of course quite capable of looking out for herself, as the reader sees when she quickly hitches up with the socially unsuitable Wilson, the big burly ''black-browned'' hospital attendant.

The comedy involved in the mistaken identity at the sanitarium, where Doctor Sanderson mistakes Veta Louise for the patient, is also a comic staple, dating back as far as the Latin New Comedy of Terence and Plautus (first century A.D.). Shakespeare also used the trope, for instance in *A Comedy of Errors, A Midsummer Night's Dream,* and *Twelfth Night*. In *Harvey,* the comedy arises in part from Dr. Sanderson's distracted interest in the pretty young nurse, which renders his judgment less than professional. Moreover, Veta hilariously mistakes the staff at the sanitarium for white slavers. Adding to the confusion is the inversion of gender roles. In *Twelfth Night,* Shakespeare's heroine, Viola, disguises herself as a young man, promptly falls in love with her boss (the Count Orsino), who thinks he loves Olivia, a young woman who fancies herself in love with the disguised Viola. As Viola sighs, ''O time, thou must untangle this, not I / It is too hard a knot for me to untie.'' In *Harvey,* Veta and Myrtle take on many stereotypically masculine attributes, active and busy, while Elwood is extremely feminized—passive, gentle, and reactive. ''My sister did all that [attempted to get Elwood committed] in one afternoon,'' he says wonderingly. ''Veta is certainly a whirlwind.'' Of course, the joke is that by the end of the play, Elwood's way wins out.

The typical comic plot is that it moves from conflict to harmony, from a state of disorder to order. However, to arrive at this order, the middle of the comedy is usually characterized by disorder in a world where all normal values have gone topsy-turvy. As critic Northrop Frye has pointed out, in Shakespearean comedy, such as *As You Like It* and *A Midsummer Night's Dream,* the increased disorder is accompanied by a move from civilized society into a so-called ''green world,'' often quite literally a forest. Here the repressive rules of normal society are relaxed, often through magic, and in the end, after much confusion, the protagonists return strengthened to a redeemed society. A similar pattern occurs in *Harvey,* which moves from the repressive world of Denver high society, to the topsy-turvy world of the insane asylum (with some off-stage visits to a few local bars), and then, much improved, back to normal society. Decency and propriety have been defeated; ''To hell with decency,'' says Dr. Chumley, ''I've got to have that rabbit!'' Moreover, the young lovers have been united, Myrtle Mae has found a man, and Veta and Dr. Chumley have admitted to their own need for an invisible friend like Harvey.

So what exactly is Harvey the rabbit supposed to signify? Apparently as accommodating as his friend Elwood, he is the perfect friend for lonely hearts everywhere. Moreover, he welcomes pleasure, as he appears to spend most of his time partying. He is also a trickster figure who vanishes and reappears as he sees fit. In fact, he is a clear descendant of the vice figure familiar from medieval and Renaissance drama, such as Falstaff, Puck, and Ariel—the latter two are also invisible. Yet in spite of the name, the Vice figure is usually reasonably good-natured, his tricks and mischief rarely cause real harm. Indeed, by the end of the play, those characters who can admit to their need for Harvey's company appear far better off than those who continue to deny him.

Thus, *Harvey*, like all comedy, is a celebration of pleasure: a victory of love over duty, freedom over restrictions, fellowship over hard work, community over isolation. City comedies of the Renaissance typically end with a feast, everyone going off to have dinner together. Likewise, Elwood is always inviting near strangers over for dinner. Characters who refuse to join in the good cheer, like Shakespeare's Malvolio or the judge in *Harvey*, are banished from the conclusion. In the final scene of the play, this theme is sounded repeatedly. Veta decides to obey her instincts and not have Elwood admitted to the asylum after the cab driver tells her that after treatment, the patients become "perfectly normal human being[s] and you know what bastards they are!" When they are still insane, they "sit back and enjoy the ride. They talk to me. . . . We have a swell time and I always get a big tip. But afterward—oh—oh. . . . They crab, crab, crab. . . . They scream at me to hurry." Moreover, thanks to Elwood's intervention, the two young lovers are united, with Miss Kelly telling Elwood, "I will never feel happier, I know it." Perhaps Elwood himself states the theme of pleasure most clearly when he recalls his mother's advice: "'In this world, Elwood, you must be oh, so smart or oh, so pleasant'. For years I was smart. I recommend pleasant. You may quote me."

Thus, the "meaning" of *Harvey* is its absence of meaning, its pretense that those who enjoy themselves and live in the moment are better off than the rest of the people who insist on taking life terribly seriously. One can certainly understand why this was a welcome message in 1944, and why it would still seem to resonate today.

Source: Kirsten Herold, in an essay for *Drama For Students*, Gale Group, 2001.

SOURCES

Craig, Pat, "Onstage Has a Good Hare Day," in *Contra Costa Times,* January 25, 2000, p. E04.

Frye, Northrop, *Anatomy of Criticism,* Princeton University Press, 1957, pp. 163–86.

Kronenberger, Louis, Review of *Harvey* in *PM,* November 2, 1944.

Levin, Harry, *Playboys [and] Killjoys,* Oxford University Press, 1987, p. 19.

Mr. Showbiz, http://www.mrshowbiz.go.com/reviews/moviereviews/movies/Harvey_1950.html (May 24, 2000).

Phelan, Kappo, "The Stage and the Screen," in *Commonweal,* Vol. 41, No. 5, November 17, 1944, p. 123.

Rhodes, Russell, in *Rob Wagner's Script,* Vol. 30, No. 694, December 16, 1944, p. 24.

Richards, Stanley, *The Most Popular Plays of the American Theatre: Ten of Broadway's Longest Running Plays,* Stein [and] Day, 1979, p. 226.

Toohey, John L., *A History of the Pulitzer Prize Plays,* The Citadel Press, 1967, pp. 199–200.

FURTHER READING

Erikson, Erik H., *Toys and Reason: Stages in the Ritualization of Experience,* W. W. Norton [and] Co., 1977.
Erikson, a world-renown psychiatrist, looks at the importance of play to the psyche. His thesis that play is a way of buffering the contact of the self with the reality of the social world might explain Elwood P. Dowd's behavior.

Frommer, Myrna Katz, and Harvey Frommer, *It Happened on Broadway: An Oral History of the Great White Way,* Harcourt Brace, 1998.
The history of the Broadway stage at the height of its greatness is told by actors, authors, producers, and others who have worked there.

Shipley, Joseph T., *The Crown Guide to the World's Best Plays,* Crown Publishers, Inc., 1986, .
A brief overview (pp. 141–2) of how *Harvey* was received when it was first produced and of its cultural significance, along with a list of revivals through the 1980s.

Simon, Neil, *Rewrites,* Touchstone Books, 1998.
More than any other contemporary playwright, Simon comes close to capturing the humorous spirit of Chase's writing. In his acclaimed autobiography he relates some of the background that is involved in mounting a comedy on Broadway.

Indian Ink

TOM STOPPARD

1994

Tom Stoppard is a leading British playwright of the twentieth century. His two-act play *Indian Ink* (1994) is based on his earlier radio play *In the Native State* and was first performed in London in 1995.

Indian Ink takes place in two different locations and time periods: India in 1930, during the struggle for national independence from British colonial rule, and England in the mid-1980s. The action shifts back and forth between these two settings without major set changes or clearly indicated transitions. The action in India concerns Flora Crewe, a British poetess, whose portrait is being painted by an amateur Indian artist. The action in England concerns the efforts of a scholar of Flora Crewe's work to gather information for a biography. Flora's surviving younger sister, Mrs. Swan, is visited first by this English scholar, and then by the son of the Indian artist. The central enigma is the question of whether or not the Indian artist painted a nude portrait of Flora, and whether or not the two had an "erotic relationship."

This play is concerned primarily with the historical and cultural struggles in India to gain independence from British Imperial rule. Indian and English characters discuss their differing perspectives on the history and meaning of British colonization of India. The play addresses themes of Empire, cultural imperialism, and nationalism.

AUTHOR BIOGRAPHY

Tom Stoppard was born Tomas Straussler, on July 3, 1937, in Zlin, Czechoslovakia (now the Czech Republic). He was the second son of Eugene and Martha Straussler. His father was a company physician for a Czech shoe manufacturer, which relocated the family to Singapore in 1939. Just before the Japanese invasion of Singapore, Tom was evacuated with his mother and older brother to Darjeeling, India. His father, who stayed behind, was killed in 1941, after the invasion. In 1946, Tom's mother married Major Kenneth Stoppard, a British army officer who was stationed in India. The family relocated to England, where Kenneth worked in the machine-tool business. After several moves throughout England, the Stoppards settled in Bristol in 1950, during which time Tom attended Dolphin preparatory school in Nottinghamshire, and then Pocklington School in Yorkshire. In 1954, when he was seventeen years old, Stoppard quit school to work for the *Western Daily Press,* a Bristol newspaper. After four years at the *Western Daily Press,* Stoppard worked as a reporter for the *Evening World,* another Bristol newspaper, from 1958 to 1960. In 1960, he moved to London, where he worked as a freelance reporter until 1963. During this time, Stoppard began writing plays, and was commissioned to write several radio and television dramas.

In 1966, his first major play, *Rosencrantz and Guildenstern are Dead,* was performed in England, garnering immediate critical acclaim and audience popularity. In 1968, he received a Tony Award and a New York Drama Critics Circle Award for best new play for *Rosencrantz and Guildenstern are Dead.* Stoppard has continued to be a leading playwright, and has since written numerous stage plays, radio and television dramas, and screenplays. In 1991, he wrote and directed the film version of *Rosencrantz and Guildenstern are Dead.* In 1965, Stoppard married Jose Ingle, with whom he has two children, Oliver, and Barnaby, and from whom he was divorced in 1972. In 1972, he married Miriam Moore-Robinson, with whom he has two sons.

Tom Stoppard

PLOT SUMMARY

Act I

In Act I, the British poetess Flora Crewe arrives in Jummapur, India, in 1930, and is greeted at the train station by Coomaraswami, the president of the local Theosophical Society. Flora is taken to stay at a guesthouse complete with a veranda and an Indian servant, Nazrul. Flora's experiences in India are narrated as a series of letters written by her to her sister Eleanor Swan, in England. Mrs. Swan sits in her garden over tea and cake in the mid-1980s with Eldon Pike, a scholar of Flora Crewe's poetry and editor of the *Collected Letters of Flora Crewe,* who is gathering information for a biography. After Flora gives a talk and answers questions for the Theosophical Society, she meets Nirad Das, an amateur artist who asks to paint her portrait while she writes. As Das paints her portrait, Flora writes poetry and letters, and the two begin to discuss the struggle of Indians to gain national independence from British colonial rule. In the 1980s setting in England, Das's son Anish Das has come to visit Mrs. Swan in her garden over tea and cake to discuss his father's portrait of Flora, which he recognized from the book cover of the *Collected Letters of Flora Crewe.* Mrs. Swan and Anish come into some conflict in discussing their differing perspectives on British colonization of India, but they remain polite and respectful of one another. In India in the 1930 setting, David Durance, a British official in the colonial government, rides up to Flora's guest house on a horse and asks her to join him at his Club.

In a 1980s setting in India, Pike arrives at the hotel where Flora had stayed, to gather more information for his biography. In the 1930s setting in India, Flora and Das continue to discuss art, politics, and culture, while Flora sits for the portrait Das is painting. One day, overcome by the heat, Flora goes into her bedroom, takes off her clothes, and gets into bed nude, covered only by a sheet. She asks Das, who is embarrassed by her nudity, to sit by her in a chair in her bedroom.

Act II

In Act II, in the 1930 India setting, Flora attends a dance at the Jummapur Cricket Club with Durance, and the two discuss the politics of British colonial rule over India. Their discussion continues as they go horseback riding together; Durance then asks Flora to marry him and she refuses. In the same setting, but in the 1980s, Dilip, an Indian man who brings him information about Flora from various sources, aids Pike. In the 1930 setting in India, the Rajah invites Flora to admire his vast collection of automobiles. The Raja then offers to make Flora a gift of a painting. In the 1980s setting in India, Pike is introduced to the grandson of the Rajah, also referred to as Rajah. The Rajah shows Pike a thank-you note from Flora for his grandfather's gift of a classic Indian nude painting. In the 1980s setting, in Mrs. Swan's garden, Anish looks at the watercolor nude from the Rajah, which Mrs. Swan has shown him, while Mrs. Swan looks at the watercolor nude of Flora, painted by Das, which Anish has shown her. In the 1930 India setting, Flora returns from the dance with Durance to learn from Das that the Theosophical Society has been suspended due to the political unrest and riots. Before leaving, Das shows Flora the miniature watercolor nude he has painted of her. In the 1980s England setting, Mrs. Swan sees Anish off, and they both agree not to tell Pike about the nude portrait of Flora painted by Das. In another flashback to India, Mrs. Swan (Nell) arrives at Flora's graveside, aided by Eric, an Englishman (whom Nell later marries).

CHARACTERS

Coomaraswami

Coomaraswami is the president of the Theosophical Society in Jummapur, India. He greets Flora upon her arrival at the train station in 1930.

Flora Crewe

Flora Crewe is an English poetess who travels by herself to India in April 1930, presumably for her health, to live and write. In India, she encounters Nirad Das, an amateur artist who paints her portrait while she writes. Flora learns from Das about the struggle among Indians for independence from British colonization. Flora's interactions with Das take on an erotic tone when, one day, overcome by the heat, she lies naked in her bed while talking to him. While in India, Flora is also courted by the British official, David Durance. Flora dies and is buried in India in June, 1930. Over fifty years later, in the mid-1980s, the scholar Eldon Pike, who has published *The Collected Letters of Flora Crewe,* is collecting information for a biography he plans to write about her. Pike attempts to determine whether or not Flora had a ''relationship'' with Das, and whether or not a nude painting of Flora by Das actually existed. After Das's death, Nirad Das, his son, finds the nude watercolor miniature in a trunk of his father's belongings.

Anish Das

Anish Das is the son of Nirad Das. In the mid-1980s, Anish visits the home of Mrs. Swan, Flora's sister, in England, to learn more about his father's portrait of Flora. Anish had seen the reproduction on the cover the of *Collected Letters of Flora Crewe,* and recognized the style as his father's. Anish tells Mrs. Swan that, after his father's death, he had found a watercolor nude portrait of a European woman, who turns out to be Flora Crewe.

Nirad Das

Nirad Das is an Indian man who first meets Flora after her lecture to the Theosophical Society in India, in 1930. Das is an amateur painter and asks to paint a portrait of Flora as she sits writing her poetry. During these painting sessions, Das and Flora discuss the politics of Indian colonization by the British Empire. Das is at first overly polite and subservient to Flora, but she encourages him to be his ''Indian'' self in her presence, and speak to her more naturally. During one painting session, Flora, overcome by the heat, ends up lying naked in bed under a sheet while Das sits uncomfortably in her bedroom. Over fifty years later, it is discovered that Das did, indeed, paint a watercolor miniature nude portrait of Flora, in addition to the portrait which appears on the cover of the published *Collected Letters of Flora Crewe.* In 1930, Das was arrested for throwing a mango during a riot in protest of

British rule over India. After his death, Anish Das, Das's son, discovers the nude portrait among his father's belongings.

Dilip

Dilip is an Indian man who attends to Pike at the hotel in India, and helps him track down information about Flora.

David Durance

David Durance is a British official in India who briefly courts Flora. He asks her to marry him, but she refuses, and it is unclear whether she chose to have an affair with him.

Nazrul

Nazrul is the servant at the home in India where Flora stays.

Eldon Pike

Eldon Pike is a scholar of Flora Crewe. He has edited the *Collected Letters of Flora Crewe* and, in the mid-1980s, is gathering research for a biography of Flora. As part of his research, Pike first visits Eleanor Swan, Flora's younger sister, and then the hotel in India where Flora stayed. Pike, while well intentioned, is thoroughly absorbed in his scholarly perspective on Flora; he continually cites facts about her life, and persistently attempts to ascertain the truth about Flora. Pike is especially interested in tracking down various paintings of Flora by various artists, famous and unknown. He is also especially interested in determining whether or not Flora had a ''relationship'' with Das, and whether or not she posed for a nude portrait by the amateur Indian painter.

Eleanor Swan

Eleanor Swan is Flora's younger sister. In the mid-1980s, Pike, who is gathering information for a biography of Flora, visits her at her home in England. She is then visited by Anish Das, the son of Nirad Das, who wishes to learn more about his father's painting of Flora. Eleanor, called Nell in her younger years, continually offers tea and cakes to her guests. She is skeptical about the value of Pike's research on her sister, but is more receptive to Anish. After Flora's death, Eleanor had traveled to India to visit her sister's grave, where she met Eric, whom she subsequently married (but who is deceased during the ''present'' time of the action).

MEDIA ADAPTATIONS

- *Indian Ink* is adapted from Stoppard's original radio play *In the Native State*, which was broadcast by the BBC in 1991.

THEMES

Empire

Perhaps the central theme of Stoppard's play is the historical, social, and cultural significance of the British Empire. Half of the play is set in India in 1930, during a period of social unrest among Indians struggling for national independence from British colonial rule. Much of the play involves two characters, one Indian, one British, in dialogue over the issue of India as a British colony. For instance, the Indian characters refer to the ''First War of Independence,'' of 1847, an historical event that the English characters know as the ''Mutiny.'' Various English characters represent different English attitudes about the politics of India. Flora, the most open-minded English character in the play, is often very aware of her presence in India as a representative of British Imperial power; in a letter to her sister describing a sight-seeing tour during which she was escorted by Indian members of the Theosophical Society, Flora employs a wry sense of humor in describing her status in India: ''I felt like a carnival float representing Empire—or, depending how you look at it, the Subjugation of the Indian People.'' David Durance, a British government official in India, as well as his fellow members of the Jummapur Cricket Club, express arrogance and disdain for Indians, which is typical of imperialist attitudes toward the people they have colonized. For instance, in the opening lines of Act II, a member of the club named only as an ''Englishman'' praises

TOPICS FOR FURTHER STUDY

- This play takes place in the historical and cultural context of the Indian struggle for independence from British colonial rule, a struggle that dates back to the 1800s. Learn more about the history of Indian colonization by Britain and the struggle for national independence, which took place during the nineteenth and twentieth centuries. What were some of the key events in the history of this struggle?

- Stoppard has been compared to such notable playwrights as Oscar Wilde, George Bernard Shaw, Samuel Beckett, and Harold Pinter. Learn more about one of these great playwrights. What are his major works? How do critics characterize his dramatic style? Are his works associated with any particular school of dramatic style?

- Characters in Stoppard's play discuss classic works of Indian art, including paintings and sculpture. Learn more about the art history of India. In what ways has Indian art been influenced by religion? What have been the major trends in twentieth-century Indian art?

- Stoppard's characters mention several great European painters of the twentieth century, including Modigliani, Picasso, Matisse, and Derain. Learn more about the works of one of these artists. What style or school of painting is he associated with? What are some of the key elements of his artistic style? What are some of his major works?

- Indian characters in Stoppard's play attempt to explain elements of the Hindu religion to the European characters. Learn more about Hinduism. What are the central tenets and beliefs of Hinduism? What is the history of the Hindu religion?

---

the writer Kipling, who was known for his racist, pro-imperialist social, and political attitudes.

Cultural Imperialism

Cultural imperialism refers to the phenomenon by which, when one culture conquers and subjugates another, the indigenous culture is decimated, and the dominant culture is imposed upon the subjugated people. In the case of the British colonization of India, the British imposed, among other things, an English educational system upon the Indian population. Educated Indians subsequently became learned in English art and literature, perhaps more so than in the literary and artistic traditions of their own culture. In many exchanges between Flora and Das, Das expresses his love of English literature; Flora questions these values on the basis that he should take more pride in his own culture and less in that of the culture that subjugates him. In an exchange between Anish and Mrs. Swan, Mrs. Swan compares the colonization of India by Britain to the conquest of Britain by the Romans and subsequent imposition of Roman culture upon British culture. Anish, however, corrects this comparison, based on the argument that India was already a highly developed culture before the arrival of Europeans: "We *were* the Romans! We were up to date when you were a backward nation. The foreigners who invaded you found a third-world country! Even when you discovered India in the age of Shakespeare, we already had our Shakespeares. And our science—architecture—our literature and art, we had a culture older and more splendid, we were rich!" Anish ends with the assertion that Britain plundered Indian culture because of its wealth: "After all, that's why you came."

Nationalism

The sentiment that inspired Indians to struggle for national independence was one of strong "nationalism." This sentiment refers to the sense of pride in Indian culture, history, and national identity. The Indian characters in Stoppard's play exhibit various degrees of nationalist pride, and an attitude of rebellion against British imperialism. The Theosophical Society, of which Flora and Das are both members, was a significant influence in the development of Indian nationalist sentiment, because of the reverence theosophy holds for traditional Indian spiritual beliefs. Flora attempts to instill in Das a sense of nationalism during her discussions with him. She tells him, "If you don't start learning to take you'll never be shot of us.... It's your country and we've got it. Everything else is bosh." And Das does eventually engage in an act of nationalist rebellion when he is arrested for throwing a mango during an anti-British riot.

STYLE

Setting

The two historical and geographical settings in Stoppard's play are central to the meaning of the play. One of the settings is Jummapur, India, in 1930, during a time of active rebellion among Indian nationalists against British imperial powers. Parts of the play are also set in this exact same location, but over fifty years later, during the mid-1980s. Throughout the play, characters refer to significant events in the history of Indian nationalist struggles. The other setting is in the private garden of an English woman in London. Setting is central to the structure and staging of the play as well, since the two main historical/geographic sets are often juxtaposed almost simultaneously. The stage is set so that the play unfolds as a series of "flashbacks" from the 1980s to 1930. Dialogue and scenes between characters in the 1980s often leads in to, is juxtaposed against, or even interspersed with, dialogue and scenes between characters in 1930.

Dialogue

Stoppard employs a variety of dialogue techniques in this play. Each scene is based primarily on dialogue between two characters, one Indian, and one English: Flora and Das, Mrs. Swan and Anish, Pike and Dilip—as well as between the two English characters Pike and Mrs. Swan. Some of the dialogue, however, is presented as Mrs. Swan, in England in the 1980s, reads various letters Flora wrote her from India in 1930. For example, the play opens with Flora sitting on a train; Flora's words open the play, but they are presented on stage as the character of Flora quoting from her own letter to her sister, even though she is not shown actually writing the letter during this sequence. In a film, the quotation of a letter over the action of the character who has written the letter would be presented as a "voice-over." Stoppard uses clever staging techniques to achieve on the live stage an effect similar to that of the cinematic voice-over. In other scenes, a character's voice is actually prerecorded, and played over the action to create an effect closer to the cinematic voice-over. Stoppard also employs unique staging of dialogue during scenes in which characters in a 1980s setting seem to be in direct dialogue with characters in a "flashback" 1930 setting. In other scenes, the dialogue of Pike, the literary scholar who is researching Flora's stay in India, functions as a series of "footnotes" to the action in a flashback. In these scenes, the action and dialogue in a 1930 setting unfolds while Pike interjects with a series of facts or explanations about Flora's life that are meant to explain what is transpiring in the "flashback."

Allusions

Stoppard's characters make reference to many historically real literary and artistic figures and works of literature and art. The list of writers includes H. G. Wells, Virginia Woolf, George Bernard Shaw (*Pygmalion*), Robert Browning, Tennyson, Dickens (*Oliver Twist*), Macaulay (*Lays of Ancient Rome*), Agatha Christie (*The Mysterious Affair at Styles*), E. M. Forster (*A Passage to India*), Shakespeare, Chaucer, Rudyard Kipling ("Gunga Din"), Ovid, and Virgil. A familiarity with these writers and their works provides the reader with a deeper understanding of the significance of these references to central themes of Stoppard's play.

HISTORICAL CONTEXT

Colonization and Independence of India

Stoppard's play takes place during a period of intense struggle on the part of Indians to gain national independence from British Imperial rule. India was a colony of the British Empire for almost a century, from 1858–1947. The history of India during this period, therefore, is one of expansion of British power in conflict with organizations, protests, rebellion, and terrorist activism among the peoples of India. Before 1848, India had been colonized and ruled by the East India Company, but power was transferred to the British crown in 1858. In 1876, Queen Victoria of England took on the additional title of Empress of India. Rebellion on the part of the Indians against European colonization was waged off and on throughout India's history of colonization. However, the first nationally organized Indian effort at achieving independence was formed in 1885, with the first meeting of the Indian National Congress. Nevertheless, Britain continued to expand its region of power in the area. In 1886, the British conquered Burma, which it added to its Indian territory. In 1906, the British government instituted a series of reforms ostensibly to increase Indian political influence. With the advent of World War I in 1914, many Indians willingly fought on the side of the British, with the expectation that their loyalty in war would result in further concessions of British power to Indian self-rule; the disappointment of this expectation following the war only served to spark further protests. Throughout the inter-war years, Indian resistance to British rule continued, with the Indian National Congress inspired by the leadership of Gandhi. In 1947, when the British Parliament voted in the Indian Independence Act, British rule was finally ceded to Indian self-rule.

Religions in India

In Stoppard's play, the Indian characters attempt to explain elements of the Hindu religion to the British characters. Das explains to Flora some of the stories and mythology of Hinduism, as well as describing to her some of the classic Indian art that illustrates these stories. The major religions of India are Muslim and Hindu. During the years of protest against British rule, particularly in the inter-war period, Indians were internally divided in their political goals along these religious lines. Gandhi worked hard to unify the two religions in the cause for independence, but his efforts were ultimately unsuccessful. Thus, when the British ceded power in 1947, India was divided into two countries—Pakistan was to be Muslim, while India (to be called the Republic of India) would be Hindu. However, the process of instituting this national division was wracked by bloody civil war between Hindus and Muslims.

Languages of India

At various points in the play, Indian characters speak to one another in Hindi. At one point, an Indian character says something to a British character in Hindi, which he completely misunderstands. With the achievement of national independence in 1947, India officially recognized 14 different languages and dialects throughout the nation, but designated Hindi as the national language, while also maintaining English as the lingua franca for government transactions.

CRITICAL OVERVIEW

Stoppard is one of the leading playwrights of the twentieth century. Anne Wright, in the *Dictionary of Literary Biography,* asserts that Stoppard "ranks as a dramatist of brilliant and original comic genius." Wright succinctly captures the scope and success of his career as a dramatist, stating that "His first major success established him as a master of philosophical farce, combining dazzling theatricality and wit with a profound exploration of metaphysical concerns. His output through more than three decades has been extensive and varied, including original plays for radio and television, screenplays for television and film, adaptations and translations of works by European dramatists, several short stories, and a novel." Wright notes that Stoppard's plays "have been heralded as major events by both audiences and critics. He is now a playwright of international reputation in Europe and the United States.... His popularity extends to both the intellectual avant-garde and the ordinary theatergoer. Since the 1960s his work has developed in other areas, from absurdist or surrealist comedy to political and even polemical drama." Wright maintains that Stoppard's "career to date confirms his importance, not merely as a theatrical phenomenon, but as a major contemporary playwright."

The work for which he is best known and most widely celebrated is the play *Rosencrantz and Guildenstern are Dead* (1964–5), which was first performed at the Edinburgh Festival in 1966, and then by the British National Theater in 1967. Rosencrantz and Guildenstern are two minor characters from Shakespeare's *Hamlet* whom Stoppard develops as his central characters. An introduction to the printed version of the play explains its central themes and major stylistic elements: "*Rosencrantz and Guildenstern* depicts the absurdity of life through these two characters who have 'bit parts' in a play not of their own making and who are capable only of acting out their dramatic destiny. They are bewil-

Felicity Kendal (as Flora Crewe), Art Malik (as Nirad Das), and Dominic Jephcott (as David Durance) in a 1995 production of Indian Ink, *performed at London's Aldwych Theatre.*

dered by their predicament and face death as they search for the meaning of their existence. While examining these themes, Stoppard makes extensive use of puns and paradox, which have since become standard devices in his plays." Stoppard received several awards for *Rosencrantz and Guildenstern are Dead,* including best new play in 1967, the Antoinette Perry ("Tony") Award for best new play in 1968, and the New York Drama Critics Circle Award for best play in 1968, as well as the Grande Prize at the 1990 Venice Film Festival for the film *Rosencrantz and Guildenstern are Dead,* which Stoppard both adapted and directed.

Indian Ink (1995) was adapted by Stoppard from his original radio play, *In the Native State,* which was broadcast by the BBC in 1991. The play was first performed at the Yvonne Arnaud Theatre in Guildford, England, and then opened at the Aldwych Theatre in London in 1995.

Stoppard's other major plays include *Jumpers* (1972), *Travesties* (1974), *The Real Thing* (1982), and *Arcadia* (1994). Stoppard has also written several highly successful screenplays, such as *Brazil* (1985, co-written with Terry Gilliam), for which he received an Academy Award nomination and the Los Angeles Critics Circle Award for Best Original Screenplay. Subsequent screenplays include *Empire of the Sun* (1987, adapted from the novel by J. G. Ballard), *The Russia House* (1989, adapted from the novel by John le Carré), and *Billy Bathgate* (1991, adapted from the novel by E. L. Doctorow).

Stoppard also wrote the screenplay for the 1998 film *Shakespeare in Love,* which swept the Academy Awards, garnering seven Oscars, including Best Picture. *Shakespeare in Love* was directed by John Madden, and stars Gwenyth Paltrow, Joseph Fiennes, Geoffrey Rush, Ben Affleck, and Judi Dench.

CRITICISM

Liz Brent

Brent has a Ph.D. in American Culture, specializing in film studies, from the University of Michigan. She is a freelance writer and teaches courses in the history of American cinema. In the

WHAT DO I READ NEXT?

- *Rosencrantz and Guildenstern are Dead* (1966) by Tom Stoppard. This comedy is Stoppard's most celebrated play, based on two minor characters from Shakespeare's *Hamlet*.

- *Jumpers* (1972) by Tom Stoppard. Stoppard's most spectacular dramatic production, this play features a troupe of gymnastic philosophers, among other zany characters.

- *Arcadia* (1994) by Tom Stoppard. This Stoppard play is set simultaneously in three different time periods: 1809, 1812, and the present.

- *The Real Thing* (1982) by Tom Stoppard. This piece is one of Stoppard's most celebrated plays. It is structured as a play-within-a-play.

- *Travesties* (1974) by Tom Stoppard. This Tony Award-winning play takes place in Zurich in 1917, where three famous revolutionaries—the Marxist leader Lenin, the British writer James Joyce, and the dadaist poet Tristan Tzara all lived simultaneously.

- *Conversations with Stoppard* (1995) by Tom Stoppard. This text is a collection of interviews between Stoppard and *New York Times* critic Mel Gussow.

---

following essay, Brent discusses cultural and historical references in Stoppard's play.

Stoppard's 1994 play *Indian Ink,* set primarily in India in 1930 during a period of intense struggle between Indian nationalists and British imperialists, makes reference to several significant historical and cultural phenomena of India and England during this period. These references include the Indian uprising of 1857, the Theosophical Society, the Bloomsbury group, the English novelists E. M. Forster and Rudyard Kipling, and the Italian artist Amedeo Modigliani. A better understanding of these references will further illuminate significant themes of the play.

In Act I, Anish Das, a young Indian man educated and residing in England, is visiting with Mrs. Swan, an elderly English woman, in her garden. In the course of their conversation, Anish mentions "the first War of Independence," to which Mrs. Swan responds, "What war was that?" Anish replies, "The Rising of 1857," to which Mrs. Swan responds, "Oh, you mean the Mutiny." In Act II, a similar exchange occurs between Flora and the Rajah. He proudly informs her that "my grandfather stood firm with the British during the First Uprising." Flora, has no idea to what he is referring, until he mentions "1857," at which points she realizes he is talking about "The Mutiny." Although they refer to it in different terms, reflecting their differing political perspectives on Indian colonial history, they are both talking about what is now referred to as the "Mutiny" or the "Great Revolt" of 1857–9. This bitter rebellion of Indian troops and citizens against the British colonial forces occupying India started on May 10, 1857. The original source of discontent among Indian soldiers in the British army was over the grease used on rifle cartridges that soldiers were required to bite in order to open; the grease was made up of a mixture of pork and beef, which was prohibited by both Hindu and Muslim religious belief. But this initial protest took on greater implications as it became a struggle for Indian national independence and gained the support of many Indian citizens. This rebellion became an all-out military revolt, during which Indian troops took control of significant sectors of the country. The British, however, ultimately defeated the Indians on June 20 of 1859. The Indian and English characters in Stoppard's play represent the different historical perspectives on this event, the English regarding it as a "mutiny" against their sovereignty in the region, and the Indians considering it the "first War" in a century-long struggle for national independence.

In the opening scene of Stoppard's play, Flora Crewe, a British poet, is greeted at the train station by the president of the local Theosophical Society, to which she later gives a talk. In Act II, Flora learns that, due to riotous rebellion in the area, the local Theosophical Society has been "suspended," presumably for its political leanings. Theosophy is a religious philosophy based on "the mystical premise that God must be experienced directly in order to be known at all," according to the *Encyclopedia Britannica*. Theosophy became internationally popular in the nineteenth and twentieth centuries. Perhaps the most significant figure in the spread of Theosophy was Helena Blavatsky, who, along with Henry Steel Olcott, founded the Theosophical Society in New York in 1875. In 1878, they moved the center of the Society to India, from which their ideas spread throughout India and Europe. Blavatsky's most influential writings include the multi-volume publications *Unveiled* (1877) and *The Secret Doctrine* (1888). Theosophy draws extensively from many Eastern religions, but especially from Indian mystical thought. In Stoppard's play, the Indian man Dilip explains to the English scholar Pike that, "Madame Blavatsky was a famous name in India, she *was* the Theosophical Society." Theosophy became important in India as a means of establishing national pride and contributing to the nationalist sentiments, which in part inspired the struggle for Indian national independence.

During a conversation with Coomaraswami, Flora mentions "Bloomsbury." She is referring to the Bloomsbury group, an unofficial affiliation of writers, intellectuals, and artists who gathered regularly in private homes located in the Bloomsbury district of London, between 1907 and 1930. According to *Encyclopedia Britannica,* the Bloomsbury group's "significance lies in the extraordinary number of talented persons associated with it." Several famous writers of the Bloomsbury group, including Virginia Woolf and E. M. Forster (1879–1970), are mentioned in Stoppard's play. References to Forster are particularly significant, as he is known for his writings on India. In a conversation between Flora and Das, Flora compares Das to a character in Forster's famous novel *A Passage to India,* and later asks his opinion of the novel. Forster wrote *A Passage to India* after having visited India in 1912–13 and again in 1921. In addition, he wrote a nonfiction book, *The Hill of the Devi* (1953), about his experiences in India. Forster is also known for his novels *A Room with a View* (1907), *Howard's End* (1910), and *Maurice* (1971), which was published posthu-

> "REFERENCE TO MODIGLIANI AS A MASTER PAINTER OF THE NUDE FEMALE FORM IN STOPPARD'S PLAY IS SIGNIFICANT TO A CENTRAL MOTIF OF THE DRAMA, WHICH IS THE RELATIONSHIP BETWEEN FLORA AND DAS AS HE EVENTUALLY PAINTS A MINIATURE NUDE PORTRAIT OF HER."

mously. The reference to Forster is significant to Stoppard's play as it invokes the literary history of English colonial fiction set in India.

In the opening scene of Act II, Flora is attending a dance at the Jummapur Cricket Club, to which she has been invited by Durance. An Englishman mentions Kipling, and recites a quote from the author: "Kipling there's a poet! 'Though I've belted you and flayed you, by the living Gawd that made you, you're a better man than I am Gunga Din!'" This reference is significant to Stoppard's play because the world best knows Rudyard Kipling (1865–1936) for his pro-imperialist writings regarding the colonization of India. Kipling was born in Bombay, India, into a British family that sent the young Kipling to school in England during much of his childhood. In 1882, Kipling moved back to India, where he worked as a journalist for the next seven years. Shortly after his return to England in 1896, Kipling was hailed as a leading British writer, and in 1907 he was the first English writer to win the Nobel Prize for Literature. His notoriety increased with the publication *Barrack-Room Ballads,* which included the poem "Gunga Din." Kipling is perhaps best known for his children's stories, *Kim* (1901) and *The Jungle Books* (1894–5), which take place in India. Stoppard's play is clearly anti-imperialist in sentiment, and the praise of Kipling by a character identified only as an "Englishman" is meant to indicate the pro-imperialist stance of the members of the Jummapur Cricket Club. These English characters, particularly Durance, function as a counterpoint to the character of Flora, a radical thinker who, despite the fact that she is English, is a supporter of Indian nationalism and a critic of British imperialism.

Although Stoppard's character of Flora Crewe is fictional, a number of references are made throughout the play that indicate that she is personally acquainted with several internationally renowned artistic, literary, and intellectual figures of her day. Flora is perhaps most closely affiliated with the modern Italian painter and sculptor Amedeo Modigliani (1884–1920). Modigliani was born in Italy, of Jewish parents, but moved to Paris as a young man in 1906 to pursue the study of art. Although he is now known as one of the most important artists of the twentieth century, Modigliani was not recognized outside of his Parisian circle of artists until after his death. In Stoppard's play, it is mentioned that Flora posed for a nude portrait by Modigliani. This portrait was later purchased and destroyed by a suitor of Flora's in a fit of jealousy, when he burned it to ashes in the bathtub of a Ritz hotel. The fictional Flora's relationship to Modigliani may be intended to refer to a real affair between Modigliani and the British poet Beatrice Hastings, between 1914–1916. The reference to a nude painting is significant to Modigliani's oeuvre, in that he is best known for about thirty large female nude paintings, which he completed between 1916–1919. His work has especially been noted for the sense of personal intimacy between the artist and his subject that is captured in his paintings. In Stoppard's play, the scholar Pike explains that Flora attended "Modigliani's first show, in Paris." This refers to the first, and only, one-man showing of Modigliani's work during his lifetime, exhibited by Berthe Weill in her gallery in Paris in 1917. This show was immediately controversial, however, because of the nude female subjects, and was closed down by the police. Reference to Modigliani as a master painter of the nude female form in Stoppard's play is significant to a central motif of the drama, which is the relationship between Flora and Das as he eventually paints a miniature nude portrait of her. Flora had made plans to sit for another nude by Modigliani, but arrived in Paris on January 23, 1920, after he had been taken to the hospital, about a week before he died of tuberculosis. (In historical reality, Modigliani's lover, the painter Jeanne Hebuterne, who was pregnant with their child, killed herself the day after his death by jumping out of a window.)

Stoppard makes a number of historical, literary, and artistic references within the dialogue of the play, each of which adds depth as well as historical and cultural relevance to his central thematic concerns regarding empire, cultural imperialism, Indian nationalism, and artistic creation.

Source: Liz Brent, in an essay for *Drama for Students*, Gale Group, 2001.

Carole Hamilton

Hamilton is an English teacher at Cary Academy, an innovative private school in Cary, North Carolina. In this essay, she explores the interwoven themes of propriety and possession as they are expressed in Tom Stoppard's Indian Ink.

In a 1995 interview with Mel Gussow, Tom Stoppard called his play *Indian Ink* "a very cosy play" but perhaps "worryingly cosy sometimes." His comment refers primarily to the play's setting in which characters interact over tea, or while having portraits made. Stoppard also implies that the seriousness of the play might be lost in coziness. Personal and political conflicts in *Indian Ink* are brought up obliquely, politely, and without being resolved. However, by interweaving three separate but related scenarios that span a critical juncture in the political relations between India and Britain, Stoppard's cozy play demonstrates how these matters inflect personal relationships. The three scenarios form a theatrical triptych that allows the viewer to see all of the action at once, in collapsed time and space. This element encourages comparison with the result that the slow subtle shifts of history appear startling and sudden. *Indian Ink* reveals a cultural shift from a society obsessed with personal propriety, overtly concerned with how people may act, to a society obsessed with possession, concerned about who may own what.

The first scenario takes place in 1930 in India between poet Flora Crewe and Indian artist Nirad Das, the second portrays a visit to her aging sister by Das's son, and the third regards the annotation of Flora's posthumous letters by Eldon Pike. The mystery of whether or not Flora and Das had an affair complicates the relationships in all three scenarios, and also affects the true ownership of certain paintings that came into Flora's possession, including the one on the cover of her *Collected Letters*. Three interrelated variations of the theme of propriety appear in the three scenarios: a theme of social propriety pervades the scenes between Flora and Das, while a theme of possession pervades the scenes between Mrs. Swan and Anish Das, and these issues merge in the theme of interpretation as Flora's biographer Eldon Pike stumbles through his investigations of her life. All three themes ultimately deal with what is proper behavior, and the events that illustrate them all stem from the initial scenario of Flora and Das.

A writer juxtaposes parallel events or relationships to draw attention to what has changed and what has remained the same. Sixty-five years separate the events narrated in *Indian Ink,* an interim that saw the decline of the British Empire, the independence of India (in 1945), and the partition of India and Pakistan (1947). These changes followed hundreds of years during which India tolerated encroaching European oppression, a cultural phenomenon at which Emily Eden expressed amazement in 1839: ''I sometimes wonder they [the Indians] do not cut all our [the Europeans'] heads off and say nothing more about it.'' Stoppard closes his play with Eden's comment, along with a description of her party's ''polite amusements'' in front of ''at least three thousand Indians who looked on'' and who ''bowed to the ground if a European came near them.'' Including this actual firsthand account, the timeline of Indian-European relations portrayed in the play encompasses over 150 years, from the golden age of British imperialism in India to its gradual exit. Momentous changes took place on the heels of Flora's visit, representing a critical juncture in Anglo-Indian relations, and, finally, in the relations between British and Indian society. The theatrical triptych in *Indian Ink* conveys how these changes inevitably affected individuals.

Two of the triptych panels comprise a parallel set of personal relationships, each being a scenario between a memsahib (the respectful term used by Indians for a white, European woman) and an Indian man. Flora Crewe, a poet traveling in India in 1930 for her health shares an intimate relationship with Nirad Das, an Indian artist with an affinity for all things British. Flora had led a scandalous life in Europe, but she is not so free in India, where strained political relations between colony and colonizer are kept under control by strict social prohibitions against interactions between whites and natives. As Dilip remarks years later about the possibility of Nirad having painted a nude portrait of her, ''In 1930, an Englishwoman, an Indian painter ... it is out of the question.'' Intimacy between Indian and European carries the power to disrupt the fragile political equilibrium. Flora and Das must neither respond to each other as man and

> *INDIAN INK...* POSES MANY COMPETING IDEOLOGIES ABOUT PERSONAL AND POLITICAL PROPRIETY, AND ABOUT THE LEGITIMATE POSSESSION OF THINGS AND OF IDEAS, WITHOUT REALLY PRIVILEGING ANY OF THEM; THE AUDIENCE IS LEFT TO MAKE UP ITS OWN MIND.''

woman, nor as artist and model, nor even as one human to another—Das's assistance at Flora's attack of breathlessness would certainly be misinterpreted by gossips. Nevertheless, drawn perhaps by the same curiosity about Indians that drove Miss Quested in *A Passage to India,* Flora risks her reputation by seeing Das alone, and Das flirts with social suicide by telling her of his nationalist sympathies. In this part of the triptych, with its theme of the propriety of personal relations, everyone, from their contemporaries to Flora's biographer, misunderstands Flora and Das's real relationship, and in the restrained social climate, they themselves misunderstand each other's intentions. By never revealing whether or not they had an affair, the scenario asks whether it is proper to proscribe how two people may conduct a relationship.

The second scenario takes place in 1985, between Flora's aging sister Mrs. Swan and Das's son, Anish Das. Though political tensions remain, the passage of time has loosened the rules of propriety that restricted Flora and Das. In the liberated 1980s, Anish Das not only has publicly painted a nude British woman, but also has married her; and he not only mentions his political sympathies, but he also openly accuses the British for incarcerating his father for his nationalist views. He is free to discuss his views; as he explains to Mrs. Swan, ''my father was a man who suffered for his beliefs and I have never had to do that.'' But despite the new liberalism, Anish cannot broach with Mrs. Swan the subject of the ownership of the portrait his father made of Flora. He verbalizes only excitement about his father's work being published, exclaiming, ''But replication! *That* is popularity! Put us on book jackets—calendars—biscuit tins!'' Questions about who receives the royalties for the image and whether the painting is properly attributed to his father's name remain unstated, but come quickly to mind to audiences familiar with contemporary debates over copyright ownership. Furthermore, the audience is prepared for this topic by the brief mention of a Modigaliani nude of Flora destroyed by a jealous boyfriend, an instance of prudish propriety overriding legitimate ownership.

Another question of legitimate ownership arises when Mrs. Swan and Anish Das show each other the paintings they have inherited. Anish has kept the nude portrait of Flora left him by his father, although it seemed valueless to him, and Mrs. Swan has held onto the erotic eighteenth-century painting of the *Gita Govinda,* her gift from the Rajah. Although neither Anish nor Mrs. Swan properly interprets or values their own inherited pictures, they each have a reason to value the one the other owns. Mrs. Swan recognizes that Eldon Pike would want the nude Flora, though she would want to hide it from him, while Anish might well understand why the Rajah's son bemoans the loss of the *Gita Govinda,* a national Indian treasure and part of a priceless and incomplete series. Under the prevailing mood of regret for imperialist transgressions, the audience might well consider it wrong not to return the painting to India. Likewise, Mrs. Swan would probably want to own the nude of Flora, to keep it out of the public eye. The Swan-Anish panel of the triptych raises but does not resolve questions of possession and legitimate ownership, nor does it resolve who should own artifacts.

In the third panel of the triptych of *Indian Ink,* Flora's former possessions filter down to new owners. The bulk of her poems and letters go to the literary bounty hunter Eldon Pike, who gobbles them up like the notoriously ravenous fish of his surname. Eating slice after slice of Mrs. Swan's cake, he easily obtains the rights to her sister's letters and her portrait, ''a treasure'' that will earn him money and fame in the literary world. Mrs. Swan withholds the erotic *Gita Govinda* from him, however, out of family modesty. Thus, the third scenario raises issues of epistemological stability, indicating how easily truth is muddied up, here, by self-interest. In addition, Pike conducts his search with the narrow aim of a speargun, missing artifacts a wide net might catch, and he fabricates the truth as he guesses what he should look for. His Indian assistant Dilip mocks Pike's quest to find the nude Flora picture, saying ''you are constructing an edifice of speculation on a smudge of paint on paper, which no longer exists.'' The Pike-Dilip triptych panel treats the postmodern mania for information, and its inherent problems of gathering and interpreting it, asking the question whether it possible to understand the past completely.

The interplay of dialogue and content across the three scenarios of *Indian Ink* imposes another complexity to the play, but also offers further insights. Glaring errors in Pike's footnotes and Mrs. Swan's obfuscation of the truth are part of a Stoppardian subtext of epistemological uncertainty. The play's many contradictions—first one perspective, then immediately another—accord with Stoppard's 1972 statement that ''I write plays because writing dialogue is the only respectable way of contradicting myself. . . . I put a position, rebut it, refute the rebuttal, and rebut the refutation.'' In *Indian Ink* he poses many competing ideologies about personal and political propriety, and about the legitimate possession of things and of ideas, without really privileging any of them; the audience is left to make up its own mind. He remains true to his reputation for raising and not resolving the big questions, such that critic Michael Billington defines the adjective ''Stoppardian'' as ''a wariness of commitment and a distrust of fixed ideologies.'' Although *Indian Ink* may seem ''cosy'' and polite, it leaves the audience troubled by important and pertinent questions about proper behavior—questions that remain as troubling today as they did sixty-five years ago when Flora did or did not have an affair with her Indian portraitist.

Source: Carole Hamilton, in an essay for *Drama for Students,* Gale Group, 2001.

Daniela Presley

Presley has an M.A. and specializes in Germanic languages, literature, and history. In the following essay, Presley discusses history, memory, and the interpretation of evidence in Tom Stoppard's Indian Ink.

Tom Stoppard has earned the reputation for being a playwright of wit and intellect, even though he has never gone to university. In *Hapgood* (1988), for example, he experiments with applying quantum physics to human behavior. In *Arcadia* (1993), he cleverly mixes literary history with mathematical chaos theory. For his next play, Stoppard revisited the material of an earlier radio play, *In the Native*

State (1991), and rewrote it as the stage play *Indian Ink* (1995). *Indian Ink* does not deal explicitly with the mathematical and scientific theories that play such a large part in *Hapgood* and *Arcadia,* but Stoppard does retain the philosophical implications these theories have on the "soft sciences" of history, literature, and sociology. Mary A. Doll, in *British and Irish Drama Since 1960* (1993), wrote about the influence of modern scientific thought on Stoppard's work: "Instead of a Newtonian universe, where problems can be solved, Stoppard ascribes to what post-modern science calls 'chaos theory.' Gaps, punctures, and breaks in sequence sabotage every logical attempt to formulate a hypothesis. Indeed, Stoppard's greatest contribution to theatre may be his concept of the indeterminacies of what it is 'to know' as a hired professional, a spectator, or even as an ordinary human being."

In *Indian Ink,* this postmodern complicating of "what it is 'to know'" takes the form of a conflict between the rigidity of academic history and the flexibility of human memory as preserved by art. Academic history, which pretends to be objective but is actually flawed by human interpretation, can offer facts, but then Stoppard calls into question the certainty of having facts at all. Stoppard suggests then that it is our duty to question our conclusions and to allow for multiple interpretations of the evidence. Memory and art allow for these multiple interpretations, and then complicate history by competing against it for popular acceptance. History strives to solve mysteries, while memory is tantalized when mysteries are left unsolved. History, as represented by the character Eldon Pike, is "accurate," public, and dry. In contrast, memory, as represented by Mrs. Swan, is imperfect, private, and alive.

Indian Ink, like *Arcadia,* is a literary mystery in which past and present coexist on stage, much like the past still exists as an underlayer of memory in the present. Stoppard often employs the convention of a mystery to demonstrate the inadequacy of human perception in interpreting evidence. Within the first minutes of the play, the American literary historian, Eldon Pike, finds a sentence in one of Flora's letters that will lead him on a hunt to India: "Perhaps my soul will stay behind as a smudge of paint on paper . . . like Radha who was the most beautiful of herdswomen, undressed for love in an empty house." Pike, as a scholar who takes the written word literally, reads "a smudge of paint on paper" as proof that a nude painting of Flora exists. He is right. But he meets opposition to this theory

> HISTORY STRIVES TO SOLVE MYSTERIES, WHILE MEMORY IS TANTALIZED WHEN MYSTERIES ARE LEFT UNSOLVED."

from Mrs. Swan, Flora's sister. After reading the sentence, Pike asks, "What do you think it means?" Mrs. Swan's response, "As much or as little as you like," shows an impatience for the literal interpretation of words that can lead to wrong conclusions.

Indian Ink is obsessed with the interpretation of the past through scraps of evidence on paper: Flora's letters and poems, a watercolor, an oil painting, a newspaper clipping. As Flora writes her letters, the moment passes and becomes history. Her letters become documents, evidence to be interpreted by the future. The play's title reminds us of the problem of interpretation. Ink is merely a liquid with the potential to convey meaning. The lines that ink forms on paper have no meaning in themselves either, but require the human brain to make sense of them.

As an example of how historical facts can be differently interpreted and remembered by different cultures, consider the conflicting vocabulary used by the Indians and the English in describing the same historical event now known as the Sepoy Rebellion. Stoppard mentions the event only briefly, but significantly he mentions it twice. Both times, the English women remember the event simply as "the Mutiny" while the Indian men refer to it either as "the first War of Independence," "the Rising of 1857," or "the First Uprising." In British history, the Indian soldiers' violent protest against British rule is interpreted as a "Mutiny," a traitorous rebellion against legal authority. Indian history, on the other hand, refers to the same event as an "Uprising," a word that holds heroic connotations of revolt against a repressive authority. Far from being an exact science, Stoppard shows how history, depending on human interpretation of so-called facts, is colored by the interpreter's cultural background, which is only one of many subjective factors that can distort a person's objectivity.

If large-scale events can be differently interpreted and remembered, how then the very private events in one woman's life? *Indian Ink* deals with history on a large scale but mostly the play is concerned with history on a very personal level. As Stoppard said in a 1995 interview with Mel Gussow, "*Indian Ink* is actually a very intimate play. It's a play of intimate scenes." Details of Flora's sex life become the mystery Pike wants to solve. If he finds the watercolor, he can prove that a relationship existed between Flora and Nirad Das, thus expanding the borders of Flora Crewe scholarship. But Mrs. Swan, as guardian of her sister's memory, tells Pike that he is "not allowed to write a book . . . biography is the worst possible excuse for getting people wrong." Mrs. Swan would rather allow her sister's poems to stand on their own and offer themselves for multiple interpretations, rather than limit them to Pike's sole interpretation. Later in India when Pike wonders whether Flora and Das had a relationship, Dilip also cautions Pike against overinterpretation. "Well, we will never know," says Dilip. "You are constructing an edifice of speculation on a smudge of paint on paper, which no longer exists."

Pike's footnotes are a running joke in the play, bridging that divide between past and present, history and memory. Pike intrudes on Flora's voice with unnecessary detail. The footnotes, which rely on Mrs. Swan's memory, pass into academic history and dissect Flora's letters. Pike strives to give Flora's words extra meaning but often only succeeds in creating confusion. Laurie Kaplan in her article in *Modern Drama* calls this "the kind of over-interpreting (which leads to misinterpreting)." For example, when Flora mentions having a dream about the Queen's Elm, Pike says, "Which Queen? What elm? Why was she dreaming about a *tree*? So this is where I come in, wearing my editor's hat. To lighten the darkness." Mrs. Swan informs Pike that the Queen's Elm is a bar, and we see that Pike's literalness threatens to pervert the intended meaning. Stoppard often makes buffoons of those characters who are rigid and overconfident in their interpretations. It is ironic that Pike, who is right about the existence of the watercolor, misinterprets the clues from the Rajah so that he will never find what he seeks.

Das explains an Indian theory of art that will hold much resonance for the play. When Flora complains that the poem she is writing holds no inspiration that day, Das tells her about *rasa:* "Rasa is juice. Its taste. Its essence. . . . Rasa is what you must feel when you see a painting, or hear music; it is the emotion which the artist must arouse in you."

All works of original artistic genius have *rasa*. Das's oil portrait of Flora has no *rasa,* no true artistic genius, because he attempts to copy the English style instead of painting from his heart. The nude watercolor has *rasa,* however, as Flora herself notices, inspired as it was by sexual attraction. It is, ironically, this true piece of art that will be hidden from Pike.

Memory and art have *rasa,* while Pike's academic history does not. Academic history is unoriginal, as Pike himself admits when he says: "This is why God made poets and novelists, so the rest of us can get published." History is a public, "accurate" record, devoid of *rasa,* while memory is private and changeable, filled with so much *rasa* that it is fluid and blurred, but cherished for that imperfection nonetheless. Scholarship reduces the *rasa* of human life to dry facts. As Mrs. Swan explains to Anish, "Mr. Pike teaches Flora Crewe. It makes her sound like a subject, doesn't it, like biology."

At the play's end, Mrs. Swan and Anish agree to protect the personal memories of their relatives by keeping the nude watercolor a secret. They do not want this private event between their families entering into the public space, represented by Pike, whose footnotes suck the *rasa* out of art. As Mrs. Swan says about the *Gita Govinda* miniature, "I didn't tell Eldon. He's not family." In *In the Native State,* Anish says he will not lock the watercolor away, but display it, "on the wall at home, and I'll tell my children too." The painting and the memory of Flora Crewe will become part of the personal history of the Das family, to be passed on like an oral legend. But even Anish will want to interpret the watercolor to prove that a relationship existed between Das and Flora. In *In the Native State,* he even uses the word "evidence" to introduce the painting. Anish interprets the vine that wraps around the tree to be proof of a sexual relationship. Mrs. Swan cautions, "Now really, Mr. Das, sometimes a vine is only a vine," paraphrasing the famous Freudian quote "sometimes a cigar is just a cigar." Mrs. Swan lives comfortably with the uncertainty of memory, while Pike seeks to solve the uncertainties in the name of scholarship.

A feeling of mourning pervades the play as memory and history compete for recognition in the present. The duality of loss and recovery is at the heart of human obsession with the past. Humans construct history to recover lost objects, to discover what really happened and preserve that truth for future generations. This reconstruction takes place on a national as well as a personal level. In complicated ways, both the Indians and the British romanticize and mourn the passing of the British Empire. Mrs. Swan keeps Indian souvenirs on her windowsill and pines for the fruit trees "at home" in India. The retired Indian soldier, "Subadar Ram Sunil Singh the toilet cleaner," keeps his British military medals on his jacket. Even on a personal level, the characters in *Indian Ink* are in mourning. Anne Wright, in her entry on Stoppard in the *Dictionary of Literary Biography,* discusses this elegiac quality: "The themes of memory, loss, and bereavement resonate at the personal level, in Anish's loss of his father and in Nell's grief for Flora and for her own dead baby, yet they connect too with the broad sweep of history in a play which is deeply nostalgic and elegiac, yet with a sharply ironic perspective on its subject." Anish's and Nell's personal losses are made more poignant by the juxtaposition on stage of past and present. While Anish and Nell mourn and remember, their dead relatives are playing out their lives just a few feet away, and yet separated from them by a gulf of time. Furthermore, while Flora mourns the loss of the Modigliani portrait, Pike mourns his inability to find the "lost" nude watercolor. For all his buffoonery, Pike's motives are not entirely self-serving, but actually touching. So enamored is he of Flora that he is excited to have his picture taken with the tree that stands where her razed bungalow once stood. He wants to recover and preserve Flora Crewe, even if this preservation threatens to make a stuffed museum piece out of her. He improvises a song based on Louis MacNeice's "Bagpipe Music," mourning the loss of evidence: "It's no go the records of the Theosophical Society, it's no go the newspaper files partitioned to ashes.... All we want is the facts and to tell the truth in our fashion." Pike represents all traditional historians who mourn the loss of objective truth.

Significantly, it is art with *rasa* that is eternal, not history. As Das says philosophically, "Well, the Empire will one day be gone like the Mughal Empire before it, and only their monuments remain .... Only in art can empires cheat oblivion, because only the artist can say, 'Look on my words, ye mighty and despair!'" History will be forgotten, but great art endures and reminds humanity of what was lost. In the final ironic moments of the play, Pike pays his respects at Flora's grave, while simultaneously, we see and hear Flora, full of vitality, reading her letter to her sister. Memory of Flora Crew is preserved in her art, even if her "true" biography and the "real" interpretation of her words will always remain a mystery.

Source: Daniela Presley, in an essay for *Drama for Students,* Gale Group, 2001.

SOURCES

Billington, Michael, "Lord Malquist and Mr. Moon," in *Critical Essays on Tom Stoppard,* edited by Anthony Jenkins, G. K. Hall, 1990, pp. 35–43, p. 38–39.

Doll, Mary A., "Stoppard's Theatre of Unknowing," in *British and Irish Drama Since 1960,* edited by James Acheson, The Macmillan Press Ltd., 1993, pp. 117–29.

Gussow, Mel, "Happiness, Chaos and Tom Stoppard," in *American Theater,* Vol. 12, No. 10, December, 1995.

Kaplan, Laurie, "In the Native State/ Indian Ink: Footnoting the Footnotes on Empire," in *Modern Drama,* Vol. 41, Issue 3, Fall, 1998.

Stoppard, Tom, *Conversations with Stoppard,* Grove Press, 1995, pp. 1–9, 117–130.

Wright, Anne, *Dictionary of Literary Biography,* Vol. 13: *British Dramatists Since World War II,* edited by Stanley Weintraub, Gale, 1982, pp. 482–500.

FURTHER READING

Beckett, Samuel, *Waiting for Godot,* Grove, 1954.
This play is one of Beckett's most well-known plays. Beckett is considered by many to be the master of the theater of the absurd. Stoppard has been compared many times in style and approach to Beckett.

Shakespeare, William, *Hamlet,* Signet Classic, 1998.
Stoppard's famous play *Rosencrantz and Gildenstern are Dead* is based on two minor characters within this famous Shakespeare tragedy.

Shaw, George Bernard, *Candida,* Penguin, 1964.
Candida is a masterpiece by the famous British playwright. Stoppard's concern for humanistic themes has often been compared to that of Shaw's.

Stoppard, Tom, *Tom Stoppard in Conversation,* University of Michigan Press, 1994.
This book is an interesting and illuminating collection of interviews with Stoppard.

Wilde, Oscar, *The Importance of Being Ernest,* Avon, 1965.
The Importance of Being Ernest is a widely popular play by the famous nineteenth-century playwright. Stoppard has been likened to Wilde for their mutual use of a quick and acerbic wit.

The Insect Play

**JOSEF CAPEK
KAREL CAPEK

1921**

Karel and Josef Capek's *The Insect Play* is one of the pair's best known and well-received collaborations. Also known as *The Insect Comedy, The World We Live In,* and *From Insect Life*, the play was published in its original Czech in 1921 as *Ze zivota hmyzu*. The play was first performed at the National Theatre in Brno, Czechoslovakia, on March 8, 1922 (some sources say February), running for about one hundred nights. *The Insect Play* made its American debut later in 1922, and its London premiere the following year. The play has been performed only intermittently since that time because of the demanding staging it requires.

The brothers Capek began work on the play in 1920. Their first collaboration after an eight-year hiatus, it would also be one of their last. *The Insect Play* was a combination of many forms, including fable, revue, and satire. All but a few of the characters are insects that are anthropomorphized (given human qualities). The brothers commented on human society in their place and time period (Czechoslovakia in the post-World War I era) via these insects. Many critics believe that the Capeks were inspired by other animal plays and short stories, including Jean Henri Fabré's *La vie des insects* (The life of insects) and *Souvenirs entomologiques,* and a story by Russian author Vsevolod Garsin, *What Never Happened.* Though *The Insect Play* has been problematic for critics from the beginning, many have found much to praise over the years. As Lucia Mauro of the *Chicago Sun-Times* wrote, when commenting on a 1999 production of the play, "their keen observations of the life cycle and poignant visions of war's futility remain relevant to this day."

AUTHOR BIOGRAPHY

Born in Male Svatonovice, Bohemia (later part of Czechoslovakia), the Capek brothers were the sons of Antonín Capek, the village doctor, and his wife, Bozena Capekova, an intellectual. Josef Capek was born in 1887, and his brother Karel followed on January 9, 1890, nearly three years later. The brothers were extremely close as children. Karel was always sickly; Josef was a strong influence and his brother's protector. Karel would be ill most of his life.

While Karel was attending boarding school, the family moved to Prague in 1907. Karel joined them there to finish high school. Despite his family's protests, Josef entered art school. The brothers began writing stories for newspapers together, especially after Karel entered Charles University in 1909. There, he studied art history, aesthetics, and philosophy, and earned his doctorate in 1915. During this time, both brothers spent some time abroad: Karel studied at universities in Paris and Berlin while Josef went to Paris. The brothers published their first book, a collection of short stories entitled *The Luminous Depths,* in 1916.

In Prague, the Capek brothers became leaders in the avant-garde movement. While Josef was on his way to becoming a renowned Czech painter, Karel worked as a journalist, began writing novels, and continued to write short stories of some renown. The brothers still collaborated, but primarily in plays. They wrote ten plays together over twenty years. The first was *The Fateful Play of Love*. This play was written in 1910 but not performed until 1919. While neither brother served in World War I, both were outspoken supporters of the burgeoning Czech nationalism.

By the 1920s, most of the brothers' work was done separately. From 1921 to 1923, Karel worked as a stage director and the dramaturg, or specialist in dramatic composition, at Prague's Vinohrady Theatre. Josef designed sets and costumes for a number of theatrical productions, and often illustrated his brother's books. Aside from their best known play, *The Insect Play* (1921), the Capeks mostly wrote their own theatrical works. In 1921, Karel's seminal play, *R.U.R.*, depicted humanity as served—to the brink of subjugation—by "Rossum's Universal Robots" and gave him international fame. Josef also wrote several plays on his own, with less success, including *The Land of Many Names* (1923).

Their last dramatic collaboration was *Adam the Creator* (1927), though they continued to produce several more plays individually after this date. Karel did not write plays again until the mid-1930s. Antifascism became the focus, especially in his 1937 play *The White Plague*. For most of the early 1930s, however, Karel wrote important novels (including the acclaimed *War with the Newts,* 1936) and travel books, returned to work as a journalist, and was involved in politics. Josef continued to share his brother's left-leaning political beliefs.

Because of Karel's illnesses (including calcification of part of his spine), he did not marry his long-time girlfriend Olga Scheinpfugová, an actress and novelist, until 1935. The Capeks' political beliefs led them in public attacks against the Nazis after the Nazis occupied Czechoslovakia. The pressure might have contributed to Karel's death in Prague. He succumbed to pneumonia on December 25, 1938, on the verge of being arrested. Josef was arrested by the Nazis and taken to the Bergen-Belsen concentration camp where he died in 1945 (probably of typhus) after being held for six years.

PLOT SUMMARY

Prologue: In the Woods

The Insect Play opens in the woods where a drunken tramp sleeps on the ground. Butterflies flit near him. His slumber is interrupted by a lepidopterist who is collecting butterflies for his scientific collection. The scientist is annoyed that the tramp's movements have scared off the insects. After the scientist leaves to continue collecting, the tramp laments that all the world is paired off into couples.

Act I: The Butterflies

The tramp finds himself in a place that caters to butterflies. As the tramp makes himself comfortable on cushions and dozes, butterflies enter. Felix, a shy poet butterfly, is looking for Iris. She comes in, followed by another male butterfly, Victor. Answering her question, Felix tells Iris that he is not in love with any female butterflies, and has not been since he was a caterpillar. In fact, Felix loves Iris, but has only watched her from a distance and written poems.

Karel Capek

Iris flirts with Felix. Victor tries to embarrass him by reciting part of a poem that Felix has recently published about sex. Iris gets rid of Victor, and continues to toy with Felix's feelings. She accuses him of loving Clytie, another female butterfly. Felix admits that he is in love with Iris. She asks him to quickly compose a poem for her, which he does, much to her pleasure.

The moment is interrupted by the appearance of Clytie and Otto, a male butterfly who is chasing her. Victor also returns. Iris embarrasses Felix by quoting the poem about sex for those present. Yet Iris also calls Felix ''clever'' when she reports that he has found a rhyme for her name. A few moments later, Iris is flirting with Victor and leads him on a chase.

Clytie asks Felix why he loves Iris. Felix denies that he does. Clytie insults Iris and flirts with Felix, then asks him to be friends, ''like two girls.'' Felix recites the beginning of a new poem for her, but she is unimpressed. Clytie's attentions turn to Otto, who begs for her love. Clytie now leads Otto away on a chase. Felix leaves alone.

The tramp feels sorry for Felix. Clytie returns to primp in the mirror. Though she does not know what a man is, Clytie tries to get the tramp to chase her. The tramp will not play her game. Clytie returns to the mirror after the rejection. Iris enters, out of breath and tells Clytie a funny story about Victor being eaten by a bird. Otto nearly met the same fate. Felix comes in and tries to read his new poem to the women. They only care about their appearance. Otto enters, and both Iris and Clytie lead him on a chase. Felix tries to get them to wait, but to no avail. The tramp calls him a fool and shoos him away.

Act II: Creepers and Crawlers

This act takes place in a sandy hillock. The tramp is half-asleep nearby, but a chrysalis interrupts his repose. It is excited because it is about to be born. It expresses this sentiment regularly throughout the act.

The action shifts to a pair of beetles, Mr. and Mrs. Beetle. They are rolling a huge ball of dirt and dung, which they call their ''capital.'' They have worked very hard to collect the ball, and are immensely proud of it. Mr. Beetle wants to immediately begin work on their next pile. Mrs. Beetle is more concerned with protecting what they already have. Mr. Beetle goes to look for a hole in which to bury it.

While he is gone, Mrs. Beetle thinks she has found a hole in an ichneumon fly's lair and enters. In the meantime, a strange beetle takes the unguarded capital. The tramp questions him, but does not prevent him from taking it. Mrs. Beetle returns and accuses the tramp of taking the pile. The tramp denies it and describes the beetle. Mrs. Beetle believes that it is her husband and goes looking for him.

The ichneumon fly returns with a dead cricket for his daughter, a larva. After feeding his daughter, the fly turns his attention to the tramp, asking if he is edible. The tramp says he is not, and the fly proceeds to regale him with the wonders of children.

Mr. Beetle returns looking for his wife. He has found a hole. The tramp tells him that his wife is looking for him and that another beetle stole their capital. Mr. Beetle is more concerned with the loss of it than his wife.

Mr. and Mrs. Cricket enter. They are moving into the home vacated by a cricket eaten by a bird. Mr. Cricket leaves to introduce himself to the neighbors. After he goes, Mrs. Cricket, who is pregnant, and the tramp talk about children. Mrs. Beetle returns and gets into an argument with Mrs. Cricket over what is more important: a dung pile or a home. Mrs. Beetle leaves again.

The fly returns, kills Mrs. Cricket, and takes her to his lair. A parasite enters, and sympathizes with the tramp's horror over the murder. The parasite believes that the fly is bad because he just stores most of what he kills while others starve. The fly considers eating the parasite, but finds him inedible. When Mr. Cricket returns, the fly quickly kills him, then leaves to look for more food. After he exits, the parasite enters the lair and eats much of what is in there, including the larva. The tramp is disgusted by all the killing.

Act III: The Ants

The chrysalis is growing more excited about being born. The tramp realizes he has sat on an ant heap. He asks the blind ant, who is counting time for the worker ants, what he has stumbled upon. The blind ant does not answer, but the chief engineer does. He is in the Ant Realm. A second engineer enters. He has come up with a more efficient way to count and get more work done.

The engineer ants have never heard of humans and inform the tramp that ants are the masters of the world ruled by a she. These ants have defeated the black and brown ants, conquered the grey ants, and are now trying to beat the yellow ants. They are doing this to rule the world and master time. The engineers are concerned with the speed of work.

An inventor ant enters. He has come up with a new war machine that will kill quickly. A messenger comes in. The southern army has had some men captured by the yellow ants, who have declared war on the Ant Realm. The ants call for arms as the yellow ants invade. The ants become soldiers led by the chief engineer, now the commander in chief and dictator. He organizes forces and readies the battle plan.

The messenger returns regularly with progress reports. The Ant Realm is losing badly to the yellow ants. Wounded ants return. The tide of the battle turns, and the yellow retreat. The chief engineer orders their destruction, and proclaims himself emperor. The tide changes again and it is the Ant Realm who retreats. The yellows invade and are victorious. The tramp kills the yellow leader.

Epilogue: Death and Life

The tramp is sleeping in the dead of night. Voices of all the insects can be heard as morning nears. The tramp strikes stones to make a spark, which lights up the forest. Moths come into the light and die. The chrysalis breaks open to reveal a moth, who dies soon after she is born. The tramp is upset by her death, and moments later is struggling with his own death.

After dawn, a woodcutter comes upon the corpse of the tramp. A woman with a baby finds both of them. The woodcutter covers the tramp, while the woman places a flower on his makeshift grave. Children sing as they go by on their way to school.

CHARACTERS

Mr. Beetle

Mr. Beetle appears primarily in Act II. He is married to Mrs. Beetle. He is very proud of his "capital," the ball/pile of dung and dirt that he and his wife have worked for some time to gather. After getting the first ball done, Mr. Beetle wants to make another, then another. Mrs. Beetle decides that they should find a deep hole to bury their first pile in so that they do not have to worry about it while making the second pile. Mr. Beetle becomes infuriated when the strange beetle steals the ball under his wife's nose. Mr. Beetle is more concerned with the location of his capital than his wife's whereabouts. Mr. Beetle represents greed.

Mrs. Beetle

Mrs. Beetle appears primarily in Act II. She is married to Mr. Beetle, and shares his enthusiasm for their "capital." It is she who suggests that they have to protect the dung ball while working on the next one. When her husband goes off to look for a hole to bury it in, Mrs. Beetle wanders in the lair of the ichneumon fly. When she looks inside for a moment, the strange beetle steals the capital. Mrs. Beetle goes looking for her husband, believing he has taken it. When she returns briefly to her original location, she argues with Mrs. Cricket over what is more important, a dung ball or a home and children. Mrs. Beetle believes the former. Like Mr. Beetle, Mrs. Beetle is greedy.

Blind Ant

The blind ant appears primarily in Act III. He continuously counts to four to keep time for the worker ants throughout the act. The quickness of his words determines the pace. The ant ignores the tramp's requests for information and only continues counting. He continues to count even after the yellow ants invade and conquer.

Chief Engineer

The chief engineer is an ant who appears primarily in Act III. He runs the Ant Realm for the mysterious "she," receiving information from the inventor and the messenger and acting on it. It is the chief engineer who answers the tramp's questions about the operation and tries to put him to work. The chief engineer directs the operation against the yellow ants, the Ant Realm's last enemy. He is power hungry, adapting his words to fit the situation and to his benefit. The chief engineer appoints himself dictator and emperor when war breaks out between his ants and the yellow ants. While he tries to win without mercy to his enemy or his men, he fails. The chief engineer only thinks in terms of work, control, and victory: nothing else matters.

A Chrysalis

The chrysalis makes her first appearance in Act II and appears though the epilogue. She is a moth waiting to be born. She looks forward to her birth, for the chrysalis believes she will do something great. She is sure the world will change because of her. However, when the moth finally emerges from the chrysalis, other moths are dying after entering the light that the tramp creates. Like her fellow moths, the chrysalis, as a newborn moth, dies only moments after she was born. The chrysalis represents the whole of the life cycle, hope in birth and suddenness of death.

Clytie

Appearing primarily in Act I, Clytie is a female butterfly. She enjoys being chased by male butterflies, especially Otto. She is also jealous of Iris, another female butterfly, and speaks disparagingly of her when she is not present. Unlike Iris, Clytie does not like poetry, even the poem Felix writes for her. She is more concerned with her appearance and flirtation. She tries to get every male, including the tramp, to chase her. Clytie is very superficial.

Mr. Cricket

Mr. Cricket appears primarily in Act II. He is married to the very pregnant Mrs. Cricket, whom he has moved to a sandy hillock. They are to take over the home of another cricket who was eaten by a bird. Mr. Cricket is loving and worried about his scared wife's well-being. When he leaves his wife to let others know where he is, she is killed by the ichneumon fly. Mr. Cricket returns himself and suffers the same fate.

Mrs. Cricket

Mrs. Cricket appears primarily in Act II. She is pregnant and married to Mr. Cricket, with whom she has moved to a sandy hillock. They are to take over the home of another cricket who was eaten by a bird. She wants to have a nice home for her new family. Mrs. Cricket is very frightened of something from the moment that she enters the hillock. After debating the merits of home versus dung heap with Mrs. Beetle, Mrs. Cricket is killed by the ichneumon fly. When her husband returns, he suffers the same fate.

Felix

Appearing primarily in Act I, Felix is a male butterfly. Unlike the other butterflies, Felix is shy and not flirtatious. He is a published poet and thinks a lot. Felix is in love with Iris, and tells her he has really only been in love one previous time. Then he was a caterpillar and only admired his love from afar. Felix tries to please both Iris and Clytie with poems. While Iris appreciates them, at least at first, Clytie does not. Felix is stymied by both butterflies and continues on as the frustrated poet.

Ichneumon Fly

The fly appears primarily in Act II. He has a lair where his daughter, the larva, lives, and where he stores the many insects he kills. The fly is only concerned with killing other edible insects and feeding his daughter. After he realizes that the tramp is inedible, the fly shares his enthusiasm for his daughter and children in general with him. The fly has no real conscious. He kills Mr. and Mrs. Cricket in front of the tramp without hesitation, and would kill both the tramp and the parasite if they were edible. The fly is despised by the parasite, who enacts a measure of revenge at the end of Act II. The parasite eats both his larva daughter and much of his store of food while the fly is off hunting for more prey.

Inventor

The inventor is an ant who appears briefly in Act III. He is proud of the fact that he has invented a war machine that can kill thousands of men continuously. He is considered a scientific genius by his fellow ants.

Iris

Appearing primarily in Act I, Iris is very flirtatious female butterfly. Like Clytie, she enjoys attention from the other male butterflies, primarily Victor and Felix, but later, Otto as well. Iris toys with Felix's feelings for her, asking him about other women he has been involved with and making him write poems for her. Iris is rather insensitive to Felix, and by the end of the act, she is brusque towards him when he tries to read a new poem to her. Iris's coldness also shows itself when she is amused that a bird eats Victor after he asks her to love him. Iris is arguably the most superficial butterfly.

Larva

The larva is the daughter of the ichneumon fly, appearing in Act II. She is bored in the lair, constantly being fed by her doting father. She is killed and eaten by the parasite at the end of the act.

A Lepidopterist

In the prologue to *The Insect Play*, the lepidopterist is collecting butterflies for his scientific collection. He is angry at the tramp for making him lose potential specimens. The lepidopterist vows revenge on the tramp, but is really more concerned with acquiring butterflies for his collection. The lepidopterist claims to love nature, but represents man's indifference to the beauty of nature.

Messenger

The messenger is an ant who appears in Act III. He reports to the chief engineer about the declaration of war by the yellow ants and continues to update him as the situation develops.

Otto

Appearing primarily in Act I, Otto is a male butterfly. He is in love with Clytie, primarily, but also flirts with Iris. Otto repeatedly tells both of them that he loves them and wants to be loved by them. He will do whatever they want him to. Otto is proud when he comes up with a rhyme for his own name, and begins to write his own poem. Otto is nearly eaten by a bird, though avoids the fate of Victor. Like most of the butterflies, Otto is superficial.

Parasite

The parasite appears primarily in Act II. He shares the tramp's distaste for the regular killings of the ichneumon fly. But the parasite is angrier about the amount of food the fly hoards while others go hungry. After the fly leaves to continue the hunt, the parasite enacts his revenge by going into the lair. The parasite eats the fly's daughter and much of his stored food. The tramp is appalled by the parasite's actions. The parasite is an opportunist.

Second Engineer

The second engineer is an ant and appears primarily in Act III. He is second in command to the chief engineer, and is his superior's "yes man." They share the same beliefs about work, war, and victory. The second engineer assists in the direction of work and war. He is wounded in the attack by the yellow ants.

Strange Beetle

The strange beetle appears in the second act. He takes Mr. and Mrs. Beetle's dung heap, their "capital," when Mrs. Beetle has entered the ichneumon fly's lair. The strange beetle is never seen again.

A Tramp

The tramp is the main character who ties the whole of *The Insect Play* together. At the beginning of the play, he is trying to sleep after drinking alcohol. He is awakened by the lepidopterist, who is collecting butterfly specimens for his collection. The tramp is the only human to observe and be a part of the action that takes place in the three acts of the play. First, the tramp dozes in the butterflies' cafe, overhearing their flirtatious, though empty, talk. He does not like their superficiality. Then the tramp witnesses the harshness of insect life through the actions of the ichneumon fly, who kills Mr. and Mrs. Cricket, and other insects, to feed his larva daughter. A parasite kills the larva and eats the fly's store of food. The tramp also witnesses the greed of Mr. and Mrs. Beetle with their pile of dung, and how this scenario ends badly. Finally, the tramp comes across an ant realm, and a war between these ants and yellow ants. The tramp kills the yellow leader after he declares victory. At the end of *The Insect Play*, the tramp worries about his death after the chrysalis, who is waiting to be born throughout the play, dies soon after her birth as a moth. This predicts the tramp's death. His body is found in the morning by the woodcutter and the woman. The tramp represents man's conscious.

Victor

Appearing primarily in Act I, Victor is a male butterfly and a lady-killer. He is primarily interested in Iris and enjoys embarrassing Felix. Victor recites a poem that Felix has recently published in front of Iris knowing that he would be uncomfortable. Victor does not like poetry. Victor's enthusiastic chasing of Iris leads to his demise. After he asks her to love him, a bird eats him. Iris is very amused by how he dies. Like most of the butterflies, Victor is superficial.

A Woman

The woman appears only in the epilogue. She is carrying her sister's baby to the infant's baptism when she comes upon the woodcutter. She believes the corpse is bad luck. Still, she places a flower on the makeshift grave the woodcutter arranges for the deceased tramp.

Peter Wood

See A Woodcutter

A Woodcutter

The woodcutter appears only in the epilogue. He is the one who finds the corpse of the dead tramp and covers it up so the school children will not see it.

THEMES

Cycle of Life

Underscored throughout *The Insect Play,* sometimes brutally, is the cycle of life. From birth, to maturity, to reproduction, and to death, all of the high points on the human life cycle are represented in the play. The chrysalis contains a female moth that cannot wait to be born. She believes she will do wondrous things for the world after her birth. However, the moth dies soon after she emerges from her chrysalis in what is a mass death of moths. During the epilogue of the play, a woman is taking her sister's newborn baby to its baptism. The butterflies in Act I represent the maturation process. They flit and flirt with each other, pairing off only temporarily. Nothing is permanent for them yet. The ants in Act III are the opposite: they are about work and being part of the community. This is a different part of the maturation process. There are several examples of reproducing adults, concerned with responsibilities. The ichneumon fly is a doting father whose only goal in life is to feed his daughter and increase the amount of food he has stored. Mr. and Mrs. Cricket are expecting baby crickets. While Mr. and Mrs. Beetle are not interested in having children, they do have their "capital" (a ball of dung and dirt) that is very precious to them and their future.

By far, the harshest part of the life cycle depicted in *The Insect Play,* however, is death. Many of the deaths are sudden and murderous. The fly kills the crickets to feed his daughter. The parasite kills the fly's larva and eats her partially as revenge, but also because he seeks food. Victor, the butterfly, comes to a nasty end. A bird eats him, much to Iris's amusement. Even the Lepidopterist collects butterflies to kill for his collection. The tramp is horrified by all these senseless deaths, but he cannot abide the yellow ants' victory over the Ant Realm. He grinds the yellow ant leader into pieces. After all the moths die—perhaps because of the light the tramp struck—he, too, takes his last breath. The Capeks depict the life cycle as endless and cruel, with moments of hope. Though the tramp has died, a baby is being baptized, children are going to school, and two adults move forward. Life may be short, but it is worth living.

Morals and Morality/Ethics/Vice

In their depiction of the insect world, the Capeks comment on human vices, morals, and ethics. All but one of the butterflies in Act I lack any depth or compassion. They tease and try to manipulate each other, worrying only about their appearance. Though Felix, the shy sensitive poet butterfly, is not as superficial as the others, he also has his weakness. Felix only cares about his poetry and what effect it might have on female butterflies. He does not write for himself, but to lure them to him. Mr. and Mrs. Beetle are the epitome of greed. They are only concerned with their "capital" (the ball of dung and dirt), and acquiring more of it. When Mrs. Beetle and the capital are missing, Mr. Beetle is more concerned with the capital than his wife. The ichneumon fly shares their obsession to a lesser degree. He kills whatever he has to so that his larva daughter is fed, and stores the rest. Though the parasite claims to sympathize with the tramp over the brutal murder of the Crickets, he too is an opportunist. As soon as the ichneumon fly leaves his lair, the parasite goes in, kills the fly's larva, and eats her as well as the rest of the fly's store of food. Those in the Ant Realm are most concerned with doing work more quickly, even though it kills one of their own. The chief engineer ant says whatever is necessary at the moment to get what he desires. He most wants power and declares himself dictator and emperor when battle breaks out between his realm and the yellow ants. The human characters also have their own moral lapses. The scientist is more concerned with capturing and killing the butterflies than how he woke the tramp up from his sleep. Though the tramp is horrified by the harsh behavior of the insects he encounters, he too kills by the end of the play. He rubs out the yellow ant leader with his heel. The Capeks use the insects' characters to illustrate negative behaviors of humankind and how these behaviors affect others.

Nature and its Meaning

Implicit in *The Insect Play* is a critique of nature and its meaning. Though the Capeks use the insects as symbolic humans, with all their problems, the meaning of nature also comes into play. The ants, for example, have some of the characteristics of real ants. Real ants have a strict division of labor, and seem to work nonstop in a certain kind of pattern. The Capeks take what they observed in nature and added human characteristics. A similar thing could be said for butterflies and the way they flit around; parasites, who live off the work of others; and so on. The Capeks seem to be saying that the ways of nature and human life are not always far apart. Nature has much to show humans about their existence.

STYLE

Setting

The Insect Play is a revue-like fable/drama set in the woods of an unspecified place and time. While the action of the prologue and epilogue takes place in "reality" with only human characters, the three acts are interlinked sketches that occur only in the mind of the tramp. Act I is set on a hill, but with cushions and a table or bar where the butterflies gather. Act II takes place on a sandy hillock with many holes for the insects to go in and out of. Act III is set inside an ant heap, where the ants work, strategize war, and fight. These settings emphasize the play's dichotomy: the tramp's reality and his fantasy, as well as the link between man and nature.

Symbolism/Characters

Nearly every character in *The Insect Play* is a symbol or has symbolic meaning. The only character that appears in each section of the play is the tramp, who represents humanity. He is the one who observes the faults of humanity as symbolized in each insect character. Though the tramp is upset by

TOPICS FOR FURTHER STUDY

- Research the history of Europe in World War I and the immediate postwar years. How do these events relate to the world the Capeks portray in Act III? Do the actions and attitudes of the Ant Realm predict subsequent events?

- Read the fables of Aesop, which often use animal characters to make their point. Compare and contrast these fables with the Capeks's play.

- Pick one of the insect species depicted in *The Insect Play* and do research into its entomology (the scientific study of insects). How do the real behaviors of insects compare to the way the Capeks depict them?

- Compare and contrast the anthropomorphized insects in *The Insect Play* with the human-like robots in Karel Capek's seminal play *R.U.R.* (1921). What does each depiction of nonhumans with human-like characteristics reveal about the authors' take on humankind?

what he sees, he does not directly intercede until he kills the yellow ant leader at the end of Act III. The tramp dies soon afterwards. The insect characters are also symbolic. The butterflies symbolize the shallowness of youth or society. The ants represent, among other things, the unquestioned loyalty to one's state, an important issue in post-World War I Europe. Some of the insects in Act II symbolize various human characteristics, especially faults. Mr. and Mrs. Beetle, for example, are greedy. The strange beetle and the parasite are opportunists ready to take advantage of another's misfortune. The ichneumon fly shares this characteristic, but is also a cold-blooded murderer.

Anthropomorphism/Fable

Anthropomorphism means to give animals, objects, or anything non-human, some of the characteristics of a human. As the previous section suggests, the Capeks have given these insects human qualities for symbolic value. But the anthropomorphic traits serve other purposes in the play as well. By using anthropomorphic characters, *The Insect Play* becomes fable-like. That is, it has some of the qualities of a fable. A fable is a fictitious story with a moral lesson that often features animals. This play touches on many moral issues and ideas—greed, the blind following of leaders, the brutality of murder, the harshness of death—using the insects, but does not have an obvious moral. Instead *The Insect Play* focuses on the implications of actions without clearly stating that one action is definitely good, while another is clearly bad, as a fable would. The authors leave the interpretation (good, bad, or a mix of both) of what is depicted up to the audience. Fables are usually written to instruct, while this play is more concerned with being thought-provoking as well as entertaining.

HISTORICAL CONTEXT

In the aftermath of World War I, Central Europe was a mess. World War I (1914–1918) had torn the area apart, and borders and countries changed. Before the war, there was a movement to create an independent state for the Czech and Slovak people. At the time, the land and people that eventually formed Czechoslovakia were a part of Austria-Hungary. Czechs shared the land with Germans, who supported the war and the Central Powers. The Czechs were generally opposed, though the opposition took time to become coordinated. Czechs were pressed into military service by Austrians to fight on the side of the Central Powers. But those that served on the Eastern Front often defected to the Russian side. At home, the Czech press was censored, and no public meetings were allowed. Those considered disloyal to Austria-Hungary's interests were often put in prison.

After 1917, when the United States officially entered the war and the Russian Revolution took place, Czech leaders sought to increase their autonomy within Austria-Hungary. A Czechoslovak army was formed to fight on the side of the Allies (including the United States and Russia). These troops participated in high-profile operations that gained sympathy for their cause. Independence now seemed possible, with the help of the Allies. Before the war ended, Czech leaders got recognition for their Czechoslovak National Council from Allied countries. This Council officially represented Czech interests at the peace conference, and declared itself a provisional government. After the Austria-Hungary Empire fell apart in October 1918, a republic was declared.

The early years of the Republic of Czechoslovakia were not easy. Immediately after the war, while the new government was being formed, borders had to be determined in the postwar peace conference. The new government got in a dispute with Poland over the partition of the Duchy of Teschen, for example. Still, Czech leaders formed a National Assembly that drafted a new, democratic constitution. This constitution was adopted on February 29, 1920. While many Czechs and Slovaks were pleased to finally have their own country, there was internal opposition to the republic. One group in particular, the Sudeten Germans, protested the constitution. They did, however, vote in elections and form political parties. Some Slovaks also had aspirations towards their own autonomous state, though others supported a close alliance with Czechs. The first strong political party in Czechoslovakia was the Social Democracy party for the first several years. After an internal split in 1920, the Republicans became the leading political party. One Republican, Antonín Svehla, was prime minister of Czechoslovakia from 1921 until 1929.

As the newly formed Czechoslovakia began to define itself internally and externally, problems in Europe were on the horizon. Though Czechoslovakia was loyal to the League of Nations (formed in the wake of World War I), and had an alliance with France and treaties with Yugoslavia and Romania, Germany proved to be the biggest stumbling block to the country's future. Though relations were somewhat cool, one event in the Germany of the early 1920s proved important: Adolf Hitler was elected chair and dictator for life of the relatively new Nazi Party. Hitler's rise to power in Germany in the late 1920s and early 1930s would eventually spell the end of Czechoslovakia in 1938. Germany occupied the country, and split it up during World War II. Later, Czechoslovakia would rise again.

CRITICAL OVERVIEW

Since the premiere of *The Insect Play* in 1922, the play has not been performed often, but it does appear every couple of decades. The demands of staging the Capeks' insect world are the primarily reason that it is only occasionally produced. Critics' reaction to the play has changed over time.

COMPARE & CONTRAST

- **1920s:** Czechoslovakia is a single, newly formed country, trying to define itself. While most Czechs support the republic, there is a Slovak independence movement.

    Today: The Czech Republic and Slovakia are now two separate countries. The countries split amicably on January 1, 1993, when the federation was dissolved.

- **1920s:** Czech writers, like Karel Capek, are in vogue throughout the literary world.

    Today: A Czech writer of some acclaim, Vaclav Havel, has served as president of Czechoslovakia, as well as the Czech Republic.

- **1920s:** Czechoslovakia, and much of Central Europe, is recovering from the effects of World War I.

    Today: The Czech Republic, Slovakia, and much of the Eastern Bloc that was previously under the rule of the Soviet Union are recovering from the effects, economic and otherwise, of communist rule. The Czech Republic is trying to become part of the larger European Economic Community.

- **1920s:** In 1921, Adolf Hitler is elected chair and dictator of the Nazi Party. He will eventually lead Germany into World War II. Hitler's rise to power in Europe leads to the end of Czechoslovakia. The United Soviet Socialist Republic (USSR) is also declared, creating one of the largest communist powers the world will ever see.

    Today: While communism is on the wane in Europe, the Soviet Union has broken up and become a democracy and the Czechs and Slovaks have their own independent countries, Nazism still has a hold over some German-speaking peoples. In Austria, a controversial politician with ties to Nazism was elected.

When the play was first produced in the United States in 1922 (as *The World We Live In*), John Corbin of the *New York Times* discussed the contemporary parallels that it was meant to evoke. Corbin included the impact of World War I and how Central European writers like the Capeks were perceived at the time. While Corbin believed that "the impression persists that it is all rather a libel on the insects," later in the review, he stated "the insects who thus represent the world are . . . but a travesty conceived in the spirit of the wartime."

Robert Allerton Parker of the *Independent* shared Corbin's mixed feelings about this production. Calling the play "puerile," Parker believed *The Insect Play* was only staged because of its Central European origins. Writers from that part of the world were in vogue, leading Parker to speculate that if an American had written it, no producer would have touched it. Parker faulted the Capeks for "this failure . . . to organize their theme with any notable dramatic efficiency. This failure, it seemed to me, was the inevitable result of a confusion of thought and intention. Were they aiming to expose the human traits in insects? Or were they revealing the entomic vices of humans?"

The Insect Play made its London debut in May 1923 under that name at the Regent Theatre. Francis Birrell of *The Nation [and] the Athenaeum* shared some of Parker's concerns. Though Birrell called the production "rare and refreshing fruit" as well as it one of the best plays he had seen in London, he had problems with it as well. He wrote, "They have, up to a point, sympathetic minds. . . . There is a gritty disillusion about their reactions which has enabled them to produce a far more healthy entertainment than is usually seen on the London stage. But one cannot help feeling they have got muddled about their aims."

The Insect Play did not have the same impact in the post-World War II period as it did in the post-World War I era. In 1948, another production was put on in New York City under the name *The Insect Comedy,* which also received mixed reviews. A *New York Times* critic wrote ''what seems to have struck another generation as powerfully interesting theatre, as profound wisdom and searching analysis, now seems only interesting.... What it had to say probably matters more than how it said it and its sentiments could easily have echoed in the minds and hearts of a world attempting to recover its balance.''

Harold Clurman of the *New Republic* and John Gassner of *Forum* echoed these sentiments. Clurman believed the play's sources—the post-World War I era and its problems—were key to understanding *The Insect Play.* Clurman wrote, ''It represents the combination of despair and fury without any foundation in specific social understanding that inevitably paves the way to another war. The play is nevertheless justified by the fact that it does reflect an atmosphere created by a painfully real historical situation.'' Gassner was one critic who believed the play was still ''timely,'' arguing that ''this strangely moving, devastatingly satirical drama, born of postwar disillusionment, a play as timely today as it was in 1921 when the world felt the same dismay over a war fought and a peace won only to be lost.''

The Insect Play was produced again in 1979 in New York City as the *The Insect Comedy* and 1999 in Chicago as *The Insect Play.* Lucia Mauro of the *Chicago Sun-Times* wrote of the latter production in contemporary terms while commenting on what many critics have talked about since the earliest productions. Calling it ''a work of operatic proportions,'' Mauro wrote, ''In this early feminist study and dark comedy, female butterflies assert their independence and acknowledge their burning passions. The Capeks also call into question the overriding belief that humans have mightier ambitions than other species.'' Mauro believed that *The Insect Play* was still relevant at the dawn of the twenty-first century.

CRITICISM

Annette Petruso

In this essay, Petruso discusses the important role of the character of the Tramp plays in The Insect Play.

Many critics have noted that Karel and Josef Capek's *The Insect Play* (1921) consists of three one-act playlets. Others have called the play a revue, a show comprised of different sketches that comment on recent events. However these critics describe the nature of *The Insect Play,* everyone agrees that one character ties the disparate acts together: The Tramp. Introduced in the prologue, the tramp could be interpreted as dreaming the play's action or as merely a device the Capeks use to link the three stories they are telling. In either case, the tramp plays a key role in *The Insect Play.* He gives the audience a human character to identify with. The tramp guides the audience through the action, commenting on it. As the play progresses, he becomes part of it. This essay looks at the crucial role the tramp has in the play, and the effect of his character on the play's tone and content.

The tramp is the only human character to appear in each part of *The Insect Play.* When he is introduced in the prologue, he is asleep with an empty bottle, implied to be liquor, at his side. The tramp is awakened by the lepidopterist, who is collecting butterflies for his scientific collection. The scientist is trying to nab a butterfly that is resting on the tramp's nose. After the scientist leaves to continue his pursuit, the tramp addresses the audience directly. He tells them that he was not drunk, but that he fell from a tree while rehearsing ''the fall of man.'' Further, the tramp declares ''I'm a man, that's what I am—a lord of creation! A great thing to be I tell yer! Now then, pass along there, my man! That's what they say to me.''

Thus, from the beginning of the play, the tramp's role is established. He identifies himself as ''man,'' not just in one way but several. The tramp may be a human man, but to his fellow human men and women, he is less than them. He is pushed aside by them. He has no home to sleep in, no job or family. Yet the tramp also claims to be ''a lord of creation.'' The tramp is a man who created these insect worlds in the woods, away from civilization. They are, perhaps, his interpretations of or perceptions of the reality of human life. This duality makes the tramp a Christ-like figure: both complex man and god. The tramp represents the human conscience, a definer of values.

Each of the three one-acts (or sketches, depending on the definition preferred) defines an aspect of human morality for the tramp. The fact that the pieces use insects makes them small morality plays: they illustrate human vices and define meritorious behavior. The human audience can see these morals more clearly because they are presented in a palat-

WHAT DO I READ NEXT?

- *Gulliver's Travels*, a novel by Jonathan Swift written in 1726, is also a social and political commentary on his era. Like *The Insect Play*, it uses fantastic characters to underscore its themes and ideas about human vice.

- *Animal Farm*, a novel by George Orwell written in 1945, also anthropomorphizes animals to comment on human society.

- *Fables and Would-Be Tales* is a collection of narrative fiction written by Karel Capek between 1925 and 1938 and published in 1946. Many of the pieces are fables that take on an animal or inanimate object's point of view.

- *What Never Happened* is a story written by Vsevolod Garsin in 1882. Many critics believe that it is a direct influence on *The Insect Play*.

- *The Fateful Game of Love*, a play written by Karel and Josef Capek in 1910, is a one-act *commedia dell'arte* on the facade of real life. It is not unlike Act I in *The Insect Play*.

---

able form. They are not seeing themselves on stage, but a version thereof. Each act is like an animated cartoon. The tales reflect an aspect of society, exaggerated to reveal a deeper message. While the goal of most cartoons is to elicit a humorous reaction, the acts of *The Insect Play* define what the tramp thinks is wrong and right with the human world.

In Act I, the tramp shows a society that has rejected him. The butterflies—vain, shallow creatures only concerned with attracting the opposite sex and outmaneuvering those of the same—intrigue him at first. But as he watches the superficial mating dance unfold, the tramp becomes disgusted. Towards the end of the act, Clytie, a female butterfly, tries to induce the tramp into chasing her. He becomes annoyed by her false interest, calling her a "'ussy" and a "'arlot" before exclaiming "Go—get a move on. I 'ate the sight of yer." The tramp sees past skin-deep beauty and empty relationships. While the act begins with him believing he has found paradise, it ends with him disparaging their lifestyle and motivation.

The tramp shows both what he respects and despises in Act II. This act is more complex than the first, with several story lines. One concerns a Mr. and Mrs. Beetle, who have worked very hard to collect what they call their "capital." This is a ball of dirt and dung, what they consider their life's savings. The tramp respects the fact that these insects actually labor. He says: "Them butterflies was gay / And foolish, yer might say: / But these 'ere beetles—lumme, / They *do* work, anyway!" Later in the act, he makes fun of their obsession with their capital after it is stolen. The beetles care more about the capital than each other.

The tramp is more troubled by the actions of the ichneumon fly. The fly kills other insects to feed his daughter, a larva. While the tramp respects the right of the fly to feed his children, he also sympathizes with the fly's victims. The tramp exclaims in the middle of the act: "That fly destroys / The cricket jest to feed 'is girls and boys; / But that pore 'armless cricket found life sweet, / Same as 'e does—No! Nature 'as me beat!" But later in the act, after the tramp observes and becomes friendly with a Mr. and Mrs. Cricket, he finds the fly's actions murderous. The fly kills them both in cold blood in front of the tramp. The tramp blames himself for not trying to help these innocent victims. The tramp expresses his horror over killing with a parasite who happens along. The parasite further condemns the fly for storing large amounts of food when other creatures are starving.

After the parasite exacts a certain amount of revenge by eating the parasite's stored food as well as his daughter, the tramp remains upset by the murders. Near the end of the act, while the parasite is in the fly's lair eating his fill, the tramp speaks

> "... DUALITY MAKES THE TRAMP A CHRIST-LIKE FIGURE: BOTH COMPLEX MAN AND GOD. THE TRAMP REPRESENTS THE HUMAN CONSCIENCE, A DEFINER OF VALUES."

three verses that explicitly compares humankind to these three kinds of creatures (beetles, crickets, and ichneumon fly), as much as he dislikes the parallels. The last line of these verses states "'oo can think straight on gin?" The tramp, as a conscience, does not always like what he sees.

The tramp still has confidence in Act III. At the beginning of the act, he exclaims, "Insec's won't work together. Man / Will. 'E can form a general plan. There's something great in 'im what fights / And perishes for the nation's rights." The tramp goes on to laud those that give up their lives for their country. His opinion changes once he sees what goes on in the Ant Realm. This sketch is about the negative effect of blind devotion to the state and to work. The ants are only concerned with how to work more quickly and efficiently for the good of the state. Unlike the insects in other sketches, some of the ants are defined by work titles: chief engineer and second engineer. (The butterflies have names, while the insects in Act II are defined by species.)

The ants want to work faster so they can take over the world. The chief engineer declares himself dictator as soon as a war has begun with their last remaining enemy, the yellow ants. The tramp takes the Ant Realm's side and hopes they win their war. But when he sees the slaughter from the battles and the injured ants, the tramp changes his mind. He identifies more with the soldiers of the Ant Realm, rather than its self-proclaimed dictator. Finally, when the yellow ants overrun the Ant Realm at the end of Act III, the tramp can no longer remain a passive observer to slaughter. He kills the yellow leader, grinding the ant with his boot. Everything the tramp has seen in *The Insect Play* has led to this moment. It is one thing to moralize through example; it is quite another to take action for one's self. His conscience has driven him to murder.

One reason for the tramp's evolution, especially after the end of Act I, might be the introduction of the chrysalis at the beginning of Act II. The chrysalis is an insect about to be born. She is excited about her forthcoming birth, and tells the tramp (and whoever else is listening) about the great things she will accomplish. While the tramp grows tired of hearing her plans, she does give him one thing none of the other insects can: hope. Her hope touches him when all the other insects disappoint him with their actions. She is possibility. She is the future. One interpretation could be that the chrysalis is the tramp's foster child. He laments his childless state several times in the play. It is as if they adopt each other as father and daughter. But like the other father-daughter relationship depicted in *The Insect Play,* it ends badly.

In the play's epilogue, it is night and the tramp is yelling in his sleep. He already fears death in the dark and seeks light. The light that comes draws and kills moths. When the chrysalis finally opens, a moth emerges, only to die a few moments later. None of her hopes or dreams are realized. Before she is born, the tramp asks "Butterflies, beetles, moths and men—why can't we all live 'appy together? The world's big enough, and life could be 'appy for everythink—if we 'ad a bit o' sense." After her death, the tramp realizes that he is going to die, though he tries to deny it. He wants to live because he knows more about what it means to be human now. But like the chrysalis/moth, he will not get the chance.

In *The Insect Play,* the tramp serves as a symbol of optimism for humankind. Despite the problems he sees exemplified by the insects, the tramp does not lose hope until he is near death. The hope that is lost is only for his future, not the rest of humanity's. The tramp wants the world to be a fair place, though his frustrations do lead to his murdering the yellow ant leader at the end of Act III. The ending of the play shows this change. Though the woodcutter who finds the tramp's corpse dismisses him as "Only a tramp," he also states that "I hope he'll be better off than we are." The woman, carrying a newborn baby, yet another symbol of a hopeful future, places a flower on his makeshift grave. Unlike the beginning of *The Insect Play,* when the scientist is angry and dismissive of the tramp, the end shows other humans being kind to their fellow man.

Source: Annette Petruso, in an essay for *Drama for Students,* Gale Group, 2001.

Joyce Hart

Hart, a former college professor, is a freelance writer. In the following essay, she focuses on the play's main author, Karel Capek, and investigates the political theory that lies beneath the veneer of humor in The Insect Play.

Although *The Insect Play* was an immediate hit on Broadway in the early 1920s, Robert Wechsler states, in *Capek in America,* that the Capeks and their play were viewed mostly as a novelty. "[Karel]Capek was from a brand new country [that] some reviewers didn't even seem to know about." According to Wechsler, the Capeks' play appealed to an audience that was "taken with the scenery and the special effects." In the 1920s the audience found the Capeks' play entertaining; they were unable, or unwilling, to go beyond the surface meaning of the dialogue. It was viewed as a comedy—something that was supposed to be taken lightly.

With the passing of time, as well as another world war, the development of the nuclear bomb, and the degradation of the environment by an industrialized world, Arthur Miller, an American playwright, has a different take on the Capek play and sense of humor. Miller believes that Karel Capek was so far ahead of his time that his contemporaries missed the point. They thought Karel's ideas were too improbable to ever come true. In his introduction to a study of the Capeks' works titled, *Toward The Radical Center,* Miller writes that while the audiences in the Capeks' time responded to the play with charming curiosity, more modern audiences view the Capeks' portrayed world as far less outrageous and far more frightening. "We have evolved into [Karel's] nightmare," Miller says, and now "when our science, shorn of moral purpose, is gradually enclosing our planet in unbreathable gases, it is time to read Capek again for his insouciant laughter, and the anguish of human blindness that lies beneath it."

The Insect Play is a play about scary things; and the least scary things in the play are the insects. The play is not about bugs, per se, but rather about the bugs in humanity: the problems, the faults, the mistakes. Karel Capek, having been an avid gardener, uses insects as an extended metaphor, expressing the foibles of humanity by giving insects a voice and exaggerating their likeness to mankind. It is the scary things in *The Insect Play* that Karel masks with his deceptive sense of humor. As Peter Kussi puts it in *Toward the Radical Center,* Karel Capek "has the gift of expressing weighty matters

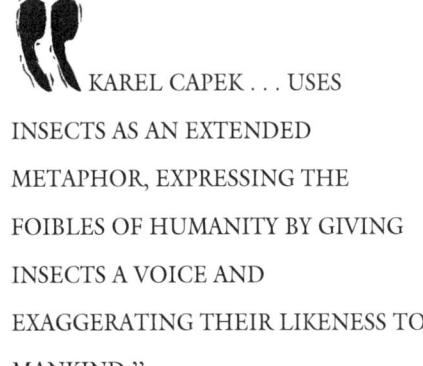

"KAREL CAPEK... USES INSECTS AS AN EXTENDED METAPHOR, EXPRESSING THE FOIBLES OF HUMANITY BY GIVING INSECTS A VOICE AND EXAGGERATING THEIR LIKENESS TO MANKIND."

in the simplest of terms, while his most casual, humorous articles and stories contain something of real substance."

The overall theme in all of Karel's works, says Kussi, is a "search for man." If this is true, then *The Insect Play* begins with what appears to be a rather shabby example of man, a tramp: unshaven, rumpled, and wobbly. But it is off this tramp that the Capeks bounce all the underlying political and social commentary. The tramp observes the other characters in the play and reflects on the absurdity of their communications and actions. Although he appears drunk, it is the tramp who has the clearest thoughts. "P'raps I am screwed," he says, but "...that ain't the only reason why I see everythink double..."

What is double in this play is not the tramp's vision, but rather the double-talk, or nonsense, of its characters. The first character that the tramp meets is the scientist, who represents one of Karel's central worries about the world. Karel was very concerned that scientists were not aware of the potentially catastrophic consequences of scientific investigations and subsequent inventions. He wrote several science fiction novels about the possible misuse of technology. So *The Insect Play* begins with a lepidopterist, or someone who studies butterflies. This scientist appears more benign than a nuclear physicist might in today's world, but Karel nonetheless presents this seemingly safe butterfly man as a cold, unemotional person who seems to be defying his own scientific end. When asked by the tramp what it is that he is doing, the lepidopterist responds: "The butterfly must be carefully killed...pinned, and...dried." And what is this all for, the tramp wants to know. "Love of nature," says the lepidopterist, then he adds, "if you loved nature as much as I did, my man . . . ,'' trailing off without finishing his statement, leaving the audience to fill in the blanks.

It is also in this opening scene that the tramp voices Karel's deepest concern: the eventual destruction of humanity. The tramp turns to the audience and says: "I know what you think . . . you think I'm screwed . . . You didn't catch me staggering, did you? I fell like a tree . . . like a hero! I was rehearsing . . . the fall of man!" This sets up the premise, and from this point to the end of the play Karel postulates the various combinations of events that might lead to mankind's eventual destruction.

The next scene is dedicated to the butterflies, a somewhat superficial and frivolous group, possibly reflecting the upper-class dilettantes of society. The act begins with poor Felix who resembles the fourteenth-century Italian poet Petrarch, who constantly wrote of his love for an unattainable woman. Felix has his own unattainable woman, Iris. Part of this scene revolves around Felix's attempts to tell Iris of his love, but the words he uses are grossly misinterpreted. Iris mistakes Felix's subtle emotional pronouncements as insults. She calls him a "rude little man" and a "cynic." "Oh, Iris," Felix says, "every one disparages the thing that he loves best." Iris' reply is: "Do you mean dark women?" In another exchange Felix tells Iris that woman is a riddle. Iris again confuses his meaning and says: "Guess it then. But not too roughly, please." Love is the first of two issues that the butterflies flit around, stopping briefly to touch, but never investing full emotion. The second topic is death.

The fatality of Felix and Iris' relationship is obvious, but it is not the only fatality in this scene. One of Iris' other, more superficial suitors is eventually eaten by a bird. He is caught in a bird's mouth much like the butterflies in the first scene were caught in the lepidopterist's net. His demise is swift and, like the lepidopterist, Iris shrugs death off lightly. In fact, death makes her laugh. She eventually flies off, leaving Felix with the tramp to listen to his poetry that, by the end of this scene, reflects the brevity not only of love, but also of life. Brevity of life is a concept that will reoccur in the play, linking one scene to the next.

The creepers and crawlers enter the stage in the next scene. They represent various forms of political systems, most obviously capitalism and communism. "Philosophically as well as politically," says Kussi, "[Karel] was a man of the center. . .The center he was aiming for was not a lukewarm middle ground between extremes. It was a radical center, radical in the original sense of the word: at the root of things." Karel did not believe in collectivism, or any type of social organization in which the individual is seen as subordinate to a social collectivity such as a state or nation. Communism, Fascism, and Nazism are all based on a type of collectivism philosophy. Neither did Karel support selfish individualism that is the underlying philosophy in extreme capitalism. Karel was a "passionate democrat and pluralist," says Kussi. "He disliked single vision and preferred to look at everything from many sides."

Some of the most obvious as well as most absurd capitalists in the third scene are the beetles. Their main goal in life is centered on gathering their precious little pile. These beetles are like dung beetles who gather cow dung in small balls and roll them into their holes in the ground. The tramp says the little pile smells, but the beetles are willing to protect their little pile with their lives. They will roll it around with them forever for they fear someone may steal it. Once they find a good hiding place, they will go find another pile that they will roll around again. They talk about this pile as if it were their child. They've watched it grow. They refer to it as a blessing from heaven. Their whole life is consumed with taking care of the pile. They care for nothing else, not even for one another. All they want is to accumulate more piles. When the unthinkable happens—another beetle steals the pile—the first beetle despairs: "Rolled it away? My pile? . . . All my little lot. All I've saved. They've killed me . . . Who cares about my wife? It's my pile they've taken."

There is also the ichneumon fly in this scene who spends his life gathering food for his larval daughter. She is spoiled and eats only the tasty parts of the crickets that her father brings home. He, on the other hand, is proud of her and does not mind all the work that she requires. As a matter of fact, the fly's whole life is consumed with work. "Up early, home late, but as long as you're doing it for some one worth doing it for, what does it matter?" says the fly.

The tramp sees that it matters. He can't figure out nature. "This 'as me fairly beat. That fly destroys but that pore 'armless cricket found life sweet, same as 'e does . . . No! Nature 'as me beat!" This is the Capeks' comment on capitalism. One capitalist nation feeds off another. To provide economic growth, a capitalist nation must find ways of making a profit, even if it is at the expense of another nation.

In contrast to capitalism is the parasite, whom the tramp calls a "Bolshie." The Bolsheviks, to whom the play is referring, were the forerunners of communism in Russia. The parasite is two-faced and at one point yells: "Down with work," but then steals from the fly who has worked to build his larder. "Down with larder," says the parasite. "Hoarding shouldn't be allowed. Eat your fill and 'ave done with it . . . Storing things is robbin' those who haven't nowhere to store. Eat your fill and have done with it and then there'd be enough for all, wouldn't there?" Later the parasite says: "why should I work when somebody else has more than he can consume?" Then a few lines later, the parasite contradicts himself with: "That's the third cricket [the fly has] had already, and me nothing. And that's what we poor working men are asked to put up with."

By the end of this scene the poor tramp is very confused. He tries hard to define man, thinking that man is better than the insects. But every time he comes up with a definition of what man is, he is reminded of the beetles, the crickets or the flies.

> But man—man's diff'rent. Folks like me an' you
> Work 'ard, real 'ard, and makes our little pile...
> Blast! I'm all mixed. *That's* what them beetles do...
>
> ... Bold—that's what man is; resolute, yer might s'y,
> If 'e wants more, 'e does 'is neighbour in ... O 'Ell!
> That makes 'im like this murd'rous fly ...

The war machine comes in the next scene as seen through the lives of the ants. Anticipating these insects, the tramp begins this act with a commentary on how men need to work together, and surrender their own, selfish desires (such as the capitalists have) to the greater good of the State. This act is Karel's reference to the worst of communism. The ants' values emphasize world power, reason, law and the interests of the whole. Everything that the ant colony does is for "Her." This "Her" is the queen ant that Karel uses as a metaphor for the State. She is "the one who orders." At first the tramp likes this concept, a kind of one for all and all for one philosophy. Unfortunately, the "all" in this anthill excludes anyone outside the given race of that particular colony. Therefore the ants believe that enemies surround them. The enemies are the black, brown, gray, and yellow ants. When the Chief Engineer declares war on the yellow ants, it is proposed that his ants are "fighting the battle of peace."

Karel inserts an inventor in this scene, taking on the scientist again. This time the scientist is the creator of the war machine. The inventor glorifies his invention: "A war machine. A vast machine, a huge one. The swiftest, most effective crusher of lives. The forefront of progress, the acme of science . . . Two hundred thousand dead . . ." When the tramp asks the ants why there must be war, the ants reply: "Because we shall have a new war machine."

The play ends with a summary of Karel's observations about life from the viewpoint of death. In the end, Karel cries out for the use of common sense. Kussi says,

> [Karel's] work radiates a firm belief in common sense. . .praise for simple folk wisdom. [Karel] counters nonsense by steadfast adherence to good sense. Such an attitude could easily become boring; [but] it is one of the glories of [Karel] that he makes the voice of reason sound lively, amusing, totally fresh . . . he writes [from] a deep-rooted center that includes reason yet reaches beyond reason to deeper springs.

The Epilogue of the play is titled "Death and Life." In this scene the tramp sees his own death coming in the form of two snails. Before leaving, the tramp reflects on all the lives, as well as the deaths of the insects:

> "Life and death—seems they're both good if we know how to treat 'em . . . why can't we all live 'appy together? The world's big enough, and life could be 'appy for everythink—if we 'ad a bit o' sense."

Source: Joyce Hart, in an essay for *Drama for Students*, Gale Group, 2001.

Liz Brent

Brent has a Ph.D. in American Culture, specializing in film studies, from the University of Michigan. She is a freelance writer and teaches courses in the history of American cinema. In the following essay, Brent discusses the allegorical meaning of the play.

In *The Insect Play*, insect society, so to speak, is represented as an allegory for human society. In particular, in Act II, Capek and Capek address their concerns with the economic struggles of, and competition between, humans through their characterization of different species of insects. Thus, the dung beetles represent the working class, the Ichneumon Fly seems to represent the entrepreneurial, or petit-bourgeoisie, middle class, and the butterflies represent the upper classes, or bourgeoisie. The play presents a highly cynical perspective on the workings of human society, made up of lives characterized by meaningless existence, greed, and hard work in the name of family.

The dung beetles represent the working masses who toil their lives away for no other reason than to amass a pitiful life savings for which there is no real purpose. The dung beetles are obsessed with their "little pile"—a ball of dung—which represents their life's work. They refer to it in terms commonly used by people to describe their hard-earned savings. The Male Beetle calls it, "Our capital. Our nest-egg. Our stock-in-trade. Our all." The Female Beetle concurs with similar descriptions, which further indicate that these two value their "pile" of dung above all else in life, although it in fact serves no purpose, except to represent an abstract notion of amassed wealth: "Oh, what a lovely little pile, what a treasure, what a beautiful little ball, what a precious little fortune." And the Male Beetle adds that it is "our only joy." The beetles further describe the lifetime of labor they have devoted to amassing this "pile." The Male Beetle continues, "To think how we've saved and scraped, toiled and moiled, denied ourselves, gone without this, stinted ourselves that—," and, the Female Beetle adds, "worked our legs off and drudged and plodded to get it together." Capek and Capek represent this "life's work" of the beetles as an allegory for the "life work" of humans, who spend their entire lives working in order to save a "nest-egg," of money. But the beetles' "nest-egg" is merely a ball of dung, and the implication is that the life savings of a hard-working human amounts to little more than a pile of dung, and has no intrinsic value. But the beetles value their pile of dung simply because they own it, just as humans tend to value their amassed life savings simply because it represents an abstract concept of wealth, or ownership, regardless of whether or not this wealth actually adds any value to the quality of human life. The Male Beetle states that, "it's fine to own something. Your property! The dream of your life! The fruit of your labors!" Not only does this amassed pile of dung smell bad and seem to have no intrinsic value, but also it brings with it a world of fear and anxiety. Once this wealth has been amassed, it serves no purpose, except as a basis for amassing more wealth. The Male Beetle states that he is "going off my head with sheer worry"; and continues, "Now we've got our little pile. I've been so much looking forward to it, and now we've got it, we'll have to make another one. Nothing but work, work, work." The Female Beetle asks, "Why another one?" to which her husband replies, "so that we can have two, of course.... Ah, just fancy, two of them. At least two. Let's say even three. You know, every one who's made one pile has to make another." It seems that, for the beetles, and, allegorically, for humans, the purpose of work is to amass wealth, and yet this only leads to more work in the service of amassing yet more wealth. The implication is that a human life, filled with hard work for the sole end of amassing more and more wealth, is ultimately meaningless.

Furthermore, the acquisition of wealth only adds more worry and anxiety, lest it be lost or stolen. The Female Beetle says "I'm scared. Suppose someone was to steal it from us." Their life's work of amassed wealth brings them no joy or pleasure, but merely fear, anxiety, and the prospect of more work. The beetles continue to describe their pile of dung in terms which humans use to describe their life savings. They call it, "Our little pile. Our joy. Our all," and "Our precious little store. Our life. Our whole concern." The pile of dung clearly represents money, as the Male Beetle refers to it as "Our precious gold," and suggests that they "invest it." When the Strange Beetle comes along to steal the "pile" of dung left by the Male and Female Beetle, he too describes it in terms which humans use to describe a life's fortune, calling it "my pile. Capital. Gold.... My treasure. You lovely nest-egg. My jewel. My all." The Vagrant (The Tramp in other versions) points out that this "gold" is actually a pile of dung when he comments that "That gold of yours smells." Capek and Capek here clearly criticize the value of material wealth, and criticize a human society that attaches such importance and worth to something so inherently worthless, and even distasteful, as money or "gold." The Strange Beetle further represents the materialism of a human society that values "possessing" material wealth, just for the sake of "owning" something. The Strange Beetle replies that, despite the fact that the pile "smells," as the Vagrant put it, "it's nice to own something."

The materialism and greed of the beetles is so extreme that the Male Beetle even values his pile of dung more than his own wife. While he speaks of the pile with the greatest of affection, his references to his wife are full of disdain and insult; he agrees with the Vagrant's description of his wife as "that old harridan.... That ugly chatterbox.... That bad-tempered, dirty rag-bag." The Male Beetle is completely unconcerned that another beetle may have taken his wife, but becomes hysterical at the idea of losing his pile. He tells the Vagrant, "I don't care what he did with my wife. But where's my pile?" When he is told that the pile has been taken, he cries, "My pile? God in heaven! Catch him! Thief! Murder! (Flings himself to the ground.) My hard-earned fortune. They've killed me. I'd rather give up my life than that ball of golden manure." Capek and Capek are here criticizing the ways in which human society values material wealth over other humans, as well as one's own life. The Vagrant sums up the allegory in which the beetles represent the working masses, whose only wish is to work hard in order to acquire material wealth, no matter how valueless. Comparing them to the butterflies, who represent the leisure classes, the Vagrant observes:

> These others at least smell of honest labor. They don't want to enjoy, they only want to possess. Something.

The Vagrant then observes the concept of the "family" as a justification for a life of meaningless labor in the service of amassing material wealth.

> You labour for others, and if you're stingy,
>
> Well, stinginess is a virtue, when it's for the family.
>
> The family has its rights, the family sanctifies everything,
>
> Even theft, if need be, for after all, there are children. That's how it is, I tell you, and that's the whole point: A man will do anything to preserve his kindred.

The view of family and children, and the role of family and children in the economic structure of human society, allegorically represented here by Capek and Capek, is extremely cynical and critical. Through the Vagrant's comments, and the examples of the Ichneumon Fly and the cricket couple, the purpose of children is presented as merely an excuse for hard work, greed, and selfishness in the service of amassing material wealth. According to this perspective, as the Vagrant comments in the quote above, "stinginess," and even "theft," are justified on the basis that it is for the children, since "the family sanctifies everything."

The first species encountered by the Vagrant who justifies greed in the name of children is the Ichneumon Fly, whose sole purpose in life is to procure food for his larva. As represented in the play, the Fly's life would be meaningless if he didn't have a child whose need for food justifies his every act. He tells the Vagrant, "When you have them, you do at least know who you're working for. If you have a child then you must strive, work, struggle. That's real life, eh? Children want to grow, to eat, to feast, to play, don't they?" The Fly even kills other insects, such as the crickets, in order to

> CAPEK AND CAPEK REPRESENT THIS 'LIFE'S WORK' OF THE BEETLES AS AN ALLEGORY FOR THE 'LIFE WORK' OF HUMANS, WHO SPEND THEIR ENTIRE LIVES WORKING IN ORDER TO SAVE A 'NEST-EGG,' OF MONEY."

feed his larvae. Because this selfishness, greed, and stinginess is justified by the importance of the child, the Fly must constantly remind himself and others of the importance of the child. The Fly comments to the Vagrant, "Children are a great joy, aren't they?" He goes on to justify his life of hard work by expressing his "pride" in his child: "I'm proud of her. Really proud. Just like her daddy, eh? . . . and I'm gossiping here, instead of getting to work. Oh, the fuss and running about. But as long as we do it for somebody, what does it matter? Aren't I right?"

The cricket couple expecting a baby are another example representing the ways in which human beings use family as an excuse to justify a life devoted to meaningless material acquisition. The cricket couple, rather than amassing a pile as their life's work, like the beetles, or spending all of their time and energy working to feed a child, put all of their efforts into their dream of owning a home in which to house their expected child. Capek and Capek, however, are making a similar social critique of human life spent in pursuit of acquiring such material possessions as a house, especially at the expense of others. The Male Cricket and Female Cricket take over the home of the cricket that has been tied up by the Fly, to be preserved for food for his larva. The cricket couple are concerned only with acquiring their own home, as the Male Cricket says, "Our little nest, our villa, our own little place, our, ha, ha, our residence." Meanwhile, they merely look in and laugh at the cricket who has been captured and tied up, interested only in their own good fortune in taking over the poor cricket's home. The Male Cricket even refers to the captured cricket's demise as a "godsend" for him and his wife. The materialism of the cricket couple in their dream of acquiring their own home is further expressed through the middle-class cliché of hanging curtains as a symbol of successful homemaking. The Male Cricket tells his wife, "We'll furnish this place beautifully. And as soon as we can manage it we'll put up some—" at which point the Female Cricket finishes his sentence with, "Curtains." Later, the Female Beetle and the Female Cricket debate the relative value of a life spent amassing a pile, and a life spent acquiring and furnishing a home to house a family. Although each values her own approach to life, they are both completely preoccupied with a life devoted to material acquisition.

> Female Beetle: And aren't you making a pile?
>
> Female Cricket: What for?
>
> Female Beetle: A pile, that for the family. That's the future. That's your whole life.
>
> Female Cricket: Oh no. My whole life is to have my own little house, my nest, a little place of my own. And curtains. And children. And to have my Cricket. My own home. That's all.
>
> Female Beetle: How can you live without a pile?
>
> Female Cricket: What would we do with it?
>
> Female Beetle: Roll it about with you everywhere. I tell you, there's nothing like a pile for holding a man.
>
> Female Cricket: Oh no, a little house.
>
> Female Beetle: A pile, I tell you.
>
> Female Cricket: A little house.

The Fly represents the most aggressive type of materialist, the entrepreneur. The Fly describes himself and his aggressive approach to obtaining food for his child, in terms similar to how successful business people are described. After he murders the pregnant Female Cricket and feeds it to his larva, he calls his act "A fine piece of work." He brags that such an accomplishment takes "expert knowledge. Enterprise. I—ni—tiative. And foresight. And love for work, let me tell you." The Fly continues in this vein: "if you want to keep alive, you've got to fight your way. There's your future. There's your family. And then, you know, there's a certain amount of ambition. A strong personality is bound to assert itself. Aren't I right?" The Fly goes on to describe such aggressive work as the stuff of a "useful life": "Make your way in the world, use the talent that's in you, that's what I call a useful life." The Fly further extols the value of such work, which involves killing and eating other insects: "And how it cheers you up, when you fulfil your duty like that. When you perform your job. When you feel that you're not living in vain. It's so elevating, isn't it?" Capek and Capek are here criticizing the aggressive nature of capitalist enterprise as based on the selfish sacrifice of other humans beings in the service of one's own economic success.

The Vagrant concludes Act II by attempting to assert that the lives of human beings are devoted to some higher purpose than that of the cruel and meaningless lives of the insects, who selfishly and greedily kill and watch each other suffer for the sake of acquiring their own material wealth, in the name of supporting a family. But the Vagrant ultimately finds himself asserting that human beings are no better than such insects, looking out only for their own material self-interests, without regard to any higher purpose or meaning in life. He concludes with a cynical message about the baseness of human endeavors, no better than those of the insects:

> Do you not hear
>
> How throughout the world feverish jowls are working,
>
> Chew-chew-chew, the blood-stained, sated smacking of lips
>
> Over the still living morsel. Life is the prey to life.

In other words, Capek and Capek imply, human beings merely prey upon one another in the pursuit of their own material gain, and without regard to the value of human life, other than their own and that of their families.

Source: Liz Brent, in an essay for *Drama for Students,* Gale Group, 2001.

SOURCES

Birrell, Francis, "The Aesthetics of Revue," in *The Nation [and] the Athenaeum,* May 19, 1923, p. 248.

Capek, Karel, and Josef Capek, *The Insect Play (And so ad infinitum),* in *R.U.R. and The Insect Play,* translated by Paul Selver, Oxford University Press, 1961, pp. 105–77.

Clurman, Harold, "A Dying Sound," in *New Republic,* June 21, 1948, pp. 28–29.

Corbin, John, "Libeling the Insects," in *New York Times,* November 1, 1922, p. 16.

Gassner, John, Review of *The Insect Comedy,* in *Forum,* July, 1948, pp. 20–22.

Mauro, Lucia, Review of *The Insect Play,* in *Chicago Sun-Times,* February 4, 1999, p. 34.

Parker, Robert Allerton, "Satire from Czecho-Slovakia," in *The Independent,* November 25, 1922, pp. 320–22.

Review of *The Insect Comedy,* in *New York Times,* May 28, 1948, p. 26.

FURTHER READING

Bradbrook, Bohuslava, *Karel Capek: In Pursuit of Truth, Tolerance, and Trust,* Sussex Academic Press, 1998.

    This critical biography considers Karel Capek's career in terms of each area he wrote in, including drama, novels, and short stories.

Harkins, William E., *Karel Capek,* Columbia University Press, 1962.

    This critical biography covers Karel Capek's life, both as a writer and a person. It also includes information on Josef Capek and the brothers' collaboration.

Makin, Michael, and Jindrich Toman, eds., *On Karel Capek,* Michigan Slavic Publications, 1992.

    This collection of essays considers the whole of Karel Capek's work from different perspectives.

Thomson, S. Harrison, *Czechoslovakia in European History,* Archon Books, 1965.

    This history of Czechoslovakia includes information on how the country came to be formed and the problems it faced in the era in which the Capeks worked.

M. Butterfly

DAVID HENRY HWANG

1988

David Henry Hwang's *M. Butterfly* is one of the most celebrated of recent American plays, and the first by an Asian-American to win universal acclaim. It was first produced in 1988 and won numerous awards, including the Tony Award for Best Play of the Year, the New York Drama Desk Award, the Outer Critics Circle Award for Best Broadway play, and the John Gassner Award for the season's outstanding new playwright. *M. Butterfly* enjoyed a popular run on Broadway and when it moved to London's Shaftsbury Theatre in 1989 it broke all box office records in the first week.

The play is based on a bizarre but true story of a French diplomat who carried on a twenty-year affair with a Chinese actor and opera singer, not realizing that his partner was in fact a man masquerading as a woman. The diplomat apparently became aware of the deception only in 1986, when he was charged by the French government with treason—it transpired that his companion had been an agent for the Chinese government, and had passed on sensitive political information that he had acquired from the diplomat. This almost unbelievable story stimulated Hwang's imagination, and from it he created a drama that plays with ideas on a grand scale and manages at the same time to be witty and entertaining. Weaving into the play many parallels with, and ultimately ironic reversals of, Puccini's opera, *Madame Butterfly,* Hwang explores the stereotypes that underlie and distort relations between Eastern and Western culture, and between men and women.

AUTHOR BIOGRAPHY

David Henry Hwang was born on August 11, 1957 in Los Angeles, California. His father, Henry Hwang, was a banker who had immigrated to the United States from Shanghai, China, in the 1940s, and his mother Dorothy, also born in China, was a pianist and music teacher. Hwang grew up in an affluent suburb of Los Angeles. He enrolled at Stanford University in 1975, where he developed an interest in playwriting. It was while he was at Stanford that he wrote his first play, *F.O.B.* The letters stand for "fresh off the boat," and the play explores the contrast in cultural attitudes between a recently arrived Chinese immigrant to California and two Chinese-American students who have long since assimilated American ways. The exploration of the interaction of Eastern and Western culture was to become a prominent theme in much of Hwang's later work.

Hwang directed a performance of *F.O.B.* at Stanford in 1978 while he was still an undergraduate. The following year the play was produced at the prestigious National Playwrights Conference at the O'Neill Theatre Center in Waterford, Connecticut. A year later it was staged Off-Broadway, to appreciative reviews. *F.O.B.* won an Obie Award as the best play of the 1980–81 off-Broadway season.

Hwang went on to study at Yale University School of Drama from 1980 to 1981, and while there, he followed the success of *F.O.B.* with two more plays that explored the Chinese-American heritage. The first was *The Dance and the Railroad* (1981), about Chinese immigrants who helped to build the transcontinental railroad in the nineteenth century. The second, *Family Devotions* (1981), explores the tensions in a modern Chinese-American family.

Hwang wrote several more plays during the next few years, including *Sound and Beauty* (1983), made up of two one-act plays, *The House of Sleeping Beauties* and *The Sound of a Voice,* both of which were set in Japan. *Rich Relations*, a comedy, followed in 1986. For the first time, Hwang chose not to write about Asian-Americans, his focus in this play being a white American family. The play was not a success, however.

After doing some writing for television, Hwang returned to the stage with *M. Butterfly,* which was first produced in Washington, D.C., in 1988 and moved to Broadway later that year. The play remains Hwang's biggest success to date. In the same year, Hwang collaborated with composer Philip Glass to create the science-fiction music drama, *One Thousand Airplanes on the Roof,* in which a character relates his experience of abduction by aliens.

Hwang continued his collaboration with Glass by writing the libretto for *The Voyage*, an opera produced at New York's Metropolitan Opera in 1992. He also adapted *M. Butterfly* for the movie screen (Warner Bros., 1993). In 1996, Hwang wrote *Of Golden Child,* which was produced at the Joseph Papp Public Theater in Washington, D.C. and moved to Broadway in 1998. The play is set in China in 1918, and deals with a Chinese family that comes increasingly under the influence of Western values.

PLOT SUMMARY

Act 1, scenes 1–3

M. Butterfly opens in present-day Paris. Rene Gallimard is in a small prison cell. He describes his monotonous daily routine, and then confides that he is no ordinary prisoner, but a celebrity. People talk about him at parties from Amsterdam to New York. Scene 2 shows three people at a party joking about Gallimard, and the joke obviously has something to do with sex. Scene 3 returns to Gallimard's cell, and he confides that he has been loved by the "Perfect Woman." He then says that to understand his story, the audience must know the opera *Madame Butterfly,* by Giacomo Puccini. He describes the opera and plays some of the music from it on his tape recorder. His old school friend Marc appears as one of the characters, and Gallimard assumes the role of Pinkerton, the American sailor who wins the heart of Butterfly, the Japanese girl, and then betrays her.

Scenes 4–5

Scene 4 flashes back to 1947, at a school in Aix-en-Provence, France. Marc tries to persuade Gallimard to accompany him to a party, promising that there will be plenty of girls available, but Gallimard refuses to go. He lacks confidence with girls. Scene 5 returns to Gallimard's cell, and Gallimard further explains the plot of *Madame Butterfly,* commenting that in real life, it is not easy to find a woman who will give herself so completely to a man. The closest to it are the girls who pose in pornographic magazines. As Gallimard pulls some of these magazines out of a crate in his cell, a pin-up girl appears, and tantalizingly disrobes. Gallimard

David Henry Hwang

resumes his exposition of the opera, as Comrade Chin plays the part of Suzuki, Butterfly's maid. Gallimard reveals that he married a woman, Helga, for career reasons rather than love. Then he reveals that when he was a diplomat in Beijing, he first saw ''her'' singing the death scene from *Madame Butterfly*. He does not explain who the woman was.

Scenes 6–10

Scene 6 takes place in Beijing in 1960, in the house of the German Ambassador. Gallimard has just watched Song Liling sing an aria from *Madame Butterfly*. He tells her he was moved by the story. Song, however, expresses little enthusiasm for it. She does, however, invite Gallimard to attend the Peking Opera. After scene 7, in which Gallimard and Helga discuss Chinese arrogance, scene 8 shows a meeting between Song and Gallimard in the streets of Beijing after Gallimard has attended the Peking Opera. Song invites him to her flat. In the next scene, Gallimard lies to his wife about having met Song, and Gallimard relates a dream in which Marc urges him to begin an affair with Song. In scene 10, Gallimard relates what happened on his first visit to Song's flat. They drink tea, and Song confesses she is afraid of scandal because she is entertaining a man in her flat, which is against Chinese custom. Gallimard believes she is afraid of him.

Scenes 11–13

In scene 11, Gallimard describes a strategy he devised to test Song. He makes no contact with her for five weeks. Marc reappears and together they recall Gallimard's first sexual experience. Then Gallimard tells the audience that after six weeks, Song began to write to him, pleading with him to visit her. He ignores this and subsequent letters, until he feels ashamed of making her suffer. In scene 12, Gallimard learns from Toulon, the French Ambassador, that he is to be promoted and will be in charge of the intelligence division. In scene 13, eight weeks after he last saw Song, he returns to her apartment and asks if she will surrender to him, just as Madame Butterfly surrendered to Pinkerton in Puccini's opera. Song is reluctant at first, but then they kiss and prepare to make love, although Song protests that she is inexperienced.

Act 2, scenes 1–4

Act two begins in the present, in Gallimard's cell. Gallimard comments about Puccini's opera. Scene 2 returns to Beijing in 1960, where Gallimard and Song now live in a flat together. Song complains about how, in Chinese society, women are kept down by men, and expresses admiration for the West. The following scene takes place a year later at the French Embassy. Toulon and Gallimard discuss Vietnam. Gallimard says that if the Americans show the will to win, the Vietnamese will submit. In scene 4, Comrade Chin asks Song to find out when the Americans plan to start bombing Vietnam. Song passes on information she has gleaned from an unsuspecting Gallimard. Chin asks why Song is wearing a dress, and Song says it is because she is in disguise.

Scenes 5–8

In scene 5, Gallimard relates the routine the couple settled into from 1961 to 1963. Song says she longs to bear Gallimard's child. In scene 6, Gallimard has an affair with Renee, a Western student he met at a party. Toulon tells Gallimard that the Americans are planning to assassinate the South Vietnamese leader, which is what Gallimard, in his diplomatic capacity, has been advising. But Toulon says that if anything goes wrong, no one will listen to Gallimard's advice again. Humiliated, Gallimard visits Song for the first time in three weeks. At first, he wants to dominate her, but these feelings disappear and he feels genuine love. Song tells him she is pregnant (she is lying), and he says he wants to marry her. In the next scene, Song tells

Chin that she needs a baby—a Chinese baby with blond hair—so she can convince Gallimard the child is his. In scene 8, Gallimard promises to divorce his wife and marry Song. Song says she is not worthy and declines. Gallimard informs the audience that Song went away to the countryside for three months, and then returned with a child.

Scenes 9–11

Scene 9 jumps forward three years, to 1966. Gallimard explains that the revolutionary situation in China made contact between Chinese and foreigners impossible. The flat the couple shared was confiscated. Gallimard is sent back to France by Toulon because of the failure of his predictions about the relationship between China and the West. During the cultural upheaval, Song is made to confess that she had been corrupted by a foreigner. She is sent to work in the fields to be "rehabilitated." In scene 10, set in 1970, Chin informs Song that she (although it is now clear that Song is really a man) is to be sent to France to spy, using Gallimard as her source of information. Scene 11 is set in Paris from 1968 to 1970. There are student demonstrations in the streets. Gallimard confesses to his wife about Song, and asks for a divorce. After Gallimard has a brief discussion with Marc, Song appears, and she and Gallimard are reunited. Some time elapses, and Song hints to the audience that she is about to undergo a transformation and that Gallimard must face the truth.

Act 3

Act 3 is set in a courthouse in Paris in 1986. Song now appears as a man, dressed in a suit. He explains that Gallimard has supported him and his "son" in Paris for fifteen years. He also says that Gallimard gave him copies of sensitive documents. The judge asks Song if Gallimard knew he was a man. Song replies, in a roundabout way, that men believe what they want to believe. In scene 2, Song tries to convince Gallimard that he, Gallimard, still loves him, even though Gallimard now knows Song is a man. Gallimard asks Song why he treated him so cruelly. Song begins slowly to remove his clothes. Donning Butterfly's robes, he tells Gallimard that he is still the same Butterfly that Gallimard loved. But Gallimard, now free of twenty years of illusion, tells Song to leave. Scene 3 returns to Gallimard's cell, in the present. To the audience, he reasserts the vision of love that he had, of the perfect Oriental woman. But he realizes that it was he, not his beloved, who sacrificed everything and was betrayed. He puts on make-up, a wig, and a kimono, and rechristens himself Madame Butterfly. Then he plunges a knife into his body, committing suicide just as Butterfly does in the opera.

CHARACTERS

Comrade Chin

Comrade Chin is the Chinese Communist Party official who instructs Song to spy. Chin unthinkingly accepts communist doctrine. As the representative of the Communist Party during the revolutionary upheavals in the 1960s, she supervises Song's confession of his offenses against party dogma.

Rene Gallimard

Gallimard is a former French diplomat who has been imprisoned for treason. His crime was passing classified documents to the Chinese, through his lover, Song. Gallimard is an unimpressive man, who by his own admission is not "witty or clever." At high school, he was voted "least likely to be invited to a party." He is uncomfortable in his relations with the opposite sex, and has had little success in romance. He married for practical reasons rather than for love. However, he still longs for a beautiful woman who will be completely devoted to him. When he thinks he has found such a woman in Song, he gains pleasure in dominating her, and behaves arrogantly and cruelly towards her. This makes him feel for the first time that he is a real man. Eventually, however, he does develop a genuine love for Song. As a diplomat, Gallimard is a failure, and is ordered back to France for giving poor advice to the French ambassador. Gallimard's greatest mistake, however, is that he fails to realize that Song, his long-time lover, is, in fact, a man. When his error is revealed at his trial, he becomes a laughingstock in France and around the world.

Helga

Helga is Gallimard's wife. While the couple lives in Beijing, she remains ignorant of Chinese culture and appears to dislike the Chinese. She is concerned that she and Gallimard seem unable to produce a child. When the couple returns to Paris, Helga is upset by the demonstrations in the street and realizes that she was happier in Beijing.

MEDIA ADAPTATIONS

- *M. Butterfly* was adapted as a film in 1993 and released by Geffen Films through Warner Brothers. Hwang wrote the screenplay and David Cronenberg directed. Jeremy Irons played Gallimard and John Lone played Song. The producer was Gabriella Martinelli.

- An audio version of the play was made in 1996, starring the original Broadway cast: John Lithgow as Gallimard and B. D. Wong as Song. It was produced by L.A. Theatre Works as part of its Audio Theatre Series.

Judge

At Gallimard's trial in Paris in 1986, the judge questions Song about his relationship with Gallimard.

Song Liling

Song is a Chinese singer and actor. Although he is a man, he plays female roles in Chinese opera, which is a traditional practice in China. When Song and Gallimard first meet, Song allows him to think that he, Song, is really a woman. Song pretends to fit the stereotype that Western men have of the submissive Oriental woman: he appears modest and retiring in a way that Gallimard finds enticing. However, Song can also be assertive in his views about how women are treated in Chinese society and of the West's prejudiced attitude to China. But all the time he is with Gallimard, Song is merely acting a part. In reality, he is using Gallimard to obtain sensitive political information, which he passes on to the Chinese government. Song shows no qualms about his deception of Gallimard, and even goes as far as acquiring a baby (supplied for him by his communist masters) and telling Gallimard the baby is theirs. When Song reveals himself as a man and testifies against Gallimard at the trial, he relates his story in a detached and unemotional manner, as if he has no real feelings in the matter. At the end of the play, he toys with the distressed Gallimard and tries to reassert his control over him.

Marc

Marc is an old school friend of Gallimard's, and his complete opposite. Whereas Gallimard was socially withdrawn in high school, Marc was the most popular student. Gallimard lacks confidence with women, but Marc has been a shameless womanizer all his life. He is married, but boasts that he cheated on his wife only six months after their wedding and has had three hundred sexual conquests in twelve years. He urges Gallimard to be aggressive in his pursuit of Song.

Renee

Renee is a student from Denmark with whom Gallimard has an affair. She is physically attractive and sexually uninhibited. She engages Gallimard in explicit discussions about the male sexual organ.

M. Toulon

Toulon is the French Ambassador in Beijing. He is a man of the world as far as sexual liaisons are concerned, and he seems impressed when he learns of Gallimard's affair with Song. In his conversations with Gallimard about state business, however, he expresses disdain for both the Chinese and the Americans. Gallimard thinks Toulon has a paternalistic attitude to his employees, regarding them all as his children.

THEMES

Race and Racism

Hwang set out to write a play that would deconstruct the race and gender stereotypes that the West has adopted in its dealings with Eastern culture. First, he had to show these stereotypes in operation. Negative Western images of the Chinese occur frequently throughout the play. Gallimard complains that the Chinese are arrogant, a view which he learned in Paris, where, according to him, it is a common belief. He and his wife also appear to despise Chinese culture, and complain about how the Chinese value its great antiquity, as if age conveyed some special distinction. And Toulon, the French Ambassador, is quick to point out that although he may live *in* China, he does not live *with* the Chinese, as if to do so would be beneath him.

Deeper than these derogatory perceptions of a foreign culture, however, is the implication that Western cultural stereotyping of the East as passive, weak, and subservient is in part responsible for

TOPICS FOR FURTHER STUDY

- Is there any truth to the suggestion made in *M. Butterfly* that Western stereotypes of the East helped to produce the American involvement in Vietnam? What was the official reason that America embarked on the Vietnam war, and what was the situation there in 1961, when much of *M. Butterfly* takes place?

- Do you think that white male readers will identify with Gallimard? Is he a sympathetic figure or someone to be despised? Is there any character in this play with whom Asian-Americans could identify?

- What was the Cultural Revolution in China, and how does Hwang make use of it in the plot of *M. Butterfly*?

- Research the experience of Asian immigrants, especially Chinese and Japanese, in the United States since the nineteenth century. Have they been, or are they still, subject to racial stereotyping by whites? What consequences do stereotypes about different races have in a multicultural society?

- Describe some of the challenges faced by interracial couples today. Is it possible for two people from different cultures to fully understand each other, or are misperceptions, as in *M. Butterfly*, inevitable?

---

international conflicts such as the Vietnam war. Gallimard, who in his role as diplomat passes on his opinions to American decision-makers, expresses the belief that "The Orientals simply want to be associated with whoever shows the most strength and power." Therefore America will succeed in Vietnam if it chooses to exercise sufficient force of will; the East will not resist. "The West has sort of an international rape mentality towards the East," explains Song in the trial scene.

The playwright hardly needs to point out the irony of Gallimard's views, since everyone in the audience will be aware of the American debacle in Vietnam, in which superior technology and powerful weaponry did not result in victory, and the Vietnamese proved to be far from passive. But Hwang points this out anyway, showing Gallimard being dismissed from his diplomatic post for giving bad advice. The year is 1966, and the war is going badly for the Americans. But even then Gallimard still mouths the platitudes that the American government was also disseminating at the time, that "the end is in sight"; it is only a matter of time before the Americans prevail. Gallimard cannot surrender the stereotype of how the East will respond to the West. This has been made plain earlier in the play when Song tells him that he cannot objectively judge his own Western values. Gallimard replies with rich dramatic irony, "I think it's possible to achieve some distance," something he manifestly fails to do in any of his opinions, feelings, or actions.

The racism also works in the other direction. Westerners are referred to as "foreign devils" more than once in the play, and the term appears to be so common and well known in China that the Westerners even use it ironically about themselves. On the other hand, Hwang suggests that many Eastern women accept the stereotype supplied to them by the West—that Western men are powerful and most to be prized. For example, one scene in the play acts out a scene from the opera *Madame Butterfly*, in which Butterfly refuses the marriage proposal of Yamadori, a Japanese prince, with the words "But he's Japanese." Suzuki, Butterfly's maid, rebukes her, reminding her that she is Japanese too. "You think you've been touched by the whitey god?" she says. (This exchange is not in Puccini's opera, but is created by the playwright.) Similarly, Song hints to Gallimard that the fascination with the paradigm of the dominant white male/submissive Oriental female is not confined to Western men. The fascination may be mutual. The implication is that blame does not lie entirely with the West. As Hwang himself said in an interview with John Lewis DiGaetani,

> The colonial power . . . has an attitude of condescension toward the East. But the East has played up to that to its short-term advantage without thinking of the long-term ill effects that reinforcing those racial stereotypes causes. I think both sides are equally guilty.

Sexism

The theme of racial and cultural stereotyping is inextricably linked to sexism and gender stereotyping. At the heart of the play is the cultural sexism displayed in Puccini's *Madame Butterfly,* which Gallimard unthinkingly accepts. When he sees Song performing the death scene from the opera, he cannot separate her from the role she is singing, and so cannot relate to her as a real individual. Because he sees only through the lens of the cultural myth of the helpless, meek, self-sacrificial Oriental woman, he is ripe for both self-deception and deception by Song.

What Gallimard fails to notice is that when he first meets Song in his female guise, Song does his best to undermine the myth, perhaps before he has decided to dupe Gallimard. The story of Butterfly is "ridiculous," Song says. He then tells Gallimard, "It's one of your favorite fantasies, isn't it? The submissive Oriental woman and the cruel white man." He tries to point out to Gallimard how objectionable the stereotype might be for an Eastern woman by giving an example in which the roles are reversed:

> What would you say if a blonde homecoming queen fell in love with a short Japanese business man? He treats her cruelly, then goes home for three years, during which time she prays to his picture and turns down marriage from a young Kennedy. Then, when she learns he has remarried, she kills herself. Now, I believe you would consider this girl to be a deranged idiot, correct? But because it's an Oriental who kills herself for a Westerner—ah!—you find it beautiful.

Although Gallimard then turns to the audience and says, "So much for protecting her in my big Western arms," Song's deconstruction of the myth does not free Gallimard from the grip of the stereotype. He continues to admire Pinkerton, the callous betrayer in Puccini's opera, saying that although an opera audience might condemn Pinkerton, few men would pass up the chance to be Pinkerton, if such an opportunity came their way. This observation about male psychology seems to be confirmed when Toulon, the French Ambassador, expresses admiration of Gallimard's affair with Song. Gallimard takes Toulon's approval to mean that he has finally managed to join a kind of "good old boys" club, admission to which seems to be granted to those men who seduce whatever women they choose and then sit together smoking and bragging about their conquests.

According to Song's explanation at the trial, the reason that Gallimard failed to discern that his lover was a man can also be attributed to the cultural stereotype imposed by the West on the East. The West thinks of itself as masculine—"big guns, big industry, big money"—while it regards the East as feminine, "weak, delicate, poor . . . but good at art, and full of inscrutable wisdom—the feminine mystique." Just as the West expects the East to submit to military force, it expects Oriental women to be submissive to Western men. Thus, the themes of racism and sexism are explicitly linked. And because of this type of thinking, even Eastern men are feminized. As Song puts it, "being an Oriental, I could never be completely a man."

At the end of the play, the playwright finally demolishes the racial and sexual stereotypes that he has been steadily exposing from the beginning. The roles of Gallimard and Song become completely reversed. Gallimard, exploited, loving, betrayed, becomes like Butterfly, while Song is revealed not only as a man but also as a calculating deceiver (like Pinkerton in *Madame Butterfly*) who was never what he appeared to be. The lesson for the audience is that stereotypes are not only dangerous, they are also false.

STYLE

Setting

M. Butterfly is set in several different places and time periods. It begins in the present, in Gallimard's prison cell in Paris. As Gallimard tells his story, the scene shifts to Beijing, China, during the decade from 1960 to 1970. Scenes are set in the German Ambassador's house, French Embassy, the French Ambassador's residence, Gallimard's apartment, Song's apartment, a Chinese opera house, and the streets of Beijing. One scene flashes back to Gallimard's schooldays in Aix-en-Provence, France, in 1947. Later scenes take place in Paris from 1966 to 1968, and in a courthouse in Paris in 1986.

Foreshadowing

As the play begins, and before a word is spoken, the playwright employs a technique known as foreshadowing, which is the presentation of an action, image, or symbol that anticipates a theme or event later in the work. In Act 1, scene 1, as Gallimard sits in his cell, the audience also sees Song upstage, behind Gallimard. Song is dressed as a beautiful woman in traditional Chinese clothing, and he/she is dancing to a piece from the Peking Opera, while Chinese percussion music plays. As Song dances, the Chinese music fades and is replaced by the music of a Western opera, *Madame Butterfly*. Song continues to dance in the Chinese style. Thus one of the main themes of the play, of a clash between two cultures, East and West, is demonstrated at the outset.

Flashbacks

The story of *M. Butterfly* ranges across two continents and more than twenty-six years. Hwang solved the problem of how to present such a lengthy and unwieldy drama by making Gallimard the narrator of his own story and adopting the device of the flashback. The flashback is a technique that presents events that took place prior to the opening scene of the play. So after the play begins in the present, in Gallimard's prison cell in Paris, it flashes back to the early days of Gallimard's love affair with Song. Most of Act 1 is presented through flashbacks. Act 2 begins once more in the present, before again flashing back as Gallimard continues the story. Finally, in Act 3, scene 3, the action returns to the present, as Gallimard prepares his own transformation into Madame Butterfly.

Structurally, then, the play rounds back on itself, ending where it began, in a prison cell, to the music of the "love duet" from the opera *Madame Butterfly*. Another structural parallelism occurs when the opening words of the play, "Butterfly, Butterfly," spoken by Gallimard as he gazes upstage at the dancing Song, are repeated as the final words of the play. However, there is a difference. The words are spoken not by Gallimard to Song, but the other way round, by Song to Gallimard. So the structure of the play, in which the ending is a reverse image of the beginning, echoes the theme, of how the expected, traditional roles of the Western man and the Oriental woman are radically reversed. (Incidentally, "Butterfly? Butterfly?" are also the last words of Puccini's opera, sung by Pinkerton as he gazes with remorse on the dying Butterfly. This gives yet another layer of reference to the ending of the play.)

Direct Address

As Gallimard tells his story, he addresses the audience directly. Many of the scenes that flash back to an earlier period are introduced by Gallimard telling the audience of how he felt at the time, what his reasoning was for his actions, what the events were that lead up to the scene. For example, in Act 1, scene 10, Gallimard sets the scene for his first meeting alone with Song in the actor's apartment by explaining how the meeting has long been delayed and confiding in the audience that he thinks Song is interested in him. Similarly, a scene often ends with Gallimard's reflections on what has just taken place, as in Act 2 scene 9, in which he speculates about Song's motives and his own state of mind.

On a number of occasions Gallimard turns to the audience and addresses it directly even in the middle of a scene. He may confide his thoughts, explain who a character is, or move the action forward with a piece of narration. An example occurs in Act 1, scene 11, when Gallimard is reading letters from Song complaining that Gallimard has failed to keep in touch. Gallimard keeps turning to the audience, commenting on the tone of the letters, and how he reacted to them.

Towards the end of the play, Gallimard's role of narration and direct address is taken over by Song. This is in keeping with the reversal of roles that occurs as the play reaches its climax.

The effect of the technique of direct address to the audience is to limit the audience's emotional involvement in the scene that is being played out in front of them. It is sometimes called a distancing device. When a character steps out of the immediate action and talks directly to the audience, the theatrical illusion is temporarily broken and the audience is reminded that they are watching a performance. The result is that the audience can view events from a more objective, or detached, point of view, rather than getting drawn into the emotional dynamics of the scene. The technique is appropriate for a play like *M. Butterfly*, which has as its purpose the deconstruction of the stereotypical romantic myth that is being acted out on stage.

COMPARE & CONTRAST

- **1960s:** The United States fights in the Vietnam war. In 1969, more than 500,000 American troops are stationed in South Vietnam. Casualties mount. More than 10,000 American soldiers are killed in Vietnam this year.

    1980s: Vietnam no longer exists as two separate, independent nations; it is one nation under communist rule.

    Today: The United States has normal diplomatic relations with communist-ruled Vietnam, but expresses frustration at the slow pace of Vietnam's economic and political reform. Vietnam continues to ask for aid in dealing with the continuing environmental and health effects of Agent Orange, a highly toxic defoliant used by U.S. forces during the Vietnam war.

- **1960s:** In 1966 China begins the Cultural Revolution, a period of upheaval that lasts until 1976, to try to rekindle revolutionary fervor amongst the young.

    1980s: In 1989, hundreds of nonviolent, pro-democracy students are massacred by Chinese troops in Beijing's Tianamen Square.

    Today: U.S. policy towards China is a major topic of political debate. Human rights activists oppose the granting of permanent trading relations with China, but probusiness groups argue that it will be good for American trade.

- **1960s:** Asian-American writers find it difficult to get their works published. Even when they succeed, their books sell poorly, are soon out of print, and are regarded, if they are noticed at all, as "minority" or "ethnic" literature.

    1980s: In the late 1980s, around the time that *M. Butterfly*, is written, there is an explosion of interest in Asian-American writing. Amy Tan's *The Joy Luck Club* (1989) becomes a best-seller, and acclaimed Asian-American writer Maxine Hong Kingston publishes her first novel, *Tripmaster Monkey: His Fake Book* (1989).

    Today: Hundreds of books by and about Asian Americans are in print. Many of them have mass-market appeal, and Asian-American writers are on the cutting edge of literary achievement.

- **1960s:** In 1965, the Immigration Act removes discriminatory quotas against immigrants from Asia. Asian immigration to the United States undergoes a rapid increase.

    1980s: Because of their economic success and strong family structures, Asian Americans are sometimes referred to as the "model minority"; some Asian Americans see this as yet another stereotype imposed on them by the dominant white culture.

    Today: According to a public policy report issued by a team of respected scholars in March 2000, Asian Americans, no matter how long they have lived in the United States, are still often perceived as an "alien presence."

HISTORICAL CONTEXT

The Vietnam War

During the early 1950s, the Western power with a vital interest in Vietnam was not the United States, but France. However, in 1954, the French were defeated by the Vietnamese at Dien Ben Phu, which ended direct French involvement in the region. It is this defeat that Ambassador Toulon alludes to in *M. Butterfly* ("It's embarrassing that we lost Indochina.").

In the Geneva Accords that followed, Vietnam was divided into two separate countries, North Vietnam and South Vietnam. Communist North Vietnam was under the leadership of Ho Chi Minh, and South Vietnam was under the nationalist, anticommunist rule of Ngo Dinh Diem, who was supported by the United States. During the administration of President Dwight Eisenhower, U.S. military advisors were sent to South Vietnam. U.S. commitment to defending South Vietnam against communist aggression from the North increased during the presidency of John F. Kennedy from 1961 to 1963.

This is the background to the incident in Act 2, scene 3 of *M. Butterfly,* in which Toulon and Gallimard discuss what is described as an American decision to begin bombing North Vietnam in 1961. Hwang has altered the chronology of the war, since the decision to bomb North Vietnam was not made until the administration of President Lyndon Johnson (1963–68). Similarly, Song's report to Comrade Chin in 1961 (Act 2, scene 4) that the United States was to increase its troops in Vietnam to 170,000 soldiers, is greatly exaggerated. It was only in December 1961, that the first direct U.S. military support for the South Vietnamese government arrived in Saigon, the capital city. Troop numbers were initially small.

By 1963, South Vietnamese leader Diem had become an unpopular despot. He was assassinated in a coup by South Vietnamese generals who acted with the tacit support of the United States. This is the incident referred to in Act 2 scene 6, when Gallimard says that he has been advising the Americans that Diem must be removed from power.

By the end of 1966, when in the play Gallimard is dismissed for wrongly predicting that the United States would win in Vietnam, the United States had 385,000 troops in the region and was heavily bombing North Vietnam. But little progress was being made in winning the war.

One factor which was always uncertain in the minds of U.S. policy makers was how China would react to any escalation of the war. This concern about Chinese intentions is reflected in Toulon's question to Gallimard (Act 2, scene 4). The United States feared that if China intervened, as it had done in the Korean War (1950–53), the war might escalate to the point where the use of nuclear weapons might have to be considered.

China's Cultural Revolution

After a civil war in China, the communists gained power in 1949. Song refers to these events in Act 1, scene 10, when he tells Gallimard that his father did not live to see the Revolution.

Nearly two decades later, in 1966, China embarked on another period of internal upheaval, known as the Cultural Revolution, which lasted until 1976. Some of the effects of this are described impressionistically by Gallimard in Act 2, scene 9. Fueled by the personality cult of Mao Zedong, the Cultural Revolution attempted a radical restructuring of Chinese society. Political leaders at all levels were purged, and large groups of communist youths, known as Red Guards, created disruption in cities as part of an officially approved struggle against what were called old ideas and customs. Schools were closed down, intellectuals and artists were denounced, and, in many cities, conditions became chaotic. This is the "continuous anarchy" that Gallimard describes in the play.

One aim of the Cultural Revolution was the complete restructuring of the educational system to make it less elitist. The goal was to eliminate the distinction between manual labor and intellectual work, and between urban and rural. Urban workers, young people, intellectuals, and artists were sent to work on farms where they engaged in physical labor and were forced to study the prevailing political ideology. This is the background of Act 2, scenes 9 and 10 in the play, when Comrade Chin holds a placard reading, "The Actor Renounces His Decadent Profession" and Song says he spent four years working on a farm from 1966 to 1970.

Cultural Stereotyping

The cultural stereotyping of Asians by the West that is a central theme of *M. Butterfly* has a long history. Peter Kwan, in his article, "Invention, Inversion and Intervention: The Oriental Woman in *The World of Suzie Wong, M. Butterfly,* and *The Adventures of Priscilla, Queen of the Desert,*" writes, "The figure of the Oriental Woman, and her relationship with the white man who becomes her lover is a theme repeatedly mined by Hollywood studios.... The Oriental Woman is meek, shy, passive, childlike, innocent and naive. She relies and is dependent on the white hero to satisfy her most basic needs and to perform the most basic tasks." Kwan draws on the work of feminist scholar Gina Marchetti, who in *Romance and the "Yellow Peril"* analyzed seventeen mainstream films, made between 1958 and 1986, which featured romantic and sexual relationships between white men and Asian women. Marchetti concluded that the "myth" of the submissive Oriental woman "endures and continues to function not only as a romantic justification for traditional female roles but also as a political legitimation of American hegemony internationally." This conclusion is a striking echo of the theme of *M. Butterfly,* in which cultural stereotyping is seen as in part responsible for the Vietnam war.

The meek Asian woman is not the only stereotype that American popular culture has imposed on the East. As Elaine H. Kim writes in *Asian-American Literature,* "The power-hungry despot, the helpless heathen, the sensuous dragon lady, the comical loyal servant, and the pudgy, desexed detective who talks about Confucius are all part of the standard American image of the Asian."

CRITICAL OVERVIEW

When *M. Butterfly* was first performed in 1988 in Washington D.C. and then on Broadway, reviews were decidedly mixed. Most critics acknowledged that Hwang was a playwright of great talent, but praise for the play was often tempered by some harsh criticism. On the positive side, Frank Rich in the *New York Times* described *M. Butterfly* as "a visionary work that bridges the history and culture of two worlds" and "as intricate as an infinity of Chinese boxes." He added that "one must [be] grateful that a play of this ambition has made it to Broadway." But Rich had some serious reservations also, writing that the play did not rise to its full power until the final act; it was marred by repetition and "its overly explicit bouts of thesis mongering" (the dramatist's tendency to pursue his central ideas in a didactic manner). Several other critics, including John Gross, in another *New York Times* review, and John Simon, in *New York* magazine, expressed a similar view.

However, William A. Henry III, in *Time,* had no such reservations, calling *M. Butterfly* "brilliant" and praising the ambitious scale of the work: "Hwang displays astonishing command of his material and craft." Henry also praised the director, John Dexter, who "fuses the presentational style of opera with confessional scenes that address the audience directly," and B. D. Wong, the actor who played Song, who moves from "hauntingly persuasive female victim ... [to] cocky and unrepentant man."

Jack Kroll in *Newsweek* was considerably less enthusiastic. While acknowledging that Hwang was a "very clever and gifted playwright," Kroll complained that Hwang "has concocted a play that consumes itself in its own cleverness, that takes so many twists and turns that it spins itself into a brilliant blur." Kroll's main objections were, first, that *Madame Butterfly,* written in 1904, was not a relevant symbol of relations between East and West in the late twentieth century; second, that the playwright offered no real insight into why Gallimard failed to realize that Song was a man; and third, the references to the Vietnam war were completely unconvincing. Kroll's conclusion was that "Hwang is a natural playwright whose desire to astonish has subverted the intellectual legitimacy of his play."

Reviews in *The Nation, The New Republic* and the *Washington Post* were mostly on the negative side. For David Richards in the *Post,* for example, Hwang pays "entirely too much attention to footnotes, ironic asides and running commentary on such issues as male sexuality and how America lost the Vietnam war (related topics in Hwang's view)." According to Richards, some of the more puzzling aspects of the affair between Gallimard and Song remain unanswered, such as "Was [Gallimard] merely the hapless victim of an astounding scheme or did he, in fact, realize deep down that he was involved in a masquerade and choose to embrace it anyway?"

Whatever may have been the reservations of some theatre critics, the fact that *M. Butterfly* won so many awards, including the Tony Award for Best Play of the Year, and was nominated for a Pulitzer Prize, shows that the play was held in considerable esteem by those qualified to judge it. And within eighteen months, *M. Butterfly* had become a hit on the international stage, with productions mounted in London, Buenos Aires, and Hamburg, and bookings already made for Paris, Brussels, Oslo, Copenhagen, Rome, Madrid, Tokyo, Tel Aviv, Sydney, Auckland, Rio de Janeiro, Mexico City, San Juan, and New Delhi. *M. Butterfly* reached an even wider audience when the film version, with screenplay written by Hwang, was released in 1993.

After drama reviewers had had their say, the more in-depth work of literary scholars and critics began to appear. Critics have used *M. Butterfly* to further explore the presence of stereotypes of Asians, both men and women, in American literature and film, and the play has been examined through a variety of interpretive frameworks, especially femi-

Anthony Hopkins (as Rene Gallimard) speaking to Glenn G. Goei (as Song Liling) in a scene from a 1989 stage production of M. Butterfly.

nist and gay. Although Hwang has written other plays since *M. Butterfly,* as well as screenplays and opera librettos, *M. Butterfly* remains his most acclaimed work.

CRITICISM

Bryan Aubrey

Bryan Aubrey, Ph.D., has published many articles on literature and drama. In this essay, he discusses sexism and the extent to which the play deconstructs the Western ideal of romantic love.

It is hardly surprising that *M. Butterfly* has proved a fertile ground for feminist critics. The play is a relentless indictment of the way men, driven by inherited, male-created cultural patterns, behave towards women. There is something deeply disturbing about Gallimard's psychology when it comes to his relations with women, and one doesn't need to be a feminist to notice it. Let's take just two examples. Every time he visits Renee, the young woman with whom he has an affair, he is excited by the knowledge that he is inflicting suffering on Song, who, Gallimard believes, is aware of his unfaithfulness. He imagines Song crying, alone and without comfort, and says, "It was her tears and her silence that excited me, every time I visited Renee." Gallimard had earlier demonstrated his cruelty in his refusal to make contact with Song, even when he knew she had a right to expect him to do so. This deliberate withdrawal also excited him: "I felt for the first time that rush of power—the absolute power of a man."

The implication in both cases is that a man who is in the grip of a culturally determined romantic and sexual fantasy will seek to shore up his own fragile sense of identity by mistreating a woman. Women must suffer because men are weak. This is hardly a pretty picture, and it is made even less savory by the fact that the playwright links sexism with politics and imperialism. For example, Renee offers the opinion that the male aggression that erupts in wars is caused by the same kind of sexual insecurity and feelings of inferiority that are the dark elements in Gallimard's own psychological make-up.

Nor is the indictment of male-female relations confined to Western culture. Hwang also has Chinese society in his sights. Song complains that women are kept down in Chinese society and denied an education, the implication being that a man is

WHAT DO I READ NEXT?

- *F.O.B.* was Hwang's first play, first produced in 1980. Set in California, it contrasts the attitudes of recent Chinese immigrants with those who were born in America, and makes use of both Western and Oriental theatrical techniques.

- *Between Worlds: Contemporary Asian-American Plays*, edited with an introduction by Misha Berson (1990), contains a selection of plays that includes Hwang's *As the Crow Flies* and *The Sound of a Voice*.

- *Asian-American Literature: A Brief Introduction and Anthology*, edited by Shawn Wong (1996), is an attractive anthology that includes essays, fiction, poetry, and drama (thirty-five pieces in all) by Asian Americans. Wong's introduction surveys the history of Asian-American literature.

- *Growing Up Asian-American: An Anthology*, edited with an introduction by Maria Hong (1993). This collection of essays, excerpts, and short stories is about the experiences of Asian Americans growing up in America. The collection covers a wide range of topics, from first love to adolescent rebellion, and also deals with Asian-American concerns about assimilation and cultural history.

- The main character in Maxine Hong Kingston's *Tripmaster Monkey: His Fake Book* (1989) is a fifth-generation Chinese American from San Francisco whose struggle to assert his own identity reveals much of how the Chinese-American experience differs from that of white Americans.

- *Liaison: The Gripping Real Story of the Diplomat Spy and the Chinese Opera Star Whose Affair Inspired M. Butterfly*, by Joyce Wadler (1993), examines the bizarre true story that gave rise to Hwang's play. Wadler draws on interviews with the two men involved, French diplomat Bernard Boursicot and Chinese opera singer Pei Pu, and many of their friends and colleagues.

- *Red Scarf Girl: A Memoir of the Cultural Revolution*, by Ji-Li Jiang (1998) is a vivid account of how the chaos of the Cultural Revolution in China in the late 1960s affected a young girl and her family, who lived in terror of arrest and detention. The book includes a foreword by David Henry Hwang.

- For those intrigued by the way the plot of *M. Butterfly* hinges on spying, Nathan Miller's *Spying for America: The Hidden History of U.S. Intelligence* (1997) is an excellent read. It covers the history of American espionage from the earliest days of the republic to the cold war and beyond.

---

threatened by a woman who may know as much as he does. Later, Song asks Chin why it is that in Chinese opera, all the women's parts are played by men. Then he answers his own question: "Only a man knows how a woman is supposed to act." In other words, women behave in ways that are culturally prescribed, and those who prescribe their conduct are men.

In the light of all this, it is clear why a feminist critic such as Chalsa Loo can refer to the play as a "revenge fantasy." As she comments in her essay, "*M. Butterfly*: A Feminist Perspective," "Women who have felt the sting of male abandonment and betrayal silently rise in applause as Butterfly's death is avenged. Gallimard, the cad, gets his due: he is betrayed, humiliated, and made miserable."

And yet the play is also much more than a revenge fantasy, because it suggests that the stereotypical perceptions that lead to the tragedy are socially constructed; they are not inherent in the nature of things. And if something is a human, cultural construct, it can also be deconstructed and something else constructed in its place. Hwang himself, in "A Conversation With David Henry

Hwang," has described his play as "an attempt to debunk the stereotypes completely by mixing them up and confusing them so much that they really become inapplicable in any meaningful sense."

The audience feels this demolition of stereotypical roles of race and gender most acutely in the immediate aftermath of the play, when the lights on stage dim and applause has not yet begun to fill the theatre. The play is over, but its effects linger in the mind. It is as if all the unconsciously imbibed, unexamined expectations of gender roles have been tossed up in the air like a pack of cards, and they have not yet landed to form a new pattern. There is a kind of imaginative space present in the collective mind of the audience, which is for a few moments free of the props, short cuts, and lazy conveniences that the human mind normally uses to classify its experience and confirm its prejudices. It is in this imaginative space that everyone in the audience is free to restructure their perceptions "from the common and equal ground we share as human beings," as Hwang put it in his Afterword to the published edition of the play.

The aesthetic response to the play, then, includes the shattering of what Western, and also, to an extent, Eastern culture has conditioned people to believe regarding race and gender roles. Does it also shatter the myth of romantic love that is also so prevalent in the Western mind? Many would say that it does—after all, look what happens to Gallimard—but is it also possible that nestling somewhere alongside all the punctured balloons of Western male imperialism, the aesthetic response to *M. Butterfly* includes a sense, in spite of everything that would seem to contradict it, of a transforming vision of love? Or is that deconstructed too?

Few critics have seen the play primarily as a love story. Perhaps in part this is because Hwang seems more interested in playing with the ideas that underlie the drama than in exploring the emotional states of the characters. There is little in the relationship between Gallimard and Song, for example, that would explain why Gallimard regards Song as the "Perfect Woman." Nor are the complexities of Gallimard's own emotions, as his relationship with Song deepens, fully explored.

However, there is no reason to doubt that Gallimard does indeed experience a genuine love for Song. And at the time he first fully conceives this love, Gallimard's character undergoes a marked transformation. This occurs well before the final, dramatic reversal of roles at the end of the play. The

> THERE IS SOMETHING DEEPLY DISTURBING ABOUT GALLIMARD'S PSYCHOLOGY WHEN IT COMES TO HIS RELATIONS WITH WOMEN, AND ONE DOESN'T NEED TO BE A FEMINIST TO NOTICE IT."

change begins in Act 2, scene 7, when Gallimard approaches Song seeking only to dominate him/her sexually. Gallimard is completely caught up in the idea that he is the arrogant Pinkerton in Puccini's *Madame Butterfly*. But then something unexpected happens:

> At the time, I only knew that I was seeing Pinkerton stalking towards his Butterfly, ready to reward her love with his lecherous hands. The image sickened me, pulled me to my knees, so I was crawling towards her like a worm. By the time I reached her, Pinkerton . . . had vanished from my heart. To be replaced by something new, something unnatural, that flew in the face of all I'd learned in the world—something very close to love.

Instead of forcing Song to strip and overpowering her, Gallimard asks for forgiveness. He is a different man now, embarking on new psychic terrain, and perhaps he now wins back some of the sympathy from the audience that his callous behavior up to that point has forfeited.

It is from this point on that Gallimard, although he does not yet realize it, starts to become Butterfly, in that he loves unthinkingly, wholly, unconditionally, no matter what the circumstances. Of course he is deluded, and nowhere in the play is it made clear exactly why or how he fails to realize that the object of his love is a male spy. And his acceptance that the baby Song presents him with is his own makes him look, to say the least, foolish. But Gallimard is at least now a fool for love, not the arrogant seducer he once fancied himself to be. Love has ensnared him, in exactly the way that Madame Butterfly in Puccini's opera had feared. She confesses to Pinkerton she has heard that in the United States, if a man catches a butterfly, "he'll pierce its heart with a needle/ And then leave it to perish!" Gallimard alludes to this when he first embarks on his cruel behavior towards Song: "Had I, too, caught a butterfly who would writhe on a needle?'' Now, in love, Gallimard has himself become the butterfly. Interestingly, in Western literature the butterfly is a traditional symbol of transformation, of the liberation of the human spirit from the fetters that bind it. Although Hwang utilizes Puccini's reversal of the traditional meaning, the more usual symbolism will surface later. Gallimard will indeed undergo a transformation.

This transformation comes in the final scene of the play. In spite of the shattering revelation that he has been deceived and betrayed by a man masquerading as a woman, Gallimard cannot shake the vision of love that he had. The romantic love for a particular individual, unable to jump the gender barrier, may have died, but the ideal of love lives on. As he begins his physical transformation into Madame Butterfly, Gallimard finally acknowledges that it is time to face the truth about Song:

> And the truth demands a sacrifice. For mistakes made over the course of a lifetime. My mistakes were simple and absolute—the man I loved was a cad, a bounder. He deserved nothing but a kick in the behind, and instead I gave him . . . all my love. Yes—love. Why not admit it all? That was my undoing, wasn't it? Love warped my judgment, blinded my eyes, rearranged the very lines on my face.

As he dons the Butterfly wig, Gallimard reaffirms his belief in his original vision of love, but this time it is fortified by his own experience and suffering:

> I have a vision. Of the Orient. That, deep within its almond eyes, there are still women. Women willing to a sacrifice themselves for the love of a man. Even a man whose love is completely without worth.

As he continues his physical transformation, Gallimard realizes that the very love he longed for he has found, not in another but in himself. He does not need any more to search for a Butterfly, for he is Butterfly. He has lived his own ideal. His own fate is proof that the vision is real. With this self-knowledge and insight, Gallimard rises at the last to the stature of a tragic hero, and Hwang invests the scene with great dramatic and emotional power.

The impression of noble sacrifice (''Death with honor is better than life . . . life with dishonor,'' Gallimard says, quoting Madame Butterfly), the playing of the Love Duet from *Madame Butterfly* rather than the music of the death scene, and the dignity of the dancers who lay the dying Gallimard ''reverently on the floor,'' all combine to create this final, moving moment. Of course, many may feel that Gallimard dies while still in the grip of a dangerous romantic illusion. Others may feel that in its own peculiar way, this moment is indeed an affirmation of a kind of transcendent, absolute vision of love, and hear in the background echoes of the deaths of other famous lovers in the Western tradition, such as Antony for his Cleopatra, Romeo for his Juliet.

The final moment in this play, however, belongs not to Gallimard but to the romantic antitype, namely Song, who is seen staring at the dead Gallimard, coolly smoking a cigarette and uttering the words ''Butterfly? Butterfly?'' The vision of love is juxtaposed with its antithesis; the myth of romantic fulfillment is deconstructed even in the moment that it reaches its most powerful expression.

So the answer to the question posed earlier—whether the aesthetic response to the play includes the sense of a transforming vision of love—is both yes and no. The dead Gallimard is proof of the power of the romantic imagination to create for itself the form of its deepest desire; the living Song is proof that in this harsh and unforgiving world, even that may not be enough.

Source: Bryan Aubrey, in an essay for *Drama for Students*, Gale Group, 2001.

Liz Brent

Brent has a Ph.D. in American Culture, specializing in film studies, from the University of Michigan. She is a freelance writer and teaches courses in the history of American cinema. In the following essay, Brent discusses the theme of male fantasies in Hwang's play.

David Henry Hwang's play *M. Butterfly* is loosely based on a true story about a French diplomat who lived for twenty years as the lover of a person he thought was a Chinese female actress but who was in fact a Chinese male spy. In his fictionalized story of love and espionage, based on this incident, Hwang's play focuses on the theme of Western male fantasies about ''Oriental'' (Asian) women. The theme of fantasy is focused on the Frenchman Rene Gallimard's perception of Song Liling as ''The Perfect Woman.'' In his ''Afterword'' to the published play, David Hwang explains that, having heard about the true story on which the play he later wrote was based, he ''concluded that the diplomat must have fallen in love, not with a person, but with a fantasy stereotype.'' Hwang goes on to explain that this ''stereotype'' is that of the ''exotic,'' submissive ''Oriental'' woman, as portrayed in the famous Puccini opera, *Madame Butterfly*.

A scene from the 1993 film adaptation of M. Butterfly, *starring Jeremy Irons (left) and John Lone.*

The motif of dream and fantasy is first invoked through Gallimard's tongue-in-cheek description of his life in a French prison, following his conviction for treason: "When I want to eat, I'm marched off to the dining room.... When I want to sleep, the light bulb turns itself off—the work of fairies. It's an enchanted space I occupy." In this description, however, he symbolically characterizes his relationship to Song Liling, a relationship based on his own personal fantasies of what "The Perfect Woman" is like, a relationship in which he occupied "an enchanted space" of his own imagination. Addressing the audience, Gallimard claims that, "I have known, and been loved by . . . the Perfect Woman." At the point when he makes this statement, Gallimard has already learned that his "Perfect Woman" was in fact a man; by insisting that Song was nonetheless "the Perfect Woman," he emphasizes the extent to which she was, to him, a fantasy of a woman all along.

Hwang's play thus begins with a portrayal of Gallimard's early perceptions of women, which are derived from the many images of pin-up girls he saw in pornographic magazines. Hwang here establishes that, from youth, Gallimard's relationship to women is purely that of fantasy images, as he has next to no experience with real women. Gallimard compares the character Madame Butterfly in Puccini's opera, who insists that she is not worth the few cents he paid for her, to the images of women in "girlie magazines": "In real life, women who put their total worth at less than sixty-six cents are quite hard to find. The closest we come is in the pages of these magazines.... For three or four dollars, you get seven or eight women." Hwang makes a strong feminist statement here by implying that the pleasure for a man in paying for a fantasy image of a woman is not so much sexual, as one of power. Gallimard explains that, when he first saw such magazines, at the age of twelve, "my body shook. Not with lust—no, with power. Here were women—a shelfful—who would do exactly as I wanted." The images of women in "girlie magazines" suggest to the man that "You can do whatever you want."

When Gallimard meets Song, she points out to him directly that the opera *Madame Butterfly* is an expression of a standard fantasy that Western culture holds about Eastern culture: "It's one of your favorite fantasies, isn't it? The submissive Oriental woman and the cruel white man." Later, as he is walking her home, Song again makes the observa-

> "... 'I HAVE KNOWN, AND BEEN LOVED BY ... THE PERFECT WOMAN.' AT THE POINT WHEN HE MAKES THIS STATEMENT, GALLIMARD HAS ALREADY LEARNED THAT HIS 'PERFECT WOMAN' WAS IN FACT A MAN; BY INSISTING THAT SONG WAS NONETHELESS 'THE PERFECT WOMAN,' HE EMPHASIZES THE EXTENT TO WHICH SHE WAS, TO HIM, A FANTASY OF A WOMAN ALL ALONG."

tion that she represents to him a white male fantasy of a woman: "We have always held a certain fascination for you Caucasian men, have we not?" Later, Song points out the extent to which a "Perfect Woman" is a creation of the male mind, a construction of a male fantasy which has little or nothing to do with real women. She comments that the reason the roles of women in the Peking Opera are always played by men is that, "only a man knows how a woman is supposed to act." The truth of this statement is confirmed when, even after Gallimard learns that Song was a man all along, he asserts that, "in China, I once loved, and was loved by, very simply, the Perfect Woman." Again, the implication is that the "Perfect Woman" does not need to be a woman at all, but simply an image which conforms to a man's fantasy.

The fantasy motif includes not just Gallimard's perceptions of Song, but also the appearance of his school friend Marc in his imagination and his dreams. Marc, who appears as a "formless spirit," encourages Gallimard to pursue Song by pointing out that she can be used like a "girlie magazine," or a sex symbol from the movies, to fulfill his fantasies of sexual power: "All your life you've waited for a beautiful girl who would lay down for you. . . . And you see them in magazines and you see them in movies. And you wonder, what's wrong with me? Will anyone beautiful ever want me?" Marc himself functions for Gallimard as a fantasy figure who gives him permission to live out his fantasies. Gallimard even compares the figure of Marc, as he appears in a dream, to the Italian movie star and sex symbol Sophia Lauren: "Other people, I've been told, have dreams where angels appear. Or dragons, or Sophia Lauren in a towel. In my dream, Marc from school appeared." Marc represents the cultural influences that encourage men to view women as sexual objects who can be purchased for the purpose of male pleasure. In Gallimard's dream, Marc refers to Gallimard's imminent conquest in the form of Song to "picking exotic women off trees"—as if women were merely pieces of fruit, to be taken and consumed, rather than individuals. Marc then reminds Gallimard of a woman named Isabelle, whom Marc apparently either paid or otherwise convinced to have sex with Gallimard, his "first experience."

Gallimard even begins to perceive "God" and the spiritual world as a justification for using Song as a means of acting on his fantasies of a love affair with "the Perfect Woman." At first, however, Gallimard's conscience tells him that his affair with Song is "evil." When he believes, for a moment, that he is about to be fired from his job as a diplomat, Gallimard says, "Just as I feared! God has seen my evil heart—" But, after he learns that, in fact, he has been given a promotion, he comes to believe that God "understands," and even desires that women be placed in the sexual service of men: "Of course! God who creates Eve to serve Adam, who blesses Solomon with his harem but ties Jezebel to a burning bed—that God is a man. And he understands! At age thirty-nine, I was suddenly initiated into the way of the world."

Once Gallimard has established an affair with Song, he further pursues women who can be used to fulfill the fantasies evoked by the "picture perfect" images of "those girls in magazines." He describes Renee, a young woman with whom he has his "first extra-extramarital affair," as "picture perfect. With a body like those girls in the magazines. If I put a tissue paper over my eyes, I wouldn't have been able to tell the difference."

The theme of fantasy and the imagination in the play is central to the question of how it could have been that Gallimard lived with Song for twenty years without discovering that "she" was actually a man. Gallimard speculates about the power of the imagination to shape and maintain a fantasy that brings "happiness." When he requests of Song that she allow him to see her completely naked, she takes the risk of offering to allow him to undress her—but he chooses not to at the last moment. From his cell, in retrospect, Gallimard reflects, "Did I not undress her because I knew, somewhere deep down, what I would find? Perhaps. Happiness is so rare that our mind can turn somersaults to protect it." Gallimard later comments on the extent to which his imagination was able to maintain the fantasy of Song as his "Butterfly," even as he sat in the witness box in men's clothing, confessing to his deception; even with the truth right before his very eyes, Gallimard states that, "even in this moment my mind remains agile, flip-flopping like a man on a trampoline."

After Gallimard is fired from his position as a French diplomat in China, he returns to France with his wife Helga. Years later, Song appears at his home in France, having been sent by Chinese authorities to continue spying activities through him. As Gallimard narrates this part of his story to the audience, Song enters onstage. Although he now knows the "truth" about Song, Gallimard continues to see her in his imagination as his idea of "the Perfect Woman." When he sees her onstage, unable to let go of this Perfect Woman in his mind's eye, he says, "My imagination is hell." Song then begins to tell the audience of her arrival in France, but Gallimard argues with her that he prefers to remember how they "embraced" their final evening together in China. When Song insists that the story move on, Gallimard argues that, since she is a figment of his imagination, she has to "do what I say!" because "I'm conjuring you up in my mind!" Song, however, responds that, now that Gallimard knows the "truth" about her, he can no longer completely control her, even as a fantasy figure; she tells him, "No matter what your eyes tell you, you can't ignore the truth. You already know too much."

During the court proceedings in which Gallimard is on trial for spying, the judge asks Song to explain how he was able to conceal from Gallimard the fact that he was a man. Song's response indicates that, as he learned from his mother, who was a prostitute, it is easy to fool a man into believing in his own fantasies because "Men always believe what they want to hear. So a girl can tell the most obnoxious lies and the guys will believe them every time— 'This is my first time'—'That's the biggest I've ever seen'—" Furthermore, Song explains that the West has always imagined itself to be masculine in relation to the East, which it imagines to be feminine. Therefore, Song explains, it was not difficult for an Asian man to convince a Western man that he is a woman—because, in the eyes of the Western world, the stereotypical "Orient" is already seen as feminine. Furthermore, Song explains, the West holds a stereotype of "Oriental" women as submissive, and so imagines the East to be both feminine and submissive to the West. Song points out that, "You expect Oriental countries to submit to your guns, and you expect Oriental women to be submissive to your men. That's why you say they make the best wives." The judge then questions Song as to why this would make it "possible" to "fool" Gallimard into thinking he was a woman. Song responds by pointing out that Gallimard was only able to perceive Song as a "fantasy," and therefore allowed his imagination to project onto her his image of the "Perfect Woman": "because when he finally met his fantasy woman, he wanted more than anything to believe that she was, in fact, a woman." Finally, Song explains that, because the West never sees the East as anything but feminine and submissive, then, "being an Oriental, I could never be completely a man."

In the final scenes of the play, the Song of Gallimard's imagination becomes confrontational toward him—he no longer passively submits to Gallimard's fantasy image of him as the "Perfect Woman." Instead, Song challenges Gallimard with the intention of undressing completely and revealing his manhood. At this point, it is as if Gallimard's imagination can no longer cooperate with his fantasy. As Song begins to undress, against Gallimard's wishes, he protests: "You're only in my mind! All this is in my mind! I order you to stop! To stop!" Gallimard then admits to Song that, "I know what you are.... A—a man." But Song replies "You don't really believe that." Gallimard then admits that, at some level, he knew the truth, but wished to postpone the unveiling of that truth in order to maintain his fantasy of Song as the Perfect Woman. He explains "I knew all the time somewhere that my happiness was temporary, my love a deception. But my mind kept the knowledge at bay. To make the wait bearable." Gallimard goes on to assert that what he loved in Song was "a perfect lie," a fantasy in which s/he was "playing a part."

Gallimard comes to realize that what he loved was not a woman, but a male fantasy of a woman: "I'm a man who loved a woman created by a man." Furthermore, Gallimard realizes that no "true" woman could ever live up to this male fantasy of a Perfect Woman, because "Everything else—simply falls short." He concludes that he prefers such fantasies as he derived from "girlie magazines" to the truth: "I've finally learned to tell fantasy from reality. And, knowing the difference, I choose fantasy." Having lived for twenty years with someone he imagined was the Perfect Woman, Gallimard says of himself "I am pure imagination," and that he in fact prefers the realm of imagination to that of reality, for "in my imagination I will remain." Having been presented with the incontrovertible truth of Song's masculinity, Gallimard chooses to return to "the world of fantasy" in which he first met Song. In these stereotyped fantasies of Eastern culture, the "Orient" is a realm of "perfect" women, who willingly submit to the dominance of men, and willingly cater to the needs of men—women, in short, who satisfy traditional male fantasies: "There is a vision of the Orient that I have. Of slender women in chong sams and kimonos who die for the love of unworthy foreign devils. Who are born and raised to be the perfect women. Who take whatever punishment we give them, and bounce back, strengthened by love, unconditionally. It is a vision that has become my life." Gallimard goes on to describe this fantasy "vision" which he had projected onto Song: "I have a vision. Of the Orient. That, deep within its almond eyes, there are still women. Women willing to sacrifice themselves for the love of a man. Even a man whose love is completely without worth."

Hwang's play presents a feminist perspective on the nature of male fantasies of the "Perfect Woman." He also addresses the issue of racial stereotyping of Asian culture as feminine and Asian women as embodying male fantasies of submissiveness and subservience. In the Afterword to the play, Hwang explains that, "The catalogues and TV spots appeal to a strain in men which desires to reject Western women for what they have become—independent, assertive, self-possessed—in favor of a more reactionary model—the pre-feminist, domesticated geisha girl." Hwang characterizes Gallimard as a man who prefers to live in a fantasy world of his imagination in which such a "Perfect Woman" loves him, rather than living in the realm of truth and reality.

Source: Liz Brent, in an essay for *Drama for Students,* Gale Group, 2001.

Jan Herman

Jan Herman provides an overview of Hwang's career and the plays that made it successful.

Being Asian-American has always been David Henry Hwang's stock in trade. Since the fall of 1978, when he wrote his first play, *FOB,* as a Stanford undergraduate and saw it open less than two years later at the prestigious New York Public Theater, the playwright has created a large and provocative body of work out of his highly charged sense of cultural identity.

Best known for *M. Butterfly,* the 1998 Tony-winning play of sexual deceit and romantic delusion that tapped into the troubled East-West history of race, ideology and alienation, Hwang has made his crucial theme the immigrant experience, a topic that has been at the heart of American theater in one way or another for nearly a century.

He's at it again with his latest play, *Golden Child,* a bittersweet memory piece based on his own family's history. But this time, it may be that he has written with more deeply felt emotion and, with the exception of *M. Butterfly,* more intellectual engagement than ever.

Directed by James Lapine, *Golden Child* has its world premiere at the Public on Nov. 17, a co-production with South Coast Repertory, which commissioned it. After closing in New York on Dec. 1, the show will transfer to the SCR Mainstage in Costa Mesa, opening Jan. 10.

"I wanted to write something detailed and less directly political than before," Hwang says of the new play. "I sort of used Chekhov as my example. But I didn't necessarily know I was going to write about my family history."

Golden Child begins with a taxi ride from Manhattan that takes us back to China of a century ago, before arriving at Kennedy Airport. Unlike most of the writer's plays, which generally have two main figures, this one has a handful.

It tells the story of the taxi passenger's great-grandfather, Tieng-Bin, a widely traveled, well-to-do merchant with three wives. He returns to China from a trip to the Philippines with a British church missionary who converts him to Christianity. Although the encounter between East and West is rather comical at first, the consequences are tragic for the great-grandfather as well as his wives and a beloved daughter, who turns out to be the passenger's maternal grandmother.

Sitting in a corner of the Time Cafe, a vast bistro on Lafayette Street down the block from the Public, Hwang has come from a rehearsal for *Golden Child,* where he left Lapine working on sound cues.

"One of the reasons for writing this play had to do with the fact that I've rejected Christianity," Hwang said. "When you're raised with a Christian fundamentalist mind-set, as I was, in order to free yourself from it you have to find something equally fundamentalist. I'm trying to take a more humanistic, complex view of how it is that my family came to the point it did in religion.

"To some extent—and this is really something I've developed more in rewrites—the story of Tieng-Bin is the story of somebody who's been raised in a Confucian tradition, which is very rigid and fundamentalist itself. Freeing himself from that, he has to find a new big stick to beat down the old big stick. Fundamentalism begets fundamentalism. I'm trying to transcend the rigidity and reactiveness that I needed, too, at a certain point in my life to become my own person."

Now 39, on the cusp of middle age, when writers are inclined to turn inward, it seems only natural for Hwang to explore his family's roots in a serious way.

"In some sense I feel like this is a play I've been writing since I was 10, when I wrote a 'novel' from stories my grandmother told me," he recounted. "It was fun to use the book as source material for something I'm doing now."

But making art of raw materials requires considerably more than a firsthand witness. In this case, his grandmother's stories only supplied the structure—that is to say, the plot of *Golden Child*. Although many events in the play mirror what he'd been told, Hwang said, he had to imagine the characters more thoroughly and invent new situations where there were gaps in his grandmother's narrative.

Hwang's mother, Dorothy, a pianist, was born in the Philippines after her family moved there from Amoy, a southern coastal town in China's Fukien province across the straits from Taiwan. She came to the United States in 1952 to study piano at USC, where she met her future husband at a dance for foreign students. But when the pair decided to marry, her wealthy family—it owned the entire Philippine General Motors franchise, among many other ventures—insisted that her fiancé convert to Christianity before they could wed.

Asked about the family's reaction to the revealing details in his plays, Hwang says he "tends to apprise them" of what to expect "because my parents go out of their way to see everything I've

> ASKED ABOUT THE FAMILY'S REACTION TO THE REVEALING DETAILS IN HIS PLAYS, HWANG SAYS HE 'TENDS TO APPRISE THEM' OF WHAT TO EXPECT 'BECAUSE MY PARENTS GO OUT OF THEIR WAY TO SEE EVERYTHING I'VE DONE. BUT I DON'T ASK THEIR PERMISSION TO USE WHAT I WANT. THEY KNOW MY REACTION: SORRY, I NEED THAT STORY.'"

done. But I don't ask their permission to use what I want. They know my reaction: Sorry, I need that story."

Hwang's Shanghai-born father, Henry, came to the U.S. in 1948 and made his mark as a Los Angeles banker in 1974, when he founded the Far East National Bank. It was the first Asian-American federally chartered national bank in the country, and the playwright has served on the board of directors. He expresses mild astonishment when it's suggested that as a writer he might have been bored by the world of high finance.

"Not necessarily!" he replied. "The bank is family business." Indeed, Far East National, whose shares are publicly traded on the American Stock Exchange, has given Hwang a kind of financial security many writers long for. His family holds the largest block of stock; his father is chief policymaker; and the company recently announced its intent to merge with a Taiwanese bank, Sinopac, sending Far East National's stock higher.

Hwang has always strived to be self-reliant, however, and he hasn't done too poorly. He gained international renown and became a millionaire several times over on the strength of *M. Butterfly*. As of last year, the play had grossed $35 million in U.S. earnings alone. In addition to the original Broadway production, which ran for nearly two years (777 performances), it had three national tours, was a hit in London's West End and had major commercial outings in almost three dozen countries. However, the play has not had productions in China or France, which figure prominently in the plot.

Hwang was also unusually precocious. He came into his own with *M. Butterfly* at the age of 30, younger than Arthur Miller (33) with *Death of a Salesman,* Tennessee Williams (36) with *A Streetcar Named Desire* or Edward Albee (34) with *Who's Afraid of Virginia Woolf?*

Like them, Hwang wrote many plays before getting to the top, including *The Dance and the Railroad, The House of Sleeping Beauties* and *The Sound of a Voice,* to name just three. Yet he insists, as always, that he has learned more from his failures— *Rich Relations,* produced off-Broadway in 1986, for example, and most recently his disastrous 1994 Broadway flop *Face Value,* which lasted just eight preview performances and never opened— than he has from his successes.

"A playwright has to have a right to fail," he said philosophically, "otherwise you're not going to get the really good works."

Hwang considers himself a "relatively quick" writer but noted, "I've gotten slower as the years have gone by. I hope it's because I'm playing more attention." He admitted, though, that writing became somewhat intimidating in the aftermath of *M. Butterfly.* Worldwide raves are a hard act to follow and he modestly said he doubts he'll "ever reach that peak again."

His first produced play, *FOB* (the title stands for "fresh off the boat"), took him just three weeks to complete, he recalled.

"It will always have a special place for me, because I wrote it before I knew how to do anything. As I get older, I find that craft is useful in the sense that it allows me to fix things more easily, to know where I'm going.

"But when it comes to that first draft, it's almost as if you have to overcome your craft to be able to get back to the original impulse. Maybe that's why it takes me a bit longer, I'm trying not to be facile. For the first draft, I don't want to take advantage of the tricks I've learned along the way."

Today, the once-divorced Hwang lives on the Upper West Side in a posh but sparely decorated apartment near Central Park with his second wife, Kathryn Layng, and their 8-month-old son, Noah.

Layng, an actress from Rockford, Ill., played the nurse for four seasons on the TV comedy-drama *Doogie Howser, M.D.* At the other end of the dramatic spectrum, she also played the brazen Renée in *M. Butterfly,* for nine months on Broadway; and she starred as the dominatrix in Hwang's kinky 1992 one-act, *Bondage,* set in an S&M parlor near Los Angeles (and produced for the Humana Festival by the Actors Theatre of Louisville in Kentucky).

Said Hwang: "I've reached a point in my life where I'm really happy. For me, the 1980s were about having a career; the 1990s are about having a life."

For all his domestic bliss, however, it's not as though he has chosen to ignore his career. If *Golden Child* is well-received both at the Public and SCR, "it's fair to say that Broadway is a possibility," director Lapine said in a separate interview.

"Naturally, a lot will depend on the critics, but I think the play will be pretty popular," said Lapine, best known for his many prize-winning collaborations with Stephen Sondheim (*Sunday in the Park With George, Into the Woods, "Passion"*) and William Finn (*Falsettos*).

"I was asked last spring about directing this," Lapine said, "which was flattering, because I've always admired David's writing. But I ended up saying no because of another project. Then they called again in August, and I'm so glad they did. I don't get offers to direct a play I haven't written or isn't a classic. This is the first one I've done.

"I love that *Golden Child* is about a culture I didn't know. And David's a total doll to work with. Very, very flexible, intellectually stimulating. He's an enthusiast in a way, even though he can be as withdrawn as I am."

Late last month, Hwang traveled to Washington, where *Golden Child* received a $50,000 grant from the annual Kennedy Center Fund for New American Plays—$10,000 to him and $40,000 to South Coast Rep for commissioning it and co-producing it.

Hwang says he owes a special debt to SCR— and particularly to its dramaturge Jerry Patch, who was one of his earliest advocates and who helped bring about the commission.

"Jerry is the first person who ever wrote me a letter of support from a real theater," the playwright explained. "This was when I went to the [Eugene

O'Neill] Playwrights Center in Connecticut to develop *FOB,* before it got on at the Public. Jerry has no memory of the letter. But I treasured it. I still have it.''

Patch, for his part, discounts any special foresight on his part.

''I thought his first play was terrific, though we couldn't do it. It knocked me out, and apparently I wrote the letter before we met. Then I met him at the O'Neill, and it was obvious by that point that he was the next thing going to happen. *FOB* was out there.''

The late producer and Public founder Joseph Papp, for whom the theater is now named, was already interested in producing it and getting interested in Hwang's next play. *The Dance and the Railroad.*

Patch returned to South Coast and told its coartistic directors, David Emmes and Martin Benson, about ''this kid who had a 250 IQ or something and was, I thought, the smartest young artist I'd ever met. The kid had a mind like a trap.

''So Hwang drives down from Los Angeles one day in 1982, and Martin and David give him this big commission,'' Patch recalled. ''It was a few thousand bucks, but that was a lot for us at the time.

''I don't think Hwang really needed the money. He drove down in a Mercedes. But it meant something to him because he was very proud of the fact that he could make his own money.''

After writing several plays already committed to other theaters, Hwang spent the next five or so years on *M. Butterfly,* which was a commercial project from the outset. Then he wrote *Face Value,* which was unmistakably meant for a New York audience—it was a satire based on the well-publicized protests about the casting of *Miss Saigon* when it came to Broadway in 1991 with a white British star as the Eurasian lead (Jonathan Pryce, who had originated the role of the Engineer in London). It also portrayed the collective howl from Asian-American performers who objected to *Miss Saigon* stereotyping their community as pimps and whores.

Because of its commission, South Coast had a first look at *Face Value,* which its officials did only *pro forma* they say, taking a pass for reasons of diplomacy (Hwang's Broadway backers had dibs on the show) and dramatic art (the show would have been too big and expensive for their nonprofit theater).

But when Hwang's agent showed *Golden Child* to Emmes and Benson, they took it. ''The plan was to start in Costa Mesa and *then* go to the Public,'' Patch said. ''The change had to do with Lapine's schedule. He had to stay in New York. Hwang really wanted him to direct, so we made the accommodation.''

Said Hwang: ''They could have been hardasses about it. But that's not their style, and I'm grateful it's not. I think they're happy. I'm happy. And I'm getting the production I want.''

Certainly, he's getting an A-team capable of taking *Golden Child* all the way. Lapine has brought on Tony-winning designers Tony Straiges (set) and Richard Nelson (lighting), among others, and the cast includes the celebrated Chinese, British-trained actress Tsai Chin, who won a 1995 Los Angeles Drama Critics Award for a featured role in Maxine Hong Kingston's *The Woman Warrior* at the Doolittle and who played Auntie Lindo in the movie of Amy Tan's *The Joy Luck Club.*

Between plays, moreover, Hwang has become a busy screenwriter. He's currently midway through the second draft of a script for a Jessica Lange picture at 20th Century Fox, based on a Russian film called *Umbrellas for Newlyweds.* He has also written screen adaptations of *Possession,* the A. S. Byatt novel, for Sydney Pollack, which hasn't been produced, and Dostoevski's *The Idiot* for Martin Scorcese.

''That's still a picture Marty intends to make,'' Hwang said. ''I love working with him. What's so great is learning about film from him and getting paid for it.''

Meanwhile, Hwang is working on another Scorsese project, *Texas Guinan,* a vehicle for Bette Midler, And he's done *The Alienist* for producer Scott Rudin, ''which is somewhere at Paramount.''

Still, the playwright hasn't had great luck in Hollywood. The two scripts that have reached the screen came and went: 1994's *Golden Gate,* about an FBI agent (Matt Dillon) obsessed with the daughter (Joan Chen) of an accused Communist he'd hounded to death during the McCarthy era, and 1993's *M. Butterfly,* which starred Jeremy Irons and John Lone, and was directed by David Cronenberg.

''The *Butterfly* screenplay was rather impressionistic,'' Hwang recalled. ''My goal was to take some of the theatrical devices and find film equivalents. At the time David had just finished editing

Naked Lunch, and I thought, 'Oh, he'll love this stuff.' But most of it didn't end up in the movie. He made something quite naturalistic.

"Movies are a director's medium, of course, and David's a great artist. He worked really hard; he had his own vision of the piece. It was just slightly different from mine. Let's leave it at that."

A trained musician who played classical violin throughout his youth and later turned to jazz, Hwang also spends some of his time working on operas. He wrote the libretto for composer Philip Glass' science-fiction music drama *1000 Airplanes on the Roof,* which premiered in Vienna in 1988 and toured the world. He also wrote the libretto for *The Voyage* (again with a score by Glass) on commission from the Metropolitan Opera, which premiered at the Met in a colossal 1992 production to commemorate the 500th anniversary of Columbus' arrival in America.

And he's about to begin the libretto of a Bright Sheng chamber opera, *The Silver River,* on commission from the Santa Fe Chamber Music Festival, where it is scheduled to open next July.

Pondering the future—the national elections were on his mind—Hwang surveyed the Time Cafe with its homey decor put together from different American decades and picked at his half-eaten gourmet pizza.

"We don't listen when it comes to race and culture in this country," he said. "We go in with our minds made up, and then we try to batter the other side with our opinions. The situation becomes either confrontational or nonsensical. There's no receptiveness, whether it's a white male complaining about reverse racism or an American Indian complaining about the Atlanta Braves.

"We strive for order in our lives, for constancy, for something to believe in," he continued. "But human experience is contradictory. In fact, our lives are a horrid tangle of ambivalences, self-delusions, accidents. In part that's what *Golden Child* is about. The attraction of any sort of fundamentalist ideology, whether it's ethnic, political or religious, is this need to have some certainty, so you can say, 'This is an unalterable truth. If I can hang my hat on this, my life will make more sense.'

"But finally all those fundamentalist efforts are doomed to fail, because life is never that simple. Face it, life is inherently complex."

Source: Jan Herman, "M. as in Metamorphosis," in *Los Angeles Times Book Review,* Vol. 3, November 3, 1996, pp. 6–7, 71.

SOURCES

Brustein, Robert, "Transcultural Blends," in *New Republic,* April 25, 1988, pp. 28–29.

"A Conversation With David Henry Hwang," in *Bearing Dreams, Shaping Visions: Asian Pacific American Perspectives,* edited by Linda A. Revilla, Gail M. Nomura, Shawn Wong, and Shirley Hune. Washington State University Press, 1993, pp. 185–191.

DiGaetani, John Louie, "M. Butterfly: An Interview with David Henry Hwang," in *Drama Review,* Vol. 33, No. 3, Fall 1989, pp. 142–43.

Henry, William A., III., "Politics and Strange Bedfellows," in *Time,* April 4, 1988, p. 74.

Hodgson, Moira, "M. Butterfly," in *Nation,* April 23, pp. 577–78.

Hwang, David Henry, "Afterword," in *M. Butterfly,* by David Henry Hwang, Penguin, 1989, pp. 94–100.

Kim, Elaine H., *Asian-American Literature: An Introduction to the Writings and Their Social Context,* Temple University Press, 1982, p. 3.

Kroll, Jack, "The Diplomat and the Diva," in *Newsweek,* April 4, 1988, p. 75.

Kwan, Peter, "Invention, Inversion and Intervention: The Oriental Woman in *The World of Suzie Wong, M. Butterfly,* and *The Adventures of Priscilla, Queen of the Desert,*" in *Asian Law Journal,* Vol. 99, 1998.

Loo, Chalsa, "*M. Butterfly*: A Feminist Perspective," in *Bearing Dreams, Shaping Visions: Asian Pacific American Perspectives,* edited by Linda A. Revilla, Gail M. Nomura, Shawn Wong, and Shirley Hune, Washington State University Press, 1993, pp. 177–180.

Marchetti, Gina, *Romance and the "Yellow Peril": Race, Sex, and Discursive Strategies in Hollywood,* University of California Press, 1994, p. 108.

Rich, Frank, "*M. Butterfly,* a Story of a Strange Love, Conflict and Betrayal," in *New York Times,* March 21, 1988, p. C13.

Richards, David, "Chinese Puzzle at the National: A Curious *M. Butterfly,*" in *Washington Post,* February 11, 1988, p. C1.

FURTHER READING

Chang, Williamson B. C., "*M. Butterfly*: Passivity, Deviousness, and the Invisibility of the Asian-American Male," in *Bearing Dreams, Shaping Visions: Asian Pacific American*

Perspectives, edited by Linda A. Revilla, Gail M. Nomura, Shawn Wong, and Shirley Hune. Washington State University Press, 1993.

> In this text, Chang argues that the play lacks a character with whom Asian males can identify because Song embodies a negative stereotype of Asians as devious and untrustworthy.

Deeney, John J., "Of monkeys and butterflies: transformation in M. H. Kingston's *Tripmaster Monkey* and D. H. Hwang's *M. Butterfly,*" in *MELUS,* Vol. 18, No. 4, Winter 1993, p. 21.

> This article is an analysis of how both works present characters seeking to transform themselves in reaction to stereotyped images that keep them from being recognized as individuals.

Gerard, Jeremy, "David Hwang: Riding on the Hyphen," in *New York Times Magazine,* March 13, 1988, pp. 44–5, 88–9.

> Gerard's article is an overview of Hwang's life and career up to *M. Butterfly,* including many observations by Hwang himself.

Henry III, William A., "When East and West Collide: David Henry Hwang Proves Bedfellows Make Strange Politics in *M. Butterfly,* a Surprise Stage Success on Three Continents." in *Time,* Vol. 134, No. 7, August 14, 1989, p. 62.

> This overview of Hwang's early life and career emphasizes the success of *M. Butterfly,* suggesting that Hwang has the potential to become the most important American dramatist since Arthur Miller.

Lyons, Bobby, "'Making His Muscles Work For Himself': An Interview with David Henry Hwang," in *The Literary Review,* Vol. 42, No. 2, Winter 1999, p. 230.

> During this interview, Hwang discusses the question of identity in his plays, including *M. Butterfly,* and notes that his work has been influenced by the plays of Sam Shepard and Anton Chekhov. Jazz has also influenced his theatrical approach.

Street, Douglas, *David Henry Hwang,* Boise State University Press, 1989.

> This book is a concise analysis of Hwang's work up to and including *M. Butterfly,* highlighting the many ways in which Hwang combines the American with the Asian experience.

Saint Joan

GEORGE BERNARD SHAW

1923

George Bernard Shaw's *Saint Joan* was first produced in New York City in 1923 and in London in 1924. Shaw published it with a long Preface in 1924. When word came out that Shaw, who was known as an irreverent jokester, was writing about a Christian saint and martyr, there were fears that he would not be able to produce something appropriate, but the early reception of the play was generally favorable, although some commentators criticized him for historical inaccuracy and for being too talky or comic. Over the years, the play, a rare tragic work in his generally comic oeuvre, has been seen as one of his greatest and most important. It has been hailed as being intellectually exciting and praised for dealing with important themes, such as nationalism, war, and the relation of the individual to society. The play solidified Shaw's reputation as a major playwright and helped win him the Nobel Prize in 1925.

Being at least in part a tragedy, though with comic moments, *Saint Joan* is part of a shift in Shaw's work from his earlier optimistic comedies to a more melancholy attitude, perhaps in part the result of his reaction to World War I.

Although he had been thinking about Joan of Arc as early as 1913, Shaw did not actually begin writing the play until 1923, three years after Joan's canonization. He consulted many earlier works on Joan, including the transcripts of her trial. In fact, he modestly said that he had done little more than reproduce Joan's own words as recorded in the transcripts; however, that statement is unfair to Shaw, who left a distinctive Shavian touch on the story of the martyred saint.

AUTHOR BIOGRAPHY

Shaw was born in Dublin on July 26, 1856. His family was of upper-class ancestry, but had fallen on hard times. Perhaps as a result, he developed a lifelong interest in poverty and other social issues. Eventually, after moving to London in 1876, he joined the Fabian Society, an organization of intellectual socialists. He wrote and lectured for the Fabians on many issues of the day, and many of his creative works, including his five unsuccessful novels and his many successful plays, dealt with such topics as slumlords, prostitution, and women's rights, usually in a light-hearted manner. His plays in general are witty and paradoxical discussions of ideas, in some ways just an extension of the political debates he liked to engage in as a member of the various debating societies to which he belonged.

Throughout his career, Shaw was known as an irreverent skeptic, and he was not a believer in any orthodox religion. However, influenced by the writings of the Norwegian playwright Henrik Ibsen, he developed a theory of what he called the Life Force: an irrational force at work in the universe that guides social evolution by entering the consciousness of certain superior individuals. Despite his socialist views, Shaw was a great believer in the importance of superior individuals or geniuses and, especially after experiencing the popular anti-German hysteria during World War I, had a low opinion of the common people and a distrust of democracy. In fact, in later years, Shaw became quite sympathetic to dictatorial regimes, such as the Soviet Union and Mussolini's Italy.

Shaw was much opposed to war, and when World War I broke out, he published an antiwar pamphlet that caused him to be greatly criticized. He was also critical of English rule in Ireland, and spoke out against the execution of the leaders of the Irish uprising against the English in 1916. He also defended Roger Casement, an Irishman executed for treason that same year.

Shaw had been thinking of writing a play about Joan of Arc for many years and finally did so at the urging of his wife in 1923, three years after Joan was canonized as a saint. The play earned him enormous prestige and contributed to his being awarded the Nobel Prize for Literature in 1925. It was also one of his last major works, though he lived for another twenty-seven years, dying at the age of 94 on November 2, 1950 in Ayot Saint Lawrence, Hertfordshire, England.

PLOT SUMMARY

Preface

Shaw begins his preface to *Saint Joan* by announcing that Joan, though a professed Catholic, was in fact one of the first Protestant martyrs as well as being an apostle of nationalism, a Napoleonic military strategist, and a forerunner of feminism. He adds that by claiming to be in direct contact with Heaven and by acting in a condescending way to men in authority, she created so much resentment that it is no wonder she was burnt.

Of course, he says, Joan was not really guilty of the charges of witchcraft and improper behavior leveled against her, but it is not necessary to prove this nowadays because posterity has vindicated her. Nowadays it is necessary not to defend Joan, but to avoid romanticizing her. She was not a pretty village lass, as some have described her, but a genius and a saint. And she was not an ignorant beggarmaid or servant girl, but came from a higher social class and was even an intellectual, despite being illiterate.

Joan's visions and voices, Shaw says, were not signs of madness, witchcraft, or sainthood, but simply the sort of inspiration that often comes to people of genius. She was quite sane, and proposed quite sensible policies, even if her imagination tricked her into thinking that those policies were being conveyed to her by visible saints. As for Joan's belief in baptism and other Catholic rites, which the modern age condemns as superstition, Shaw says that we have our own superstitious beliefs (such as the "gospel" of scientists like Louis Pasteur and belief in the Oedipus complex).

Shaw criticizes earlier writers for saying Joan's judges were corrupt scoundrels. On the contrary, he says, her trial was as fair as modern trials, perhaps even more fair. It was the later trial, the one that exonerated her, that was corrupt.

Shaw argues that since Joan refused to accept the authority of the Catholic Church, the Church was within its rights to excommunicate her; that

George Bernard Shaw

would have been a reasonable punishment. However, to burn her was a horrifying thing that cannot be defended.

On the other hand, Shaw says, if the Church had merely excommunicated Joan and allowed her to continue to promote her views outside the Church, that would have meant tolerating a danger to society, and societies have the right to refuse to tolerate such dangers. Society is founded on intolerance, he says, though he also says that all improvements result from tolerance, especially tolerance of apparent heresies like Joan's—because heretics, if they are persons of genius, promote views superior to those found in organizations. Shaw adds that toleration increases and decreases depending on circumstances, and says that the modern era is not necessarily more tolerant than the Middle Ages.

Shaw ends his Preface by saying he has presented the Middle Ages more accurately than Shakespeare did, but adds that he has deliberately introduced some anachronisms to make the events intelligible. He also rejects suggestions that the philosophical portions and the Epilogue of the play be cut.

Scene I

Scene I opens in a castle in France in 1429. Robert de Baudricourt is berating his steward because the hens are not laying eggs. The steward blames Joan, whom Robert has refused to see. He now decides to see her, and she convinces him to supply her with a horse and armor, and some men, so that she can go convince the Dauphin to raise the siege of Orléans, with the ultimate goal of driving the English out of France. Joan tells Robert that this is the will of God as conveyed to her in messages she receives from Saints Margaret and Catherine. Robert thinks Joan may be mad, but also thinks that her talk of doing God's will may inspire the troops. Immediately after he agrees to help her, the steward rushes in to say that the hens have started laying again.

Scene II

Joan arrives at the court of Charles, the Dauphin. Charles is being bullied by his advisers, but insists on seeing Joan, about whom he has received a glowing report from Robert. There is also news of another of Joan's supposed miracles: causing the death of a soldier who refused to stop swearing.

Joan arrives at court and is able to recognize Charles even though he has changed places with one of his courtiers. Joan gets Charles alone and is able to inspire him to authorize her to take control of the army to raise the siege at Orléans.

Scene III

Joan arrives at Orléans eager to lead the troops into battle. Dunois, the commander, tells her they cannot attack until the wind changes. Joan agrees to pray for such a change, and before they can even get to the church, the wind does change.

Scene IV

The Earl of Warwick, the English chaplain de Stogumber, and Bishop Cauchon meet in a tent in the English camp to discuss recent English defeats and the role Joan played in them. Stogumber demands that Joan be executed as a witch. Cauchon says she is a heretic rather than a witch; his main concern is with the threat her individualist views pose to the power of the Church. Warwick is concerned that Joan's views would strengthen the royalty at the expense of the feudal aristocracy. Though calmer than Stogumber, Warwick is set on executing Joan and pressures Cauchon to agree. Cauchon balks at being used this way and says he wants to make sure that Joan's soul is saved.

Scene V

Charles has just been crowned in the cathedral at Rheims, thanks to Joan. Joan now advises him that they should continue the war and take Paris. Charles and his advisers are appalled. Even Joan's friend Dunois tells her that she is being reckless. The Archbishop accuses her of the sin of pride, which he says will lead to her destruction as in a Greek tragedy. He adds that if she persists in setting herself up above the Church and the military, she will find herself alone. Joan says she will be no more alone than France is or God is, and she will have the love of the common people to support her.

Scene VI

The trial scene. Rouen castle, 1431. Several of the judges and assessors do their best to convince Joan to recant to save herself, but she obstinately refuses to pledge absolute obedience to the Church. Only when threatened with execution does she change her mind, saying it is only sensible to avoid being burnt. But when she realizes that she will still be imprisoned for life, she tears up her recantation and is led away to the stake. The Inquisitor, who had warned the court of the seriousness of Joan's heresy, now tells Cauchon that Joan was innocent. Stogumber, who was furious when it seemed Joan might escape burning, and who all along has demanded the harshest penalties for her, stumbles in from the execution full of remorse. He says he never realized what he was actually demanding when he called for her execution. The Executioner enters to tell Warwick that Joan's heart would not burn. Warwick wonders if they have heard the last of her.

Epilogue

It is now twenty-five years after the execution. Charles is brought news that a second trial has exonerated Joan, and then Joan herself appears to him in a dream, along with many of the other characters from the play. A gentleman from 1920 appears, announcing that Joan has been made a saint. Everyone kneels before Joan and praises her. She asks if they would like her to come back to life. Disconcerted, they all say that would not be a good idea. Joan is soon left alone, and wonders when the world will be ready to receive God's saints.

CHARACTERS

Archbishop of Rheims

A political prelate who bullies the Dauphin and is shrewdly cynical about miracles. He is moved at first by Joan, but later reproaches her for pride, seeing her views as a threat to the Church.

Bluebeard

Bluebeard is Gilles de Rais. A frivolous young courtier, sporting a dyed blue beard.

Peter Cauchon

Cauchon, the Bishop of Beauvais, presides over Joan's trial along with the Inquisitor. Earlier, he discussed Joan's fate with Warwick, her other major antagonist. Unlike Warwick, however, Cauchon in Shaw's play (as opposed to the Cauchon of history) is scrupulously fair and merciful, and sincerely wants to save Joan's soul. However, he is also seriously concerned about the threat posed to the Church by her belief in her private judgment. At the trial, he strives to get Joan to recant and is disappointed when she refuses to declare absolute obedience to the Church.

The Chaplain

See John de Stogumber

Charles

Called the Dauphin (that is, heir to the throne), but actually he is already king, though not yet crowned. He is a timid young man, reluctant even to try being brave and assertive against the bullies at court, but Joan puts some spirit in him for a while, getting him to support her plans for raising the siege at Orleans and crowning him in the cathedral at Rheims. When she wants to attack Paris, however, he reverts to timidity and will not support her; instead, he is eager to sign a treaty. In the Epilogue, however, he seems stronger again: he is called Charles the Victorious and leads his men into battle. But he remains skeptical of idealists who try to change the world.

Clerical Gentleman

The Clerical Gentleman arrives back in 1456 from the year 1920 to announce that Joan has been made a saint.

MEDIA ADAPTATIONS

- Shaw himself drafted a screenplay for *Saint Joan* in the 1930s, but no movie was made of it, owing to pressure from the Catholic Church. Shaw's screenplay, edited by Bernard F. Dukore, was published in 1968 by the University of Washington Press.

- A movie version of the play was later made based on a screenplay by Graham Greene. Directed by Otto Preminger, this 1957 version starred Jean Seberg as Joan, Richard Widmark as the Dauphin, Richard Todd as Dunois, Anton Walbrook as Cauchon, and John Gielgud as Warwick.

- There was also a television version of the play in 1967, starring Geneviève Bujold as Joan and Roddy McDowall as the Dauphin.

- The Media Resources Center at the University of California at Berkeley lists a version of the play read by Siobhan McKenna as Saint Joan.

John D'Estivet

The prosecutor at Joan's trial, D'Estivet is defensive about the proceedings, declaring that they are not motivated by hate, and saying that everything has been done to give Joan a chance to escape execution.

The Dauphin

See Charles

Robert de Baudricourt

The local squire where Joan lives; Joan's father owes allegiance to him. Though blustery, he is a weak man and is easily convinced by Joan to give her the men and horses that she wants.

Richard de Beauchamp

See Earl of Warwick

de Courcelles

Courcelles is a priest who serves as an assessor at Joan's trial. He is earnest and strict in his adherence to the rules and advocates torturing Joan, not so much out of bloodthirstiness as because it is customary.

Bertrand de Poulengey

A dreamy gentleman, vassal to de Baudricourt. A convert to Joan's cause.

John de Stogumber

Stogumber, the chaplain to the Cardinal of Winchester in England, is Joan's most vehement antagonist, largely because, like her, he is a nationalist, only on the English rather than the French side. He excitedly demands that she be burned as a witch for her part in the recent defeats suffered by the English and says he would like to strangle her with his own hands. But when he actually sees her burnt, he undergoes a remorseful transformation and becomes a preacher against violence, warning people not to advocate extreme measures whose nature they do not truly understand.

Jack Dunois

Commander of the French troops at Orléans. A dedicated soldier and wise strategist, known as the Bastard of Orléans, he adopts Joan's ideas about waging war for a national cause rather than for feudal ransoms. He becomes Joan's friend, but also becomes resentful of her when she seems to forget that his military leadership played a role in their joint victories.

Earl of Warwick

An English nobleman and one of Joan's major antagonists. He is much more suave and diplomatic than the English chaplain, de Stogumber, but just as dedicated to having Joan executed. He has none of the scruples expressed by Bishop Cauchon; he will pay lip service to saving Joan's soul, but he wants to make sure the Church condemns her body to be burned. He sees Joan as a threat to his side in the war and as a more general threat to the power of the feudal aristocracy.

The Executioner

The Executioner reports to Warwick after the execution that Joan's heart would not burn.

The Inquisitor

This is John Lemaître, the mild and elderly but firm agent of the Holy Inquisition who presides over Joan's trial with Cauchon. He is impatient with the assessors who want to bring trivial charges against Joan. He focuses on the heresy charge, and makes a long speech warning of the dangers of heresy.

Joan

Known also as the Maid, Joan is the dominant figure in the play. Even when she is offstage, the other characters discuss her, and when she is in the scene, she takes charge: she knows what she wants and at least in the first half of the play is able to achieve it.

Joan is no frail, delicate woman, and has little interest in traditional womanly things; instead, she wants to be a soldier and she has a large political goal: to free her country from the presence of the English. She is also extremely pious and believes she is being directed by saints to carry out God's will. She is strong-willed, persistent, and inspirational; she is even able to lend courage to the timid Dauphin. Perhaps because she is still not even twenty, she is brashly impatient, even reckless, and does not understand all the ways of the world. She is surprised that her achievements inspire resentment and does not understand why she is condemned as a heretic. She has a touch of genius about her, but she is also a bit naïve.

La Hire

A captain in the army and a loyal follower of Joan's. He is as eager as she is for battle.

La Trémouille

Lord Chamberlain at the Dauphin's court and commander of his army. He bullies the Dauphin. He has difficulty reading and is not as shrewd as the Archbishop.

Martin Ladvenu

The most compassionate of the assessors at Joan's trial. He draws up the recantation statement and gets her to sign it in an attempt to save her life.

The Maid

See Joan

Soldier

The soldier shows up in the Epilogue to report that although his generally sinful life has condemned him to hell, he gets a day off each year for having given Joan two sticks as a cross before she was burnt.

Steward

De Baudricourt's steward. He cringes before his master, but is inspired by Joan.

THEMES

Treatment of Geniuses and Saints

What the play seems to demonstrate is that the world is not very accepting of exceptional people like Joan. Joan has accomplished great things: won the battle of Orléans and several other battles, inspired the French troops, put courage into Charles and gotten him crowned as king, and so forth. And yet she encounters resentment from those she helps and is eventually condemned to death as a heretic for refusing to accept the absolute authority of the Church. Her mystical connection to the saints in Heaven might have been regarded as something admirable, but instead she is killed for it. When she is safely dead, people worship her, but those same people flee in horror at the suggestion that she might come back to life, just as her supporters fled in her lifetime when she proposed to push past a certain point. The point seems to be that we are uncomfortable with exceptional individuals; we may tolerate them for a while, but in the end we wish to be rid of them—though once we are rid of them, we find it safe to speak admiringly of them.

Individualism Versus Authority

The play poses difficult questions about the relation of individualism and authority. On the one hand, there is the supreme individualist, Joan, who follows her private judgment in defiance of the authorities. Joan is such a charismatic figure in the play that it is hard not to side with her and then to want to side with the individualist, rebellious approach to life. Shaw does say in his Preface that individual geniuses see more than others and are of a higher caliber than the leaders of organizations. On the other hand, in the same Preface, discussing

TOPICS FOR FURTHER STUDY

- Read some biographical material on Joan of Arc. In what ways does Shaw's Joan differ from the Joan of history?

- Compare Shaw's treatment of Joan with the way she is portrayed by other writers (e.g., Mark Twain, Andrew Lang, Voltaire). Also, look at how Shaw (in his Preface) says these other writers portray Joan; is he fair to the other writers?

- In what circumstances is it appropriate to defy the authorities in Joan's manner? If a citizen disagrees with government spending policies, does s/he have the right to refuse to pay taxes? Would it have been proper to disobey the apartheid laws in South Africa or the anti-Semitic laws in Nazi Germany, or to defy the tanks in Tienanmen Square? How about protesting against the Vietnam War?

- To what extent do Joan's own failings contribute to her downfall? To what extent do external forces cause her downfall?

- Is Joan a failure in the end? Does she achieve something? What?

- Whose side is Shaw on in the play? Joan's? The Church and Cauchon's? Both? Neither? Explain.

---

the characters of William Shakespeare, he associates individualism with selfishness and irresponsibility. And in the play itself (in Scene IV), Bishop Cauchon warns that Joan's doctrine of individual judgment will lead to the triumph of "every ignorant laborer or dairymaid" over "The Church's accumulated wisdom and knowledge and experience, its councils of learned, venerable pious men." Perhaps individual judgment is to be respected only when it is the judgment of an exceptional individual like Joan, when it is the judgment of a genius or a saint, but, as Cauchon says in the Epilogue, human beings cannot distinguish saints from heretics.

Nationalism and War

Joan is associated with the doctrine of nationalism several times, especially with the idea that France should be for the French, England for the English, and so forth. She is also associated with modern approaches to warfare, renouncing the old, feudal ways in which ransoms were sought, in favor of a more serious, dedicated approach, in which soldiers fight to the death for a cause such as nationalism. Because of Joan's charismatic appeal, the temptation is to support what she supports: these new attitudes to nations and war. On the other hand, the other highly nationalist character in the play, Stogumber, is portrayed as a dangerous extremist. And Bishop Cauchon, in Scene IV, says that nationalism leads to war and destruction. Again, it is hard to know which side Shaw wants his audience to be on.

Feminism

One of the charges against Joan is that she dresses in men's clothes and engages in traditional male pursuits, notably soldiering. Shaw in his Preface is dismissive of historians who do not think women capable of genius in the "traditional masculine departments," and the play seems to speak in favor of a woman's right to pursue whatever career and lifestyle she chooses and not to be bound by traditional notions of women's roles.

Miracles, Faith, and Sainthood

The miracles in the play are all capable of rational explanation: hens stop and start laying eggs for a variety of reasons; natural causes can explain the shift in the wind; and as the Archbishop says, Joan's ability to distinguish Charles from Bluebeard may merely mean that she has heard them described. But whether they have a supernatural basis or not, Joan's miracles do inspire faith and win her followers. It is Joan's ability to inspire that is perhaps her most miraculous power; putting enough courage into Charles so that he lets himself be crowned king is a large-scale miracle, as Joan says herself. It seems that what is truly miraculous is the inner power of a genius like Joan, who can move men and change the course of history.

STYLE

Setting

Saint Joan is set in France in the period 1429–1431, with an epilogue set in 1456. Four of the scenes are set in castles in the northern part of the country, including the castle occupied by the court of the Dauphin in Chinon and the castle in Rouen where Joan's trial takes place. One scene takes place in the cathedral at Rheims where Charles is crowned, another takes place on the banks of the Loire River in the French military camp across from Orleans, and one (the so-called Tent Scene) takes place in a tent in the English camp.

Structure and Tone

In his Preface, Shaw suggests that his play is divided into three parts: "the romance of [Joan's] rise, the tragedy of her execution, and the comedy of the attempts of posterity to make amends for that execution." The first three scenes depict the rise, showing Joan's successes and "miracles" in a lively manner. In the next three scenes, the play becomes darker: Joan's enemies plot against her, her friends desert her, and she is put to death. The Epilogue for the most part restores the light tone of the early scenes as it depicts Joan's posthumous triumph, but it does end on a plaintive note, with another desertion of Joan.

Genre

There has been much debate about whether Shaw's play is a comedy or a tragedy. It certainly has elements of both. There are humorous, even farcical moments, as in the opening scene about the hens that will not lay eggs, or the moment when Robert de Baudricourt looks up apprehensively to see if there really is a halo over his head. There is a jaunty tone in the opening scenes and again in the Epilogue, but a much darker tone in between, and Joan's death can be seen as the fall of a tragic hero.

On the other hand, the play does not end with her death, but with a mostly light-hearted presentation of her posthumous vindication. At least one critic has said that the play is best described as a tragicomedy.

In his Preface, Shaw calls the play a tragedy, but mainly in an attempt to distinguish it from melodrama. His point is that he is not telling a story of evil villains and a pure saint, as in a melodrama; instead, he wants to show how a murder can be committed by "normally innocent people," that is, by honorable characters who are not villains. He also notes that there is an element of comedy in the tragedy.

If the play is a tragedy, at least in part, then there is the question of whether Joan is a tragic hero in the traditional sense of being a character of high standing who falls because of some tragic error she commits. Joan is not of high social standing, but she does rise to a powerful position, and she is accused in the play itself (by the Archbishop) of suffering from one of the traditional tragic flaws of Greek drama: hubris, or pride. She herself admits to vanity in wearing a gold coat into her final battle, an action that made her easily singled out and captured. And especially in the later scenes she does seem to lose some of her earlier humility and become a bit overbearing: giving orders to the Archbishop instead of falling on her knees before him. Of course, she has been brash and self-confident all along; those are some of her strengths, but it is typical of tragedy to have the hero's tragic error stem from his own strengths. Joan has other flaws as well: her inexperience and simplicity, her impatience, and what seems like an excessive enjoyment of soldiering. These may all be said to bring her down. However, the play's emphasis is actually less on the personal errors committed by Joan and more on the sociopolitical forces that surround her. The Church, the English, and the feudal aristocracy want her removed; they are the main causes of Joan's fall, along with the desertion of Joan by her supposed friends in the French camp.

Symbols

The fact that Joan's heart will not burn suggests that, as is said at the end of Scene VI, her execution is not really the end of her. And indeed Joan reappears in the Epilogue in a sort of resurrection.

This quasi-resurrection of Joan makes her seem something like Christ. And there are other suggestions in the play that Joan functions as a Christ figure: more than once it is suggested that a character may play the role of Judas in relation to her; Stogumber says the onlookers who laughed at her burning would have laughed at Christ; and in the Epilogue, on hearing that it took the burning of Joan to save Stogumber, Bishop Cauchon wonders if a Christ must perish in every age to save those (like Stogumber) who lack imagination.

Anachronisms and Discussions

Saint Joan features long philosophical discussions typical of Shaw, most notably in the Tent Scene, in which characters use historical terms like Protestantism and nationalism that were not yet in use. Shaw's purpose in using these devices is, as he says in the Preface, to help the audience to better understand the medieval period and the forces at work that bring Joan down.

HISTORICAL CONTEXT

Joan and Her Times

Shaw follows the historical record fairly closely in describing Joan's career. Just like the Joan in the play, the real Joan of Arc was a farmer's daughter who, dressed in men's clothes and aided by Robert de Baudricourt, won the ear of the Dauphin and was instrumental in lifting the siege of Orléans. This action is generally seen as the turning point in the Hundred Years' War (1337–1453) between England and France; England at that point controlled most of northern France, but after triumphing at Orléans in 1429, the French went on to push the English almost completely out of the country.

The Hundred Years' War, though it began in part because of the complications arising from feudal landholding in which English kings held lands in France as vassals of the French king, led to the growth of nationalism, the strengthening of royal power, and the weakening of the feudal nobility and the whole feudal system—the very things Warwick fears in the play.

While Warwick fears nationalism, Cauchon fears Protestantism, a force that did not really exist until a century after the time of Joan. But there were forerunners of the Protestant Reformation even before Joan's time, most notably the Englishman John Wyclif (1328–1384) and the Czech Jan Hus (1369–1415), both of whom Cauchon mentions (in Scene IV). Wyclif and Hus both questioned the ultimate authority of the Church, somewhat like the way Shaw has Joan question its authority, although Wyclif and Hus subordinated the Church to Scripture rather than to mystical contact with saints in Joan's manner, and modern critics say Joan did not intend to be a reformer or to challenge the Church's role in the way that Wyclif and Hus did.

Shaw and His Times

Shaw wrote *Saint Joan* at the same time that T. S. Eliot, James Joyce, and other modernists were writing in experimental forms about an incomprehensible universe, but Shaw was no modernist. Indeed, it is a curious fact about his Preface that in it he more than once compares life in Joan's time with life in the nineteenth century, as if he were still writing in the nineteenth century instead of in 1924.

Shaw was very much a man of the nineteenth century, influenced by one of the major nineteenth-century beliefs: socialism, in its Fabian form. Fabian socialism, which became influential in England in the 1880s and 1890s, advocated a gradual, non-revolutionary reorganization of society to create a utopian society in which poverty and excessive individualism, profit-making, and competition would be eliminated.

Of course, Shaw could not help but be influenced by developments in the early years of the twentieth century, and he was especially affected by World War I. The first World War was notable for the large-scale destruction and loss of life that it caused and also for the nationalistic propaganda associated with it. J. L. Wisenthal, in *Shaw's Sense of History,* says Shaw's negative feelings about World War I are reflected in *Saint Joan,* for instance, in Cauchon's remark in Scene IV about how the division of united Christendom into nations would cause the world to perish in war.

In 1916, Irish rebels led a short-lived uprising (the Easter Rebellion) against British rule in Ireland. The rebellion was suppressed and its leaders executed, much to the dismay of Shaw. In *Saint Joan,* the struggle to push the English out of France may echo the Irish struggle to push the British out of Ireland.

In 1917, the Bolsheviks came to power in the Russian Revolution and dedicated themselves to establishing socialism in Russia by whatever means necessary, including methods reminiscent of the

COMPARE & CONTRAST

- **1400s:** The Hundred Years' War, and increases in royal power and economic development, lead to the growth of national feeling and modern nation-states.

  1923: World War I, which itself resulted from nationalist clashes, gives rise to a number of new nation-states, encouraging national rivalries.

  Today: With the end of the cold war, which had suppressed many nationalist rivalries, old and new conflicts between nations and ethnic groups have come to the fore.

- **1400s:** The Catholic Church is the dominant religious and political force in the Western World.

  1923: The Catholic Church retains its dominant religious role in some parts of the Western World, including France and southern Europe, but elsewhere (England, the United States) it has no such dominant status.

  Today: The Catholic Church, like other churches, has tried to modernize itself to broaden its appeal in an increasingly secular age.

- **1400s:** In the traditional medieval world, individuals have few rights.

  1923: In the capitalist democracies, individual rights are enshrined in law and the economy, but various socialist groups call for putting collective rights ahead of individual ones, a philosophy that the Communist Party in the newly formed Soviet Union is trying to put into practice.

  Today: With the collapse of the Soviet Union and the disappearance of most socialist states and movements, capitalist individualism holds sway in much of the world, though kept in check to a certain extent by governmental regulation and certain political movements, such as environmentalism.

- **1400s:** In the traditional medieval world, women have few political or economic rights, and are confined to a few traditional roles.

  1923: Women have won some property rights, and some have won the right to vote; some women have entered traditional male spheres, but the division into male and female spheres remains largely intact.

  Today: Feminism has had a large impact on Western culture. Women have entered more and more traditionally male occupations; laws have been enacted guaranteeing them equality or priority in employment; many no longer feel obliged to follow the traditional paths of marriage and motherhood, or seek to combine such paths with professional careers.

---

medieval Inquisition. Shaw was quite sympathetic to the Bolshevik enterprise, and even sent Lenin, the Bolshevik leader, an autographed copy of *Back to Methuselah,* the play he wrote before *Saint Joan.* Arnold Silver, in *Saint Joan: Playing with Fire,* suggests that there is sympathy for the Inquisition in *Saint Joan* because of Shaw's growing sympathy for the dictatorial methods being used in Russia.

In 1903, Emmeline Pankhurst founded the Women's Social and Political Union to win the right to vote for women. Over the next decade this group (called suffragettes) picketed and protested, winning partial voting rights for women by 1918. There is no evidence that Shaw modeled Joan on Pankhurst or her followers, but the belief in equal rights for women that underlay the woman's suffrage movement also underlies Shaw's play.

CRITICAL OVERVIEW

Even before *Saint Joan* first appeared on stage, it inspired commentary. At least one critic worried about how Joan would fare in the hands of an irreverent writer like Shaw, but when he finally saw the play he was pleased by Shaw's treatment of the subject. The play had successful first runs in New York in 1923 and in London in 1924, running for 214 and 244 performances respectively. An early production in Paris was also a great success, even though Shaw had previously not been very popular in France. However, Shaw himself was not pleased with the French production because it made Joan a weaker, more victimized character than he had envisioned her to be. There were also successful early productions in Berlin, Moscow, Madrid, and Tokyo. Overall, *Saint Joan,* though something of a departure from Shaw's usual comic output, solidified his reputation as a great playwright.

On the other hand, the early critics did not all write favorably about the new play. There was a great deal of negative comment about Shaw's use of history: many historical inaccuracies were pointed out, and his anachronistic use of terms like Protestantism and nationalism was criticized. The well-known medieval historian Johan Huizinga said Shaw had not succeeded in reproducing the medieval atmosphere, despite his claims to have done so in his Preface. Many critics disliked the Epilogue, saying its comic character did not fit the tragic events depicted in the preceding scene. One critic, though, said it was the tragic events that did not fit; seeing the play primarily as a comedy, he said the Epilogue was appropriate, but Joan's execution was out of place.

The mix of comedy and tragedy in the play inspired criticism, as did some of the more farcical elements in the story. The French critics, who generally praised the play, found the comic depiction of Charles and his court unacceptable. Shaw himself referred to the opening comic scenes as "flapdoodle" (in a letter cited by Nicholas Grene in *George Bernard Shaw's Saint Joan*), but he said *Saint Joan* was generally "a magnificent play" (in another letter, cited by Stanley Weintraub in *Saint Joan Fifty Years After*) and an "act of respect" for Joan (cited by James Graham in *Saint Joan Fifty Years After*).

Other commentators have also found much to praise in the play. In *Saint Joan Fifty Years After,* Desmond MacCarthy wrote in awe of how the play lifted the audience on "waves of emotion to be dashed on thought." He called it intellectually exciting and emotionally moving. The Italian playwright Luigi Pirandello praised its poetic emotion, though he found Joan's character too simple and preferred the character of Stogumber, a view not held by many, Stogumber being seen by others as too extreme to be believable. Later writers have also praised the play, seeing it either as Shaw's greatest, or at least his most important, play because it deals effectively with important themes. Some have even ranked it with Shakespeare's tragedies. It is also seen as being part of a new development in Shaw's work, a shift towards a more melancholy, less optimistic attitude, coupled with a friendlier attitude towards authority, all this stemming in part from his reaction to World War I.

The play itself had no problems with the censors, unlike Shaw's earlier play *Mrs. Warren's Profession.* However, a screenplay of *Saint Joan* that Shaw drafted in the 1930s was never produced because the Catholic Church put pressure on the Hollywood censors not to approve it.

The issue of whether the play is a tragedy or a comedy has exercised many commentators. Some see it as a traditional tragedy with Joan causing her own downfall because of the hubris of which she stands accused by the Archbishop. Others say that Shaw does not agree with the Archbishop and that Joan's pride is a positive quality in the play. One critic, while unsure whether Joan's pride qualifies as a tragic flaw, says the play is a tragedy in the Greek manner because Fate, in the form of the social forces arrayed against Joan, brings about the catastrophe. Another critic, noting how the fairly happy ending in the Epilogue follows the unhappy ending of the previous scene, suggests that what Shaw has produced is a tragicomedy.

The critics have also disagreed about whose side Shaw is on in the play: Joan's or her opponents'. Eric Bentley writes that Shaw is actually on both sides. Arnold Silver says Joan represents the younger, rebellious Shaw, while Cauchon is the older, more authoritarian Shaw. But most critics see Shaw as being on Joan's side.

CRITICISM

Sheldon Goldfarb

Goldfarb has a Ph.D. in English and has published two books on the Victorian author William Makepeace Thackeray. In the following essay, he

Jean Seberg (left) as Joan of Arc in the 1957 film adaptation of Saint Joan.

discusses the underlying philosophy of Shaw's Saint Joan.

Saint Joan is full of surprises. The first surprise is that a nonreligious writer like Shaw (at least nonreligious in a conventional Christian sense) should even write on a topic like this: the martyrdom of a Christian saint. Indeed, when it was first announced that Shaw, the "professional iconoclast," was writing on Saint Joan, at least one critic worried that the play would not be properly reverent. And critics in France, before the French version opened, were similarly nervous about how the irreverent Irishman would treat their national heroine.

But the critics were all satisfied, at least on this point: Shaw, the mocking non-Christian, produced a completely sympathetic portrait of a Christian saint. Except in a way the saint is less Christian than Shavian: Shaw's Joan does hear Heavenly voices, it is true, and ends up a martyr, but she is no shrinking, timid victim (except in the French production, which displeased Shaw immensely). She is an active warrior saint, keen to go into battle, strong and clever, ready with a pert reply when challenged. For instance, when told (in Scene I) that the voices she says are from God actually come from her imagination, she says: "Of course. That is how the messages from God come to us." Commentators have disapproved of this line, saying the historical Joan would never have spoken like that. Probably true. But the line is very revealing about the nature of the Shavian Joan: she is as witty as her creator, a genius just like him, though a somewhat untutored genius, whose inexperience contributes to her downfall.

Not that it is clear that even an experienced genius can triumph in our world. As Shaw says in his Preface, even the experienced Socrates was forced to drink hemlock. The world cannot tolerate its geniuses; superior men and women make others feel inferior and resentful, and so the superior ones end up being condemned to die, just as Joan is condemned to die by the Catholic Church and its Holy Office of the Inquisition.

But here is another surprise from Shaw. In both the Preface and the play itself, Shaw is at pains to say that Joan received a fair trial at the hands of the Church. He goes out of his way to present a flattering portrait of Cauchon, one of her chief judges, even though the historical record suggests he was unscrupulous and corrupt, not the merciful and fair-minded defender of the Church that Shaw makes him out to be. How can Shaw, the professional rebel and defender of Joan, be sympathetic to the Inquisition, that instrument for suppressing individual rights,

WHAT DO I READ NEXT?

- *Caesar and Cleopatra* (1901), an earlier historical play by Shaw, focuses on the heroism of Julius Caesar.

- *Major Barbara* (1905) is another play by Shaw about a heroic female: this time, an official in the Salvation Army and a social reformer.

- *Androcles and the Lion* (1912) is a play by Shaw about miracles, martyrs, and Christians.

- *Personal Recollections of Joan of Arc* is Mark Twain's loving portrayal of Joan, first published in 1896.

- *The Maid of Orléans* is Voltaire's irreverently ribald account of Joan's story, first published as *La pucelle d'Orléans* in 1755.

- *Joan of Lorraine* (1946) is a play about Joan by the American playwright Maxwell Anderson.

- *Saint Joan of the Stockyards* (1931) is a play by Bertolt Brecht that combines elements of Shaw's *Saint Joan* and his *Major Barbara*. Brecht's Joan is a member of the Salvation Army trying to do good in Chicago during the Depression.

- *Henry VI, Part One* (1623), by William Shakespeare, is about the Hundred Years' War and contains a negative portrayal of Joan.

---

for maintaining dictatorial rule, and stamping out new thoughts, the instrument that sent Joan to her death?

According to Louis Crompton, in *George Bernard Shaw's Saint Joan,* Shaw is not actually sympathetic to the Inquisition at all; he is merely warning us that individuals may believe themselves to be right and still do evil things: "the most nefarious institutions and their administrators always seem perfectly justified in their own eyes and in the eyes of most onlookers."

But Shaw is actually more sympathetic to the Inquisition than Crompton suggests, saying in his Preface not that Joan was executed by a nefarious institution but by "normally innocent people in the energy of their righteousness." And though Shaw says that executing Joan was a horrible action, he suggests that the Church was within its rights to punish her in some way, perhaps to excommunicate her, because societies have the right to set down laws and have them obeyed: "society must always draw a line somewhere between allowable conduct and insanity or crime, in spite of the risk of mistaking sages for lunatics and saviors for blasphemers." He even says, "We must persecute, even to the death."

In *Saint Joan: Playing with Fire,* Arnold Silver sees this persecuting side of Shaw as reflecting his growing disillusionment with democracy and his simultaneous attraction to dictatorial regimes like that of Lenin's Bolsheviks in Russia. It is certainly true—and this is another surprise—that Shaw takes a shot at democracy in his Preface, saying, somewhat bizarrely, that the Catholic Church is in practice a democracy, and therefore flawed, because the process of selecting bishops, cardinals, and the Pope is one of "selection and election . . . of the superior by the inferior (the cardinal vice of democracy)." The result is that the leaders of the Church cannot match geniuses like Joan who are self-selected rather than elected by their inferiors.

But what is notable here is that Shaw is calling the Church, the persecuting agency, a democracy. He is not contrasting dictatorship and democracy; he is associating the two. The actual contrast in the play is between the dictatorial orders of a democratic organization like the Church, on the one hand, and the rights of individuals on the other. It may be commonplace nowadays to associate individual rights with democracy, but Shaw is actually placing these two concepts in opposition to each other. On the one hand, there is the democratic organization of the Church, representing the people and society as a whole, and on the other hand there are individuals with their own private interests. What Shaw is doing is opposing collective rights to individual rights, and saying in his Preface that in many cases society is justified in putting its collective rights ahead of individual rights. This sounds like Shaw the socialist speaking, not necessarily Shaw the lover of dictators.

As a socialist, Shaw was impatient with individual rights and individualism. In the Preface, in his discussion of Shakespeare's plays, he specifically derides the individualism of the middle classes. He describes Shakespeare's characters as being "individualist, sceptical, self-centred . . . and selfish . . . without public responsibilities of any kind" and says that "that is why they seem natural to our middle classes, who are comfortable and irresponsible at other people's expense."

Shaw also seems critical of the individual rights of the working classes, another surprise, given that as a socialist, one would expect him to be supportive of the rights of laboring people. However, Shaw was never that close to the masses; instead of joining the proletarian Social Democratic Foundation in the 1880s, he joined the intellectual socialists in the Fabian Society. And as noted above, he was no great fan of the power of "inferiors" to elect their superiors. It is notable that, in his Preface, Shaw goes out of his way to emphasize that his heroine is not a mere laborer, but comes from a higher social class. And in the play itself (in Scene IV), Cauchon worries that Joan's assertion of the right to follow her private judgment may lead to the thrusting aside of the Church and its accumulated wisdom "by every ignorant laborer or dairymaid." This will lead, he adds, to blood and fury and devastation as well as to national conflict and destructive war.

Now, this is Cauchon speaking, not Shaw, but Cauchon's two speeches on these topics are so powerful that they seem to reflect Shaw's own views, and indeed, they meet with no rebuttal in the play.

All of this leads to seeing the following set of conflicting attitudes in the play. On the one hand, Shaw seems to be asserting the right of society through institutions like the Church to set down laws that must be obeyed and to persecute "even to the death" those who break those laws. Shaw seems to be strongly asserting the collective rights of society against individual rights, and seems to be opposed to allowing such rights to either the selfish

> WHAT SHAW IS DOING IS OPPOSING COLLECTIVE RIGHTS TO INDIVIDUAL RIGHTS, AND SAYING IN HIS PREFACE THAT IN MANY CASES SOCIETY IS JUSTIFIED IN PUTTING ITS COLLECTIVE RIGHTS AHEAD OF INDIVIDUAL RIGHTS."

middle classes or the ignorant working classes. He also seems to be attacking nationalism and the horrors of war.

At the same time, he has created a very sympathetic heroine who stands preeminently for individual rights, at least for her own right to judge God's will for herself in accordance with her private visions. Moreover, this heroine is a strong nationalist who wants France for the French as well as an advocate for a more serious, that is, a more destructive, approach to warfare.

How can these contradictory ideas be reconciled? How can Shaw be both for and against individual rights, for and against nationalism and war?

Some, like Eric Bentley, in *Bernard Shaw,* say that in fact Shaw was on both sides of the individual rights issues. Arnold Silver says that there are two Shaws in the play: the young, rebellious supporter of individualism (represented by Joan) and the older, grimmer supporter of authoritarianism (represented by Cauchon). On the issue of nationalism and war, J. L. Wisenthal, in *Shaw's Sense of History,* says Shaw supported Joan's spirit and power but not the causes she used that spirit and power to advance.

There is something in all these views, especially in Wisenthal's. There is a sense in the play (and the Preface) that Shaw supports Joan because she is a genius, one of those rare people who help advance the "creative evolution" of the human race. From one perspective, then, as Wisenthal says, it matters less what specific policies Joan favored; the point is that such geniuses are important leaders for others to follow. It may also be that Shaw, who saw history as progressing through stages, accepted the nationalist stage promoted by Joan as a necessary stage in humanity's progressive development. Or he may simply have been thinking of the society of his own day: in Shaw's view, modern society had to be transformed; he was a supporter of those who can transform societies; and therefore he would be drawn to Joan because she was one of those who brought about a transformation, even if the specific nature of that transformation was not one he favored. In other words, Shaw was in favor of rebels and geniuses and that he would support them whatever specific proposals they were advocating.

This support for geniuses also may be the key to explaining the apparent contradiction between Shaw's support for Joan's individual rights and his opposition to individual rights for others. Shaw's basic philosophical attitude as it emerges from this play seems to be the following: There are a few self-selected geniuses in the world who see further and probe deeper than other people, and whose ideas are more advanced than those to be found in organizations representing the people at large. It is important to respect, tolerate, and even celebrate these geniuses, for it is through them that society advances. Society's organizations should give them free rein.

At the same time, the bulk of the population, not being geniuses, should not have the same rights as the geniuses. The "ignorant" working classes and the "selfish" middle classes should follow the rules established by society's organizations.

So there should be order and discipline for the majority (imposed by organizations representing the majority) and free rein for the small minority of geniuses. Unfortunately, this system is not often found. It is hard to recognize a genius, for one thing. As Cauchon says in the Epilogue, "mortal eyes cannot distinguish the saint from the heretic." Or perhaps it is not so much that geniuses cannot be recognized as that they inspire fear, as Shaw says in his Preface. Then instead of following them, the people or their organizations put them to death. After they are dead, they may be worshipped, as Joan is in the Epilogue, which suggests something hopeful, but if the genius threatens to return to life, as Joan does, the ordinary people are most unhappy. As Charles says in the Epilogue, "If you could bring her back to life, they would burn her again within six months."

Still, Joan does triumph in a way. Though burnt at the stake and not wanted back on earth, the causes she advocated do win out. The English are pushed out of France, warfare becomes more modern, and the individualism she represents in Shaw's play becomes the dominant ideology of Western society. Shaw's geniuses may exert influence even though they die; there is thus some optimism present even though the play ends with Joan's lament about the earth not being ready to receive God's saints. The saints may rule from Heaven.

Source: Sheldon Goldfarb, in an essay for *Drama for Students,* Gale Group, 2001.

John Stewart Collis

Collis argues that Saint Joan *is not only a "religious play," but also a play about "military Genius."*

We turn to *Saint Joan*. It is generally regarded as a very religious play. True, there are many clergymen in it and a lot of talk about God and much wrangling over theology, but it is very difficult to understand how Joan of Arc qualified as a saint. She was a military genius. This is very rare, even among men—can you think of a military genius during World War I? For an uneducated country girl to have possessed it is extraordinary indeed. But what has this to do with religion? The French novelist, Huysmans, has expressed the regret that Joan of Arc ever rose to wrest France from the Normans who were seeking to preserve her racial and prehistoric unity with England, and thus handed her over to Charles VII and his southerners. The advantage of the union of France and England for the world generally would have been incalculable (and incidentally, the Mediterranean population of France and the Mediterranean population of Ireland would have rendered impossible an 'Irish question'). And indeed, anyone today walking across the soil of France between Passchendaele and the Somme, knowing that beneath his feet lie nearly a million British dead who were comrades of the French, might well endorse this view. At any rate the claim seems to me by no means outrageous that when the peasant girl from Lorraine with her hallucinations galvanized into action the nerveless arms of Charles she inflicted a blow upon the progress of the modern world which may never have been exceeded.

It is hard to see exactly where her sainthood comes in. She was a martyr, certainly, to outward cruelty and inward folly. I am fond of the Epilogue because of its splendid rhetoric. But it is confusing. Near the end the various parties praise Joan. Each in turn kneels in praise. Indeed they give her a very good hand. But when she asks if they would like her to come back to earth, each makes an excuse and discreetly withdraws. We are supposed to think ill

A scene from the film Saint Joan.

of them for this. But why should they want her back? She was not a saviour with a gospel of salvation; she was not a philosopher with a solution to the riddle of the world; she was not a moralist with a message for mankind. She was a soldier. Why should they want her back unless they had some military coup in mind? When they have all departed she has the nerve to kneel down in a holy manner and to ask God how long it must be before this beautiful earth is ready to receive its saints.

Source: John Stewart Collis, "Religion and Philosophy," in *The Genius of Shaw: A Symposium,* edited by Michael Holroyd, Holt, Rinehart and Winston, 1979, p. 86.

Eldon C. Hill

Saint Joan is said to be the "climax" of Shaw's career. Hill explores this concept through examination of the play.

Though in form *Back to Methuselah* and Shaw's next play stand in sharp contrast, they are similar in two ways—both reflect the pressures of the war period on their creator and both deal with religious themes. Shaw once said *Saint Joan* would not have been written had he not visualized the subject as relevant to "a world situation in which we see whole peoples perishing and dragging us toward the abyss which has swallowed them, all for want of any grasp of the political forces that move civilization."

Other authors had written of the Maid, among them, Shakespeare, Voltaire, Southey, Schiller, Andrew Lang, Mark Twain, Tom Taylor, Percy MacKaye; but Shaw did not learn much from these predecessors in the field. He felt that Voltaire and Shakespeare did Joan an injustice. Mark Twain's *Personal Recollections of Joan of Arc* Shaw regarded as a romantic creation, "an unimpeachable American school teacher in armor." He learned little, if anything, from Twain's book. The direct source of the play is T. Douglas Murray's *Jeanne D'Arc,* a work that centers on Joan's shrewdness and courage in her trial. On reading it, Mrs. Shaw urged her husband to write a play about the subject, and he readily acceded. It was the second time her direct suggestion bore fruit, the first being *The Doctor's Dilemma.* Shaw not only read Murray's account, he also thoroughly studied the case in Quichert's transcription of the trial in 1431 and the rehabilitation proceeding in 1456.

In its form, *Saint Joan* is a chronicle play like *Caesar and Cleopatra,* which it resembles also in having as its central figure a character with the attributes of a Superman. Joan exemplifies the

> INDUBITABLY, JOAN IS ONE OF SHAW'S GREAT EVOCATIONS. 'SHE IS,' AS AN ASTUTE GERMAN CRITIC DECLARES, 'THE LAST AND MOST RADIANT IN THE LONG GALLERY OF WOMEN THAT TESTIFY TO HIS DEEP REVERENCE FOR THE HIGH FUNCTION OF THE FEMININE ELEMENT IN LIFE.'"

strength, the faith, and the wisdom of Shaw's concept of the race that must supersede *homo sapiens* through Creative Evolution if civilization is to be saved. *Saint Joan* is also like *Caesar and Cleopatra* in presenting a main character to whom all the other persons in the play—most of them types—are contributory. Just as Britannus, Rufio, Appollodorus, and even Cleopatra herself are significant chiefly in letting Caesar shine in all his glory and wisdom, so De Baudricourt, Warwick, Dunois, De. Stozomber, Cauchin, the Inquisitor, the Dauphin, and all the others keep the spotlight on Joan. So skillfully does Shaw write, that she is (in Louis L. Martz's words) "the simple cause of every other word and action in the play."

Shaw describes her in the preface as a peasant girl, soldier, "Protestant martyr," yet "a professed and most pious Catholic." She was also "one of the first apostles of nationalism, and the first French practitioner of Napoleonic realism in warfare." "The pioneer of rational dressing for women," Shaw continues, "she refused to accept the specific woman's lot, and dressed and fought and lived as men did." She defied popes and patronized kings. "As her actual condition was pure upstart, there were only two opinions about her. One was that she was miraculous: The other that she was unbearable."

She was a Protestant because she insisted that her religion came from God, not from the Church, as she trusted her inner Voices rather than the traditional dogmas of Catholicism. This left the Church with nothing to do, as Shaw said, "but to burn her or canonize Wycliff and Hus." Shaw had no doubt of her sanity. "Joan must be judged as a sane woman in spite of her voices," he said, "because they never gave her any advice that might not have come to her from her mother wit exactly as gravitation came to Newton." Like Shaw's Caesar, she was a natural, unpretentious person. She spoke in dialect at times and called the future king Lad and Charlie, thereby showing her disregard for titles, officialdom, and worldly station. Her naturalness in speech and behavior (indeed, she talks and acts like a twentieth-century young woman) is part of her charm and appeal.

Though Shaw creates her as a person without sexual attraction or interest, he is careful not to make his Joan a supernatural, self-mortifying saint. Gallant and heroic as she is, she is not the all-perfect protagonist. Charismatic, she has strong power over men "from her uncle to the king, the archbishop, and the military General Staff." She is not without human weaknesses such as stubbornness, conceit; and she has a marked pride in what she conceives to be her God-given capabilities. Shaw portrays her as neither a melodramatic victim nor a romantic heroine.

As there is no conventional heroine in *Saint Joan,* neither are there any villains. In all his dramas Shaw presents his characters, as he saw his contemporaries and historical figures, as mixtures of both good and evil. Accordingly, Joan's judges are not portrayed as incarnations of malice that are bent on sending her to the stake. The Catholic Church is not the villain, and nowhere in the play does Shaw condemn or ridicule the Church, as he sometimes does in his earlier polemical writings. In the trial scene, which is central, Shaw presents both sides of the case, a fact which Eric Bentley praises as adding power to the drama.

Saint Joan is Shaw's nearest approach to tragedy; but it is not tragic in the classical or Shakespearean sense; it is more like the tragicomedies of Ibsen or Chekhov. The controversial epilogue, which brings Joan back to earth for her 1920 canonization, detracts from the tragic effect. Moreover, just as in *Hedda Gabler,* society is to blame for the tragedy of a wasted life; and Shaw makes it clear that the tragedy lies not so much in Joan's fate as in the failure of her society—the establishment of Church and State—to accept and understand her. Indubitably, Joan is one of Shaw's great evocations. "She is," as an astute German critic declares, "the last and most radiant in the long gallery of women that testify to his deep reverence for the high function of the feminine element in life."

This play is the climax of Shaw's career. Though he lived on for more than half a century, nothing that he did afterward is of comparable importance.

Source: Eldon C. Hill, "The Climax of a Career," in *George Bernard Shaw,* Twayne Publishers, 1978, pp. 131–33.

SOURCES

Bentley, Eric, *Bernard Shaw, 1856–1950,* New Directions, 1957.

Crompton, Louis, "A Hagiography of Creative Evolution," in *George Bernard Shaw's Saint Joan,* edited by Harold Bloom, Chelsea House, 1987, p. 47.

Graham, James, "Shaw on *Saint Joan,*" in *Saint Joan Fifty Years After,* edited by Stanley Weintraub, Louisiana State University Press, 1973, p. 17.

Grene, Nicholas, "Shavian History," in *George Bernard Shaw's Saint Joan,* edited by Harold Bloom, Chelsea House, 1987, p. 121.

Huizinga, Johan, "Bernard Shaw's *Saint Joan,*" in *Saint Joan Fifty Years After,* edited by Stanley Weintraub, Louisiana State University Press, 1973, p. 54–85.

MacCarthy, Desmond, "*St Joan:* The Theme and the Drama," in *Saint Joan Fifty Years After,* edited by Stanley Weintraub, Louisiana State University Press, 1973, p. 31–38.

Pirandello, Luigi, "Bernard Shaw's *St Joan,*" in *Saint Joan Fifty Years After,* edited by Stanley Weintraub, Louisiana State University Press, 1973, p. 23–28.

Shaw, George Bernard, *Saint Joan: A Chronicle Play in Six Scenes and an Epilogue,* edited by Dan H. Laurence, Penguin, 1957.

Silver, Arnold, *Saint Joan: Playing with Fire,* Twayne, 1993.

Weintraub, Stanley, "Bernard Shaw's Other Saint Joan," in *Saint Joan Fifty Years After,* edited by Stanley Weintraub, Louisiana State University Press, 1973, p. 233.

Wisenthal, J. L., *Shaw's Sense of History,* Clarendon, 1988.

FURTHER READING

Allmand, C. T., *The Hundred Years War: England and France at War, 1300–1450,* Cambridge University Press, 1988.
   This text provides information on the historical background to Joan's career.

Bloom, Harold, ed., *George Bernard Shaw's 'Saint Joan,'* Chelsea House, 1987.
   Bloom's book is a collection of essays on the play dating from 1955 through 1984.

Gies, Frances, *Joan of Arc: The Legend and the Reality,* Harper and Row, 1981.
   Gies presents a study of Joan's life and the literature about her.

Holroyd, Michael, *Bernard Shaw,* 5 vols., Chatto and Windus, 1988–1992.
   Holroy's book is the major modern biography of Shaw.

Irvine, William, *The Universe of G. B. S.,* Russell [and] Russell, 1968 (first published in 1949).
   Irvine's work is a study of Shaw's philosophical and political views.

Silver, Arnold, *Saint Joan: Playing with Fire,* Twayne, 1993.
   In this book, Silver gives a full-length study of the play.

Weintraub, Stanley, ed., *Saint Joan Fifty Years After,* Louisiana State University Press, 1973.
   Weintraub assembles a collection of essays on Shaw's play. This book includes several early reviews and essays from the 1920s.

Shadowlands

WILLIAM NICHOLSON

1989

That the core love story of William Nicholson's *Shadowlands* has staying power seems undeniable. The account of the unusual relationship between British author and scholar C. S. Lewis, who wrote on Christianity and literature, and also wrote the *Narnia Chronicles* many other children's books, and Joy Davidman Gresham, an American poet and self-described Jewish-Communist-Christian, has been told in three mediums. Nicholson originally wrote it as a television movie for the BBC in 1986 before adapting it for the stage in 1989 and for a feature-length film, which garnered an Academy Award nomination in 1993.

The theatrical production of *Shadowlands* debuted at Theatre Royal in Plymouth, England on October 5, 1989. The production later ran for approximately a year in London, winning the *London Evening Standard*'s award for Best Play of 1990. *Shadowlands* made its New York premiere on November 11, 1990, at the Brooks Atkinson Theatre on Broadway. This production ran for about 180 performances.

Critics were sharply divided on *Shadowlands*. While many agreed that the play was very meaningful and tapped into powerful emotions about the nature of life, death, love, and suffering, others believed it was trite and inaccurate, if not sappy. But even critics that had problems with the play reported that *Shadowlands* had a cathartic effect on audiences, often leaving them in tears. For example, an

unnamed critic in *Variety* questioned why the play even was written. The critic writes, "it is not clear why Lewis' musings or his 10 year relationship with Davidman needs to be staged. The story is both tragic and difficult." Yet other critics found much to praise. Gerald Nachman of the *San Francisco Chronicle* states "*Shadowlands* poses classic questions about God, pain and love, but mostly it makes you determined to embrace life. You can't ask much more of play than that."

AUTHOR BIOGRAPHY

Nicholson was born in England in 1948. During Nicholson's childhood, his father worked as a doctor in Africa, while his mother raised the family (which included two sisters) in Sussex. Raised as a Catholic, Nicholson attended prep schools and public schools, mostly all-male boarding schools, in Great Britain before entering Cambridge University.

After graduating from Cambridge in the mid-1970s, Nicholson became a graduate trainee at the BBC (British Broadcasting Corporation). For the next ten years, he wrote, directed, and produced over fifty documentaries for the network. Nicholson also executive produced several television series.

While working for the BBC, Nicholson pursued his dream to become a novelist. He wrote each morning before going to work, eventually producing eight novels. However, Nicholson could find no publishers and he abandoned this goal. Instead, in the mid-1980s, he turned to writing dramatic scripts for television.

In 1985, he wrote a fifty-three-minute movie, called *Shadowlands,* about children's author and religious writer C. S. Lewis's relationship with American Joy Gresham. The movie, which aired on the BBC, met with positive reviews. Nicholson began writing many biographical dramas, influenced by techniques he learned as a documentarian.

Nicholson began writing screenplays in 1986 with his first feature, *New World.* He continued to work in television. In 1987, he wrote another drama for British television entitled *Life Story,* which was later aired in the United States under the titles of *Double Helix* and *The Search for the Double Helix.*

In 1989, Nicholson expanded his writing career to the stage. He adapted his television movie *Shadowlands* into a successful play in 1989. Nicholson would only produce a few more stage plays in his career. They included *Map of the Heart* and 1999's *Retreat from Moscow,* the latter being influenced by the failure of his own parents' marriage.

Primarily, Nicholson focused on screenplays. In 1993, he adapted his stage play for *Shadowlands* into a major motion picture. He received an Academy Award nomination for Best Adapted Screenplay. Other movie scripts that he wrote or adapted include *Sarafina!* (1992, based on a stage play); *Nell* (1994, with Mark Handley, a fellow playwright), *First Knight* (1995), *Firelight* (1997), and *Gladiator* (2000, coauthor). Nicholson also tried his hand at directing with the script *Firelight.*

Much of what Nicholson wrote for television in the 1990s was biographical in nature. For HBO, he wrote *A Private Matter* (1992) based on the true experiences of a children's show hostess who traveled to Sweden to get an abortion. In 1996, Nicholson penned *Crime of the Century* about the Lindburgh baby kidnapping trial for HBO. By 1998, eleven of his nineteen dramatic scripts were based on true stories or people's lives.

Nicholson never forgot his desire to write books. Influenced in part by his work on C. S. Lewis, Nicholson published his first children's book, *The Wind Singer* (2000), part of a planned trilogy called *The Wind on Fire Trilogy.* Nicholson resides in England with his wife, Virginia Bell, and their three children.

PLOT SUMMARY

Act One

Shadowlands opens with a monologue by C. S. "Jack" Lewis. He addresses the audience as if they were attending a lecture. He talks about how much he knows about pain, love, and suffering, and why God lets tragedies happen to people. Lewis argues that God does not want us to be happy, but rather, he wants us to be worthy of love. He believes that suffering is God's love in action.

In an Oxford dining hall, Lewis sits with his elder brother, Major Warner "Warnie" Lewis, and several colleagues from the university. They discuss how women are different. Lewis' friends chide him for his vast experience with women, especially since he is defending them in this conversation.

Lewis tells them about his correspondence with women. As the group breaks up, a slightly drunk Warnie begins to recite poetry. Lewis leads him home. They discuss their friends, revealing the brothers' close relationship.

Lewis sits at his desk in his study in the morning, reading and writing letters, including a letter for a Mrs. Joy Gresham. It seems she has been writing many letters to Lewis and they have had an extensive correspondence. Lewis tells Warnie that he is curious about her. The letter indicates that she is coming to England and wants to meet the brothers. Lewis seeks his brother's advice about meeting Mrs. Gresham in a hotel. Warnie is not helpful, but Lewis decides that they will go.

At the tea room of an Oxford hotel, Lewis and Warnie meet Mrs. Gresham and her eight-year-old son Douglas. Warnie still is not sure about the situation. Douglas tells Lewis that he does not look like he should. The polite conversation is a bit tense, especially after Mrs. Gresham tells Lewis that his letters are the most important thing in her life. They talk about Lewis' religious writings. Mrs. Gresham talks about her religious experiences, including her transitions from Judaism to communism to Christianity. Warnie asks Mrs. Gresham about her poetry; she says that she only used to be a poet. Mrs. Gresham shows that she understands Lewis' thought processes. As Mrs. Gresham and Douglas move to leave, Lewis invites them to have tea at his home before they leave England.

Before the tea at Lewis and Warnie's home, Lewis tells his brother that he enjoys talking to Mrs. Gresham. They both still wonder about her and her motivations. When Mrs. Gresham arrives, she and Lewis discuss literature as Douglas reads a book. Lewis prevails upon her to recite one of her poems. Lewis is surprised by it. They discuss her poem and how personal experience and pain inflect their writing. Lewis tells her about how he was hurt by his mother's death from cancer when he was eight years old. As Mrs. Gresham (now called Joy as she and Lewis are on a first name basis) and Douglas leave, Lewis invites them to spend Christmas at his home.

Later, at a pre-Christmas party at Lewis' home, his colleagues from Oxford meet Joy. The colleagues are rather condescending to Joy, but she stands up for herself. Some of his colleagues believe that Lewis has found his soulmate. Joy soon leaves the party and reads a distressing letter. In the meantime, Lewis' colleagues speak disparagingly of her to him. He does not really care. After they leave, Joy tells Lewis that her husband has written a letter in which he indicates that he has fallen in love with another women and wants a divorce. Joy also confides that her husband has an alcohol problem. Joy decides to give him what he wants. Lewis promises to be her friend.

After Joy and Douglas have gone back to the United States, Lewis implies to his brother that he misses her. One of his colleagues, Christopher Riley, visits. He antagonizes Lewis over Joy and their unusual friendship. Riley leaves, and Lewis returns to work. A few moments later, Joy comes in unannounced. She and Douglas have moved to Oxford, much to Lewis' surprise. He tells her that he is glad to see her. Later, at Joy's new house, Lewis helps her unpack. Joy tells Lewis that while her husband did not like her moving to Britain, it is cheaper to live there than the States. Joy asks him if he minds that she has moved there. He does not, and they confirm the importance of their friendship.

At Lewis' house, Warnie again asks Lewis about the nature of his relationship with Mrs. Gresham. Lewis says that they are merely good friends, though he has agreed to marry her so she can stay in England. Lewis calls it "technically" marrying her. No one will know about the arrangement. The scene moves to the Registry Office where Joy and Lewis marry, with Warnie as the witness. It is an uncomfortable ceremony. Later, Lewis visits Joy at her home. They are comfortable in their secret: everyone thinks they are having an affair, when in fact they are married and are having no affair at all. As Lewis leaves, Joy has a pain in her leg and crumples to the floor.

Act II

At the beginning of Act II, Lewis again speaks to the audience. Without naming Joy, he tells them that she has bone cancer and is in pain. He again talks about faith and suffering. Warnie and Douglas enter. Lewis tells his brother that Joy is not well. While Douglas visits his mother in the hospital, Joy's doctor tells Lewis that she will probably die soon. After Warnie takes Douglas to tea, Lewis visits Joy himself. Joy wants to know the truth about her condition, which Lewis tell her only after being prodded. Lewis admits that he does not want to lose her. Joy tells him that she loves him, but he cannot say it back.

Lewis runs into his colleagues in a street. They are apologetic to the distressed man. He asks Harry Harrington, a chaplain, to marry them in a religious ceremony. Harrington declines because she is divorced. Returning to Joy's bedside, Lewis tells her that he wants to marry her in this way and that he is afraid of losing her. She agrees. They have the ceremony in her hospital bed, with Douglas and Warnie present. Some time passes. Joy's doctor and Lewis talk. The progress of Joy's disease has slowed. Lewis and Joy's visit shows how close they have grown.

Warnie, Lewis, and the Oxford colleagues talk. Lewis tells them that Joy is getting better. The scene returns to the hospital room. Joy can now manage a few steps, and the doctor expects her to live for some time. Lewis soon takes Joy (and Douglas) to his home. Joy and Lewis continue their intellectual banter before deciding to honeymoon in Greece. The action shifts to Greece, where Joy and Lewis are in a hotel. Lewis remains stiff, but Joy tries to loosen him up. They discuss their happiness.

About three years later, Lewis tells Douglas that his mother is going to die. At her bedside, Lewis and Joy talk about dying. Lewis promises to take care of Douglas, and tells her that he loves her. The scene moves forward in time to the high table at the dining hall. Harrington, Riley, and others talk about Joy's funeral. Lewis joins them, but soon leaves when they do not understand his pain. Lewis comforts Douglas, and both cry in each other's arms. *Shadowlands* ends with Lewis continuing his talk on human suffering. He realizes that pain is part of happiness.

CHARACTERS

Mrs. Joy Davidman Gresham

Joy Gresham is an American woman in her late thirties, the mother of one son, Douglas. Born Jewish, Joy later became a communist, then a Christian. She also was a poet who once won a national prize that she shared with Robert Frost. Gresham is having problems with her marriage to a fellow writer in the United States. By the beginning of the play, her correspondence with Lewis has become the most important thing in her life. On a trip to England with her son, she meets Lewis and finds that even in person they have an intellectual kinship that grows into a strong friendship. After meeting him in a hotel for tea, then accepting his invitation to come to tea at his house and staying there for Christmas as well, Gresham divorces her husband and moves to Oxford. Joy soon discovers that she has bone cancer and is dying. Her friendship deepens into love, a feeling the repressed Lewis comes to share. Though she gets a three-year reprise from her disease that allows her and Lewis to take a honeymoon to Greece and live in their love together for a while, Joy dies before the play's end.

Douglas Gresham

Douglas is the eight-year-old son of American writers Joy and Bill Gresham. Douglas is very close to his mother, and obeys her without question. Like his mother, Douglas is a fan of Lewis' books. For him, however, the *Narnia Chronicles* are favorites. When he first meets Lewis on a trip to England with his mother, Lewis disappoints Douglas. As Lewis and Joy grow closer, Douglas becomes somewhat close to Warnie, Lewis' brother, and Lewis as well. When Joy becomes ill, Douglas follows the course of action prescribed by the hero in Lewis' *The Magician's Nephew*. Unlike in the book, Douglas' mother dies. It is only when Lewis comforts him that Douglas can cry for his mother's death. After her death, he is to be raised by Lewis and Warnie.

Harry Harrington

Harrington is a chaplain at Oxford and a close friend of Lewis'. Like many of Lewis' colleagues, Harrington does not approve of his relationship with Joy. Not as overtly offensive as Riley, Harrington encourages others to express their negative feelings

MEDIA ADAPTATIONS

- *Shadowlands* was based on a television movie written by Nicholson and aired on the BBC in 1986. It later aired on PBS and A&E. It featured Claire Bloom as Joy Gresham and Joss Ackland as Lewis.

- A feature film version was produced in 1993 with a script by Nicholson. Directed by Sir Richard Attenborough, the film featured Debra Winger as Joy and Anthony Hopkins as Lewis.

on the subject. Though Joy is dying, Harrington will not perform a religious wedding ceremony for his friend. Harrington does perform her funeral, but admits he just said what he thought Lewis needed to hear.

Jack Lewis
See C. S. Lewis

C[live] S[taples] Lewis
Lewis is the central character in *Shadowlands*. He is an Oxford scholar and professor in his late fifties. An expert in English literature, Lewis is also the author of religious writing and famous children's books, including the *Narnia Chronicles*. A rather cold man at the beginning of the play, Lewis is also deeply religious and already pondering the meaning of life, death, pain, and suffering. He lives with his brother, Warnie, in a bachelor-type existence that is turned upside down when one of his pen pals physically comes into his life. American Joy Gresham is unlike any woman he has ever known. They first meet when she, while on a trip to England, visits him in Oxford. Then, he invites her to his home for tea and, later, Christmas. While there is an intellectual kinship, it develops into love after Joy returns to England permanently. Lewis realizes that he loves Joy, which changes his life. Their marriage ends with Joy's death from cancer. Through her suffering in the last years of her life, Lewis learns that with happiness comes pain.

Major Warner Lewis
Warnie is the elder brother of Jack Lewis. Like his brother, Warnie is a bachelor. They live together in Lewis' house, with Warnie talking care of his brother's domestic needs. Lewis also takes care of his brother as well. Throughout Act I, Warnie is suspicious of Joy and her motivations, but goes along with what his brother wants. As Lewis grows closer to Joy and becomes a different person, Warnie too begins to like and care about Joy and her son. He and Douglas seem to be particularly close. Warnie and Lewis depend greatly on each other, and their closeness helps Lewis deal with his pain and suffering.

Christopher Riley
Riley is one of Lewis' colleagues at Oxford, a fellow don. Riley is rather pushy and condescending, especially about women. When he says something implicitly offensive to Joy, she does not hesitate to put him in his place, much to Lewis' delight. Riley does not approve of Lewis' relationship to Joy, and tries to show it at every opportunity.

Warnie
See Major Warner Lewis

THEMES

Love and Passion/Change and Transformation
At the beginning of *Shadowlands,* both Joy and Lewis are rather unhappy in their own way. Joy is stuck in a bad marriage. Her husband, Bill, is an alcoholic and has had numerous liaisons during their marriage. She finds solace only in Lewis' letters to her and in his published books. When she comes to England on vacation with her son, Douglas, Joy finally meets the man behind the letters. They grow closer, though Lewis is much more stiff and formal than she is. But after Joy moves to England, and Lewis marries her "technically" so she can stay in the country, their relationship deepens. It blooms into love when Joy becomes ill with bone cancer, and Lewis and Joy realize that they will soon be losing each other. Joy says "I love you" first, much to Lewis' discomfort, but Lewis soon comes to share her feelings. It is he who insists on another wedding, a religious ceremony, between Joy and himself. Through their passionate feelings for each other, each grows as a person, though Lewis' transformation is more drastic and obvious. He loosens up and is not afraid to express how he feels for Joy to his disapproving colleagues at Oxford. Even after Joy dies, Lewis continues to undergo change. Previously unable to cry, Lewis lets loose while comforting Douglas, who also lets the tears flow. By the end of the play, Lewis has been profoundly changed. Joy also has found the kind of passionate, intellectual love she wanted.

Pain and Suffering
The other side of love and passion is pain and suffering. Lewis discovers that with love comes pain. It is only when Joy learns she is suffering from bone cancer, has a tumor in her breast, and breaks her hip that she and Lewis grow truly close and fall passionately in love. At first, Joy and Lewis believe she will die right away, but the disease's progres-

sion slows, giving them three years together. Hanging over this time is the inevitability of Joy's death. Both Joy and Lewis do not like the pain or the suffering. Joy, in particular, believes it is unfair that she becomes ill when she finds her soulmate. As religious people, it is hard for them to understand why God is making them suffer, especially considering all that Joy has already gone through. But by the end of *Shadowlands,* Lewis understands why and accepts that pain comes with happiness. Joy also comes to terms with this dichotomy before her death.

God and Religion

Both Lewis and Joy are practicing, faithful Christians. Lewis has written religious works and gives talks on the subject. Indeed, at the beginning of *Shadowlands* in Lewis' first monologue, he introduces the idea that with happiness and pleasure comes pain and suffering. He argues that it is God's way of loving his creations. In the actual action of the play, Lewis and Joy's relationship with God is addressed and analyzed. Lewis does not like that Joy has to suffer with her illness, that he has found love late in life but has to lose it. Yet he finds solace in prayer, he tells a colleague at one point, because it changes him. The experience teaches him about God. Lewis also has problems with the rules of religion. His friend Harry Harrington will not officiate at his wedding because Joy is divorced and it is against tenets of his religion. Lewis has rationalized the marriage and finds another minister to perform the ceremony. Joy also talks about her religious feelings and experiences. In the middle of Act I, she tells Lewis about a particularly dark moment in her marriage to Bill Gresham when she felt the presence of God coming to her in her hour of need. By Act II, her beliefs are tested by her illness, but she sees her temporary (three-year) recovery as a miracle and takes what she can get.

STYLE

Setting

Shadowlands is a drama set in the 1950s. Much of the action is confined to Oxford, England, except for a brief scene in Act II that takes place at a hotel in Greece. Most of the scenes in Oxford are set in Lewis' world: a lecture room, his home and study, the main dining hall at Oxford, and the surrounding streets. When Lewis and Joy first meet, they have

TOPICS FOR FURTHER STUDY

- Research grief management techniques for both children and adults. How could such techniques have helped both Douglas and Lewis deal with Joy's illness and death?

- Compare and contrast the character of Lewis with Hamlet in William Shakespeare's play *Hamlet*. Discuss how both men handle their tendency towards indecision.

- Watch the 1986 BBC version of *Shadowlands* that Nicholson wrote before the stage version. Compare the two versions, focusing on how the characters of Lewis and Joy evolved.

- Research the social and cultural history of the University of Oxford, especially the institution's dons. Did this insular society contribute to Lewis' problematic character at the beginning of the play?

tea at a hotel with Douglas and Warnie. After Joy moves to Oxford, she has her own home with Douglas, where Lewis visits. So that Joy can stay in England, she and Lewis marry in an uncomfortable scene in the local Registry Office. When Joy becomes sick, many of their most intimate scenes take place in her hospital room. *Shadowlands* only leaves Oxford for Joy and Lewis' honeymoon in Greece during a temporary reprise in her illness. These settings underscore what Lewis' life was like before Joy and after, and how events have profoundly changed him.

Staging/Transitions within Acts

Within each act in *Shadowlands,* Nicholson has numerous small scenes with clever staging that underline the play's themes and the characters. It is the staging that often defines the transitions between these scenes. The stage directions call for the stage to be divided in two by a translucent screen. The screen defines an inner area and an outer area. Only certain kinds of scenes take place in the inner area: the scenes in the Oxford dining hall; Lewis' study and home, except for one towards the end of Act I when Joy goes into another room during the Christmas party and reads a letter from her husband who wants a divorce; Joy's home in Oxford; the Registry office; and Joy's hospital room. Others take place in the outer area in front of the screen: Lewis' monologues; scenes on the street where characters are walking; the hotel tea room; certain scenes in Lewis' house, especially those in which the outside world is intruding on Lewis; the corridor outside of Joy's hospital room; the scene in Greece. The scenes in front of the screen generally signify the outside world, while those inside are more personal and deep. Changes in lighting also define the passage of time and the change of scene.

Another staging device is a large wardrobe at the back of the stage, looming over the proceedings primarily in the stage's inner area. The wardrobe itself refers to a series of children's books written by Lewis, the Narnia books, including *The Lion, the Witch and the Wardrobe*. Douglas is already a fan of Lewis' books and carries around *The Magician's Nephew* with him. After his mother has tea at the hotel with Lewis and Warnie in the middle of Act I, Douglas effects a transition in the scene by ringing the bell on the table, as a character in the book does. This makes the screen rise and Douglas walks into the world of Narnia inside the wardrobe. He returns to the other world in the wardrobe in Act II during the religious ceremony that marries his mother and Lewis. Douglas is reenacting the story line from *The Magician's Nephew,* though this time the magic apple does not cure the mother permanently.

Monologue

At the beginning of each act in *Shadowlands* as well at the end of the play, Lewis delivers a monologue to the audience. It is done in the form of a talk or lecture, as Lewis gave these often in his lifetime. These monologues reveal much about Lewis' character, motivations, and how he changes over the course of the play. The topic of his talk does not change. It is about human "love, pain and suffering," and the role God plays (or does not play) in it. During the first monologue at the beginning of Act I, Lewis believes that suffering is God's "love in action." He seems to talk of such pain in a detached tone. At the beginning of Act II, Lewis continues the same train of thought in his lecture, but questions suffering from a more personal place. At the end of the play, Lewis has been completely transformed by suffering and his monologue is barely a talk, but more of a conversation with himself. He is quieter and more reflective about his relationship with Joy. God is not directly mentioned.

HISTORICAL CONTEXT

Philosophy of Political Leadership

The decade of the 1950s had much in common with the late 1980s in British history. For much of the 1950s and into the early 1960s, Great Britain was ruled by a Conservative government. Winston Churchill was prime minister from 1951 to 1955, Anthony Eden from 1955 to 1957, and Harold Macmillan from 1957 to 1963. The country was still recovering from the effects of World War II, and while there were some prosperity and expansion, much of it was illusionary until the end of decade. Still, high interest rates limited growth. Also, in 1957, Great Britain declined to join the European Economic Community (EEC), a burgeoning organization designed to regionalize trade and other economic concerns.

By 1989, the Conservatives were again entrenched in power, as they had been since 1979. They only had one prime minister in that time period: Margaret Thatcher. In 1988, after winning her third general election, she had become the longest continually serving prime minister. Under her leadership in the 1980s, Great Britain had eradicated the social welfare state that had been built up after World War II. Most major industries (such as coal mining) were denationalized and much of the power of trade unions was taken away. Like her Conservative predecessors, Thatcher opposed Great Britain becoming part of the European-wide currency.

Despite her best efforts, Thatcher did not totally dismantle the welfare state. Pensions and the National Health Service (NHS) remained, though they were reorganized in 1982 and 1988 to increase efficiency and accountability. Because of a sluggish economy, many were dependent on welfare at this time. Thatcher was forced out of power in late 1990 when she tried to put a uniform poll tax on British citizens in place of local property taxes. This proposal led to riots in London and other parts of the country, and Thatcher lost the support of her own Conservative party. She was replaced by a fellow Conservative, John Major.

Education

Only about four percent of all British, and less than three percent of British working class adoles-

COMPARE & CONTRAST

- **1950s:** The Labour Party is in power throughout 1951, though the Conservative Party rules Great Britain for the rest of the decade.

  Today: The Conservative Party is in power through much of the 1990s, until the Labour Party returns in the late 1990s.

- **1950s:** At Oxford, women and men have separate colleges. There is not talk of allowing women and men into some of the same colleges until the mid-1960s.

  Today: Since the mid-1970s, at least some of the previously all-male colleges admit women, though the women's colleges fear they might return to secondary status again.

- **1950s:** Great Britain is still recovering from the devastating effects of World War II on its economy, infrastructure, and people. Food is rationed until 1954, while coal is rationed until 1958.

  Today: Fully recovered from World War II with no rationing, Great Britain still has economic problems but looks to the future in Europe with a common currency.

- **1950s:** At the beginning of the decade, less than a third of those who reside in Great Britain own their home. Few homes contain featured televisions, washing machines, and refrigerators.

  Today: Nearly 70 percent of those residing in Great Britain own their home. Since the consumer boom of the 1960s and 1970s, most homes contain "luxury" items such as televisions, washing machines, and refrigerators.

---

cents, went to university by the late 1950s, a percentage that was much less than the United States and other countries in Europe. By the late 1980s, more British students went to university, but the proportion relative to the population did not change much. Education was a way to become socially mobile, but few were in the position to take advantage of it.

While in office, the Thatcher-led government worked to reform the government-sponsored educational system. Before these changes, a test given at the age of eleven determined what kind of comprehensive school they would attend. About 88 percent of British children attended these schools. Kenneth Backer created a national curriculum for schools with the Education Act of 1988. More vocational programs and technical colleges were also created in the late 1980s and 1990s to give young people more educational options. By the end of the decade, many more mature students went to university, about 237,000 towards the end of the decade.

To become truly part of Great Britain's elite (leaders in government, industry, and banking), however, it seemed that one had to attend public schools (comparable to U.S. private schools) such as Eton. By 1988, 119,002 were in such public schools, where just over 95,000 were in such schools at the end of the 1950s. Fees over that period had greatly increased, limiting their access even further. Since many products of public schools went on to Oxford, Cambridge, and other select universities, educational opportunity greatly determined who would be in power and determine policy in Great Britain.

CRITICAL OVERVIEW

Since its earliest productions, *Shadowlands* has split critics. While many believe the play is a powerful study of the human condition that left audiences openly weeping, some have questioned the authenticity of this portrayal of C. S. Lewis and Joy Gresham. Several critics highlighted inaccuracies, such as the fact that Joy really had two sons, not one, and that both Lewis and Joy were much more difficult people than Nicholson's portrayal suggests. Many compared the stage play to the original BBC television movie, somewhat unfavorably.

Of an initial British production in the Queen's Theatre on London's West End, John James of the *Times Educational Supplement* wrote, "William Nicholson's witty, humane script brings them both to theatrical life so truthfully that we are caught up in their autumnal romance." The unnamed critic of *Financial Times* argued, "The play describes but does not illustrate. We never know why this bumbling bachelor falls in love, if not through pity." Still, this critic concluded, "For all its ultimate evasiveness, it deserves to flourish." Claire Armistead of *New Statesman and Society* believed Nicholson skimmed on the truth for dramatic purposes. She wrote, "in the interests of portraying their romance on stage William Nicholson's four-tissue weepie makes only cursory mention of his arrogance and her waspishness."

Some of these same issues came to the fore when *Shadowlands* made its New York debut in late 1990. Frank Rich of the *New York Times* believed, "How you feel about *Shadowlands* depends a great deal on your degree of Anglophilia. The play . . . has little more intellectual or emotional depth than a tear-jerker set in a two-car-garage suburbia, but it does boast a certain rarefied British atmosphere." Rich's colleague at the *New York Times* David Richards saw the play as part of a trend towards tear-jerkers. He wrote that *Shadowlands* "represents the tear-jerker in full glory, and I say that admiringly. Oh, you can look down your nose at it and accuse it of middlebrow pretensions, if you wish. You can fault it for not always sidestepping the clichés of love and regret, for saying nothing that hasn't been said before. But in the end, you'll probably conclude that your reservations count for precious little."

Many New York critics still expressed reservations. Howard Kissel of the *Daily News* wrote "You sense that Nicholson has been extremely careful about the words he puts in Lewis' mouth, and that much has been culled from Lewis' own writing. Such genial wit is the chief virtue of this rather plodding account of their lives together, which tells us very little about either of them." Mimi Kramer of the *New Yorker* also had problems with the way the characters were drawn, as did other critics. Comparing it to the previously aired television movie, she wrote "What's missing from this stage version is any sense that Joy had a life apart from Lewis—she seems to be merely a woman obsessed with C. S. Lewis, a celebrity seeker—and any sense of the world she was invading." Further, Kramer argued, "*Shadowlands* seems to suggest that what makes the events it recounts tragic is the fact that it happened to C. S. Lewis."

Kramer's sentiments were echoed by other critics. Jan Stuart of *New York Newsday* argued that "*Shadowlands* is a sterling example of that uniquely British hybrid, the polemical soap opera. It is so artfully constructed that you may not be able to tell whether you are being lured into its fundamentalist ideology with prime-time melodrama or vice versa. And it is so skillfully acted that you probably won't care." Some critics had similar problems with how themes and settings were handled. Gerald Weales of *Commonweal* wrote, "A rather unusual love story, then, the play . . . is really about grief, pain and Christian faith. At least, it toys with those ideas." Though Clive Barnes of the *New York Post* found much to praise about the play, he writes "The play is full of bright speeches—some more convincing than others—and offers a quaint and cozy view of Oxford Academic life that admittedly has more the tone of friendly caricature than reality."

Though many critics were critical of aspects of *Shadowlands,* there were a few who unabashedly praised it. John Beaufort of *Christian Science Monitor* believed that "because of the depth of love that has been expressed and shared, it is not a depressing play. Much of this is due to Nicholson's wit and style as a dramatist." Edwin Wilson of *Wall Street Journal* wrote that the play "is a rarity on Broadway: a well-crafted drama with a strong emotional appeal. Based on the life of writer C. S. Lewis, William Nicholson's play is a most unusual love story, but all the more affecting for that."

CRITICISM

Annette Petrusso

In this essay, Petrusso compares and contrasts the stage version of Shadowlands *with its feature film counterpart.*

While both the stage play and film versions of *Shadowlands* were written by the same author, William Nicholson, they each present the story differently. This is due in part to the nature of each genre. Dramatic stage plays only have limited set-

Nigel Hawthorne as C. S. Lewis in a 1989 production of Shadowlands, *performed at London's Queens Theatre.*

ting possibilities and are focused primarily on dialogue. Movies are generally more visual than stage plays because they are not constrained by the demands of the theater. Film scripts also can be constructed differently than stage plays, which affects the flow of action, dialogue, and character development. Some of these differences are apparent when comparing the stage play to the movie version of *Shadowlands*.

In the play version of *Shadowlands,* Nicholson calls for a symbolic staging. The stage is to be divided into two areas (inner and outer) by a translucent screen. Some action takes place in front of it. Other times, the screen rises, revealing Lewis' study, Joy's hospital room, the main dining hall at Oxford, and other places. These places are Lewis' intimate surroundings, where most of his personal transformation take place.

Also dominating the stage, in the scenes that take place inside Lewis' study, is a giant wardrobe. This wardrobe refers to the famous wardrobe in Lewis' *Narnia Chronicles,* a series of children's books. The wardrobe is the portal to a parallel world. It symbolizes a number of things to Lewis, and to Joy Gresham's son Douglas, including Lewis' books and their themes and, for both, the loss of their mother. In a highly symbolic moment in Act I, Douglas actually goes into the wardrobe and disappears. In Act II, during the religious ceremony, which unites his bed-ridden mother and Lewis in marriage, Douglas again goes through the wardrobe to the Other World. He retrieves the magic apple, as described in Lewis' *The Magician's Nephew,* in hopes it will cure his sick mother just as it does in the book. Joy's bone cancer does go into remission, but she still dies at the end of the play.

The movie has a much richer visual text, though this *Shadowlands* has much in common with the stage play. Because there is no stage, the screen and its symbolism has been eliminated. The film takes viewers to Oxford and its hallowed halls, to train stations full of smoke and steam, to all corners of Lewis' home, to Joy's small place in England, and to the hospital during Joy's illness and treatment. By actually seeing the period settings, the world in which Lewis and Joy lived becomes clearer. The audience sees how they interact with their environment as well as many other people. It also gives the filmmakers the opportunity to make visual symbols stronger and deeper.

One aspect does not change: the wardrobe continues to play an important role in the movie, but

WHAT DO I READ NEXT?

- *Grief Observed*, a nonfiction book written by C. S. Lewis in 1961 (originally published under the pen name N. W. Clerk), is about how Joy Gresham's death affected him.

- *The Magician's Nephew* (1955), book six in C. S. Lewis' *Narnia Chronicles*, is the book that Douglas Gresham reads in *Shadowlands* and which underscores its themes.

- *The Wind Singer* is a children's book written by Nicholson in 2000 about a parallel world not unlike Narnia.

- *The Lion, the Witch and the Wardrobe* (1950), book one in C. S. Lewis' *Narnia Chronicles*, also prominently features a wardrobe and is mentioned in *Shadowlands*.

- *84 Charing Cross Road*, based on material by Helene Hanff and published in 1983, is a play that was adapted for the stage by James Roose-Evans. At its center is an unusual romance between an unlikely man and woman.

---

more for Douglas than Lewis. In the movie, the wardrobe—the actual one from Lewis' childhood nursery—sits in his attic. When Douglas first comes to visit Lewis' home, Warnie, Lewis' brother and housemate, shows it to him on a tour of the attic. Douglas and Joy later return to stay for Christmas. At this time, Douglas sneaks up there and opens the wardrobe, hoping to find the portal to the parallel world, as Lewis wrote in his Narnia books. Douglas is rather disappointed that this wardrobe has a solid back instead of an open gateway. Lewis discovers him there, which leads to a conversation about Douglas's alcoholic father. At the end of the movie, after Joy has died, Lewis finds Douglas in the attic, staring at the wardrobe. Though Lewis tells him of his mother's death, Douglas is more upset that the wardrobe does not ''work,'' that there is no portal. It leads to both of them crying in each other's arms over their loss of Joy. Lewis also cries for the death of his own mother when he was a boy, a feeling he has apparently kept inside since the age of eight.

Another contrasting aspect of the play versus the movie is how characters are portrayed and developed. One criticism of the play that seems corrected in the movie is the development of secondary characters such as Warnie and Douglas. In reviewing the original Broadway production of *Shadowlands,* Frank Rich of the *New York Times* wrote, ''the Lewises' fraternal bond, like the plays' other important secondary relationship, between Joy's son and Lewis, is so sketchily drawn that it cannot carry the dramatic weight it must in the evening's waning scenes.'' In the play, Douglas and Warnie are only in a handful of scenes and are barely developed as individuals. Warnie is merely a directionless man with a small alcohol problem who takes care of his brother's every need. Douglas comes off as a young boy who lives in a fantasy world and obeys his mother without question. He is upset at her death, but their closeness does not seem obvious.

In the movie, both Warnie and Douglas are still secondary to Lewis and Joy, but Warnie seems more like Lewis' equal. They have a housekeeper who takes care of them, and Warnie has his own desk in the study. While Lewis still looks to Warnie for opinions and approval as he does extensively in the play, Warnie's support seems more respected and real. Douglas's character is even better developed than Warnie's in the film version. Douglas is not merely an obedient boy-machine who only breaks down in the end as in the play. While he is still very affectionate, he shows more anger about being in England away from his home and father, and his mother's illness and death. He is scared when his mother comes home to die. In addition to the wardrobe scenes described above, the very end of the movie shows Lewis and Douglas together walking through the nearby countryside with a dog in tow. This gives some closure to about the issue of what happens to Douglas after his mother dies. The play does not say that Douglas lived with his stepfather until Lewis himself died a few years later.

Both Joy and Lewis are also better and more completely developed in the movie than in the play version of *Shadowlands*. Mimi Kramer of the *New Yorker* argued that in the play version, Joy only existed in terms of Lewis. She was an obsessed fan who met him and invaded his world. The play does include facts about Joy—she has a husband in New York who asks for a divorce in Act I, she used to be a poet who once won a national poetry award, and she moved to Oxford because it would a cheaper place to live far from her now ex-husband. Yet every scathing remark Joy makes, whether it be to one of Lewis' boorish colleagues or Lewis himself, is ultimately for Lewis' benefit and entertainment. Nothing pithy comes from Joy outside of that relationship.

While the majority of the film, and even more of the play, is interaction between Joy and Lewis, in the movie, Joy does have a more separate and individual character. In the movie, she does not move to Oxford, but to London. Lewis is forced to take a train to see her. When she enters a hospital, it is in London as well, so Lewis must journey to her. Only when Joy leaves the hospital after her cancer is in remission does she move to Oxford to live with Lewis. (Douglas apparently starts staying with them as soon as his mother becomes ill.) One critic of the play wrote that Joy seemed like the cat and Lewis the mouse she was hunting. In the play, Joy blurts out her feelings and Lewis holds back, keeping his rein on their relationship. In the movie, they are more balanced. Though Joy still does not have much of a life outside of Lewis in the movie, she seems more fleshed out, affectionate, and independent. More importantly, Lewis is portrayed much differently in the movie, which in turn changes how Joy's character is defined.

At the center of both the play and the movie is the enigmatic character of Lewis, the writer many people are familiar with because of his Narnia books, religious writing, and works on English literature. In the play, Lewis is depicted as an indecisive man who cannot admit his affection for Joy in any capacity until she becomes very ill with cancer and death seems imminent. He is rather cold, and his life seems to consist only of his relationship

> "THE FILM TAKES VIEWERS TO OXFORD AND ITS HALLOWED HALLS, TO TRAIN STATIONS FULL OF SMOKE AND STEAM, TO ALL CORNERS OF LEWIS' HOME, TO JOY'S SMALL PLACE IN ENGLAND, AND TO THE HOSPITAL DURING JOY'S ILLNESS AND TREATMENT."

with his Oxford colleagues and with Warnie. At the beginning of the play, Joy is merely an interesting pen pal. The situation changes as he and Joy meet in a hotel tea room, at her request. Though Lewis invites her and her son to come to his house for tea, and then to stay for Christmas, Lewis seems very out of touch with his feelings. He does not cry until the end when Warnie essentially forces him to comfort the distraught Douglas.

The *Shadowlands* movie makes Lewis much more human from the start and gives him different forums in which to express his humanity. The play limits Lewis' interactions to Warnie, his colleagues, Joy (and illness-related people like doctors), and Douglas. In addition to those people, the movie also shows Lewis with students he teaches at Oxford. There is a very minor, but very important, subplot involving one of his students, named Whistler. The subplot shows what effect Joy has had on Lewis' life.

At the beginning of the movie, Whistler does not get along with Lewis when he tries to start an intellectual fight at a tutorial. The student later sleeps during another tutorial led by Lewis. Lewis catches Whistler stealing books, and offers him a loan, which the student turns down. By this point, Lewis has spent Christmas with Joy before she returns to the States. After Joy has moved back to England and the couple has married "technically" so that she can stay in the country, she attends a graduation ceremony with him. Afterwards they fight. Joy criticizes him for dealing only with those weaker than him or those who indulge certain parts of him, and she storms off. Lewis is befuddled by her claim. Then Lewis learns that Whistler is dropping out of school, which makes him wonder what it is everyone wants from him. Joy discovers she has cancer, and Lewis learns to love. After the religious wedding ceremony, Lewis runs into Whistler on the train. Lewis has mellowed and asks probing questions about Whistler's father, about whom the pair have already conversed. Whistler is working as a teacher, which makes Lewis proud. By the end of the movie, Lewis has a new student to teach. This time he does not verbally or intellectually intimidate, but listens to and interacts with the student.

There are many other differences between the stage and film versions of *Shadowlands,* including the key components of the core story as described here. Neither version is superior to the other, but the film gives Lewis and Joy's unusual love story a firmer visual foundation and deepens many of the characters. Both versions capture a wealth of emotions and show how hard it can be to suffer through love and loss.

Source: Annette Petrusso, in an essay for *Drama for Students,* Gale Group, 2001.

Richard Alleva

A comparison between the play an the movie is given in this review by Richard Alleva.

I reviewed the stage play, *Shadowlands,* three years ago (*Crisis* February 1991), praised it, but issued a warning that I now repeat re Richard Attenborough's film adaptation. "Let devotees of the life and works of Clive Staples 'Jack' Lewis go to . . . *Shadowlands* . . . forewarned though not necessarily forearmed. If they go to sniff out omissions and distortions of facts, they will have a field day. But they won't have as good a time as those who attend the play to discover what idea, what compelling image the playwright William Nicholson perceived in . . . Lewis's marriage to Joy Davidman, and how close Nicholson comes to realizing that image theatrically."

The stage version is made of sterner stuff than the new film. In the play's first scene, Jack Lewis, delivering a lecture, addresses the question of why God makes or lets us suffer. His answer, "the blows of God's chisel, which hurt us so much, are what make us perfect," is something that Lewis believes intellectually but doesn't feel with his entire being. By the final curtain, because of the suffering he has undergone, Lewis faces the audience as a transfigured man, prepared, even longing to undergo his own death because only death can release him from the "shadowlands" of earthly life into the higher reality of heaven where he will be reunited with Joy. Head knowledge has become heart knowledge. The stage play, when well performed (as it certainly was on Broadway with Jane Alexander and Nigel Hawthorne), provides a deeply spiritual experience.

Not so the movie. Artfully directed, photographed, and played, it is a poignant, funny-sad movie that can provoke an instant nostalgia for the dreaming spires of Oxford even in the breasts of those who have never been anywhere near Oxford. But it is also about as untranscendent as any film about C. S. Lewis could possibly be. Quite a feat, that. How did Attenborough and Nicholson bring it off?

The lineaments of the plot are the same. Jack, self-trapped in the forlorn bachelorhood he shares with his brother, Warnie, and in the academic routine he shares with a bunch of academic stiffs (no Tolkein, no Owen Barfield, no Hugo Dyson on view in this movie, since any suggestion of bracing intellectual companionship would queer Nicholson's dramaturgical pitch), encounters an American, Jewish, ex-Communist, soon-to-be-divorcee Joy Davidman Gresham, marries her to give her British citizenship, then marries her before God when her first bout with cancer makes him realize how much he loves her. Joy has a seemingly miraculous remission, then succumbs. Lewis is left to spend the rest of his life. . .how?

The answer given by this movie indicates how a spiritual experience has been yanked sharply down to earth. In the early scenes, Lewis is still seen delivering his lectures about pain being the chisel-blows of God, and this statement is still perceived as an untested, purely cerebral concept. But, at the conclusion, Lewis does not affirm his belief as now verified by his experience. Instead, he quotes a remark of Joy's, "the pain now is part of the happiness then." This Lewis isn't braced for the afterlife by the heartbreak of Joy's death. Rather, he has accepted suffering (as J. W. N. Sullivan said Beethoven did) "as one of the great structural lines of human life." Earthly happiness is worth the suffering we undergo when we lose the bringer of happiness. I found this conclusion quite as poignant as that of the play's but not quite so grand. Oddly enough, it makes Lewis's fiercely held Christian beliefs quite inessential to the main dramatic action. After all, an atheist or agnostic can learn to accept earthly suffering in the same way that this movie's

Anthony Hopkins (as C. S. Lewis) and Debra Winger (as Joy Gresham) in a scene from the 1993 film adaptation of Shadowlands.

version of Lewis does. There is no wholehearted acceptance of the strokes of God's chisel at this movie's fade-out, no more talk of Shadowlands.

Another way Nicholson diminishes the spiritual aspect of his story is by deleting the scene in which Joy tells Jack Lewis of her first apprehension of God's existence. Though many of Joy's qualities attracted Lewis, he would obviously be especially drawn by her personal experience of the holy. And since Joy came to her conversion after a long period of Communist commitment, we may well wonder how this transformation came about. But the script never answers this question and Lewis never even raises it. A breathtaking omission in light of who Lewis and Davidman were in real life, yet a logical omission considering the kind of movie Attenborough and Nicholson want to make. For *Shadowlands* is no longer the story of the romantic union of two equally life-perplexed, God-seeking individuals, perfectly matched in intellect and mettlesome high spirits. It is now the story of an overgrown teddy bear, lovably bookish and unworldly, who is rescued from emotional suffocation and his own virginity by a warmhearted, tough-tender earth mother who shatters his routine, skewers his narrow-minded colleagues, and takes him on a motor tour of the English countryside. Let's face it: this *Shadowlands* is really the latest rendition of *Goodbye, Mr. Chips.*

And a nice rendition it is. Richard Attenborough's direction is the best work of his career. It's as if the intimacy of the story had reined in Attenborough's penchant for visual fustian and incoherent storytelling. Each directorial stroke makes its point succinctly.

Following his triumph in *The Remains of the Day,* Anthony Hopkins's Jack Lewis comes across as The Butler Escapes. For, like Stevens in *The Remains of the Day,* Nicholson's version of Lewis is a man who has fashioned his own leash and wears it with conviction. In researching this role, Hopkins must have read Lewis's confession that emotional safe-playing was his greatest temptation. Hopkins has zeroed in on that trait and amplified it. This Jack Lewis is an overgrown boy who keeps his eyes on the carpet in the presence of an attractive female. This virginal, flustered quality is the keynote of the first three quarters of the performance. Later, when Lewis is moved to passion, first by the love of Joy, then by anger at her death, Hopkins's specialty—staccato bursts of emotion issuing out of a seemingly passive exterior—comes into play and makes viewers sit up wide-awake in the knowledge that

> "THE STAGE PLAY, WHEN WELL PERFORMED (AS IT CERTAINLY WAS ON BROADWAY WITH JANE ALEXANDER AND NIGEL HAWTHORNE), PROVIDES A DEEPLY SPIRITUAL EXPERIENCE."

there is more to this man's character than they had suspected. And so another triumph is added to Hopkins's seemingly unbreakable chain of triumphs.

But Debra Winger's triumph is bigger. While Hopkins tailors Lewis to match his peculiar strengths as an actor, Winger extends the boundaries of her talent to encompass Joy. Though too pretty and still too young for the role, she bestows the best sort of amnesia on the viewer. She wipes out her own backlog of characterizations and makes you accept this woman as the only Debra Winger you have ever seen. Nicholson has given Joy a few too many wisecracks, but Winger never lets us forget the emotional neediness that deploys those wisecracks like SOS signals. When Jack casually asks his Yuletide guest if her husband is looking after himself for Christmas, Winger raps out "Yes!" with a speed and fierceness that bespeak a world of marital woe.

So, by all means, go see *Shadowlands* but be prepared to take it on its own terms. This is a C. S. Lewis biopic for secular humanists in search of a good cry. I believe they constitute a sizable audience.

Source: Richard Alleva, "Shadowlands," in *Commonweal*, Vol. 121, No. 2, January 28, 1994, pp. 22–23.

Time

In the following, an overview explaining the main points of the film are given.

When we meet him, C. S. Lewis (Anthony Hopkins) is giving rather smug lectures about the blessed necessity for suffering in our life: "Pain is God's megaphone to rouse a deaf world," he happily informs his listeners.

But what does Lewis—Oxford don, literary critic, fairy-tale writer, Christian apologist—actually know about the ordinary hurts of ordinary life? Or, for that matter, about life as most people know it? His beloved mother died when he was a child, and for decades he has lived in withdrawn bachelorhood. Snuggled up in a charming book-lined cottage with his brother Warnie (the excellent Edward Hardwicke), he is sage but distant with his students, witty but somewhat abstract with his colleagues at the high table.

The man needs shaking up. And Joy Gresham (Debra Winger) is just the woman to do it. She's an American, something of a poet, something of an imposition. But she's also someone any writer is bound to cherish, a knowledgeable fan. They meet for tea; she and her eight-year-old son (she's in the midst of a messy divorce) return for Christmas; and eventually they settle in London. Bemusement soon gives way to concern. Lewis marries her so she can stay in England, but true love does not happen until she falls ill with cancer. A period of remission offers them the opportunity for an idyll. That brief happiness, followed by the pain of her death, does indeed "rouse" Lewis. But in ways deeper and more mysterious than he formerly gabbled about.

Shadowlands is, in essence, a true story, though screenwriter William Nicholson, adapting his own play, admits that given Lewis' reticence, he has had to imagine much of what went on in the relationship with Gresham. And reticent is the word for Richard Attenborough's film version. But that's a virtue, not a defect, when your setting is English academia (no one has more persuasively captured its manners) and your subject is mortality. There is something very moving in the understated way that these people confront it, something very sweetly believable in their courtship and in the brief bliss they shared. Hopkins gets to do what he could not in *The Remains of the Day,* shake off repression, and Winger is awfully good too; there is a steady pressure in her forcefulness that is never flashy or abrasive. They—the entire movie—are strong, unsentimental, exemplary.

Source: "Shadowlands," in *Time,* Vol. 142, No. 27, December 27, 1993, p. 72.

Mimi Kramer

Kramer points out the flaws in Shadowlands *and explores the personalities of the different characters.*

Shadowlands, the William Nicholson play about C. S. Lewis, which ran for a year in London in a production directed by Elijah Moshinsky and starring Nigel Hawthorne and Jane Lapotaire, has just opened at the Brooks Atkinson Theatre. It turns out to be a major disappointment. Like the television film of the same name, which Mr. Nicholson wrote for the BBC, the play tells the story of Lewis's strange, doomed love affair with the minor American poet Joy Davidman Gresham. Anyone who has seen the movie version of *Shadowlands* (it has been broadcast on PBS and on the Arts and Entertainment cable network) knows how poignantly and affectingly this story can be told. She was a married woman with two children (boys), a Jewish convert to Christianity, and a former Communist, who, having initiated a correspondence with Lewis, sought an introduction to him on a visit to England, which she undertook when her marriage appeared to be failing. Eventually, she was divorced (her husband had left her for another woman), and she moved lock, stock, and barrel to Oxford (with the two boys), whereupon Lewis agreed to marry her for immigration purposes. She became the love of his life, and soon afterward died of bone cancer.

I have no idea what Joy was really like, or how Jane Lapotaire portrayed her in the West End production. But Claire Bloom, who played the role, opposite Joss Ackland, in the television movie, was beautiful, charming, and graceful, with a kind of lively-mindedness that made it perfectly clear why a celebrated author and academic might have turned, for love and friendship, to a Jewish American intellectual divorcée. Jane Alexander, who plays Joy, opposite Mr. Hawthorne, in the current production, brings to the role a combination of toughness and tartness that has served her well in other roles, but for lively-mindedness she substitutes belligerence, which reduces the relationship to a hackneyed conflict between American brashness and Oxford inhibition. Moreover, where Bloom was gawky only in approaching passion, Alexander is gawky in everything. (She seems to come onstage limping.) This, along with a certain freeness of the hands and upper torso, seems to be her way of getting the idea of Jewishness across. Owing partly to a quality of abrasiveness that Alexander brings to the role (something that A. N. Wilson, in fact, attributes to Joy in his new biography of Lewis, which is discussed elsewhere in this issue), and owing partly to Nicholson's script, which doesn't give the relationship between the two people much time to develop, Joy appears to be plotting: she seems to have designs on Lewis.

> "BUT WHAT DOES LEWIS—OXFORD DON, LITERARY CRITIC, FAIRY-TALE WRITER, CHRISTIAN APOLOGIST—ACTUALLY KNOW ABOUT THE ORDINARY HURTS OF ORDINARY LIFE? OR, FOR THAT MATTER, ABOUT LIFE AS MOST PEOPLE KNOW IT?"

What's missing from this stage version is any sense that Joy had a life apart from Lewis—she seems to be merely a woman obsessed with C. S. Lewis, a celebrity-seeker—and any sense of the world she was invading. The film used pictures and tiny gestures to establish a moral context and ambience: a world of middle-aged men who talk to each other without looking up from their books. It juxtaposed scenes of Lewis reading, lecturing to students, and strolling through Magdalen deer park with references to and images from the sacred and secular medieval literature Lewis taught and studied. Nicholson's script for the stage version substitutes Robert Louis Stevenson for Guillaume de Lorris and Chrétien de Troyes; it has Paul Sparer, Robin Chadwick, Hugh A. Rose, and Edmund C. Davys (playing a collection of stereotypical dons and vicars) spouting some sort of ghastly parody of high-table conversation; and it vulgarizes everything that in the film was subtle. As for Mark Thompson's set, its only nod to the idea of Oxford is a vaguely Gothic front panel that moves endlessly up and down, up and down, allowing stagehands to get ready for the next scene.

Joy's younger son, Douglas, was in his teens when his mother died. The movie fudges this a bit, making him a child of eight or nine, and fair enough: the movie wants to offer a parallel between Joy's children and Lewis and his older brother, who lost their mother when Lewis was nine. It suggests visually that those two little boys might very easily become those two middle-aged men. In the movie, though, Lewis's brother, Warnie, was played by an actor whose puffy, feline face—he was like a maiden aunt—presented an image of passionlessness and sterility. Michael Allinson, who plays Warnie in the

> JANE ALEXANDER, WHO PLAYS JOY, OPPOSITE MR. HAWTHORNE, IN THE CURRENT PRODUCTION, BRINGS TO THE ROLE A COMBINATION OF TOUGHNESS AND TARTNESS THAT HAS SERVED HER WELL IN OTHER ROLES, BUT FOR LIVELY-MINDEDNESS SHE SUBSTITUTES BELLIGERENCE, WHICH REDUCES THE RELATIONSHIP TO A HACKNEYED CONFLICT BETWEEN AMERICAN BRASHNESS AND OXFORD INHIBITION."

current production, cuts a rather dapper figure. He's tall and distinguished—like an American's dream of the romantic English gentleman. Moreover, since the play reduces the number of Joy's children to one, the trumped-up parallel between Douglas and Lewis has to be pounded home verbally.

Douglas Gresham, who seems to have been involved with *Shadowlands* at every phase of its development, from screen to stage, has provided a program note for the current production in which he says that the play "comes closer to the truth" than anything else he has read "about the nature of my stepfather's relationship with my mother." The film version made some sort of spiritual sense out of the dilemma that Lewis's Neo-platonic relationship with Joy posed to his Neo-platonic Christianity. But the play, which purports to answer the question "If God loves us, why does he allow us to suffer so much?," succeeds only in Broadwayizing everything. "Her death," Douglas Gresham writes of his mother, "taught him . . . that in the very deepest despair there is hope and when by grief the entire universe is suddenly emptied, there is God."

The movie script gave bigger play to what may have been Lewis's true final comment on life as symbolized by Joy's bone cancer: "This is a mess, and that is all there is to it." Cancer *is* a mess, and the stories of people who die from it don't usually get made into a play. *Shadowlands* seems to suggest that what makes the events it recounts tragic is the fact that they happened to C. S. Lewis. Given that Mr. Hawthorne, who hasn't the authority or the presence to play Lewis with any depth or complexity, is a television star before anything else (he plays the shady secretary in the popular series "Yes, Minister" and "Yes, Prime Minister"), the whole thing has the feel of a tourist trap—the sort of play that gets mounted in London with the idea of capitalizing on America's love for anything having to do with Oxford or England.

Source: Mimi Kramer, "Shady Doings," in *New Yorker*, November 26, 1990, p. 124–125.

William A. Henry, III

The tragedy portrayed in this play is described by Henry as a "metaphysical dilemma."

For almost every person of religious conviction, the most harrowing test of faith comes with the suffering and death of a loved one. It is hard to believe in a just and kind God who allows innocent people to suffer the physical agonies of dying or the mental agonies of being parted. Yet it is precisely at these moments that religious belief can be most comforting. Being sure that apparently pointless grief does serve some higher purpose, even if one cannot yet divine what it is, may enable a depressed mourner to get himself through the despondency of the day.

That metaphysical dilemma lies at the heart of *Shadowlands,* a new Broadway play that personalizes the issue in the life of Clive Staples Lewis, a distinguished literary scholar and one of the 20th century's foremost popular writers on Christian theology. When Lewis was nine, his mother died of cancer. When he was 61, his wife Joy died of the same disease. Both were racked with pain; both endured the false hope of brief remission; both left behind baffled, brittle sons. Part of Lewis plainly believed these horrors somehow reflected the Almighty's benevolent hand. Another part of him, the play argues, never could. That led him to escape into writing another kind of literature for which he is remembered: children's fables such as *The Lion, the Witch and the Wardrobe.* He yearned, it is suggested, for a healing magic he could not find in the everyday world.

Writers' lives rarely yield good drama. Their work is mostly done silently and alone. They live out their fantasies more openly on the page than in company. They often thwart relationships with others because they view everyone as "material." *Shadowlands* might seem doubly doomed because it also embraces disease-of-the-week pathos of a kind that TV generally does better. The plot focuses almost entirely on Lewis' relationship with Joy, whom he met and married—less to live as man and wife than to enable her and her offspring by a prior marriage to stay in Britain—after a half-century of hearty bachelorhood. The script is far more graphic about her symptoms (her hip "snapped like a frozen twig") than about whether this marriage of convenience ripened into sexual love, and its overall view of Lewis as a near monk clashes with a recent biography. Moreover, the play is lumbered with Lewis' fellow Oxford dons, middle-aged men joking about women in an awed, distant, prepubescent way that may resonate for audiences in London, where the show originated, but does not for American theatergoers.

Yet *Shadowlands* does work. William Nicholson, adapting his 1984 TV drama, finds a wealth of delicate metaphor in the imagery of the title, a reference to Lewis' assertion that true life is inner life or afterlife and what happens on earth a mere shadow existence. He prospers by Jane Alexander's blunt, practical, meticulously underplayed Joy and by Nigel Hawthorne's epic performance, reminiscent of Ralph Richardson at his finest, as Lewis. Shuffling and shambling, looking as if forever surrounded by muddy acres and faithful hounds, Hawthorne is the embodiment of an older, surer England coming to grips with a new world that is not so much brave as demanding of bravery. He makes theological abstractions breathe—and weep.

Source: William A. Henry, III, "Shadowlands," in *Time,* Vol. 136, No. 22, November, 19, 1990, p. 106.

SOURCES

Armistead, Claire, "Visions of Love," in *New Statesman & Society,* February 9, 1990, p. 42.

Barnes, Clive, "Stars Shine in *Shadowlands,*" in *New York Post,* November 12, 1990.

Beaufort, John, Review of *Shadowlands,* in *Christian Science Monitor,* November 4, 1990.

James, John, "Improbable Attachment," in *Times Educational Supplement,* November 3, 1989, p. 33.

Kissel, Howard, "Tepid Tea, Anyone?: *Shadowlands* Conveys Little About Its Celebrated Subjects," in *Daily News,* November 12, 1990.

Kramer, Mimi, "Shady Doings," in *New Yorker,* November 26, 1990, pp. 124–25.

Nachman, Gerald, "Drama of Oxford Don in Love," in *San Francisco Chronicle,* November 27, 1990, p. E1.

Nicholson, William, *Shadowlands,* Fireside Theatre, 1989.

Review of *Shadowlands,* in *Financial Times,* October 24, 1989, p. 25.

Review of *Shadowlands,* in *Variety,* November 12, 1990, p. 68.

Rich, Frank, Review of *Shadowlands,* in *New York Times,* November 12, 1990, p. C11.

Richards, David, "Why Breaking Up Is Hard to Do," in *New York Times,* November 18, 1990, sec. 2, p. 5.

Stuart, Jan, "Probing the Humanity of C. S. Lewis," in *New York Newsday,* November 12, 1990.

Weales, Gerald, "Partially Observed," in *Commonweal,* February 8, 1991, pp. 99–100.

Wilson, Edwin, Review of *Shadowlands,* in *Wall Street Journal,* November 23, 1990.

FURTHER READING

Finkle, David, "For C. S. Lewis, Does Love Conquer All?" in *New York Times,* November 4, 1990, pp. H1, H5.
   This article gives background on the relationship between Lewis and Gresham, how Nicholson came to write both the television movie and play, and the stage production.

Green, V. H. H. *A History of Oxford University,* B. T. Batsford, Ltd., 1974.
   This nonfiction book gives the historical background at the institution where Lewis taught for many years and is used as a setting in *Shadowlands*.

Gresham, Douglas H., *Lenten Lands,* Macmillan, 1998.
   This book by Joy Gresham's son who is a character in *Shadowlands,* describes his perspective on the relationship between his mother and Lewis.

Wilson, A. N., *C. S. Lewis: A Biography,* Collins, 1990.
   This is the definitive biography of Lewis and includes information about his relationship with Gresham.

Slave Ship

AMIRI BARAKA
1967

Amiri Baraka's play *Slave Ship: A Historical Pageant* was first produced at the Spirit House theater in Newark, New Jersey, in 1967, and first published in 1969, by Jihad, the publishing house founded by Baraka himself. The play has been noted for its successful embodiment of the politics of black nationalism, the aesthetics of the Black Arts Movement, and the principals of "revolutionary theater" put forth by Baraka through his founding of the Black Repertory Theater in Harlem in 1965.

Slave Ship is a one-act play that takes place during distinct historical experiences in African-American history: aboard a slave ship during the Middle Passage from Africa to America, during a plantation-era uprising, and in the era of the civil rights movement. Baraka's play utilizes the representation of African-American history as a means of forging a communal African-American identity through the preservation of African cultural roots. The use of music throughout the play is central to this theme of African-American cultural identity and communal solidarity. Critics have noted the use of music in conjunction with audience participation in a communal dance to create a ritualistic drama through which theater is intended to inspire political action.

AUTHOR BIOGRAPHY

Floyd Gaffney, in the *Dictionary of Literary Biography,* has compared Amiri Baraka (also known as LeRoi Jones or Imamu Amiri Baraka) to W. E. B. Dubois and Richard Wright as "one of the twentieth century's most prolific and persistent social and moral critics of black experience in America." Baraka's political and literary career can be divided into three separate phases: a Beat Movement poet in the 1950s, a black nationalist poet, dramatist, essayist, and music historian in the 1960s, and a Marxist/Socialist writer and activist in the 1970s.

Baraka was born Everett Leroy Jones, on October 7, 1934, in Newark, New Jersey, into an educated, middle-class African-American family. His father, Coyette LeRoy Jones, was a postal worker, and his mother, Anna Lois Russ Jones, was a social worker. He graduated from Barringer High School in 1951, spent a year at Rutgers University, and then transferred to Howard University, in Washington, D.C., which he attended from 1952 to 1954. Baraka, however, quit school to join the U.S. Air Force, where he spent three years stationed in Puerto Rico as a weatherman and gunner, from 1954 to 1957. He was dishonorably discharged. Baraka once stated in an interview that, while his experiences at a predominantly black university taught him about the "Negro sickness," by which he referred to the prevailing effort to assimilate into white culture, his experiences in the armed forces taught him the "white sickness" of racism. In 1957, Baraka moved to the Lower East Side in New York City, where he became engaged with writers and intellectuals of the (mostly white) bohemian Beat Movement, such as Allen Ginsberg, who were concentrated in the East Village of Manhattan. Baraka worked at various small, alternative publishing and magazine businesses, as well as at a bookstore, and attended courses in Comparative Literature at Colombia University. It was during this time that Baraka met Hettie Roberta Cohen, a white Jewish woman, whom he married in 1958, and with whom he had two children. His first collection of poetry, *Preface to a Twenty Volume Suicide Note,* was published in 1961, by Totem Press, a publishing company which he had founded in 1959.

In 1960, Baraka was invited to Cuba, along with other African-American writers, to celebrate the anniversary of Fidel Castro's 1953 Marxist Revolution. Exposure to many politically committed writers in Cuba had a profound affect on Baraka's political, and therefore literary, orientation. Whereas Baraka's Beat poetry had been generally apolitical, his writing became consciously politicized as he adopted a black nationalist political stance. Baraka's social history of blues and jazz music, *Blues People: Negro Music in White America* (1964), continues to be regarded as a seminal work of historical and musicological scholarship. In 1964, Baraka won notoriety and critical acclaim for his highly political play, *Dutchman.* His growing identification with black nationalism, which characterizes the second phase of his literary/political career, led to his divorce from his white wife and his move to Harlem shortly after the assassination of Malcolm X in 1965. There, he founded the Black Arts Repertory Theater in 1965, married a black woman, Sylvia Robinson, in 1966, and, in 1968, converted to Islam and changed his name to Imamu Amiri Baraka, which means "blessed spiritual leader"; his wife accordingly changed her name to Amina Baraka. In 1974, Baraka began the third major phase of his literary and political career when he declared himself a Marxist-Leninist, rejecting black nationalism, and dropping the religious title of "Imamu" from his name. His own account of his life is recorded in *The Autobiography of LeRoi Jones* (1984).

Baraka continued to be a presence in American mass culture when, in 1991, he protested the portrayal of Malcolm X in Spike's Lee's film, *X,* and when he appeared as a homeless poet in the movie *Bulworth* in 1998. Baraka retired from the State University of New York at Stonybrook and became Professor Emeritus in 1999, on his sixty-fifth birthday.

PLOT SUMMARY

Baraka's one-act play opens in darkness. A variety of sounds and smells are emitted to the audience in order to represent the "atmosfeeling" of life in the hold of a slave ship. The sounds include that of the sea, and the boat rocking, as well as the sounds of the suffering of the enslaved Africans, and the sounds of the white slave traders. The smells are meant to create an atmosphere of "life processes going on anyway," and include "urine" and "ex-

Amiri Baraka

crement." A light comes up on two white sailors chatting idly about the "riches" to be had from the slave trade in America, above the "drone of terror" from the hold below them. While the stage is still in almost complete darkness, the sounds of the enslaved Africans on the ship continue, and begin to include the sounds of humming, and chanting, as well as the voices of the suffering Africans, calling out to their gods. The sailors above them laugh and point at the suffering Africans. From the ship's hold, one man cries out that a woman has killed her baby and herself. The sounds of another African woman being assaulted and raped by a white sailor are heard. The sounds of an African man struggling with the white man in defense of the raped African woman are also heard. Throughout, the sounds of African women humming can be heard almost continuously.

The second section of the play takes place on a Southern plantation in America. A character referred to as "The Old Tom," is described as "a shuffling 'Negro.'" He dances and shuffles in a show of self-deprecation, speaking subserviently to "massa," as the two White Men, dressed as plantation owners, continue laughing. A group of enslaved African Americans plan a revolt in discussion with the Preacher, as the Old Tom looks on.

The Old Tom then reports the planned revolt to the white slave masters in exchange for a couple of pork chops. The revolt is staged in darkness, the struggle indicated only by sounds.

In the third section, a Preacher in a business suit, referred to as the New Tom, gives a speech, intended to placate the white men, advocating integration. A man approaches the Preacher and lays the bloody corpse of a baby at his feet. As the Preacher continues his speech, which turns into jabbering nonsense, he attempts to kick the corpse behind him. The voice of the White Man is heard pleading for his life as he is killed in revolt. The African-American characters, as a group, begin to dance to modern jazz music. The stage directions indicate that the cast is to invite members of the audience to dance, creating a ''party'' atmosphere. Amidst this festive, ritualized dancing, which indicates a celebration of successful revolt, the head of the Preacher is thrown into the center of the dancers. The stage then goes black.

CHARACTERS

1st Man
The speaker identified as 1st Man is described as "Prayer—husband of Dademi." He is heard onstage as one of the Africans imprisoned in the hold of the slave ship. He can be heard praying to an African god through his misery.

1st Woman
The speaker identified as 1st Woman is described as "Prayer." She is heard onstage as one of the Africans imprisoned in the slave ship. She is heard praying to an African god in her misery.

2nd Man
The speaker identified as 2nd Man is described as "Curser." He is heard onstage as one of the Africans imprisoned in the hold of the slave ship. He curses the disembodied voices of the White Men for their abuse of the Africans.

2nd Woman
The speaker identified as 2nd Woman is described as "Screamer—attacked." She is one of the

Africans imprisoned in the hold of the slave ship. Her voice is heard onstage as the woman who is raped by one of the white sailors on the slave ship.

3rd Man

The speaker identified as the 3rd Man is described as ''Struggler.'' He is heard onstage as one of the Africans imprisoned in the slave ship He attempts to fend off the white man who rapes one of the African women.

3rd Woman

The speaker identified as 3rd Woman is described as ''with child.'' She is one of the Africans imprisoned in the hold of the slave ship. Her voice can be heard onstage as the other enslaved Africans note that she has killed her baby and herself while on the ship. Later in the play, during the plantation scene and the revolt scene, her voice can be heard, as the stage directions indicate, ''whispering after death.''

New Tom

The character identified as New Tom is the preacher who attempts to talk in a dignified fashion to the white man and preaches assimilation to his fellow African Americans. In the final moments of the play, the severed head of the preacher is thrown amidst the dancing and ''party'' atmosphere in celebration of the revolt. Some critics have pointed out that this character seems to represent the Reverend Martin Luther King, Jr., known for his advocacy of the harmonious integration of whites and blacks in America. Baraka's black nationalist sentiments, as expressed through this play, are critical of the integrationist approach represented by Martin Luther King.

Old Tom Slave

The character identified as Old Tom Slave appears in the segment of the play that is set on a plantation. He represents the enslaved African Americans who kowtowed to white authority in acts of self-degradation for the purpose of gaining favor. The Old Tom Slave betrays his fellow African Americans when he reports to the white plantation owners that a revolt is being planned. He betrays his African-American community in exchange for a couple of pork chops which are thrown to him by the White Men.

White Men

The White Men are presented sometimes as disembodied voices, but at other points are actually seen onstage. In the first part of the play, they appear in sailor uniforms, and represent the white sailors on the slave ship. In the next part of the play, the stage directions indicate that these same white actors are now seen with hats that indicate that they are plantation owners.

THEMES

Black Nationalism

Slave Ship was first produced during Baraka's literary and political phase of black nationalist sentiment. The play expresses a black nationalist perspective through the interlocking thematic concerns of African-American history, African-American community, and African-American identity. A strong sense of African-American communal identity is expressed through the play's representation of the seminal experience of African Americans—the ''Middle Passage'' to America via ''slave ships,'' enforced accommodation to the oppressive conditions of slavery, whether through ''Uncle Tomism'' or attempted revolt, and contemporary struggles for racial equality. The play emphasizes the power of African-American community, as the African and African-American characters maintain their communal solidarity despite the efforts of white oppressors to disperse community and disband families. This strong sense of African-American community is expressed in the play through the persistence of African cultural roots throughout the history of oppression. The survival of African culture throughout African-American history is most strongly expressed in the play through the use of music: from the Yoruba songs of the enslaved Africans during the Middle Passage to the contemporary jazz music that accompanies the final ritual revolt and celebration. Baraka's stage directions also indicate the expression of contemporary African-American identity through the survival of African culture when he coins a phrase in instructing the actors to lead the

TOPICS FOR FURTHER STUDY

- Baraka was very influential in the development of the Black Arts Movement, especially in drama, through his founding of the Black Arts Repertory Theater and his many dramatic works. Learn more about recent developments in the area of African-American dramatic production. Who are the important African-American playwrights today, and what are their most important plays? What are the titles of some of the important works by these writers? What theaters throughout the U.S. are devoted to producing works by African-American writers? To what extent are the principles of the Black Arts Movement still practiced today? What developments have occurred in the literary aesthetics and political orientation of African-American dramatists?

- Baraka's play *Slave Ship* is unique and innovative in part due to its unusual stage directions and characterization. Perform a scene from the play with a group of students. What kinds of choices do you make in your interpretation of the stage directions? In what ways does performing a scene illuminate the meaning and impact of the play?

- During the 1950s, Baraka was associated with the writers of the Beat Movement, a primarily white, bohemian, literary orientation most commonly associated with the poet Allen Ginsberg (especially for his poem *Howl*) and the novelist Jack Kerouac (especially for his novel *On the Road*). Learn more about the Beat Movement, the writers associated with it, and the works they produced. What aesthetic principles did they put forth? What were the social or political implications of the literary aesthetics of the Beat Movement?

- During an important phase of his literary and political career, Baraka was dedicated to the political philosophy of black nationalism and the religion of Islam. Learn more about black nationalism, and its association with Islam. What is the history of black nationalism? What are some of the fundamental political values held by black nationalists? Who are some of the important figures in the black nationalist movement? What is your own opinion of black nationalism as a political philosophy and movement?

- The third phase of Baraka's literary and political career was characterized by his orientation to a Marxist-Socialist political philosophy. Learn more about Karl Marx and Marxist political theory. What are the fundamental social and political values put forth by Marxism? What is your own opinion of Marxism as a political philosophy?

---

audience in a "Boogalooyoruba" dance. Baraka's advocacy of African-American identity through black nationalism is represented by his dramatic celebration of African-American communal solidarity via the persistence of African historical roots as expressed by contemporary African-American culture.

Racial Oppression

Baraka's one-act play, subtitled "a history pageant," presents a series of "historical tableaux" representing the conditions of slavery in the history of African Americans: the transportation of enslaved Africans on "slave ships" across the "Middle Passage" to America, the conditions of slavery on the Southern plantation, and the continuing struggle for racial equality. The white characters in the play include the disembodied voices of white slave traders on the slave ship, who laugh at the horrible conditions of the Africans they have captured and rape an African woman. Harry Elam Jr. comments on the effectiveness of the staging of the White Voices in expressing the conditions of racial oppression: "This offstage White Voice, an invisible but extremely tangible symbol of the powerful psychological and sociological effects of white oppression, hovers above the play, inhibiting black interaction. Implicitly and explicitly, the representation of the White Voice critiques and comments on the power of representation. Although not physically present, the White Voice is powerfully represented.'' Elam has also observed that ''the oppressive socioeconomic conditions of black American life inform and were informed by the symbolism'' of the play. He goes on to explain that the play's representation of history is designed to emphasize the continuation of racial oppression beyond the official emancipation of slaves: ''The play's action compressed the horrors of the Middle Passage and the degradations of centuries under white racist hegemony into succinct stage moments. *Slave Ship's* representational account of black history flowed from slavery to civil rights, omitting any record of emancipation. This deliberate omission emphasized that oppressive conditions for blacks have been continuous.''

Assimilation

Baraka's play, which embodies the cultural and political values of black nationalism, is vehemently anti-assimilationist. The harshest criticism within the play is reserved for the African Americans who represent ''Uncle Tom-ism''—dancing and singing for the benefit of the white master in an act of self-degradation and denial of their African-American communal identity. Tejumola Olaniyan points out that, in keeping with the values of black nationalism, ''the 'Toms,' who veered away from the group, lose both ways: they are not only treated with contempt and condescension by the oppressors they ally with, but they are also the first to be consumed by the people's wrath. The play is unsparing in their condemnation.'' In fact, the African-American preacher advocating integration is beheaded in the play's finale revolt and ritual. Several critics have pointed out that the preacher may have been intended to represent Martin Luther King, Jr., the highly influential civil rights activist whom some African Americans considered to be a pawn of white America in his advocacy of integration.

STYLE

Audience Participation and Ritual

One of the innovative elements of Baraka's play is the encouragement of audience participation. During the final sequence, actors step down from the stage and invite audience members to participate in a celebratory dance. Floyd Gaffney describes the overall effect of this final sequence and it thematic implications: ''The final moments of the drama bring members of the cast together in a communion of singing 'When We Gonna Rise' and dancing 'a new-old dance, Boogalooyoruba line.' The celebration moves beyond the footlights into the theater, involving black spectators in this gesture of unified consciousness. The severed head of the preacher is thrown onto the dance floor, abruptly reminding audience members that the struggle continues in the community, the nation, and, ultimately, in the world. Critics have observed the ritualistic element of the play, as it culminates in this final dance involving the audience. As Tejumola Olaniyan notes, ''It is not a 'play' as such but, more appropriately, a presentational, gigantic ritual, a pageant.'' Harry J. Elam Jr. praises the theatrical production of *Slave Ship* as an ''effective strategy'' of what he calls ''ritualistic protest theater.''

Sounds and Smells

Nilgun Anadolu-Okur describes the colorful use of sound, as well as the unusual use of actual smells, to dramatize central themes of the play: ''To reenact the horrors of enslavement, drums, rattles, tambourines, ship bells and horns, gun shots and whip cracks, the sound of the waves, the smell of the open sea, incense, urine, and excrement are utilized, adding more weight to the realistic imagery.'' Gaffney describes the significance of sound to thematic concerns throughout the play, explaining that ''The ritual of sound provides cohesion through which the slaves appeal to and abandon their African deities. Humming and singing of spirituals occur as the pageant shifts to slavery in America. . . . The contemporary phase of the ritual juxtaposes the voice of the integrationist preacher against that of the nationalist fighter, which is metaphorically extended into the 'new voice of freedom' heard through the wailing of a saxophone.'' Kimberly W. Benston observes that, ''The experience of the play . . . is less one of watching than of listening.''

Plot

Benston discusses the absence of a traditional plot line from Baraka's play as an aesthetic choice intended to more powerfully express his central thematic concerns. Benston notes that, ''*Slave Ship* has no definite plot,'' and that ''There is very little use of discursive speech and almost no dialogue,'' but that ''Every theatrical device is directed toward creating an 'atmosphere of feeling,' one appropriate to a slave ship, the attendant horrors of the Middle

Passage, and the grim consequences that comprise the history of the Afro-American experience.'' Thus, Benston explains that ''With the abandonment of traditional plot, Baraka moves us along these historical and mystical paths by a series of tableaux and symbolic actions.''

Set Design

Harry J. Elam Jr. discusses the significance of the set design of one particular production of *Slave Ship* to its central thematic concerns. Elam notes that Gilbert Moses, the set designer, ''attempted to transform the performance space into a slave ship— a critical, historical site of black degradation and collective social memory.'' Elam goes on to say that ''As a historical site of unconscionable racial violence, the slave ship potently communicated to its spectators an African-American heritage of struggle and survival.''

HISTORICAL CONTEXT

African-American Literary Movements

Twentieth-century African-American literature has been characterized by two important literary movements: The Harlem Renaissance and the Black Arts Movement. The Harlem Renaissance, also referred to as the New Negro Movement, designates a period during the 1920s in which African-American literature flourished among a group of writers concentrated in Harlem, New York. Important writers and works of the Harlem Renaissance include James Weldon Johnson, who wrote the novel *Autobiography of an Ex-Colored Man* (1912); Claude McKay, who wrote the bestselling novel *Home to Harlem* (1928); Langston Hughes, who wrote the poetry collection *The Weary Blues* (1926); and Wallace Thurman, who wrote the novel *The Blacker the Berry* (1929). This period of incredible literary output diminished when the Great Depression of the 1930s affected the financial status of many African-American writers. The Black Arts Movement, also referred to as the Black Aesthetic Movement, which flourished during the 1960s and 70s, embodied values derived from black nationalism, promoting politically and socially significant works, often written in black English vernacular. Important writers of the Black Arts Movement, in addition to Baraka, include Eldridge Cleaver, Angela Davis, Alice Walker, and Toni Morrison.

African-American Theater

Baraka's play is an important work in the history of African-American dramatic literary production. Dramatic works by African-American writers in the nineteenth century include *King Shotaway* (1823), by William Henry Brown, the first known play by an African-American writer; *The Escape: or, A Leap for Freedom* (1858), by William Wells Brown, the first play by an African-American writer to be published; and *Rachel* (1916), by Anglina W. Grimke, the first successful stage play by an African-American writer. Dramatic works and stage productions by African Americans in the twentieth century were influenced by important literary movements, such as the Harlem Renaissance and the Black Arts Movement. The development of Black Theater in the first half of the twentieth century was inspired by the Harlem Renaissance, and included the establishment of theaters devoted to black productions in major cities throughout the United States. The most prominent black theaters by mid-century were the American Negro Theater and the Negro Playwrights' Company. In the post-World War II era, black theater became more overtly political and more specifically focused on celebrating African-American culture. One of the most prominent works to emerge from this period was the 1959 play, *A Raisin in the Sun,* by Lorraine Hansberry. The Black Arts Movement, which emerged in the 1960s, led to the establishment in 1965 of the Black Repertory Theater in Harlem, initiated by Baraka. Baraka's award-winning 1964 play *Dutchman* is among the most celebrated dramatic works of this period. Ntozake Shange's 1977 *for colored girls who have considered suicide/when the rainbow is enuf* used an experimental dramatic format to address issues facing African-American women. In the 1980s, August Wilson emerged as one of the most important African-American playwrights, with his play *Ma Rainey's Black Bottom* (1985), set in Chicago in the 1920s, about a blues singer and her band.

The Beat Movement

During the 1950s, Baraka became associated with the literary and cultural aesthetics of the Beat Movement. Writers of the Beat Movement were concentrated in San Francisco and Greenwich Village, New York City, and included, most prominently, Allen Ginsberg (1926–1997), best known for his poem *Howl* (1956), and Jack Kerouac (1922–1969), best known for his novel *On the Road* (1957). Beat Movement aesthetics were apolitical, but were associated with such cultural practices as jazz music, drugs, sexual experimentation, and Zen

COMPARE & CONTRAST

- **1920s:** The Harlem Renaissance is the celebrated African-American literary movement that inspires many great African-American writers to an unprecedented literary output.

  1950s: The Beat Movement in poetry is primarily made up of white writers, but is influenced by the African-American musical tradition of jazz, and is influential to such celebrated African-American writers such as Amiri Baraka.

  1960s: The Black Arts Movement, inspired by the Civil Rights Movement and Black Nationalism, promotes an artistic aesthetic based in African-American culture.

- **1823:** *King Shotaway*, by James Brown, is the first known play written by an African American.

  1858: *The Escape: Or, a Leap for Freedom*, by William Wells Brown, is the first *published* play by an African-American writer.

  1916: *Rachel*, by Angelina W. Grimke, is the first successful stage play by an African-American writer.

  1959: *A Raisin in the Sun*, by Lorraine Hansberry, is the most prominent and widely celebrated play by an African-American writer.

  1965: The Black Repertory Theatre, established by Amiri Baraka for the production of African-American dramatic works, initiates the Black Arts Movement in drama.

  1977: *For colored girls who have considered suicide, when the rainbow is enuf*, by Ntozake Shange, is a successful, experimental play, inspired by the Black Arts Movement, and written by a black feminist writer.

  1985: *Ma Rainey's Black Bottom*, by August Wilson, is the most celebrated play by an African-American writer.

- **1518–1845:** The Middle Passage refers to the route across the Atlantic Ocean from Africa to the Americas—a journey that takes from three weeks to three months and that brings millions of enslaved Africans to be sold into bondage. There are a recorded fifty-five mutinies among the slaves against the slave traders during the Middle Passage.

  1861–1865: The American Civil War results in the complete abolition of slavery in the United States.

  1964: An extensive Civil Rights Act is passed by Congress, declaring various forms of racial discrimination illegal.

Buddhism. Beat poets advocated a free-flowing, loosely structured use of language, sometimes borrowing from the rhythms of jazz music. Other important writers to emerge from the Beat Movement include William Burroughs and Gary Snyder.

CRITICAL OVERVIEW

Baraka has been a leading figure in the development of African-American literature and thought during the twentieth century. Kimberly W. Benston states that Baraka "is one of the most intriguing, controversial, and enigmatic figures in modern letters." Benston goes on to say that "Baraka entered the American consciousness not merely as a writer but as an event, a symbolic figure somehow combining the craft and insights of Euro-American radicalism with the rebellious energies of young Afro-America." William J. Harris describes the extensive influence of Baraka on American literature: "Acting as an energetic artist-critic-spokesman, Baraka almost single-handedly changed both the nature and the form of post-World War II Afro-American literature. In addition to being a prime influence on other poets and dramatists of his time, Baraka has also created an original body of work that belongs in the forefront of innovative avant-garde writing, regardless of ethnic background. As a contemporary American artist Baraka must be ranked with the likes of John Coltrane, Ralph Ellison, Norman Mailer, Toni Morrison, and Thomas Pynchon.'' Harris goes on to describe the extent of Baraka's continuing influence on African-American artistic production throughout the 1990s, stating that ''In essence, Baraka and the Black Arts Movement have had a profound and lasting philosophical and aesthetic impact on all postintegrationist black art; they have turned black art from other-directed to ethnically centered. Thus the contemporary Afro-American artist writes out of his or her own culture and, moreover, is self-consciously an Afro-American.''

Baraka's influence on African-American theater has been extensive. Nilgun Anadolu-Okur notes that ''At the height of the Black Arts movement Baraka was considered both the theoretician and the practitioner of a new outlook in theater, with his radical propositions engendered in the Revolutionary Theater.'' In addition to founding the Black Repertory Theater in Harlem in 1965, Baraka has written influential essays on the aesthetic values of black theater, as well as numerous stage plays, most notably, in 1964, the highly celebrated *Dutchman*. Benston says of Baraka's influence on theater:

> From the ground-breaking manifesto 'The Revolutionary Theatre' (1964) to his post-nationalist notes on The Motion of History, Baraka has insisted on a theatre that energetically seeks new forms, new intensity, and new language to present and be a part of our constantly changing culture.

Baraka's own dramatic works have embodied these values, as Benston observes that, ''no single body of plays is more resolutely exploratory than Baraka's.''

Critics point to the political implications of Baraka's dramatic productions, particularly *Slave Ship*, as embodied in the aesthetic values of what Baraka called ''revolutionary theater.'' Anadolu-Okur comments that Baraka's ''ultimate concern has always been with the political functions of drama,'' observing that Baraka's drama ''was targeted to educate the masses and his people to reclaim their historical consciousness, aesthetic and philosophical assets that spring from the center of Africanness. Renewal of the self and the employment of the new self to acquire a better means of existence became Baraka's fundamental message in his plays.'' Benston asserts that in the production of *Slave Ship*, ''the objectives of the 'revolutionary theater' are fully realized.'' Tejumola Olaniyan, noting that *Slave Ship* is ''perhaps the most discussed of Baraka's plays'' of his black nationalist period, observes the ways in which it stands out from his previous plays up to this point: ''It is thematically the most reflective, a deep introspective exploration of the origins of the present struggles for black self-fashioning.... Thus far more than we could say of the other plays, the audience assumed is largely black, and this assumption is woven into the very fabric of the play.''

Baraka subtitled *Slave Ship* ''A Historical Pageant,'' and critics have commented on the political implications of Baraka's representation of African-American history. Olaniyan observes that, ''The brief successive 'scenes' are like pages in a history book of a people under an imposed, dehumanizing condition.'' Baraka uses historical reference as a means of defining a contemporary African-American communal identity based on the survival of African cultural roots. Anadolu-Okur notes that the play ''is historical in content, but it uses history metaphorically; in other words a historical dateline is used as a symbol for the present, and enslavement is a current event.'' In discussing a specific stage production of *Slave Ship*, Harry J. Elam Jr. observes that, ''As a historical site of unconscionable racial violence, the slave ship potently communicated to its spectators an African-American heritage of struggle and survival.'' Benston notes that, ''At every stage of his evocation of Afro-American history, Baraka insists upon the survival of aboriginal African communalism in the black slave population.'' This representation of history ultimately asserts the values of a black nationalist identity. Discussing the final action of the play, in which audience members are invited to participate in a communal dance on stage with the actors, Benston asserts that through the play's ''final rite ... the entire assembled black community dons the mask of its ancient spirit and comes to full life as a potent, physical manifestation of the forgotten, but historically nourished, national power. In *Slave Ship*, the black nation promptly transforms itself into history, for the imitation of suffering has conferred on it a collective past and assigned it a triumphant future.'' Elam comments on the political implications of the play's ending with audience participation, stating that ''Baraka intends for this final moment of *Slave Ship* to induce the spectators' participation and compel their activism.'' Elam concludes ''*Slave Ship*, in its finale, jolts the audience back into the uncertain 1960s reality, in which victory over white oppression has yet to be achieved."

Critics further praise *Slave Ship* for its use of music as a means of asserting the values of the Black Arts Movement, which celebrate communal African-American identity through African-American cultural practices. According to Benston, "*Slave Ship* is the most successful dramatic work to emerge from the Black Arts Movement precisely because it 'reclaims' and utilizes the musical base of the Afro-American genius. Baraka galvanizes a communal response to his vision by calling upon collective creation and participation in the play's musical life." Benston goes on to state that "The genius of Baraka's play lies in the manner in which the complex black music aesthetic is given precise theatrical embodiment."

Critics discuss the emphasis in *Slave Ship* on theatrical techniques other than standard narrative and dialogue. Benston notes "Whereas Baraka's earlier plays were characterized by long, illuminating orations, in *Slave Ship* he emphasizes in every way concrete aspects of pain, the heavy reality of chains, the screams and smells of degradation. There is horror but there is also life, and we feel it all." Elam comments on the impact of these elements of the play: "Because the plot and character delineation of *Slave Ship* were so sparse, the other elements of the production increased in significance. The performance of *Slave Ship* emphasized gestures and symbols over the spoken word. Spectacle, music, sounds, and smells all combined to bring audience and performers together in an atmosphere of intense feeling."

CRITICISM

Liz Brent

Brent has a Ph.D. in American Culture, specializing in film studies, from the University of Michigan. She is a freelance writer and teaches courses in the history of American cinema. In the following essay, Brent discusses the use of innovative dramatic style in Baraka's play.

Over thirty years after its initial production and publication, Baraka's one-act play *Slave Ship: A Historical Pageant* continues to strike the reader with its variety of experimental stylistic and technical elements as a dramatic work. Experimental dramatic technique in this play includes a rich texture of overlapping sounds, as well as smells (a highly unusual element of dramatic productions), and audience participation. As *Slave Ship* is neither plot-driven nor character-oriented, nor dialogue-centered, much of the written play consists of stage directions; the stylistic elements of Baraka's written stage directions are extremely expressive and sound, at times, like poetry. In addition, Baraka makes use in his stage directions of nonverbal phonetic indications of musical sounds, as well as made-up words, and expressive phrases that indicate the "atmosfeeling" of a particular scene, rather than concrete directions indicating action.

In the stage directions for the play's opening sequence, Baraka introduces several of these experimental stylistic elements and dramatic techniques. Most notably, Baraka provides stage directions indicating the emission of a variety of odors discernible to the audience:

> Whole theater in darkness. Dark. For a long time. Occasional sound, like ship groaning, squeaking, rocking. Sea smells. In the dark. Keep people in the dark, and gradually odors of the sea, and sounds of the ship, creep up. Burn incense, but make a significant, almost stifling, smell come up. Urine. Excrement. Death. Life processes going on anyway. Eating. These smells and cries, the slash and tear of the lash, in a total atmosfeeling, gotten some way.

In these stage directions, Baraka indicates the emission of the smells of the sea, incense, urine, and excrement. While most of these smells are intended to invoke the realistic conditions of Africans in the hold of a slave ship, the smell of incense adds an expressive element into the mix. Clearly, Baraka does not mean to imply that the inside of a slave ship ever smelled of incense. Rather, the incense seems intended to invoke an element of ritual, which can be associated with the Africans who hold on to their traditional cultural and spiritual practices, despite the oppressive conditions of the slave ship. (Although it may not be historically accurate that African cultures utilized incense in ritual, the effect on a contemporary American audience could certainly evoke associations with non-Western religious practice.) The sound equivalent of the incense is the expressive sounds of African drumming overlapping the realistic sounds within the slave ship. Thus, Baraka uses odors both to represent realistic conditions of a slave ship, and to invoke expressionistic associations with traditional African culture and spirituality. The implication is that traditional

WHAT DO I READ NEXT?

- *Dutchman* (1964) is Baraka's award-winning, critically acclaimed, first professional dramatic production, about racial conflict as expressed by a white woman toward a black man on a subway train.

- *Preface to a Twenty Volume Suicide Note . . .* (1961) is Baraka's first volume of poetry, published by Totem Press, which Baraka founded in 1959. It reflects the literary aesthetics of his Beat Movement phase.

- *Blues People: Negro Music in White America* (1963) is Baraka's highly regarded social history of blues and jazz music in the U.S. and in African-American culture.

- *The LeRoi Jones/Amiri Baraka Reader* (1991), edited by William J. Harris, is a collection of important works and excerpts from all three phases of Baraka's career.

- *Transbluency: The Selected Poems of Amiri Baraka/LeRoi Jones (1961-1995)* (1996) is a recent collection of important poems from throughout Baraka's career.

- *The Autobiography of LeRoi Jones/Amiri Baraka* (1984; reprinted in 1997) is Baraka's autobiography, written during a prison sentence for his activity during a political protest.

- *Image of the Tiger: Essays by Amiri Baraka* (1993), edited by Thornton Dial, is a collection of important essays from throughout Baraka's career.

African culture survived the Middle Passage within the hearts and minds and spirits of the enslaved Africans, even if specific cultural practices did not literally survive the passage to America.

Baraka also uses expressionistic stage directions to indicate the use of smells and sounds onstage when he includes in his list of concrete sounds and smells, ''Death.'' Clearly, the producer of the stage play is here asked by the playwright to represent abstract concepts like ''death'' through the concrete use of sounds and smells directed at the theater spectator. To express the abstract qualities that the stage directions are designed to impress upon a theater audience, Baraka in fact makes up an entirely new word: ''atmosfeeling.'' He ends these opening stage directions, both concrete and expressive, by indicating that these theatrical effects are intended to add up to ''a total atmosfeeling.'' Furthermore, Baraka's stage directions make it clear that he leaves up to the producer of the stage play the exact, concrete means by which this effect, and these abstract associations, are to be conveyed to the audience, for he concludes that this ''atmosfeeling'' is to be ''gotten some way.''

Throughout the play, Baraka uses expressive, poetically articulated stage directions to indicate the abstract ''atmosfeeling'' to be conveyed at various points. Baraka constructs phrases that read like poetry in that they privilege the expression of feeling, atmosphere, or abstract concepts over clear or concrete description. For instance, in the first sequence, which takes place in the slave ship, Baraka describes the sounds emitting from the darkness as ''the long stream of different wills, articulated as screams, grunts, cries, etc.'' ''The long stream of different wills'' is clearly a poetic image that does not describe a concrete sound or image, but has abstract implications. The ''long stream'' seems to refer in part to the vast number of Africans brought across the ''Middle Passage'' over a period of several centuries of slave trade. The mention of ''different wills'' suggests the ways in which the enslaved Africans and African Americans continued to exert their own individuality and will, despite the extremely oppressive conditions under which they were forced to live. In another stage direction indicating the sounds of the slave ship, Baraka uses the poetic phrase ''the moans of pushed-together agony.'' Baraka also uses expressive, poetic phrasing to describe the expressions on the faces of the white sailors on the slave ship, who appear "grinning their vices."

Baraka's stage directions for the musical sounds that permeate the play are also often poetic, expressive, and abstract. In a sequence shortly after the sounds of the slave revolt, Baraka's stage directions call for the sound of drums, "drums of fire and blood, briefly loud and smashing against the dark." Baraka also makes use of nonverbal phonetic letter combinations to indicate the sounds of drumming as well as of human voices. During the plantation sequence, the stage directions first indicate the sounds of African drumming through primarily descriptive language that indicates both the concrete sounds and the cultural associations meant to be invoked by these sounds: "drums of ancient African warriors come up ... hero-warriors.... Black dancing in the dark, with bells, as if free, dancing wild old dances." Baraka goes on, however, to reproduce the actual drumming sounds through the rhythmic phrasing of phonetically spelled sounds: "Bam Boom Bam Booma Bimbam boomama boom beem bam." Such phonetic sound descriptions are indicated later when Baraka describes the sounds of the slave revolt, which include: "AIEEEEEEEEIEIEIEEEE." Baraka combines phonetically indicated sounds with poetic description in his stage directions for the sounds of "humming" which permeate much of the play:

> (humming starts ... hmmmmm, hmmm, like old black women humming for three centuries in the slow misery of slavery ... hmmmmmmmm, hmmmmmmmmmmm)

And later, but still on the slave ship:

> (... Soft drums, and the constant, almost maddening, humming ... hmmmmmmmmmmmmm ... like mad old nigger ladies humming forever in deathly patience ... hmmmmmmm hmmmmmmmmm hmmmmmmmmm.)

Baraka makes further use of poetic language in the dialogue of the "New Tom," the modern day black Preacher calling for integration. Several critics have observed that this "New Tom" Preacher, wearing the garb of a business suit, is meant to represent the Reverend Martin Luther King, Jr., an extremely influential figure in the civil rights movement who advocated integration and harmonious relations between black and white. Baraka, a black nationalist when he wrote this play, is rather blatantly comparing Martin Luther King to the "Old Tom" who dances and shuffles in an act of self-

> "... BARAKA MAKES USE IN HIS STAGE DIRECTIONS OF NONVERBAL PHONETIC INDICATIONS OF MUSICAL SOUNDS, AS WELL AS MADE-UP WORDS, AND EXPRESSIVE PHRASES THAT INDICATE THE 'ATMOSFEELING' OF A PARTICULAR SCENE, RATHER THAN CONCRETE DIRECTIONS INDICATING ACTION."

deprecation in hopes of gaining favor with the white man. Critics have also pointed out the similarities in the Preacher's advocacy of "non-violence" and "integration" to the well-known rhetoric of Martin Luther King's civil rights writings, speeches, and political actions. But Baraka's critique of the racial politics represented by Martin Luther King is further developed through the Preacher's speech to the white man. The Preacher is described as "jabbering senselessly to the white man," but his "senseless" jabber, in the skillful hands of Baraka's poetic sensibilities, is crafted to express Baraka's strong anti-integrationist feelings at the time he wrote this play.

> Preacher—Yasss, we understand ... the problem. And, personally, I think some agreement can be reached. We will be non-violent ... to the last ... because we understand the dignity of pruty mcbonk and the greasy ghost. Of course diddy rip to bink, of vout juice. And penguins would do the same. I have a trauma. That the gold sewers wont integrate. Present fink. I have an enema ... a trauma, on the coaster with your wife bird-crap.

And, after the bloody corpse of the dead baby has been laid at his feet:

> Preacher—Uhhherrr ... as I was sayin' ... Mas'un ... Mister Tastyslop ... We kneegrows are ready to integrate ... the blippy rump of stomach bat has corrinked a lip to push the thimble. Yass. Yass. Yass ...

Baraka here introduces a plethora of made up nonsense "words," and phrases, such as, "diddy rip to bink, of vout juice," and "the blippy rump of stomach bat has corrinked a lip to push the thimble." But, in the midst of this "nonsense" Baraka has crafted poetic phrases that may be interpreted, like poetry, through their associations, rather than their (lack of) literal sense. There are several elements of this "senseless jabber" that *do* make sense in the historical context of Martin Luther King's famous "I Have a Dream" speech. In place of "I have a dream," Baraka's "New Tom" Preacher states that, "I have a trauma," and, later, "I have an enema . . . a trauma. . ." Exchanging "trauma" and "enema" for "dream," Baraka transforms King's idealistic message of hope in regard to the future of racial relations in the United States into a very different message. The scatological associations of "I have an enema" imply a very harsh criticism of King's dream—one that many who consider King to be a great figure in American history would certainly find offensive: that King's "dream," from Baraka's perspective at the time the play was written, was unrealistic. The substitution of "trauma" for "dream" changes the focus of the speech from that of hope for the future, to that of the expression of the "traumatic" suffering caused by centuries of slavery—that slavery was a national "trauma" that cannot so easily be overcome. The Preacher's statement, "I have a trauma. That the gold sewers wont integrate," further develops this critique in a sentence that at first seems like nonsense, but that can be interpreted, like poetry, through the associations evoked by the words. Throughout the play, the white man has been associated with "s—t" in the slave ship, the Africans call the white slave traders "s—t eaters"—and, by association, with "sewers." The white men are also associated with wealth, as acquired through the slave trade, when one of the sailors on the slave ship says that "riches be ours." The "gold sewers," then, refer to the white oppressors who have amassed the wealth symbolized by "gold" from the exploitation of African-Americans. Thus, while Martin Luther King's "dream" is of integration between black and white, Baraka's message is that this "dream" is, symbolically *full of s—t*, because the white oppressors, who benefit financially from a racist society, "won't integrate."

Thus, Baraka's innovative play *Slave Ship* is noteworthy for its expressive, poetic stage directions and experimental staging, designed above all to create an "atmosfeeling" of racial relations in America in accordance with Baraka's black nationalist sentiments at the time the play was written.

Source: Liz Brent, in an essay for *Drama for Students,* Gale Group, 2001.

Harry J. Elam, Jr.

In the following essay, Elam discusses the depiction of Slave Ship *as a presentation of "the survival of African culture."*

In the performance of *Slave Ship* playwright Baraka and director Gilbert Moses also sought to connect the cultural past with their immediate social struggle. They created images and action that infused the present historical moment with symbols of African cultural heritage. Through sparse dialogue, music, sound, and movement, *Slave Ship* chronicles African-American history from Africa through the middle passage to the civil rights and black power struggles of the 1960s and 1970s. The symbolism in Moses's production of *Slave Ship* emphasized the survival of African culture, spirituality, and communalism in African-American experience. Yoruba dialect was spoken during the first twenty minutes of the play, while the beating of African drums remained constant throughout. As the action moved from the roots of black civilization in Africa through slavery to the 1960s, the characters continued to chant and speak phrases in Yoruba and pray to African deities. This visual portrayal of African cultural retention informed the spectators that, despite the pressures from white America to conform, African traditions continued to survive in African-American culture and experience.

Because the plot and character delineation of *Slave Ship* were so sparse, the other elements of the production increased in significance. The performance of *Slave Ship* emphasized gestures and symbols over the spoken word. Spectacle, music, sounds, and smells all combined to bring audience and performers together in an atmosphere of intense feeling. Created by jazz musician Archie Shepp and director Gil Moses, the music covered the historical spectrum of black music, from African drums to jazz to rhythm and blues. This music suffused the entire production, intensifying the emotional impact of onstage moments. Critic John Lahr in the *Village Voice* called the production "genuine musical theater." Kimberly Benston asserted that the music in *Slave Ship* "is thus the strength, memory, power, triumph affirmation—the entire historical and mythical process of Afro-American being." As suggested by both Lahr's and Benston's comments, the music acted as much more than background. The conjunction of historical and contemporary African and African-American musical styles symbolized and reaffirmed the African presence in the African-American cultural continuum.

As in *Quinta Temporada,* the action of *Slave Ship* was not real but, rather, symbolic re-presenting, re-producing meanings for its audience. Paul Carter Harrison noted, in his response to the performance of *Slave Ship,* that the director ''Moses was able to heighten our sensitivity to the context of oppression without duplicating the experience in a static representation of reality, as in a natural life photograph; instead he relied upon our response to inform the spirit of outrage.'' Rather than realism, Moses employed powerful stage symbols. Turner writes that ritual symbols act as ''instigators and products of temporal sociocultural processes.'' Correspondingly, the oppressive socioeconomic conditions of black American life inform and were informed by the symbolism of *Slave Ship.* The play's action compressed the horrors of the middle passage and the degradations of centuries under white racist hegemony into succinct stage moments. *Slave Ship's* representational account of black history flowed from slavery to civil rights, omitting any record of emancipation. This deliberate omission emphasized that oppressive conditions for blacks have been continuous.

Baraka and Moses also used action and images within *Slave Ship* to challenge and transform conventional social and cultural meanings. Like *The Prayer Meeting, Slave Ship* contested the legitimacy of and the black spectators' faith in traditional black religion. Baraka visually associated the civil rights ministry, the legacy of Dr. Martin Luther King Jr., with betrayal and complicity, by having the Uncle Tom house slave of the early slavery scenes and the assimilationist black preacher in later scenes portrayed by the same performer. When the preacher first appeared, the stage directions read: ''Now lights flash on, and preacher in modern business suit stands with hat in his hand. He is the same Tom as before.'' Audiences close to and familiar with the achievements of the immensely popular Dr. King could potentially have found such an association troubling. Still, the signs and symbols connected with the black preacher in *Slave Ship* transformed the meanings embodied in the image of the black preacher-as-civil rights crusader. The depiction of the black preacher in *Slave Ship* worked to, as Jean and John Comaroff suggest, ''make new meanings, new ways of knowing,'' out of established images.

The transformation of the Uncle Tom slave into the black preacher called into question the preacher's credibility within the black liberation struggle. As a result, the representation of the preacher in *Slave*

> THROUGH SPARSE DIALOGUE, MUSIC, SOUND, AND MOVEMENT, *SLAVE SHIP* CHRONICLES AFRICAN-AMERICAN HISTORY FROM AFRICA THROUGH THE MIDDLE PASSAGE TO THE CIVIL RIGHTS AND BLACK POWER STRUGGLES OF THE 1960S AND 1970S.''

Ship reads not as a symbol of black pride and authority but, rather, as a caricature in the minstrel tradition, a stereotype of accommodation. According to the stage directions, ''He [the preacher] tries to be, in fact, assumes he is, dignified, trying to hold his shoulders straight, but only succeeds in giving his body an odd slant like a diseased coal chute''. With the guidance of these stage directions as well as the language that Baraka creates for this character, the performer who played the preacher presented him as a demeaning and deferential ''Steppin Fetchit''-like character. The play remakes the nonviolent preacher as an accommodating obstacle to the black liberation cause.

With newly awakened political consciousness and militancy, the other black characters onstage rise en masse and murder the black preacher. The execution of the preacher visually dramatized the need of the gathered black spectators to eliminate from their own consciousness any tendency to accommodate oppression. Significantly, the black masses execute the preacher in the same stage area previously used as a slave auction block. Their violent actions transform the space and exorcise the negative vestiges of slavery. The transformations of space and of the complacent black masses into militant activists symbolized for the audience that oppressive circumstances could be overcome, ''transformed,'' through collective revolutionary action.

The killing of the black preacher is followed by the symbolic execution of an offstage ''White Voice.'' This offstage White Voice, an invisible but extremely tangible symbol of the powerful psychological and sociological effects of white oppression, hovers above the play, inhibiting black interaction.

Implicitly and explicitly, the representation of the White Voice critiques and comments on the power of representation. Although not physically present, the White Voice is powerfully represented. At one point the White Voice announces to the onstage black masses: "I'm God. You can't kill white Jesus God. I got long blond blow hair. I don't even wear a wig. You love the way I look. You want to look like me!" These words underline racist representations and assumptions that have conditioned the treatment of blacks by whites and have also constrained blacks' self-image. By controlling the representational apparatus, the dominant culture has perpetuated its values and superiority. As a result, some blacks have internalized their inferiority and accepted and coveted everything white, including, according to *Slave Ship*, the concept of a white, blue-eyed, blond-haired "Jesus" god. The play charges the oppressive United States, capitalist system with the perpetuation of a spiritually bankrupt Christian ethos that promotes and legitimizes racism.

The black masses literally destroy and disempower the White Voice, symbolically deconstructing its representational authority. Subdued by the oncoming black onslaught, the White Voice changes from confident disdain to fearful pleading and finally to screams of horror. Simultaneously, other black cast members remove an effigy of Uncle Sam with a cross around his neck—a grotesque representation of the connection between the Christian ethic and U.S. capitalism—from the upstage wall and smash it. By controlling the representational apparatus of *Slave Ship*, Baraka empowers the black masses and black cultural representations. Through the execution of the White Voice the visible and invisible hegemony of the dominant culture and cultural representations is symbolically expunged.

Slave Ship explicitly invites the black spectators to become participants in this symbolic overthrow of the White Voice. Chanting "When we gonna rise. Rise, rise, rise cut the ties, Black man rise", they cross out into the audience, shaking hands with the black audience members, challenging and encouraging black audience members to stand, to join with them in the chant and in their attack on the White Voice. This antistructural interpolation is at once inside and outside the action of the play. It is both creative and destructive as it allows for the improvisational flexibility of the performers and destroys the conventional boundaries between stage and spectators. Through this antistructural trope *Slave Ship* moves toward Benston's notion of methexis, the ritualistic and communal helping out. The participatory and symbolic action—the chanting and shaking of hands—encouraged audience members to commune, to help out.

The finale of *Slave Ship*, like the ending of *Quinta Temporada*, is antistructural. It attempts to induce further audience participation and to compel its audience to act. After the onstage black masses kill the White Voice in *Slave Ship*, they invite black spectators up onto the stage to dance with the performers to the jazz music of Archie Shepp. This action reinforces the celebratory and communal bond between spectators and performers. Together actors and audience become participants in a collective ritual, a "tribal" ceremony of spiritual and social significance. Just when the party reaches some loose improvisation, Baraka calls for the head of the Uncle Tom preacher to be thrown into the center of the dance floor. This symbolic, antistructural act transformed the atmosphere of the theatrical event. The shocking introduction of the preacher's head abruptly shifts the mood of the action. In a manner similar to Antonin Artaud and his Theater of Cruelty, Baraka bombards his audience with violent, cruel images. Rather than purging spectators of the propensity to act—the expected response to violent images that Artaud articulated in *Theater and Its Double*—Baraka intends for this final moment of *Slave Ship* to induce the spectators' participation and compel their activism. Baraka reminds the audience through this powerful image of the unfulfilled legacy of the civil rights movement.

Source: Harry J. Elam, Jr., "Rehearsing the Revolution Onstage," in *Taking It to the Streets: The Social Protest Theater of Luis Valdez and Amiri Baraka,* University of Michigan Press, 1997, pp. 86–87, 93.

Tejumola Olaniyan

Olaniyan explores the themes of Slave Ship, *through the "origins of the present struggles for black self-fashioning."*

Slave Ship (1967), perhaps the most discussed of Baraka's plays of this period, has a significantly different orientation. It is thematically the most reflective, a deep introspective exploration of the origins of the present struggles for black self-fashioning, a genealogy of, to paraphrase Chinua Achebe, how, where, and when the rain began to beat us. Thus far more than we could say of the other plays, the audience assumed is largely black, and this assumption is woven into the very fabric of the play.

It is not a "play" as such but, more appropriately, a presentational, gigantic ritual, a pageant. It has no defined plot. Dialogue or discursive language is spare and very sparse. The series of scenes or tableaux are juxtaposed with drumming, singing, dancing, laughing, screaming, wailing, miming, and various theatrical devices: sounds of the sea, chains, and whips, smells, dramatic light shifts, and so on—atmosphere ceases to be a mere backdrop for the action but a character in its own right:

> Whole theater in darkness.... Occasional sound, like groaning, squeaking, rocking. Sea smells. Burn incense ... make a significant, almost stifling smell come up. Pee. S—t. Death. Life processes ... Eating. Those smells and cries, the slash and tear of the lash, in a total atmosfeeling, African drums like the worship of some Orisha. Obatala. Mbwanga rattles of the priests.... Rocking of the slave ship ... sounds ... of people, dropped down in the darkness, frightened, angry, mashed together in common terror.

This "historical pageant," as the playwright calls it, attempts to show its African-American audience their origin and the direction to be taken in the present. It dramatizes the ordeal of Africans from the time of capture as slaves, through the horrors of the Middle Passage, to slavery in the New World, and finally to liberation.

The contradictions arising from the historical black-white encounter still define the moving force of the action but, unlike the calculatingly crafted rhetorical and confrontational bombast of the earlier plays, *Slave Ship* simply shows the negative effects of the encounter on the victims and proceeds with its more urgent task of celebrating their courage and community, especially as these traits resist total disintegration through alien invasion to betrayal of kin. A critic, Stefan Brecht, also notes this crucial turn in Baraka and contemplates its implication:

> This play is devoted to showing the evil done (& suffered), not the evil doer. On the contrary: it neglects him. It focuses on the good, though on its destruction.... This play's principles being profoundly humanitarian, if the course of action it suggests carries the day, the outlook, even for us, i.e., for the survivors among us, is hopeful.

The play's identified task is made poignant by a series of oppositions that seem to be its basic principle of composition: the screams and wails of agony of the slaves versus the satisfied, voluminous laughter of the slavemasters: "We head West! ... (Long laughter) Black gold in the West. We got our full cargo"; courageous women killing themselves and their children in order to escape the ignominy of slavery versus the white slavemasters looking on

> *SLAVE SHIP ... IS THEMATICALLY THE MOST REFLECTIVE, A DEEP INTROSPECTIVE EXPLORATION OF THE ORIGINS OF THE PRESENT STRUGGLES FOR BLACK SELF-FASHIONING, A GENEALOGY OF, TO PARAPHRASE CHINUA ACHEBE, HOW, WHERE, AND WHEN THE RAIN BEGAN TO BEAT US."*

and laughing in blissful contentment; the slaves' degrading condition versus their intact humanity and fellow feeling; drums of ancient African warriors versus images of detestable "yassa massa" sellouts; rebellion versus betrayal; and so on.

These oppositions, generously bathed in affective music and evocative oppressive atmosphere, tug insistently on the audience's emotional chord. The brief successive "scenes" are like pages in a history book of a people under an imposed, dehumanizing condition. This condition is not static but evinces a clear, unmistakable—though many times lost and recaptured—progression, from origin to elimination. The protagonist in this movement is the people, as a collective: the characters are not only anonymous but non-individualized, and their effectiveness is shown to be most potent only in that unity. A united African-American community, we remember, is central to nationalist thought. The renegades, the "Toms," who veered away from the group, lose both ways: they are not only treated with contempt and condescension by the oppressors they ally with, but they are also the first to be consumed by their people's wrath. The play is unsparing in their condemnation:

> (... *speaking in the pseudo-intelligent patter he uses for the boss. He tries to be, in fact, assumes he is, dignified, trying to hold his shoulders straight, but only succeeds in giving his body an odd slant like a diseased coal chute*)
>
> PREACHER: Yass, understand ... the problem. And, personally, I think some agreement can be reached. We will be nonviolenk ... to the last. ...

(*Scream ... moans ... drums ... mournful death-tone.... The preacher looks, head turned just slightly, as if embarrassed, trying still to talk to the white man. Then, one of the black men, out of the darkness, comes and sits before the Tom, a wrapped-up bloody corpse of a dead burned baby as if they had just taken the body from a blown-up church, sets the corpse in front of the preacher. Preacher stops. Looks up at "person" he's Tomming before, then, with his foot, tries to push baby's body behind him, grinning, and jeffing, all the time, showing teeth, and being "dignified"*)

Central to the play then is an exploration of the dynamics of collective self-construction inscribed in the African-American experience.

At the beginning, the slaves are Africans held captive and carted away from their land. Their wailings and invocations are replete with references to spaces that had been intimate parts of their lives, that had defined and given them an identity: Shango, Obatala, Ifanami, and so on. With whips, chains, and time, *captives* are broken to submission as slaves, and there is a concomitant loss of a self-directed sense of self: "Now the same voices, as if transported in time to the slave farms, call names, English slave names" and metaphysical spaces like Luke, John, Jesus. But the slaves deny the planters' hegemony any completeness. A subversive "New-sound saxophone" by the slaves begins a new tune, drawing on aboriginal memory to forge a self-reflexive, hybrid identity: "sounds of slave ship, saxophone and drums," and "a new-old dance, Boogalooyoruba line...." The resistant character of the new subjectivity is testified to by the fact that what the new music and dance articulate are "sounds of people picking up. Like dead people rising." The play's final call is for the destruction of all enemies, black or white, and the eradication of the existing condition of oppression.

Source: Tejumola Olaniyan, "LeRoi Jones/Amiri Baraka: The Motion of History," in *Scars of Conquest/Masks of Resistance: The Invention of Cultural Identities in African, African-American, and Caribbean Drama*, Oxford University Press, 1995, pp. 82–84.

Lloyd W. Brown

In the following essay, Brown argues that the strength of the play lies in the "audio-visual impact of its materials."

Slave Ship, (1967), "a historical pageant," is one of Baraka's more successful experiments in ritual drama. The plot is minimal. It consists of images, dances, and pantomime together with sporadic dialogue; all is designed to dramatize the physical and psychic experiences of slavery from the holds of the slave ships to contemporary American society. The play's real strength lies in the audiovisual impact of its materials. Much of the action takes place in darkness or half-light. This suggests the hold of a slave ship, and the relative lack of lighting accentuates the variety of sounds upon which Baraka builds his themes and his dramatic effect—African drums, humming of the slaves, cries of children and their mothers, shouts of slave drivers, and cracking sounds of the slaver master's whip.

The succession of audiovisual forms is integral to the pattern of ritual upon which Baraka bases his historical pageant. The sights and sounds of the slave ship remain throughout, but they alternate from time to time with other forms which depict successive stages of black American history—the plantation of the slaveholder, the nonviolent civil rights movement, and the black nationalist movement. History itself becomes a succession of rituals, particularly the ritual of suffering which gives way after repeated cycles to the new rituals of racial assertion and cultural awakening. The music which dominates the play is integral to the ritualistic pageantry of history. At first the main sounds are those of the African drum, accentuating the fresh African memories of the new slaves. Then as the plot moves toward the contemporary period the sounds of the African drum are gradually integrated with the musical forms that evolved in black American history since slavery. And this musical progression culminates in the blues and jazz idioms both as forms of protest and as the celebration of black nationalism. By a similar token the humming of the slaves in the holds of the slave ships gradually gives way to the sounds of protest and eventual triumph.

But throughout all of this the audience is always in touch with the persistent sounds and sights of the slave ship itself, for this is the setting that remains for the duration of the play, and the subsequent historical epochs are actually superimposed upon it in sequence. The historical pageant is, therefore, both progressive in direction (moving from slavery to the black nationalism of the 1970s) and circular (reinforcing a sense of the moral and social continuities of the society: the slavery of the past exerts a powerful influence on the circumstances of the present). Moreover, the persistence of the slave ship images has the effect of defining history itself as movements (progressive and cyclical) through time. Similarly the ritualistic forms of the play (dance, chant, and pantomime) are each a microcosm of the historical process: each synthesizes the materials inherited from a previous generation with the experiences of the contemporary period. And by extension this kind of synthesis characterizes the play as a whole. As a pageant that combines past and present experiences, traditional forms and new materials, it reenacts the historical process as Baraka defines it.

Source: Lloyd W. Brown, "Drama," in *Amiri Baraka,* Twayne Publishers, 1980, pp. 161–62.

SOURCES

Anadolu-Okur, Nilgun, *Contemporary African-American Theater,* Garland, 1997, pp. 94, 97–9.

Benston, Kimberly W., ed., "Introduction" to *Imamu Amiri Baraka (LeRoi Jones): A Collection of Critical Essays,* Prentice-Hall, 1978, pp. 1, 14.

———, "Vision and Form in Slave Ship," in *Imamu Amiri Baraka (LeRoi Jones): A Collection of Critical Essays,* edited by Kimberly W. Benston, Prentice-Hall, 1978, pp. 174–176, 178–81.

Elam, Harry J., Jr., *Taking It to the Streets: The Social Protest Theater of Luis Valdez and Amiri Baraka,* University of Michigan Press, 1997, pp. 74, 77, 86–88, 93–4.

Floyd, Gaffney, "Amiri Baraka," in *Dictionary of Literary Biography,* Vol. 38, edited by Thadius M. Davis, Gale, 1985, pp. 6, 18.

Harris, William J., ed., in collaboration with Amiri Baraka, *The LeRoi Jones/Amiri Baraka Reader,* Thunder's Mouth Press, 1991, p. xvii.

Olaniyan, Tejumola, *Scars of Conquest/Masks of Resistance,* Oxford University Press, 1995, pp. 82–84.

FURTHER READING

Anadolu-Okur, Nilgun, *Contemporary African-American Theater: Afrocentricity in the Works of Larry Neal, Amiri Baraka, and Charles Fuller,* Garland Publishing, 1997.
   This text is an analysis of the impact of three important African-American playwrights in the historical context of Black Theater movements.

Baraka, Amiri, ed., *Confirmation: An Anthology of African-American Women,* Morrow, 1983.
   This book is seen as a collection of important writings by African-American women.

———, *Eulogies,* Marsilio Publishers, 1996.
   This work is a collection of eulogies given by Baraka for the funerals of many famous African-American writers, musicians, and intellectuals, including Malcolm X, John Coltrane, James Baldwin, Miles Davis, and Toni Cade Bambara.

Baraka, Amiri, and Larry Neal, eds., *Black Fire: An Anthology of Afro-American Writing,* Morrow, 1968.
   Baraka is a contributor as well as editor of this landmark anthology in African-American literary history.

Elam, Harry J., Jr., *Taking It to the Streets: The Social Protest Theater of Luis Valdez and Amiri Baraka,* University of Michigan Press, 1997.
   Elam's book provides an interesting comparative analysis of the political impact of dramatic productions by Amiri Baraka and Luis Valdez.

Olaniyan, Tejumola, *Scars of Conquest/Masks of Resistance: The Invention of Cultural Identities in African, African-American, and Caribbean Drama,* Oxford University Press, 1995.
   Olaniyan's book is a discussion of dramatic performances as political acts of forging "cultural identity" through artistic production.

Reilly, Charlie, ed., *Conversations with Amiri Baraka,* University of Mississippi Press, 1994.
   This work is a collection of previously published interviews with Baraka by various writers.

> "... THE RITUALISTIC FORMS OF THE PLAY (DANCE, CHANT, AND PANTOMIME) ARE EACH A MICROCOSM OF THE HISTORICAL PROCESS: EACH SYNTHESIZES THE MATERIALS INHERITED FROM A PREVIOUS GENERATION WITH THE EXPERIENCES OF THE CONTEMPORARY PERIOD."

The Sleep of Reason

ANTONIO BUERO VALLEJO

1970

The Sleep of Reason (*El sueno de la razon*) was first performed in 1970 and remains the principal work by which Antonio Buero Vallejo is known in the United States. Buero Vallejo's play is just one of many in his works devoted to criticizing Spain's long struggle to institute increased freedoms of speech and political action. *The Sleep of Reason* takes place in the Spain of 1823, just after the French invaded Spain to put the Spanish king, Ferdinand VII, back on the throne (the monarchy was thrown out of power for a three-year period called the Liberal Triennium), and focuses on the king's obsession to punish those he thinks oppose and threaten him. One man stands out: former painter to the king and one of the world's great painters, Francisco Goya (1746–1828). Not only is Goya a Liberal, a member of the Spanish faction opposed to unlimited powers of church and crown, but he has recently offended the king in a letter intercepted in the mail.

From one side *The Sleep of Reason* is a study in imperial repression. But more importantly, the work explores the effects of repression, threat, and intimidation on individuals, most importantly in this case, on Goya. The painter lives in fear of the political consequences of his affiliations, and as a direct or indirect result, exhibits a number of symptoms—from increased insecurity accompanying diminished sexuality, to auditory and visual hallucinations. Buero Vallejo's play is a timeless case study situated in political and psychological history.

Reflecting this depiction of both outer political and inner psychological states is the most memorable feature of *The Sleep of Reason:* the multimedia staging called for by the author. Like most plays it consists of actors in costume and props. But more impressively, the play is staged against the backdrop of large projections of Goya's puzzling and threatening Black Paintings (c.1820–1823), the amplified sounds of Goya's heartbeats and hallucinations, and the live fantasia of sinister dream figures dressed in grotesque costume. The combination of these effects as early as 1970 led one critic to call *The Sleep of Reason* the first work of ''total theater'' by a Spanish author.

AUTHOR BIOGRAPHY

Antonio Buero Vallejo was born September 29, 1916, in Guadalajara, Spain, just east of Madrid. Buero Vallejo's father, a military engineer, owned a sizable collection of plays and drama journals. These inspired the young Buero Vallejo to stage his own plays in which he mimicked imaginary battles dressed, for example, as D'Artagnan of Alexandre Dumas' *Three Musketeers* (1844), sang old ballads, and read and recited dialogue. Buero Vallejo and his friends progressed into constructing elaborate sets of complete towns with wooden boxes as houses and ''actors'' made of cardboard. Shifting the props, they acted out legends of the wild west, stories of outer space travel, or fairy tales. But young Buero Vallejo wanted to be a painter, partially from an intense interest in the great Spanish painter, Diego Velazquez (1599–1660). At eighteen, Buero Vallejo enrolled in Madrid's San Fernando School of Fine Arts. When the Spanish Civil War erupted in 1936, Buero Vallejo ceased study to enlist with the Loyalists as a medic. At the war's end, in 1939, he was sentenced to death but the sentence was commuted, then reduced to six years. At twenty-nine, in 1946, Buero Vallejo was freed. He made a living, though meager, selling his paintings, but eventually switched to theater. By 1949, he had written several plays and had won two important awards. His one-act play *The Words in the Sand* won the Friends of the Quinteros Award and his *Story of a Stairway* won the prestigious Lope de Vega Prize. These awards and the production of his work established Buero Vallejo as the first socially conscious dramatist since the Spanish Civil War.

Buero Vallejo's success exposed him to the hostility and censorship of critics aligned with the Fascist government of Francisco Franco. Buero Vallejo experienced difficulty in getting some of his plays by the censors, especially those with political themes. Examples of such plays include *Adventure in Grey,* an allegory of the Spanish Civil War written around 1949 but not performed until 1963, and a history of police torture, *The Double Case History of Doctor Valmy,* which, though performed in England, was not performed or published in Spain until 1970. Buero Vallejo's trouble with censors dogged him, even though his target was the Spain of over one hundred years ago.

Buero Vallejo has received numerous prizes, among them the Maria Rolland Prize (1956, 1958, 1960), Nacional de Teatro Prize (1957, 1958, 1959, 1980), Fundacion March prize (1959), Critica de Barcelona Prize (1960), El Espectador y la Critica prize (1967, 1970, 1974, 1977, 1981, 1984, 1986), Leopoldo Cano Prize (1968, 1972, 1974, 1975, 1977), Mayte Prize (1974), Cervantes prize (1986), Medalla de Oro al Merito en las Bellas Artes (1993), and the Nacional de las Letras Prize (1996). One of Buero Vallejo's most recent plays, *Mission to the Deserted Town,* had its premiere at Madrid's Teatro Espanol in October, 1999. The play concerns the rescue of an El Greco painting during the Spanish Civil War. In January 1999 there was a major revival of his 1974 play, *The Foundation,* the production having toured as far as Buenos Aires. Buero Vallejo died on April 29, 2000, in Madrid, Spain, of a stroke.

PLOT SUMMARY

Act I

It is December 1823 and Spain's King Ferdinand VII is in Madrid. Ferdinand discusses past, present, and future with his advisor, Francisco Tadeo Calomarde. Ferdinand has just been restored to the throne with help from the French, and he and Calomarde discuss what to do with his political enemies, the Liberals. Of special note is the letter that the king's men have intercepted. It is from Francisco Goya to a friend. The letter contains words against Ferdinand, and for this Calomarde wants Goya hanged. Ferdinand appears calm and instructs Calomarde to arrange two meetings: first, with the commander-general of the Royal Volunteers, the king's army/police; second, with Don Jose

Antonio Buero-Vallejo

Duaso y Latre, a priest and chaplain to the king. Suspense is aroused as a result of Ferdinand's order to Calomarde not to allow Father Duaso and the commander-general to see each other.

Scene two opens at the home of Goya, formerly the king's painter. Goya lives with his mistress/housekeeper, Leocadia Zorilla Weiss, who is legally married to someone else, but now estranged. Because Goya is deaf, he speaks to Leocadia in sign language, who signs back. Goya is, for unknown reasons, worried about his daughter and chastises Leocadia for allowing her to go out. When Goya goes out to look for Mariquita, Eugenio Arrieta, Goya's friend and physician, enters and discusses the old painter alone with Leocadia. She tells Arrieta that Goya is insane. His paintings, says Leocadia, are a sure sign. In one painting, she thinks she is the model for a woman beheading a man (*Judith and Holofernes*), and is upset at the obscenity of another in which a man masturbates while two women look on (*The Busybodies*). Dr. Arrieta questions Leocadia, a woman less than half Goya's age, about her and Goya's sex life. Arrieta learns that Goya—now seventy-six years old—formerly had a robust sex drive that is now diminished. Arrieta finds that Leocadia also believes Goya crazy because he is unafraid of persecution by King Ferdinand. Leocadia says with all the king's banishments, whippings, and executions of Liberals (those wanting to rein in the monarchy), Goya, a Liberal, should be fearful and escape. That he refuses indicates madness. When Goya enters and sees the doctor, Goya confirms he is unafraid, even though he has just seen—having just returned from seeking his daughter—the Royal Volunteers near the house. Goya then talks to Arrieta about his paintings. Goya remarks that he was formerly brought before the Inquisition (1478–1834), the infamous Catholic court, to account for painting a nude. Goya then confides he is hearing things and wonders if it means that his hearing is on the mend (throughout the play, Goya has auditory hallucinations heard by the audience over a sound system, but unheard by the characters). The doctor replies that Goya's hearing is not returning, that Goya is indeed, irrevocably deaf. Leocadia now returns with news the king has decreed new repressive measures threatening Liberals and other enemies of the crown, but she only tells Arrieta. Then Goya tells the doctor he has seen flying men who Goya hopes will "put an end to all the cruelties in the world." Arrieta advises Goya to escape but Goya says he must remain. The scene ends with Leocadia urging Goya to flee Spain.

Scene three opens in Goya's home with Leocadia speaking with Gumersinda Goicoechea, Goya's daughter-in-law. Gumersinda tells Leocadia she refuses to hide Goya from Ferdinand. When Gumersinda leaves, Goya tells Leocadia that he believes she is having an affair with a Royal Volunteer stationed near the estate. She denies it. Father Duaso arrives, sent by Ferdinand. There is some tension between Arrieta (who has also entered) and Duaso, who are, politically, on opposite sides. Goya now enters with news that someone has painted a threatening cross and written "heretic" on the door of his house. Duaso indicates that this kind of harassment will stop if Goya to apologizes to Ferdinand. Goya refuses. As Duaso leaves, a rock, with a threatening note attached, breaks through a window. Still, Goya refuses to leave.

Act II

The king is speaking to Father Duaso, who is reporting on his trip to Goya's. Duaso argues for Goya's safety, but Ferdinand is far more interested in Goya's submission. Though Ferdinand will not actively demand it, he does seem pleased that Goya feels somewhat threatened. Ferdinand affirms he will not rescind the decree making an assault against the property of Liberals pardonable for the reason that he wants to keep the Liberals afraid. Duaso is instructed to visit Goya again on December 23, but told not to arrive before 8:00. Ferdinand does not say why.

Goya is alone but listening to the voices in his head, especially that of his daughter, Mariquita. Mariquita tells him to look for the button from a Royal Volunteer's uniform amongst Leocadia's belongings. Mariquita fills Goya with suspicions of Leocadia having an affair. When Leocadia enters, Goya reveals his suspicion and shows her a button from an officer's uniform. She denies any affair, but says an officer did give it to her outside the house and promised to return to get it. Goya doubts Leocadia's story. Arrieta interrupts them and Leocadia exits. Goya tells Arrieta there have been no more threats since Arrieta last visited (Goya wonders to himself if Leocadia's affair has kept the threats away). Goya is also worried that the letter he sent has not been answered. By scene's end, Goya finally receives a letter from his friend asking why Goya has not written. Goya suddenly realizes his letter has been intercepted.

On December 23 at Father Duaso's, the father and Doctor Arrieta are conferring before going to Goya's. Arrieta says that Goya's letter was intercepted and that he wants Duaso to convince Goya he is in mortal danger. Arrieta knows that the king has told Duaso not to leave before 8:00 but convinces Duaso that this indicates Goya could be in danger. Duaso agrees and both leave to try and save Goya.

At his home, Goya is dreaming. In his dream, he hears the voices of demons, part animal, part human (the audience is able to see them) accusing Goya of crimes and tormenting him. When he awakes, he hears beating at the door. Five Royal Volunteers have broken in. They tie Goya in a chair and place him on mock trial. Then they beat him. After, the sergeant rapes Leocadia, with Goya a helpless witness. When the Volunteers leave, Goya accuses Leocadia of having collaborated with the Volunteers. Goya threatens to shoot her, but comes to realize his jealousy has been a sign of his own weakness. As Leocadia ushers him out, Gumersinda enters and Goya (showing he has come to his senses) asks her for asylum. She refuses, saying it will put her family in danger. Angry, he slaps her. Then, as with Leocadia, Goya blames himself, realizing his reason has been sleeping. Duaso and Arrieta now enter too late to save Goya and Leocadia. To make up for what he has done, Duaso promises to provide Goya with temporary asylum until Goya can escape to France.

CHARACTERS

Eugenio Arrieta

Eugenio Arrieta is Francisco de Goya's friend and physician. In Marion Peter Holt's translation of *The Sleep of Reason,* Buero Vallejo describes Arrieta as "between fifty-five and sixty. He is vigorous but gaunt. His blond hair is turning gray; he hides his incipient baldness by combing his hair forward; he has a large cranium and the sharp features of an ascetic; he has a gentle and melancholy look." Arrieta is Goya's loyal friend, risking his safety by associating with Goya, and by urging Father Duaso, the king's chaplain, to provide asylum for Goya. Arrieta, though verbally careful, shows dissatisfaction with Ferdinand's repressive practices, especially censorship.

Francisco de Goya

Francisco Goya (1746–1828) (also called Francho) is one of the world's great painters and the play's main character. Depicted as a genius beyond the understanding of those around him, Goya is thought by his mistress, Leocadia, to be going mad: Goya imagines voices and sounds, believes in messianic flying men, imagines Leocadia to be having an affair with a soldier, refuses to believe he in danger from the king, and paints what Leocadia thinks of as horrid and obscene paintings. Goya is, however, under multiple pressures: he is aging and losing confidence in his once robust sexuality, has been isolated from friends, family, and the palace, and is now concerned the king might endanger him. This point in Goya's life marks the end of a three-year project of fourteen paintings—now called the Black Paintings—on the walls of two rooms of his home. Their subject matter concerns—depending on the interpretation one reads—either fear or courage in the face of threat. At different times during the course of the play, one, two, or three paintings are projected onstage so as to be seen by the audience. They serve as both backdrop to the action and conversational fodder for the characters. As for Goya, Buero Vallejo's characterization of him is not altogether praiseworthy. Though Goya is under intense pressures, he places his associates in danger by arrogantly believing that the king would not dare harm him, the "great Goya." When proved wrong,

Goya, to his credit, finally realizes his mistake and reforms his actions.

Don Jose Duaso y Latre

Father Duaso is King Ferdinand's recently hired chaplain in charge of censoring publications. Characteristic of a new employee, Duaso is naïve, unsuspecting of the king's will to vengeance. Duaso, though politically opposed to Goya, is a long-lasting acquaintance, and so does not want Goya harmed by Ferdinand. On assignment from the king, Duaso tries to convince Goya to prostrate himself before Ferdinand and come back to work as the king's painter. Goya refuses, and Duaso realizes too late that Goya, as a result of his defiance, is in mortal danger from the king. Duaso agrees to provide asylum for Goya, asks the king to forgive the painter, and gives him leave to go to France. Though not part of the play, the real-life Duaso was successful.

Ferdinand VII

Ferdinand is Spain's repressive king, a figure more cunningly despicable than Calomarde. Thanks to the French, Ferdinand has recently been reinstated to the throne after three years of exile. Now he is out to revenge himself on Liberals, Masons, Jews, and others who had opposed his absolute authority. Ferdinand wants Goya, not only because Goya is a defiant Liberal who once served him, but because Goya has insulted him in an intercepted letter. The king concocts a plan to make Goya pay: Ferdinand sends soldiers to Goya's home, to beat and humiliate him, and then rape Goya's mistress, Leocadia. Ferdinand's plan is mostly successful: Goya decides to apologize to the king and seek the king's permission to leave Spain. However, it is not known whether Goya remained defiant by refusing to once again serve the king as court painter.

Francho

See Francisco de Goya

Gumersinda Goicoechea

Gumersinda is Goya's daughter-in-law, married to Goya's only surviving child. Not fond of Goya (she calls him Leocadia's "master"), she does not want to offer him asylum, nor bring her children to see him. Leocadia believes Gumersinda and Goya's son (her husband) want Goya to die so they can inherit his estate. While Buero Vallejo does not reveal whether this is true, his depiction of Gumersinda makes it quite possible.

Mariquita

See María Weiss

Francisco Tadeo Calomarde

Calomarde is the king's advisor. He wants Goya hanged for insults to the king found in a letter to Goya's friend. Buero Vallejo describes Calomarde: "He appears to be fifty and is also dressed in dark colors. His hair tousled over a smooth forehead; two shining little eyes gleam in his sheep-like features." The description is of an evil and fawning man, a sheepish sycophant to a lion king, but ruthless to anyone opposing the king.

Various Dream Figures

These are various animal and carnival figures of Goya's dream, tormenting him with a trial and beatings. They consist of a bat figure, a cat figure, a horned figure, and two pig figures. They are both shadows of Goya's thoughts and "foreshadows" of the break-in by the Royal Volunteers.

Volunteers of the Royal Army

The sergeant of the Volunteers gave Leocadia a metal button saying he would return to get it. When Goya finds it amongst Leocadia's things, he believes she is having an affair with him. Near the end of the play, the sergeant and four soldiers break into Goya's home on orders from Ferdinand. They loot and break up the house, humiliate Goya by subjecting him to a mock trial, beat him, and then rape Leocadia. Before leaving, the sergeant threatens Goya with a return visit.

María Weiss

The Voice of María (also known as Mariquita) is one of Leocadia's two children. She appears as a disembodied voice that makes Goya paranoid. Mariquita's voice urges Goya to suspect Leocadia of an affair with a soldier. Mariquita was born after Goya became deaf. Partially because he regrets never having heard her voice, he hallucinates it (Goya and his wife, Josefa Bayeu, probably had seven children but only one survived). It is usually believed that Mariquita was the issue of Leocadia and Goya.

Leocadia Zorrilla Weiss

Leocadia is Goya's mistress and housekeeper. She is estranged from her husband but takes care of the two children, María and Guillermo. María is now thought to have been Goya's child. Leocadia and Goya are having problems because he refuses to believe the king seeks vengeance on him. Leocadia is sure of it, and is proved painfully right when Ferdinand sends his men to humiliate her and Goya. Goya suspects Leocadia of having an affair with a soldier, probably because his imagination is stirred up by loss of his sexual appetite and its accompanying insecurities. Leocadia is the play's smartest character: she is the only one who fears the king's wrath and power completely. Her perspicacity is, however, fruitless since her loyalty to Goya keeps her with him and makes her a victim of rape by a sergeant of the Royal Volunteers.

THEMES

Repression and Fear

The characters of *The Sleep of Reason* can be divided into two categories: repressors and the repressed. The repressors are both real and unreal. The real repressors are King Ferdinand VII, Calomarde, and the soldiers of the Royal Volunteers. They are engaged in the same project: intimidation of the Spanish populace to force political compliance. Methods of intimidation include banishments, beatings, and executions. While Calomarde is clearly evil in machination, the soldiers are evil in practice. Calomarde wants Goya hanged for insulting the king in a private letter to a friend and the soldiers break in and loot Goya's home, beat and humiliate him, and rape Goya's mistress. The king's depravity is far more subtle, primarily because others execute his orders while he speaks quietly and embroiders flowers (somewhat like the archenemy stroking a white cat in a James Bond film). Ferdinand masterminds the plan to teach Goya fear and humility, sends the soldiers to dress Goya in the costume of the "penitents" on trial before the Inquisition, and then subject him and Leocadia to torment.

The unreal repressors appear in Goya's dream as animal figures subjecting a sleeping Goya to humiliations nearly identical with those suffered at the hands of the soldiers. These dream figures (bat, cat, horned figure, and two pigs) are five, the same number as the Royal Volunteers. The bat-man is a composite figure combining the Inquisitional judge and the sergeant of the Royal Volunteers; the cat figure, a composite figure of Leocadia and Calomarde; the horned figure represents both death and the king; and the two pigs are Royal Volunteers. The only major difference between dream and real-

TOPICS FOR FURTHER STUDY

- Compare and contrast two historical periods: the period just after Ferdinand's restoration to the Spanish throne in 1823, and the time of Franco's takeover of Spain after its civil war (1936–1939). Then, investigate the late sixties in Spain for events that could have immediately led to Buero writing *The Sleep of Reason*.

- Study the history of Spain from the 1800s to the present. Focus on attempts to limit the power of church and crown in order to establish greater freedoms and increased political input. Present your findings as a "Democracy Chronology" or "Democracy Timeline."

- After studying the Black Paintings, provide reasons for their projection at particular times in *The Sleep of Reason*. Present these findings to your class showing the paintings as either slides or plates from books.

- Provide your class with a history of twentieth-century Spanish theater up to *The Sleep of Reason*. Supplement your paper with a timeline copied on a transparency for display on an overhead projector.

ity is Leocadia: in Goya's dream, transmuted by his suspicious nature, she is a repressor, but in the rape scene, she is a victim.

The repressed figures are Goya, Leocadia, Gumersinda, and Doctor Arrieta. Of these Gumersinda is the most difficult with whom to sympathize—her actions appear motivated by selfishness. Goya also is not entirely sympathetic, since his arrogance is the cause of Leocadia's rape and the threatening crucifix painted on Arrieta's door.

Only one figure is left—Father Duaso. He is a more complex person because he operates on the side of the repressors, but retains sympathy with the victimized. The reason Duaso teeters between repressor and repressed is largely the product of his naivete: Duaso cannot imagine the king would take such extreme measures to subdue Goya, an innocent, old man that no longer represents an important threat. By the time Duaso realizes his mistake, he has himself become a repressor.

Sanity versus Insanity

Was Goya insane? Leocadia plainly thinks so. She calls Goya's *The Busybodies* obscene since it pictures a masturbator; *Judith and Holofernes* paranoid (since she thinks it depicts her as Judith cutting off the head of Goya as Holofernes); lastly, she claims Goya told her that she was the "witch" in *Asmodea*. She also knows that Goya hears voices. Her strongest reason for thinking Goya insane is his fearlessness of the king's persecution. Buero Vallejo stands behind most of Leocadia's claims. In the first case, she knows Goya gratifies himself, though it is not clear whether Leocadia thinks masturbation, or its depiction, is obscene. The second related point of debate is whether the obscenity (wherever it lies) indicates insanity. Buero Vallejo leaves this to readers. Next, Leocadia's claim that she is Judith is borne out in Goya's dream where she nearly beheads him with a knife. And finally, Goya does call Leocadia a witch, though his comment does not refer to *Asmodea*. As to hearing voices there is little doubt, since Goya tells Arrieta he hears them. The most damning of Leocadia's claims about Goya's madness—that he is not afraid when he should be—is proven painfully true. Still, do these lapses of judgment prove him foolish or insane?

Apart from Leocadia's judgments, other factors might lead readers to think Goya insane. He believes he has seen flying men but cannot decide whether they will be good or evil when they intervene in human affairs, as he assumes they will. Is this visionary, Goya seeing into a future when humans fly, or delusional, a product of messianic hope? Finally, there exists the issue of Goya's paranoia about Leocadia having an affair. Because he has found the sergeant's button, Goya's suspicion is not completely unfounded. But after the soldiers rape Leocadia and beat and humiliate him, Goya persists in his paranoia believing she has invited the soldiers in. If this is madness, is it temporary since he soon realizes his mistake? And one final question: If none of these—obscenity, auditory and visual hallucinations, foolish arrogance, and severe paranoia—in and of themselves bespeak insanity, what about all of them combined? By leaving the question unanswered, Buero Vallejo might be indicating that madness is not the most important issue.

STYLE

Setting

The Sleep of Reason takes place in Madrid during the month of December 1823, ending December 23. There are three locales in the play: the king's palace in Madrid, Goya's estate (quinta del sordo, house of the deaf), and Father Duaso's quarters in Madrid. Goya's estate and the king's palace are located across the Manzanares River from each other, close enough to be seen through a spyglass. All scenes take place inside.

Literary Devices

Foreshadowing is the most prominent device. Its most memorable employment is in Goya's dream, when animal monsters subject him to torture, trial, and humiliation. This is just before Goya wakes up and is subjected to the same treatment by soldiers of the Royal Volunteers. Allegory is another device: the events of Spain in 1823 refer to Franco's Spain (1939–70) and, partially, to Buero Vallejo's own story when he was jailed after the Spanish Civil War (1936–39). Symbolism and allegory abound in Goya's Black Paintings, complex and opaque enough to occupy the contents of numerous books and studies. The play is a combination of modes: historical and realistic because it depicts primarily real events and real people, but also fantastic since it indicates the inner state of the painter, his auditory hallucinations, his amplified heartbeats, and the terrifying phantasmagoria of his dreams.

Dialogue

The play has no soliloquies and almost all dialogue is between two people: Ferdinand and Caloverde, Goya and Leocadia, Leocadia and Gumersinda, Duaso and Arrieta, and so on. The dialogue's most unusual feature is that much is signed, Goya being deaf. It is, however, characters speaking to Goya who use it, and rarely Goya himself, since he is deaf but not mute. The other prominent aspect of the dialogue is that the disembodied voices are of two sorts: those of real persons like Mariquita, or of males and females from the paintings. These are heard by Goya and no one else onstage.

Set and Sound

Set and sound are the most distinctive aspect of Buero Vallejo's multimedia production. Not only are there sets with props and costumed characters, but Goya's paintings are projected onstage, timed to coincide with applicable dialogue or events. The paintings are employed as objects for characters' discussion, or as "silent" accompaniment to happenings on stage. While the play has no music, there is plenty of projected sound: not only characters' lines, but a profusion of words from disembodied voices and sounds thrown into the auditorium. These are primarily Goya's auditory hallucinations and heartbeats. One final aspect of the sound is its absence: when characters sign, only traces of speech are seen. Such multimedia aspects make Buero Vallejo's play larger than the stage, as large as the theater.

Movement

Movement is not a large part of this play except when Goya and Leocadia are violated by the five soldiers of the Royal Volunteers and shortly thereafter when Goya and Leocadia quarrel. Movement mostly arises in terms of successive paintings projected onstage, and sign language performed primarily by Leocadia, Arrieta, and Gumersinda.

HISTORICAL CONTEXT

The victor of the Spanish Civil War (1936–39)—aided by Hitler's Germany and Mussolini's Italy—was the far Right Nationalist general, Francisco Franco. Franco defeated the leftist-radical Republican Popular Front which had, six months before the war, gained power in legal elections. Franco's rule (1939–75) was characterized in the early years by repressive military tribunals, political purges, suppression of regional languages and cultures, censorship (which affected some of Buero Vallejo's plays), and economic woe for most of the populace. Franco imprisoned former Republican, also known as Loyalist, soldiers in camps where many were starved while they awaited court martial. Members of labor syndicates and the Popular Front were also threatened with trials. The Popular Front originated in 1935 with Stalin, who advocated a strategy of "popular front" alliances between socialists and communists throughout the world to fight fascism, especially Franco. As was the case in Ferdinand's Spain, Freemasonry was considered one of the most heinous crimes. An estimated one million people went to prison. Thousands were condemned to death and executed. Mussolini's son-in-law, Count Ciano, visited Spain in the summer of 1939 and reported that 200 to 250 executions took place every day in Madrid, 150 in Barcelona, 80 in Seville. It is estimated that approximately 200,000 people were executed from 1939 to 1941, when state killings started tapering off. Many of the jailed were freed after hard labor ruined their health or their place in civil society was destroyed. Buero Vallejo, himself, had been a medic with the Popular Front Republicans and was imprisoned after the war for six years. During his imprisonment, Spain entered World War II, sending 40,000 troops to fight with the Axis powers (Germany, Italy, Japan) against the Allies (Britain, France, the Soviet Union, the United States). When the war began going badly for Axis, Spain declared its neutrality, but sent raw materials to the Allies. As a result, Spain escaped sanctions by the Allies after the war.

Franco's hold on power, while successful, was not without opposition from monarchists led by Don Juan, heir of Alfonso XIII, king of Spain (1886–1931), and from communist guerilla attacks. During this period, the Catholic Church controlled Spain's education and the country existed as an autarky (self-sufficient state) out of choice and because it was excluded from the United Nations until 1955. In 1953, an agreement establishing four United States military bases in Spain supplied Franco with the money to hold down oppositional elements. A concordat with the Pope gave Franco added respectability.

Franco played his allies—the Falange (the ruling party), monarchists, and Catholics—one against the other in order to promote those he knew were loyal to him and to keep rightist factions in balance. From the left, political opposition mounted from student protests and workers, and from unsuccessful attempts by the Communist Party of Spain to form a united front against Franco. Meanwhile, Spain suffered from inflation, a growing deficit, and workers' strikes. Devaluation of European currencies brought about the Stabilization Plan (1959), which forced Franco to abandon the economic nationalism, protectionism, and state intervention characteristic of autarky. The opening of Spain to international trade and a subsequent encouragement of private enterprise in 1963 brought Spain out of economic doldrums. Tourism, foreign investment, and wages increased. The mass migration from country to city resulted in a dramatic drop—from 42 percent in 1960 to 20 percent in 1976—in the agricultural workforce. Spain was becoming industrialized. But the only substantial cultural result of industrialization and wealth was the Press Law (1966), enabling greater freedom of the press. Meanwhile, workers kept up the pressure, forming their

COMPARE & CONTRAST

- **1823:** Goya finishes his fourteen Black Paintings on the walls of his home, quinta del sordo, in Madrid.

  1969: Vito Acconci's *Conversion* ushers in "body art" with an attempt to conceal his body's masculinity, partially by burning the hair off his body and hiding his genitals.

  1970: Jose Gudiol publishes his four volume work, *Goya: 1746–1828, Biografia, estudio analitico y catalogo de sus pinturas*, in Barcelona.

  Today: All the Black Paintings—now existing as oil on canvas—have been restored and hang in Madrid's Prado Museum.

- **1823:** After the French enter Spain to restore Ferdinand VII to the Spanish throne, Major Rafael de Riego, who in 1820 had initiated a Liberal constitutional revolution against the monarchy, is publicly humiliated and then executed for treason on November 7. In addition, Ferdinand begins intense repression of Liberals.

  1969: Following intensifying protests over the government's treatment of political prisoners and the suspicious death of a student in police custody, Spain's dictator, Francisco Franco, suspends civil liberties for three months. Freedom of expression and assembly, the right to choose one's residence, immunity from search and seizure of private homes without a warrant, and the right to have charges brought within seventy-two hours of arrests are all abrogated. Professors and students are targeted for jailing and deportation. About 700 people are imprisoned.

  Today: Spain is a parliamentary democracy with universal suffrage.

- **1823:** The Catholic Church, in collaboration with King Ferdinand VII, gains renewed control over Spain.

  1970s: The Church and Franco's government begin a separation of church and state.

  Today: Though Spain is ninety-nine-percent Roman Catholic, church and state have become entirely separate.

---

own organizations—particularly Workers Commissions—to negotiate claims of unfair pay and plan strikes. Workers even began to get sympathy from certain groups within the Church, particularly younger priests.

Throughout Spain, regional nationalisms proved intractable. Most important was Basque nationalism in northern Spain, which also began to gain the sympathy of the clergy. With the Burgos trials of members of the ETA (from the Basque, "Basque Homeland and Liberty"—the combat wing of the Basque party) for terrorism in 1970, Franco's government found itself discredited abroad. In the 1960s, new problems arose over Franco's successor. Franco wanted Juan Carlos to be instated as king and head of state but this did not happen. In June 1973, Luis Carrero Blanco, another of Franco's men, was named head of state. By December, Blanco was dead, assassinated by the ETA. Another premier, Carlos Arias Navarro, succeeded him as the first civilian ruler since the Spanish Civil War. Franco died November 20, 1975, and was succeeded by King Juan Carlos I. Because of Juan Carlos, Spain actively moved toward increased internationalization and liberalization to the point where, today, Spain has become a member of the European Economic Community.

CRITICAL OVERVIEW

As multifaceted and multilayered as Buero Vallejo's play is the history of its critical reception. Unlike controversies surrounding some plays, *The Sleep of Reason* does not fire controversy, but research and analysis. Shortly after *The Sleep of Reason* first appeared in 1970, Ricardo Domenech, in "Notas sobre *El sueno de la razon*," points out that the epoch of civil discord under Ferdinand VII resembles the period during and immediately following the Spanish Civil War; the play is therefore both historical and contemporary. Domenech also draws parallels between Ferdinand and Goya: Ferdinand embroiders and Goya paints, and both use spyglasses to view each other across the Manzanares River running through Madrid. In the same year, Juan Emilio Aragones, in "Goya, pintor baturro y liberal," calls the work the first spectacle of "total theater" by a Spanish author. "Total" refers to the play's use of audio and visual projections, and the depiction of Goya's inner and outer life. In "*El sueno de la razon* de Antonio Buero Vallejo," Angel Fernandez-Santos notices that the play contains elements of each of three major forms of contemporary theater—participation, distancing, and the absurd—all of them combined in satiric and macabre scenes like the dispute between Leocadia and Gumersinda. In 1970, John Kronik points out that Goya's criticism of a reality which does not correspond to ideals is the result not of hate, but of love. Two years later, in a more lengthy analysis of *The Sleep of Reason,* Robert B. Nicholas continues the observations of Domenech on the parallels between Ferdinand and Goya. Nicholas views both characters as dominated by fear. John Dowling subsequently picks up on Nicholas's motif of fear but places it in the black paintings in which terror and irrationality are combined.

The most important text in English on Buero Vallejo's life and works is Martha Halsey's *Antonio Buero Vallejo*. She observes a thread running through Buero Vallejo's work until the early seventies: "In *The Sleep of Reason,* as in the preceding two plays [*A Dreamer for a People* and *Las Meninas*], Buero Vallejo dramatizes certain negative moments in Spain's history to illustrate problems whose essence and reality are still present today and to point out the need for tolerance and intelligence. In these plays, no less than in *Story of a Stairway, Today's a Holiday,* and *The Cards Face Down,* we see the tragedy of present-day Spain." Lastly, in the introduction to Buero Vallejo's *Three Plays: The Sleep of Reason, The Foundation, and In the Burning Darkness,* Marion Peter Holt writes that "Buero Vallejo's Goya is a visionary. Not only is he an artist of genius but he sees beyond the present reality to a more enlightened future, though his associates view his musings on benevolent flying men as another manifestation of dementia." Holt sums up *The Sleep of Reason* this way: "no modern work for the stage has dealt more compellingly with the effects of terror and intimidation on the creative mind in a repressive society."

CRITICISM

Chris Semansky

Semansky teaches literature and writing at Portland Community College. In the following essay, he discusses the genesis of Goya's engraving and the role of Buero Vallejo's title, The Sleep of Reason *in his play by the same name.*

Francisco Goya's *The Sleep of Reason Produces Monsters* (El sueno de la razon produce monstruos, 1799) has—theorizes Eleanor A. Sayre in her and Perez Sanchez's *Goya and the Spirit of Enlightenment*—at least two possible antecedents. The first is Charles Monnet's engraved frontispiece for Jean-Jacques Rousseau's *Philosophie,* volume two (1793). In Monnet's engraving, reason can be said to issue from the eye of God in the form of light beaming down on the desk and person of Rousseau, philosopher-muse of the French Revolution (1789). Rousseau is intensely awake, hand-to-head, deep in active thought as Lady Liberty stands near and splayed-open books and papers lie at Rousseau's feet. While dreams do not have a role in this engraving, Rousseau did write *Reveries d'un promeneur solitaire* (*Daydreams of a Solitary Stroller,* 1776–78). Rousseau shares other loosely related features with Goya: Rousseau was threatened by a king, suffered a long-term physical ailment like Goya's deafness, was known as a famous paranoid, and, as a young man, was apprenticed to an engraver.

According to Sayre, the other inspiration for Goya's *The Sleep of Reason Produces Monsters* was an engraving, *Quevedo Dreaming* in volume one (1699) of the works of the famous Spanish satiric poet, Francisco de Quevedo y Villegas (1580–1645). In 1639, Quevedo, while in Italy, was accused of having slipped into the Italian king's napkin a satiric poem against the royal favorite, the count-duke of Olivares. As a result, Quevedo was imprisoned in the monastery of San Marcos in Leon from 1639 to 1643. Upon release, his health was ruined. Quevedo's alleged poem is suggestive of Goya's intercepted letter in *The Sleep of Reason,* and Quevedo's imprisonment (1639–43)

WHAT DO I READ NEXT?

- *The Origins of Totalitarianism* is a set of three historical essays by Hannah Arendt, twentieth-century German philosopher. The original manuscript was first published in 1949. The three works in the series are *Totalitarianism*, *anti-Semitism*, and *Imperialism*. For those mystified by state-sanctioned acts of large-scale cruelty—like those of Ferdinand VII or Francisco Franco—*Totalitarianism* is a crucial text.

- *How It Is* is a 1964 tragi-comedy by Samuel Beckett, one of the twentieth-century's great novelists and playwrights. The work is a hellish, hallucinatory journey of near blindness and deafness, a complex and unparalleled maze of torture and hallucination.

- *The Wretched of the Earth* is a 1963 study by the French-Algerian psychoanalyst, Frantz Fanon. This powerful examination of the role of violence in imperialistic oppression and the psychology of those suffering under its heel is a classic of revolutionary literature.

- *The Interpretation of Dreams*, by Sigmund Freud, was first published in English translation in 1913. Freud regarded this work as his most valuable. His study begins with a history of dream interpretation until 1900, moving to what Freud called the "dream-work," a description of the dream's modes of operation.

- *The History of Hell*, by Alice K. Turner, from 1993 is a book of color plates and text charting the geography and populations of hell from the clay tablets found in the Tigris-Euphrates valley and written almost four thousand years ago to what Turner calls "the age of Freud." The book's pictures of hell make a fine compliment to Goya's black paintings.

---

could remind one of Buero Vallejo's imprisonment (1939–46). In the Quevedo engraving, a sitting, slumbering Quevedo leans—head on hand—on his desk in what seems like a library. On the table is an unfurled sheet with two of Quevedo's works listed, the pertinent one being *Los Suenos de Don Francisco de Quevedo*. In the engraving, Quevedo's dreams and work appear to be almost the same. Sayre is certain Goya read Quevedo's *Dreams* and that it played an important role in the creation of Goya's own series, *Caprichos,* of which Goya's *The Sleep of Reason Produces Monsters* is part. Quevedo had written that from his dreams he learned there was little difference between demons and humans. Partially inspired by Quevedo, Goya made twenty-eight or more sketches of his own *Dreams* as preparation for the *Caprichos*. In *Dreams*, humans were transformed into animals, monsters, or witches. Of this series, two pen and ink drawings over chalk (they were to be sketches for the frontispiece to the *Dreams* series) served as preliminary sketches to the *The Sleep of Reason Produces Monsters*. Both of the preliminary sketches show Goya asleep at drawing table or desk, forehead upon folded arms. In the earlier of the two, numerous animals, demons, and Goya himself populate his dreams. In the second of the pair, there are only animals: bat, cat, and owl figures. All of these are night-creatures, creatures often associated with evil, falsehood, and ignorance, often opposed to a light long associated with goodness, truth, and knowledge. In the margin below the second sketch, Goya wrote: "The author dreaming. His only purpose is to banish harmful ideas commonly believed, and with this work of *Caprichos* to perpetuate the solid testimony of Truth."

In Goya's aquatint, *The Sleep of Reason Produces Monsters,* from which Buero Vallejo took the name of his play, Goya is still asleep at his table. On the table's side can be seen the title of the work. Behind the sleeping Goya are bats, owls, a black cat, and what Sayre calls a lynx. All of these creatures appear to represent enemies of light and its metaphors. The lynx, however, likely serves as Goya's keen-eyed guide through the darkness, in order to "perpetuate the solid testimony of Truth." At the end of Sayre's short essay on *The Sleep of Reason Produces Monsters,* she collects various interpretations:

> Prado: "Imagination forsaken by Reason [sic] begets impossible monsters: united with her, she is the mother of the arts and the source of their wonders." Sanchez: "When Reason falls asleep, all is filled with phantoms and monstrous visions." Stirling: "The sleep of Reason begets monsters, and one must be a lynx to decipher their meaning." Simon: "When men deafen themselves to the cry of Reason, the world is filled with visions."

It is perhaps obvious that the above interpretations are similar, interpretations with which Rousseau and Quevedo would likely agree.

It may be noteworthy that Buero Vallejo has left off the predicate, "produces monsters," from the title to his play *The Sleep of Reason.* Perhaps it was simply to avoid duplication of Goya's title, or to keep the reference to Goya's title less obvious. But there might be another reason: Buero Vallejo was more ambivalent than Goya about what the "sleep of reason" produced. To test this theory, it might be useful, before addressing Goya, to briefly examine the other major characters in whom it can be said "reason sleeps": Calomarde, Ferdinand, Duaso Y Latre, and Leocadia. Calomarde and Ferdinand are never seen sleeping, but their reason appears sleepy in this sense: they believe that revenge will rid them of more enemies than it will produce or inflame. The monsters they "produce" are the five Royal Volunteers, their number and actions almost exactly corresponding to the monsters of Goya's dream. Father Duaso's reason can also be said to sleep: he is unaware that his political employer, the crown, is capable of such extreme brutality. Father Duaso does not "produce" monsters but enables the monsters running and representing Spain. This is the reason Goya says that Spain is "A country at the edge of the grave, whose reason sleeps."

Leocadia's reason might be said to sleep because Doctor Arrieta believes she is overwrought, that Goya's behavior is driving her toward madness. Without Buero Vallejo judging Leocadia negatively, he might seem to agree. Leocadia is depicted as hysterical, maybe even paranoid, her major motivation for action being fear. She is so overpowered by fear that she understands it as the pinnacle of sanity, portraying Goya's fearlessness as sanity's opposite. While overwhelming fear (at least in the United States) is often thought a kind of sickness, an

> **"QUEVEDO HAD WRITTEN THAT FROM HIS DREAMS HE LEARNED THERE WAS LITTLE DIFFERENCE BETWEEN DEMONS AND HUMANS."**

impediment to confidence, ambition, and success, Buero Vallejo's Leocadia exhibits a fear that is well founded—and she pays for ignoring it when she and Goya are brutalized by the king's men. Was Buero Vallejo asserting that Leocadia's "unreasonable" fear was in fact reasonable, that sometimes what may seem like a sleeping reason is the opposite? Still, while Leocadia might have exhibited the sanity of insanity, was her reason awake when she thought Goya's asleep?

The nature and meaning of reason are uncertain even with Goya himself, whose reason can be said to sleep and not sleep. Was it not asleep when, wide-awake, Goya ignored Leocadia's seemingly unreasonable fears of royal revenge? Was it not asleep, when Goya, fully awake, suspected Leocadia of collaboration and an affair with the sergeant of the Royal Volunteers? And finally, was his reason not napping when wide-awake, he heard the voice of Mariquita urging him to suspect Leocadia of betrayal? But while Goya's reason slept in terms of reading Ferdinand's intentions, he was not provided with information about the king's edict pardoning those who would violate the property of Liberals. And Goya was right that Leocadia had contact with the sergeant who gave her his button. On these counts, Goya's reason was only partially asleep, combined as it was with imagination. And what of Goya's dream when his reason is supposed to be fully asleep? While he did dream a monstrous Leocadia-as-Judith, armed with a knife to cut off his head which proved to be untrue, he did produce animal monsters that were amazingly accurate foreshadowings of the Royal Volunteers. Thus, while Goya's dreams produced monsters, they were not wholly monstrous since a great deal of the dream came true.

Goya's flying men are a final issue. Were they the product of reason or its slumbering? When Goya first mentions them to Arrieta they seem presentiments of a hundred years into the future. But as Goya continues, he invests the flyers with messianic qualities: "they'll come down. To finish off the king and put an end to all the cruelties in the world. Maybe one day they'll descend like a shining army and knock on every door. With blows so thunderous . . . that even I will hear them." Goya does end up hearing them: between dream and waking the flying men turn out to be those avenging angels, the Royal Volunteers, come to continue, rather than "put an end to all the cruelties in the world," and "knocking so loud that even I [Goya] can hear them." By play's end, Goya shows he has understood the irony: "Will the flyers come? And if they come, won't they treat us like dogs?" In Goya's waking visions—while reason slumbered—the flying men appeared almost like angels yet they turned out to be monsters.

Buero Vallejo has added an important variation to Goya's less complicated title, *The Sleep of Reason Produces Monsters,* a complication nearer the Prado Museum's interpretation: "Imagination forsaken by Reason begets impossible monsters: united with her, she is the mother of the arts and the source of their wonders." Buero Vallejo might have stated his interpretation as follows: While the sleep of reason may or may not produce monsters, only during wakefulness can a sleeping reason empower them.

Source: Chris Semansky, in an essay for *Drama for Students,* Gale Group, 2001.

SOURCES

Aragones, Emilio, "Goya, pintor baturro y liberal," in *La Estafa Literaria,* No. 438, February 15, 1970, p. 36.

Buero Vallejo, Antonio, *Three Plays: The Sleep of Reason, The Foundation, and In the Burning Darkness,* translated and introduced by Marion Peter Holt, Trinity University Press, 1985, pp. xiv, xii.

Domenech, Ricardo, "Notas sobre *El sueno de la razon*" in *Primer Acto,* No. 117, February 1970, p. 8.

Dowling, John, "Buero Vallejo's Interpretation of Goya's 'Black Paintings,'" in *Hispania* Vol. 56, No. 2, 1973, pp. 449–57.

Fernandez-Santos, Angel, "Sobre *El sueno de la razon de Antonia Buero Vallejo,*" in *Insula,* No. 280, March, 1970, p. 15.

Halsey, Martha, *Antonio Buero Vallejo,* Twayne, 1973, p. 124.

Kronik, John W., "Buero Vallejo y su *sueno de la razon,*" in *El Urogallo,* Nos. 5–6, October-November-December, 1970, p. 156.

Nicholas, Robert B., *The Tragic Stages of Antonio Buero Vallejo,* 1972, No. 23 in the series, Estudios de Hispanofila, Department of Romance Languages, University of North Carolina, p. 96–97.

FURTHER READING

Bertrand, Louis, and Sir Charles Petrie, *The History of Spain, Part I and II,* Dawsons of Pall Mall, 1969.
> Bertrand and Petrie's work is broken up into short periods for focus and easy digestion. It also contains ancillary materials: maps, several genealogies of royal lines, and a list of important events.

Gudiol, Jose, *Goya 1746–1828,* Tudor Publishing Company, 1971.
> This four-volume work has all of Goya's work in large plates, usually showing both the whole work and often several details. Most plates are in black and white. When looking for the black paintings, prepare to be confused by titles not used by Buero Vallejo.

London, John, *Reception and Renewal in Modern Spanish Theatre: 1939–63,* W. S. Maney, 1997.
> London tackles international theater's impact on Spanish theater. Buero Vallejo's first major play, *Historia de una escalera* gets much attention from London as he calls it one of Spain's two most important post-Civil War plays.

Muller, Priscilla E., *Goya's 'Black' Paintings,* Hispanic Society of America, 1984.
> Muller is an incredible critic doing exhaustive research into the possible and best interpretations of Goya's ambiguous series, made even more difficult to interpret because of decay. Her ambitious attempt is not only to see these works as a series but a series in a particular order of placement on the walls of Goya's home, the quinta del sordo.

Perez, Sanchez, Alfonso E. Sayre, and Eleanor A. Sayre, *Goya and the Spirit of Enlightenment,* Bullfinch Press, 1989.
> For all other works besides the black paintings, this is the best volume for both plates and interpretation. Find *The sleep of reason produces monsters* on p. 115.

Spike Heels

THERESA REBECK
1990

Theresa Rebeck's *Spike Heels* was the first play by this multitalented writer to gain wide notice. Originally staged as a workshop piece by the New York Stage and Film Company at Vassar College in Poughkeepsie, New York, in 1990, the play was first produced in New York at the Second Stage Theatre in 1992. That first production starred the well-known movie actor Kevin Bacon as Edward. The play explores issues of sexual harassment, the control and use of women, self-determination and identity, and changing expectations of men in a feminist era. Its discussion of sexual harassment was particularly timely, coming as it did soon after Anita Hill was hostilely questioned by Congress about her assertions that Supreme Court nominee Clarence Thomas had harassed her. Although the important New York critics were not universally fond of the play, it was a success in that over the next decade it was produced all over the country. As Rebeck has gone on to fame and recognition as a screenwriter for television and film, the play remains an important early milestone in her career as well as an intelligent examination of issues that are as important today as they were in 1990.

AUTHOR BIOGRAPHY

Theresa Rebeck has had success writing for television, film, and the theater. Originally from the

Cincinnati, Ohio, area, Rebeck moved to Boston to attend college and graduated from Brandeis University. While writing plays, Rebeck began also to write for television for such shows as *Brooklyn Bridge* and *Dream On* and later for the critically acclaimed show *NYPD Blue*. Rebeck won a Writer's Guild award in 1995 for the *NYPD Blue* episode ''Girl Talk.'' At the same time she was also having success with her screenwriting career, and coauthored the screenplay for the major motion picture version of Louise Fitzhugh's book *Harriet the Spy*. ''Theatre, film, and television,'' she once remarked, ''are all modes of storytelling, and many of us are fortunate enough to move freely among them without feeling that we've 'left' or need to 'go back' to one or the other. In fact, if the theatre is to avoid a brain drain, this type of fluidity is increasingly necessary.'' Because of her versatility, she is an inspiration to many young screenwriters today.

PLOT SUMMARY

Act I, Scene 1

Spike Heels opens in Andrew's apartment. Georgie, his neighbor, arrives home from work in a foul mood. She is wearing her work clothes, including a pair of spike-heeled shoes. She changes her clothes in front of Andrew, which makes him uncomfortable. As she complains to Andrew, she lets him know that her boss, Edward, has made unwanted sexual advances to her and threatened to rape her. Andrew gets very angry, and Georgie tries to seduce him, unsuccessfully. When Andrew lets Georgie know that he has informally given Edward permission to pursue her, Georgie gets furious and storms out.

Act I, Scene 2

The second scene also takes place in Andrew's apartment, one day later. Edward arrives unexpectedly, dropping by to see his friend before picking up Georgie for their date, and Andrew lets him know that he is not welcome. Andrew and Edward argue about Edward's conduct toward Georgie. Georgie arrives, dressed provocatively, and Andrew gets Edward to leave for a minute so that he can talk to Georgie. As he tries to remove her spike heels, they kiss passionately. He pulls away. Georgie and Andrew argue about their relationship and Andrew, in anger, lets it slip that he believes that he ''made her.'' Deeply offended and angered, Georgie returns to her apartment to wait for Edward.

Act II, Scene 1

The second act takes place in Georgie's apartment. Scene 1 opens later the same night. Georgie and Edward have returned to her apartment and are making out on the couch. She is attempting to seduce him but he resists, and wants to talk with her about her relationship with Andrew. When she refuses, he becomes insulting and she gets upset. They are interrupted by a pounding on the door: it is Lydia, who is very angry, thinking that Georgie is having an affair with Andrew. Edward leaves, and Lydia and Georgie discuss Lydia's relationship with Andrew, who has just postponed their wedding. They end up dancing with each other but stop when there is a pounding on the door—it is Edward and Andrew. Edward convinces Andrew to tell Georgie he loves her. This upsets both Lydia and Georgie, and the two women leave.

Act II, Scene 2

As the scene opens, the two men are waking up in Georgie's apartment. They continue discussing the events of the previous night and Andrew admits that he and Lydia had slept together while she was still together with Edward. Georgie returns, and after getting Edward to leave, Andrew expresses his feelings to Georgie again, but she rejects him. Andrew leaves, Edward returns, and the play ends with Georgie and Edward discussing whether they will become involved with each other.

CHARACTERS

Andrew

Andrew is a professor of political philosophy at a small college in Boston. He lives alone in an apartment and has befriended his neighbor Georgie, appointing himself her ''teacher.'' He is engaged to be married to Lydia. As the play opens, Andrew is fastidious, cautious, and tends not to take risks. However, during the course of the play he becomes less restrained because of Georgie's influence on him.

Edward

Edward is an old friend of Andrew's. Their personalities are very different, though; Edward is aggressive, extroverted, demanding, and at times a little sleazy. He is a criminal defense lawyer and, as a favor to Andrew, has hired Georgie to be his secretary even though she has not attended college. He dated Andrew's fiancée, Lydia, before Andrew began dating her.

Georgie

Georgie is Andrew's neighbor and Edward's secretary. She comes from a working-class background and has not attended college. She is lusty, earthy, sarcastic, and fatalistic, especially in her relationships with men. Six months before the play begins, Andrew has decided to become her friend and to try to diminish her self-destructive tendencies. In befriending her, Andrew has also tried to "improve" her by giving her books to read and encouraging her to speak more properly. She has responded to Andrew's friendship by falling in love with him.

Lydia

Lydia is Andrew's fiancée and Edward's ex-girlfriend. She is from an old, upper-class Boston family. In many ways, she is described as the opposite of Georgie, and the characters talk about her a great deal before she ever actually appears. Edward describes her as cold and unemotional, and Andrew wants to keep her pure, in a way. When she does appear, she is quite fiery, convinced that Georgie is trying to steal Andrew from her. Georgie comes to like her when she sees that Lydia is not the "vampire" Edward has portrayed her to be.

THEMES

Power

One of the most important themes of *Spike Heels* is power. Each of the characters has a form of power and attempts to wield it, with results that are not what the character was hoping for. Andrew's power is as a teacher—he is a college professor, and taking the role of the teacher in his relationships is natural to him—and he uses this power to "mold" Georgie into a different person. Although he wants to feel that he is simply helping her, at one point in the play his true feelings come out: "I made you better than that," he tells Georgie. Edward also has power as a lawyer and as a boss, and he uses it crudely in an attempt to get Georgie to sleep with him. Georgie has little power, she feels, and therefore uses her sexual attractiveness (symbolized by her spike heels) and her foul mouth to establish her power. Lydia, the most powerless character of the play, in the outside world would have a great deal of power due to the fact that she is from an old, established family and presumably has a great deal of money.

The irony of the play is that each character's use of power backfires. Andrew wants to establish an enduring relationship with Georgie through his tutoring and, later, wants that relationship to become romantic, but, by laying bare the mechanism of his power over her, he loses her. Edward's use of power—his sexual harassment—backfires, and he must use another form of power (his ability to grant her a raise) to win her back. When Georgie tries to use her sexual power with Andrew and Edward, they both reject her. And Lydia's only exercise of power, her arrival at Georgie's apartment, gains her nothing and may have helped in her losing her fiancée.

Male and Female Roles

At the heart of the play's plot are the differing roles that men and women play in society. In this play, as is often true in society at large, the men have the power and the women are acted upon by that power. Andrew takes the role of the father or teacher figure, directing Georgie's life—telling her what to read, how to talk, even where to work. Edward plays the role of boss and of sexual predator. He is aggressive, insulting, and demanding. By contrast, the women are acted upon. Georgie realizes halfway through the play that Andrew and Edward were treating her like a commodity that they trade between themselves—Andrew gives Edward permission to come on to Georgie, and Edward seems to feel that Andrew's permission is more important than Georgie's interest or even acquiesence. Lydia, as well, is acted upon—like Georgie she is traded between the men, and she is also subject to the approval of her (presumably male-dominated) family.

The genders' differing relations to sexuality are also important themes in *Spike Heels,* and this difference is nowhere better illustrated than in Rebeck's use of the symbol of the spike-heel shoes. At the very beginning of the play, Georgie storms into Andrew's apartment, complaining about how uncomfortable the shoes are. She argues to Andrew that the only reason women wear such impractical shoes is that they make women's legs more attrac-

TOPICS FOR FURTHER STUDY

- Andrew accuses Edward of "sexual harassment" in his treatment of Georgie. What is sexual harassment? Why is it such an important and controversial issue? Research sexual harassment, concentrating on the difficulties of constructing a legal definition and of enforcement.

- Why does Georgie decide to be with Edward instead of Andrew? Think about this question in terms of the development of each character: where does each character begin and what does each character learn in the course of the play?

- How is social class important in this play? Each character represents a different social class, and to some extent has stereotypical aspects of that class. How does Rebeck use our expectations of how someone of a particular class behaves, and how do the action of the play and the changing relationships between the characters undermine those expectations?

- In *Spike Heels*, Theresa Rebeck alludes a number of times to George Bernard Shaw's play *Pygmalion*. The Pygmalion story did not originate or end with Shaw, however; it is originally a Greek myth, and Shaw's story has been reworked a number of times, most famously as the musical play *My Fair Lady*. Read the Greek myth and Shaw's play or see the movie of the musical and discuss how Rebeck changes the story. What are the changes she works in the structure of the story, and how does this give her play different meanings than the other stories?

---

tive. Yet for all of her feminist consciousness of this, she still wears them because she feels that being sexually attractive is her only way to have power. She must embrace the role of temptress that the shoes give her in order to have any power. Andrew, who wants to remake her and diminish her sexuality, tells her to stop wearing them, but later in the play he admits that he, too, finds the shoes attractive. Lydia also examines the shoes curiously. She does not rely on her sexuality to obtain power, and both disdains and envies women who do. "I guess you don't wear them for comfort," she tells Georgie. "You wear them for other reasons. You wear them because they make your legs look amazing."

STYLE

Setting

Spike Heels is set in two apartments in contemporary Boston. The play does not make much use of the city; however, Rebeck cleverly structures the play in two parts, and the division is also indicated by the locations of the two acts. The first act is set in Andrew's apartment, the second in Georgie's. As the play examines very carefully some important differences between men and women, setting the two acts in apartments belonging to the two sexes allows the setting to mirror the theme. Rebeck also uses music to contribute to the theme and to reinforce our impressions of the characters, indicating in the text what music should be playing in each apartment—classical in Andrew's, Elvis Costello in Georgie's.

Character Development

The play is in large part about self-discovery and the way that we grow to understand and learn new things about other people, and Rebeck uses the development of her characters to reinforce that theme. With the exception of Georgie, all of the characters in the play are both presented to us and described to us by other characters while they are offstage. We get a very negative impression of Lydia before she ever arrives on the stage—Edward describes her as a vampire—but when she does show up she is much more animated and sympathetic than we suspected she would be. Edward seems like a monster in the first scene, but when he makes his first appearance he is less so (although he is certainly unsympathetic and arrogant). Andrew appears quite sympathetic when he is presented directly to us, but when he is off-stage—when Edward or Lydia is talking to Georgie about him—we learn things about him that are unflattering. Rebeck's use of direct and indirect characterization underscores her point that we cannot make hard and fast judgments about people based solely on how they first appear.

Symbolism

As indicated by the play's title, the most important symbol in the play is Georgie's spike-heeled shoes. The spike heels represent a number of aspects of women's roles in contemporary society—as sex object, sexual predator, working woman, and homebody. As the play opens, Georgie arrives at Andrew's apartment, complaining about how badly her spike heels hurt her. Women on the job, Rebeck indicates, are expected to dress attractively or even in a way that accentuates their sexuality. Men's work clothes hide the body, she suggests; why do women's emphasize their bodies? In addition, women must endure pain to appear professional or attractive. High-heeled shoes, worn consistently over a lifetime, can cause permanent malformation of the foot, and the spike-heeled shoes (taller and, because of their narrow heels, transmitting more impact to the foot) are especially dangerous for that.

Women are expected to wear high heels to work, but spike-heeled shoes, connoting sexuality, are rarely appropriate for work. So why does Georgie wear them? Georgie is from a working-class family and has little experience with the white-collar world. The fact that she wears these shoes to work indicates her inexperience in the business world. And, as a secretary, she feels powerless. Sexuality has always been her source of power, and the spike heels represent her sexual power—something that Lydia comments on. Georgie uses the spike heels to lure Andrew and Edward, but they limit her, make her just a sexual object. In that sense, when she doffs them—as she does on stage—it emphasizes her powerlessness and her lack of a defined place in the world. But, as she says herself, the spike heels are also an entirely nonsexual way for her to obtain power. "I like the way they make my legs look kind of dangerous," she tells Edward and Andrew. "And I like being tall. I like being able to look you both in the eyes. It's the only chance I get, when I'm wearing these things."

HISTORICAL CONTEXT

The 1970s were a time of great change for American women. Through the turbulence of the 1960s, women's roles in American society went largely unquestioned. Even the revolutionaries of the period dismissed questions of women's liberation and feminism. But, led by such theorists, writers, and political figures as Simone de Beauvoir, Betty Friedan, Gloria Steinem, and Bella Abzug, women in the 1970s began to demand different treatment.

There has been much talk about the "Sexual Revolution" in American society. Although it is very difficult to make generalizations about such a vast transformation of social attitudes, we can confidently say that beginning in the 1920s and lasting into the 1950s a small but increasingly vocal minority of Americans wanted their Puritanical culture to talk frankly about sex. The "carefree" 1920s were characterized by groups of young people who had much different attitudes toward sex than did any generation in American history—for the first time, sex was being regarded not simply as a dirty secret for married people to keep but as a recreational activity. In the 1950s, a decade whose image today is dominated by middle-class American values, the movie star Marilyn Monroe and the magazine publisher Hugh Hefner, among many others, forced America to confront its hypocrisy about sexuality. And in the 1960s, the various countercultural groups of young people often made sexual liberation or "free love" part of their program.

But for all of the changes in American attitudes toward sex, American attitudes towards women had changed little. This "Sexual Revolution" often made women into sexual objects, existing only for the pleasure of promiscuous men. Even the invention of the birth control pill, which allowed women to experiment sexually without fear of pregnancy, was a mixed blessing for women in some ways. Tired of the disdainful attitude toward women demonstrated by the self-described radicals of the 1960s, Friedan and Steinem organized a women's movement that sought to secure equal treatment for women in society. One of the most difficult problems this movement faced was how to fight for the sexual freedom of women without seeming to make women into "tramps" or "sluts." There was no model in Western culture for the woman who was in control of her own sexuality; as Steinem often pointed out, Western women were inevitably portrayed as virgins, whores, or mothers, with no other roles available to them.

American society spent much of the 1970s and 1980s debating the question of women's liberation. What were appropriate roles for women at home? In the workplace? How should a woman use her sexuality? By the early 1990s, most jobs and careers were open to women, although a "glass ceiling" often existed that effectively prevented women from advancing to executive positions in government or business. An especially thorny and enduring problem was sexual harassment, or unwanted sexual advances at work, especially those made by a male superior to a female employee. Many men dismissed the issue, but the legal scholar Catherine MacKinnon—mentioned by Edward in *Spike Heels*—helped draft legislation to define such conduct and make it illegal.

In 1991, many women's frustrations about sexual harassment came to the fore in the so-called "Anita Hill case." President Bush had nominated Judge Clarence Thomas to serve on the Supreme Court, and, during his confirmation process in the United States Senate, a lawyer who had worked under Thomas, Anita Hill, accused the judge of sexually harassing her during the time they worked together. The stories Hill told of Thomas's behavior were very familiar to millions of women, but the Senators questioning her in the hearings concentrated instead on Hill's sexual history, her conduct, even her clothes. The Senators' obliviousness to the seriousness and pervasiveness of sexual harassment in many women's lives, and their tendency to "blame the victim," caused those women to conclude publicly that "they [the Senators specifically, but in a larger sense men in general] just don't get it."

Rebeck draws on women's problematic, expanded sexual freedom and on the issue of sexual harassment in her play. Georgie uses her sexuality as a way to establish power, but her sexuality apparently backfires. In the play, though, we see that Edward and Andrew have been treating her like a commodity, almost as if they have traded her—something they have done before—for Lydia. The thorny issues of sexual harassment, women's liberation, and changing gender roles are at the heart of *Spike Heels*.

CRITICAL OVERVIEW

Theresa Rebeck's play *Spike Heels*, exploring issues of love, gender roles, sex, and sexual harassment, did not receive great reviews when it was initially produced but has since been produced to acclaim all over the country. When the play was first staged in New York in 1992, Rebeck was already known in the New York theatre world for her one-act plays, but *Spike Heels* was her biggest success to date.

In the world of contemporary American theatre, the most important city is New York. Although many plays have their initial productions in small theatres around the country, it is not until they are produced in New York that they are taken seriously. And as befits New York's central place in theatre, the theatre critics for the city's most influential daily newspaper, the *New York Times*, have become America's leading theatre critics. Frank Rich, at that time the paper's head critic, could make or break a play by his review.

Rich attended the 1992 staging of *Spike Heels*, starring Kevin Bacon, and was unimpressed. He saw the play as a modernization of the "glossy Hollywood comedies of the unabashedly sexist 1950s" in which the men, not the women, are "virgins and tramps. The idea is wicked and promising." But, Rich felt, "the play is a letdown." Rich found the dialogue excessively profane, writing that "the lines that are not funny frequently try to get by on scatological bombast." The play was too heavy-handed, he continues: "When really stuck, the playwright takes to pounding in her points. There is too much talk about how men view women as property, or want to be in control of every situation, or try to pass themselves off as sensitive even as they are being manipulative."

When the play was staged the following year in Boston, the *Globe's* critic Louise Kennedy was similarly unimpressed, but for different reasons. The play's cardinal sin, for Kennedy, is that for a comedy, it just is not funny. "It just isn't any fun," she gripes. "Every character . . . is unbelievably annoying. The actors are not well-served by the script's ridiculous plot twists and implausible shifts in character." Kennedy also felt that in this ostensibly feminist-minded play, Rebeck undermined her own feminist principles. "Maybe it's hysterical to have a woman threatened with rape by her boss, then turn around and go out to dinner with him to make his best friend jealous, then declare her love for the best friend, then have a fleeting bonding session with the friend's fiancée, then windup going back to the harassing snake. If it really does sound fun to you, go anyway—maybe you can tell me what I'm missing.''

Similarly negative was Alvin Klein, who reviewed a Stamford, Connecticut, production in the *New York Times* in 1993. ''In case the audience doesn't figure out that *Spike Heels* is a contemporary, multicultural *Pygmalion* knockoff, don't worry; one is bopped over the head with that allusion. There is more he says-she says attitudinizing here than an organized forum on the gender wars can accommodate, but hardly enough wit, balance, sense of craft or coherence to sustain a play.'' Klein also disliked what he saw as the ultimately antifeminist contradiction of the play, writing that Georgie's success at the end is really a ''Pyrrhic victory . . . back to square one.''

Later reviewers in other cities were more enthusiastic. Reviewing the Victory Theatre's production of *Spike Heels* in Burbank, California, Madeleine Shaner of *Backstage* wrote that the ''delightfully fresh play is like a sip of sparkling champagne after a steady diet of city water . . . funny, touching, crazy, unpredictable, and as insightful as it is entertaining.'' In 1994, Nelson Pressley of the *Washington Times* compared the play with Shaw's *Pygmalion*, calling it ''Shavian with blue language'' and praising the play's ''wry characters and nervy, earthy dialogue.'' ''Miss Rebeck is a writer to watch,'' he concludes.

CRITICISM

Greg Barnhisel

Barnhisel holds a Ph.D. in American literature. In the following essay, he discusses the structure of the play and how that structure relates to and helps construct its themes of gender relations.

Theresa Rebeck's play *Spike Heels* is a humorous meditation on contemporary gender roles and romantic relationships. It explores feminism, sexual harassment in the workplace, the teacher-student relationship, and even social class. Some of its critics have taken the play to task for undermining its own feminist message or simply for not being funny. Whatever its shortcomings, though, *Spike Heels* boasts a sophisticated structure that Rebeck expertly uses to reinforce the themes of the play.

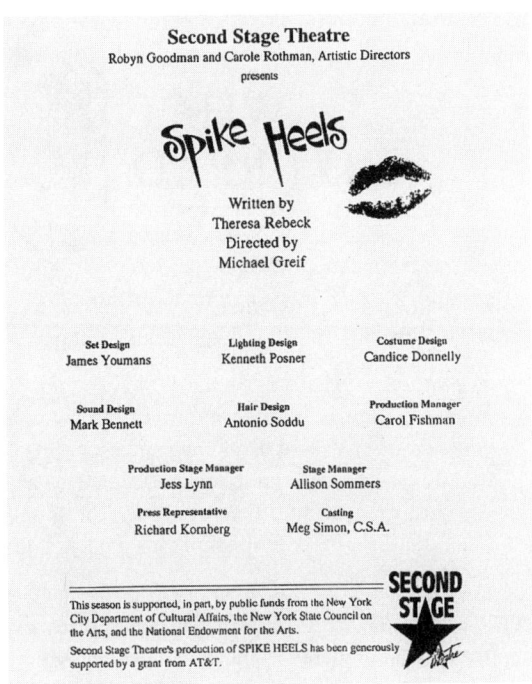

A playbill for the Second Stage Theatre production of Spike Heels.

Rebeck's play does an effective job of anatomizing and questioning gender roles and the easy dualisms into which we divide the world. Although it does rely perhaps too heavily on stock characters, it is an interesting, and at times even funny, updating of Bernard Shaw's famous story.

Rebeck structures her play as a complex of dualities. Everything works in opposed pairs that are turned upside down or switched at some point before or during the play's action. Most obvious of the pairs are the two sexes. Although there is no transsexuality (i.e., nobody actually switches genders), one of the attributes that the play gives to the characters does get switched: at the start of the play, the two males are friends and the two females rivals, but by the end, Andrew and Edward are fighting and rivals for Georgie, while Georgie and Lydia strike up a friendship and their rivalry disappears when Georgie rejects Andrew.

The roles that the genders are supposed to play are also implicated in this complex of dualities. The male characters, Andrew and Edward, represent two poles of stereotypical male behavior. Andrew is the teacher, the father figure, but he is also almost utterly asexual. When Georgie returns from work at the opening of the play, she quickly sheds her

WHAT DO I READ NEXT?

- *Theresa Rebeck: Collected Plays* (1999) collects all of Rebeck's full-length and one-act plays.

- *Pygmalion* is George Bernard Shaw's classic 1913 retelling of the Greek myth. In Shaw's play, a sophisticated London professor bets a friend that he can remake an uneducated, working-class city girl into the very model of upper-class gentility. In accomplishing his goal, he falls in love with her.

- *Oleanna* (1992), a play by David Mamet, explores sexual harassment, as well. But where Rebeck's play takes a comic look at the aftermath of workplace harassment, Mamet's play is a more serious examination of sexual harassment on a college campus.

---

clothes, walking out to the front room in only her underwear, but Andrew shows no temptation, even when she makes it clear to him that she would like to have sex with him. In a way, he is slightly feminized (at least in relation to Edward) because of his passivity and even by his choice of drinks—tea or zinfandel, as opposed to the Scotch the rest of the characters drink. He also wants her to minimize her own sexuality; "you're making a spectacle of yourself," he tells her. He is dry and pretentious, dropping names of philosophers like Hegel and Nietzsche and quoting James Joyce—"history is a nightmare from which I am trying to awake"—when discussing Georgie's personal problems. Yet even though he is not an aggressive male in the way that Edward is, he is still stereotypically male in the way that he attempts to control Georgie. He is "remaking" her, much like the professor of George Bernard Shaw's play *Pygmalion*. But Georgie resists: "I'm confused, but I do know that I don't want to be the person you keep trying to make me."

Edward, by contrast, is the young wolf, the tomcat, the aggressive male. He is an outspoken lawyer, an obnoxious "snake," as one of the play's reviewers calls him, and a sexual predator. But he, also, has his identity undermined over the course of the story. When Georgie comes on to him, he refuses her. The playwright seems to be suggesting that Edward can only be sexual when he is the aggressor—Lydia's statement that "he always wants it," when taken with Edward's description of Lydia as cold and passive, reinforces this. Frank Rich, of the *New York Times,* felt that Rebeck was reacting to, and reversing, the "glossy Hollywood comedies of the unabashedly sexist 1950s" in which women are always "virgins and tramps." This would be yet another example of Rebeck's transformed dualisms—Andrew as the virgin who leaves his fiancée for the exciting and dangerous woman from another social class, Edward as the tramp who in the end acts like the virgin.

Given Rich's formulation, the women would have to then be respectable, if boring, suitors and rakish, rebellious, earthy interlopers. At first glance, this is exactly what they are. Lydia is almost a stock character when described by Edward and Andrew—the character of Lilith from the television show *Cheers* is an example of this type—and Georgie is, as well. But when Lydia arrives she is warmer, more fiery and emotional than we would have suspected. Georgie, the character who is at the center of the play, transcends her stereotypical role, as well. The women, who are traditionally under the control of men, gain control in this play to some extent. In the end, nobody is in control: the end of the play is a negotiation. As Georgie says, "it's always about what you guys want. And I'm just like some thing just spinning in the middle of it all. I can't even think, you know?"

The women also embody the class dualisms common in American drama in stock ways. Lydia, the upper-class woman, is initially portrayed as dry, cold, and condescending. Georgie fears her because she represents the qualities that she feels Andrew is trying to cultivate in her, and when she mockingly tries on Lydia's dress Andrew gets very upset—he resents the way she is undercutting the distinction between the two women. Georgie is figured as working class in many ways: she is profane and crude, she is sexually loose, she is street-smart but not (yet) book-smart, she is aggressive and extroverted. Both men comment dismissively and insultingly on her working-class upbringing, also.

The relationships around which the play revolves are also structured as a series of amorphous dualities. The play encompasses numerous kinds of emotional relationships. There is a relationship that definitely existed in the past and definitely ended then: Lydia and Edward. There is a relationship that could have existed in the past but definitely ends during the play: Georgie and Andrew. There is a relationship that definitely existed in the past and may end during the play: Lydia and Andrew. There is a relationship that does not exist during the play but may in the future: Georgie and Edward. There is a relationship that existed in the past and will continue to exist in the future: Andrew and Edward. There is even a relationship that is merely suggested, even though it neither existed in past nor will exist in the future: Lydia and Georgie, who are friendly and even dance "erotically" until the fighting men enter Georgie's apartment.

The play captures these relationships at a point at which they are being transformed in ways that also transform the people involved. During the course of the 36 hours of the play, an engagement ends, two people admit their unrequited love for another, a sexual Lothario finds his sex drive absent, and one long-term friendship is severely tested. The dualisms of the play extend to its setting. The play takes place in two apartments in the same building, apartments that are, in the words of the stage directions, "identical . . . but in all particulars different." The apartments share the same space but they are distinguished from each other by music, degree of mess, and appearance of lived-in comfort.

But in the end, for all of the shifting identities and roles that the characters take on during the play, at the end the situation really changes very little. Georgie's last scene, in which she rejects Andrew and "negotiates" the terms of a potential relationship with Edward, is clearly intended to show her coming into "ownership" of her life. Ironically, Andrew may have succeeded in remaking her, for at this point she is more in control than at any other point in the play. But the resolution is troubling, even if it does show Georgie coming into her own. The viewers or readers question Georgie perhaps more than the playwright does—what is this woman doing, getting involved with a man who threatened to rape her? Yes, she is intending to do this on her own terms, but the issue (of rape and sexual harassment) brought up earlier is so serious, and tossed away so flippantly, that we question if the playwright is simply wrapping things up artificially. Edward tells her that he is not the "enemy," but this is unconvincing. He is still a jerk, an arrogant grasper who has threatened her—and who is, let us not forget, still her boss.

> "THIS WOULD BE YET ANOTHER EXAMPLE OF REBECK'S TRANSFORMED DUALISMS—ANDREW AS THE VIRGIN WHO LEAVES HIS FIANCEE FOR THE EXCITING AND DANGEROUS WOMAN FROM ANOTHER SOCIAL CLASS, EDWARD AS THE TRAMP WHO IN THE END ACTS LIKE THE VIRGIN."

Rebeck's play does an effective job of anatomizing and questioning gender roles and the easy dualisms into which we divide the world. Although it does rely perhaps too heavily on stock characters, it is an interesting, and at times even funny, updating of Bernard Shaw's famous story. But for all of its feminist overtones, it does not really transcend the gender roles of the Hollywood comedies to which Frank Rich alludes. Yes, at first the men do play the traditionally female roles—but the end of the play brings us back to the old model, in which a rakish man gets the girl and the frigid woman is quickly and patly written off. Perhaps this is just another overturned dualism, in which Rebeck at first plays with but ultimately reaffirms the gender roles of Hollywood and the pre-feminist United States.

Source: Greg Barnhisel, in an essay for *Drama for Students*, Gale Group, 2001.

Carole Hamilton

Hamilton is an English teacher at Cary Academy, an innovative private school in Cary, North Carolina. In the following essay, she discusses "power feminism" and Rebeck's Spike Heels.

In his essay "Power and Knowledge," Michel Foucault wrote, "What makes power hold good, what makes it accepted, is simply the fact that it doesn't only weigh on us as a force that says no, but that it traverses and produces things, it induces pleasure, forms knowledge, produces discourse." Foucault means that power, even dominant power, is not bad, but actually enticing. Recent feminists have adopted the Foucaultian idea of power as both attractive and compatible with pleasure, in a new form of feminism called "power feminism." The term "power feminism" was coined by Naomi Wolf, who offers it as a healthy alternative to the "victim feminism" that focuses on paternalistic oppression and denies women's sexuality. Victim feminism concerns itself with retribution against oppressive males, and victim feminists act militant by effacing their femininity. Wolf is applauded by Camille Paglia, the outrageously outspoken academic who calls herself the "Feminist Fatale," whose shocking book *Sexual Personae* (1990) led many erstwhile feminists to revamp their beliefs. With Paglia, many contemporary feminists no longer find sexiness incompatible with power, or with feminist thinking. Paglia considers the nineties to be a time of "feminist reform." In the shifting arena of gender politics, every woman must come to terms with her own sense of sexuality and the ways in which she interacts with men. Theresa Rebeck's play *Spike Heels* showcases one woman grappling with issues of beauty, intelligence, and sexuality in the post-women's-movement era. Her play explores the confusion that surrounds sexual relations as young women negotiate a new brand of feminism, one that embraces sexuality and feminine attractiveness, as well as power.

The play's title, *Spike Heels,* portends an attitude toward the bondage of style that women endure in the interest of pleasing and enticing men. In this regard, the play manifests "victim feminism," which finds fault with the trappings of the cultural oppression of women. The uncomfortable spike heel shoes, Andrew tells Georgie, "look like some sort of medieval torture device." However, in the next breath he says that wearing them has put her "in a bad mood." Thus, on one hand Andrew seems enlightened (in "victim feminist" terms) in his view that women should not abuse their bodies to look attractive; but on the other hand, his trivialization of her distress as "a bad mood" marks him as hopelessly chauvinistic. A feminist of the 1970s or 1980s would find fault with Andrew for his apparent insincerity. He further condemns himself by his paternalistic attitude toward her. Georgie suffers from social and gender bondage, according to Andrew. Georgie discovers that he has made a "pygmalion" project of her, hoping through books and conversation to transform her street-wise smarts to sophisticated intellectualism. "I am your teacher," he tells her. He wishes she were calm; "there's no peace in you," he complains, and he adds, "I made you better than this." He wants to raise her up from her lower class life, where she "came home drunk after every shift sleeping with every guy who looked at you." He presents his re-make project as social philanthropy, but he expects her to make herself a tabula rasa for his ideas. Georgie resents this. It does not take book learning for her to recognize that his project is not an altruistic one; "this is about sex!" she exclaims as she departs for her rendezvous with Edward. She objects to his usurping her own authority, and retaliates by enticing Edward to sleep with her, to make Andrew jealous, "to teach you something for a change, you could learn from me." Tired of being "in the receiver's position," she takes control over her own body and mind. She also does so without feeling compromised by her body, and without the necessity of denying the power of her feminine sexuality. Her tactic is ultimately successful, as it breaks Andrew out of his reformer's mode and puts him on her level.

Both social and the sexual issues are played out over the spike heels. Andrew begs her to let him take off the heels she wears for the date with Edward. Andrew thinks they look "sad and ridiculous," but Edward says "it's perfectly delightful" that they let her look men in the eye. The question becomes, are the spike heels a form of gender bondage imposed by men, or are they an equalizing weapon Georgie can use so that her "legs look kind of dangerous"? For Georgie, the shoes express the new feminism, that allows her to use her feminine beauty in the service of achieving equality with men. As Camille Paglia summed it up in a 1997 essay, "Since Madonna, younger women no longer feel that makeup and sexy outfits are incompatible with feminism." Georgie wants to wear the spike heels to entice and thereby regain control with Edward. She succeeds with him through a combination of powerful attractiveness and giving in. She returns to clean out her desk and then submits to his authority in a public showdown when he demands that she come to his office. "It's like this dare it's like this f—ing dare, and everyone goes real quiet, just waiting to see what I'm gonna do," Georgie tells Andrew. As a reward for giving in, Edward gives her a $2,000 raise and makes a dinner date. To Andrew, accepting a date with someone who threatened to rape her is absurd. But she is using Edward as a pawn in her game with Andrew. The power of the spike heels, combined with the knowledge that she is using him, proves emasculating for Edward, however. After dinner, in her apartment, he suddenly withdraws from their embrace and engages in a series of power struggles with her: over her loud music (which he turns down), over what to drink (tea and not scotch), over making love (the ultimate power struggle). Edward objects to Georgie's lack of "subtlety," because he prefers to take the role of aggressor. He desperately seeks control, washing her dishes, using her toothbrush. In his attempt to recover the dominant position, he refuses to go when she tells him to leave. He tells Andrew, "This woman makes Godzilla look like a Barbie doll." Rather it is the reverse. A Barbie doll has taken on the power of Godzilla, and is in the process of deciding whether to use it for destruction or for good in the gender wars.

The Status of the Gender Wars in Spike Heels

The spike heels figure in the final scene, when Georgie brandishes them as a weapon. Though to Edward they are "delightful," he leaves it up to Georgie whether she keeps them. "Do whatever you want," he tells her about the shoes, and regarding their relationship, he defers too: "I accept your terms." He has "gone through" a lot of women, as Andrew reminds him. Edward is the male, profligate Mary Magdalene to her Christ, a male prostitute reformed by her truth. Her endorsement of the Jehovah's Witnesses as "nerdy," with a message of "Resurrection" that is "nice," is not accidental, nor is the fact that she offers their books to Edward. She is a prophet—of the new sexuality. Andrew massages her feet, in the ritual stance of a disciple towards his master, but she decides to "negotiate" a relationship with Edward, who never had a civilizing mission for her and who accepts her terms.

Women's relations with other women are also affected by the new feminism. Georgie adopts Lydia into her sisterhood. But because Lydia is a "vampire," one who (symbolically) drinks blood, she must be transformed. First Lydia drinks Georgie's scotch, thus replacing blood with the drink that breaks down social barriers. Now she is open to change. Next, Lydia tries on the spike heels. While wearing them, the women discover another connection besides loving Andrew: through Edward, who used to date Lydia. Georgie chastises Lydia for feeling superior to people like herself, from a lower class, saying "shame on you." When the two dance together, they discover a mutual eroticism that is not lesbian, but rather an appreciation of feminine sexuality. They nearly decide not to let the men in when they knock. Georgie is tired of "spinning" around trying to be what men want. The victim feminists

> THE QUESTION BECOMES, ARE THE SPIKE HEELS A FORM OF GENDER BONDAGE IMPOSED BY MEN, OR ARE THEY AN EQUALIZING WEAPON GEORGIE CAN USE SO THAT HER 'LEGS LOOK KIND OF DANGEROUS'?"

bonded through mutual resentment against men. Power feminists share that bond, plus the bond of appreciating each other sexually. It is not that competition does not exist between women, any more than it does for men, as evidenced by Andrew and Edward's relationship.

This new generation of women are both threatening and enticing to men. The threat is partially because these women resist pygmalion makeovers, but it also consists in a confusing form of feminine power, power that entices. This power is as enticing and confusing to the women who wield it, as it is to the men learning to relate to power feminists, feminists of the real world. As Camille Paglia says, it is now time to "shift the center of gravity away from academic feminism toward real-life issues." Theresa Rebeck's play *Spike Heels* takes the feminist movement to a new ground, away from books and shaved eyebrows, back to the streets, bars, jobs, and bedrooms, where women appreciate and use their power of enticement. Now at stake is the negotiation of the terms of relations between women and between women and men, as the play aptly demonstrates.

Source: Carole Hamilton, in an essay for *Drama for Students*, Gale Group, 2001.

Rena Korb

Korb has a master's degree in English literature and creative writing and has written for a wide variety of educational publishers. In the following essay, she examines issues of objectification and power in relationships between the sexes.

On her date with Edward, Georgie wears her gold spike heels; these shoes function as the central

> EVERY REFERENCE THE MEN MAKE TO GEORGIE—AND TO WOMEN IN GENERAL—SHOW THAT THEY BELIEVE IN A WOMAN AS OBJECT, NOT AS AN INDIVIDUAL BEING, WHETHER SHE BE A PROTEGE, A SECRETARY, OR A SEX SYMBOL."

symbol of Theresa Rebeck's plays *Spike Heels*. Georgie wears these shoes to make her more sexy, but as she says immediately after putting them on, when she "staggers" after rising to her feet, "I haven't worn these things for a while and you have to get used to them, you know? It's kind of like walking on stilts." Georgie's admission suggests not just the physical lengths to which women go to entice men, but also suggests to the communiques and relationships that are played out by the play's four characters. Georgie, Edward, Andrew, and Lydia all are walking a symbolic tightrope, crossing over the chasm of stereotypes to try to reach each other and form meaningful connections. As Marsha Mason writes in her introduction to *Women Playwrights, The Best Plays of 1992,* Rebeck "pounds, picks and chisels away at the mountain of sexism and class with Georgie's spike heels." This empowerment is not freely given, however. Georgie earns it by coming face to face with Andrew and Edward's treatment of her.

Throughout the play, Andrew and Edward clearly perceive of Georgie as an object to be desired, subdued, and possessed. Georgie recognizes this truth early on: "You gave me to him?" she asks Andrew, speaking of Edward. Although Andrew protests, explaining that Edward only spoke of her because he thought a relationship might exist between the two, the ensuing conversation between the men demonstrates their attitude toward women. Every reference the men make to Georgie—and to women in general—show that they believe in a woman as object, not as an individual being, whether she be a protege, a secretary, or a sex symbol. Edward openly acknowledges this, reminding Andrew, "I got clearance from you, pal."

Andrew realizes that the way they are talking about Georgie is wrong. He reminds Edward, and himself, that Georgie "is not some thing we can pass around between us," but he continues to participate in the conversation, showing that he does not truly believe his own admonition. While it is Edward who openly shows his objectification of Georgie, Andrew's protests are feeble. For example, when Edward says, "[Y]ou'd prefer that no one else had her?," Andrew responds to Edward's use of language—"everything sounds so sleazy coming out of your mouth"—instead of the message inherent in his words.

The challenge between the men is who will win control of Georgie—under whose domination she will submit. The bet that they make symbolizes this.

Edward: How much time you do you need?

Andrew: I don't.

Edward: It took me five minutes to get her to come back. How much time do you need to get her to quit again?

Georgie: *(Knocking.)* Hey, are you guys in there?

Edward: Ten minutes? Will that do?

Andrew: You know, Lydia really is right about you.

Edward: I'll give you fifteen. That's ten more than I had. And I'll bet you, you still can't do it. How about it, Andrew?

Andrew: I'm not going to bet you

Georgie: *(Pounding.)* You guys

Edward: You're on. . . .

This exchange shows the basic relationship between the men: Edward proposes some "sleazy" idea, and Andrew protests, but not enough to put a halt to Edward's proposition. Indeed, when Georgie enters Andrew's apartment, Andrew sets about to get her to leave her job. His strategies start off with his promise to be of further assistance to her: "I can get you another job," he tells her. "Last night I called some people in the department and found some leads." When that does not work—as Georgie points out "I can take care of myself: I been doing it for years"—Andrew appeals to her emotions. "Last night you said you were in love with me," he says, implying that because she loves him, she should do what he wants her to. Finally, Andrew resorts to pointing out that she is going out on this date with Edward, and dressing sexy and seductively, in order to make him jealous. Georgie, however, points out that, while she may be hoping to do so, these men render her essentially powerless. "I live in a whole different world from you," she says. "I'm in the receiver's position. I do what you guys tell me to:

whether it's reading books or f——g. I always manage to do what you say. That's the way we survive."

Source: Rena Korb, in an essay for *Drama for Students,* Gale Group, 2001.

SOURCES

Kennedy, Louise, Review of *Spike Heels,* in *Boston Globe,* May 8, 1993, p. 27.

Klein, Alvin, Review of *Spike Heels,* in *New York Times,* Connecticut Edition, November 14, 1993, p. 18.

Pressley, Nelson, Review of *Spike Heels,* in *Washington Times,* September 21, 1994, p. C16.

Rich, Frank, Review of *Spike Heels,* in *New York Times,* June 5, 1992, p. C3.

Shaner, Madeleine, Review of *Spike Heels,* in *Backstage,* December, 1999.

FURTHER READING

MacKinnon, Catharine, *Only Words,* Harvard University Press, 1993.
> MacKinnon examines sexual harassment and explores the legal issues involved with legislating against it.

——, *Sexual Harassment of Working Women: A Case of Sex Discrimination,* Yale University Press, 1979.
> *Sexual Harassment of Working Women* is one of the first works to identify sexual harassment as a social problem that needs to be addressed.

Phelps, Timothy M., and Helen Winternitz, *Capitol Games: Clarence Thomas, Anita Hill, and the Story of a Supreme Court Nomination,* Hyperion, 1992.
> This work is a long and careful look at the Anita Hill case and its effects on American society and politics.

Glossary of Literary Terms

A

Abstract: Used as a noun, the term refers to a short summary or outline of a longer work. As an adjective applied to writing or literary works, abstract refers to words or phrases that name things not knowable through the five senses. Examples of abstracts include the *Cliffs Notes* summaries of major literary works. Examples of abstract terms or concepts include "idea," "guilt" "honesty," and "loyalty."

Absurd, Theater of the: See *Theater of the Absurd*

Absurdism: See *Theater of the Absurd*

Act: A major section of a play. Acts are divided into varying numbers of shorter scenes. From ancient times to the nineteenth century plays were generally constructed of five acts, but modern works typically consist of one, two, or three acts. Examples of five-act plays include the works of Sophocles and Shakespeare, while the plays of Arthur Miller commonly have a three-act structure.

Acto: A one-act Chicano theater piece developed out of collective improvisation. *Actos* were performed by members of Luis Valdez's Teatro Campesino in California during the mid-1960s.

Aestheticism: A literary and artistic movement of the nineteenth century. Followers of the movement believed that art should not be mixed with social, political, or moral teaching. The statement "art for art's sake" is a good summary of aestheticism. The movement had its roots in France, but it gained widespread importance in England in the last half of the nineteenth century, where it helped change the Victorian practice of including moral lessons in literature. Oscar Wilde is one of the best-known "aesthetes" of the late nineteenth century.

Age of Johnson: The period in English literature between 1750 and 1798, named after the most prominent literary figure of the age, Samuel Johnson. Works written during this time are noted for their emphasis on "sensibility," or emotional quality. These works formed a transition between the rational works of the Age of Reason, or Neoclassical period, and the emphasis on individual feelings and responses of the Romantic period. Significant writers during the Age of Johnson included the novelists Ann Radcliffe and Henry Mackenzie, dramatists Richard Sheridan and Oliver Goldsmith, and poets William Collins and Thomas Gray. Also known as Age of Sensibility

Age of Reason: See *Neoclassicism*

Age of Sensibility: See *Age of Johnson*

Alexandrine Meter: See *Meter*

Allegory: A narrative technique in which characters representing things or abstract ideas are used to convey a message or teach a lesson. Allegory is typically used to teach moral, ethical, or religious lessons but is sometimes used for satiric or political purposes. Examples of allegorical works include Edmund Spenser's *The Faerie Queene* and John Bunyan's *The Pilgrim's Progress.*

Allusion: A reference to a familiar literary or historical person or event, used to make an idea more easily understood. For example, describing someone as a "Romeo" makes an allusion to William Shakespeare's famous young lover in *Romeo and Juliet.*

Amerind Literature: The writing and oral traditions of Native Americans. Native American literature was originally passed on by word of mouth, so it consisted largely of stories and events that were easily memorized. Amerind prose is often rhythmic like poetry because it was recited to the beat of a ceremonial drum. Examples of Amerind literature include the autobiographical *Black Elk Speaks,* the works of N. Scott Momaday, James Welch, and Craig Lee Strete, and the poetry of Luci Tapahonso.

Analogy: A comparison of two things made to explain something unfamiliar through its similarities to something familiar, or to prove one point based on the acceptedness of another. Similes and metaphors are types of analogies. Analogies often take the form of an extended simile, as in William Blake's aphorism: "As the caterpillar chooses the fairest leaves to lay her eggs on, so the priest lays his curse on the fairest joys."

Angry Young Men: A group of British writers of the 1950s whose work expressed bitterness and disillusionment with society. Common to their work is an anti-hero who rebels against a corrupt social order and strives for personal integrity. The term has been used to describe Kingsley Amis, John Osborne, Colin Wilson, John Wain, and others.

Antagonist: The major character in a narrative or drama who works against the hero or protagonist. An example of an evil antagonist is Richard Lovelace in Samuel Richardson's *Clarissa,* while a virtuous antagonist is Macduff in William Shakespeare's *Macbeth.*

Anthropomorphism: The presentation of animals or objects in human shape or with human characteristics. The term is derived from the Greek word for "human form." The fables of Aesop, the animated films of Walt Disney, and Richard Adams's *Watership Down* feature anthropomorphic characters.

Anti-hero: A central character in a work of literature who lacks traditional heroic qualities such as courage, physical prowess, and fortitude. Anti-heros typically distrust conventional values and are unable to commit themselves to any ideals. They generally feel helpless in a world over which they have no control. Anti-heroes usually accept, and often celebrate, their positions as social outcasts. A well-known anti-hero is Yossarian in Joseph Heller's novel *Catch-22.*

Antimasque: See *Masque*

Antithesis: The antithesis of something is its direct opposite. In literature, the use of antithesis as a figure of speech results in two statements that show a contrast through the balancing of two opposite ideas. Technically, it is the second portion of the statement that is defined as the "antithesis"; the first portion is the "thesis." An example of antithesis is found in the following portion of Abraham Lincoln's "Gettysburg Address"; notice the opposition between the verbs "remember" and "forget" and the phrases "what we say" and "what they did": "The world will little note nor long remember what we say here, but it can never forget what they did here."

Apocrypha: Writings tentatively attributed to an author but not proven or universally accepted to be their works. The term was originally applied to certain books of the Bible that were not considered inspired and so were not included in the "sacred canon." Geoffrey Chaucer, William Shakespeare, Thomas Kyd, Thomas Middleton, and John Marston all have apocrypha. Apocryphal books of the Bible include the Old Testament's Book of Enoch and New Testament's Gospel of Peter.

Apollonian and Dionysian: The two impulses believed to guide authors of dramatic tragedy. The Apollonian impulse is named after Apollo, the Greek god of light and beauty and the symbol of intellectual order. The Dionysian impulse is named after Dionysus, the Greek god of wine and the symbol of the unrestrained forces of nature. The Apollonian impulse is to create a rational, harmonious world, while the Dionysian is to express the irrational forces of personality. Friedrich Nietzche uses these terms in *The Birth of Tragedy* to designate contrasting elements in Greek tragedy.

Apostrophe: A statement, question, or request addressed to an inanimate object or concept or to a nonexistent or absent person. Requests for inspiration from the muses in poetry are examples of apostrophe, as is Marc Antony's address to Caesar's corpse in William Shakespeare's *Julius Caesar*: "O, pardon me, thou bleeding piece of earth, That I am meek and gentle with these butchers!. . . Woe to the hand that shed this costly blood!. . . ''

Archetype: The word archetype is commonly used to describe an original pattern or model from which all other things of the same kind are made. This term was introduced to literary criticism from the psychology of Carl Jung. It expresses Jung's theory that behind every person's "unconscious," or repressed memories of the past, lies the "collective unconscious" of the human race: memories of the countless typical experiences of our ancestors. These memories are said to prompt illogical associations that trigger powerful emotions in the reader. Often, the emotional process is primitive, even primordial. Archetypes are the literary images that grow out of the "collective unconscious." They appear in literature as incidents and plots that repeat basic patterns of life. They may also appear as stereotyped characters. Examples of literary archetypes include themes such as birth and death and characters such as the Earth Mother.

Argument: The argument of a work is the author's subject matter or principal idea. Examples of defined "argument" portions of works include John Milton's *Arguments* to each of the books of *Paradise Lost* and the "Argument" to Robert Herrick's *Hesperides.*

Aristotelian Criticism: Specifically, the method of evaluating and analyzing tragedy formulated by the Greek philosopher Aristotle in his *Poetics.* More generally, the term indicates any form of criticism that follows Aristotle's views. Aristotelian criticism focuses on the form and logical structure of a work, apart from its historical or social context, in contrast to "Platonic Criticism," which stresses the usefulness of art. Adherents of New Criticism including John Crowe Ransom and Cleanth Brooks utilize and value the basic ideas of Aristotelian criticism for textual analysis.

Art for Art's Sake: See *Aestheticism*

Aside: A comment made by a stage performer that is intended to be heard by the audience but supposedly not by other characters. Eugene O'Neill's *Strange Interlude* is an extended use of the aside in modern theater.

Audience: The people for whom a piece of literature is written. Authors usually write with a certain audience in mind, for example, children, members of a religious or ethnic group, or colleagues in a professional field. The term "audience" also applies to the people who gather to see or hear any performance, including plays, poetry readings, speeches, and concerts. Jane Austen's parody of the gothic novel, *Northanger Abbey,* was originally intended for (and also pokes fun at) an audience of young and avid female gothic novel readers.

Avant-garde: A French term meaning "vanguard." It is used in literary criticism to describe new writing that rejects traditional approaches to literature in favor of innovations in style or content. Twentieth-century examples of the literary *avant-garde* include the Black Mountain School of poets, the Bloomsbury Group, and the Beat Movement.

B

Ballad: A short poem that tells a simple story and has a repeated refrain. Ballads were originally intended to be sung. Early ballads, known as folk ballads, were passed down through generations, so their authors are often unknown. Later ballads composed by known authors are called literary ballads. An example of an anonymous folk ballad is "Edward," which dates from the Middle Ages. Samuel Taylor Coleridge's "The Rime of the Ancient Mariner" and John Keats's "La Belle Dame sans Merci" are examples of literary ballads.

Baroque: A term used in literary criticism to describe literature that is complex or ornate in style or diction. Baroque works typically express tension, anxiety, and violent emotion. The term "Baroque Age" designates a period in Western European literature beginning in the late sixteenth century and ending about one hundred years later. Works of this period often mirror the qualities of works more generally associated with the label "baroque" and sometimes feature elaborate conceits. Examples of Baroque works include John Lyly's *Euphues: The Anatomy of Wit,* Luis de Gongora's *Soledads,* and William Shakespeare's *As You Like It.*

Baroque Age: See *Baroque*

Baroque Period: See *Baroque*

Beat Generation: See *Beat Movement*

Beat Movement: A period featuring a group of American poets and novelists of the 1950s and 1960s—including Jack Kerouac, Allen Ginsberg, Gregory Corso, William S. Burroughs, and Lawrence Ferlinghetti—who rejected established social and literary values. Using such techniques as stream of consciousness writing and jazz-influenced free verse and focusing on unusual or abnormal states of mind—generated by religious ecstasy or the use of drugs—the Beat writers aimed to create works that were unconventional in both form and subject matter. Kerouac's *On the Road* is perhaps the best-known example of a Beat Generation novel, and Ginsberg's *Howl* is a famous collection of Beat poetry.

Black Aesthetic Movement: A period of artistic and literary development among African Americans in the 1960s and early 1970s. This was the first major African-American artistic movement since the Harlem Renaissance and was closely paralleled by the civil rights and black power movements. The black aesthetic writers attempted to produce works of art that would be meaningful to the black masses. Key figures in black aesthetics included one of its founders, poet and playwright Amiri Baraka, formerly known as LeRoi Jones; poet and essayist Haki R. Madhubuti, formerly Don L. Lee; poet and playwright Sonia Sanchez; and dramatist Ed Bullins. Works representative of the Black Aesthetic Movement include Amiri Baraka's play *Dutchman,* a 1964 Obie award-winner; *Black Fire: An Anthology of Afro-American Writing,* edited by Baraka and playwright Larry Neal and published in 1968; and Sonia Sanchez's poetry collection *We a BaddDDD People,* published in 1970. Also known as Black Arts Movement.

Black Arts Movement: See *Black Aesthetic Movement*

Black Comedy: See *Black Humor*

Black Humor: Writing that places grotesque elements side by side with humorous ones in an attempt to shock the reader, forcing him or her to laugh at the horrifying reality of a disordered world. Joseph Heller's novel *Catch-22* is considered a superb example of the use of black humor. Other well-known authors who use black humor include Kurt Vonnegut, Edward Albee, Eugene Ionesco, and Harold Pinter. Also known as Black Comedy.

Blank Verse: Loosely, any unrhymed poetry, but more generally, unrhymed iambic pentameter verse (composed of lines of five two-syllable feet with the first syllable accented, the second unaccented). Blank verse has been used by poets since the Renaissance for its flexibility and its graceful, dignified tone. John Milton's *Paradise Lost* is in blank verse, as are most of William Shakespeare's plays.

Bloomsbury Group: A group of English writers, artists, and intellectuals who held informal artistic and philosophical discussions in Bloomsbury, a district of London, from around 1907 to the early 1930s. The Bloomsbury Group held no uniform philosophical beliefs but did commonly express an aversion to moral prudery and a desire for greater social tolerance. At various times the circle included Virginia Woolf, E. M. Forster, Clive Bell, Lytton Strachey, and John Maynard Keynes.

Bon Mot: A French term meaning "good word." A *bon mot* is a witty remark or clever observation. Charles Lamb and Oscar Wilde are celebrated for their witty *bon mots*. Two examples by Oscar Wilde stand out: (1) "All women become their mothers. That is their tragedy. No man does. That's his." (2) "A man cannot be too careful in the choice of his enemies."

Breath Verse: See *Projective Verse*

Burlesque: Any literary work that uses exaggeration to make its subject appear ridiculous, either by treating a trivial subject with profound seriousness or by treating a dignified subject frivolously. The word "burlesque" may also be used as an adjective, as in "burlesque show," to mean "striptease act." Examples of literary burlesque include the comedies of Aristophanes, Miguel de Cervantes's *Don Quixote,*, Samuel Butler's poem "Hudibras," and John Gay's play *The Beggar's Opera.*

C

Cadence: The natural rhythm of language caused by the alternation of accented and unaccented syllables. Much modern poetry—notably free verse—deliberately manipulates cadence to create complex rhythmic effects. James Macpherson's "Ossian poems" are richly cadenced, as is the poetry of the Symbolists, Walt Whitman, and Amy Lowell.

Caesura: A pause in a line of poetry, usually occurring near the middle. It typically corresponds to a break in the natural rhythm or sense of the line but is sometimes shifted to create special meanings or rhythmic effects. The opening line of Edgar Allan Poe's "The Raven" contains a caesura following "dreary": "Once upon a midnight dreary, while I pondered weak and weary...."

Canzone: A short Italian or Provencal lyric poem, commonly about love and often set to music. The *canzone* has no set form but typically contains five or six stanzas made up of seven to twenty lines of eleven syllables each. A shorter, five- to ten-line "envoy," or concluding stanza, completes the poem. Masters of the *canzone* form include

Petrarch, Dante Alighieri, Torquato Tasso, and Guido Cavalcanti.

Carpe Diem: A Latin term meaning "seize the day." This is a traditional theme of poetry, especially lyrics. A *carpe diem* poem advises the reader or the person it addresses to live for today and enjoy the pleasures of the moment. Two celebrated *carpe diem* poems are Andrew Marvell's "To His Coy Mistress" and Robert Herrick's poem beginning "Gather ye rosebuds while ye may. . . ."

Catharsis: The release or purging of unwanted emotions— specifically fear and pity—brought about by exposure to art. The term was first used by the Greek philosopher Aristotle in his *Poetics* to refer to the desired effect of tragedy on spectators. A famous example of catharsis is realized in Sophocles' *Oedipus Rex,* when Oedipus discovers that his wife, Jacosta, is his own mother and that the stranger he killed on the road was his own father.

Celtic Renaissance: A period of Irish literary and cultural history at the end of the nineteenth century. Followers of the movement aimed to create a romantic vision of Celtic myth and legend. The most significant works of the Celtic Renaissance typically present a dreamy, unreal world, usually in reaction against the reality of contemporary problems. William Butler Yeats's *The Wanderings of Oisin* is among the most significant works of the Celtic Renaissance. Also known as Celtic Twilight.

Celtic Twilight: See *Celtic Renaissance*

Character: Broadly speaking, a person in a literary work. The actions of characters are what constitute the plot of a story, novel, or poem. There are numerous types of characters, ranging from simple, stereotypical figures to intricate, multifaceted ones. In the techniques of anthropomorphism and personification, animals—and even places or things— can assume aspects of character. "Characterization" is the process by which an author creates vivid, believable characters in a work of art. This may be done in a variety of ways, including (1) direct description of the character by the narrator; (2) the direct presentation of the speech, thoughts, or actions of the character; and (3) the responses of other characters to the character. The term "character" also refers to a form originated by the ancient Greek writer Theophrastus that later became popular in the seventeenth and eighteenth centuries. It is a short essay or sketch of a person who prominently displays a specific attribute or quality, such as miserliness or ambition. Notable characters in literature include Oedipus Rex, Don Quixote de la Mancha, Macbeth, Candide, Hester Prynne, Ebenezer Scrooge, Huckleberry Finn, Jay Gatsby, Scarlett O'Hara, James Bond, and Kunta Kinte.

Characterization: See *Character*

Chorus: In ancient Greek drama, a group of actors who commented on and interpreted the unfolding action on the stage. Initially the chorus was a major component of the presentation, but over time it became less significant, with its numbers reduced and its role eventually limited to commentary between acts. By the sixteenth century the chorus—if employed at all—was typically a single person who provided a prologue and an epilogue and occasionally appeared between acts to introduce or underscore an important event. The chorus in William Shakespeare's *Henry V* functions in this way. Modern dramas rarely feature a chorus, but T. S. Eliot's *Murder in the Cathedral* and Arthur Miller's *A View from the Bridge* are notable exceptions. The Stage Manager in Thornton Wilder's *Our Town* performs a role similar to that of the chorus.

Chronicle: A record of events presented in chronological order. Although the scope and level of detail provided varies greatly among the chronicles surviving from ancient times, some, such as the *Anglo-Saxon Chronicle,* feature vivid descriptions and a lively recounting of events. During the Elizabethan Age, many dramas— appropriately called "chronicle plays"—were based on material from chronicles. Many of William Shakespeare's dramas of English history as well as Christopher Marlowe's *Edward II* are based in part on Raphael Holinshead's *Chronicles of England, Scotland, and Ireland.*

Classical: In its strictest definition in literary criticism, classicism refers to works of ancient Greek or Roman literature. The term may also be used to describe a literary work of recognized importance (a "classic") from any time period or literature that exhibits the traits of classicism. Classical authors from ancient Greek and Roman times include Juvenal and Homer. Examples of later works and authors now described as classical include French literature of the seventeenth century, Western novels of the nineteenth century, and American fiction of the mid-nineteenth century such as that written by James Fenimore Cooper and Mark Twain.

Classicism: A term used in literary criticism to describe critical doctrines that have their roots in ancient Greek and Roman literature, philosophy, and art. Works associated with classicism typically exhibit restraint on the part of the author, unity of design and purpose, clarity, simplicity, logical organization, and respect for tradition. Examples of literary classicism include Cicero's prose, the dramas of Pierre Corneille and Jean Racine, the poetry of John Dryden and Alexander Pope, and the writings of J. W. von Goethe, G. E. Lessing, and T. S. Eliot.

Climax: The turning point in a narrative, the moment when the conflict is at its most intense. Typically, the structure of stories, novels, and plays is one of rising action, in which tension builds to the climax, followed by falling action, in which tension lessens as the story moves to its conclusion. The climax in James Fenimore Cooper's *The Last of the Mohicans* occurs when Magua and his captive Cora are pursued to the edge of a cliff by Uncas. Magua kills Uncas but is subsequently killed by Hawkeye.

Colloquialism: A word, phrase, or form of pronunciation that is acceptable in casual conversation but not in formal, written communication. It is considered more acceptable than slang. An example of colloquialism can be found in Rudyard Kipling's *Barrack-room Ballads:* When 'Omer smote 'is bloomin' lyre He'd 'eard men sing by land and sea; An' what he thought 'e might require 'E went an' took—the same as me!

Comedy: One of two major types of drama, the other being tragedy. Its aim is to amuse, and it typically ends happily. Comedy assumes many forms, such as farce and burlesque, and uses a variety of techniques, from parody to satire. In a restricted sense the term comedy refers only to dramatic presentations, but in general usage it is commonly applied to nondramatic works as well. Examples of comedies range from the plays of Aristophanes, Terrence, and Plautus, Dante Alighieri's *The Divine Comedy,* Francois Rabelais's *Pantagruel* and *Gargantua,* and some of Geoffrey Chaucer's tales and William Shakespeare's plays to Noel Coward's play *Private Lives* and James Thurber's short story "The Secret Life of Walter Mitty."

Comedy of Manners: A play about the manners and conventions of an aristocratic, highly sophisticated society. The characters are usually types rather than individualized personalities, and plot is less important than atmosphere. Such plays were an important aspect of late seventeenth-century English comedy. The comedy of manners was revived in the eighteenth century by Oliver Goldsmith and Richard Brinsley Sheridan, enjoyed a second revival in the late nineteenth century, and has endured into the twentieth century. Examples of comedies of manners include William Congreve's *The Way of the World* in the late seventeenth century, Oliver Goldsmith's *She Stoops to Conquer* and Richard Brinsley Sheridan's *The School for Scandal* in the eighteenth century, Oscar Wilde's *The Importance of Being Earnest* in the nineteenth century, and W. Somerset Maugham's *The Circle* in the twentieth century.

Comic Relief: The use of humor to lighten the mood of a serious or tragic story, especially in plays. The technique is very common in Elizabethan works, and can be an integral part of the plot or simply a brief event designed to break the tension of the scene. The Gravediggers' scene in William Shakespeare's *Hamlet* is a frequently cited example of comic relief.

Commedia dell'arte: An Italian term meaning "the comedy of guilds" or "the comedy of professional actors." This form of dramatic comedy was popular in Italy during the sixteenth century. Actors were assigned stock roles (such as Pulcinella, the stupid servant, or Pantalone, the old merchant) and given a basic plot to follow, but all dialogue was improvised. The roles were rigidly typed and the plots were formulaic, usually revolving around young lovers who thwarted their elders and attained wealth and happiness. A rigid convention of the *commedia dell'arte* is the periodic intrusion of Harlequin, who interrupts the play with low buffoonery. Peppino de Filippo's *Metamorphoses of a Wandering Minstrel* gave modern audiences an idea of what *commedia dell'arte* may have been like. Various scenarios for *commedia dell'arte* were compiled in Petraccone's *La commedia dell'arte, storia, technica, scenari,* published in 1927.

Complaint: A lyric poem, popular in the Renaissance, in which the speaker expresses sorrow about his or her condition. Typically, the speaker's sadness is caused by an unresponsive lover, but some complaints cite other sources of unhappiness, such as poverty or fate. A commonly cited example is "A Complaint by Night of the Lover Not Beloved" by Henry Howard, Earl of Surrey. Thomas Sackville's "Complaint of Henry, Duke of Buckingham" traces the duke's unhappiness to his ruthless ambition.

Conceit: A clever and fanciful metaphor, usually expressed through elaborate and extended comparison, that presents a striking parallel between two seemingly dissimilar things—for example, elaborately comparing a beautiful woman to an object like a garden or the sun. The conceit was a popular device throughout the Elizabethan Age and Baroque Age and was the principal technique of the seventeenth-century English metaphysical poets. This usage of the word conceit is unrelated to the best-known definition of conceit as an arrogant attitude or behavior. The conceit figures prominently in the works of John Donne, Emily Dickinson, and T. S. Eliot.

Concrete: Concrete is the opposite of abstract, and refers to a thing that actually exists or a description that allows the reader to experience an object or concept with the senses. Henry David Thoreau's *Walden* contains much concrete description of nature and wildlife.

Concrete Poetry: Poetry in which visual elements play a large part in the poetic effect. Punctuation marks, letters, or words are arranged on a page to form a visual design: a cross, for example, or a bumblebee. Max Bill and Eugene Gomringer were among the early practitioners of concrete poetry; Haroldo de Campos and Augusto de Campos are among contemporary authors of concrete poetry.

Confessional Poetry: A form of poetry in which the poet reveals very personal, intimate, sometimes shocking information about himself or herself. Anne Sexton, Sylvia Plath, Robert Lowell, and John Berryman wrote poetry in the confessional vein.

Conflict: The conflict in a work of fiction is the issue to be resolved in the story. It usually occurs between two characters, the protagonist and the antagonist, or between the protagonist and society or the protagonist and himself or herself. Conflict in Theodore Dreiser's novel *Sister Carrie* comes as a result of urban society, while Jack London's short story "To Build a Fire" concerns the protagonist's battle against the cold and himself.

Connotation: The impression that a word gives beyond its defined meaning. Connotations may be universally understood or may be significant only to a certain group. Both "horse" and "steed" denote the same animal, but "steed" has a different connotation, deriving from the chivalrous or romantic narratives in which the word was once often used.

Consonance: Consonance occurs in poetry when words appearing at the ends of two or more verses have similar final consonant sounds but have final vowel sounds that differ, as with "stuff" and "off." Consonance is found in "The curfew tolls the knells of parting day" from Thomas Grey's "An Elegy Written in a Country Church Yard." Also known as Half Rhyme or Slant Rhyme.

Convention: Any widely accepted literary device, style, or form. A soliloquy, in which a character reveals to the audience his or her private thoughts, is an example of a dramatic convention.

Corrido: A Mexican ballad. Examples of *corridos* include "Muerte del afamado Bilito," "La voz de mi conciencia," "Lucio Perez," "La juida," and "Los presos."

Couplet: Two lines of poetry with the same rhyme and meter, often expressing a complete and self-contained thought. The following couplet is from Alexander Pope's "Elegy to the Memory of an Unfortunate Lady": 'Tis Use alone that sanctifies Expense, And Splendour borrows all her rays from Sense.

Criticism: The systematic study and evaluation of literary works, usually based on a specific method or set of principles. An important part of literary studies since ancient times, the practice of criticism has given rise to numerous theories, methods, and "schools," sometimes producing conflicting, even contradictory, interpretations of literature in general as well as of individual works. Even such basic issues as what constitutes a poem or a novel have been the subject of much criticism over the centuries. Seminal texts of literary criticism include Plato's *Republic,* Aristotle's *Poetics,* Sir Philip Sidney's *The Defence of Poesie,* John Dryden's *Of Dramatic Poesie,* and William Wordsworth's "Preface" to the second edition of his *Lyrical Ballads.* Contemporary schools of criticism include deconstruction, feminist, psychoanalytic, poststructuralist, new historicist, postcolonialist, and reader- response.

D

Dactyl: See *Foot*

Dadaism: A protest movement in art and literature founded by Tristan Tzara in 1916. Followers of the movement expressed their outrage at the destruction brought about by World War I by revolting against numerous forms of social convention. The Dadaists presented works marked by calculated madness and flamboyant nonsense. They stressed total freedom of expression, commonly through primitive displays of emotion and illogical, often senseless, poetry. The movement ended shortly after the war, when it was replaced by surrealism. Proponents of Dadaism include Andre Breton, Louis Aragon, Philippe Soupault, and Paul Eluard.

Decadent: See *Decadents*

Decadents: The followers of a nineteenth-century literary movement that had its beginnings in French aestheticism. Decadent literature displays a fascination with perverse and morbid states; a search for novelty and sensation—the "new thrill"; a preoccupation with mysticism; and a belief in the senselessness of human existence. The movement is closely associated with the doctrine Art for Art's Sake. The term "decadence" is sometimes used to denote a decline in the quality of art or literature following a period of greatness. Major French decadents are Charles Baudelaire and Arthur Rimbaud. English decadents include Oscar Wilde, Ernest Dowson, and Frank Harris.

Deconstruction: A method of literary criticism developed by Jacques Derrida and characterized by multiple conflicting interpretations of a given work. Deconstructionists consider the impact of the language of a work and suggest that the true meaning of the work is not necessarily the meaning that the author intended. Jacques Derrida's *De la grammatologie* is the seminal text on deconstructive strategies; among American practitioners of this method of criticism are Paul de Man and J. Hillis Miller.

Deduction: The process of reaching a conclusion through reasoning from general premises to a specific premise. An example of deduction is present in the following syllogism: Premise: All mammals are animals. Premise: All whales are mammals. Conclusion: Therefore, all whales are animals.

Denotation: The definition of a word, apart from the impressions or feelings it creates in the reader. The word "apartheid" denotes a political and economic policy of segregation by race, but its connotations— oppression, slavery, inequality—are numerous.

Denouement: A French word meaning "the unknotting." In literary criticism, it denotes the resolution of conflict in fiction or drama. The *denouement* follows the climax and provides an outcome to the primary plot situation as well as an explanation of secondary plot complications. The *denouement* often involves a character's recognition of his or her state of mind or moral condition. A well-known example of *denouement* is the last scene of the play *As You Like It* by William Shakespeare, in which couples are married, an evildoer repents, the identities of two disguised characters are revealed, and a ruler is restored to power. Also known as Falling Action.

Description: Descriptive writing is intended to allow a reader to picture the scene or setting in which the action of a story takes place. The form this description takes often evokes an intended emotional response—a dark, spooky graveyard will evoke fear, and a peaceful, sunny meadow will evoke calmness. An example of a descriptive story is Edgar Allan Poe's *Landor's Cottage,* which offers a detailed depiction of a New York country estate.

Detective Story: A narrative about the solution of a mystery or the identification of a criminal. The conventions of the detective story include the detective's scrupulous use of logic in solving the mystery; incompetent or ineffectual police; a suspect who appears guilty at first but is later proved innocent; and the detective's friend or confidant— often the narrator—whose slowness in interpreting clues emphasizes by contrast the detective's brilliance. Edgar Allan Poe's "Murders in the Rue Morgue" is commonly regarded as the earliest example of this type of story. With this work, Poe established many of the conventions of the detective story genre, which are still in practice. Other practitioners of this vast and extremely popular genre include Arthur Conan Doyle, Dashiell Hammett, and Agatha Christie.

Deus ex machina: A Latin term meaning "god out of a machine." In Greek drama, a god was often lowered onto the stage by a mechanism of some kind to rescue the hero or untangle the plot. By extension, the term refers to any artificial device or coincidence used to bring about a convenient and simple solution to a plot. This is a common device in melodramas and includes such fortunate circumstances as the sudden receipt of a legacy to save the family farm or a last-minute stay of execution. The *deus ex machina* invariably rewards the virtuous and punishes evildoers. Examples of *deus ex machina* include King Louis XIV in Jean-Baptiste Moliere's *Tartuffe* and Queen Victoria in *The Pirates of Penzance* by William Gilbert and Arthur Sullivan. Bertolt Brecht parodies the abuse of such devices in the conclusion of his *Threepenny Opera.*

Dialogue: In its widest sense, dialogue is simply conversation between people in a literary work; in its most restricted sense, it refers specifically to the speech of characters in a drama. As a specific literary genre, a "dialogue" is a composition in which characters debate an issue or idea. The Greek philosopher Plato frequently expounded his theories in the form of dialogues.

Diction: The selection and arrangement of words in a literary work. Either or both may vary depending on the desired effect. There are four general types of diction: "formal," used in scholarly or lofty writing; "informal," used in relaxed but educated conversation; "colloquial," used in everyday speech; and "slang," containing newly coined words and other terms not accepted in formal usage.

Didactic: A term used to describe works of literature that aim to teach some moral, religious, political, or practical lesson. Although didactic elements are often found in artistically pleasing works, the term "didactic" usually refers to literature in which the message is more important than the form. The term may also be used to criticize a work that the critic finds "overly didactic," that is, heavy-handed in its delivery of a lesson. Examples of didactic literature include John Bunyan's *Pilgrim's Progress,* Alexander Pope's *Essay on Criticism,* Jean-Jacques Rousseau's *Emile,* and Elizabeth Inchbald's *Simple Story.*

Dimeter: See *Meter*

Dionysian: See *Apollonian and Dionysian*

Discordia concours: A Latin phrase meaning "discord in harmony." The term was coined by the eighteenth-century English writer Samuel Johnson to describe "a combination of dissimilar images or discovery of occult resemblances in things apparently unlike." Johnson created the expression by reversing a phrase by the Latin poet Horace. The metaphysical poetry of John Donne, Richard Crashaw, Abraham Cowley, George Herbert, and Edward Taylor among others, contains many examples of *discordia concours.* In Donne's "A Valediction: Forbidding Mourning," the poet compares the union of himself with his lover to a draftsman's compass: If they be two, they are two so, As stiff twin compasses are two: Thy soul, the fixed foot, makes no show To move, but doth, if the other do; And though it in the center sit, Yet when the other far doth roam, It leans, and hearkens after it, And grows erect, as that comes home.

Dissonance: A combination of harsh or jarring sounds, especially in poetry. Although such combinations may be accidental, poets sometimes intentionally make them to achieve particular effects. Dissonance is also sometimes used to refer to close but not identical rhymes. When this is the case, the word functions as a synonym for consonance. Robert Browning, Gerard Manley Hopkins, and many other poets have made deliberate use of dissonance.

Doppelganger: A literary technique by which a character is duplicated (usually in the form of an alter ego, though sometimes as a ghostly counterpart) or divided into two distinct, usually opposite personalities. The use of this character device is widespread in nineteenth- and twentieth- century literature, and indicates a growing awareness among authors that the "self" is really a composite of many "selves." A well-known story containing a *doppelganger* character is Robert Louis Stevenson's *Dr. Jekyll and Mr. Hyde,* which dramatizes an internal struggle between good and evil. Also known as The Double.

Double Entendre: A corruption of a French phrase meaning "double meaning." The term is used to indicate a word or phrase that is deliberately ambiguous, especially when one of the meanings is risque or improper. An example of a *double entendre* is the Elizabethan usage of the verb "die," which refers both to death and to orgasm.

Double, The: See *Doppelganger*

Draft: Any preliminary version of a written work. An author may write dozens of drafts which are revised to form the final work, or he or she may write only one, with few or no revisions. Dorothy Parker's observation that "I can't write five words but that I change seven" humorously indicates the purpose of the draft.

Drama: In its widest sense, a drama is any work designed to be presented by actors on a stage. Similarly, "drama" denotes a broad literary genre that includes a variety of forms, from pageant and spectacle to tragedy and comedy, as well as countless types and subtypes. More commonly in modern usage, however, a drama is a work that treats serious subjects and themes but does not aim at the grandeur of tragedy. This use of the term originated with the eighteenth-century French writer Denis Diderot, who used the word *drame* to designate his plays about middle- class life; thus "drama" typically features characters of a less exalted stature than those of tragedy. Examples of classical dramas include Menander's comedy *Dyscolus* and Sophocles' tragedy *Oedipus Rex.* Contemporary dramas include Eugene O'Neill's *The Iceman Cometh,* Lillian Hellman's *Little Foxes,* and August Wilson's *Ma Rainey's Black Bottom.*

Dramatic Irony: Occurs when the audience of a play or the reader of a work of literature knows something that a character in the work itself does not know. The irony is in the contrast between the intended meaning of the statements or actions of a character and the additional information understood by the audience. A celebrated example of dramatic irony is in Act V of William Shakespeare's *Romeo and Juliet,* where two young lovers meet their end as a result of a tragic misunderstanding. Here, the audience has full knowledge that Juliet's apparent "death" is merely temporary; she will regain her senses when the mysterious "sleeping potion" she has taken wears off. But Romeo, mistaking Juliet's drug-induced trance for true death, kills himself in grief. Upon awakening, Juliet discovers Romeo's corpse and, in despair, slays herself.

Dramatic Monologue: See *Monologue*

Dramatic Poetry: Any lyric work that employs elements of drama such as dialogue, conflict, or characterization, but excluding works that are intended for stage presentation. A monologue is a form of dramatic poetry.

Dramatis Personae: The characters in a work of literature, particularly a drama. The list of characters printed before the main text of a play or in the program is the *dramatis personae.*

Dream Allegory: See *Dream Vision*

Dream Vision: A literary convention, chiefly of the Middle Ages. In a dream vision a story is presented as a literal dream of the narrator. This device was commonly used to teach moral and religious lessons. Important works of this type are *The Divine Comedy* by Dante Alighieri, *Piers Plowman* by William Langland, and *The Pilgrim's Progress* by John Bunyan. Also known as Dream Allegory.

Dystopia: An imaginary place in a work of fiction where the characters lead dehumanized, fearful lives. Jack London's *The Iron Heel,* Yevgeny Zamyatin's *My,* Aldous Huxley's *Brave New World,* George Orwell's *Nineteen Eighty-four,* and Margaret Atwood's *Handmaid's Tale* portray versions of dystopia.

E

Eclogue: In classical literature, a poem featuring rural themes and structured as a dialogue among shepherds. Eclogues often took specific poetic forms, such as elegies or love poems. Some were written as the soliloquy of a shepherd. In later centuries, "eclogue" came to refer to any poem that was in the pastoral tradition or that had a dialogue or monologue structure. A classical example of an eclogue is Virgil's *Eclogues,* also known as *Bucolics.* Giovanni Boccaccio, Edmund Spenser, Andrew Marvell, Jonathan Swift, and Louis MacNeice also wrote eclogues.

Edwardian: Describes cultural conventions identified with the period of the reign of Edward VII of England (1901-1910). Writers of the Edwardian Age typically displayed a strong reaction against the propriety and conservatism of the Victorian Age. Their work often exhibits distrust of authority in religion, politics, and art and expresses strong doubts about the soundness of conventional values. Writers of this era include George Bernard Shaw, H. G. Wells, and Joseph Conrad.

Edwardian Age: See *Edwardian*

Electra Complex: A daughter's amorous obsession with her father. The term Electra complex comes from the plays of Euripides and Sophocles entitled *Electra,* in which the character Electra drives her brother Orestes to kill their mother and her lover in revenge for the murder of their father.

Elegy: A lyric poem that laments the death of a person or the eventual death of all people. In a conventional elegy, set in a classical world, the poet and subject are spoken of as shepherds. In modern criticism, the word elegy is often used to refer to a poem that is melancholy or mournfully contemplative. John Milton's "Lycidas" and Percy Bysshe Shelley's "Adonais" are two examples of this form.

Elizabethan Age: A period of great economic growth, religious controversy, and nationalism closely associated with the reign of Elizabeth I of England (1558-1603). The Elizabethan Age is considered a part of the general renaissance—that is, the flowering of arts and literature—that took place in Europe during the fourteenth through sixteenth centuries. The era is considered the golden age of English literature. The most important dramas in English and a great deal of lyric poetry were produced during this period, and modern English criticism began around this time. The notable authors of the period—Philip Sidney, Edmund Spenser, Christopher Marlowe, William Shakespeare, Ben Jonson, Francis Bacon, and John Donne—are among the best in all of English literature.

Elizabethan Drama: English comic and tragic plays produced during the Renaissance, or more narrowly, those plays written during the last years of and few years after Queen Elizabeth's reign. William Shakespeare is considered an Elizabethan dramatist in the broader sense, although most of his work was produced during the reign of James I. Examples of Elizabethan comedies include John Lyly's *The Woman in the Moone,* Thomas Dekker's *The Roaring Girl, or, Moll Cut Purse,* and William Shakespeare's *Twelfth Night.* Examples of Elizabethan tragedies include William Shakespeare's *Antony and Cleopatra,* Thomas Kyd's *The Spanish Tragedy,* and John Webster's *The Tragedy of the Duchess of Malfi.*

Empathy: A sense of shared experience, including emotional and physical feelings, with someone or something other than oneself. Empathy is often used to describe the response of a reader to a literary character. An example of an empathic passage is William Shakespeare's description in his narrative poem *Venus and Adonis* of: the snail, whose tender horns being hit, Shrinks backward in his shelly cave with pain. Readers of Gerard Manley Hopkins's *The Windhover* may experience some of the physical sensations evoked in the description of the movement of the falcon.

English Sonnet: See *Sonnet*

Enjambment: The running over of the sense and structure of a line of verse or a couplet into the following verse or couplet. Andrew Marvell's "To His Coy Mistress" is structured as a series of enjambments, as in lines 11-12: "My vegetable love should grow/Vaster than empires and more slow."

Enlightenment, The: An eighteenth-century philosophical movement. It began in France but had a wide impact throughout Europe and America. Thinkers of the Enlightenment valued reason and believed that both the individual and society could achieve a state of perfection. Corresponding to this essentially humanist vision was a resistance to religious authority. Important figures of the Enlightenment were Denis Diderot and Voltaire in France, Edward Gibbon and David Hume in England, and Thomas Paine and Thomas Jefferson in the United States.

Epic: A long narrative poem about the adventures of a hero of great historic or legendary importance. The setting is vast and the action is often given cosmic significance through the intervention of supernatural forces such as gods, angels, or demons. Epics are typically written in a classical style of grand simplicity with elaborate metaphors and allusions that enhance the symbolic importance of a hero's adventures. Some well-known epics are Homer's *Iliad* and *Odyssey,* Virgil's *Aeneid,* and John Milton's *Paradise Lost.*

Epic Simile: See *Homeric Simile*

Epic Theater: A theory of theatrical presentation developed by twentieth-century German playwright Bertolt Brecht. Brecht created a type of drama that the audience could view with complete detachment. He used what he termed "alienation effects" to create an emotional distance between the audience and the action on stage. Among these effects are: short, self-contained scenes that keep the play from building to a cathartic climax; songs that comment on the action; and techniques of acting that prevent the actor from developing an emotional identity with his role. Besides the plays of Bertolt Brecht, other plays that utilize epic theater conventions include those of Georg Buchner, Frank Wedekind, Erwin Piscator, and Leopold Jessner.

Epigram: A saying that makes the speaker's point quickly and concisely. Samuel Taylor Coleridge wrote an epigram that neatly sums up the form: What is an Epigram? A Dwarfish whole, Its body brevity, and wit its soul.

Epilogue: A concluding statement or section of a literary work. In dramas, particularly those of the seventeenth and eighteenth centuries, the epilogue is a closing speech, often in verse, delivered by an actor at the end of a play and spoken directly to the audience. A famous epilogue is Puck's speech at the end of William Shakespeare's *A Midsummer Night's Dream.*

Epiphany: A sudden revelation of truth inspired by a seemingly trivial incident. The term was widely used by James Joyce in his critical writings, and the stories in Joyce's *Dubliners* are commonly called "epiphanies."

Episode: An incident that forms part of a story and is significantly related to it. Episodes may be either self-contained narratives or events that depend on a larger context for their sense and importance. Examples of episodes include the founding of Wilmington, Delaware in Charles Reade's *The Disinherited Heir* and the individual events comprising the picaresque novels and medieval romances.

Episodic Plot: See *Plot*

Epitaph: An inscription on a tomb or tombstone, or a verse written on the occasion of a person's death. Epitaphs may be serious or humorous. Dorothy Parker's epitaph reads, "I told you I was sick."

Epithalamion: A song or poem written to honor and commemorate a marriage ceremony. Famous examples include Edmund Spenser's

"Epithalamion" and e. e. cummings's "Epithalamion." Also spelled Epithalamium.

Epithalamium: See *Epithalamion*

Epithet: A word or phrase, often disparaging or abusive, that expresses a character trait of someone or something. "The Napoleon of crime" is an epithet applied to Professor Moriarty, arch-rival of Sherlock Holmes in Arthur Conan Doyle's series of detective stories.

Exempla: See *Exemplum*

Exemplum: A tale with a moral message. This form of literary sermonizing flourished during the Middle Ages, when *exempla* appeared in collections known as "example-books." The works of Geoffrey Chaucer are full of *exempla*.

Existentialism: A predominantly twentieth-century philosophy concerned with the nature and perception of human existence. There are two major strains of existentialist thought: atheistic and Christian. Followers of atheistic existentialism believe that the individual is alone in a godless universe and that the basic human condition is one of suffering and loneliness. Nevertheless, because there are no fixed values, individuals can create their own characters—indeed, they can shape themselves—through the exercise of free will. The atheistic strain culminates in and is popularly associated with the works of Jean-Paul Sartre. The Christian existentialists, on the other hand, believe that only in God may people find freedom from life's anguish. The two strains hold certain beliefs in common: that existence cannot be fully understood or described through empirical effort; that anguish is a universal element of life; that individuals must bear responsibility for their actions; and that there is no common standard of behavior or perception for religious and ethical matters. Existentialist thought figures prominently in the works of such authors as Eugene Ionesco, Franz Kafka, Fyodor Dostoyevsky, Simone de Beauvoir, Samuel Beckett, and Albert Camus.

Expatriates: See *Expatriatism*

Expatriatism: The practice of leaving one's country to live for an extended period in another country. Literary expatriates include English poets Percy Bysshe Shelley and John Keats in Italy, Polish novelist Joseph Conrad in England, American writers Richard Wright, James Baldwin, Gertrude Stein, and Ernest Hemingway in France, and Trinidadian author Neil Bissondath in Canada.

Exposition: Writing intended to explain the nature of an idea, thing, or theme. Expository writing is often combined with description, narration, or argument. In dramatic writing, the exposition is the introductory material which presents the characters, setting, and tone of the play. An example of dramatic exposition occurs in many nineteenth-century drawing-room comedies in which the butler and the maid open the play with relevant talk about their master and mistress; in composition, exposition relays factual information, as in encyclopedia entries.

Expressionism: An indistinct literary term, originally used to describe an early twentieth-century school of German painting. The term applies to almost any mode of unconventional, highly subjective writing that distorts reality in some way. Advocates of Expressionism include dramatists George Kaiser, Ernst Toller, Luigi Pirandello, Federico Garcia Lorca, Eugene O'Neill, and Elmer Rice; poets George Heym, Ernst Stadler, August Stramm, Gottfried Benn, and Georg Trakl; and novelists Franz Kafka and James Joyce.

Extended Monologue: See *Monologue*

F

Fable: A prose or verse narrative intended to convey a moral. Animals or inanimate objects with human characteristics often serve as characters in fables. A famous fable is Aesop's "The Tortoise and the Hare."

Fairy Tales: Short narratives featuring mythical beings such as fairies, elves, and sprites. These tales originally belonged to the folklore of a particular nation or region, such as those collected in Germany by Jacob and Wilhelm Grimm. Two other celebrated writers of fairy tales are Hans Christian Andersen and Rudyard Kipling.

Falling Action: See *Denouement*

Fantasy: A literary form related to mythology and folklore. Fantasy literature is typically set in nonexistent realms and features supernatural beings. Notable examples of fantasy literature are *The Lord of the Rings* by J. R. R. Tolkien and the Gormenghast trilogy by Mervyn Peake.

Farce: A type of comedy characterized by broad humor, outlandish incidents, and often vulgar subject matter. Much of the "comedy" in film and television could more accurately be described as farce.

Feet: See *Foot*

Feminine Rhyme: See *Rhyme*

Femme fatale: A French phrase with the literal translation "fatal woman." A *femme fatale* is a sensuous, alluring woman who often leads men into danger or trouble. A classic example of the *femme fatale* is the nameless character in Billy Wilder's *The Seven Year Itch,* portrayed by Marilyn Monroe in the film adaptation.

Fiction: Any story that is the product of imagination rather than a documentation of fact. characters and events in such narratives may be based in real life but their ultimate form and configuration is a creation of the author. Geoffrey Chaucer's *The Canterbury Tales,* Laurence Sterne's *Tristram Shandy,* and Margaret Mitchell's *Gone with the Wind* are examples of fiction.

Figurative Language: A technique in writing in which the author temporarily interrupts the order, construction, or meaning of the writing for a particular effect. This interruption takes the form of one or more figures of speech such as hyperbole, irony, or simile. Figurative language is the opposite of literal language, in which every word is truthful, accurate, and free of exaggeration or embellishment. Examples of figurative language are tropes such as metaphor and rhetorical figures such as apostrophe.

Figures of Speech: Writing that differs from customary conventions for construction, meaning, order, or significance for the purpose of a special meaning or effect. There are two major types of figures of speech: rhetorical figures, which do not make changes in the meaning of the words, and tropes, which do. Types of figures of speech include simile, hyperbole, alliteration, and pun, among many others.

Fin de siecle: A French term meaning "end of the century." The term is used to denote the last decade of the nineteenth century, a transition period when writers and other artists abandoned old conventions and looked for new techniques and objectives. Two writers commonly associated with the *fin de siecle* mindset are Oscar Wilde and George Bernard Shaw.

First Person: See *Point of View*

Flashback: A device used in literature to present action that occurred before the beginning of the story. Flashbacks are often introduced as the dreams or recollections of one or more characters. Flashback techniques are often used in films, where they are typically set off by a gradual changing of one picture to another.

Foil: A character in a work of literature whose physical or psychological qualities contrast strongly with, and therefore highlight, the corresponding qualities of another character. In his Sherlock Holmes stories, Arthur Conan Doyle portrayed Dr. Watson as a man of normal habits and intelligence, making him a foil for the eccentric and wonderfully perceptive Sherlock Holmes.

Folk Ballad: See *Ballad*

Folklore: Traditions and myths preserved in a culture or group of people. Typically, these are passed on by word of mouth in various forms—such as legends, songs, and proverbs— or preserved in customs and ceremonies. This term was first used by W. J. Thoms in 1846. Sir James Frazer's *The Golden Bough* is the record of English folklore; myths about the frontier and the Old South exemplify American folklore.

Folktale: A story originating in oral tradition. Folktales fall into a variety of categories, including legends, ghost stories, fairy tales, fables, and anecdotes based on historical figures and events. Examples of folktales include Giambattista Basile's *The Pentamerone,* which contains the tales of Puss in Boots, Rapunzel, Cinderella, and Beauty and the Beast, and Joel Chandler Harris's Uncle Remus stories, which represent transplanted African folktales and American tales about the characters Mike Fink, Johnny Appleseed, Paul Bunyan, and Pecos Bill.

Foot: The smallest unit of rhythm in a line of poetry. In English-language poetry, a foot is typically one accented syllable combined with one or two unaccented syllables. There are many different types of feet. When the accent is on the second syllable of a two syllable word (con- *tort*), the foot is an "iamb"; the reverse accentual pattern (*tor* -ture) is a "trochee." Other feet that commonly occur in poetry in English are "anapest", two unaccented syllables followed by an accented syllable as in inter-*cept*, and "dactyl", an accented syllable followed by two unaccented syllables as in *su*-i- cide.

Foreshadowing: A device used in literature to create expectation or to set up an explanation of later developments. In Charles Dickens's *Great Expectations,* the graveyard encounter at the beginning of the novel between Pip and the escaped convict Magwitch foreshadows the baleful atmosphere and events that comprise much of the narrative.

Form: The pattern or construction of a work which identifies its genre and distinguishes it from other genres. Examples of forms include the different genres, such as the lyric form or the short story form, and various patterns for poetry, such as the verse form or the stanza form.

Formalism: In literary criticism, the belief that literature should follow prescribed rules of construction, such as those that govern the sonnet form. Examples of formalism are found in the work of the New Critics and structuralists.

Fourteener Meter: See *Meter*

Free Verse: Poetry that lacks regular metrical and rhyme patterns but that tries to capture the cadences of everyday speech. The form allows a poet to exploit a variety of rhythmical effects within a single poem. Free-verse techniques have been widely used in the twentieth century by such writers as Ezra Pound, T. S. Eliot, Carl Sandburg, and William Carlos Williams. Also known as *Vers libre*.

Futurism: A flamboyant literary and artistic movement that developed in France, Italy, and Russia from 1908 through the 1920s. Futurist theater and poetry abandoned traditional literary forms. In their place, followers of the movement attempted to achieve total freedom of expression through bizarre imagery and deformed or newly invented words. The Futurists were self-consciously modern artists who attempted to incorporate the appearances and sounds of modern life into their work. Futurist writers include Filippo Tommaso Marinetti, Wyndham Lewis, Guillaume Apollinaire, Velimir Khlebnikov, and Vladimir Mayakovsky.

G

Genre: A category of literary work. In critical theory, genre may refer to both the content of a given work—tragedy, comedy, pastoral—and to its form, such as poetry, novel, or drama. This term also refers to types of popular literature, as in the genres of science fiction or the detective story.

Genteel Tradition: A term coined by critic George Santayana to describe the literary practice of certain late nineteenth- century American writers, especially New Englanders. Followers of the Genteel Tradition emphasized conventionality in social, religious, moral, and literary standards. Some of the best-known writers of the Genteel Tradition are R. H. Stoddard and Bayard Taylor.

Gilded Age: A period in American history during the 1870s characterized by political corruption and materialism. A number of important novels of social and political criticism were written during this time. Examples of Gilded Age literature include Henry Adams's *Democracy* and F. Marion Crawford's *An American Politician*.

Gothic: See *Gothicism*

Gothicism: In literary criticism, works characterized by a taste for the medieval or morbidly attractive. A gothic novel prominently features elements of horror, the supernatural, gloom, and violence: clanking chains, terror, charnel houses, ghosts, medieval castles, and mysteriously slamming doors. The term ''gothic novel'' is also applied to novels that lack elements of the traditional Gothic setting but that create a similar atmosphere of terror or dread. Mary Shelley's *Frankenstein* is perhaps the best-known English work of this kind.

Gothic Novel: See *Gothicism*

Great Chain of Being: The belief that all things and creatures in nature are organized in a hierarchy from inanimate objects at the bottom to God at the top. This system of belief was popular in the seventeenth and eighteenth centuries. A summary of the concept of the great chain of being can be found in the first epistle of Alexander Pope's *An Essay on Man,* and more recently in Arthur O. Lovejoy's *The Great Chain of Being: A Study of the History of an Idea.*

Grotesque: In literary criticism, the subject matter of a work or a style of expression characterized by exaggeration, deformity, freakishness, and disorder. The grotesque often includes an element of comic absurdity. Early examples of literary grotesque include Francois Rabelais's *Pantagruel* and *Gargantua* and Thomas Nashe's *The Unfortunate Traveller,* while more recent examples can be found in the works of Edgar Allan Poe, Evelyn Waugh, Eudora Welty, Flannery O'Connor, Eugene Ionesco, Gunter Grass, Thomas Mann, Mervyn Peake, and Joseph Heller, among many others.

H

Haiku: The shortest form of Japanese poetry, constructed in three lines of five, seven, and five syllables respectively. The message of a *haiku* poem usually centers on some aspect of spirituality and provokes an emotional response in the reader. Early masters of *haiku* include Basho, Buson,

Kobayashi Issa, and Masaoka Shiki. English writers of *haiku* include the Imagists, notably Ezra Pound, H. D., Amy Lowell, Carl Sandburg, and William Carlos Williams. Also known as *Hokku.*

Half Rhyme: See *Consonance*

Hamartia: In tragedy, the event or act that leads to the hero's or heroine's downfall. This term is often incorrectly used as a synonym for tragic flaw. In Richard Wright's *Native Son,* the act that seals Bigger Thomas's fate is his first impulsive murder.

Harlem Renaissance: The Harlem Renaissance of the 1920s is generally considered the first significant movement of black writers and artists in the United States. During this period, new and established black writers published more fiction and poetry than ever before, the first influential black literary journals were established, and black authors and artists received their first widespread recognition and serious critical appraisal. Among the major writers associated with this period are Claude McKay, Jean Toomer, Countee Cullen, Langston Hughes, Arna Bontemps, Nella Larsen, and Zora Neale Hurston. Works representative of the Harlem Renaissance include Arna Bontemps's poems "The Return" and "Golgotha Is a Mountain," Claude McKay's novel *Home to Harlem,* Nella Larsen's novel *Passing,* Langston Hughes's poem "The Negro Speaks of Rivers," and the journals *Crisis* and *Opportunity,* both founded during this period. Also known as Negro Renaissance and New Negro Movement.

Harlequin: A stock character of the *commedia dell'arte* who occasionally interrupted the action with silly antics. Harlequin first appeared on the English stage in John Day's *The Travailes of the Three English Brothers.* The San Francisco Mime Troupe is one of the few modern groups to adapt Harlequin to the needs of contemporary satire.

Hellenism: Imitation of ancient Greek thought or styles. Also, an approach to life that focuses on the growth and development of the intellect. "Hellenism" is sometimes used to refer to the belief that reason can be applied to examine all human experience. A cogent discussion of Hellenism can be found in Matthew Arnold's *Culture and Anarchy.*

Heptameter: See *Meter*

Hero/Heroine: The principal sympathetic character (male or female) in a literary work. Heroes and heroines typically exhibit admirable traits: idealism, courage, and integrity, for example. Famous heroes and heroines include Pip in Charles Dickens's *Great Expectations,* the anonymous narrator in Ralph Ellison's *Invisible Man,* and Sethe in Toni Morrison's *Beloved.*

Heroic Couplet: A rhyming couplet written in iambic pentameter (a verse with five iambic feet). The following lines by Alexander Pope are an example: "Truth guards the Poet, sanctifies the line,/ And makes Immortal, Verse as mean as mine."

Heroic Line: The meter and length of a line of verse in epic or heroic poetry. This varies by language and time period. For example, in English poetry, the heroic line is iambic pentameter (a verse with five iambic feet); in French, the alexandrine (a verse with six iambic feet); in classical literature, dactylic hexameter (a verse with six dactylic feet).

Heroine: See *Hero/Heroine*

Hexameter: See *Meter*

Historical Criticism: The study of a work based on its impact on the world of the time period in which it was written. Examples of postmodern historical criticism can be found in the work of Michel Foucault, Hayden White, Stephen Greenblatt, and Jonathan Goldberg.

Hokku: See *Haiku*

Holocaust: See *Holocaust Literature*

Holocaust Literature: Literature influenced by or written about the Holocaust of World War II. Such literature includes true stories of survival in concentration camps, escape, and life after the war, as well as fictional works and poetry. Representative works of Holocaust literature include Saul Bellow's *Mr. Sammler's Planet,* Anne Frank's *The Diary of a Young Girl,* Jerzy Kosinski's *The Painted Bird,* Arthur Miller's *Incident at Vichy,* Czeslaw Milosz's *Collected Poems,* William Styron's *Sophie's Choice,* and Art Spiegelman's *Maus.*

Homeric Simile: An elaborate, detailed comparison written as a simile many lines in length. An example of an epic simile from John Milton's *Paradise Lost* follows: Angel Forms, who lay entranced Thick as autumnal leaves that strow the brooks In Vallombrosa, where the Etrurian shades High over-arched embower; or scattered sedge Afloat, when with fierce winds Orion armed Hath vexed the Red-Sea coast, whose waves o'erthrew Busiris and his Memphian chivalry, While with perfidious hatred they pursued The sojourners of

Goshen, who beheld From the safe shore their floating carcasses And broken chariot-wheels. Also known as Epic Simile.

Horatian Satire: See *Satire*

Humanism: A philosophy that places faith in the dignity of humankind and rejects the medieval perception of the individual as a weak, fallen creature. ''Humanists'' typically believe in the perfectibility of human nature and view reason and education as the means to that end. Humanist thought is represented in the works of Marsilio Ficino, Ludovico Castelvetro, Edmund Spenser, John Milton, Dean John Colet, Desiderius Erasmus, John Dryden, Alexander Pope, Matthew Arnold, and Irving Babbitt.

Humors: Mentions of the humors refer to the ancient Greek theory that a person's health and personality were determined by the balance of four basic fluids in the body: blood, phlegm, yellow bile, and black bile. A dominance of any fluid would cause extremes in behavior. An excess of blood created a sanguine person who was joyful, aggressive, and passionate; a phlegmatic person was shy, fearful, and sluggish; too much yellow bile led to a choleric temperament characterized by impatience, anger, bitterness, and stubbornness; and excessive black bile created melancholy, a state of laziness, gluttony, and lack of motivation. Literary treatment of the humors is exemplified by several characters in Ben Jonson's plays *Every Man in His Humour* and *Every Man out of His Humour*. Also spelled Humours.

Humours: See *Humors*

Hyperbole: In literary criticism, deliberate exaggeration used to achieve an effect. In William Shakespeare's *Macbeth,* Lady Macbeth hyperbolizes when she says, ''All the perfumes of Arabia could not sweeten this little hand.''

I

Iamb: See *Foot*

Idiom: A word construction or verbal expression closely associated with a given language. For example, in colloquial English the construction ''how come'' can be used instead of ''why'' to introduce a question. Similarly, ''a piece of cake'' is sometimes used to describe a task that is easily done.

Image: A concrete representation of an object or sensory experience. Typically, such a representation helps evoke the feelings associated with the object or experience itself. Images are either ''literal'' or ''figurative.'' Literal images are especially concrete and involve little or no extension of the obvious meaning of the words used to express them. Figurative images do not follow the literal meaning of the words exactly. Images in literature are usually visual, but the term ''image'' can also refer to the representation of any sensory experience. In his poem ''The Shepherd's Hour,'' Paul Verlaine presents the following image: ''The Moon is red through horizon's fog;/ In a dancing mist the hazy meadow sleeps.'' The first line is broadly literal, while the second line involves turns of meaning associated with dancing and sleeping.

Imagery: The array of images in a literary work. Also, figurative language. William Butler Yeats's ''The Second Coming'' offers a powerful image of encroaching anarchy: Turning and turning in the widening gyre The falcon cannot hear the falconer; Things fall apart. . . .

Imagism: An English and American poetry movement that flourished between 1908 and 1917. The Imagists used precise, clearly presented images in their works. They also used common, everyday speech and aimed for conciseness, concrete imagery, and the creation of new rhythms. Participants in the Imagist movement included Ezra Pound, H. D. (Hilda Doolittle), and Amy Lowell, among others.

In medias res: A Latin term meaning ''in the middle of things.'' It refers to the technique of beginning a story at its midpoint and then using various flashback devices to reveal previous action. This technique originated in such epics as Virgil's *Aeneid.*

Induction: The process of reaching a conclusion by reasoning from specific premises to form a general premise. Also, an introductory portion of a work of literature, especially a play. Geoffrey Chaucer's ''Prologue'' to the *Canterbury Tales,* Thomas Sackville's ''Induction'' to *The Mirror of Magistrates,* and the opening scene in William Shakespeare's *The Taming of the Shrew* are examples of inductions to literary works.

Intentional Fallacy: The belief that judgments of a literary work based solely on an author's stated or implied intentions are false and misleading. Critics who believe in the concept of the intentional fallacy typically argue that the work itself is sufficient matter for interpretation, even though they may concede that an author's statement of purpose can be useful. Analysis of William Wordsworth's *Lyri-*

cal Ballads based on the observations about poetry he makes in his "Preface" to the second edition of that work is an example of the intentional fallacy.

Interior Monologue: A narrative technique in which characters' thoughts are revealed in a way that appears to be uncontrolled by the author. The interior monologue typically aims to reveal the inner self of a character. It portrays emotional experiences as they occur at both a conscious and unconscious level. images are often used to represent sensations or emotions. One of the best-known interior monologues in English is the Molly Bloom section at the close of James Joyce's *Ulysses.* The interior monologue is also common in the works of Virginia Woolf.

Internal Rhyme: Rhyme that occurs within a single line of verse. An example is in the opening line of Edgar Allan Poe's "The Raven": "Once upon a midnight dreary, while I pondered weak and weary." Here, "dreary" and "weary" make an internal rhyme.

Irish Literary Renaissance: A late nineteenth- and early twentieth-century movement in Irish literature. Members of the movement aimed to reduce the influence of British culture in Ireland and create an Irish national literature. William Butler Yeats, George Moore, and Sean O'Casey are three of the best-known figures of the movement.

Irony: In literary criticism, the effect of language in which the intended meaning is the opposite of what is stated. The title of Jonathan Swift's "A Modest Proposal" is ironic because what Swift proposes in this essay is cannibalism—hardly "modest."

Italian Sonnet: See *Sonnet*

J

Jacobean Age: The period of the reign of James I of England (1603-1625). The early literature of this period reflected the worldview of the Elizabethan Age, but a darker, more cynical attitude steadily grew in the art and literature of the Jacobean Age. This was an important time for English drama and poetry. Milestones include William Shakespeare's tragedies, tragi-comedies, and sonnets; Ben Jonson's various dramas; and John Donne's metaphysical poetry.

Jargon: Language that is used or understood only by a select group of people. Jargon may refer to terminology used in a certain profession, such as computer jargon, or it may refer to any nonsensical language that is not understood by most people. Literary examples of jargon are Francois Villon's *Ballades en jargon,* which is composed in the secret language of the *coquillards,* and Anthony Burgess's *A Clockwork Orange,* narrated in the fictional characters' language of "Nadsat."

Juvenalian Satire: See *Satire*

K

Knickerbocker Group: A somewhat indistinct group of New York writers of the first half of the nineteenth century. Members of the group were linked only by location and a common theme: New York life. Two famous members of the Knickerbocker Group were Washington Irving and William Cullen Bryant. The group's name derives from Irving's *Knickerbocker's History of New York.*

L

Lais: See *Lay*

Lay: A song or simple narrative poem. The form originated in medieval France. Early French *lais* were often based on the Celtic legends and other tales sung by Breton minstrels—thus the name of the "Breton lay." In fourteenth-century England, the term "lay" was used to describe short narratives written in imitation of the Breton lays. The most notable of these is Geoffrey Chaucer's "The Minstrel's Tale."

Leitmotiv: See *Motif*

Literal Language: An author uses literal language when he or she writes without exaggerating or embellishing the subject matter and without any tools of figurative language. To say "He ran very quickly down the street" is to use literal language, whereas to say "He ran like a hare down the street" would be using figurative language.

Literary Ballad: See *Ballad*

Literature: Literature is broadly defined as any written or spoken material, but the term most often refers to creative works. Literature includes poetry, drama, fiction, and many kinds of nonfiction writing, as well as oral, dramatic, and broadcast compositions not necessarily preserved in a written format, such as films and television programs.

Lost Generation: A term first used by Gertrude Stein to describe the post-World War I generation of American writers: men and women haunted by a sense of betrayal and emptiness brought about by the destructiveness of the war. The term is commonly applied to Hart Crane, Ernest Hemingway, F. Scott Fitzgerald, and others.

Lyric Poetry: A poem expressing the subjective feelings and personal emotions of the poet. Such poetry is melodic, since it was originally accompanied by a lyre in recitals. Most Western poetry in the twentieth century may be classified as lyrical. Examples of lyric poetry include A. E. Housman's elegy "To an Athlete Dying Young," the odes of Pindar and Horace, Thomas Gray and William Collins, the sonnets of Sir Thomas Wyatt and Sir Philip Sidney, Elizabeth Barrett Browning and Rainer Maria Rilke, and a host of other forms in the poetry of William Blake and Christina Rossetti, among many others.

M

Mannerism: Exaggerated, artificial adherence to a literary manner or style. Also, a popular style of the visual arts of late sixteenth-century Europe that was marked by elongation of the human form and by intentional spatial distortion. Literary works that are self-consciously high-toned and artistic are often said to be "mannered." Authors of such works include Henry James and Gertrude Stein.

Masculine Rhyme: See *Rhyme*

Masque: A lavish and elaborate form of entertainment, often performed in royal courts, that emphasizes song, dance, and costumery. The Renaissance form of the masque grew out of the spectacles of masked figures common in medieval England and Europe. The masque reached its peak of popularity and development in seventeenth-century England, during the reigns of James I and, especially, of Charles I. Ben Jonson, the most significant masque writer, also created the "antimasque," which incorporates elements of humor and the grotesque into the traditional masque and achieved greater dramatic quality. Masque-like interludes appear in Edmund Spenser's *The Faerie Queene* and in William Shakespeare's *The Tempest*. One of the best-known English masques is John Milton's *Comus*.

Measure: The foot, verse, or time sequence used in a literary work, especially a poem. Measure is often used somewhat incorrectly as a synonym for meter.

Melodrama: A play in which the typical plot is a conflict between characters who personify extreme good and evil. Melodramas usually end happily and emphasize sensationalism. Other literary forms that use the same techniques are often labeled "melodramatic." The term was formerly used to describe a combination of drama and music; as such, it was synonymous with "opera." Augustin Daly's *Under the Gaslight* and Dion Boucicault's *The Octoroon, The Colleen Bawn,* and *The Poor of New York* are examples of melodramas. The most popular media for twentieth-century melodramas are motion pictures and television.

Metaphor: A figure of speech that expresses an idea through the image of another object. Metaphors suggest the essence of the first object by identifying it with certain qualities of the second object. An example is "But soft, what light through yonder window breaks?/ It is the east, and Juliet is the sun" in William Shakespeare's *Romeo and Juliet*. Here, Juliet, the first object, is identified with qualities of the second object, the sun.

Metaphysical Conceit: See *Conceit*

Metaphysical Poetry: The body of poetry produced by a group of seventeenth-century English writers called the "Metaphysical Poets." The group includes John Donne and Andrew Marvell. The Metaphysical Poets made use of everyday speech, intellectual analysis, and unique imagery. They aimed to portray the ordinary conflicts and contradictions of life. Their poems often took the form of an argument, and many of them emphasize physical and religious love as well as the fleeting nature of life. Elaborate conceits are typical in metaphysical poetry. Marvell's "To His Coy Mistress" is a well-known example of a metaphysical poem.

Metaphysical Poets: See *Metaphysical Poetry*

Meter: In literary criticism, the repetition of sound patterns that creates a rhythm in poetry. The patterns are based on the number of syllables and the presence and absence of accents. The unit of rhythm in a line is called a foot. Types of meter are classified according to the number of feet in a line. These are the standard English lines: Monometer, one foot; Dimeter, two feet; Trimeter, three feet; Tetrameter, four feet; Pentameter, five feet; Hexameter, six feet (also called the Alexandrine); Heptameter, seven feet (also called the "Fourteener" when the feet are iambic). The most common English meter is the iambic pentameter, in which each line contains ten syllables, or five iambic feet, which individually are composed of an unstressed syllable followed by an accented syllable. Both of the following lines from Alfred, Lord Tennyson's

"Ulysses" are written in iambic pentameter: Made weak by time and fate, but strong in will To strive, to seek, to find, and not to yield.

Mise en scene: The costumes, scenery, and other properties of a drama. Herbert Beerbohm Tree was renowned for the elaborate *mises en scene* of his lavish Shakespearean productions at His Majesty's Theatre between 1897 and 1915.

Modernism: Modern literary practices. Also, the principles of a literary school that lasted from roughly the beginning of the twentieth century until the end of World War II. Modernism is defined by its rejection of the literary conventions of the nineteenth century and by its opposition to conventional morality, taste, traditions, and economic values. Many writers are associated with the concepts of Modernism, including Albert Camus, Marcel Proust, D. H. Lawrence, W. H. Auden, Ernest Hemingway, William Faulkner, William Butler Yeats, Thomas Mann, Tennessee Williams, Eugene O'Neill, and James Joyce.

Monologue: A composition, written or oral, by a single individual. More specifically, a speech given by a single individual in a drama or other public entertainment. It has no set length, although it is usually several or more lines long. An example of an "extended monologue"—that is, a monologue of great length and seriousness—occurs in the one-act, one-character play *The Stronger* by August Strindberg.

Monometer: See *Meter*

Mood: The prevailing emotions of a work or of the author in his or her creation of the work. The mood of a work is not always what might be expected based on its subject matter. The poem "Dover Beach" by Matthew Arnold offers examples of two different moods originating from the same experience: watching the ocean at night. The mood of the first three lines— The sea is calm tonight The tide is full, the moon lies fair Upon the straights. . . . is in sharp contrast to the mood of the last three lines— And we are here as on a darkling plain Swept with confused alarms of struggle and flight, Where ignorant armies clash by night.

Motif: A theme, character type, image, metaphor, or other verbal element that recurs throughout a single work of literature or occurs in a number of different works over a period of time. For example, the various manifestations of the color white in Herman Melville's *Moby Dick* is a "specific" *motif*, while the trials of star-crossed lovers is a "conventional" *motif* from the literature of all periods. Also known as *Motiv* or *Leitmotiv*.

Motiv: See *Motif*

Muckrakers: An early twentieth-century group of American writers. Typically, their works exposed the wrongdoings of big business and government in the United States. Upton Sinclair's *The Jungle* exemplifies the muckraking novel.

Muses: Nine Greek mythological goddesses, the daughters of Zeus and Mnemosyne (Memory). Each muse patronized a specific area of the liberal arts and sciences. Calliope presided over epic poetry, Clio over history, Erato over love poetry, Euterpe over music or lyric poetry, Melpomene over tragedy, Polyhymnia over hymns to the gods, Terpsichore over dance, Thalia over comedy, and Urania over astronomy. Poets and writers traditionally made appeals to the Muses for inspiration in their work. John Milton invokes the aid of a muse at the beginning of the first book of his *Paradise Lost:* Of Man's First disobedience, and the Fruit of the Forbidden Tree, whose mortal taste Brought Death into the World, and all our woe, With loss of Eden, till one greater Man Restore us, and regain the blissful Seat, Sing Heav'nly Muse, that on the secret top of Oreb, or of Sinai, didst inspire That Shepherd, who first taught the chosen Seed, In the Beginning how the Heav'ns and Earth Rose out of Chaos. . . .

Mystery: See *Suspense*

Myth: An anonymous tale emerging from the traditional beliefs of a culture or social unit. Myths use supernatural explanations for natural phenomena. They may also explain cosmic issues like creation and death. Collections of myths, known as mythologies, are common to all cultures and nations, but the best-known myths belong to the Norse, Roman, and Greek mythologies. A famous myth is the story of Arachne, an arrogant young girl who challenged a goddess, Athena, to a weaving contest; when the girl won, Athena was enraged and turned Arachne into a spider, thus explaining the existence of spiders.

N

Narration: The telling of a series of events, real or invented. A narration may be either a simple narrative, in which the events are recounted chronologically, or a narrative with a plot, in which the account is given in a style reflecting the author's artistic concept of the story. Narration is sometimes used as a synonym for "storyline." The recounting of scary stories around a campfire is a form of narration.

Narrative: A verse or prose accounting of an event or sequence of events, real or invented. The term is also used as an adjective in the sense "method of narration." For example, in literary criticism, the expression "narrative technique" usually refers to the way the author structures and presents his or her story. Narratives range from the shortest accounts of events, as in Julius Caesar's remark, "I came, I saw, I conquered," to the longest historical or biographical works, as in Edward Gibbon's *The Decline and Fall of the Roman Empire,* as well as diaries, travelogues, novels, ballads, epics, short stories, and other fictional forms.

Narrative Poetry: A nondramatic poem in which the author tells a story. Such poems may be of any length or level of complexity. Epics such as *Beowulf* and ballads are forms of narrative poetry.

Narrator: The teller of a story. The narrator may be the author or a character in the story through whom the author speaks. Huckleberry Finn is the narrator of Mark Twain's *The Adventures of Huckleberry Finn.*

Naturalism: A literary movement of the late nineteenth and early twentieth centuries. The movement's major theorist, French novelist Emile Zola, envisioned a type of fiction that would examine human life with the objectivity of scientific inquiry. The Naturalists typically viewed human beings as either the products of "biological determinism," ruled by hereditary instincts and engaged in an endless struggle for survival, or as the products of "socioeconomic determinism," ruled by social and economic forces beyond their control. In their works, the Naturalists generally ignored the highest levels of society and focused on degradation: poverty, alcoholism, prostitution, insanity, and disease. Naturalism influenced authors throughout the world, including Henrik Ibsen and Thomas Hardy. In the United States, in particular, Naturalism had a profound impact. Among the authors who embraced its principles are Theodore Dreiser, Eugene O'Neill, Stephen Crane, Jack London, and Frank Norris.

Negritude: A literary movement based on the concept of a shared cultural bond on the part of black Africans, wherever they may be in the world. It traces its origins to the former French colonies of Africa and the Caribbean. Negritude poets, novelists, and essayists generally stress four points in their writings: One, black alienation from traditional African culture can lead to feelings of inferiority. Two, European colonialism and Western education should be resisted. Three, black Africans should seek to affirm and define their own identity. Four, African culture can and should be reclaimed. Many Negritude writers also claim that blacks can make unique contributions to the world, based on a heightened appreciation of nature, rhythm, and human emotions—aspects of life they say are not so highly valued in the materialistic and rationalistic West. Examples of Negritude literature include the poetry of both Senegalese Leopold Senghor in *Hosties noires* and Martiniquais Aime-Fernand Cesaire in *Return to My Native Land.*

Negro Renaissance: See *Harlem Renaissance*

Neoclassical Period: See *Neoclassicism*

Neoclassicism: In literary criticism, this term refers to the revival of the attitudes and styles of expression of classical literature. It is generally used to describe a period in European history beginning in the late seventeenth century and lasting until about 1800. In its purest form, Neoclassicism marked a return to order, proportion, restraint, logic, accuracy, and decorum. In England, where Neoclassicism perhaps was most popular, it reflected the influence of seventeenth- century French writers, especially dramatists. Neoclassical writers typically reacted against the intensity and enthusiasm of the Renaissance period. They wrote works that appealed to the intellect, using elevated language and classical literary forms such as satire and the ode. Neoclassical works were often governed by the classical goal of instruction. English neoclassicists included Alexander Pope, Jonathan Swift, Joseph Addison, Sir Richard Steele, John Gay, and Matthew Prior; French neoclassicists included Pierre Corneille and Jean-Baptiste Moliere. Also known as Age of Reason.

Neoclassicists: See *Neoclassicism*

New Criticism: A movement in literary criticism, dating from the late 1920s, that stressed close textual analysis in the interpretation of works of literature. The New Critics saw little merit in historical and biographical analysis. Rather, they aimed to examine the text alone, free from the question of how external events—biographical or otherwise—may have helped shape it. This predominantly American school was named "New Criticism" by one of its practitioners, John Crowe Ransom. Other important New Critics included Allen Tate, R. P. Blackmur, Robert Penn Warren, and Cleanth Brooks.

New Negro Movement: See *Harlem Renaissance*

Noble Savage: The idea that primitive man is noble and good but becomes evil and corrupted as he becomes civilized. The concept of the noble savage originated in the Renaissance period but is more closely identified with such later writers as Jean-Jacques Rousseau and Aphra Behn. First described in John Dryden's play *The Conquest of Granada,* the noble savage is portrayed by the various Native Americans in James Fenimore Cooper's "Leatherstocking Tales," by Queequeg, Daggoo, and Tashtego in Herman Melville's *Moby Dick,* and by John the Savage in Aldous Huxley's *Brave New World.*

O

Objective Correlative: An outward set of objects, a situation, or a chain of events corresponding to an inward experience and evoking this experience in the reader. The term frequently appears in modern criticism in discussions of authors' intended effects on the emotional responses of readers. This term was originally used by T. S. Eliot in his 1919 essay "Hamlet."

Objectivity: A quality in writing characterized by the absence of the author's opinion or feeling about the subject matter. Objectivity is an important factor in criticism. The novels of Henry James and, to a certain extent, the poems of John Larkin demonstrate objectivity, and it is central to John Keats's concept of "negative capability." Critical and journalistic writing usually are or attempt to be objective.

Occasional Verse: poetry written on the occasion of a significant historical or personal event. *Vers de societe* is sometimes called occasional verse although it is of a less serious nature. Famous examples of occasional verse include Andrew Marvell's "Horatian Ode upon Cromwell's Return from England," Walt Whitman's "When Lilacs Last in the Dooryard Bloom'd"— written upon the death of Abraham Lincoln—and Edmund Spenser's commemoration of his wedding, "Epithalamion."

Octave: A poem or stanza composed of eight lines. The term octave most often represents the first eight lines of a Petrarchan sonnet. An example of an octave is taken from a translation of a Petrarchan sonnet by Sir Thomas Wyatt: The pillar perisht is whereto I leant, The strongest stay of mine unquiet mind; The like of it no man again can find, From East to West Still seeking though he went. To mind unhap! for hap away hath rent Of all my joy the very bark and rind; And I, alas, by chance am thus assigned Daily to mourn till death do it relent.

Ode: Name given to an extended lyric poem characterized by exalted emotion and dignified style. An ode usually concerns a single, serious theme. Most odes, but not all, are addressed to an object or individual. Odes are distinguished from other lyric poetic forms by their complex rhythmic and stanzaic patterns. An example of this form is John Keats's "Ode to a Nightingale."

Oedipus Complex: A son's amorous obsession with his mother. The phrase is derived from the story of the ancient Theban hero Oedipus, who unknowingly killed his father and married his mother. Literary occurrences of the Oedipus complex include Andre Gide's *Oedipe* and Jean Cocteau's *La Machine infernale,* as well as the most famous, Sophocles' *Oedipus Rex.*

Omniscience: See *Point of View*

Onomatopoeia: The use of words whose sounds express or suggest their meaning. In its simplest sense, onomatopoeia may be represented by words that mimic the sounds they denote such as "hiss" or "meow." At a more subtle level, the pattern and rhythm of sounds and rhymes of a line or poem may be onomatopoeic. A celebrated example of onomatopoeia is the repetition of the word "bells" in Edgar Allan Poe's poem "The Bells."

Opera: A type of stage performance, usually a drama, in which the dialogue is sung. Classic examples of opera include Giuseppi Verdi's *La traviata,* Giacomo Puccini's *La Boheme,* and Richard Wagner's *Tristan und Isolde.* Major twentieth-century contributors to the form include Richard Strauss and Alban Berg.

Operetta: A usually romantic comic opera. John Gay's *The Beggar's Opera,* Richard Sheridan's *The Duenna,* and numerous works by William Gilbert and Arthur Sullivan are examples of operettas.

Oral Tradition: See *Oral Transmission*

Oral Transmission: A process by which songs, ballads, folklore, and other material are transmitted by word of mouth. The tradition of oral transmission predates the written record systems of literate society. Oral transmission preserves material sometimes over generations, although often with variations. Memory plays a large part in the recitation and preservation of orally transmitted material. Breton lays, French *fabliaux,* national epics (including the Anglo-Saxon *Beowulf,* the Spanish *El Cid,* and the Finnish *Kalevala*), Native American myths and legends, and African folktales told by plantation slaves are examples of orally transmitted literature.

Oration: Formal speaking intended to motivate the listeners to some action or feeling. Such public speaking was much more common before the development of timely printed communication such as newspapers. Famous examples of oration include Abraham Lincoln's "Gettysburg Address" and Dr. Martin Luther King Jr.'s "I Have a Dream" speech.

Ottava Rima: An eight-line stanza of poetry composed in iambic pentameter (a five-foot line in which each foot consists of an unaccented syllable followed by an accented syllable), following the abababcc rhyme scheme. This form has been prominently used by such important English writers as Lord Byron, Henry Wadsworth Longfellow, and W. B. Yeats.

Oxymoron: A phrase combining two contradictory terms. Oxymorons may be intentional or unintentional. The following speech from William Shakespeare's *Romeo and Juliet* uses several oxymorons: Why, then, O brawling love! O loving hate! O anything, of nothing first create! O heavy lightness! serious vanity! Mis-shapen chaos of well-seeming forms! Feather of lead, bright smoke, cold fire, sick health! This love feel I, that feel no love in this.

P

Pantheism: The idea that all things are both a manifestation or revelation of God and a part of God at the same time. Pantheism was a common attitude in the early societies of Egypt, India, and Greece—the term derives from the Greek *pan* meaning "all" and *theos* meaning "deity." It later became a significant part of the Christian faith. William Wordsworth and Ralph Waldo Emerson are among the many writers who have expressed the pantheistic attitude in their works.

Parable: A story intended to teach a moral lesson or answer an ethical question. In the West, the best examples of parables are those of Jesus Christ in the New Testament, notably "The Prodigal Son," but parables also are used in Sufism, rabbinic literature, Hasidism, and Zen Buddhism.

Paradox: A statement that appears illogical or contradictory at first, but may actually point to an underlying truth. "Less is more" is an example of a paradox. Literary examples include Francis Bacon's statement, "The most corrected copies are commonly the least correct," and "All animals are equal, but some animals are more equal than others" from George Orwell's *Animal Farm*.

Parallelism: A method of comparison of two ideas in which each is developed in the same grammatical structure. Ralph Waldo Emerson's "Civilization" contains this example of parallelism: Raphael paints wisdom; Handel sings it, Phidias carves it, Shakespeare writes it, Wren builds it, Columbus sails it, Luther preaches it, Washington arms it, Watt mechanizes it.

Parnassianism: A mid nineteenth-century movement in French literature. Followers of the movement stressed adherence to well-defined artistic forms as a reaction against the often chaotic expression of the artist's ego that dominated the work of the Romantics. The Parnassians also rejected the moral, ethical, and social themes exhibited in the works of French Romantics such as Victor Hugo. The aesthetic doctrines of the Parnassians strongly influenced the later symbolist and decadent movements. Members of the Parnassian school include Leconte de Lisle, Sully Prudhomme, Albert Glatigny, Francois Coppee, and Theodore de Banville.

Parody: In literary criticism, this term refers to an imitation of a serious literary work or the signature style of a particular author in a ridiculous manner. A typical parody adopts the style of the original and applies it to an inappropriate subject for humorous effect. Parody is a form of satire and could be considered the literary equivalent of a caricature or cartoon. Henry Fielding's *Shamela* is a parody of Samuel Richardson's *Pamela*.

Pastoral: A term derived from the Latin word "pastor," meaning shepherd. A pastoral is a literary composition on a rural theme. The conventions of the pastoral were originated by the third-century Greek poet Theocritus, who wrote about the experiences, love affairs, and pastimes of Sicilian shepherds. In a pastoral, characters and language of a courtly nature are often placed in a simple setting. The term pastoral is also used to classify dramas, elegies, and lyrics that exhibit the use of country settings and shepherd characters. Percy Bysshe Shelley's "Adonais" and John Milton's "Lycidas" are two famous examples of pastorals.

Pastorela: The Spanish name for the shepherds play, a folk drama reenacted during the Christmas season. Examples of *pastorelas* include Gomez

Manrique's *Representacion del nacimiento* and the dramas of Lucas Fernandez and Juan del Encina.

Pathetic Fallacy: A term coined by English critic John Ruskin to identify writing that falsely endows nonhuman things with human intentions and feelings, such as "angry clouds" and "sad trees." The pathetic fallacy is a required convention in the classical poetic form of the pastoral elegy, and it is used in the modern poetry of T. S. Eliot, Ezra Pound, and the Imagists. Also known as Poetic Fallacy.

Pelado: Literally the "skinned one" or shirtless one, he was the stock underdog, sharp-witted picaresque character of Mexican vaudeville and tent shows. The *pelado* is found in such works as Don Catarino's *Los effectos de la crisis* and *Regreso a mi tierra.*

Pen Name: See *Pseudonym*

Pentameter: See *Meter*

Persona: A Latin term meaning "mask." *Personae* are the characters in a fictional work of literature. The *persona* generally functions as a mask through which the author tells a story in a voice other than his or her own. A *persona* is usually either a character in a story who acts as a narrator or an "implied author," a voice created by the author to act as the narrator for himself or herself. *Personae* include the narrator of Geoffrey Chaucer's *Canterbury Tales* and Marlow in Joseph Conrad's *Heart of Darkness.*

Personae: See *Persona*

Personal Point of View: See *Point of View*

Personification: A figure of speech that gives human qualities to abstract ideas, animals, and inanimate objects. William Shakespeare used personification in *Romeo and Juliet* in the lines "Arise, fair sun, and kill the envious moon,/ Who is already sick and pale with grief." Here, the moon is portrayed as being envious, sick, and pale with grief—all markedly human qualities. Also known as *Prosopopoeia.*

Petrarchan Sonnet: See *Sonnet*

Phenomenology: A method of literary criticism based on the belief that things have no existence outside of human consciousness or awareness. Proponents of this theory believe that art is a process that takes place in the mind of the observer as he or she contemplates an object rather than a quality of the object itself. Among phenomenological critics are Edmund Husserl, George Poulet, Marcel Raymond, and Roman Ingarden.

Picaresque Novel: Episodic fiction depicting the adventures of a roguish central character ("picaro" is Spanish for "rogue"). The picaresque hero is commonly a low-born but clever individual who wanders into and out of various affairs of love, danger, and farcical intrigue. These involvements may take place at all social levels and typically present a humorous and wide-ranging satire of a given society. Prominent examples of the picaresque novel are *Don Quixote* by Miguel de Cervantes, *Tom Jones* by Henry Fielding, and *Moll Flanders* by Daniel Defoe.

Plagiarism: Claiming another person's written material as one's own. Plagiarism can take the form of direct, word-for- word copying or the theft of the substance or idea of the work. A student who copies an encyclopedia entry and turns it in as a report for school is guilty of plagiarism.

Platonic Criticism: A form of criticism that stresses an artistic work's usefulness as an agent of social engineering rather than any quality or value of the work itself. Platonic criticism takes as its starting point the ancient Greek philosopher Plato's comments on art in his *Republic.*

Platonism: The embracing of the doctrines of the philosopher Plato, popular among the poets of the Renaissance and the Romantic period. Platonism is more flexible than Aristotelian Criticism and places more emphasis on the supernatural and unknown aspects of life. Platonism is expressed in the love poetry of the Renaissance, the fourth book of Baldassare Castiglione's *The Book of the Courtier,* and the poetry of William Blake, William Wordsworth, Percy Bysshe Shelley, Friedrich Holderlin, William Butler Yeats, and Wallace Stevens.

Play: See *Drama*

Plot: In literary criticism, this term refers to the pattern of events in a narrative or drama. In its simplest sense, the plot guides the author in composing the work and helps the reader follow the work. Typically, plots exhibit causality and unity and have a beginning, a middle, and an end. Sometimes, however, a plot may consist of a series of disconnected events, in which case it is known as an "episodic plot." In his *Aspects of the Novel,* E. M. Forster distinguishes between a story, defined as a "narrative of events arranged in their time- sequence," and plot, which organizes the events to a "sense of causality." This definition closely mirrors Aristotle's discussion of plot in his *Poetics*.

Poem: In its broadest sense, a composition utilizing rhyme, meter, concrete detail, and expressive language to create a literary experience with emotional and aesthetic appeal. Typical poems include sonnets, odes, elegies, *haiku,* ballads, and free verse.

Poet: An author who writes poetry or verse. The term is also used to refer to an artist or writer who has an exceptional gift for expression, imagination, and energy in the making of art in any form. Well-known poets include Horace, Basho, Sir Philip Sidney, Sir Edmund Spenser, John Donne, Andrew Marvell, Alexander Pope, Jonathan Swift, George Gordon, Lord Byron, John Keats, Christina Rossetti, W. H. Auden, Stevie Smith, and Sylvia Plath.

Poetic Fallacy: See *Pathetic Fallacy*

Poetic Justice: An outcome in a literary work, not necessarily a poem, in which the good are rewarded and the evil are punished, especially in ways that particularly fit their virtues or crimes. For example, a murderer may himself be murdered, or a thief will find himself penniless.

Poetic License: Distortions of fact and literary convention made by a writer—not always a poet—for the sake of the effect gained. Poetic license is closely related to the concept of "artistic freedom." An author exercises poetic license by saying that a pile of money "reaches as high as a mountain" when the pile is actually only a foot or two high.

Poetics: This term has two closely related meanings. It denotes (1) an aesthetic theory in literary criticism about the essence of poetry or (2) rules prescribing the proper methods, content, style, or diction of poetry. The term poetics may also refer to theories about literature in general, not just poetry.

Poetry: In its broadest sense, writing that aims to present ideas and evoke an emotional experience in the reader through the use of meter, imagery, connotative and concrete words, and a carefully constructed structure based on rhythmic patterns. Poetry typically relies on words and expressions that have several layers of meaning. It also makes use of the effects of regular rhythm on the ear and may make a strong appeal to the senses through the use of imagery. Edgar Allan Poe's "Annabel Lee" and Walt Whitman's *Leaves of Grass* are famous examples of poetry.

Point of View: The narrative perspective from which a literary work is presented to the reader. There are four traditional points of view. The "third person omniscient" gives the reader a "godlike" perspective, unrestricted by time or place, from which to see actions and look into the minds of characters. This allows the author to comment openly on characters and events in the work. The "third person" point of view presents the events of the story from outside of any single character's perception, much like the omniscient point of view, but the reader must understand the action as it takes place and without any special insight into characters' minds or motivations. The "first person" or "personal" point of view relates events as they are perceived by a single character. The main character "tells" the story and may offer opinions about the action and characters which differ from those of the author. Much less common than omniscient, third person, and first person is the "second person" point of view, wherein the author tells the story as if it is happening to the reader. James Thurber employs the omniscient point of view in his short story "The Secret Life of Walter Mitty." Ernest Hemingway's "A Clean, Well-Lighted Place" is a short story told from the third person point of view. Mark Twain's novel *Huck Finn* is presented from the first person viewpoint. Jay McInerney's *Bright Lights, Big City* is an example of a novel which uses the second person point of view.

Polemic: A work in which the author takes a stand on a controversial subject, such as abortion or religion. Such works are often extremely argumentative or provocative. Classic examples of polemics include John Milton's *Aeropagitica* and Thomas Paine's *The American Crisis.*

Pornography: Writing intended to provoke feelings of lust in the reader. Such works are often condemned by critics and teachers, but those which can be shown to have literary value are viewed less harshly. Literary works that have been described as pornographic include Ovid's *The Art of Love,* Margaret of Angouleme's *Heptameron,* John Cleland's *Memoirs of a Woman of Pleasure; or, the Life of Fanny Hill,* the anonymous *My Secret Life,* D. H. Lawrence's *Lady Chatterley's Lover,* and Vladimir Nabokov's *Lolita.*

Post-Aesthetic Movement: An artistic response made by African Americans to the black aesthetic movement of the 1960s and early '70s. Writers since that time have adopted a somewhat different tone in their work, with less emphasis placed on the disparity between black and white in the United States. In the words of post-aesthetic authors such as Toni Morrison, John Edgar Wideman, and Kristin Hunter, African Americans are portrayed as looking inward for answers to their own questions, rather than always looking to the outside world. Two well-known examples of works produced as part of the post-aesthetic movement are the Pulitzer Prize-winning novels *The Color Purple* by Alice Walker and *Beloved* by Toni Morrison.

Postmodernism: Writing from the 1960s forward characterized by experimentation and continuing to apply some of the fundamentals of modernism, which included existentialism and alienation. Postmodernists have gone a step further in the rejection of tradition begun with the modernists by also rejecting traditional forms, preferring the anti-novel over the novel and the anti-hero over the hero. Postmodern writers include Alain Robbe-Grillet, Thomas Pynchon, Margaret Drabble, John Fowles, Adolfo Bioy-Casares, and Gabriel Garcia Marquez.

Pre-Raphaelites: A circle of writers and artists in mid nineteenth-century England. Valuing the pre-Renaissance artistic qualities of religious symbolism, lavish pictorialism, and natural sensuousness, the Pre-Raphaelites cultivated a sense of mystery and melancholy that influenced later writers associated with the Symbolist and Decadent movements. The major members of the group include Dante Gabriel Rossetti, Christina Rossetti, Algernon Swinburne, and Walter Pater.

Primitivism: The belief that primitive peoples were nobler and less flawed than civilized peoples because they had not been subjected to the tainting influence of society. Examples of literature espousing primitivism include Aphra Behn's *Oroonoko: Or, The History of the Royal Slave,* Jean-Jacques Rousseau's *Julie ou la Nouvelle Heloise,* Oliver Goldsmith's *The Deserted Village,* the poems of Robert Burns, Herman Melville's stories *Typee, Omoo,* and *Mardi,* many poems of William Butler Yeats and Robert Frost, and William Golding's novel *Lord of the Flies.*

Projective Verse: A form of free verse in which the poet's breathing pattern determines the lines of the poem. Poets who advocate projective verse are against all formal structures in writing, including meter and form. Besides its creators, Robert Creeley, Robert Duncan, and Charles Olson, two other well-known projective verse poets are Denise Levertov and LeRoi Jones (Amiri Baraka). Also known as Breath Verse.

Prologue: An introductory section of a literary work. It often contains information establishing the situation of the characters or presents information about the setting, time period, or action. In drama, the prologue is spoken by a chorus or by one of the principal characters. In the ''General Prologue'' of *The Canterbury Tales,* Geoffrey Chaucer describes the main characters and establishes the setting and purpose of the work.

Prose: A literary medium that attempts to mirror the language of everyday speech. It is distinguished from poetry by its use of unmetered, unrhymed language consisting of logically related sentences. Prose is usually grouped into paragraphs that form a cohesive whole such as an essay or a novel. Recognized masters of English prose writing include Sir Thomas Malory, William Caxton, Raphael Holinshed, Joseph Addison, Mark Twain, and Ernest Hemingway.

Prosopopoeia: See *Personification*

Protagonist: The central character of a story who serves as a focus for its themes and incidents and as the principal rationale for its development. The protagonist is sometimes referred to in discussions of modern literature as the hero or anti-hero. Well-known protagonists are Hamlet in William Shakespeare's *Hamlet* and Jay Gatsby in F. Scott Fitzgerald's *The Great Gatsby.*

Protest Fiction: Protest fiction has as its primary purpose the protesting of some social injustice, such as racism or discrimination. One example of protest fiction is a series of five novels by Chester Himes, beginning in 1945 with *If He Hollers Let Him Go* and ending in 1955 with *The Primitive.* These works depict the destructive effects of race and gender stereotyping in the context of interracial relationships. Another African American author whose works often revolve around themes of social protest is John Oliver Killens. James Baldwin's essay ''Everybody's Protest Novel'' generated controversy by attacking the authors of protest fiction.

Proverb: A brief, sage saying that expresses a truth about life in a striking manner. ''They are not all cooks who carry long knives'' is an example of a proverb.

Pseudonym: A name assumed by a writer, most often intended to prevent his or her identification as the author of a work. Two or more authors may work together under one pseudonym, or an author may use a different name for each genre he or she publishes in. Some publishing companies maintain "house pseudonyms," under which any number of authors may write installations in a series. Some authors also choose a pseudonym over their real names the way an actor may use a stage name. Examples of pseudonyms (with the author's real name in parentheses) include Voltaire (Francois-Marie Arouet), Novalis (Friedrich von Hardenberg), Currer Bell (Charlotte Bronte), Ellis Bell (Emily Bronte), George Eliot (Maryann Evans), Honorio Bustos Donmecq (Adolfo Bioy-Casares and Jorge Luis Borges), and Richard Bachman (Stephen King).

Pun: A play on words that have similar sounds but different meanings. A serious example of the pun is from John Donne's "A Hymne to God the Father": Sweare by thyself, that at my death thy sonne Shall shine as he shines now, and hereto fore; And, having done that, Thou haste done; I fear no more.

Pure Poetry: poetry written without instructional intent or moral purpose that aims only to please a reader by its imagery or musical flow. The term pure poetry is used as the antonym of the term "didacticism." The poetry of Edgar Allan Poe, Stephane Mallarme, Paul Verlaine, Paul Valery, Juan Ramoz Jimenez, and Jorge Guillen offer examples of pure poetry.

Q

Quatrain: A four-line stanza of a poem or an entire poem consisting of four lines. The following quatrain is from Robert Herrick's "To Live Merrily, and to Trust to Good Verses": Round, round, the root do's run; And being ravisht thus, Come, I will drink a Tun To my *Propertius*.

R

Raisonneur: A character in a drama who functions as a spokesperson for the dramatist's views. The *raisonneur* typically observes the play without becoming central to its action. *Raisonneurs* were very common in plays of the nineteenth century.

Realism: A nineteenth-century European literary movement that sought to portray familiar characters, situations, and settings in a realistic manner. This was done primarily by using an objective narrative point of view and through the buildup of accurate detail. The standard for success of any realistic work depends on how faithfully it transfers common experience into fictional forms. The realistic method may be altered or extended, as in stream of consciousness writing, to record highly subjective experience. Seminal authors in the tradition of Realism include Honore de Balzac, Gustave Flaubert, and Henry James.

Refrain: A phrase repeated at intervals throughout a poem. A refrain may appear at the end of each stanza or at less regular intervals. It may be altered slightly at each appearance. Some refrains are nonsense expressions—as with "Nevermore" in Edgar Allan Poe's "The Raven"—that seem to take on a different significance with each use.

Renaissance: The period in European history that marked the end of the Middle Ages. It began in Italy in the late fourteenth century. In broad terms, it is usually seen as spanning the fourteenth, fifteenth, and sixteenth centuries, although it did not reach Great Britain, for example, until the 1480s or so. The Renaissance saw an awakening in almost every sphere of human activity, especially science, philosophy, and the arts. The period is best defined by the emergence of a general philosophy that emphasized the importance of the intellect, the individual, and world affairs. It contrasts strongly with the medieval worldview, characterized by the dominant concerns of faith, the social collective, and spiritual salvation. Prominent writers during the Renaissance include Niccolo Machiavelli and Baldassare Castiglione in Italy, Miguel de Cervantes and Lope de Vega in Spain, Jean Froissart and Francois Rabelais in France, Sir Thomas More and Sir Philip Sidney in England, and Desiderius Erasmus in Holland.

Repartee: Conversation featuring snappy retorts and witticisms. Masters of *repartee* include Sydney Smith, Charles Lamb, and Oscar Wilde. An example is recorded in the meeting of "Beau" Nash and John Wesley: Nash said, "I never make way for a fool," to which Wesley responded, "Don't you? I always do," and stepped aside.

Resolution: The portion of a story following the climax, in which the conflict is resolved. The resolution of Jane Austen's *Northanger Abbey* is neatly summed up in the following sentence: "Henry and Catherine were married, the bells rang and every body smiled."

Restoration: See *Restoration Age*

Restoration Age: A period in English literature beginning with the crowning of Charles II in 1660 and running to about 1700. The era, which was characterized by a reaction against Puritanism, was the first great age of the comedy of manners. The finest literature of the era is typically witty and urbane, and often lewd. Prominent Restoration Age writers include William Congreve, Samuel Pepys, John Dryden, and John Milton.

Revenge Tragedy: A dramatic form popular during the Elizabethan Age, in which the protagonist, directed by the ghost of his murdered father or son, inflicts retaliation upon a powerful villain. Notable features of the revenge tragedy include violence, bizarre criminal acts, intrigue, insanity, a hesitant protagonist, and the use of soliloquy. Thomas Kyd's *Spanish Tragedy* is the first example of revenge tragedy in English, and William Shakespeare's *Hamlet* is perhaps the best. Extreme examples of revenge tragedy, such as John Webster's *The Duchess of Malfi,* are labeled "tragedies of blood." Also known as Tragedy of Blood.

Revista: The Spanish term for a vaudeville musical revue. Examples of *revistas* include Antonio Guzman Aguilera's *Mexico para los mexicanos,* Daniel Vanegas's *Maldito jazz,* and Don Catarino's *Whiskey, morfina y marihuana* and *El desterrado.*

Rhetoric: In literary criticism, this term denotes the art of ethical persuasion. In its strictest sense, rhetoric adheres to various principles developed since classical times for arranging facts and ideas in a clear, persuasive, appealing manner. The term is also used to refer to effective prose in general and theories of or methods for composing effective prose. Classical examples of rhetorics include *The Rhetoric of Aristotle,* Quintillian's *Institutio Oratoria,* and Cicero's *Ad Herennium.*

Rhetorical Question: A question intended to provoke thought, but not an expressed answer, in the reader. It is most commonly used in oratory and other persuasive genres. The following lines from Thomas Gray's "Elegy Written in a Country Churchyard" ask rhetorical questions: Can storied urn or animated bust Back to its mansion call the fleeting breath? Can Honour's voice provoke the silent dust, Or Flattery soothe the dull cold ear of Death?

Rhyme: When used as a noun in literary criticism, this term generally refers to a poem in which words sound identical or very similar and appear in parallel positions in two or more lines. Rhymes are classified into different types according to where they fall in a line or stanza or according to the degree of similarity they exhibit in their spellings and sounds. Some major types of rhyme are "masculine" rhyme, "feminine" rhyme, and "triple" rhyme. In a masculine rhyme, the rhyming sound falls in a single accented syllable, as with "heat" and "eat." Feminine rhyme is a rhyme of two syllables, one stressed and one unstressed, as with "merry" and "tarry." Triple rhyme matches the sound of the accented syllable and the two unaccented syllables that follow: "narrative" and "declarative." Robert Browning alternates feminine and masculine rhymes in his "Soliloquy of the Spanish Cloister": Gr-r-r—there go, my heart's abhorrence! Water your damned flower-pots, do! If hate killed men, Brother Lawrence, God's blood, would not mine kill you! What? Your myrtle-bush wants trimming? Oh, that rose has prior claims— Needs its leaden vase filled brimming? Hell dry you up with flames! Triple rhymes can be found in Thomas Hood's "Bridge of Sighs," George Gordon Byron's satirical verse, and Ogden Nash's comic poems.

Rhyme Royal: A stanza of seven lines composed in iambic pentameter and rhymed *ababbcc*. The name is said to be a tribute to King James I of Scotland, who made much use of the form in his poetry. Examples of rhyme royal include Geoffrey Chaucer's *The Parlement of Foules,* William Shakespeare's *The Rape of Lucrece,* William Morris's *The Early Paradise,* and John Masefield's *The Widow in the Bye Street.*

Rhyme Scheme: See *Rhyme*

Rhythm: A regular pattern of sound, time intervals, or events occurring in writing, most often and most discernably in poetry. Regular, reliable rhythm is known to be soothing to humans, while interrupted, unpredictable, or rapidly changing rhythm is disturbing. These effects are known to authors, who use them to produce a desired reaction in the reader. An example of a form of irregular rhythm is sprung rhythm poetry; quantitative verse, on the other hand, is very regular in its rhythm.

Rising Action: The part of a drama where the plot becomes increasingly complicated. Rising action leads up to the climax, or turning point, of a drama. The final "chase scene" of an action film is generally the rising action which culminates in the film's climax.

Rococo: A style of European architecture that flourished in the eighteenth century, especially in France. The most notable features of *rococo* are its extensive use of ornamentation and its themes of lightness, gaiety, and intimacy. In literary criticism, the term is often used disparagingly to refer to a decadent or over-ornamental style. Alexander Pope's "The Rape of the Lock" is an example of literary *rococo*.

Roman a clef: A French phrase meaning "novel with a key." It refers to a narrative in which real persons are portrayed under fictitious names. Jack Kerouac, for example, portrayed various real-life beat generation figures under fictitious names in his *On the Road.*

Romance: A broad term, usually denoting a narrative with exotic, exaggerated, often idealized characters, scenes, and themes. Nathaniel Hawthorne called his *The House of the Seven Gables* and *The Marble Faun* romances in order to distinguish them from clearly realistic works.

Romantic Age: See *Romanticism*

Romanticism: This term has two widely accepted meanings. In historical criticism, it refers to a European intellectual and artistic movement of the late eighteenth and early nineteenth centuries that sought greater freedom of personal expression than that allowed by the strict rules of literary form and logic of the eighteenth-century neoclassicists. The Romantics preferred emotional and imaginative expression to rational analysis. They considered the individual to be at the center of all experience and so placed him or her at the center of their art. The Romantics believed that the creative imagination reveals nobler truths—unique feelings and attitudes—than those that could be discovered by logic or by scientific examination. Both the natural world and the state of childhood were important sources for revelations of "eternal truths." "Romanticism" is also used as a general term to refer to a type of sensibility found in all periods of literary history and usually considered to be in opposition to the principles of classicism. In this sense, Romanticism signifies any work or philosophy in which the exotic or dreamlike figure strongly, or that is devoted to individualistic expression, self-analysis, or a pursuit of a higher realm of knowledge than can be discovered by human reason. Prominent Romantics include Jean-Jacques Rousseau, William Wordsworth, John Keats, Lord Byron, and Johann Wolfgang von Goethe.

Romantics: See *Romanticism*

Russian Symbolism: A Russian poetic movement, derived from French symbolism, that flourished between 1894 and 1910. While some Russian Symbolists continued in the French tradition, stressing aestheticism and the importance of suggestion above didactic intent, others saw their craft as a form of mystical worship, and themselves as mediators between the supernatural and the mundane. Russian symbolists include Aleksandr Blok, Vyacheslav Ivanovich Ivanov, Fyodor Sologub, Andrey Bely, Nikolay Gumilyov, and Vladimir Sergeyevich Solovyov.

S

Satire: A work that uses ridicule, humor, and wit to criticize and provoke change in human nature and institutions. There are two major types of satire: "formal" or "direct" satire speaks directly to the reader or to a character in the work; "indirect" satire relies upon the ridiculous behavior of its characters to make its point. Formal satire is further divided into two manners: the "Horatian," which ridicules gently, and the "Juvenalian," which derides its subjects harshly and bitterly. Voltaire's novella *Candide* is an indirect satire. Jonathan Swift's essay "A Modest Proposal" is a Juvenalian satire.

Scansion: The analysis or "scanning" of a poem to determine its meter and often its rhyme scheme. The most common system of scansion uses accents (slanted lines drawn above syllables) to show stressed syllables, breves (curved lines drawn above syllables) to show unstressed syllables, and vertical lines to separate each foot. In the first line of John Keats's *Endymion,* "A thing of beauty is a joy forever:" the word "thing," the first syllable of "beauty," the word "joy," and the second syllable of "forever" are stressed, while the words "A" and "of," the second syllable of "beauty," the word "a," and the first and third syllables of "forever" are unstressed. In the second line: "Its loveliness increases; it will never" a pair of vertical lines separate the foot ending with "increases" and the one beginning with "it."

Scene: A subdivision of an act of a drama, consisting of continuous action taking place at a single time and in a single location. The beginnings and endings of scenes may be indicated by clearing the stage of actors and props or by the entrances and exits of important characters. The first act of William Shakespeare's *Winter's Tale* is comprised of two scenes.

Science Fiction: A type of narrative about or based upon real or imagined scientific theories and technology. Science fiction is often peopled with alien creatures and set on other planets or in different dimensions. Karel Capek's *R.U.R.* is a major work of science fiction.

Second Person: See *Point of View*

Semiotics: The study of how literary forms and conventions affect the meaning of language. Semioticians include Ferdinand de Saussure, Charles Sanders Pierce, Claude Levi-Strauss, Jacques Lacan, Michel Foucault, Jacques Derrida, Roland Barthes, and Julia Kristeva.

Sestet: Any six-line poem or stanza. Examples of the sestet include the last six lines of the Petrarchan sonnet form, the stanza form of Robert Burns's "A Poet's Welcome to his love-begotten Daughter," and the sestina form in W. H. Auden's "Paysage Moralise."

Setting: The time, place, and culture in which the action of a narrative takes place. The elements of setting may include geographic location, characters' physical and mental environments, prevailing cultural attitudes, or the historical time in which the action takes place. Examples of settings include the romanticized Scotland in Sir Walter Scott's "Waverley" novels, the French provincial setting in Gustave Flaubert's *Madame Bovary,* the fictional Wessex country of Thomas Hardy's novels, and the small towns of southern Ontario in Alice Munro's short stories.

Shakespearean Sonnet: See *Sonnet*

Signifying Monkey: A popular trickster figure in black folklore, with hundreds of tales about this character documented since the 19th century. Henry Louis Gates Jr. examines the history of the signifying monkey in *The Signifying Monkey: Towards a Theory of Afro-American Literary Criticism,* published in 1988.

Simile: A comparison, usually using "like" or "as", of two essentially dissimilar things, as in "coffee as cold as ice" or "He sounded like a broken record." The title of Ernest Hemingway's "Hills Like White Elephants" contains a simile.

Slang: A type of informal verbal communication that is generally unacceptable for formal writing. Slang words and phrases are often colorful exaggerations used to emphasize the speaker's point; they may also be shortened versions of an often-used word or phrase. Examples of American slang from the 1990s include "yuppie" (an acronym for Young Urban Professional), "awesome" (for "excellent"), wired (for "nervous" or "excited"), and "chill out" (for relax).

Slant Rhyme: See *Consonance*

Slave Narrative: Autobiographical accounts of American slave life as told by escaped slaves. These works first appeared during the abolition movement of the 1830s through the 1850s. Olaudah Equiano's *The Interesting Narrative of Olaudah Equiano, or Gustavus Vassa, The African* and Harriet Ann Jacobs's *Incidents in the Life of a Slave Girl* are examples of the slave narrative.

Social Realism: See *Socialist Realism*

Socialist Realism: The Socialist Realism school of literary theory was proposed by Maxim Gorky and established as a dogma by the first Soviet Congress of Writers. It demanded adherence to a communist worldview in works of literature. Its doctrines required an objective viewpoint comprehensible to the working classes and themes of social struggle featuring strong proletarian heroes. A successful work of socialist realism is Nikolay Ostrovsky's *Kak zakalyalas stal* (*How the Steel Was Tempered*). Also known as Social Realism.

Soliloquy: A monologue in a drama used to give the audience information and to develop the speaker's character. It is typically a projection of the speaker's innermost thoughts. Usually delivered while the speaker is alone on stage, a soliloquy is intended to present an illusion of unspoken reflection. A celebrated soliloquy is Hamlet's "To be or not to be" speech in William Shakespeare's *Hamlet*.

Sonnet: A fourteen-line poem, usually composed in iambic pentameter, employing one of several rhyme schemes. There are three major types of sonnets, upon which all other variations of the form are based: the "Petrarchan" or "Italian" sonnet, the "Shakespearean" or "English" sonnet, and the "Spenserian" sonnet. A Petrarchan sonnet consists of an octave rhymed *abbaabba* and a "sestet" rhymed either *cdecde, cdccdc,* or *cdedce*. The octave poses a question or problem, relates a narrative, or puts forth a proposition; the sestet presents a solution to the problem, comments upon the narrative, or applies the proposition put forth in the octave. The Shakespearean sonnet is divided into three quatrains and a couplet rhymed *abab cdcd efef gg*. The couplet provides an epigrammatic comment on the narrative or problem put forth in the quatrains. The Spenserian sonnet uses three quatrains and a couplet like the Shakespearean, but links their three rhyme schemes in this way: *abab bcbc cdcd ee*. The Spenserian sonnet develops its theme in two parts like the Petrarchan, its final six lines resolving a problem, analyzing a narrative, or applying a proposition put forth in its first eight lines. Examples of sonnets can be found in Petrarch's *Canzoniere,* Edmund Spenser's *Amoretti,* Elizabeth Barrett

Browning's *Sonnets from the Portuguese,* Rainer Maria Rilke's *Sonnets to Orpheus,* and Adrienne Rich's poem "The Insusceptibles."

Spenserian Sonnet: See *Sonnet*

Spenserian Stanza: A nine-line stanza having eight verses in iambic pentameter, its ninth verse in iambic hexameter, and the rhyme scheme ababbcbcc. This stanza form was first used by Edmund Spenser in his allegorical poem *The Faerie Queene.*

Spondee: In poetry meter, a foot consisting of two long or stressed syllables occurring together. This form is quite rare in English verse, and is usually composed of two monosyllabic words. The first foot in the following line from Robert Burns's "Green Grow the Rashes" is an example of a spondee: Green grow the rashes, O

Sprung Rhythm: Versification using a specific number of accented syllables per line but disregarding the number of unaccented syllables that fall in each line, producing an irregular rhythm in the poem. Gerard Manley Hopkins, who coined the term "sprung rhythm," is the most notable practitioner of this technique.

Stanza: A subdivision of a poem consisting of lines grouped together, often in recurring patterns of rhyme, line length, and meter. Stanzas may also serve as units of thought in a poem much like paragraphs in prose. Examples of stanza forms include the quatrain, *terza rima, ottava rima,* Spenserian, and the so-called *In Memoriam* stanza from Alfred, Lord Tennyson's poem by that title. The following is an example of the latter form: Love is and was my lord and king, And in his presence I attend To hear the tidings of my friend, Which every hour his couriers bring.

Stereotype: A stereotype was originally the name for a duplication made during the printing process; this led to its modern definition as a person or thing that is (or is assumed to be) the same as all others of its type. Common stereotypical characters include the absent-minded professor, the nagging wife, the troublemaking teenager, and the kindhearted grandmother.

Stream of Consciousness: A narrative technique for rendering the inward experience of a character. This technique is designed to give the impression of an ever-changing series of thoughts, emotions, images, and memories in the spontaneous and seemingly illogical order that they occur in life. The textbook example of stream of consciousness is the last section of James Joyce's *Ulysses.*

Structuralism: A twentieth-century movement in literary criticism that examines how literary texts arrive at their meanings, rather than the meanings themselves. There are two major types of structuralist analysis: one examines the way patterns of linguistic structures unify a specific text and emphasize certain elements of that text, and the other interprets the way literary forms and conventions affect the meaning of language itself. Prominent structuralists include Michel Foucault, Roman Jakobson, and Roland Barthes.

Structure: The form taken by a piece of literature. The structure may be made obvious for ease of understanding, as in nonfiction works, or may be obscured for artistic purposes, as in some poetry or seemingly "unstructured" prose. Examples of common literary structures include the plot of a narrative, the acts and scenes of a drama, and such poetic forms as the Shakespearean sonnet and the Pindaric ode.

Sturm und Drang: A German term meaning "storm and stress." It refers to a German literary movement of the 1770s and 1780s that reacted against the order and rationalism of the enlightenment, focusing instead on the intense experience of extraordinary individuals. Highly romantic, works of this movement, such as Johann Wolfgang von Goethe's *Gotz von Berlichingen,* are typified by realism, rebelliousness, and intense emotionalism.

Style: A writer's distinctive manner of arranging words to suit his or her ideas and purpose in writing. The unique imprint of the author's personality upon his or her writing, style is the product of an author's way of arranging ideas and his or her use of diction, different sentence structures, rhythm, figures of speech, rhetorical principles, and other elements of composition. Styles may be classified according to period (Metaphysical, Augustan, Georgian), individual authors (Chaucerian, Miltonic, Jamesian), level (grand, middle, low, plain), or language (scientific, expository, poetic, journalistic).

Subject: The person, event, or theme at the center of a work of literature. A work may have one or more subjects of each type, with shorter works tending to have fewer and longer works tending to have more. The subjects of James Baldwin's novel *Go Tell It on the Mountain* include the themes of father-son relationships, religious conversion, black life, and sexuality. The subjects of Anne Frank's

Diary of a Young Girl include Anne and her family members as well as World War II, the Holocaust, and the themes of war, isolation, injustice, and racism.

Subjectivity: Writing that expresses the author's personal feelings about his subject, and which may or may not include factual information about the subject. Subjectivity is demonstrated in James Joyce's *Portrait of the Artist as a Young Man,* Samuel Butler's *The Way of All Flesh,* and Thomas Wolfe's *Look Homeward, Angel.*

Subplot: A secondary story in a narrative. A subplot may serve as a motivating or complicating force for the main plot of the work, or it may provide emphasis for, or relief from, the main plot. The conflict between the Capulets and the Montagues in William Shakespeare's *Romeo and Juliet* is an example of a subplot.

Surrealism: A term introduced to criticism by Guillaume Apollinaire and later adopted by Andre Breton. It refers to a French literary and artistic movement founded in the 1920s. The Surrealists sought to express unconscious thoughts and feelings in their works. The best-known technique used for achieving this aim was automatic writing—transcriptions of spontaneous outpourings from the unconscious. The Surrealists proposed to unify the contrary levels of conscious and unconscious, dream and reality, objectivity and subjectivity into a new level of "super-realism." Surrealism can be found in the poetry of Paul Eluard, Pierre Reverdy, and Louis Aragon, among others.

Suspense: A literary device in which the author maintains the audience's attention through the buildup of events, the outcome of which will soon be revealed. Suspense in William Shakespeare's *Hamlet* is sustained throughout by the question of whether or not the Prince will achieve what he has been instructed to do and of what he intends to do.

Syllogism: A method of presenting a logical argument. In its most basic form, the syllogism consists of a major premise, a minor premise, and a conclusion. An example of a syllogism is: Major premise: When it snows, the streets get wet. Minor premise: It is snowing. Conclusion: The streets are wet.

Symbol: Something that suggests or stands for something else without losing its original identity. In literature, symbols combine their literal meaning with the suggestion of an abstract concept. Literary symbols are of two types: those that carry complex associations of meaning no matter what their contexts, and those that derive their suggestive meaning from their functions in specific literary works. Examples of symbols are sunshine suggesting happiness, rain suggesting sorrow, and storm clouds suggesting despair.

Symbolism: This term has two widely accepted meanings. In historical criticism, it denotes an early modernist literary movement initiated in France during the nineteenth century that reacted against the prevailing standards of realism. Writers in this movement aimed to evoke, indirectly and symbolically, an order of being beyond the material world of the five senses. Poetic expression of personal emotion figured strongly in the movement, typically by means of a private set of symbols uniquely identifiable with the individual poet. The principal aim of the Symbolists was to express in words the highly complex feelings that grew out of everyday contact with the world. In a broader sense, the term ''symbolism'' refers to the use of one object to represent another. Early members of the Symbolist movement included the French authors Charles Baudelaire and Arthur Rimbaud; William Butler Yeats, James Joyce, and T. S. Eliot were influenced as the movement moved to Ireland, England, and the United States. Examples of the concept of symbolism include a flag that stands for a nation or movement, or an empty cupboard used to suggest hopelessness, poverty, and despair.

Symbolist: See *Symbolism*

Symbolist Movement: See *Symbolism*

Sympathetic Fallacy: See *Affective Fallacy*

T

Tale: A story told by a narrator with a simple plot and little character development. Tales are usually relatively short and often carry a simple message. Examples of tales can be found in the work of Rudyard Kipling, Somerset Maugham, Saki, Anton Chekhov, Guy de Maupassant, and Armistead Maupin.

Tall Tale: A humorous tale told in a straightforward, credible tone but relating absolutely impossible events or feats of the characters. Such tales were commonly told of frontier adventures during the settlement of the west in the United States. Tall tales have been spun around such legendary heroes as Mike Fink, Paul Bunyan, Davy Crockett, Johnny Appleseed, and Captain Stormalong as well as the real-life William F. Cody and Annie Oakley. Literary use of tall tales can be found in Washington Irving's *History of New York,* Mark Twain's *Life on the Mississippi,* and in the German R. F. Raspe's *Baron Munchausen's Narratives of His Marvellous Travels and Campaigns in Russia.*

Tanka: A form of Japanese poetry similar to *haiku.* A *tanka* is five lines long, with the lines containing five, seven, five, seven, and seven syllables respectively. Skilled *tanka* authors include Ishikawa Takuboku, Masaoka Shiki, Amy Lowell, and Adelaide Crapsey.

Teatro Grottesco: See *Theater of the Grotesque*

Terza Rima: A three-line stanza form in poetry in which the rhymes are made on the last word of each line in the following manner: the first and third lines of the first stanza, then the second line of the first stanza and the first and third lines of the second stanza, and so on with the middle line of any stanza rhyming with the first and third lines of the following stanza. An example of *terza rima* is Percy Bysshe Shelley's ''The Triumph of Love'': As in that trance of wondrous thought I lay This was the tenour of my waking dream. Methought I sate beside a public way Thick strewn with summer dust, and a great stream Of people there was hurrying to and fro Numerous as gnats upon the evening gleam,. . .

Tetrameter: See *Meter*

Textual Criticism: A branch of literary criticism that seeks to establish the authoritative text of a literary work. Textual critics typically compare all known manuscripts or printings of a single work in order to assess the meanings of differences and revisions. This procedure allows them to arrive at a definitive version that (supposedly) corresponds to the author's original intention. Textual criticism was applied during the Renaissance to salvage the classical texts of Greece and Rome, and modern works have been studied, for instance, to undo deliberate correction or censorship, as in the case of novels by Stephen Crane and Theodore Dreiser.

Theater of Cruelty: Term used to denote a group of theatrical techniques designed to eliminate the psychological and emotional distance between actors and audience. This concept, introduced in the 1930s in France, was intended to inspire a more intense theatrical experience than conventional theater allowed. The ''cruelty'' of this dramatic theory signified not sadism but heightened actor/audience involvement in the dramatic event. The theater of cruelty was theorized by Antonin Artaud in his *Le Theatre et son double* (*The Theatre and Its Double*), and also appears in the work of Jerzy Grotowski, Jean Genet, Jean Vilar, and Arthur Adamov, among others.

Theater of the Absurd: A post-World War II dramatic trend characterized by radical theatrical innovations. In works influenced by the Theater of the absurd, nontraditional, sometimes grotesque characterizations, plots, and stage sets reveal a meaningless universe in which human values are irrelevant. Existentialist themes of estrangement, absurdity, and futility link many of the works of this movement. The principal writers of the Theater of the Absurd are Samuel Beckett, Eugene Ionesco, Jean Genet, and Harold Pinter.

Theater of the Grotesque: An Italian theatrical movement characterized by plays written around the ironic and macabre aspects of daily life in the World War I era. Theater of the Grotesque was named after the play *The Mask and the Face* by Luigi Chiarelli, which was described as ''a grotesque in three acts.'' The movement influenced the work of Italian dramatist Luigi Pirandello, author of *Right You Are, If You Think You Are.* Also known as *Teatro Grottesco.*

Theme: The main point of a work of literature. The term is used interchangeably with thesis. The theme of William Shakespeare's *Othello*—jealousy—is a common one.

Thesis: A thesis is both an essay and the point argued in the essay. Thesis novels and thesis plays share the quality of containing a thesis which is supported through the action of the story. A master's thesis and a doctoral dissertation are two theses required of graduate students.

Thesis Play: See *Thesis*

Three Unities: See *Unities*

Tone: The author's attitude toward his or her audience may be deduced from the tone of the work. A formal tone may create distance or convey politeness, while an informal tone may encourage a friendly, intimate, or intrusive feeling in the reader. The author's attitude toward his or her subject matter may also be deduced from the tone of the words he or she uses in discussing it. The tone of John F. Kennedy's speech which included the appeal to ''ask not what your country can do for you'' was intended to instill feelings of camaraderie and national pride in listeners.

Tragedy: A drama in prose or poetry about a noble, courageous hero of excellent character who, because of some tragic character flaw or *hamartia*, brings ruin upon him- or herself. Tragedy treats its subjects in a dignified and serious manner, using poetic language to help evoke pity and fear and bring about catharsis, a purging of these emotions. The tragic form was practiced extensively by the ancient Greeks. In the Middle Ages, when classical works were virtually unknown, tragedy came to denote any works about the fall of persons from exalted to low conditions due to any reason: fate, vice, weakness, etc. According to the classical definition of tragedy, such works present the "pathetic"—that which evokes pity—rather than the tragic. The classical form of tragedy was revived in the sixteenth century; it flourished especially on the Elizabethan stage. In modern times, dramatists have attempted to adapt the form to the needs of modern society by drawing their heroes from the ranks of ordinary men and women and defining the nobility of these heroes in terms of spirit rather than exalted social standing. The greatest classical example of tragedy is Sophocles' *Oedipus Rex*. The "pathetic" derivation is exemplified in "The Monk's Tale" in Geoffrey Chaucer's *Canterbury Tales*. Notable works produced during the sixteenth century revival include William Shakespeare's *Hamlet, Othello,* and *King Lear.* Modern dramatists working in the tragic tradition include Henrik Ibsen, Arthur Miller, and Eugene O'Neill.

Tragedy of Blood: See *Revenge Tragedy*

Tragic Flaw: In a tragedy, the quality within the hero or heroine which leads to his or her downfall. Examples of the tragic flaw include Othello's jealousy and Hamlet's indecisiveness, although most great tragedies defy such simple interpretation.

Transcendentalism: An American philosophical and religious movement, based in New England from around 1835 until the Civil War. Transcendentalism was a form of American romanticism that had its roots abroad in the works of Thomas Carlyle, Samuel Coleridge, and Johann Wolfgang von Goethe. The Transcendentalists stressed the importance of intuition and subjective experience in communication with God. They rejected religious dogma and texts in favor of mysticism and scientific naturalism. They pursued truths that lie beyond the "colorless" realms perceived by reason and the senses and were active social reformers in public education, women's rights, and the abolition of slavery. Prominent members of the group include Ralph Waldo Emerson and Henry David Thoreau.

Trickster: A character or figure common in Native American and African literature who uses his ingenuity to defeat enemies and escape difficult situations. Tricksters are most often animals, such as the spider, hare, or coyote, although they may take the form of humans as well. Examples of trickster tales include Thomas King's *A Coyote Columbus Story,* Ashley F. Bryan's *The Dancing Granny* and Ishmael Reed's *The Last Days of Louisiana Red.*

Trimeter: See *Meter*

Triple Rhyme: See *Rhyme*

Trochee: See *Foot*

U

Understatement: See *Irony*

Unities: Strict rules of dramatic structure, formulated by Italian and French critics of the Renaissance and based loosely on the principles of drama discussed by Aristotle in his *Poetics.* Foremost among these rules were the three unities of action, time, and place that compelled a dramatist to: (1) construct a single plot with a beginning, middle, and end that details the causal relationships of action and character; (2) restrict the action to the events of a single day; and (3) limit the scene to a single place or city. The unities were observed faithfully by continental European writers until the Romantic Age, but they were never regularly observed in English drama. Modern dramatists are typically more concerned with a unity of impression or emotional effect than with any of the classical unities. The unities are observed in Pierre Corneille's tragedy *Polyeuctes* and Jean-Baptiste Racine's *Phedre.* Also known as Three Unities.

Urban Realism: A branch of realist writing that attempts to accurately reflect the often harsh facts of modern urban existence. Some works by Stephen Crane, Theodore Dreiser, Charles Dickens, Fyodor Dostoyevsky, Emile Zola, Abraham Cahan, and Henry Fuller feature urban realism. Modern examples include Claude Brown's *Manchild in the Promised Land* and Ron Milner's *What the Wine Sellers Buy.*

Utopia: A fictional perfect place, such as "paradise" or "heaven." Early literary utopias were included in Plato's *Republic* and Sir Thomas More's

Utopia, while more modern utopias can be found in Samuel Butler's *Erewhon,* Theodor Herzka's *A Visit to Freeland,* and H. G. Wells' *A Modern Utopia.*

Utopian: See *Utopia*

Utopianism: See *Utopia*

V

Verisimilitude: Literally, the appearance of truth. In literary criticism, the term refers to aspects of a work of literature that seem true to the reader. Verisimilitude is achieved in the work of Honore de Balzac, Gustave Flaubert, and Henry James, among other late nineteenth-century realist writers.

Vers de societe: See *Occasional Verse*

Vers libre: See *Free Verse*

Verse: A line of metered language, a line of a poem, or any work written in verse. The following line of verse is from the epic poem *Don Juan* by Lord Byron: "My way is to begin with the beginning."

Versification: The writing of verse. Versification may also refer to the meter, rhyme, and other mechanical components of a poem. Composition of a "Roses are red, violets are blue" poem to suit an occasion is a common form of versification practiced by students.

Victorian: Refers broadly to the reign of Queen Victoria of England (1837-1901) and to anything with qualities typical of that era. For example, the qualities of smug narrowmindedness, bourgeois materialism, faith in social progress, and priggish morality are often considered Victorian. This stereotype is contradicted by such dramatic intellectual developments as the theories of Charles Darwin, Karl Marx, and Sigmund Freud (which stirred strong debates in England) and the critical attitudes of serious Victorian writers like Charles Dickens and George Eliot. In literature, the Victorian Period was the great age of the English novel, and the latter part of the era saw the rise of movements such as decadence and symbolism. Works of Victorian literature include the poetry of Robert Browning and Alfred, Lord Tennyson, the criticism of Matthew Arnold and John Ruskin, and the novels of Emily Bronte, William Makepeace Thackeray, and Thomas Hardy. Also known as Victorian Age and Victorian Period.

Victorian Age: See *Victorian*

Victorian Period: See *Victorian*

W

Weltanschauung: A German term referring to a person's worldview or philosophy. Examples of *weltanschauung* include Thomas Hardy's view of the human being as the victim of fate, destiny, or impersonal forces and circumstances, and the disillusioned and laconic cynicism expressed by such poets of the 1930s as W. H. Auden, Sir Stephen Spender, and Sir William Empson.

Weltschmerz: A German term meaning "world pain." It describes a sense of anguish about the nature of existence, usually associated with a melancholy, pessimistic attitude. *Weltschmerz* was expressed in England by George Gordon, Lord Byron in his *Manfred* and *Childe Harold's Pilgrimage,* in France by Viscount de Chateaubriand, Alfred de Vigny, and Alfred de Musset, in Russia by Aleksandr Pushkin and Mikhail Lermontov, in Poland by Juliusz Slowacki, and in America by Nathaniel Hawthorne.

Z

Zarzuela: A type of Spanish operetta. Writers of *zarzuelas* include Lope de Vega and Pedro Calderon.

Zeitgeist: A German term meaning "spirit of the time." It refers to the moral and intellectual trends of a given era. Examples of *zeitgeist* include the preoccupation with the more morbid aspects of dying and death in some Jacobean literature, especially in the works of dramatists Cyril Tourneur and John Webster, and the decadence of the French Symbolists.

Cumulative Author/Title Index

A

Abe Lincoln in Illinois
  (Sherwood): V11
Aeschylus
  Prometheus Bound: V5
  Seven Against Thebes: V10
Ajax (Sophocles): V8
Albee, Edward
  Three Tall Women: V8
  Tiny Alice: V10
  *Who's Afraid of Virginia
    Woolf?*: V3
  The Zoo Story: V2
The Alchemist (Jonson): V4
All My Sons (Miller): V8
The Amen Corner (Baldwin): V11
American Buffalo (Mamet): V3
Angels in America (Kushner): V5
Anonymous
  Everyman: V7
Anouilh, Jean
  Antigone: V9
  Ring Around the Moon: V10
Antigone (Sophocles): V1
Arcadia (Stoppard): V5
Arden, John
  Serjeant Musgrave's Dance: V9
Aristophanes
  Lysistrata: V10
Ayckbourn, Alan
  A Chorus of Disapproval: V7

B

The Bacchae (Euripides): V6
The Balcony (Genet): V10
The Bald Soprano (Ionesco): V4
Baldwin, James
  The Amen Corner: V11
Baraka, Amiri
  Dutchman: V3
  Slave Ship: V11
Barnes, Peter
  The Ruling Class: V6
Barrie, J(ames) M.
  Peter Pan: V7
Barry, Philip
  The Philadelphia Story: V9
The Basic Training of Pavlo Hummel
  (Rabe): V3
Beckett, Samuel
  Krapp's Last Tape: V7
  Waiting for Godot: V2
Behan, Brendan
  The Hostage: V7
The Birthday Party (Pinter): V5
Blood Relations (Pollock): V3
Blood Wedding (García Lorca): V10
Blue Room (Hare): V7
Boesman & Lena (Fugard): V6
Bolt, Robert
  A Man for All Seasons: V2
Bond, Edward
  Lear: V3
  Saved: V8
Brecht, Bertolt
  *The Good Person of
    Szechwan*: V9
  *Mother Courage and Her
    Children*: V5
  The Threepenny Opera: V4
Brighton Beach Memoirs
  (Simon): V6
The Browning Version (Rattigan): V8

Buero Vallejo, Antonio
  The Sleep of Reason: V11
Buried Child (Shepard): V6
Burn This (Wilson): V4
Bus Stop (Inge): V8

C

Capek, Josef
  The Insect Play: V11
Capek, Karel
  The Insect Play: V11
  R.U.R.: V7
Carballido, Emilio
  I, Too, Speak of the Rose: V4
The Caretaker (Pinter): V7
Cat on a Hot Tin Roof
  (Williams): V3
The Chairs (Ionesco): V9
Chase, Mary
  Harvey: V11
Chekhov, Anton
  The Cherry Orchard: V1
  The Three Sisters: V10
  Uncle Vanya: V5
The Cherry Orchard (Chekhov): V1
Children of a Lesser God
  (Medoff): V4
The Children's Hour (Hellman): V3
Childress, Alice
  Trouble in Mind: V8
  The Wedding Band: V2
A Chorus of Disapproval
  (Ayckbourn): V7
Christie, Agatha
  The Mousetrap: V2
Come Back, Little Sheba (Inge): V3

Coward, Noel
  Hay Fever: V6
  Private Lives: V3
Crimes of the Heart (Henley): V2
The Crucible (Miller): V3
Cyrano de Bergerac (Rostand): V1

D

Dancing at Lughnasa (Friel): V11
Death and the King's Horseman
  (Soyinka): V10
Death and the Maiden
  (Dorfman): V4
Death of a Salesman (Miller): V1
Delaney, Shelagh
  A Taste of Honey: V7
Doctor Faustus (Marlowe): V1
A Doll's House (Ibsen): V1
Dorfman, Ariel
  Death and the Maiden: V4
Driving Miss Daisy (Uhry): V11
Dutchman (Baraka): V3

E

Edward II (Marlowe): V5
Electra (Sophocles): V4
The Elephant Man (Pomerance): V9
Eliot, T. S.
  Murder in the Cathedral: V4
The Emperor Jones (O'Neill): V6
Entertaining Mr. Sloane (Orton): V3
Equus (Shaffer): V5
Euripides
  The Bacchae: V6
  Iphigenia in Taurus: V4
  Medea: V1
Everyman (): V7

F

Fences (Wilson): V3
Fiddler on the Roof (Stein): V7
Fierstein, Harvey
  Torch Song Trilogy: V6
Fool for Love (Shepard): V7
*for colored girls who have
  considered suicide/when the
  rainbow is enuf* (Shange): V2
Ford, John
  'Tis Pity She's a Whore: V7
The Foreigner (Shue): V7
Friel, Brian
  Dancing at Lughnasa: V11
The Front Page (MacArthur): V9
Fugard, Athol
  Boesman & Lena: V6
  *"Master Harold"... and the
    Boys*: V3
  Sizwe Bansi is Dead: V10
Fuller, Charles H.
  A Soldier's Play: V8

Funnyhouse of a Negro
  (Kennedy): V9

G

García Lorca, Federico
  Blood Wedding: V10
  The House of Bernarda Alba: V4
Genet, Jean
  The Balcony: V10
The Ghost Sonata (Strindberg): V9
Ghosts (Ibsen): V11
Gibson, William
  The Miracle Worker: V2
Glaspell, Susan
  Trifles: V8
The Glass Menagerie (Williams): V1
Glengarry Glen Ross (Mamet): V2
Goldsmith, Oliver
  She Stoops to Conquer: V1
The Good Person of Szechwan
  (Brecht): V9
Gorki, Maxim
  The Lower Depths: V9
The Great God Brown
  (O'Neill): V11
Guare, John
  The House of Blue Leaves: V8

H

The Hairy Ape (O'Neill): V4
Hammerstein, Oscar
  The King and I: V1
Hansberry, Lorraine
  A Raisin in the Sun: V2
Hare, David
  Blue Room: V7
  Plenty: V4
Hart, Moss
  Once in a Lifetime: V10
  You Can't Take It with You: V1
Harvey (Chase): V11
Havel, Vaclav
  The Memorandum: V10
Hay Fever (Coward): V6
Hecht, Ben
  The Front Page: V9
Hedda Gabler (Ibsen): V6
The Heidi Chronicles
  (Wasserstein): V5
Hellman, Lillian
  The Children's Hour: V3
  The Little Foxes: V1
Henley, Beth
  Crimes of the Heart: V2
Highway, Tomson
  The Rez Sisters: V2
The Homecoming (Pinter): V3
The Hostage (Behan): V7
Hot L Baltimore (Wilson): V9
The House of Bernarda Alba (García
  Lorca): V4

The House of Blue Leaves
  (Guare): V8
Hughes, Langston
  Mule Bone: V6
Hurston, Zora Neale
  Mule Bone: V6
Hwang, David Henry
  M. Butterfly: V11

I

I, Too, Speak of the Rose
  (Carballido): V4
Ibsen, Henrik
  A Doll's House: V1
  Ghosts: V11
  Hedda Gabler: V6
  Peer Gynt: V8
  The Wild Duck: V10
The Iceman Cometh (O'Neill): V5
The Importance of Being Earnest
  (Wilde): V4
Indian Ink (Stoppard): V11
Inge, William
  Bus Stop: V8
  Come Back, Little Sheba: V3
  Picnic: V5
Inherit the Wind (Lawrence
  and Lee): V2
The Insect Play (Capek): V11
Ionesco, Eugène
  The Bald Soprano: V4
  The Chairs: V9
Iphigenia in Taurus (Euripides): V4

J

Jarry, Alfred
  Ubu Roi: V8
Jesus Christ Superstar (Webber and
  Rice): V7
Jonson, Ben(jamin)
  The Alchemist: V4
  Volpone: V10

K

Kaufman, George S.
  Once in a Lifetime: V10
  You Can't Take It with You: V1
Kennedy, Adrienne
  Funnyhouse of a Negro: V9
The Kentucky Cycle
  (Schenkkan): V10
The King and I (Hammerstein and
  Rodgers): V1
Kopit, Arthur
  *Oh Dad, Poor Dad, Mamma's
    Hung You in the Closet and
    I'm Feelin' So Sad*: V7
Krapp's Last Tape (Beckett): V7
Kushner, Tony
  Angels in America: V5

L

Lady Windermere's Fan (Wilde): V9
Lawrence, Jerome
　　Inherit the Wind: V2
Lear (Bond): V3
Lee, Robert E.
　　Inherit the Wind: V2
The Little Foxes (Hellman): V1
Long Day's Journey into Night
　　(O'Neill): V2
Look Back in Anger (Osborne): V4
The Lower Depths (Gorki): V9
Lysistrata (Aristophanes): V10

M

M. Butterfly (Hwang): V11
MacArthur, Charles
　　The Front Page: V9
Major Barbara (Shaw): V3
Mamet, David
　　American Buffalo: V3
　　Glengarry Glen Ross: V2
　　Speed-the-Plow: V6
Man and Superman (Shaw): V6
A Man for All Seasons (Bolt): V2
Marat/Sade (Weiss): V3
Marlowe, Christopher
　　Doctor Faustus: V1
　　Edward II: V5
"Master Harold"... and the Boys
　　(Fugard): V3
McCullers, Carson
　　The Member of the Wedding: V5
Medea (Euripides): V1
Medoff, Mark
　　Children of a Lesser God: V4
The Member of the Wedding
　　(McCullers): V5
The Memorandum (Havel): V10
Miller, Arthur
　　All My Sons: V8
　　The Crucible: V3
　　Death of a Salesman: V1
The Miracle Worker (Gibson): V2
Miss Julie (Strindberg): V4
A Month in the Country
　　(Turgenev): V6
Mother Courage and Her Children
　　(Brecht): V5
Mourning Becomes Electra
　　(O'Neill): V9
The Mousetrap (Christie): V2
Mule Bone (Hurston and
　　Hughes): V6
Murder in the Cathedral (Eliot): V4

N

Nicholson, William
　　Shadowlands: V11
'night, Mother (Norman): V2
The Night of the Iguana
　　(Williams): V7
No Exit (Sartre): V5
Norman, Marsha
　　'night, Mother: V2

O

The Odd Couple (Simon): V2
Odets, Clifford
　　Waiting for Lefty: V3
Oedipus Rex (Sophocles): V1
*Oh Dad, Poor Dad, Mamma's Hung
　　You in the Closet and I'm
　　Feelin' So Sad* (Kopit): V7
Once in a Lifetime (Kaufman and
　　Hart): V10
O'Neill, Eugene
　　The Emperor Jones: V6
　　The Great God Brown: V11
　　The Hairy Ape: V4
　　The Iceman Cometh: V5
　　*Long Day's Journey into
　　　Night*: V2
　　Mourning Becomes Electra: V9
Orton, Joe
　　Entertaining Mr. Sloane: V3
　　What the Butler Saw: V6
Osborne, John
　　Look Back in Anger: V4
Our Town (Wilder): V1

P

Peer Gynt (Ibsen): V8
Peter Pan (Barrie): V7
The Philadelphia Story (Barry): V9
The Piano Lesson (Wilson): V7
Picnic (Inge): V5
Pinter, Harold
　　The Birthday Party: V5
　　The Caretaker: V7
　　The Homecoming: V3
Pirandello, Luigi
　　*Right You Are, If You Think You
　　　Are*: V9
　　*Six Characters in Search of an
　　　Author*: V4
Plenty (Hare): V4
Pollock, Sharon
　　Blood Relations: V3
Pomerance, Bernard
　　The Elephant Man: V9
Private Lives (Coward): V3
Prometheus Bound (Aeschylus): V5
Pygmalion (Shaw): V1

R

R.U.R. (Capek): V7
Rabe, David
　　*The Basic Training of Pavlo
　　　Hummel*: V3
　　Streamers: V8
A Raisin in the Sun (Hansberry): V2
Rattigan, Terence
　　The Browning Version: V8
The Real Thing (Stoppard): V8
Rebeck, Theresa
　　Spike Heels: V11
The Rez Sisters (Highway): V2
Rice, Tim
　　Jesus Christ Superstar: V7
Right You Are, If You Think You Are
　　(Pirandello): V9
Ring Around the Moon
　　(Anouilh): V10
Rodgers, Richard
　　The King and I: V1
*Rosencrantz and Guildenstern Are
　　Dead* (Stoppard): V2
Rostand, Edmond
　　Cyrano de Bergerac: V1
The Ruling Class (Barnes): V6

S

Saint Joan (Shaw): V11
Salome (Wilde): V8
Sartre, Jean-Paul
　　No Exit: V5
Saved (Bond): V8
Schenkkan, Robert
　　The Kentucky Cycle: V10
School for Scandal (Sheridan): V4
Serjeant Musgrave's Dance
　　(Arden): V9
Seven Against Thebes
　　(Aeschylus): V10
Shadowlands (Nicholson): V11
Shaffer, Peter
　　Equus: V5
Shange, Ntozake
　　*for colored girls who have
　　　considered suicide/when the
　　　rainbow is enuf*: V2
Shaw, George Bernard
　　Major Barbara: V3
　　Man and Superman: V6
　　Pygmalion: V1
　　Saint Joan: V11
She Stoops to Conquer
　　(Goldsmith): V1
Shepard, Sam
　　Buried Child: V6
　　Fool for Love: V7
　　True West: V3
Sheridan, Richard Brinsley
　　School for Scandal: V4
Sherwood, Robert E.
　　Abe Lincoln in Illinois: V11
Shue, Larry
　　The Foreigner: V7
Simon, Neil
　　Brighton Beach Memoirs: V6
　　The Odd Couple: V2

Six Characters in Search of an Author (Pirandello): V4
Sizwe Bansi is Dead (Fugard): V10
The Skin of Our Teeth (Wilder): V4
Slave Ship (Baraka): V11
The Sleep of Reason (Buero Vallejo): V11
Smith, Anna Deavere
   Twilight: Los Angeles, 1992: V2
A Soldier's Play (Fuller): V8
Sophocles
   Ajax: V8
   Antigone: V1
   Electra: V4
   Oedipus Rex: V1
Soyinka, Wole
   Death and the King's Horseman: V10
Speed-the-Plow (Mamet): V6
Spike Heels (Rebeck): V11
Stein, Joseph
   Fiddler on the Roof: V7
Stoppard, Tom
   Arcadia: V5
   Indian Ink: V11
   The Real Thing: V8
   Rosencrantz and Guildenstern Are Dead: V2
Streamers (Rabe): V8
A Streetcar Named Desire (Williams): V1
Strindberg, August
   The Ghost Sonata: V9
   Miss Julie: V4

T

A Taste of Honey (Delaney): V7
The Three Sisters (Chekhov): V10
Three Tall Women (Albee): V8
The Threepenny Opera (Brecht): V4
Tiny Alice (Albee): V10
'Tis Pity She's a Whore (Ford): V7
Torch Song Trilogy (Fierstein): V6
Trifles (Glaspell): V8
Trouble in Mind (Childress): V8
True West (Shepard): V3
Turgenev, Ivan
   A Month in the Country: V6
Twilight: Los Angeles, 1992 (Smith): V2

U

Ubu Roi (Jarry): V8
Uhry, Alfred
   Driving Miss Daisy: V11
Uncle Vanya (Chekhov): V5

V

Valdez, Luis
   Zoot Suit: V5
Vidal, Gore
   Visit to a Small Planet: V2
Visit to a Small Planet (Vidal): V2
Volpone (Jonson): V10

W

Waiting for Godot (Beckett): V2
Waiting for Lefty (Odets): V3
Wasserstein, Wendy
   The Heidi Chronicles: V5
Webber, Andrew Lloyd
   Jesus Christ Superstar: V7
The Wedding Band (Childress): V2
Weiss, Peter
   Marat/Sade: V3
What the Butler Saw (Orton): V6
Who's Afraid of Virginia Woolf? (Albee): V3
The Wild Duck (Ibsen): V10
Wilde, Oscar
   The Importance of Being Earnest: V4
   Lady Windermere's Fan: V9
   Salome: V8
Wilder, Thornton
   Our Town: V1
   The Skin of Our Teeth: V4
Williams, Tennessee
   Cat on a Hot Tin Roof: V3
   The Glass Menagerie: V1
   The Night of the Iguana: V7
   A Streetcar Named Desire: V1
Wilson, August
   Fences: V3
   The Piano Lesson: V7
Wilson, Lanford
   Burn This: V4
   Hot L Baltimore: V9

Y

You Can't Take It with You (Kaufman and Hart): V1

Z

The Zoo Story (Albee): V2
Zoot Suit (Valdez): V5

Nationality/Ethnicity Index

African American

Baldwin, James
   The Amen Corner: V11
Baraka, Amiri
   Dutchman: V3
   The Slave Ship: V11
Childress, Alice
   Trouble in Mind: V8
   The Wedding Band: V2
Fuller, Charles H.
   A Soldier's Play: V8
Hansberry, Lorraine
   A Raisin in the Sun: V2
Hughes, Langston
   Mule Bone: V6
Hurston, Zora Neale
   Mule Bone: V6
Kennedy, Adrienne
   Funnyhouse of a Negro: V9
Shange, Ntozake
   for colored girls who have considered suicide/when the rainbow is enuf: V2
Smith, Anna Deavere
   Twilight: Los Angeles, 1992: V2
Wilson, August
   Fences: V3
   The Piano Lesson: V7

American

Albee, Edward
   Three Tall Women: V8
   Tiny Alice: V10
   Who's Afraid of Virginia Woolf?: V3
   The Zoo Story: V2
Baldwin, James
   The Amen Corner: V11
Baraka, Amiri
   Dutchman: V3
   Slave Ship: V11
Barry, Philip
   The Philadelphia Story: V9
Chase, Mary
   Harvey: V11
Childress, Alice
   Trouble in Mind: V8
   The Wedding Band: V2
Eliot, T. S.
   Murder in the Cathedral: V4
Fierstein, Harvey
   Torch Song Trilogy: V6
Fuller, Charles H.
   A Soldier's Play: V8
Gibson, William
   The Miracle Worker: V2
Glaspell, Susan
   Trifles: V8
Guare, John
   The House of Blue Leaves: V8
Hammerstein, Oscar
   The King and I: V1
Hansberry, Lorraine
   A Raisin in the Sun: V2
Hart, Moss
   Once in a Lifetime: V10
   You Can't Take It with You: V1
Hecht, Ben
   The Front Page: V9
Hellman, Lillian
   The Children's Hour: V3
   The Little Foxes: V1
Henley, Beth
   Crimes of the Heart: V2
Hurston, Zora Neale
   Mule Bone: V6
Hwang, David Henry
   M. Butterfly: V11
Inge, William
   Bus Stop: V8
   Come Back, Little Sheba: V3
   Picnic: V5
Kaufman, George S.
   Once in a Lifetime: V10
   You Can't Take It with You: V1
Kopit, Arthur
   Oh Dad, Poor Dad, Mamma's Hung You in the Closet and I'm Feelin' So Sad: V7
Kushner, Tony
   Angels in America: V5
Lawrence, Jerome
   Inherit the Wind: V2
Lee, Robert E.
   Inherit the Wind: V2
MacArthur, Charles
   The Front Page: V9
Mamet, David
   American Buffalo: V3
   Glengarry Glen Ross: V2
   Speed-the-Plow: V6
McCullers, Carson
   The Member of the Wedding: V5
Medoff, Mark
   Children of a Lesser God: V4
Miller, Arthur
   All My Sons: V8
   The Crucible: V3
   Death of a Salesman: V1

Norman, Marsha
  'night, Mother: V2
Odets, Clifford
  Waiting for Lefty: V3
O'Neill, Eugene
  The Emperor Jones: V6
  The Great God Brown: V11
  The Hairy Ape: V4
  The Iceman Cometh: V5
  Long Day's Journey into Night: V2
  Mourning Becomes Electra: V9
Pomerance, Bernard
  The Elephant Man: V9
Rabe, David
  The Basic Training of Pavlo Hummel: V3
  Streamers: V8
Rebeck, Theresa
  Spike Heels: V11
Rodgers, Richard
  The King and I: V1
Schenkkan, Robert
  The Kentucky Cycle: V10
Shange, Ntozake
  for colored girls who have considered suicide/when the rainbow is enuf: V2
Shepard, Sam
  Buried Child: V6
  Fool for Love: V7
  True West: V3
Sherwood, Robert E.
  Abe Lincoln in Illinois: V11
Shue, Larry
  The Foreigner: V7
Simon, Neil
  Brighton Beach Memoirs: V6
  The Odd Couple: V2
Smith, Anna Deavere
  Twilight: Los Angeles, 1992: V2
Stein, Joseph
  Fiddler on the Roof: V7
Uhry, Alfred
  Driving Miss Daisy: V11
Valdez, Luis
  Zoot Suit: V5
Vidal, Gore
  Visit to a Small Planet: V2
Wasserstein, Wendy
  The Heidi Chronicles: V5
Wilder, Thornton
  Our Town: V1
  The Skin of Our Teeth: V4
Williams, Tennessee
  Cat on a Hot Tin Roof: V3
  The Glass Menagerie: V1
  The Night of the Iguana: V7
  A Streetcar Named Desire: V1
Wilson, August
  Fences: V3
  The Piano Lesson: V7
Wilson, Lanford
  Burn This: V4
  Hot L Baltimore: V9

Argentinian

Dorfman, Ariel
  Death and the Maiden: V4

Bohemian (Czechoslovakian)

Capek, Karel
  The Insect Play: V11

Canadian

Highway, Tomson
  The Rez Sisters: V2
Pollock, Sharon
  Blood Relations: V3

Chilean

Dorfman, Ariel
  Death and the Maiden: V4

Czechoslovakian

Capek, Josef
  The Insect Play: V11
Capek, Karel
  The Insect Play: V11
  R.U.R.: V7
Havel, Vaclav
  The Memorandum: V10
Stoppard, Tom
  Indian Ink: V11

English

Arden, John
  Serjeant Musgrave's Dance: V9
Ayckbourn, Alan
  A Chorus of Disapproval: V7
Barnes, Peter
  The Ruling Class: V6
Bolt, Robert
  A Man for All Seasons: V2
Bond, Edward
  Lear: V3
  Saved: V8
Christie, Agatha
  The Mousetrap: V2
Coward, Noel
  Hay Fever: V6
  Private Lives: V3
Delaney, Shelagh
  A Taste of Honey: V7
Ford, John
  'Tis Pity She's a Whore: V7
Goldsmith, Oliver
  She Stoops to Conquer: V1
Hare, David
  Blue Room: V7
  Plenty: V4
Jonson, Ben(jamin)
  The Alchemist: V4
  Volpone: V10
Marlowe, Christopher
  Doctor Faustus: V1
  Edward II: V5
Nicholson, William
  Shadowlands: V11
Orton, Joe
  Entertaining Mr. Sloane: V3
  What the Butler Saw: V6
Osborne, John
  Look Back in Anger: V4
Pinter, Harold
  The Birthday Party: V5
  The Caretaker: V7
  The Homecoming: V3
Rattigan, Terence
  The Browning Version: V8
Rice, Tim
  Jesus Christ Superstar: V7
Shaffer, Peter
  Equus: V5
Stoppard, Tom
  Arcadia: V5
  The Real Thing: V8
  Rosencrantz and Guildenstern Are Dead: V2
Webber, Andrew Lloyd
  Jesus Christ Superstar: V7

French

Anouilh, Jean
  Antigone: V9
  Ring Around the Moon: V10
Genet, Jean
  The Balcony: V10
Jarry, Alfred
  Ubu Roi: V8
Rostand, Edmond
  Cyrano de Bergerac: V1
Sartre, Jean-Paul
  No Exit: V5

German

Brecht, Bertolt
  The Good Person of Szechwan: V9
  Mother Courage and Her Children: V5
  The Threepenny Opera: V4
Weiss, Peter
  Marat/Sade: V3

Greek

Aeschylus
  Prometheus Bound: V5
  Seven Against Thebes: V10

Aristophanes
  Lysistrata: V10
Euripides
  The Bacchae: V6
  Iphigenia in Taurus: V4
  Medea: V1
Sophocles
  Ajax: V8
  Antigone: V1
  Electra: V4
  Oedipus Rex: V1

Hispanic
Valdez, Luis
  Zoot Suit: V5

Irish
Beckett, Samuel
  Krapp's Last Tape: V7
  Waiting for Godot: V2
Behan, Brendan
  The Hostage: V7
Friel, Brian
  Dancing at Lughnasa: V11
Shaw, George Bernard
  Major Barbara: V3
  Man and Superman: V6
  Pygmalion: V1
  Saint Joan: V11
Sheridan, Richard Brinsley
  School for Scandal: V4
Wilde, Oscar
  The Importance of Being Earnest: V4
  Lady Windermere's Fan: V9
  Salome: V8

Italian
Pirandello, Luigi
  Right You Are, If You Think You Are: V9
  Six Characters in Search of an Author: V4

Mexican
Carballido, Emilio
  I, Too, Speak of the Rose: V4

Native Canadian
Highway, Tomson
  The Rez Sisters: V2

Nigerian
Soyinka, Wole
  Death and the King's Horseman: V10

Norwegian
Ibsen, Henrik
  A Doll's House: V1
  Ghosts: V11
  Hedda Gabler: V6
  Peer Gynt: V8
  The Wild Duck: V10

Romanian
Ionesco, Eugène
  The Bald Soprano: V4
  The Chairs: V9

Russian
Chekhov, Anton
  The Cherry Orchard: V1
  The Three Sisters: V10
  Uncle Vanya: V5
Gorki, Maxim
  The Lower Depths: V9
Turgenev, Ivan
  A Month in the Country: V6

Scottish
Barrie, J(ames) M.
  Peter Pan: V7

South African
Fugard, Athol
  Boesman & Lena: V6
  "Master Harold"... and the Boys: V3
  Sizwe Bansi is Dead: V10

Spanish
Buero Vallejo, Antonio
  The Sleep of Reason: V11
García Lorca, Federico
  Blood Wedding: V10
  The House of Bernarda Alba: V4

Swedish
Strindberg, August
  The Ghost Sonata: V9
  Miss Julie: V4

Subject/Theme Index

*Boldface terms appear as subheads in Themes section.

1950s
   Slave Ship: 229-231
1980s
   Indian Ink: 146-148

A

Abandonment
   The Amen Corner: 21-23
Abstinence
   Saint Joan: 280
Africa
   Dancing at Lughnasa: 38-40, 43-44, 51-52
Alcoholism, Drugs, and Drug Addiction
   Harvey: 134-135
Allegory
   The Great God Brown: 122, 124-125
   The Insect Play: 178-179
American Dream
   The Great God Brown: 113
American Midwest
   Abe Lincoln in Illinois: 2-4, 10-11
American Northeast
   Abe Lincoln in Illinois: 9-11
   Driving Miss Daisy: 59, 62, 64, 66, 68
   M. Butterfly: 200, 203
   Saint Joan: 273, 278-279

American South
   Driving Miss Daisy: 59, 62, 64-65
Anger
   The Amen Corner: 36
Anthropomorphism
   The Insect Play: 162, 169-170
Asia
   M. Butterfly: 184-192, 199-202
Assimilationism
   The Sleep of Reason: 247
Atonement
   Ghosts: 98-99

B

Betrayal
   The Great God Brown: 113
Betrayal
   The Great God Brown: 108, 110, 113, 115
   M. Butterfly: 182-183, 188
Biography
   Abe Lincoln in Illinois: 12-16
Black Arts Movement
   The Amen Corner: 27-29
   The Sleep of Reason: 248-251
Black Nationalism
   The Sleep of Reason: 245
Bloomsbury Group
   Indian Ink: 154-155

C

Capitalism
   The Insect Play: 176-177

Change
   Dancing at Lughnasa: 42
Change and Transformation
   The Great God Brown: 114
Childhood
   Dancing at Lughnasa: 55-56
   Ghosts: 78-79, 82-84
Christianity
   Dancing at Lughnasa: 39, 43-44, 54-55
   Slave Ship: 224, 226, 229, 232
Civil Rights
   Driving Miss Daisy: 62, 65-66
   The Sleep of Reason: 247, 249, 254-256
Colonialism
   Indian Ink: 146-147, 150-152
Comedy
   Harvey: 143-145
   Shadowlands: 213, 216
Communism
   M. Butterfly: 190-191
Courage
   Abe Lincoln in Illinois: 17
   Shadowlands: 211, 213
Creativity
   The Great God Brown: 117, 119
Crime and Criminals
   Driving Miss Daisy: 59, 62, 65-66
   Ghosts: 85-86
   The Insect Play: 179
Cruelty
   The Sleep of Reason: 247-248, 251, 255-256
Cultural Imperialism
   Indian Ink: 150

Subject/Theme Index

Cycle of Life
  The Insect Play: 168

D

Dance
  Dancing at Lughnasa: 38-40, 45-50, 53-56
  The Sleep of Reason: 244, 246-247
Death
  Abe Lincoln in Illinois: 7
Death
  Abe Lincoln in Illinois: 2-3, 9, 11-12
  The Amen Corner: 22-23
  The Great God Brown: 110, 116
  The Insect Play: 164-165, 169-170, 176-177
  M. Butterfly: 188-189
  Shadowlands: 211-214, 218-220
  Slave Ship: 226-229, 234-235
Deceit
  Ghosts: 95-97
Deception
  Ghosts: 81
Dialogue
  Indian Ink: 149, 151
  Spike Heels: 266-267
Dictatorship
  Shadowlands: 218-219
Disease
  Ghosts: 77, 79, 81-87
Doubt and Ambiguity
  Abe Lincoln in Illinois: 7
Drama
  Abe Lincoln in Illinois: 7-8, 12, 14-16
  The Amen Corner: 27-30, 34
  Dancing at Lughnasa: 38, 44-46
  Driving Miss Daisy: 59, 66-67
  Ghosts: 96, 99-100, 104-106
  The Great God Brown: 115-117, 121-123
  Harvey: 136, 143, 145
  Indian Ink: 152-153
  The Insect Play: 169, 171-172
  M. Butterfly: 189, 192, 200, 202-204
  Slave Ship: 224, 229, 232-233
  The Sleep of Reason: 247-250
  Spike Heels: 267, 269
  Saint Joan: 273, 278-279
Dreams and Visions
  Ghosts: 93-94, 104-105
  Harvey: 141-142
  M. Butterfly: 196-198
  The Sleep of Reason: 254
  Spike Heels: 261, 263, 265-266, 270-272
Duty and Responsibility
  Abe Lincoln in Illinois: 3-4, 12
  Ghosts: 89-90

E

Emotions
  Abe Lincoln in Illinois: 11-12
  Dancing at Lughnasa: 38, 42, 45, 54, 56
  Ghosts: 88-89, 97-98, 103-105
  The Great God Brown: 115, 117
  Harvey: 134
  Indian Ink: 160
  The Insect Play: 176
  M. Butterfly: 189, 195-196
  Shadowlands: 216
  Slave Ship: 224, 232, 236-238
Empire
  Indian Ink: 149
Eternity
  The Great God Brown: 124
Europe
  The Amen Corner: 21-23
  Dancing at Lughnasa: 39-40, 44-49, 52
  Ghosts: 77, 83-87, 106
  The Great God Brown: 110, 113, 116
  Harvey: 134-135
  Indian Ink: 147-148, 151-156
  The Insect Play: 169-171
  M. Butterfly: 183, 185, 189-190
  Shadowlands: 206, 208-209, 213-216
  Slave Ship: 224, 226-235
  Spike Heels: 261-263, 267-269
Evil
  The Amen Corner: 31-32, 36
  Ghosts: 86, 93, 96, 98-99, 105-106
Execution
  Shadowlands: 209, 213, 216
Expressionism
  The Great God Brown: 108, 114-116

F

Farm and Rural Life
  Abe Lincoln in Illinois: 1, 3-4, 10
  Dancing at Lughnasa: 38-39, 43
Fear and Terror
  Ghosts: 88-90, 96-98
  Spike Heels: 260, 262-263, 266, 269, 271
Feminism
  Shadowlands: 212
Feminism
  M. Butterfly: 193-194
  Saint Joan: 276-278, 282-283
Film
  Abe Lincoln in Illinois: 11-13
  Dancing at Lughnasa: 48-50
  Harvey: 133, 135-137
  Indian Ink: 152-153
  M. Butterfly: 203-204
  Slave Ship: 232-237, 240

Folklore
  The Insect Play: 162, 169-170
  Spike Heels: 271-272
Friendship
  Driving Miss Daisy: 62
  Harvey: 131

G

Gender Roles
  M. Butterfly: 195
  Saint Joan: 278-279
Generosity
  Driving Miss Daisy: 72-73
Ghost
  Ghosts: 77, 83, 87-88, 96-98, 104, 106
God and Religion
  Slave Ship: 229
God
  The Amen Corner: 35-36
  The Great God Brown: 113-114, 118-119, 125
  M. Butterfly: 198
  Slave Ship: 225, 229-230, 237
Greed
  The Insect Play: 168-170, 179-180
Grief and Sorrow
  Indian Ink: 160-161
Growing Old
  Driving Miss Daisy: 63
Guilt
  Ghosts: 95-98

H

Happiness and Gaiety
  Ghosts: 95, 97-100
  The Insect Play: 179-180
  Slave Ship: 225-240
Harlem Renaissance
  The Amen Corner: 27-28
  The Sleep of Reason: 249
Hatred
  Ghosts: 95
  The Great God Brown: 110, 114, 117-119
  Spike Heels: 262, 265, 269
Heaven
  The Amen Corner: 35-36
  Shadowlands: 211, 220
Heritage and Ancestry
  Ghosts: 101-102, 106
Heroism
  Abe Lincoln in Illinois: 17
  Ghosts: 100
  The Great God Brown: 121
  Harvey: 144
  Shadowlands: 213, 217, 219
History
  Abe Lincoln in Illinois: 1, 12
  The Amen Corner: 28

Subject/Theme Index

Dancing at Lughnasa: 42-44
Driving Miss Daisy: 67
Indian Ink: 146, 149-152, 159-161
M. Butterfly: 192
Shadowlands: 212-213
Slave Ship: 230
The Sleep of Reason: 242, 245-248
Spike Heels: 260, 268-269
Saint Joan: 278

Honor
Ghosts: 77, 92-93

Hope
The Insect Play: 174

Human Condition
Ghosts: 101-102

Human Traits
The Insect Play: 171

Humiliation and Degradation
Spike Heels: 265-266

Humility
M. Butterfly: 188, 191-192, 197, 199-200

Humor
Driving Miss Daisy: 74
Harvey: 136, 143-144
Indian Ink: 152-153
Shadowlands: 206, 213, 216

I

Identity
The Great God Brown: 113

Imagery and Symbolism
The Amen Corner: 30, 32, 35-36
Ghosts: 83-84
The Great God Brown: 114, 116
Harvey: 133-134
The Insect Play: 175, 177
Slave Ship: 233
The Sleep of Reason: 247-249, 255-256

Imagination
Harvey: 126, 132-135, 141-143
M. Butterfly: 197-200

Imperialism
Indian Ink: 146, 149-151, 155-156

Individualism versus Authority
Shadowlands: 211

Insanity
Harvey: 127-128, 133, 143-145
Spike Heels: 263, 266, 269

Irony
Indian Ink: 160-161
M. Butterfly: 187, 192

J

Judaism
Driving Miss Daisy: 59, 61-62, 68, 72-73

K

Killers and Killing
The Insect Play: 165, 168-169, 174
M. Butterfly: 188, 190
Shadowlands: 211

Kindness
The Great God Brown: 109-110, 117

Knowledge
Ghosts: 105-106

L

Landscape
Dancing at Lughnasa: 53-56
M. Butterfly: 201-203

Law and Order
Abe Lincoln in Illinois: 1, 3, 8-11
Driving Miss Daisy: 65-66
Spike Heels: 262, 266-268

Literary Criticism
Harvey: 143

Literary Movements
The Amen Corner: 27
The Sleep of Reason: 248

Loneliness
The Great God Brown: 108, 110, 113-114

Love
The Amen Corner: 25

Love and Passion/Change and Transformation
Slave Ship: 228

Love and Passion
Abe Lincoln in Illinois: 3, 10-12
The Amen Corner: 23, 25, 29-30
Dancing at Lughnasa: 49, 51-52
Ghosts: 89-90, 96, 99
The Great God Brown: 109-110, 118-119
Harvey: 141-145
The Insect Play: 164, 172, 175-176
M. Butterfly: 185, 188-189, 195-196, 199-200, 203-204
Slave Ship: 225-226, 229-230, 239-240

Loyalty
Ghosts: 81

Loyalty
Ghosts: 81-82
The Insect Play: 178-180
Spike Heels: 267

M

Male and Female Roles
Saint Joan: 275

Marriage
Abe Lincoln in Illinois: 3, 7
Ghosts: 77, 79, 82-84, 89
Slave Ship: 228-229

Martyr
Shadowlands: 206-207, 217

Materialism
The Great God Brown: 123-124

Memory
Dancing at Lughnasa: 41

Memory and Reminiscence
Dancing at Lughnasa: 38-43, 55-56
Indian Ink: 160-161

Mental Instability
Harvey: 129, 134

Middle Ages
Shadowlands: 208, 214-216

Middle Class
Ghosts: 94-96

Middle East
Indian Ink: 146-152, 155-158

Miracle
Shadowlands: 208, 212-213

Miracles, Faith, and Sainthood
Shadowlands: 212

Monarchy
The Amen Corner: 25, 27-28
Driving Miss Daisy: 62, 66
Shadowlands: 208, 211, 213-214
The Sleep of Reason: 254
Spike Heels: 260-263, 266-269, 272

Money and Economics
Ghosts: 78-79
The Insect Play: 177-180
M. Butterfly: 202-203

Monologue
Dancing at Lughnasa: 38-41
Slave Ship: 225, 229-230

Moral Corruption
Ghosts: 82

Morals and Morality/Ethics/Vice
The Insect Play: 168

Morals and Morality
The Amen Corner: 30, 32, 35
Ghosts: 82, 84-86, 94-106
The Insect Play: 169-170, 174, 178-180

Murder
The Insect Play: 165, 168-170

Music
The Amen Corner: 21-23, 29-34
Dancing at Lughnasa: 39-40, 43, 45-49, 53-56
Driving Miss Daisy: 73
M. Butterfly: 182-185, 188-189, 192-201
The Sleep of Reason: 242, 244-245, 248-249, 253-258

Mystery and Intrigue
Indian Ink: 159-161

Myths and Legends
Abe Lincoln in Illinois: 1, 9, 11-12
The Great God Brown: 123-124
M. Butterfly: 189, 191-192

N

Narration
  Dancing at Lughnasa: 55-56
Nationalism
  Indian Ink: 150
Nationalism and Patriotism
  Indian Ink: 146, 150-151
  Shadowlands: 207, 212, 214-216
  The Sleep of Reason: 242, 245-250
Nationalism and War
  Shadowlands: 212
Nature and its Meaning
  The Insect Play: 169
Nature
  Abe Lincoln in Illinois: 9
  Ghosts: 93
  The Insect Play: 169
Nietzschean Philosophy
  The Great God Brown: 117, 119
Nomadic Life
  The Insect Play: 178-180
North America
  Abe Lincoln in Illinois: 3-4, 10-11
  M. Butterfly: 191-192

P

Pagan
  Dancing at Lughnasa: 38-39, 43, 46-55
Paganism
  Dancing at Lughnasa: 42
Pain and Suffering
  Slave Ship: 228
Painting
  Harvey: 141-142
  Indian Ink: 147-148, 156-161
  Spike Heels: 261-263, 266-272
Paranormal
  Ghosts: 95
Perception
  Ghosts: 101-104
  M. Butterfly: 182, 187-188, 192
Permanence
  Dancing at Lughnasa: 53, 55-56
  Saint Joan: 277-278
Persecution
  Ghosts: 79, 83, 86, 94, 98-100
  Shadowlands: 218-219
  Spike Heels: 265-266
  Saint Joan: 283
Personal Identity
  The Great God Brown: 108, 110, 113-115
  The Sleep of Reason: 245-247, 251
Personification
  The Sleep of Reason: 242, 247-248, 251

Philosophical Ideas
  The Great God Brown: 123
Plants
  Indian Ink: 146-161
Plot
  Ghosts: 96-97, 101-102
  The Great God Brown: 124-125
  The Sleep of Reason: 248, 251
Poetry
  Ghosts: 100-102, 106
  The Insect Play: 163-164
Point of View
  Ghosts: 102, 104
Politicians
  Abe Lincoln in Illinois: 1-4, 9, 11-12, 15-16
  Driving Miss Daisy: 66
Politics
  Abe Lincoln in Illinois: 1-4, 8-11
  The Amen Corner: 27-28
  Driving Miss Daisy: 65-66
  Ghosts: 86
  Indian Ink: 147-150, 154-158
  The Insect Play: 171, 175-176
  M. Butterfly: 184, 187, 190-192
  Shadowlands: 218-219
  Slave Ship: 231
  The Sleep of Reason: 242, 245, 247-250
  Spike Heels: 260-262, 267-268
Poverty
  The Amen Corner: 25
Power
  Saint Joan: 275
Pride
  Shadowlands: 209, 213, 216
Protestantism
  Shadowlands: 207, 214, 216
Psychology and the Human Mind
  Dancing at Lughnasa: 53
  Ghosts: 99-100
  The Great God Brown: 114-116
  Harvey: 127-128, 133-139
  Indian Ink: 160
  The Sleep of Reason: 246
  Spike Heels: 260-261

R

Race and Prejudice
  Driving Miss Daisy: 62
Race and Racism
  M. Butterfly: 186
Race
  The Amen Corner: 22, 25, 27-29
  Driving Miss Daisy: 59, 62, 64-66, 70, 72-73
  M. Butterfly: 185-186, 189-191
  The Sleep of Reason: 245-251, 255-256
Racial Oppression
  The Sleep of Reason: 246

Racism and Prejudice
  The Amen Corner: 22, 25, 28
  Driving Miss Daisy: 59, 61-62, 65-67
  M. Butterfly: 186-188
Realism
  Ghosts: 83-84, 102, 104, 106
  The Great God Brown: 114-116
Recreation
  The Insect Play: 171, 179
Religion
  The Amen Corner: 25
Religion and Religious Thought
  The Amen Corner: 21-23, 30-33, 36
  Dancing at Lughnasa: 46, 49, 52, 54-56
  The Great God Brown: 114, 117, 121
  Shadowlands: 207, 215, 220-222
  Slave Ship: 228-230
  The Sleep of Reason: 251, 255
Repression and Fear
  Spike Heels: 265
Revenge
  Ghosts: 95
Roman Catholicism
  Dancing at Lughnasa: 49, 51-54
  Shadowlands: 215-216
  Spike Heels: 267-268

S

Saints
  Shadowlands: 206-209, 212-214, 220-221
Sanity and Insanity
  Harvey: 132
Sanity versus Insanity
  Spike Heels: 266
Science and Technology
  Harvey: 133
Science and Technology
  Dancing at Lughnasa: 46-49
  Harvey: 141-142
  Indian Ink: 159-160
  The Insect Play: 177
Search For Knowledge
  The Amen Corner: 33-34
  Ghosts: 103-106
Sentimentality
  The Great God Brown: 115
Setting
  Abe Lincoln in Illinois: 9
  The Amen Corner: 21, 29
  Dancing at Lughnasa: 43-44
  Ghosts: 94
  The Great God Brown: 114-115
  Indian Ink: 146-148
  Slave Ship: 229, 232
Sex and Sexuality
  Dancing at Lughnasa: 46, 49
  Ghosts: 77, 79, 82, 84-86

M. Butterfly: 198
Spike Heels: 260, 262, 266, 268
Saint Joan: 273-283

Sexism
M. Butterfly: 188

Sexual Abuse
Spike Heels: 263, 265-266

Sickness
Ghosts: 77, 79, 82-83
Slave Ship: 228-229, 234-235

Sin
The Amen Corner: 30-31, 36
Ghosts: 77, 82-84, 92-93, 99
The Insect Play: 168, 171

Slavery
Abe Lincoln in Illinois: 3-4, 9-11
The Sleep of Reason: 243-255, 258

Social Order
The Insect Play: 178-179

Socialism
Shadowlands: 214-215

Soul
The Great God Brown: 120-121

Spiritual Leaders
The Amen Corner: 21-23, 26-27
Ghosts: 79, 81-84, 88-90, 102-104
The Sleep of Reason: 247, 253-256

Spirituality
Dancing at Lughnasa: 53, 55-56

Sports and the Sporting Life
Abe Lincoln in Illinois: 2-3, 10
The Amen Corner: 22, 25
The Insect Play: 164-165, 179-180

Storms and Weather Conditions
Abe Lincoln in Illinois: 3, 7, 9

Structure
Abe Lincoln in Illinois: 9, 15
Driving Miss Daisy: 64
Saint Joan: 279

Success and Failure
The Great God Brown: 113

Success and Failure
The Great God Brown: 108, 113, 116

Suspense
Ghosts: 101, 103

T

Time and Change
M. Butterfly: 195-196

Tone
Shadowlands: 213

Tragedy
Ghosts: 94-95, 99-102
Shadowlands: 206, 209, 213, 216

Treatment of Geniuses and Saints
Shadowlands: 211

U

Understanding
Ghosts: 101

Upper Class
Spike Heels: 261-263, 266-267, 271-272

V

Victim and Victimization
Ghosts: 83

W

War and Peace
Abe Lincoln in Illinois: 7

War, the Military, and Soldier Life
Abe Lincoln in Illinois: 1-2, 7-8, 11
Driving Miss Daisy: 62, 64-65
Harvey: 135
Indian Ink: 149, 152, 154
The Insect Play: 163, 165, 169-172, 177
M. Butterfly: 184, 187-188, 191-192
Shadowlands: 207-209, 212-215, 220-221
Spike Heels: 262-263, 266-269

Wealth
The Insect Play: 178-180

Wildlife
Indian Ink: 146-148, 151, 156-162
The Insect Play: 168-170

World War I
The Insect Play: 162, 169-172
Shadowlands: 214-216

World War II
Harvey: 134-135
The Insect Play: 171

Z

Zeitgeist
Ghosts: 105